LAW, RELIGION, AND HEALTH IN THE UNITED STATES

Should religious physicians be required to disclose their beliefs to patients? How should we think about institutional conscience in the health care setting? How should health care providers deal with families with religious objections to the withdrawal of treatment? These are but a few of the pressing questions at the intersection of law, religion, and health in the United States. The law can generate conflict between religion and health, but it can also act as a tool for the religious accommodation and protection of conscience. This book explores both angles, bringing together expert authors from a variety of perspectives and disciplines to offer insights on what the public discourse gets right and wrong, how policymakers might respond, and what future unanticipated conflicts may emerge. It not only tackles issues of academic interest, but also real-world conflicts with the capacity to touch the lives of any one of us – patient or physician, secular or devout.

Holly Fernandez Lynch is Executive Director of the Petrie-Flom Center for Health Law Policy, Biotechnology, and Bioethics at Harvard Law School, Massachusetts and a faculty member at the Harvard Medical School Center for Bioethics. She is the author of *Conflicts of Conscience in Health Care: An Institutional Compromise* (2008) and co-editor of *Nudging Health: Health Law and Behavioral Economics* (2016), *FDA in the Twenty-First Century: The Challenges of Regulating Drugs and New Technologies* (2015), and *Human Subjects Research Regulation: Perspectives on the Future* (2014).

I. Glenn Cohen is a Professor at Harvard Law School, Massachusetts and Faculty Director of the Petrie-Flom Center. He is one of the world's leading experts on the intersection of bioethics and the law, as well as health law. He has authored or co-edited eight books and has published more than eighty articles in venues like *The New England Journal of Medicine*, *JAMA: The Journal of the American Medical Association*, *Nature*, and the *Harvard Law Review*.

Elizabeth Sepper is an Associate Professor at Washington University School of Law. She is an expert in health law and religious liberty law. She has written extensively on conscientious refusals to provide reproductive and end-of-life care, and conflicts between religion and antidiscrimination laws with articles in top law journals, including the *Columbia Law Review*, *Virginia Law Review*, and *Indiana Law Journal*.

Law, Religion, and Health in the United States

Edited by

HOLLY FERNANDEZ LYNCH
Harvard Law School

I. GLENN COHEN
Harvard Law School

ELIZABETH SEPPER
Washington University School of Law

CAMBRIDGE
UNIVERSITY PRESS

One Liberty Plaza, 20th Floor, New York, NY 10006, USA

Cambridge University Press is part of the University of Cambridge.

It furthers the University's mission by disseminating knowledge in the pursuit of education, learning, and research at the highest international levels of excellence.

www.cambridge.org
Information on this title: www.cambridge.org/9781316616543
DOI: 10.1017/9781316691274

© Cambridge University Press 2017

This publication is in copyright. Subject to statutory exception and to the provisions of relevant collective licensing agreements, no reproduction of any part may take place without the written permission of Cambridge University Press.

First published 2017

Printed in the United States of America by Sheridan Books, Inc.

A catalogue record for this publication is available from the British Library.

Library of Congress Cataloging-in-Publication Data
Names: Lynch, Holly Fernandez, editor. | Cohen, I. Glenn, editor. | Sepper, Elizabeth, editor.
Title: Law, religion, and health in the United States / edited by Holly Fernandez Lynch, I. Glenn Cohen, Elizabeth Sepper.
Description: New York: Cambridge University Press, 2017. |
Includes bibliographical references and index.
Identifiers: LCCN 2017008238 | ISBN 9781107164888 (hardback) | ISBN 9781316616543 (paperback)
Subjects: LCSH: Freedom of religion – United States. | Health Care Reform – United States. | Christian ethics – United States. | Religious health facilities – United States. | Catholic Church – United States – Doctrines. | Medicine – Religious aspects.
Classification: LCC KF4783.L387 2017 | DDC 342.7308/52–dc23
LC record available at https://lccn.loc.gov/2017008238

ISBN 978-1-107-16488-8 Hardback
ISBN 978-1-316-61654-3 Paperback

Cambridge University Press has no responsibility for the persistence or accuracy of URLs for external or third-party internet websites referred to in this publication and does not guarantee that any content on such websites is, or will remain, accurate or appropriate.

To Bill, for your unending patience and support.

– H. F. L.

To Eddie Soloway, the good soldier.

– I. G. C.

To Navid, through thick and thin, rant and rave.

– E. S.

Contents

Contributors		*page* xi
Foreword by Martha Minow		xv
Acknowledgments		xxi
	Introduction: Law, Religion, and Health in the United States Elizabeth Sepper, Holly Fernandez Lynch, and I. Glenn Cohen	1
	PART I: TESTING THE SCOPE OF LEGAL PROTECTIONS FOR RELIGION IN THE HEALTH CARE CONTEXT	19
1	Religious Liberty, Health Care, and the Culture Wars Douglas Laycock	21
2	From *Smith* to *Hobby Lobby*: The Transformation of the Religious Freedom Restoration Act Diane L. Moore and Eric M. Stephen	34
3	The HHS Mandate Litigation and Religious Health Care Providers Adèle Keim	47
4	Not Your Father's Religious Exemptions: The Contraceptive-Coverage Litigation and the Rights of Others Gregory M. Lipper	60
5	Recent Applications of the Supreme Court's Hands-Off Approach to Religious Doctrine: From *Hosanna-Tabor* and *Holt* to *Hobby Lobby* and *Zubik* Samuel J. Levine	75

PART II: LAW, RELIGION, AND HEALTH CARE INSTITUTIONS: INTRODUCTION ... 87

6 A Corporation's Exercise of Religion: A Practitioner's Experience ... 90
   Melanie Di Pietro

7 The Natural Person as the Limiting Principle for Conscience: Can a Corporation Have a Conscience If It Doesn't Have an Intellect and Will? ... 103
   Ryan Meade

8 Contracting Religion ... 113
   Elizabeth Sepper

9 Mission Integrity Matters: Balancing Catholic Health Care Values and Public Mandates ... 125
   David M. Craig

PART III: LAW, RELIGION, AND HEALTH INSURANCE: INTRODUCTION ... 139

10 Religious Exemptions to the Individual Mandate: Health Care Sharing Ministries and the Affordable Care Act ... 143
    Rachel E. Sachs

11 Bosses in the Bedroom: Religious Employers and the Future of Employer-Sponsored Health Care ... 154
    Holly Fernandez Lynch and Gregory Curfman

PART IV: PROFESSIONAL RESPONSIBILITIES, RELIGION, AND HEALTH CARE: INTRODUCTION ... 169

12 Religious Outliers: Professional Knowledge Communities, Individual Conscience Claims, and the Availability of Professional Services to the Public ... 173
    Claudia E. Haupt

13 A Common Law Duty to Disclose Conscience-Based Limitations on Medical Practice ... 187
    Nadia N. Sawicki

Contents

	PART V: THE IMPACT OF RELIGIOUS OBJECTIONS ON THE HEALTH AND HEALTH CARE OF OTHERS: INTRODUCTION	199
14	Conscientious Objection, Complicity, and Accommodation Amy J. Sepinwall	203
15	How Much May Religious Accommodations Burden Others? Nelson Tebbe, Micah Schwartzman, and Richard Schragger	215
16	"A Patchwork Array of Theocratic Fiefdoms?" RFRA Claims Against the ACA's Contraception Mandate as Examples of the New Feudalism Mary Anne Case	230
17	Unpacking the Relationship Between Conscience and Access Robin Fretwell Wilson	242
	PART VI: A CASE STUDY – RELIGIOUS BELIEFS AND THE HEALTH OF THE LGBT COMMUNITY: INTRODUCTION	259
18	Religious Convictions About Homosexuality and the Training of Counseling Professionals: How Should We Treat Religious-Based Opposition to Counseling About Same-Sex Relationships? Susan J. Stabile	263
19	Reclaiming Biopolitics: Religion and Psychiatry in the Sexual Orientation Change Therapy Cases and the Establishment Clause Defense Craig J. Konnoth	276
	PART VII: ACCOUNTING FOR PATIENTS' RELIGIOUS BELIEFS: INTRODUCTION	289
20	Brain Death Rejected: Expanding Legal Duties to Accommodate Religious Objections Thaddeus Mason Pope	293
21	Accommodating Miracles: Medical Futility and Religious Free Exercise Teneille R. Brown	306

22	Putting the Insanity Defense on Trial: Understanding Criminality in the Context of Religion and Mental Illness Abbas Rattani and Jemel Amin Derbali	319
23	Religion as a Controlling Interference in Medical Decision Making by Minors Jonathan F. Will	332

PART VIII: RELIGION AND REPRODUCTIVE HEALTH CARE: INTRODUCTION — 345

24	Regulating Reasons: Governmental Regulation of Private Deliberation in Reproductive Decision Making B. Jessie Hill	348
25	Religion and Reproductive Technology I. Glenn Cohen	360
26	Religion and the Unborn Under the First Amendment Dov Fox	372

PART IX: RELIGION, LAW, AND PUBLIC HEALTH: INTRODUCTION — 383

27	Race, Religion, and Masculinity: The HIV Double Bind Michele Goodwin	387
28	The Intersection of Law, Religion, and Infectious Disease in the Handling and Disposition of Human Remains Aileen Maria Marty, Elena Maria Marty-Nelson, and Eloisa C. Rodriguez-Dod	399
29	When Religion Pollutes: How Should Law Respond When Religious Practice Threatens Public Health? Jay Wexler	411

Index — 423

Contributors

Noa Ben-Asher, LL.B., LL.M., J.S.D. Professor of Law, Elisabeth Haub School of Law at Pace University.

Teneille R. Brown, J.D. Professor, S.J. Quinney College of Law, University of Utah; Adjunct Professor, Division of Medical Ethics, University of Utah.

Mary Anne Case, J.D. Arnold I. Shure Professor of Law, University of Chicago Law School.

I. Glenn Cohen, J.D. Professor of Law and Faculty Director of the Petrie-Flom Center for Health Law Policy, Biotechnology, and Bioethics, Harvard Law School.

David M. Craig, M.T.S., M.A., Ph.D. Professor of Religious Studies and Adjunct Faculty in Philanthropic Studies, Indiana University – Purdue University Indianapolis.

Gregory Curfman, M.D. Editor in Chief, Harvard Health Publications; Assistant Professor of Medicine and Lecturer in Health Care Policy, Harvard Medical School; Assistant in Medicine, Massachusetts General Hospital; Affiliated Faculty, Petrie-Flom Center for Health Law Policy, Biotechnology, and Bioethics, Harvard Law School; Senior Advisor and Physician-Scholar in Residence, Solomon Center for Health Law and Policy, Yale Law School.

Jemel Amin Derbali, J.D. Co-founder, Wise Systems.

Melanie Di Pietro, S.C., J.D., J.C.D. Founder and Co-Director, Seton Center for Religiously Affiliated Non-Profit Corporations, Seton Hall Law School (Formerly: Distinguished Practitioner in Residence and Professor, Seton Hall Law School).

Richard H. Fallon Jr., J.D. Story Professor of Law, Harvard Law School.

Dov Fox, D.Phil., J.D., LL.M. Associate Professor of Law and Director of the Center for Health Law Policy and Bioethics, University of San Diego School of Law.

Michele Goodwin, J.D., LL.M. Chancellor's Professor of Law and Director of the Center for Biotechnology and Global Health Policy, University of California, Irvine School of Law.

Claudia E. Haupt, M.A., Ph.D., LL.M. J.S.D. Candidate, Columbia Law School; Resident Fellow, Information Society Project, Yale Law School.

B. Jessie Hill, J.D. Associate Dean for Academic Affairs and Judge Ben C. Green Professor of Law, Case Western Reserve University School of Law.

Adèle Keim, J.D. Counsel, Becket — Religious Liberty for All.

Craig J. Konnoth, M.Phil., J.D. Sharswood Fellow and Lecturer in Law, University of Pennsylvania Law School; Senior Fellow, Leonard Davis Institute of Health Economics, University of Pennsylvania; Rudin Fellow, Division of Medical Ethics, NYU Langone Medical Center.

Douglas Laycock, J.D. Robert E. Scott Distinguished Professor of Law, Class of 1963 Research Professor in Honor of Graham C. Lilly and Peter W. Low, and Professor of Religious Studies, University of Virginia School of Law.

Samuel J. Levine, J.D., Rabbinical Ordination, LL.M. Professor of Law and Director of the Jewish Law Institute, Touro College Jacob D. Fuchsberg Law Center.

Gregory M. Lipper, J.D. Partner, Clinton Brook & Peed (Formerly: Senior Litigation Counsel, Americans United for Separation of Church and State).

Holly Fernandez Lynch, J.D., M.Bioethics Executive Director, Petrie-Flom Center for Health Law Policy, Biotechnology, and Bioethics, Harvard Law School; Faculty, Center for Bioethics, Harvard Medical School.

Aileen Maria Marty, M.D. Professor and Clinical Lab Director, Florida International University, Herbert Wertheim College of Medicine.

Elena Maria Marty-Nelson, J.D., LL.M. Associate Dean for Diversity, Inclusion, and Public Impact and Professor of Law, Nova Southeastern University, Shepard Broad College of Law.

Ryan Meade, J.D. Director of Regulatory Compliance Studies and Visiting Professor of Law, Beazley Institute for Health Law and Policy, Loyola University Chicago School of Law.

Martha Minow, Ed.M., J.D. Morgan and Helen Chu Dean and Professor of Law, Harvard Law School; Member, Faculty of Education, Harvard Graduate School of Education.

Christine Mitchell, M.T.S., M.S. Executive Director, Center for Bioethics, Harvard Medical School.

Diane L. Moore, M.Div., D.Min., Ph.D. Director of Religious Literacy Project, Senior Lecturer on Religious Studies and Education, and Senior Fellow at the Center for the Study of World Religions, Harvard Divinity School.

Thaddeus Mason Pope, M.A., J.D., Ph.D. Professor of Law and Director of the Health Law Institute, Mitchell Hamline School of Law; Adjunct Professor, Australian Centre for Health Law Research, Queensland University of Technology; Adjunct Associate Professor, Alden March Bioethics Institute, Albany Medical College; Affiliate Faculty, University of Minnesota Center for Bioethics; Visiting Professor of Medical Jurisprudence, School of Medicine, St. George's University.

Ahmed Ragab, M.D., Ph.D. Richard T. Watson Associate Professor of Science and Religion and Director of Science, Religion, and Culture Program, Harvard Divinity School; Affiliate Associate Professor, Department of the History of Science, Harvard University.

Abbas Rattani, M.Be., M.D. Candidate, Meharry Medical College School of Medicine.

Eloisa C. Rodriguez-Dod, M.B.A., J.D. Professor of Law, Florida International University College of Law.

Marc A. Rodwin, M.A., J.D., Ph.D. Professor of Law, Suffolk University Law School.

Mindy Jane Roseman, J.D., Ph.D. Director, Gruber Program for Global Justice and Women's Rights, Yale Law School.

Nadia N. Sawicki, J.D., M.Bioethics Professor of Law and Academic Director of the Beazley Institute for Health Law and Policy, Loyola University Chicago School of Law.

Rachel E. Sachs, J.D., M.P.H. Associate Professor of Law, Washington University School of Law.

Richard Schragger, M.A., J.D. Perre Bowen Professor of Law and Joseph C. Carter, Jr. Research Professor of Law, University of Virginia School of Law.

Micah Schwartzman, D.Phil., J.D. Professor of Law, University of Virginia School of Law.

Amy J. Sepinwall, M.A., J.D., Ph.D. James G. Campbell, Jr. Memorial Term Assistant Professor, Department of Legal Studies and Business Ethics, The Wharton School, University of Pennsylvania.

Elizabeth Sepper, J.D., LL.M. Associate Professor of Law, Washington University School of Law.

Susan J. Stabile, J.D. Distinguished Senior Fellow, University of St. Thomas School of Law; Adjunct Instructor in Theology, St. Catherine University.

Eric M. Stephen, M.A., M.T.S., Ph.D. Candidate, Harvard University.

Nelson Tebbe, J.D., Ph.D. Professor of Law, Brooklyn Law School; Visiting Professor of Law, Cornell Law School.

Robert D. Truog, M.D., M.A. Frances Glessner Lee Professor of Medical Ethics, Anaesthesia, & Pediatrics and Director of the Center for Bioethics, Harvard Medical School; Senior Associate in Critical Care Medicine, Boston Children's Hospital; Executive Director, Institute for Professionalism & Ethical Practice; Chair, Harvard University Embryo Stem Cell Research Oversight Committee.

Jay Wexler, M.A., J.D. Professor of Law, Boston University School of Law.

Jonathan F. Will, J.D., M.A. Associate Dean for Academic Affairs and Faculty Development, Professor of Law, and Founding Director of the Bioethics and Health Law Center, Mississippi College School of Law; Affiliate Faculty, Center for Bioethics and Medical Humanities, University of Mississippi Medical Center.

Robin Fretwell Wilson, J.D. Roger and Stephanie Joslin Professor of Law, Director of the Family Law and Policy Program, and Director of the Epstein Health Law and Policy Program, University of Illinois College of Law.

Foreword

Martha Minow

This volume of essays demonstrates both the range of contemporary health issues generating conflicts reflecting religious concerns, and the power and limitations of reasoned arguments in resolving those conflicts. Flash points between religion and medicine involve whether physicians and other health care professionals can assist individuals who choose to die; whether parents can refuse public health vaccinations for their children; and access to contraception, reproductive technologies, and abortion. The issues engage individuals, as well as institutions and groups. May a religiously affiliated hospital avoid engaging in practices deemed out-of-bounds by the relevant religion and even decline to make referrals to other providers? May religiously identified employers decline to provide employees with access to contraceptives through their health plans?

Complicating each of these difficult subjects is the fact that they inevitably involve not just one person, but also the relationship between the affected individual and others, ranging from intimate family members to the larger society. Whose interests or values should govern? Each issue potentially puts health care providers in the middle of conflicts between family members and between groups in society. Physician involvement in hastening death, exemptions from mandated vaccinations, and reproductive choice can also generate conflicts between duties to individual patients and adherence to the providers' own conscience and professional norms. And increasing recognition of the potential role of religious and spiritual dimensions in patient healing and well-being makes attentiveness to religion matter, even from a purely health care vantage point.[1]

---

[1] This foreword draws upon Martha Minow, "Religion, Medicine, and Law: How to Heal When Values Conflict", George W. Gay Lecture (November 3, 2016), which, in turn, reflected Hannah Solomon-Strauss's excellent research assistance and comments, and invaluable comments from Stephen Carter, Glenn Cohen, Charles Fried, Atul Gawande, Newton Minow, Robert Mnookin, Joe Singer, Mira Singer, Vicky Spelman, and Mark Tushnet. Helpful resources include *Religion as a Social Determinant of Public Health* (Ellen L. Idler ed., 2014); Christina M. Puchalsky, Ethical

None of these issues is especially new, and yet they appear to be generating heightened attention and debate, at least within the United States. Why may this be the case? I offer these possible explanations:

1) Political and social movements have focused on religiously inflected issues for the past several decades to mobilize voters and to alter public policies. Particular issues for the past several decades have involved the status and autonomy of women, the nature of families, and the rights of LGBTQ individuals. All of this makes health care simply one of many sectors caught up in the particular cultural and religious disputes that now sweep in employers, florists, photographers, hotels, and other service providers.

2) Constitutional law has changed after the Supreme Court, in 1990, cut back on the accommodations for free exercise of religion; Congress and many states responded with legislation reinstating it. In *Employment Division v. Smith*, the Supreme Court overturned several decades of accommodation for individuals' religious beliefs and ruled that a general rule that does not target religious beliefs or practices can stand without exemptions.[2] Perhaps the Court was unsympathetic to the particular claims in the case, which involved two Native Americans seeking unemployment benefits after losing their jobs due to ingesting peyote in a religious ritual; intentional possession of peyote was a crime under state law. The Court suggested that a legislative response could provide accommodations, but probably did not expect the groundswell of popular sentiment, producing federal and state statutes rejecting the Court's whole approach in the *Smith* case. Faced now with statutory language calling for accommodations, public actors including judges, educators, and hospital administrators encounter disputes over particular situations and the scope of required accommodations. Because the United States Constitution both protects free exercise of religion and bans government establishment of religion, navigating the space for individual conscience without erecting a government endorsement of religion is tricky business. And religious questions raise potential clashes between minority rights and majority views.

3) Changes in medical technologies and in the practices for delivering health care involve teams of nurses, doctors, technicians, insurers, and others giving more visibility, greater access, and more regulated record keeping around decisions that in the past took place in the more private consultations of patient and doctor; other changes bring new technologies into play for prolonging life, affecting reproductive practices, and permitting discussion and

---

Concerns and Boundaries in Spirituality and Health, 11 Virtual Mentor 804 (2009); Stephen G. Post, The Perennial Collaboration of Medicine and Religion, 11 Virtual Mentor 807 (2009).

[2] *Emp't Div. v. Smith*, 494 U.S. 872 (1990).

debate on the internet and elsewhere by individuals concerned, for example, about vaccinations.

4) Expansions of the government's role in medical care and insurance – with the Affordable Care Act a prime example – have produced more regulations and institutional oversight, creating more visibility of and opportunities for potential conflicts with religious practices.

5) Some religious groups have become more engaged in political conflicts and litigation over aspects of secular culture and government practices.[3]

6) Junk science and even antipathy to science certainly have fueled opposition to vaccinations (especially based on apparently unfounded fears that the measles, mumps, and rubella vaccine causes autism), even as new technologies imaging fetal life have affected the politics of reproduction and abortion.[4]

7) Disputes over religion and medical issues, like many other societal conflicts, have landed in the hands of lawyers and judges, framed by litigation, adversarial politics, and allergy to compromise. Because lawsuits require casting issues in terms of competing arguments, seeking a definitive answer – yes or no – to a complaint by a plaintiff, middle or compromise positions are not possible inside the courts, and the adversarial framing affects discussions and resolutions outside the courts.

8) Individual choice is not only a deep American value, but also the solvent of intergroup conflict. On questions over how best to raise children, whether children should learn a language other than English, whether women should change their name upon marriage, and even what religion to adopt are treated largely as questions of individual choice in the United States, whereas comparable decisions in other countries are subject to more collective or governmental policies. Americans, compared with people in other nations, fall on the far end of scales valuing individualism and ascribing events to individual effort.[5]

9) Medical ethics have, over time, shifted from reliance on medical expertise to individual choice, rather than to expert medical judgment.[6] This shift

---

[3] See Darren Dochuk, *From Bible Belt to Sunbelt: Plain-Folk Religion, Grassroots Politics, and the Rise of Evangelical Conservatism* (2010); Matthew Avery Sutton, *American Apocalypse: A History of Modern Evangelicalism* (2014).

[4] See A Case of Junk Science, Conflict and Hype, 9 Nature Immunology 1317 (2008); Lisa Wade, How Fetal Photography Changed the Politics of Abortion, Sociological Images (November 7, 2014), https://thesocietypages.org/socimages/2014/11/07/visualizing-the-fetus/ [https://perma.cc/7WGY-63PB].

[5] Martha Minow, We, the Family: Constitutional Rights and American Families, 74 J. Am. Hist. 959 (1987); Richard Wike, 5 Ways Americans and Europeans are Different, Pew Research Center (April 19, 2016), www.pewresearch.org/fact-tank/2016/04/19/5-ways-americans-and-europeans-are-different/ [https://perma.cc/2TG3-EJXM].

[6] Nancy Neveloff Dubler, A "Principled Resolution": The Fulcrum for Bioethics Mediation, Law & Contemp. Probs., Summer 2011, at 177, 179–80 (2011).

reflects concern over the power imbalances in encounters between physicians and patients and in the responses of hospitals and medical centers to risks of malpractice suits. The shift strengthens philosophic, legal, and pragmatic endorsement of individual patient choice and consent.[7]

The thoughtful and diverse essays gathered in this volume reflect deep learning and sincere efforts to make progress in resolving the disagreements or persuading readers about how to proceed. There are tough and unresolved questions, such as:

1) What is the test for determining when an assertion of religious free exercise deserves constitutional concern – whenever a religious objector says so? When the objector's sincerity is established? When the objector can point to a recognized religious doctrine? When the religious practice is singled out for restriction?
2) What kind of countervailing concerns justify denying claims for religious exemptions – preserving life? Public health? According with standard medical practice? Protecting rights of third-parties?
3) When should courts have the final word, and when should legislatures? What room is and should there be for compromise or settlement of religious claims concerning health care? And;
4) Does repeated reliance on courts to resolve conflicts over religion and health care offer a path toward resolution or instead a kind of repetition compulsion, exacerbating conflict and eroding respect for law?

With deep respect for the efforts of the individual authors and the editors, I hope this work receives serious attention. I also hope readers start with the recognition that discerning "right answers" may not be possible when there are religiously-motivated conflicts over medical care. The conflicts reach to the very notion of what is "right" and who can and should make definitive and legitimate determinations. Ours is a nation that requires separation of religion and government, so any decision by law will be made according to secular lights. Perhaps ironically, this very commitment to separating religion and government has accompanied the flourishing of distinctive religious communities and pluralism in America. The United States has fostered vibrant religious traditions but also many individuals switching religions or developing their own religious beliefs.[8] Even among those who identify with a religion, a vast variety of religious teachings and practices characterizes the United States. Observers who used to predict that secularization follows modernization

---

[7] Id.
[8] Michael Lipka, 10 Facts About Religion in America, Pew Research Center (August 27, 2015), www.pewresearch.org/fact-tank/2015/08/27/10-facts-about-religion-in-america/ [https://perma.cc/9NYH-2YAR].

have shifted to emphasize that it is pluralism – multiple groups, with contrasting beliefs – that has grown.[9]

Conflicts with public policies mount amid such pluralism. There is no neutral point of view when religious views come into play on public policy questions. It is difficult for policy makers to incorporate all possible religious views in setting general rules and procedures. Even the option of a secular approach, leaving choice to individuals, does not seem neutral to those who feel a particular choice is itself immoral, or who view the resort to individual choice as disrespect for religious viewpoints. Wikipedia, a crowd-sourcing Internet encyclopedia, aims for neutrality but has come to an impasse in the definition of abortion, the entry for which was adjusted some 6,000 times. The "edit war" prompted the site's administrators, at least briefly, to close off discussion.[10] When disputes reflecting religious views come to legislatures, majorities can win, but courts are then entrusted with hearing objections.

Deferring to individual choice can be an attractive solution, yet legally protected choices to secure physician assistance in ending one's life, to avoid otherwise mandated vaccination, or to pursue contraception and abortion are not neutral options. Permitting such choices means allowing people to engage in conduct to which many object and which may harm them or others. A nation that seeks to promote individual liberty inevitably allows, and even supports, many choices to which people may object and which may even bring about harm.

But the choices involving medical care implicate symbolic and practical dimensions of life itself. To permit individuals to seek to accelerate death with medical help is to make death a choice, and doing so, to some, devalues life itself.[11] The deepest sources of meaning, purpose, truth, and morality are at issue, as well as the values and character of society. Yet, disallowing medical assistance to patients who wish to hasten death consigns individuals to suffering. Any framework allowing health care professionals to accelerate an individual's death runs risks of abuse, and great care must accompany such efforts to protect those who are vulnerable due to their physical, mental, emotional, financial, or familial situations. Allowing an employer to

---

[9] See Eboo Patel, In Promoting Campus Diversity, Don't Dismiss Religion, Chronicle of Higher Education, The Chronicle of Higher Education (March 11, 2015), www.chronicle.com/article/In-Promoting-Campus-Diversity/228427/?cid=at&utm_source=at&utm_medium=en [https://perma.cc/83HF-MFLM]; Gene Veith, Not Secularism but Pluralism, Patheos Blog (March 16, 2015), www.patheos.com/blogs/geneveith/2015/03/not-secularism-but-pluralism/ [https://perma.cc/6WEX-RUK4].

[10] Marshall Poe, A Closer Look at the Neutral Point of View (NPOV), Atlantic (September 2006), www.theatlantic.com/magazine/archive/2006/09/a-closer-look-at-the-neutral-point-of-view-npov/305120/ [https://perma.cc/36XD-BXHA].

[11] See Martha Minow, Which Question? Which Lie? Reflections on the Physician-Assisted Suicide Cases, 1997 Sup. Ct. Rev. 1 (1997).

opt out of provision of contraceptives burdens choices – constitutionally protected choices – of employees whose own quality of life and meaning are at issue.

Let's be frank. For people with lingering illnesses, massively compromised health care, and grave suffering; for people with unwanted pregnancies; for parents with religious objections to vaccines, whose neighbors have children especially vulnerable to the illness that the vaccine can prevent, there are no great options. Individual accommodations offer individuals some semblance of control or some acknowledgement of competing principles that may not be well-captured by general rules. Without individualized accommodations, lawyers, medical providers, judges and voters will continue to debate when the presumption of individual choice should be overcome because of significant harms to others or limitations of the chooser. Perhaps new forms of mediation would avoid limiting decisions to either-or choices and afford avenues for navigating conflicts between religion and health care. Thoughtful and respectful discussions are crucial. Let's proceed with humility in the face of conflicts we cannot resolve for all times and places.

Acknowledgments

A book like this is the result of the hard work of many. We are very thankful for the help. We thank our student line editors, Eleanor Davis, Noah Heinz, Jessica Goodman, and Ariel Teshuva, who worked tirelessly to bring this manuscript to fruition. We are also grateful to Crissy Hutchison-Jones and Justin Leahey for their administrative support in putting on the conference that gave rise to this book, as well as the conference's sponsors: the Petrie-Flom Center for Health Law Policy, Biotechnology, and Bioethics at Harvard Law School and the Center for Bioethics at Harvard Medical School, with support from the Oswald DeN. Cammann Fund. Finally, we thank the contributors for their wonderful contributions.

Introduction: Law, Religion, and Health in the United States

Elizabeth Sepper, Holly Fernandez Lynch, and I. Glenn Cohen

Within the covers of the Bible are the answers for all the problems men face.
– Ronald Reagan

I do not feel obliged to believe that the same God who has endowed us with sense, reason, and intellect has intended us to forgo their use.
– Galileo Galilei

What types of health care institutions ought to be allowed to exercise religion or conscience? Should corporations with religious owners be permitted to deny insurance coverage for contraception or reproductive technologies? How should providers, institutions, and the law respond to religious beliefs expressed by patients or patients' families when they resist modern medical practice with regard to definitions of death, expectation of miracles, or refusal of treatment? When should the law demand that health care professionals disclose their religious beliefs or refer patients whom they cannot counsel for religious reasons – and, more generally, how should the law respond when religious objections in the health care sphere threaten to harm or burden others? What impact might religion have on public health law and interventions, or even the environment? These are but a few of the questions (and potential conflicts) at the intersection of law, religion, and health that are becoming increasingly pressing in our current historical moment.

This volume highlights the complex ways in which these three topics collide. The collisions are ubiquitous, but they may not present as a straightforward conflict between government and believers. Instead, they tend to occur in a complicated web of relationships involving health professionals, patients, and institutions (as diverse as employers, insurers, and hospitals), all of which may hold their own religious (or opposing secular) beliefs and raise religious objections. While religious conflict is certainly not unique to the United States, this country does present a unique environment, combining secular foundations with levels both of religious and moral pluralism and of religious devotion that stand out among developed nations. From Jehovah's Witnesses who refuse life-saving blood transfusions to certain Ultra-Orthodox Jews who suck blood out of the penis as part of traditional male circumcision, from Caribbean religious practitioners who employ the ritualistic use of mercury to Christians who oppose contraceptives, people in the United States hold every possible variety of religious belief (including none at all). The law understandably refuses to examine the validity of these wide-ranging beliefs and offers the same legal protection across the board. But the protection of religious believers in this country is not absolute, resulting in the need to grapple with a variety of potential conflicts.

Many of these conflicts have been brought to the fore by the landmark 2014 U.S. Supreme Court decision, *Burwell v. Hobby Lobby Stores, Inc.*[1] That case (and related litigation ongoing at the time this volume went to press) not only addressed the specific issue of employers' religious objections to covering contraceptives in employee insurance plans, but also central, unresolved issues in law and religion doctrine that affect health generally and remain important no matter the fate of the contraceptives coverage mandate in the Trump administration.

Spurred by these developments, we brought together leading academics, practitioners, and advocates to consider religion and law within the context of the health care system, bioethics, and public health. The conference, organized by the Petrie-Flom Center for Health Law Policy, Biotechnology, and Bioethics at Harvard Law School, attracted hundreds of thought leaders from across the nation. The result of that discussion – and later debates – is memorialized in the 29 chapters that follow.

The contributors to this volume grapple with many issues at the core of ongoing debates – the definition of health care providers' professional responsibility, the challenges of creating dialogue between religious and secular worldviews, the scope of religious choice by parents for their sick children, and many more. They come from a diverse set of backgrounds and methodologies, including philosophy, public health, law, theology, and medicine. Moreover, they reflect a diversity of perspectives. Often they offer competing visions of what success in balancing religion and health would look like and the best ways to achieve it in law and policy.

In order to provide some common ground for the chapters in this volume, and to avoid the repetition that would inevitably occur if each chapter had to recapitulate the relevant background law, we set the stage in this introduction for what is to come. Many readers will already be familiar with the U.S. legal standards applicable to religious conflicts, but we hope to provide a brief overview for others without this background knowledge.

[1] 134 S. Ct. 2751 (2014).

First, it is essential to recognize that there are both constitutional and statutory protections for religious liberty, and that these protections are found in varying forms at the federal and state levels. The First Amendment to the U.S. Constitution states, in part, that "Congress shall make no law respecting an establishment of religion, or prohibiting the free exercise thereof."[2] Between 1963 and 1990, the Supreme Court interpreted the Free Exercise Clause as offering relatively extensive protection where a law imposed a substantial burden on the free exercise of religion. Under this standard, the government had to demonstrate that the law was *necessary* to advance a *compelling* government interest; if it failed on either prong, the law would be declared unconstitutional.[3] In 1990, however, the Supreme Court held in *Employment Division v. Smith* that neutral laws of general applicability – those that do not specifically target religion and apply equally to believers and nonbelievers – do not merit mandatory religious accommodation even when they burden free exercise, so long as they bear a *rational* relationship to a *legitimate* government interest.[4] The result was that the Supreme Court significantly lowered the bar that laws had to meet in order to survive a constitutional Free Exercise challenge.

In response to the Court's decision in *Smith*, Congress passed the Religious Freedom Restoration Act of 1993 (RFRA) with the support of religious and secular leaders on the political left and right.[5] The law's stated purpose was to restore the compelling interest test with explicit reference to pre-*Smith* Supreme Court precedent. Under RFRA, the federal government may "substantially burden a person's exercise of religion only if it demonstrates that application of the burden to the person – (1) is in furtherance of a compelling governmental interest; and (2) is the least restrictive means of furthering that compelling governmental interest."[6]

After the Supreme Court made clear in 1997 that RFRA applied only to action by the federal government, many states passed similar laws of their own.[7] Twenty-one states currently have what are known as "state RFRAs."[8] Beyond these state statutes, state constitutional provisions also safeguard religious exercise, sometimes more broadly than the federal Constitution.

---

[2] U.S. Const. amend. I.
[3] See *Sherbert v. Verner*, 374 US 398 (1963); *Wisconsin v. Yoder*, 406 US 205 (1972).
[4] 494 U.S. 872 (1990).
[5] 42 U.S.C. §2000bb (1993). For further discussion, see Diane L. Moore and Eric M. Stephen, Ch. 2, this volume.
[6] Id. at § 2000bb-1(b).
[7] *City of Boerne v. Flores*, 521 U.S. 507 (1997) (holding that RFRA's original extension to the states exceeded Congress's power).
[8] National Conference of State Legislatures, State Religious Freedom Restoration Acts (October 15, 2015), available at www.ncsl.org/research/civil-and-criminal-justice/state-rfra-statutes.aspx [https://perma.cc/Z8LW-XCDV].

Because plaintiffs face a lower burden under RFRA than the Constitution (where the *Smith* standard still holds), it is RFRA – and not the First Amendment – that is central to recent litigation in which plaintiffs have sought to challenge various legal requirements as unacceptably infringing their religious beliefs and/or practices. Indeed, the Supreme Court's decision in *Hobby Lobby* addressed the application of RFRA to the government's regulation requiring insurance coverage of contraceptives. Since challenges to the contraceptive mandate are central to many of the chapters in the book, it is worth discussing in greater detail here. As discussed later, it is unclear that the mandate will survive the political process regardless of what happens in court, but it nonetheless offers an important case study of religious conflict with law. We suspect that such conflicts will become increasingly important in the health care space, either by way of laws promoting access to health care services or laws accommodating religious objections to them.

The controversy over the contraceptive mandate originated with the Affordable Care Act's (ACA) so-called "employer mandate," encouraging (most) large employers with fifty or more full-time employees to extend health insurance to their employees.[9] If the employer decides not to provide health insurance and at least one full-time employee enrolls in a health plan and qualifies for a subsidy on one of the government-run exchanges, the employer must pay $2000 per year for *each* of its full-time employees.[10] The ACA also imposes regulations on health insurance plans sponsored by employers. Of particular relevance, all plans must cover "preventive care and screenings" for women without cost-sharing in the form of co-payments, co-insurance, or deductibles.[11] If an employer subject to the mandate provides health insurance, but fails to cover women's preventive care, it will face a $100-per-day tax for each insured individual.[12] Thus, employers face penalties if they choose not to offer health insurance at all, or if they fail to offer the right type of coverage. Based on a review of evidence-based preventive services for women's health and well-being, the U.S. Department of Health and Human Services (HHS) interpreted the ACA's requirement regarding "preventive care and screenings" to mean that insurance plans must cover – without cost to beneficiaries – a wide range of contraceptive methods, including oral contraceptives, intrauterine devices, emergency contraception, and sterilization, as well as patient counseling and education about these options.[13]

---

[9] 26 U.S.C. § 4980H (2012).
[10] Id. at §§4980H(a),(c)(1).
[11] 42 U.S.C §300gg–13(a)(4).
[12] 26 U.S.C. §§4980D(a)-(b).
[13] Group Health Plans and Health Insurance Issuers Relating to Coverage of Preventive Services Under the Patient Protection and Affordable Care Act, 76 Fed. Reg. 46621-01 (August 3, 2011) (to be codified at 45 C.F.R. pt. 147).

Following several revisions, but prior to *Hobby Lobby* and related cases, the HHS rule – which became known as the contraceptives mandate – was to work as follows. It granted an *exemption* to "churches, their integrated auxiliaries, and conventions or associations of churches, as well as the exclusively religious activities of any religious order."[14] These entities did not have to abide by the mandate at all or take any steps to avoid it. The rule also provided an *accommodation* for nonprofit religious organizations, such as certain universities and hospitals.[15] To be accommodated, an organization had to (1) oppose providing contraceptives coverage under the mandate for religious reasons; (2) be organized and operate as a nonprofit entity; (3) hold itself out as a religious organization; and (4) self-certify that it met these criteria. Eligible organizations had to provide notice of their objection to their health insurance issuer, which was then required to provide separate payments for contraceptives for women in the health plan at no cost to the women *or* to the organization.[16] Accommodated organizations did not have to contract, arrange, pay, or refer for contraceptive coverage.[17] Their employees, however, still had access to contraceptive coverage without cost to them.[18] A similar accommodation was available for eligible organizations using self-insured health plans run by third-party administrators.[19]

Compliance with the mandate was expected of all other employers – including all for-profit entities. Several for-profit corporations with religious owners subsequently filed suit under RFRA, requesting exemption from the mandate, and eventually reached the Supreme Court in consolidated cases brought by chain store Hobby Lobby and cabinet manufacturer Conestoga Wood.

The Court's analysis of their claims proceeded in four steps, resulting in a 5–4 decision. First came the threshold question of whether for-profit corporations count as "persons" capable of exercising religion under RFRA. Relying on the near-universal acceptance that RFRA's use of the word "persons" includes nonprofit corporations, the Court determined that "persons" should equally encompass for-profit corporations.[20] It concluded that – like religious nonprofits – closely held, secular for-profit corporations can equally "further[] individual religious freedom" of individuals united in the enterprise.[21]

As RFRA requires, the Court then evaluated whether: (1) the mandate imposed a substantial burden on the objecting corporations' free exercise rights; (2) the

---

[14] Group Health Plans and Health Insurance Issuers Relating to Coverage of Preventive Services under Patient Protection and Affordable Care Act, 78 Fed. Reg. 8456, 8461 (February 6, 2013).
[15] Id. at 8462.
[16] Id.
[17] Id.
[18] Id.
[19] Id. at 8463.
[20] *Burwell v. Hobby Lobby Stores, Inc.*, 134 S. Ct. 2751 at 2769 (2014).
[21] Id.

government had a compelling interest in the mandate; and (3) the government had less restrictive alternatives. The majority determined that the objecting corporations were indeed substantially burdened by the mandate, because they faced a choice between paying potentially large tax penalties for noncompliance and violating their religious beliefs.[22] It was irrelevant that they were not required themselves to buy or use contraceptives, as they sincerely objected to being complicit in helping pay, arrange, or contract for those services. The dissent, in contrast, concluded that the "connection between the [owners'] religious objections and the contraceptive coverage requirement is too attenuated to rank as substantial."[23]

The Court assumed, without deciding, that the governmental interest in guaranteeing cost-free access to contraceptives was compelling.[24] It then assessed whether the mandate was the least restrictive means of furthering that interest and concluded that the mandate did not satisfy RFRA's "exceptionally demanding" least-restrictive-means standard.[25] Because the government had accommodated nonprofit religious organizations, the Court determined that it could equally accommodate for-profit corporations.[26] But the Court refused to confirm that the accommodation – which at that time required notification to the employer's insurer – "complie[d] with RFRA for purposes of all religious claims" – leaving the door open to contemporaneous litigation by nonprofits against the accommodation itself.[27]

In July 2015, in response to the Supreme Court's *Hobby Lobby* decision, HHS issued a new version of the rule that allowed certain closely held for-profit entities the same accommodation available to eligible religious nonprofits.[28] The new rule also provided an alternative accommodation mechanism, permitting employers to notify HHS in writing of their religious objection, rather than deliver a specific form to their insurance issuer or third-party administrator.[29]

Despite this expansion, several employers continued to object, claiming that the required process under the accommodation still substantially burdened religious exercise in two ways. First, they argued, submitting notice directly to the insurance issuer, third-party administrator, or even the government simply triggers another party to engage in the objectionable activity without removing the employer entirely from the chain of complicity.[30] Second, they claimed that their religious convictions forbid them from contracting with companies that will provide free coverage for

---

[22] Id. at 2775–7.
[23] Id. at 2799 (Ginsburg, J., dissenting).
[24] Hobby Lobby, 134 S. Ct. at 2780.
[25] Id. (citing *City of Boerne v. Flores*, 521 U.S. 507, 532 (1997)).
[26] Id. at 2782.
[27] Id.
[28] Group Health Plans and Health Insurance Issuers Relating to Coverage of Preventive Services under Patient Protection and Affordable Care Act, 80 Fed. Reg. 41323–4 (July 14, 2015).
[29] Id. at 41323.
[30] See, e.g., *Priests for Life v. U.S. Dep't of Health & Human Servs.*, 772 F.3d 229, 237 (D.C. Cir. 2014).

the contraceptive services, so it is problematic for them to retain relationships with these insurance companies and third-party administrators at all.[31] Thus, the objecting employers sought an outright exemption, rather than an accommodation, arguing that the government has ample alternative means to provide access to cost-free contraceptives to their employees without burdening employers' religious exercise.

In response to these claims, eight out of nine appellate courts to hear the cases concluded that no substantial burden on religious exercise existed under the accommodation.[32] The accommodation, they decided, excused objecting employers from any involvement; private insurers' compliance with their own legal obligations to offer contraceptive coverage did not substantially burden the plaintiffs.[33]

In its October 2015 term, the Supreme Court took up a number of these accommodation cases, consolidated under the name *Zubik v. Burwell*.[34] After oral argument, however, having taken the unusual step of proposing a possible alternative process for accommodation from the mandate and requesting supplemental briefing on that alternative, the Court issued a unanimous per curiam opinion remanding the cases to the appellate courts with the instruction to afford the parties "an opportunity to arrive at an approach going forward that accommodates petitioners' religious exercise while at the same time ensuring that women covered by petitioners' health plans 'receive full and equal health coverage, including contraceptive coverage.'"[35] The Court took great pains to provide a list of matters it was explicitly *not* deciding, such as "whether petitioners' religious exercise has been substantially burdened, whether the Government has a compelling interest, or whether the current regulations are the least restrictive means of serving that interest."[36] While many attributed the decision not to rule on the merits to the fact that the Court had an even number of justices following the death of Justice Scalia, there is significant dispute as to what the Court did or did not signal through its opinion.[37]

---

[31] See, e.g., *Univ. of Notre Dame v. Burwell*, 743 F.3d 547, 557 (7th Cir. 2014).

[32] *Eternal Word Television Network, Inc. v. Sec'y of U.S. Dep't of Health & Human Servs.*, 756 F.3d 1339 (11th Cir. Feb. 18, 2016); *Catholic Health Care Sys. v. Burwell*, 796 F.3d 207 (2d Cir. 2015); *Little Sisters of the Poor Home for the Aged, Denver, Colo. v. Burwell*, 794 F.3d 1151 (10th Cir. 2015); *E. Texas Baptist Univ. v. Burwell*, 793 F.3d 449 (5th Cir. 2015); *Geneva Coll. v. Sec'y U.S. Dep't of Health & Human Servs.*, 778 F.3d 422, 427 (3d Cir. 2015); *Priests for Life v. U.S. Dep't of Health & Human Servs.*, 772 F.3d 229, 2523 (D.C. Cir. 2014); *Mich. Catholic Conference & Catholic Family Servs. v. Burwell*, 755 F.3d 372, 389 (6th Cir. 2014); *Univ. of Notre Dame v. Burwell*, 743 F.3d 547 (7th Cir. 2014). Only the Eighth Circuit decided a substantial burden exists. *Sharpe Holdings, Inc. v. U.S. Dep't of Health & Human Servs.*, 801 F.3d 927 (8th Cir. 2015).

[33] See, e.g., *Wheaton College v. Burwell*, 791 F.3d 792, 795 (2015).

[34] 136 S. Ct. 444 (2015).

[35] *Zubik v. Burwell*, 136 S. Ct. 1557 (2016) (per curiam).

[36] Id.

[37] For a variety of views, see ScotusBlog, *Zubik v. Burwell Symposium*, available at www.scotusblog.com/category/zubik-v-burwell-symposium/ [https://perma.cc/9CUN-9EDH] (last visited May 26, 2016).

As this volume goes to press, much is in flux. Months after the remand, the Obama administration announced that the parties had found no ground for compromise and it had concluded that no feasible approach would satisfy the religious objectors.[38] The accommodation, therefore, would not be altered further unless by court order. The *Zubik* line of cases – and the issues of substantial burden, compelling interest, and potential alternatives – thus may return to the Court shortly in the same, or similar, posture. With Justice Neil Gorsuch now sitting on the Court, the prior deadlock is likely to be broken. Alternatively, through the notice and comment process, the Trump administration may propose a new women's preventive services rule that either expands the exemption to any religious objector or altogether removes the requirement to cover some, or all, contraceptives; President Trump signed an executive order on May 4, 2017, indicating an intention to make it easier for objectors to avoid covering women's preventive care, including contraceptives, in employee health plans. Finally, federal law related to health care may change. With political power shifting to the Republican Party in 2017, now controlling both Congress and the Presidency, GOP promises to repeal the Affordable Care Act have become plausible. If the underlying employer mandate were repealed, litigation over the contraceptives mandate would be moot; objecting employers could simply avoid providing any insurance coverage at all.

Irrespective of the path that the contraceptive challenges ultimately take, important questions addressed in the chapters that follow remain open, including how far the government must and should go to accommodate religious believers in the health care sphere and beyond. The volume begins with several chapters that frame the issues and explain what is and was at stake in the contraceptive litigation, comprising Part I of the book, Testing the Scope of Legal Protections for Religion in the Health Care Context.

Douglas Laycock, a leading scholarly voice in religious freedom debates, argues that much of the scholarly and popular discussion of *Hobby Lobby* and *Zubik* is misguided. He defends *Hobby Lobby* as a narrow decision but is skeptical of the claim for accommodation in *Zubik*. His chapter, *Religious Liberty, Health Care, and the Culture Wars*, tries to divide the world between "real issues" – for example, religious pharmacists who face demands for emergency contraception and religious schools that seek to terminate the employment of individuals who use in vitro fertilization – and "hypothetical issues" envisioned by Justice Ginsburg in dissent in *Hobby Lobby* and by others that he claims "have never happened, and are not likely to happen."

---

[38] U.S. Dep't of Labor, Employee Benefits Security Administration, *FAQs About Affordable Care Act Implementation* Part 36 (January 9, 2017), available at www.dol.gov/sites/default/files/ebsa/about-ebsa/our-activities/resource-center/faqs/aca-part-36.pdf.

In this category, he argues, are employers refusing to insure blood transfusions, antidepressants, vaccinations, and the like. Along the way he discusses duties to refer on the part of religious physicians and issues relating to religious hospital concentration in a market.

In *From* Smith *to* Hobby Lobby: *The Transformation of the Religious Freedom Restoration Act*, Diane L. Moore and Eric M. Stephen next explore the social and political shifts that took place between RFRA's passage in 1993 and the Hobby Lobby ruling in 2014. Adopting a cultural studies lens, they argue that RFRA's ambiguity on what constitutes a compelling interest was not accidental but instead meant "to adapt and respond to ever changing understandings of rights and justice . . . allow[ing] for a multiplicity of interpretations to be produced whenever there exist differences of opinion over what should be considered socially just." Through a close examination of the alliances and litigation strategy giving rise to *Hobby Lobby*, they argue that the case and its progeny may best be understood as *both* a legal attempt to countenance developing theological understandings of complicity that have gained prominence due to several faith communities' rising anxieties over evolving social norms, *and also* a politically motivated attempt to mobilize those theological concerns in the interest of party politics and neoliberal economics.

Lawyers on opposing sides of the *Hobby Lobby* case and follow-on litigation square off in the chapters that follow. First, Adèle Keim, Counsel for the Becket Fund for Religious Liberty, argues that religious diversity is good for American health care and that the "background legal principles that have allowed religiously-motivated health care to serve so many people so effectively for so long" are worth defending. Her chapter, *The HHS Mandate Litigation and Religious Health Care Providers*, focuses on the third-party harm arguments raised by the government and others in the litigation. She discusses shifts in the argument from *Hobby Lobby* to *Zubik* and ultimately maintains that these arguments fail "to account for the harm to patients and the broader community that would be caused by pushing religiously-motivated providers out of U.S. health care through inadequate respect for their religious conscience."

On the other side is Gregory M. Lipper, previously Senior Litigation Counsel at Americans United for Separation of Church and State. Lipper's chapter, *Not Your Father's Religious Exemptions: The Contraceptive-Coverage Litigation and the Rights of Others*, seeks to distinguish "garden-variety religious exemptions," such as the right to grow a beard or use certain burial rituals, which do not impose harms on third parties, from those required by *Hobby Lobby*, which he characterizes as providing "a free-exercise right to restrict the benefits and thus to control behavior of others – requiring exemptions that deprive tens of thousands of women of important medical coverage." He also argues that there were reasons to doubt the sincerity of the religious claims in the case, that the case and its progeny harm both women and religion, and that the (non)decision in *Zubik* is particularly troubling.

Finally, in *Recent Applications of the Supreme Court's Hands-Off Approach to Religious Doctrine: From* Hosanna-Tabor *and* Holt *to* Hobby Lobby *and* Zubik, Samuel J. Levine argues that the Supreme Court's hands-off approach to religious liberty claims explains the somewhat unsatisfying and often contentious nature of the Supreme Court's religious liberty cases, including challenges to the contraceptive mandate. While the religious liberty doctrine under the First Amendment and RFRA requires consideration of religious claims, the Court's hands-off approach simultaneously precludes judges from evaluating and deciding questions of religion. Levine shows that, in articulating hands-off approaches in recent cases, the Court has failed to clarify conceptual issues and to resolve practical problems and thus may have rendered religious liberty tests unworkable for the government and lower courts.

As this part shows, courts, policy makers, and members of the public continue to struggle over fundamental questions that implicate health – such as whether and to what extent participation in the health care or health insurance system makes one complicit in others' health care decisions; what it means for a law to substantially burden religious exercise; when and how religious beliefs can be accommodated so as to avoid harming third parties; and what these cases tell us about our employer-based health insurance system. The contraceptive litigation, however, is just the latest and most high-profile manifestation of the vast and deep intersection between law, religion, and health in the United States, which this book explores.

The remainder of the book is divided into parts relating to various institutions in the health care system (e.g., insurance, hospitals) and various areas of health law (e.g., reproductive rights and technologies, public health). Part II of the book, Law, Religion, and Health Care Institutions, is introduced with an essay by Christine Mitchell.

In Part II's first chapter, *A Corporation's Exercise of Religion: A Practitioner's Experience*, Sister Melanie Di Pietro seeks to press back against attempts to dilute the religious character of the religious nonprofit health care corporation. Using examples from a published case study of the SSM Health Care System, Di Pietro argues that a Roman Catholic religious health care corporation exercises religion because Catholic theology requires that "worship and sacrament are inseparable from service" and "is implemented in the structure and operation of the corporation whose theology of mission is openness to 'work in harmony with others' to serve persons wherever they are encountered." She argues for the importance of a legal framework that is sufficiently inclusive of the beliefs of adherents of those religious traditions that operate health care corporations.

In his chapter, *The Natural Person as the Limiting Principle for Conscience: Can a Corporation Have a Conscience If It Doesn't Have an Intellect and Will?*, Ryan Meade urges precision in the use of conscience-speak in contemporary discussions over corporate religious exemptions for health care institutions and employers. He distinguishes between conscience, which represents an act or judgment, and religion, which may inform but is not necessary to conscience. Through recourse to philosophy of the mind and linguistic analysis, Meade argues that conscience requires a mind and a capacity to reason that humans have, but corporations ultimately lack.

Next, in *Contracting Religion*, Elizabeth Sepper highlights the growing trend of health care institutions (and their providers) being bound by Catholic restrictions on care, even when they are not truly Catholic hospitals. This occurs through both vertical and horizontal integration of health care systems, and can even extend beyond periods of direct religious ownership, for example through subsequent sales contracts that demand compliance even from nonreligious purchasers. Sepper notes the ways in which this development challenges the traditional perception of religious institutions and their treatment by the law, and points out the serious concerns raised by these contractually imposed limitations on care, most critically, restricted patient access.

The last chapter in Part II, *Mission Integrity Matters: Balancing Catholic Health Care Values and Public Mandates* by David M. Craig, proposes a standard of organizational religious mission integrity as an alternative to *Hobby Lobby*'s adoption of an individual religious belief standard. This alternative standard focuses on the degree to which an organization's stated religious mission and values have been integrated into its operations and, Craig argues, more accurately reflects the cooperative practice of individuals' beliefs in organizational exercise of religion. He then applies his approach to *Hobby Lobby* and *Zubik*, as well as to Internal Revenue Service mandates that require nonprofit hospitals to provide uncompensated care.

Part III of the book, Law, Religion, and Health Insurance, is introduced through an essay by Marc A. Rodwin. Rachel E. Sachs's chapter in this part, *Religious Exemptions to the Individual Mandate: Health Care Sharing Ministries and the Affordable Care Act*, illuminates the role health care sharing ministries play in the health care system. As Sachs shows, these Christian ministries set membership, care coverage, and reimbursement in accordance with religious values and distinguish themselves from insurance companies. Sachs contends that health care sharing ministries both share and resist ideals of health insurance embodied in the ACA. Their preference for personal responsibility over health promotion may, she suggests, lead to their instability or permit their success – offering a natural experiment for empiricists interested in insurance theory.

Next, Holly Fernandez Lynch and Gregory Curfman utilize the *Hobby Lobby* case as one more reason to eliminate the employer-based health care system that has become so entrenched in the United States. In their chapter, *Bosses in the Bedroom: Religious Employers and the Future of Employer-Sponsored Health Care*, they examine the proper scope of religion in the workplace as expressed by employers, as well as the implications for employees' health care. They argue that RFRA is "capable of facilitating an appropriate balance between the religious beliefs of employers and their employees[,]" and that "employers with a conscience" ought to be generally encouraged. However, employers ought to have no place in their employees' bedrooms, and the system that has let them in ought to be changed.

Holly Fernandez Lynch also introduces Part IV, Professional Responsibilities, Religion, and Health Care. In its first chapter, *Religious Outliers: Professional Knowledge Communities, Individual Conscience Claims, and the Availability of Professional Services to the Public*, Claudia E. Haupt draws a novel distinction between professionals who deviate from the profession's mainstream beliefs while staying within the profession's knowledge community – what she calls "internal outliers" – and those who deviate from the profession for exogenous, often religious, reasons – what she calls "external outliers." This distinction allows us to better understand why some types of professional refusals of care may be acceptable and even in line with what patients could reasonably expect, whereas religion-based refusals by external outliers truly deviate from professional duties and the responsibility to provide professional services to the public.

Nadia N. Sawicki argues in her chapter, *A Common Law Duty to Disclose Conscience-Based Limitations on Medical Practice*, that even when health care providers and institutions are protected from having to *perform* medical services to which they have religious or otherwise conscientious objections, they ought to be required to at least *disclose* those objections and the limitations on care they will be willing to provide as part of the informed consent process. She suggests that no legal changes may be needed to impose such a duty, as it may already be contemplated by existing common law duties to disclose provider characteristics and interests that might be material to a patient's decision. In the alternative, Sawicki indicates that a statutory duty on health care institutions to make sure that patients are aware of conscience-based limitations on care provided by the institution, or by particular providers within the institution, would be welcome.

Next, Part V, The Impact of Religious Objections on the Health and Health Care of Others, is introduced by an essay by Richard H. Fallon Jr. In Part V's first chapter, *Conscientious Objection, Complicity, and Accommodation*, Amy J. Sepinwall takes up the question of how the religious liberty doctrine should approach claims of complicity – that is, that the law requires the involvement of a religious adherent in the wrongdoing of third parties. She first argues that claims of complicity should be treated with great deference. She then contends that whether these claims should yield an exemption should depend, in significant part, on whether third parties would incur an undue burden as a result. Current doctrine, Sepinwall says, inadequately takes third-party interests into account. She articulates a test that ensures courts consider third-party concerns and requires balancing burdens on religious adherents against burdens on both the government and affected third parties.

Next, Nelson Tebbe, Micah Schwartzman, and Richard Schragger defend the rule that governments should avoid harm to third parties when granting religious accommodations in their chapter, *How Much May Religious Accommodations Burden Others?* Critics commonly object that third-party harms cannot always render religious accommodations unconstitutional, because many permissible exemptions have negative effects on others. Tebbe, Schwartzman, and Schragger argue that the third-party harm principle does have limits. Where the interference with religious freedom is significant and the burden on others is slight, accommodations ought to be upheld. They contend that Title VII of the Civil Rights Act offers a standard for balancing religious accommodation and third-party interests. Title VII accommodates religious employees, but it bars accommodations that result in an "undue hardship" on employers or other employees. The authors suggest that the undue hardship standard might prove helpful outside the employment context in conflicts involving reproductive health care, insurance coverage for transplants, and LGBT equality.

Mary Anne Case's chapter, "*A Patchwork Array of Theocratic Fiefdoms?" RFRA Claims Against the ACA's Contraception Mandate as Examples of the New Feudalism*, argues that the Affordable Care Act is a paradigmatic example of what she calls the "new feudalism," in which "an individual's legal rights, including rights of access to goods and services in the health care context, may turn out to be increasingly, rather than decreasingly, a function of his hierarchical attachments, such as those to a state, employer, church, or family." She argues the way this new feudalism becomes entrenched through the Supreme Court's decisions in *Hobby Lobby* and *Zubik*. She also contends that many of the cases applying RFRA in the health care setting instantiate not only the new feudalism, but indeed the "new patriarchy."

By contrast, Robin Fretwell Wilson's chapter, *Unpacking the Relationship Between Conscience and Access*, seeks to find common ground between those seeking to protect conscience in health care and those worried about access to health care. Focusing in particular on conscience clauses, she argues that it is "possible to balance conscience and access in at least some cases by using common-sense devices, such as notice, parity rules, protections conditioned on not causing harm, and thickened duties to transfer pregnant women in distress." At the same time, defenders of conscientious objection in health care must recognize that some forms of protection – most notably federal efforts to insulate conscience against encroachment by state authorities with "super conscience clauses" – will hobble attempts to accommodate access concerns and thus should be disfavored.

Part VI focuses on a particular case study, Religious Beliefs and the Health of the LGBT Community, contextualized by an introductory essay by Noa Ben-Asher. In her chapter in this part, *Religious Convictions About Homosexuality and the Training of Counseling Professionals: How Should We Treat Religious-Based Opposition to Counseling About Same-Sex Relationships?*, Susan J. Stabile explores the question of whether and how counseling education should accommodate students' religious objections to counseling gays. Looking to court decisions and shifts in the counseling profession's views of homosexuality, she explains that existing ethical norms, requiring affirmation of sexual identity, stand in tension with some students' religious beliefs. Faced with such conflicts, Stabile argues, we should seek compromise. To protect the interests of patients while accommodating religion, she suggests that objecting counseling students might earn limited certification, allowing them to practice only in settings where they would not inflict harm, and be required to disclose any limitations on the counseling relationship.

Reclaiming Biopolitics: Religion and Psychiatry in the Sexual Orientation Change Therapy Cases and the Establishment Clause Defense comes at the issue from a very different direction. In this chapter, Craig J. Konnoth explores the rise of psychotherapy as a professional, scientific, and secular discipline and the subsequent backlash from Christian evangelical activists, who combined explicitly religious aims with psychotherapeutic methods. Because sexual orientation change efforts (SOCE) originate in fundamentalist Christian counseling, Konnoth contends, SOCE should be understood as a form of religious ministry. With this understanding, the denial of state licenses – a government resource – to psychotherapists who seek to practice SOCE vindicates Establishment Clause concerns and avoids government endorsement of religious practice. Konnoth concludes that professional psychiatry should clearly define appropriate practice to ensure patients' goals are not abridged.

Robert D. Truog introduces Part VII, Accounting for Patients' Religious Beliefs. In the first chapter in this part, *Brain Death Rejected: Expanding Legal Duties to Accommodate Religious Objections*, Thaddeus Mason Pope argues that states ought to accommodate religious objections to the determination of death by neurological criteria. Typically, determination of brain death results in cessation of any further treatment, as the patient is now deemed to be a corpse. However, the law in four states currently requires at least some accommodation of families who have religious objection to withdrawal of care following diagnosis of brain death, allowing either some short-term continuation of care or indefinite continuation. Pope recognizes that states have a significant interest in a uniform standard for the determination of death, but proposes that limited accommodation of alternative views is appropriate because accommodation has already worked in several states, relatively few cases of such an objection are likely to arise, and reasonable disagreement exists about the value-laden concept of brain death.

In *Accommodating Miracles: Medical Futility and Religious Free Exercise*, Teneille R. Brown explores the tension created by patients' families demanding the continuation of life-support efforts that clinicians have deemed medically futile in order to allow families to pray for a miracle or other religious intervention. Brown describes medical futility statutes that in several states permit futile care to be withheld or withdrawn, and assesses the likelihood that these statutes could survive challenges by religious believers under state Religious Freedom Restoration Acts. She concludes that they could, as a legal matter, but also suggests that when patients and their families seek religious miracles at the end of life, a variety of spiritual counseling and psychological support is needed – and preferable to continuing futile care indefinitely.

In their chapter, *Putting the Insanity Defense on Trial: Understanding Criminality in the Context of Religion and Mental Illness*, Abbas Rattani and Jemel Amin Derbali address the challenging question of whether courts are equipped to handle questions of mental illness and culpability in instances where mentally ill defendants may use religious rhetoric as defense and when pathology blurs culpability. They explore how objective versus subjective views of wrongfulness in the application of the insanity defense affect its application to cases of religious delusion, and they grapple with the idea that delusion and mental illness may make people susceptible to religious extremism – thus obscuring analysis of their mental state.

In the final chapter in this part, *Religion as a Controlling Interference in Medical Decision-Making by Minors*, Jonathan F. Will probes the circumstances under which minors ought to be permitted to refuse medical intervention on the basis of religious beliefs. He notes that parents cannot refuse life-saving medical interventions for their children, but in some cases, minors can overcome the presumption of their incompetence to make medical decisions for themselves. In these situations, Will argues, it is essential to make sure that a minor's refusal of treatment is truly autonomous, rather than the result of inappropriate controlling influence by others. There is no clear-cut test for such a determination, but Will suggests that more voluntariness and more evidence ought to be required as the risks of refusing treatment become greater to the minor.

Part VIII focuses on Religion and Reproductive Health Care, and is introduced through an essay by Mindy Jane Roseman. *Regulating Reasons: Governmental Regulation of Private Deliberation in Reproductive Decision-Making*, by B. Jessie Hill, kicks off this part, addressing the permissible role of government in considering, protecting, or regulating individual reasons for various health-related decisions. She contrasts the general protection of religious reasons under federal and state Religious Freedom Restoration Acts against the possible interference with constitutionally protected private decisions in the context of abortion and parental authority. The chapter concludes that while "the government may seek to force deliberation, to share information, and possibly even to influence the decision-making process in some ways, it cannot cross the line from influence to coercion."

Thus, the right to privacy in certain types of health-related decision making must be understood to have privileged constitutional status, such that it should override individual religious claims in most circumstances.

In his chapter, *Religion and Reproductive Technology*, I. Glenn Cohen discusses four distinct areas in which religion intersects with reproductive technologies, and their legal implications. First, he addresses religiously motivated denials of reproductive technology services to same-sex couples and single individuals, assessing the permissibility of such denials under laws protecting freedom of religion and laws protecting against discrimination. Next, Cohen explains the role of Christian groups pressing for the "adoption" of embryos leftover following in vitro fertilization procedures, including laws to facilitate the practice, and the relationship of such pressure to the "personhood movement." The religious push to recognize embryos as "persons" with full legal status is the third area Cohen addresses, with significant implications not only for abortion but also access to various reproductive technologies. Finally, Cohen concludes with a discussion of religious influences on legal disputes over leftover embryos, in particular the notion that such disputes should be adjudicated based on the "best interests of the child," which would presumptively favor the parent seeking implantation and birth.

In Dov Fox's chapter, *Religion and the Unborn Under the First Amendment*, he argues that laws protecting embryos and fetuses can survive the claim that they violate the Establishment Clause even if they coincide with religious reasons. Fox articulates three types of religious reasons that the government may not endorse – compulsions of faith, promises of salvation, and obedience to God – but argues that laws protecting the unborn can be justified by broader visions about what makes society good. Given that laws often involve value judgments, laws protecting the unborn may be legitimate under the Establishment Clause, although they may nonetheless face other types of constitutional problems.

The final part of this book, Religion, Law, and Public Health, is introduced by Ahmed Ragab. Michele Goodwin's chapter, *Race, Religion, and Masculinity: The HIV Double Bind*, examines the scourge of HIV/AIDS in the African American community and illuminates the intersections of race, religion, and homosexuality. Goodwin argues that a growing number of Black Americans face a double bind, caught between the demands of their health and the strictures of their religion. Because of taboos within the Black church, congregants with HIV/AIDS may face rejection by the institution central to their communities. In particular, men who have sex with men stand the risk of being alienated and ostracized and accordingly may attempt to conform to ideals of masculinity. The double bind for these Black Americans raises questions about how to reconcile identity as HIV positive or homosexual with membership in the Black church.

In *The Intersection of Law, Religion, and Infectious Disease in the Handling and Disposition of Human Remains*, Aileen Maria Marty, Elena Maria Marty-Nelson, and Eloisa C. Rodriguez-Dod argue that outbreaks of highly infectious diseases expose the urgent need for laws governing the disposal of human remains that safeguard public health, show respect for survivors, and manifest sensitivity to religious rites. Because scientific approaches to burial often conflict with religious customs, governments may exacerbate a public health crisis if they are inadequately sensitive to such customs. In the United States, the authors contend, the legal regime appears unprepared to both protect the public from infection and respect religious practices related to burial. They accordingly urge the adoption of policies for culturally and religiously appropriate burials and the education of and outreach to religious communities in preparation for future outbreaks.

Finally, Jay Wexler's chapter, *When Religion Pollutes: How Should Law Respond When Religious Practice Threatens Public Health?*, takes up the issue of religious practices that pollute the environment and threaten public health. Wexler focuses on two case studies: the ritual sprinkling of liquid mercury in the homes of practitioners of Caribbean religions in U.S. cities; and old-order Amish farming and sanitary practices that produce agricultural runoff pollution and contaminate water in the mid-Atlantic states. In confronting such problems, the government faces both constitutional and prudential constraints. In lieu of a top-down, command-and-control regulatory approach, Wexler argues, the government should implement strategies focused on collaboration, education, and outreach to foster religious group buy-in to environmental goals.

CONCLUSION

The chapters in this book describe, analyze, and evaluate the myriad new and enduring challenges at the intersection of law, health, and religion. They intervene in areas of legal change and medical advances. The fundamental issues are the same as they have always been – balancing religious liberty against equality, health needs against spiritual commitments, oversight against autonomy, collective against individual. But tensions today are undoubtedly high.

Collectively, these chapters offer insights on where religion and health law intermingle, what the legal doctrine gets right and wrong, how public policy might respond, and what future unanticipated conflicts may emerge. With health care reform up for grabs again and religious freedom law in flux, the chapters here chart a course toward where we should be going and provide guideposts for evaluating current and future proposals for reform. Whatever happens in the near future, it is very clear that the intersection of religion and health care will vex the law for years to come.

PART I

Testing the Scope of Legal Protections for Religion in the Health Care Context

1

Religious Liberty, Health Care, and the Culture Wars

Douglas Laycock

The Supreme Court's decision in *Hobby Lobby* inspired a large and vehement reaction, including the conference on which this volume is based. Most of the reaction has been overreaction. Neither *Hobby Lobby*, nor religious liberty more generally, is a significant threat to American health care.

Hobby Lobby and its follow-on case, *Zubik v. Burwell*, are summarized in the Introduction to this volume. After briefly highlighting some of the key take-aways from those two cases, I will turn to other alleged conflicts between religious liberty and health care. Some of these are real; others are imaginary, found only in parades of horribles from opponents of religious liberty. Finally, I consider appropriate limits on religious exemptions in the health care context.

1. CONTRACEPTION

I begin by summarizing three points that I have elaborated elsewhere. First, *Hobby Lobby* arose because, for the first time in American history, government required adherents of the nation's largest religions to violate core religious teachings.[1] Also for the first time, government refused exemption to conscientious objectors who believed they were being asked to cooperate in killing. The *Hobby Lobby* plaintiffs believe that the drugs and devices at issue sometimes prevent the implantation in the uterus of a fertilized egg, thus killing what they believe to be a very young human being. Their views may appear idiosyncratic; most Americans would not characterize such a very early termination of a pregnancy as a killing, or even as an

---

[1] The points in this paragraph are developed and documented in Douglas Laycock, "The Campaign Against Religious Liberty", in *The Rise of Corporate Religious Liberty* 231, 232–4 (Micah Schwartzman et al. eds., 2015).

I am grateful to Douglas Rogers and Eric Backman for research assistance. All websites cited were last visited on February 22, 2017.

abortion. But the owners of Hobby Lobby believed that they were being asked to pay for killings, and such an extraordinary burden on conscience is entitled to respect. It was these unprecedented demands on what are now our largest religious minorities that escalated the conflict between religion and government and provoked the litigation.

Second, there was ample precedent for exempting businesses.[2] Statutory exemptions from performing or assisting with abortions, or with assisted suicides, protect incorporated for-profit hospitals, hospices, and medical practices. Exemptions for kosher slaughter protect incorporated for-profit slaughterhouses. Both sides in the House of Representatives understood the language of the Religious Freedom Restoration Act to protect incorporated for-profit businesses; this was common ground in a 1999 debate on whether to exclude most civil-rights claims from a bill with language substantially identical to that of RFRA.

Third, the decision in *Hobby Lobby* is narrow.[3] The case was decided on the ground that the government could provide free emergency contraception without making the employer pay for it, contract for it, or arrange for it. The employer's health insurer, or its third-party administrator in self-insured plans, must provide free contraception with segregated funds and segregated communications to insured employees. The insurers are expected to recoup their costs through the savings from fewer pregnancies; the third-party administrators are passing the costs on to the government.[4]

This solution, which the government had developed for religious nonprofits, could also be made available to for-profits. The Court said that, if this were done, the impact on employees would be "precisely zero."[5] The government has now extended this solution to closely held for-profit businesses. Numbers for insured plans are not available, but the government represented in 2016 that it was paying for free contraception for 624,000 employees of conscientious objectors with self-insured plans, that the fraction of these employees receiving free contraception matched what would be actuarially expected in the general population, and that this less restrictive solution was working smoothly.[6]

Hobby Lobby did *not* say that whenever government exempts nonprofit religious organizations, it must also exempt for-profit businesses. Rather, it said that when government has available a solution that fully serves its interest and imposes no costs on employees, it must use that solution, rather than burden religious liberty. And

---

[2] The points in this paragraph are developed and documented id. at 234–8.
[3] The points in this paragraph are developed and documented id. at 238–42.
[4] I analyze this solution in greater detail in Douglas Laycock, *Religious Liberty and the Culture Wars*, 2014 U. Ill. L. Rev. 839, 851–63.
[5] *Burwell v. Hobby Lobby Stores, Inc*, 134 S. Ct. 2751, 2760 (2014).
[6] Supplemental Reply Brief for Respondents at 4, 10 n.8, *Zubik v. Burwell*, 136 S. Ct. 1557 (2016).

Hobby Lobby did *not* say that employers get a RFRA exemption even though some employees must do without benefits promised to them by the law. That would be a different case and, at least in *Hobby Lobby*, Justice Kennedy pretty clearly signaled opposition to that.

Some religious nonprofits object that this solution is inadequate. They demand not just an exemption for themselves, but also a right to prevent their secular insurers from providing contraception. It is no surprise that after *Hobby Lobby* and before *Zubik*, eight of nine courts of appeals to consider the remaining objections to this accommodation upheld the regulations.

But in *Zubik*, the Supreme Court appears to have been deadlocked. It issued a remand order urging the parties to settle.[7] The Court claimed that "[b]oth petitioners and the Government now assert," in supplemental briefing, that it is "feasible" to provide free contraception through petitioners' insurance companies without requiring any notice from petitioners. The Court acknowledged that "there may still be areas of disagreement between the parties on issues of implementation," but claimed that the importance of these disagreements was unclear. The parties "should be afforded an opportunity to arrive at an approach going forward that accommodates petitioners' religious exercise while at the same time ensuring that women covered by petitioners' health plans 'receive full and equal health coverage, including contraceptive coverage.'"[8] The Court explicitly disclaimed any view on the merits of any issue in the case; Justices Sotomayor and Ginsburg, concurring, emphasized this disclaimer while clearly signaling their own view of the merits.

The Court's order appeared to be an attempt to buy time, pending the confirmation of a ninth Justice. The disagreements "on issues of implementation" were deal breakers – demands from the religious organizations that the government said are entirely unworkable and, in some ways, illegal.[9] Unless one or both sides cave in negotiations, these cases will come back to the Court unchanged. Both sides held firm during the Obama Administration, but the Trump Administration's position remains to be seen. It threatens to repeal the Affordable Care Act, which would end this dispute; it might also repeal the contraceptive mandate or settle the *Zubik* cases on the religious organizations' terms.

The rather desperate order in *Zubik* may imply that the Court was divided four–four on the merits; it at least implies that one or more Justices hoped to avoid deciding. This apparent deadlock surprised me. A decision for the religious nonprofits here would cause the decision in *Hobby Lobby* to come unglued. And the religious

---

[7] *Zubik v. Burwell*, 136 S. Ct. 1557 (2016).
[8] *Id.* at 1560.
[9] Compare Supplemental Brief for Petitioners at 6 (demanding separate insurance policies and separate enrollment processes), with Supplemental Reply Brief for the Respondents 3–6, 8–9 (rejecting these demands as illegal and an obstacle to women actually receiving contraception).

organizations' claim of burden is much weaker than other claims of burden that the Court has rejected.[10]

The employers in *Hobby Lobby* were required to pay, contract, and arrange for drugs and devices that they believed to be abortifacients. The employers in *Zubik* do not have to pay, contract, or arrange for anything that they object to. That seems to be a fundamental difference. But it is not a difference that changed the bottom line for the interest groups lined up on each side in both cases, and perhaps it did not matter to any Justice.

If the ultimate decision in *Zubik* leaves women without seamless access to free contraception, then parts of the criticism the Court received after *Hobby Lobby* will finally have some basis in fact. But we are not there yet, and I still think that those who would take us there do not have the votes on the Supreme Court. Justice Kennedy still seems unlikely in the end to vote for an outcome that deprives women of free contraception.

If President Trump gets a second appointment to the Court, then in all likelihood, Kennedy would no longer be the swing vote, and decisions depriving employees of benefits would become much more likely. Or Trump and his allies could repeal the right to free contraception by legislation or regulation, for reasons that may have nothing to do with religious liberty, and the issue would never come back to the Court. Religious liberty subject to the compelling-interest test is not a threat to American health care. Donald Trump may be.

2. OTHER HEALTH CARE ISSUES, REAL AND IMAGINED

A. *Real Issues*

Another health care issue that has actually been litigated is emergency contraception at pharmacies. But as of 2012, forty-two states had imposed no requirements with respect to this issue, and six had imposed rules short of requiring that all pharmacies stock and supply emergency contraception.[11]

When forty-eight states have, at most, a less restrictive rule, and forty-two states impose no requirement at all, it is hard to imagine a compelling government interest for the two outliers.[12] The problem is not that none of the other states care about

---

[10] See Brief of Baptist Joint Committee for Religious Liberty as Amicus Curiae in Support of Respondents at 8–11, 21–6, Zubik.

[11] *Stormans, Inc. v. Selecky*, 854 F. Supp. 2d 925, 935 (W.D. Wash. 2012), rev'd on other grounds sub nom. *Stormans, Inc. v. Wiesman*, 794 F.3d 1064 (9th Cir. 2015), cert. denied, 136 S. Ct. 2433 (2016).

[12] See *Holt v. Hobbs*, 135 S. Ct. 853, 866 (2015) (relying on practice of "vast majority of States and the Federal Government" permitting prisoners to grow beards, and holding that defendant prison system had failed to show why it could not do the same).

providing the full range of pharmaceuticals to their citizens; it is that none of them find it necessary to burden constitutional rights to achieve that goal. What is it that makes such means necessary in the outlier states?

Religious pharmacists in Illinois won an exemption under the Illinois Conscience Act.[13] But the Washington rule was upheld against a constitutional challenge in the Ninth Circuit, and the Supreme Court denied certiorari.[14] The underlying issue is of obvious importance, but the state claimed that it was not squarely presented, and the Court may not have wanted to decide a fundamental issue about the meaning of the Free Exercise Clause with only eight Justices.

The trial court in the Washington case found that pharmacies are generally not required to stock any particular drug and that no pharmacy could possibly stock all available drugs.[15] Despite much effort and many test shoppers, plaintiffs failed to show that anyone had been unable to get timely emergency contraception.[16] Of those pharmacies that did not stock emergency contraception, fewer than 10 percent offered religious reasons; the rest offered business reasons.[17] Conscientiously objecting pharmacies who refuse to stock emergency contraception are no threat to the timely availability of emergency contraception.

Washington law had long protected business discretion about what drugs to stock, and newly amended rules were said not to change that, except for religious objections to emergency contraception.[18] Religious reasons would be singled out for prohibition. This was more a matter of regulatory intent and enforcement policy than of the text of the rules. The "Stocking Rule" says that a pharmacy "must maintain at all times a representative assortment of drugs in order to meet the pharmaceutical needs of its patients."[19] The "Delivery Rule," adopted in 2007, says that pharmacies must deliver prescribed drugs, subject to several exceptions, one of which is "[u]navailability of the drug or device despite good faith compliance with" the Stocking Rule.[20]

In the forty-year history of the Stocking Rule, no pharmacy has ever been cited for violating it.[21] The Stocking Rule does not require pharmacies to stock all drugs – such a requirement would be impossible. So it is not clear from the text of the

---

[13] *Morr-Fitz, Inc. v. Quinn*, 976 N.E.2d 1160 (Ill. App. Ct. 2012), appeal dis'd, 982 N.E.2d 770 (Ill. 2013).
[14] *Stormans, Inc. v. Wiesman*, 794 F.3d 1064 (9th Cir. 2015), cert. denied, 136 S. Ct. 2433 (2016). This case and the broader issues it raises are discussed at greater length in Douglas Laycock and Steven T. Collis, *Generally Applicable Law and the Free Exercise of Religion*, 95 Neb. L. Rev. 1 (2016).
[15] Stormans, 854 F. Supp. 2d at 933–4.
[16] Id. at 946–51.
[17] Id. at 949.
[18] Id. at 940–6, 952–61.
[19] Wash. Admin. Code § 246-869-150(1).
[20] Wash. Admin. Code § 246-869-010.
[21] Stormans, 854 F. Supp. 2d at 934.

regulations that the Delivery Rule changed anything. But the history of the Delivery Rule's creation is clear; it is understood and intended to provide a basis for penalizing conscientious refusals to deliver emergency contraception.[22]

The state said that it prohibited pharmacies from acting on the basis of secular conscience as well as religious conscience. But that added nothing; despite substantial effort, it could not find even one pharmacy with secular conscientious objections to emergency contraception.[23] And, assuming it found one somewhere, a law that applies only to religion and to one rare and closely analogous case is still very far from generally applicable.

Yet the Ninth Circuit held that this targeted regulation is a neutral and generally applicable law,[24] subject only to rational-basis review under the Free Exercise Clause as interpreted in *Employment Division v. Smith*.[25] There are at least three major problems with the court's analysis. First, when considering whether the regulations prohibit any secular reasons for failing to stock and deliver drugs, the court myopically focused on the bare text of the regulations, largely ignoring the interpretation revealed by the enforcement history and refusing to consider the drafting history. If the court had considered reality instead of the bare text, as it had already done in deciding that the regulations prohibit conscience-based refusals to stock and deliver, it would have concluded that the regulations prohibit these conscience-based refusals – and almost nothing else.

Second, and more fundamentally, the court said that business reasons for not stocking or delivering drugs make sense and, therefore, do not detract from the general applicability of the rules.[26] That is, business reasons for not stocking a drug are good reasons, sufficient to justify a decision not to stock, but religious reasons are bad reasons, insufficient to justify a decision not to stock. This is precisely the negative "value judgment" about religion that the Free Exercise Clause prohibits.[27]

In *Sherbert v. Verner*,[28] South Carolina occasionally found acceptable secular reasons for an employee to refuse work and seek unemployment compensation instead. Explaining *Sherbert* in *Smith*, the Court said that because there were "at least some" secular exceptions to the eligibility rules, there had to be a religious exception as

---

[22] Id. at 956–9.
[23] Id. at 982–3.
[24] Stormans, 794 F.3d at 1075–84.
[25] 494 U.S. 872 (1990).
[26] Stormans, 794 F.3d at 1080.
[27] *Fraternal Order of Police v. City of Newark*, 170 F.3d 359, 366 (3d Cir. 1999) (Alito, J.); see *Church of the Lukumi Babalu Aye, Inc. v. City of Hialeah*, 508 U.S. 520, 537–8 (1993) (holding that city "devalues religious reasons for killing [animals] by judging them to be of lesser import than nonreligious reasons").
[28] 374 U.S. 398 (1963).

well.[29] In *Church of the Lukumi Babalu Aye, Inc. v. City of Hialeah*, the city and state recognized a long list of permitted secular reasons for killing animals.[30] In both *Sherbert* and *Lukumi*, the permitted secular reasons were perfectly sensible; they were not bad reasons. But exceptions for those reasons required a similar exception for religious reasons for refusing jobs or killing animals.

A rule that permits an act when done for secular reasons but prohibits the same or analogous acts when done for religious reasons discriminates against religious reasons. Such a rule may conceivably be justified by a compelling government interest, but it is not neutral and generally applicable as the Court applied that concept in *Smith* and *Lukumi*. By treating the legitimacy of business reasons for not filling prescriptions as going to general applicability instead of to justification, the Ninth Circuit substituted rational-basis review for compelling-interest review.

Third, the Ninth Circuit approved a formula for discriminatory enforcement. The court said it was irrelevant that the rules had never been enforced against anyone but the plaintiff, because the Pharmacy Commission followed a policy of "complaint-driven enforcement."[31] There had been "many complaints" against the plaintiff, and hardly any complaints against anyone else. So the court validated a multiyear campaign by ideologically motivated activists to drive one small pharmacy out of business because the activists found its religious practices unacceptable.

In vitro fertilization is another morally contested treatment, because unused embryos are often discarded in the process.[32] I am not aware of any litigation about insurance plans. Only nine or ten states require insurance plans to cover *in vitro* fertilization, and four of those specifically exempt employers with religious objections.[33] This is one context where protecting the very serious religious-liberty claim may bar access to a particular treatment for employees.

There has been employment litigation about teachers in Catholic schools who undergo *in vitro* fertilization in violation of morals clauses in their employment contracts. That litigation has not gone well for the schools.[34] But both schools

---

[29] Smith, 494 U.S. at 884.
[30] Lukumi, 508 U.S. at 543–4 (noting that fishing, hunting, extermination, euthanasia, and medical research were all permitted reasons for killing animals).
[31] Stormans, 794 F.3d at 1083–4.
[32] For the question whether conscientiously objecting physicians may be required to provide this treatment, and other related issues, see I. Glenn Cohen, Ch. 25, Religion and Reproductive Technology, this volume.
[33] National Conference of State Legislatures, State Laws Related to Insurance Coverage for Infertility Treatment, available at www.ncsl.org/research/health/insurance-coverage-for-infertility-laws [https://perma.cc/36J9-3E3C] (current through June 2014).
[34] *Herx v. Diocese of Fort Wayne-South Bend*, 2015 WL 1013783 (N.D. Ind. March 9, 2015) (upholding jury verdict for employee); *Dias v. Archdiocese of Cincinnati*, 2013 WL 360355 (S.D. Ohio January 30, 2013) (denying cross motions for summary judgment).

appear to have relied only on employment-law defenses, and failed to offer a RFRA defense.

The widespread exemptions from vaccination laws are never based on general guarantees of religious liberty. Rather, forty-seven state legislatures have enacted specific exemptions from vaccination requirements. All of these exemptions include religious beliefs,[35] and sixteen include personal or philosophical beliefs.[36]

A claim for exemption from vaccination laws under a state RFRA would present an easy case under the compelling-interest test. Most obviously, unvaccinated children, who are far too young to decide for themselves, are exposed to risks of serious diseases. Moreover, there is a large pseudo-scientific movement seeking exemption. When large numbers of people claim exemption, a virus can spread in the population and put everyone at risk. Even those who are vaccinated are no longer safe, because no vaccine is 100-percent effective. And some people cannot be vaccinated because of compromised immune systems or for other medical reasons. So those who refuse vaccination endanger those around them. These are the reasons most often cited in opposition to exemptions.[37]

Beyond these familiar and sufficient reasons is a serious collective-action problem. It is in the interest of anyone with the slightest qualms about vaccination to have everyone else vaccinated and to be exempt himself; he would be protected without incurring whatever risk he perceives. But that outcome is unachievable; allowing these would-be free riders to claim exemption soon results in many people unvaccinated, not just one. The antivaccination movement has many adherents, all with strong incentives to claim any religious exemption that is available either honestly or, more often, falsely.[38] The existence of widespread secular incentives to false claims is a reason to refuse exemptions that has visibly influenced judicial decisions under the compelling-interest test.[39]

The larger point illustrated by the vaccination example is that legislatures are *not* better than courts at assessing the public interest with respect to religious

---

[35] Hope Lu, Note, *Giving Families Their Best Shot: A Law-Medicine Perspective on the Right to Religious Exemptions from Mandatory Vaccination*, 63 Case W. Res. L. Rev. 869, 886 nn.119–20, 914 (2013) (collecting these statutes).

[36] Id. at 886 n.121. California repealed its exemption after Lu compiled her list. 2015 Cal. Legis. Serv. ch. 35, § 4.

[37] See, e.g., Dorit Rubinstein Reiss & Lois A. Weithorn, *Responding to the Childhood Vaccination Crisis: Legal Frameworks and Tools in the Context of Parental Vaccination Refusal*, 63 Buff. L. Rev. 881 (2015) (summarizing medical evidence and reviewing legal arguments).

[38] Dorit Rubinstein Reiss, *Thou Shalt Not Take the Name of the Lord Thy God in Vain: Use and Abuse of Religious Exemptions from School Immunization Requirements*, 65 Hastings L.J. 1551, 1570–88 (2014) (collecting anecdotal and survey evidence suggesting that most claims to religious motivations for refusing vaccination are false).

[39] See Douglas Laycock, *Church and State in the United States: Competing Conceptions and Historic Changes*, 13 Ind. J. Global Legal Stud. 503, 534 (2006) (applying this analysis to cases refusing exemptions to military draft, tax collection, and school desegregation).

exemptions.[40] It is hard to imagine a court getting this so wrong.[41] But nearly every state legislature has gotten it wrong, and many of them have protected not just religious conscience, but anyone who wants to free-ride, reads crackpot science, or objects for any other reason.

B. Hypothetical Issues

The other claims that people have imagined have never happened, and are not likely to happen. Justice Ginsburg envisioned employers refusing to insure blood transfusions, antidepressants, vaccinations, or medicines derived from pigs.[42] Or maybe Christian Science employers would refuse to provide any medical insurance at all. But all of these are medical treatments that various religious groups refuse to accept for themselves. Few of these religious groups believe that these treatments harm innocent third parties, let alone that they kill babies. These religious teachings are quite unlike the teaching at issue in *Hobby Lobby*.

Christian Scientists have long lobbied for the exemptions they need. They are seeking a legislative exemption from the Affordable Care Act's individual mandate;[43] they do not want to buy health insurance for themselves, which would go unused. They have such an exemption in Massachusetts,[44] which enacted the original state plan on which the Affordable Care Act was modeled.

They have not sought exemption from the employers' obligation to provide insurance for their employees. Their bill does not address that issue, and the Church's website expresses no opposition to the employer mandate.[45] Gary Jones, Manager of the Church's Federal Office, confirmed in a conversation that the Church does not object to providing health insurance for employees who want it.[46] He said that the Church's headquarters has long provided coverage for either Christian Science

---

[40] See Douglas Laycock, A *Syllabus of Errors*, 105 Mich. L. Rev. 1169, 1172–7 (2007) (responding to this claim at greater length).

[41] See *Workman v. Mingo Cnty. Bd. of Educ.*, 419 F. App'x 348, 352–4 (4th Cir. 2011) (upholding vaccination requirement under compelling-interest standard; collecting cases); cf. *Prince v. Massachusetts*, 321 U.S. 158, 166–7 (1944) ("The right to practice religion freely does not include the right to expose the community or the child to communicable disease").

[42] *Burwell v. Hobby Lobby Stores, Inc.*, 134 S. Ct. 2751, 2805 (2014) (Ginsburg, J., dissenting).

[43] The bill is H.R. 1201 in the 115th Congress, available at www.congress.gov/bill/115th-congress/house-bill/1201/text?r=1 [https://perma.cc/F5BE-YLVP].

[44] Mass. Gen. L. ch. 111M, § 3 (2014).

[45] Healthcare and the Affordable Care Act, available at www.christianscience.com/member-resources/committee-on-publication/u.s.-federal-office/healthcare-and-the-affordable-care-act-aca [https://perma.cc/9WA7-VZVQ].

[46] Conversation with Gary Jones (November 7, 2015). The Federal Office works to protect Christian Science from adverse effects of federal law. See U.S. Federal Office, available at http://christianscience.com/member-resources/committee-on-publication/u.s.-federal-office [https://perma.cc/65EL-FMU2].

treatment or standard medical treatment, as each employee chooses, and he is not aware of any Christian Science business person resisting employee health insurance on religious grounds.

Similar reasoning applies to Jehovah's Witnesses and blood transfusions. It is extremely important to Jehovah's Witnesses not to have a blood transfusion themselves; so far as I understand their teaching, they have no reason to refuse to provide blood transfusions for others.[47] As a general matter, "they do not believe that they have a right to impose their values on persons outside their community."[48] Whatever the explanation, I know of no litigation about excluding blood transfusions from health insurance plans.

And so it is with all the other hypothetical claims. They have not happened. They are not likely to happen. And if they ever do, the claim to exemption will look rather different. The Obama Administration believed that contraception pays for itself in avoided pregnancies, and this belief enabled it to find a solution that may not be available with respect to anything else. Making the insurers pay on the side either would not work, because few or none of these other medical treatments will pay for themselves, or it would work, in which case employees can be protected without burdening employers. And if employees have to actually do without these other forms of medical care, that would be a very different case from *Hobby Lobby*.

C. Limits to Religious Liberty in the Health Care Context

Sometimes there is a compelling interest in limiting religious liberty. Reasonable people can debate just where the line should be drawn. But sensible lines are possible, and they show that granting exemptions where possible does not make it impossible to refuse exemptions where serious harm would result.

Most of these limiting principles are illustrated by *Means v. U.S. Conference of Catholic Bishops*.[49] Represented by the American Civil Liberties Union, Means sued the Catholic bishops and their health care leadership in a case arising out of egregious alleged facts. She says that her water broke in the eighteenth week of pregnancy, and that she was told at a Catholic hospital that no treatment was possible, misled about her condition and about the prognosis for her and the baby, and not referred elsewhere. The baby had almost no chance of surviving, and the usual

---

[47] See M. James Penton, *Apocalypse Delayed: The Story of Jehovah's Witnesses* 153–4, 202–6 (1985) (explaining the teachings on blood); Charles H. Barron, "Blood Transfusions, Jehovah's Witnesses, and the American Patients' Rights Movement," in *Alternatives to Blood Transfusion in Transfusion Medicine* (Alice Maniatis, et al. eds., 2011) (explaining the teaching and reviewing the evolution of U.S. law and medical practice protecting the right to refuse blood transfusions).
[48] Penton, supra note 47, at 152.
[49] 836 F.3d 643 (6th Cir. 2016).

treatment would have been to terminate the pregnancy. Means had no car; the hospital is the only one in the county. Of course, she lost the baby; she also suffered painful and dangerous complications caused or aggravated by the futile effort to prolong the pregnancy. All this is according to the complaint.[50]

The bishops' lawyers said that these alleged facts would actually violate Catholic teaching if true;[51] the ACLU filed church statements ambiguously suggesting otherwise.[52] The trial court dismissed the complaint without resolving this dispute and without deciding what had happened.[53]

Neither the hospital nor its physicians were named as defendants. The claim was that the bishops and their health care leadership issued Ethical and Religious Directives for Catholic health care, that these Directives were binding on Catholic hospitals, and that these Directives caused the hospital and its doctors to withhold necessary care from the plaintiff. The alleged negligence lay in the content of the Ethical and Religious Directives.

The trial court dismissed the complaint against the bishops for lack of jurisdiction; the national organization of bishops named as a defendant had no minimum contacts with Michigan. The court dismissed the complaint against the health care leadership on two grounds: that they owed no duty to individual patients under Michigan law, and that the court could not adjudicate plaintiff's claim without resolving disputes about the Directives and associated religious doctrine. The court said that it would be "competent to address whether the medical care provided" by the hospital was negligent or was medical malpractice. But it could not decide that the religious teachings of the Catholic Church were negligent.[54] This distinction seems right.

The court of appeals affirmed the jurisdictional holding about the bishops; with respect to the health care leadership, it affirmed on the state-law ground that even under the plaintiff's allegations, the Ethical Directives had not proximately caused her any injury.[55]

If we imagine instead a straightforward suit against the hospital and the doctors on these alleged facts, the religious-liberty issues would be rather modest. *If the facts were as alleged* – local monopoly, deliberate deception of an unsophisticated patient, known and substantial risk of harm to that patient – there would be multiple

---

[50] Complaint ¶¶ 12–52, No. 1:15-cv-00353RHB (W.D. Mich. November 29, 2013), ECF No. 1.
[51] Defendant United States Conference of Catholic Bishops, Inc.'s Motion to Dismiss Pursuant to Federal Rule of Civil Procedure 12(b)(2) at 6–7, ECF No. 23.
[52] Plaintiff's Brief in Opposition to Defendant USCCB's Motion to Dismiss for Lack of Personal Jurisdiction, Exhibit 3, ECF No. 29-4.
[53] *Means v. U.S. Conference of Catholic Bishops*, 2015 WL 3970046 (W.D. Mich. June 30, 2015), aff'd, 836 F.3d 643 (6th Cir. 2016).
[54] *Means*, 2015 WL 3970046 at *13.
[55] 836 F.3d 643, 652–3 (6th Cir. 2016).

grounds for rejecting any claim of right for the hospital to do what it allegedly did. These grounds can exist independently of each other, and in less extreme circumstances. Many abortion or health care conscience statutes do not take account of these problems.

First, there will sometimes be a duty to refer elsewhere. Some conscientious objectors are willing to tell patients where religiously prohibited services are available; some are not. There are cases in which the information is so widely available, and any need for great haste so lacking, that there is no compelling interest in requiring a referral. But that is not every case, or even most cases.

The medical professional is a specialist, with vastly greater information than the typical patient. The patient may be unsophisticated, lacking in information, and lacking knowledge of where and how to search for answers. If a doctor told Means that no treatment was possible, and there was nothing to do but wait, she would have no reason to suspect otherwise. Medical ethics, or the standard of care, probably impose an obligation to tell a patient that other providers would offer a different course of treatment.[56] Or the government may impose such an obligation by regulation. A compelling government interest in preventing avoidable medical harm to patients would support such a requirement.

Second, and closely related, there is an obligation not to deliberately mislead a patient to prevent her from considering alternatives. When a doctor says that nothing can be done, even though he knows that there are standard treatments available elsewhere, he is engaged in deliberate deception.

Third, medical providers must respond to medical emergencies. A federal statute requires providers to either treat the emergency patient, or stabilize the patient until it is safe to transfer her elsewhere – and it creates a private right of action.[57] The ACLU did not allege a claim under this statute. There are surely few occasions in which an immediate abortion is medically necessary and there is no time to refer or transfer the patient elsewhere. There may be some, and *Means* may have been one.

Finally, and most controversially, monopolies matter. In a regime of individual liberty with respect to both sex and religion, one has a presumptive right to live by one's own moral commitments. One does not have a right to use a monopoly position to block others from exercising the same liberty, because we must define our liberties in such a way that the same liberties are available to all. If you want to

---

[56] Cf. Richard M. Patterson, *Harney's Medical Malpractice* §§ 5.7–5.8 at 207–21 (5th ed. 2011) (discussing duty to refer to specialist when physician is unable to provide needed care and duty not to neglect a patient after once undertaking her care); see also *Brownfield v. Daniel Freeman Marina Hosp.*, 256 Cal. Rptr. 240, 245 (Cal. Ct. App. 1989) (stating, in dictum and in conclusory fashion, that a Catholic hospital had a duty to inform a rape victim about emergency contraception).

[57] 42 U.S.C. § 1395dd (2012).

maximize your own liberty, you should stay out of chokepoints where you can cut off the liberty of others.

It follows that Catholic hospitals should not seek, and should not be permitted to acquire, local monopolies over women's health care. Yet Catholic monopolies over hospital care already exist in some places, and the economic pressures to continued consolidation of hospitals are strong.[58] Solutions are possible; much reproductive health care can be provided in community clinics, and few abortions are performed in hospitals anyway. Hospital-level reproductive care needs to be carved out of Catholic hospitals with local monopolies, delegated to independent contractors, or allowed to proceed in some other way. Many bishops understandably resist such arrangements. But if it were clearly settled that the price of monopoly is forfeiture of religious liberty, bishops would likely become more flexible about avoiding or undoing their monopolies.

There is a similar issue with respect to refusing end-of-life care in Catholic hospitals. But the alternative of nursing homes and hospices greatly eases the Catholic monopoly.

The point of such inquiries is to identify those few cases where the government interest is truly compelling, screening out all the cases where other solutions are possible. Women are entitled to reproductive health care. But they are not entitled to receive it from conscientious objectors unless there is no alternative. Conscientious objectors are generally entitled not to participate in medical procedures they find immoral. But they are not entitled to inflict affirmative harm, or use their monopoly position and control of information to prevent patients from receiving the procedure elsewhere.

If we are to continue living with each other in relative peace and equality, then we must find solutions that give women the health care they need and that, to the maximum extent possible, spare conscientious objectors from violating deeply held religious commitments. Such solutions are possible. What is lacking is mutual tolerance and political will.

---

[58] See generally Elizabeth Sepper, Ch. 8, Contracting Religion, this volume. Professor Sepper and I disagree on many things, and I suspect that she would impose the same burdens on religious liberty with or without a monopoly. For me, monopoly is a reason to override a presumptive liberty.

2

From *Smith* to *Hobby Lobby*

The Transformation of the Religious Freedom Restoration Act

Diane L. Moore and Eric M. Stephen

On November 16, 1993, over two hundred of the nation's most renowned religious leaders and political activists gathered outside the White House in anticipation as President William Jefferson Clinton took his seat behind a small desk on the South Lawn to enact the federal Religious Freedom Restoration Act (RFRA). Shortly before formally signing the measure into law, President Clinton delivered a brief speech in which he remarked at the near-unanimous and deeply bipartisan support the bill had in Congress, describing it as a stirring testament to the commitment Americans across the political and religious spectrum hold for religious liberty. "We all have a shared desire here to protect perhaps the most precious of all American liberties, religious freedom," Clinton stated, taking further note of the strange set of bedfellows that came together to champion RFRA's passage – from left-leaning organizations such as the American Civil Liberties Union (ACLU) and Americans United for the Separation of Church and State (AU), to those on the right, including the National Association of Evangelicals (NAE) and the Home School Legal Defense Association (HSLDA). "Even in the legislative process," Clinton quipped, "miracles can happen."[1]

Twenty-four years after its passage, however, RFRA's polyannaish aura has faded. No longer do most commentators view the act as a symbol of the American people's unified and unwavering fidelity to the goals and aspirations of the First Amendment. Instead, RFRA is today situated in the American public conscience as a key battleground on which the nation's political and religious communities spar over how religious freedom is to be properly understood within the American constitutional experiment. In the wake of the Supreme Court's landmark decision in *Burwell v. Hobby Lobby*[2] and the subsequent passage of a deeply partisan state RFRA in

---

[1] William J. Clinton, *Remarks on Signing the Religious Freedom Restoration Act of 1993* (November 16, 1993) (transcript available online by Gerhard Peters and John T. Woolley, The American Presidency Project www.presidency.ucsb.edu/ws/?pid=46124 [https://perma.cc/MF5T-44GF]).

[2] 134 S. Ct. 2751 (2014). The case is discussed in greater depth in this volume's Introduction.

Indiana that many pundits viewed as little more than antigay posturing on the part of conservative activists, progressive organizations such as the ACLU have even formally renounced their support for RFRA, arguing that the act has matured into a partisan legal weapon for the so-called 'Religious Right.'

In the three years since *Hobby Lobby* forced RFRA back into the political spotlight, a number of significant questions have emerged surrounding *how* this fragile bipartisan and interfaith coalition collapsed so divisively, and *what* social and political factors have allowed RFRA's religious exemption provision to be leveraged in such controversial ways. Expanding on a spate of recent scholarship that has begun to address these concerns, this chapter seeks to employ a cultural studies approach to examine the role of religion in American law and politics, especially as it relates to issues of contraception, abortion, and reproductive health care access more broadly. Guided by such a framework, this chapter will explore the social and political shifts that took place between RFRA's near-unanimous passage in 1993 and the Court's highly controversial 2014 ruling in *Hobby Lobby* by examining first the social and cultural conditions present in the early 1990s, and then, second, how they had changed in politically and theologically significant ways by the early decades of the twenty-first century. In doing so, this chapter will not only further elaborate on the work of other scholars who have noted the theological concerns of litigants, but also highlight the efforts of neoliberal economic actors and conservative political leaders in building a formidable alliance against the Affordable Care Act and other progressive legislation.

1. *SMITH* AND ITS DISCONTENTS: EXPLORING THE RISE OF RFRA FROM A CULTURAL STUDIES PERSPECTIVE

As one author of this chapter has described elsewhere, a cultural studies approach to the academic study of religion presumes that "religion is a social/cultural phenomenon that is embedded in human political, social, and cultural life," and as such "religion shapes and is shaped by the social [and] historical contexts out of which particular religious expressions and influences emerge."[3] This is to say, the methods and theories developed out of a cultural studies framework help us to recognize that religion is not an ahistorical phenomenon capable of being studied in isolation. Instead, drawing from a diverse set of disciplines including sociology, social theory, literary theory, and cultural anthropology, this approach acknowledges and examines the significance of the cultural context in which specific expressions of religious

---

[3] Diane L. Moore, "High Stakes Ignorance: Religion, Education, and the Unwitting Reproduction of Bigotry," in *Civility, Religious Pluralism, and Education* 113 (Vincent F. Biondo III and Andrew Fiala eds., 2014).

faith surface and transform – including the political, social, and economic aspects of a given cultural moment.

Critical to the cultural studies approach as applied to an analysis of religious belief are three guiding assertions: (1) that religions are internally diverse, as opposed to uniform; (2) that religions evolve and change over time, as opposed to remaining static; and, (3) that religious influences are embedded into all dimensions of cultural life, as opposed to being discrete, isolated, and "private" systems of belief.[4] All three of these theoretical claims prove integral in helping us to understand what factors help give rise to specific religious expressions; how the worldviews produced by those faith commitments inform how believers position themselves in relation to others in a society; and, finally, what is at stake socially, ethically, and politically for those who adhere to a given expression of faith. This approach, therefore, allows us to paint a more robust and nuanced picture of how interpretations of RFRA have both been informed by and also reciprocally helped produce contemporary understandings of religious liberty in the United States, particularly as they relate to questions of birth control and religious exemptions.

To do so, we must first begin by inquiring into the circumstances that prompted federal RFRA legislation in the closing decade of the twentieth century. As described in more depth in the Introduction to this volume, the Supreme Court had, prior to 1990, routinely adjudicated constitutional claims implicating the Free Exercise Clause of the First Amendment by employing a judicial "balancing test" first developed in *Sherbert v. Verner*.[5] According to this "*Sherbert* Test," so long as a claimant demonstrates that he or she holds a sincere religious belief that has been substantially burdened by a state action that is otherwise facially neutral toward religious faith,[6] it becomes the responsibility of the state to then demonstrate that its action both furthered a compelling interest and was narrowly tailored to further that interest using the least restrictive means possible. If the state fails to satisfy either judicial demand, the petitioning religious community may then be able to receive an exemption from – or an accommodation to – the state action under question. Thus, in many ways, the *Sherbert* Test was intended to provide a legally practical middle-ground between two constitutional extremes: to avoid either striking down all facially neutral legislation that has the unintended effect of burdening the religious practice of some, or ignoring outright the Constitution's commitment to religious liberty in all but the most blatant cases of intentional religious discrimination.

---

[4] See Diane L. Moore, *Guidelines for Teaching about Religion in K-12 Public Schools in the United States*, American Academy of Religion, available at www.aarweb.org/sites/default/files/pdfs/Publications/epublications/AARK-12CurriculumGuidelines.pdf [https://perma.cc/5ZBN-M742].

[5] 374 U.S. 398 (1963).

[6] For a more in-depth exploration of determinations of "sincere belief" within free exercise litigation, see Greg Lipper, Ch. 4, this volume.

Given that many in the legal community considered *Sherbert* to be settled law and relatively uncontroversial, it came as a great shock to a number of scholars, judges, and religious leaders alike when five members of the Court chose to significantly curtail *Sherbert*'s applicability in their 1990 *Employment Division v. Smith*[7] decision. In *Smith*, two Native American men in Oregon were fired from their positions as counselors at a drug rehabilitation clinic for ingesting small amounts of the entheogen peyote as part of a religious ceremony and then subsequently denied unemployment benefits because they were dismissed for misconduct.

Although many legal observers thought the case to involve a rather straightforward judicial question addressing a potential religious exemption to a state drug law under *Sherbert*, Justice Antonin Scalia, writing for the Court's majority, went so far as to reject the very notion that *Sherbert* was controlling precedent. Painting a rather disjointed picture of the Court's Free Exercise jurisprudence,[8] Scalia instead argued that prior applications of *Sherbert* addressed cases in which "hybrid rights" – that is, cases implicating free exercise as well as at least one other constitutional right, such as free speech – were involved.[9] In cases such as *Smith* that touch only upon the Free Exercise Clause, by contrast, the Court need only affirm that the state action under scrutiny is "neutral" and "generally applicable."[10] "The right of free exercise," Scalia opined, "does not relieve an individual of the obligation to comply with a valid and neutral law of general applicability on the ground that the law proscribes (or prescribes) conduct that his religion prescribes (or proscribes)."[11] Instead, Scalia suggested, a more appropriate avenue for the respondents to take here would be an appeal to the legislature.

Thus, in less than twenty pages of text, the majority opinion in *Smith* "reevaluated what many believed were decades of settled free exercise jurisprudence," and "stunned individuals in the religious and civil liberties communities" who had "expected, at worst, a decision denying the respondents' request for unemployment compensation because of the state's compelling interest in controlling drug use."[12] In quick succession after the opinion was released in April 1990, a number of prominent legal commentators voiced their outrage. Constitutional law scholar William Bentley Ball, for example, called the decision a "constitutional fault of San Andreas

---

[7] 494 U.S. 872 (1990). Justice Sandra Day O'Connor concurred in the opinion of the Court using the *Sherbert* Test, however, making the Court's overall decision 6–3.
[8] For a critique of the majority opinion's logic, see Catherine Cookson, "A Critique of the Court's Free Exercise Clause Jurisprudence in the U.S. Supreme Court Case of *Employment Division v. Smith*," in *Regulating Religion: The Courts and the Free Exercise Clause* 118–48 (2001).
[9] 494 U.S. 872, 882 (1990).
[10] Id. at 880.
[11] Id. at 879.
[12] Carolyn N. Long, *Religious Freedom and Indian Rights: The Case of Oregon v. Smith* 190, 197 (2000).

proportions,"[13] and Douglas Laycock, a leading contemporary on religious liberty and a contributor to this volume, likewise protested that "[t]he opinion appears to be inconsistent with the original intent, inconsistent with the constitutional text, inconsistent with doctrine under other constitutional clauses, and inconsistent with precedent."[14]

Soon thereafter, a group of fifty-five scholars and legal analysts filed an ultimately unsuccessful brief to the Court advocating for a rehearing of the case. At roughly the same time, religious and civil liberties groups mobilized to form the Coalition for the Free Exercise of Religion (CFER) in May 1990. Chaired by the director of the Washington office of the ACLU, Morton Halperin, the coalition cut across political and religious lines, ultimately amassing interest from sixty-six faith organizations. In addition to large, ecumenical Protestant bodies such as the liberal National Council of Churches (NCC) and the more conservative National Association of Evangelicals (NAE), less politically powerful groups such as the National Sikh Center, the Native American Church of North America, B'nai B'rith, the American Humanist Association, and the Church of Scientology International also joined in support.[15] When the petition for rehearing was formally rejected in June of 1990, CFER's legal team began looking to the Enforcement Clause of the Fourteenth Amendment to assert that Congress might be able to pass legislation to correct the perceived damage done by *Smith*.

By the end of July, a draft bill entitled the Religious Freedom Restoration Act of 1990 was introduced to the House of Representatives under Representative Stephen Solarz (D-NY), having accumulated thirty-four other co-sponsors from both sides of the aisle. On October 26, Chair of the Senate Judiciary Committee Joseph R. Biden (D-DE) and ranking minority leader Orrin G. Hatch (R-UT) introduced a companion bill to that in the House. Shortly thereafter, Layock joined constitutional scholars Michael McConnell and Edward McGlynn Gaffney to pen "An Open Letter to the Religious Community," urging bipartisan and unanimous support for the legislation and arguing that it stands as "the best practicable means of correcting a grave interpretative error by the Supreme Court, and will help ensure that all Americans,

---

[13] William Bentley Ball, "High Court Goes Cold on Religious Liberty," L.A. Times, April 22, 1990, available at http://articles.latimes.com/1990-04-22/opinion/op-87_1_religious-liberty [https://perma.cc/W7QH-KG86].

[14] Douglas Laycock, *The Supreme Court's Assault on Free Exercise and the Amicus Brief That Was Never Filed*, 8 J. L. & Religion 99, 99–114 (1990).

[15] For a full list of the religious organizations comprising CFER, see Baptist Joint Committee for Religious Liberty, *The Religious Freedom Restoration Act: 20 Years of Protecting our First Freedom*, 6 (2003) available at http://perma.cc/J9QY-K98F (reproducing a Letter from Oliver S. Thomas, October 20, 1993).

whatever their religious faith, will be protected in their exercise of religion, as the framers and ratifiers of our Constitution intended them to be."[16]

Yet despite this display of political bipartisanship and seeming legal concordance, it took Congress almost three years to successfully pass RFRA. In large part, this was due to a moderately successful attack on the bill by the National Right to Life Committee (NRLC) on the grounds that the legislation might create a new avenue for abortion litigation at a time when the future of *Roe v. Wade*[17] appeared tenuous. The $13 million operating budget of NRLC provided the organization with enough political muscle to bring the U.S. Catholic Conference to publicly oppose the legislation as well, and stunned President George H.W. Bush into silence on the matter entirely. Both liberally minded civil liberties groups including the ACLU and other religious communities with strong pro-life positions such as the Church of Jesus Christ of Latter-Day Saints responded in defense of RFRA, but to little avail.[18]

By early 1993, however, the tide had begun to turn. The newly elected President Bill Clinton and his Attorney General Janet Reno together changed the White House's tune by voicing their support for the measure. Perhaps more importantly, the Supreme Court released its mildly pro-choice opinion in *Planned Parenthood v. Casey*[19] in June 1992, which brought the NRLC and the Catholic Conference to concede that the right to reproductive health care access would not soon be unmoored from its Fourteenth Amendment foothold. After developing some compromise language in a Senate report that would accompany the bill, both groups finally endorsed RFRA. Reintroduced to the House by Representative Chuck Schumer (D-NY), RFRA passed by a unanimous voice vote on May 11, 1993, and the Senate affirmed a slightly amended version of the bill on October 27 by a vote of 97-3. Then, on November 16 of that same year, President Clinton signed one of the most bipartisan and interfaith bills in the nation's history into federal law.[20]

Put simply, then, the Religious Freedom Restoration Act of 1993 was the product of years of work on the part of legal scholars, political leaders, and an interfaith coalition of religious organizations frustrated by the Court's decision in *Smith*

---

[16] Edward McGlynn Gaffney, Douglas Laycock, and Michael W. McConnell, *An Open Letter to the Religious Community*, reprinted in First Things, (March 1991) available at www.firstthings.com/article/1991/03/004-an-open-letter-to-the-religious-community [https://perma.cc/3UU6-BZ5K].

[17] 410 U.S. 113 (1973).

[18] For a broader discussion of legislative deliberations about the act's applicability to abortion, see Douglas Laycock and Oliver S. Thomas, *Interpreting the Religious Freedom Restoration Act*, 73 Tex. L. Rev. 209, 231–8 (1994).

[19] 505 U.S. 833 (1992).

[20] Given the scope of this chapter, the discussion above only focused on pro-life critiques of RFRA. However, it is important to also note that concerns of federalism, separation of powers, and the application of RFRA in settings such as prisons also animated myriad congressional deliberations and legal debates. For discussion, see Long, supra note 12, at 179–250.

and concerned that this new judicial precedent would gravely restrict religious liberty rights in America. To militate against a perceived threat to the free exercise of religion that arose in a particular cultural moment, these groups together devised a legal mechanism that would explicitly "restore" the *Sherbert* standard, one that would be held to constitutionally apply to all *federal* legislation.[21] Absent from RFRA, however, were specific articulations of how to determine what constitutes a "compelling state interest" or exactly how courts ought to go about adjudging which "less restrictive means" are pragmatically possible or legally mandated. While this ambiguity undoubtedly allows for the legislation to adapt and respond to ever-changing understandings of rights and justice, it also allows for a multiplicity of interpretations to be produced whenever there exist differences of opinion over what should be considered socially just. And, as a cultural studies approach helps underscore, such differences of opinion pervade American political discourse.

2. RELIGIOUS LIBERTY TODAY: *HOBBY LOBBY*, RFRA, AND THE CONTEMPORARY POLITICAL CLIMATE

In the cultural context of the early 1990s, the spirit of bipartisanship and interfaith cooperation captured in CFER and its efforts to pass RFRA proves to be particularly noteworthy in its own right. Indeed, it was during the very same time that RFRA was being considered in Congress that sociologist James Davison Hunter published his 1991 bestselling book *Culture Wars: The Struggle to Define America*, helping to popularize the term 'culture wars' in American political discourse. Tracing its origins to at least as far back as the 1960s, Hunter's work invoked the phrase to describe what he saw to be the American public's increasing hyperpolarization on a number of "hot-button" social issues – most notably women's rights, LGBT equality, and the separation of church and state. Within a year of Hunter's publication, presidential hopeful Pat Buchanan – who had just made a strong though unsuccessful primary challenge from the right to incumbent president George H.W. Bush – would stand before the Republican National Convention in 1992 and similarly declare, "There is a religious war going on in this country. It is a cultural war, as critical to

---

[21] Cf. *City of Bourne v. Flores*, 521 U.S. 507 (1997); *Gonzales v. O Centro Espirita Beneficente Uniao do Vegetal*, 546 U.S. 418 (2006) (limiting RFRA's applicability to federal legislation). In *Hobby Lobby*, Justice Samuel Alito suggested that "RFRA did more than merely restore the balancing test" used in *Sherbert* by "provid[ing] even broader protection for religious liberty than was available under those decisions," 134 S. Ct. 2751, 2761 (2014). This position, however, has been largely refuted by legal scholars. See, e.g., Martin S. Lederman, *Reconstructing RFRA: The Contested Legacy of Religious Freedom Restoration*, 125 Yale L.J. F. 416, 428–33 (2016).

the kind of nation we shall be as the Cold War itself. For this war is for the soul of America."[22]

Though a number of scholars have rightly criticized the academic utility of employing a rhetoric of violence to describe the tumultuous debates currently animating American public discourse,[23] its sustained use by scholars, politicians, and faith leaders alike strongly suggests that its social logic continues to resonate deeply with many Americans. To be sure, the contemporary debates that have arisen surrounding RFRA and the recent *Hobby Lobby* decision cannot be understood without exploring this cultural context in greater detail, as Douglas Laycock points out in his contribution to this volume. Expanding on Laycock's points, a cultural studies approach also demands that we ask what reciprocal relationships existed in this period between systems of faith and other political, social, and economic phenomena that may have helped influence contemporary interpretations of RFRA as well.

With regard to questions of abortion, contraception, and reproductive health care more specifically, it is important to first note that, for a majority of the twentieth century, birth control was considered to be an almost exclusively "Catholic issue."[24] Indeed, even the Southern Baptist Convention (SBC) – today one of the most vocal "pro-life" religious organizations in the country – adopted a resolution in 1971 "call[ing] upon Southern Baptists to work for legislation that will allow the possibility of abortion under such conditions as rape, incest, clear evidence of severe fetal deformity, and ... damage to the emotional, mental, and physical health of the mother."[25] At roughly the same time, by contrast, Pope Paul VI's 1968 encyclical *Humanae Vitae* explicitly reaffirmed the long-held Church position that the primary purpose of sexual activity was procreation, and thus any attempt to inhibit that aim – save for forms of "natural family planning" that in no way affect sexual partners' fertility or the overall fecundity of sexual intercourse – stood in violation of God's natural law. Yet while anti-birth control campaigns may be viewed at that time as overwhelmingly Catholic when compared against other faiths, rank-and-file American Catholics – particularly an emerging middle-class of Catholic women – often held attitudes that diverged markedly from official Church doctrine, betraying American Catholicism's own internal diversity on the matter.[26]

---

[22] Patrick J. Buchanan, 1992 Republican National Convention Speech (August 17, 1992) (transcript available online at Patrick J. Buchanan Official Website, http://buchanan.org/blog/1992-republican-national-convention-speech-148 [https://perma.cc/RZP5-8Y6A]).

[23] E.g., Andrew Hartman, *A War for the Soul of America: A History of the Culture Wars* 285 (2015) ("The logic of the culture wars has been exhausted. The metaphor has run its course.").

[24] For a discussion of the distinctly Catholic nature of early campaigns against contraception and abortion, see generally John T. McGreevy, *Catholicism and American Freedom: A History* 127–65 (2003).

[25] Resolution on Abortion: St. Louis, Missouri – 1971, Southern Baptist Convention (available at www.sbc.net/resolutions/13/resolution-on-abortion [https://perma.cc/6PH5-6TU5]).

[26] See McGreevy, supra note 24, at 246 (noting that, in the United States, "[m]ost Catholic couples rejected the teaching [in *Humanae Vitae*] or ignored it").

Soon enough, however, Catholic antiabortion and anticontraception activists would find a sympathetic ear. Throughout much of the 1970s, theologically conservative Protestants – at the encouragement of leading theologians such as Jerry Falwell and Francis Schaeffer – were beginning to once again participate in the federal political process, an arena they had largely abandoned after the infamous Scopes Trial of 1925 in favor of local politics and grassroots organizing. In time, a loose coalition of politically conservative faith communities with overlapping theological and political interests – including much of America's Catholic leadership and a number of Protestant denominations often collapsed together under the label "evangelical" – would eventually come together to create a politically significant voting bloc described today as the "Religious Right."[27] And abortion proved an easy target for conservative Protestant groups comprising the Religious Right, as it symbolized perfectly what they perceived to be the precipitous moral decay of America caused by women's liberation, the sexual revolution, and increasing liberalism on social issues generally. In 1978, Falwell delivered his first antiabortion sermon before a Protestant evangelical audience, and in 1979 Schaeffer cohosted a five-part film series entitled *Whatever Happened to the Human Race?* with soon-to-be Surgeon General C. Everett Koop, which helped inculcate antiabortion attitudes among evangelical parishioners more broadly. Thus, in short, by the time RFRA was being discussed in Congress, Catholics no longer found themselves alone on one side of the "abortion debate," but were joined by conservative Protestant groups whose theologies were quickly shifting in order to better advocate for the return of traditional gender roles and sexual norms in American society.

As a number of contributors to this volume have also recognized,[28] theological concerns surrounding complicity in the purportedly sinful acts of others have become a critical issue for these religious groups, helping to inspire not only a rapidly expanding wave of "health care refusal laws" but also the litigation strategy employed in *Hobby Lobby*, described by legal scholars Douglas NeJaime and Reva Siegel as a "complicity-based conscience claim."[29] To be sure, questions of

---

[27] While the phrase "Religious Right" continues to carry valence in American popular discourse, it is important not to presume that this loose coalition of conservative faith communities is theologically monolithic. Moreover, we must also recognize that the Protestant communities that self-identify with the now theo-political label "evangelical" are overwhelmingly white – even though myriad African-Americans evince faith commitments consistent with Protestant evangelicalism – suggesting that intersections exist between religion and race in the contemporary use of this identity category. For discussion, see Marla Frederick McGlathery and Traci Griffin, "'Becoming Conservative, Becoming White?': Black Evangelicals and the Para-Church Movement," in *This Side of Heaven: Race, Ethnicity, and Christian Faith* (Robert J. Priest and Alvaro L. Nieves eds., 2007).

[28] See, e.g., the contributions by Claudia Haupt, Amy Sepinwell, and Robin Fretwell Wilson, this volume.

[29] Douglas NeJaime and Reva B. Siegel, *Conscience Wars: Complicity-Based Conscience Claims in Religion and Politics*, 124 Yale L.J. 2516, 2519 (2015).

complicity have long been central to the ethical teachings of a number of faith traditions. Returning to the Catholic position, for example, the *Catechism of the Catholic Church* formally states: "We have a responsibility for the sins committed by others when we cooperate in them: by participating directly and voluntarily in them; by ordering, advising, praising, or approving them; by not disclosing or not hindering them when we have an obligation to do so; [or] by protecting evil-doers."[30] And, as an amicus brief submitted by sixty-seven Catholic theologians in *Hobby Lobby* further notes, cooperation is "sometimes permissible" and may be adjudged using "several objective criteria," such as the moral gravity of the wrongdoing, the directness of the believer's involvement, and the relevant doctrine of the Church.[31] Notably, while these theologians argue in their brief that the ACA's contraceptive requirement does indeed force religious employers to materially cooperate in sin, the nonprofit organization Catholics for Choice filed an amicus brief in subsequent litigation holding that Catholics' own lived experiences and commitments to other principles such as human dignity supersede formal doctrines of cooperation. As such, they assert "as a matter of their deep Catholic faith that all employees are equally entitled to coverage of contraceptive services."[32] To be sure, positions on complicity are similarly diverse within Protestant traditions, Jewish thought, and other religions as well. Without full elaboration on the precise contours of these theological debates, suffice to say that concerns over complicity continue to be a serious theological preoccupation within and across faith traditions today.

While theological questions surrounding the nature and scope of complicity undoubtedly helped provoke some individuals' sincerely held religious objections to the ACA's contraception requirement, a cultural studies perspective also demands that we ask what cultural conditions produced this theological concern, and what other political and economic factors were also involved. Perhaps most relevant on this score is the fact that "political leaders are encouraging the faithful to assert complicity claims."[33] While legal and political interest in the outcome of such litigation is less than surprising, it is important to also note that such claims are not being leveraged equally by both sides of the aisle. As legal scholar Kara

---

[30] Catechism of the Catholic Church, pt. 5, ¶ 1868. United States Catholic Conference, Inc. available at www.catholicculture.org/culture/library/catechism/cat_view.cfm?recnum=5102 [https://perma.cc/2P9H-A9A6].

[31] Brief of 67 Catholic Theologians and Ethicists as Amici Curiae in Support of Hobby Lobby Stores, Inc., and *Conestoga Wood Specialties Corp. Buwell v. Hobby Lobby*, 573 U.S. ___ (2014). (Nos. 13-354 & 13-356), 8.

[32] Brief of Catholics for Choice et al., as Amici Curiae in support of respondents. *Zubik v. Burwell*, 578 U.S. ___ (2016). (Nos. 14-1418, 14-1453, 14-1505, 15-35, 15-105, 15-119 & 15-191), 10.

[33] NeJaime and Siegel, supra note 29, at 2542.

Loewentheil rightly recognizes, although "the logic of [religious] exemptions cannot be cabined to a particular set of political or normative goals," claimants have been overwhelmingly conservative and "political progressives have been slower to embrace this strategy."[34]

Although a more comprehensive evaluation of the intersections between Republican politics and socially conservative Christian movements is beyond the scope of this chapter, suffice to say that conservative political actors may be viewed as contributing to this discourse in at least two significant ways. First, at the level of rhetoric, the Republican Party has long played on the frustrations and anxieties of conservative religious groups in an attempt to thwart progressive legislation, particularly that which they perceive to be inappropriately expanding federal power or breaking down established social norms. To wit, the Republican Party's 2012 platform explicitly states: "The most offensive instance in [the] war on religion has been the [Obama] Administration's attempt to compel faith-related institutions, as well as believing individuals, to contravene their deeply held religious, moral, or ethical beliefs regarding health services, traditional marriage, or abortion."[35] While this position may indeed be read as acknowledging and reaffirming the attitudes of the party's constituents, it may also be seen as working to manufacture that attitude as well by further reifying "culture war" rhetoric and inappropriately vilifying a Democratic president as blithely indifferent to the nation's commitment to religious liberty.

Second, at the level of action, conservative political strategists also had a strong role to play in defining the parameters of the *Hobby Lobby* case itself. As the owners of the craft store indicated in their complaint, it was the Becket Fund for Religious Liberty – which has members contributing to this volume – that first approached the general counsel of Hobby Lobby in 2012 to alert them of the ACA's contraception requirement and inquire whether they would be interested in filing suit.[36] Though the organization maintains that it supports "religious rights of people from 'A to Z,' from Anglicans to Zoroastrians,"[37] and notably represented a Muslim RFRA claimant in the recent, less controversial case of *Holt v. Hobbs*,[38] several commentators have nonetheless noted a decisively conservative shift in their understanding and

---

[34] Kara Loewentheil, *The Satanic Temple, Scott Walker, and Contraception: A Partial Account of Hobby Lobby's Implications for State Law*, 9 Harv. L. & Pub. Pol'y Rev. 118, 124 (2015).

[35] Republican Platform 2012: We Believe in America, Republican National Convention (2012), 12, available at http://perma.cc/QM2E-5CPV.

[36] See NeJaime and Siegel, supra note 29, at 2551–2 for further elaboration.

[37] Our Mission, The Becket Fund for Religious Liberty, www.becketfund.org/our-mission/ [https://perma.cc/WCX2-7EFL] (last visited June 16, 2016).

[38] 135 S. Ct. 853 (2015).

advocacy of religious liberty.[39] Indeed, the Becket Fund – together with the conservative Christian organization Alliance Defending Freedom – was instrumental in crafting the legal strategy used in *Hobby Lobby* and also represented the Catholic organization Little Sisters of the Poor in a follow-up case to *Hobby Lobby* that would have expanded complicity claims even further. The fact that the Becket Fund has received large financial contributions from DonorsTrust, a nonprofit donor-advised fund strongly connected to conservative figureheads Charles and David Koch, also exposes important questions surrounding the relative role of neoliberal economic interests in this case, particularly given that *Hobby Lobby* greatly expanded corporate personhood rights as well.[40]

In short, these political, legal, and economic actors have been able to capitalize on the fact that religious exemptions provided in RFRA can operate as "both sincere expressions of religious commitment and effective strategies for advancing particular political or normative goals."[41] As such, *Hobby Lobby* and its progeny may best be understood as *both* a legal attempt to countenance developing theological understandings of complicity that have gained prominence due to several faith communities' rising anxieties over evolving social norms, *and also* a politically motivated attempt to mobilize those theological concerns in the interest of party politics and neoliberal economics. It is through such strategic articulations of complicity-based conceptions of accommodation in cases such as *Hobby Lobby* that RFRA has thus become a political battleground for the ongoing "culture wars" that are still pervading the American political climate.

CONCLUSION

By utilizing a cultural studies framework that meaningfully recognizes the social, political, and economic forces present in a given historical moment that help to produce and restructure theological claims, this chapter has sought to demonstrate that *Hobby Lobby* did not occur in a vacuum. Instead, striking shifts have occurred in how RFRA was popularly understood and valued between 1993 and 2014 – shifts that may be explained not only by theological innovation, but also by the work of economic and political actors who encouraged and helped finance litigation for reasons not exclusively related to religious belief. When viewed in this light, the *Hobby Lobby* decision may be better understood as just one significant flashpoint in

---

[39] See Amelia Thomson-DeVeaux, *The Spirit and the Law: How the Becket Fund Became the Leading Advocate for Corporations' Religious Rights*, The American Prospect Longform (July/August 2014), available at http://perma.cc/UJ9S-4A9N.
[40] For further discussion of these economic connections, see Id.
[41] Loewentheil, supra note 34, at 118.

a broader set of debates and controversies that has brought networks of economic, political, and religious actors with overlapping interests into conversation in a "culture wars" environment. And, given the centrality of questions surrounding abortion and contraception in this "culture wars" context, it is clear that the health care profession will thus continue to be affected by an ebb and flow of litigation seeking to mobilize RFRA to advance normative social aims.

3

The HHS Mandate Litigation and Religious Health Care Providers

Adèle Keim

Religious institutions are "near the epicenter of American philanthropy: they absorb well over half of all private charitable contributions, and account for a disproportionate share of the private voluntary effort."[1] This contribution is particularly evident in health care, which was pioneered by religious organizations – like the Catholic nuns who founded the first hospital in North America – and remains deeply shaped by religious organizations today.

There are at least two background principles that have allowed religious health care providers to flourish for so long. The first is that the law allows them to operate as religious communities by selecting leaders and employees based on a shared commitment to their religious mission. The second is that the law protects them in the religiously sensitive areas surrounding the taking of a human life – particularly with respect to providing abortions and administering the death penalty.

The U.S. Department of Health and Human Services rule requiring employers to provide and in many cases pay for contraceptives, including the "morning after" and "week after" pills (described in the introduction to this volume) undermined both of these principles. This rule, also known as the "HHS Mandate" is often defended in terms of harm to third parties, defined narrowly as employees. But this account of third-party harm is incomplete. Rules that have the effect of forcing religious health care providers to choose between following the law and following their faith harm not only their employees but also the people they serve. The Supreme Court was correct to reject the government's third-party harm arguments in *Burwell v. Hobby*

---

[1] Lester Salamon, *America's Nonprofit Sector: A Primer* 149 (2nd ed. 1999), quoted in Stephen Monsma & Stanley Carlson-Thies, *Free to Serve* 8–9 (2015).

The author thanks Mark Rienzi, Associate Professor, The Catholic University of America, Columbus School of Law and Senior Counsel, the Becket Fund for Religious Liberty, for his invaluable comments. The author has represented religious objectors to the U.S. Health and Human Services' contraceptive mandate in *Hobby Lobby v. Sebelius*, 134 S. Ct. 2751 (2014), *Little Sisters of the Poor v. Burwell*, 794 F.3d 1151 (10th Cir. 2015), and *Zubik v. Burwell*, 136 S. Ct. 1557 (2016), among others.

48   Adèle Keim

Lobby, and to press the government to find a way to more fully accommodate religious health care providers like the Little Sisters of the Poor in *Zubik*. Failing to do so would have constricted the space that allows religious individuals and communities to contribute to the common good. And that would have been a loss for everyone.

The first section of this chapter discusses the important role of religious communities in U.S. health care and the background legal principles that have allowed religiously-motivated health care to serve so many people, so effectively, for so long. The second section addresses the third-party harm arguments raised by the government and its allies, and traces the ways these arguments shifted between *Hobby Lobby* (decided in 2014) and *Zubik* (decided in 2016). The chapter concludes by reflecting on the ways that the third-party harm arguments made in both rounds of the HHS Mandate litigation failed to account for the harm to patients and the broader community that would be caused by pushing religiously motivated providers out of U.S. health care through inadequate respect for their religious conscience.

1. RELIGIOUS DIVERSITY IS GOOD FOR HEALTH CARE

When discussing religion in contemporary U.S. health care, it is wise to step back and reflect on the contributions of religious people to the health infrastructure we enjoy today.

- The oldest hospital in North America is the Hôtel-Dieu in Quebec; it was founded by an all-women religious order that ran it until the 1960s.[2]
- Jews founded hospitals in New York, St. Louis, and Cincinnati in the 1850s, in part as a response to widespread anti-Semitism.[3]
- Seventh-day Adventists pioneered holistic medicine in the nineteenth century – emphasizing diet, exercise, and rest during an era when many mainstream medical treatments did more harm than good.[4]

---

[2] Greg J. Humbert, "Catholic Hospitals in Canada," in *A Compendium of the Catholic Health Association of Canada* I-1 (2011), available at www.chac.ca/about/history/docs/compendium_hospitals.pdf [https://perma.cc/8RRK-VL3P] ("Founded in 1639, Hôtel-Dieu de Québec is the oldest and therefore the first hospital in North America."). The Hôtel-Dieu was run by religious women from the 1630s until the 1960s; in 1995 it was taken over by the government of Québec. CHUQ, L'Hôtel-Dieu de Québec, Info Capsule, available at www.chuq.qc.ca/fr/le_chuq/nos_etablissements/hdq/ [www.chuq.qc.ca/fr/le_chuq/nos_etablissements/hdq/ [https://perma.cc/5JRW-WGMH]; Catholic Hospitals in Canada at I-2.

[3] See, e.g., Edward Halperin, *The Rise and Fall of the American Jewish Hospital*, 87 History of Academic Medicine 610 (2012).

[4] Heritage Battle Creek, *The Battle Creek Idea*, available at www.heritagebattlecreek.org/index.php?option=com_content&view=article&id=95&Itemid=73 [https://perma.cc/FNM5-L2GF]; Adventist Health System, History, available at www.adventisthealthsystem.com/page.php?section=about&page=history [https://perma.cc/8CM2-D78M] (linking Battle Creek with contemporary holistic health practices in Adventist health care).

It would be a mistake to think that all of this religious involvement in health care is simply a fading relic of an age when government was inadequate to the task. Perhaps the best-known examples are Catholic: according to the Catholic Health Association, one in six patients in the United States is cared for in Catholic hospitals.[5] Indeed, according to one 2013 study, "[n]ot-for-profit, church-owned hospitals save more lives, release patients from the hospital sooner, and have better overall patient satisfaction ratings" than for-profit and government hospitals.[6] Other examples abound:

- Hospitals founded by American Jews in the 1850s provided critical training opportunities for Jewish doctors in the 1920s and 30s when many other facilities turned them away.[7] Catholic teaching hospitals fill the same role for Catholic and other pro-life medical students today.
- In the decades after the Civil War, Congress granted the Little Sisters of the Poor money to care for elderly emancipated slaves and others;[8] today they continue to care for the elderly poor of all faiths in thirty U.S. nursing homes and in more than thirty countries around the world.[9]
- The Seventh-day Adventist church continues its holistic approach in hospitals, clinics and hospice care serving ten million people a year.[10] The Adventists' distinctive holistic approach has led contemporary researchers to study U.S. Adventists, who live an average of ten years longer than other Americans.[11]

The United States enjoys a flourishing nonprofit health care sector. But that cannot be taken for granted.

---

[5] Catholic Health Association of the United States, *Facts & Statistics* (January 2016), available at www.chausa.org/about/about/facts-statistics [https://perma.cc/MQ6P-9QUZ]. The ACLU has asserted that this success threatens access to emergency abortions in some parts of the U.S. and has sued to force Catholic hospitals to perform abortions. See *ACLU Announces Lawsuit Against Catholic Hospital System* (October 1, 2015), available at www.aclu.org/news/aclu-announces-lawsuit-against-catholic-hospital-system-failing-provide-emergency-medical-care [https://perma.cc/2EZW-JZAL]. Their lawsuit was dismissed by the district court, but litigation continues. See American Civil Liberties Union v Trinity Health Corp., No. 15-cv-12611 (E.D. Mich. April 11, 2016).
[6] CHAUSA, *Facts & Statistics*, supra note 4.
[7] Halperin, supra note 2, at 611.
[8] See, e.g., *Investigation of Charities and Reformatory Institutions in D.C. Part 1* at 391–2 (1897) (noting that from 1873–84, Congress and the D.C. government had appropriated $55,000 to the Little Sisters' D.C. home and observing that the home served the "aged … without distinction of color or creed").
[9] Little Sisters of the Poor, *Directory of Homes*, available at www.littlesistersofthepoor.org/locations/u-s-homes/ [https://perma.cc/UXH6-GLSW].
[10] Adventist Health Care, available at www.sdahealthcare.org/ [https://perma.cc/X86A-EDEN] (10 million patients a year).
[11] Peter Bowes, *Loma Linda: The secret to a long healthy life?*, BBC News, December 8, 2014, available at www.bbc.com/news/magazine-30351406 [https://perma.cc/3KMQ-MJ46] (average lifespan increased by 10 years).

There are at least two background conditions that have been critical to the flourishing of nonprofit religious care, both of which are under challenge by the HHS Mandate. The first is this: religious nonprofits – including hospitals, clinics, and nursing homes – are allowed to operate as *communities* of faith. In part what this looks like is that religious organizations may choose leaders and employees that share their faith. This basic right is protected in major civil rights laws like Title VII[12] and has been repeatedly recognized by the Supreme Court.[13] And this community-forming right extends not only to churches, which enjoy particular First Amendment protection, but also to hospitals, schools, and religious health care providers like the Little Sisters of the Poor.[14] The ability to choose likeminded employees that transmit their values has enabled religious health care providers to preserve their mission and continue to make distinctive contributions to U.S. health care over time.

The second condition is this: As covered in several other chapters in this volume (Laycock, Cohen, etc.), American law works to avoid widespread and foreseeable conflicts of conscience. And the law is particularly sensitive towards conscientious objections to the taking of human life.[15]

The paradigmatic example of the second condition is the death penalty. Objections to participating in executions are widespread. In 1994, Justice Blackmun announced that he would "no longer tinker with the machinery of death."[16] The same year, Congress exempted any federal employee or contractor from being coerced to participate in an execution.[17] In March 2015, the American Pharmacists Association followed other major medical associations and adopted a policy discouraging its members from providing the drugs used to administer lethal injections.[18] In short,

---

[12] 42 U.S.C. § 2000e-1 ("This subchapter shall not apply to an employer with respect ... to a religious corporation, association, educational institution, or society with respect to the employment of individuals of a particular religion to perform work connected with the carrying on by such corporation, association, educational institution, or society of its activities.").

[13] See, e.g., *Hosanna-Tabor Evangelical Lutheran Church & School v. EEOC*, 132 S. Ct. 694, 710 (2012); *Corp. of Presiding Bishop v. Amos*, 483 U.S. 327, 336 (1987); *Nat'l Labor Relations Bd. v. Catholic Bishop of Chi.*, 440 U.S. 490 (1979).

[14] See generally 42 U.S.C. § 2000e-1 (exempting "religious corporation[s], association[s], educational institution[s]" and "societ[ies]"); see also Hosanna-Tabor, 132 S. Ct. at 699 (church-operated school); Amos, 483 U.S. at 330 (church-operated gymnasium).

[15] See generally Mark L. Rienzi, *The Constitutional Right Not to Kill*, 62 Emory L.J. 121 (2012).

[16] *Callins v. Collins*, 510 U.S. 1141, 1145 (1994) ("From this day forward, I no longer shall tinker with the machinery of death.").

[17] 18 U.S.C. §3597 (b) (1994).

[18] American Pharmacists Association, *APhA House of Delegates Adopts Policy Discouraging Pharmacist Participation in Execution* (March 30, 2015), available at www.pharmacist.com/apha-house-delegates-adopts-policy-discouraging-pharmacist-participation-execution [https://perma.cc/SE3W-K7YR]; see generally Death Penalty Information Center, *Lethal Injection: Statements Medical*, available at www.deathpenaltyinfo.org/lethal-injection-statements-medical [https://perma.cc/SX2Q-WRDW] (collecting statements from the American Medical Association, the American Board of

the United States gives health care providers who object to involvement in the death penalty wide berth.[19]

This approach is wise. When we fail to accommodate health care providers' consciences, the consequences can be perverse. For example, Illinois passed a rule requiring all pharmacists to dispense emergency contraception regardless of whether they believed that these drugs could result in the intentional taking of a human life.[20] When adopting the policy, then-Governor Blagojevich announced that its purpose was to "stop religion from 'stand[ing] in the way' of dispensing drugs, and force pharmacies to 'fill prescriptions without making moral judgments.'"[21] As a direct result of Illinois' rule, at least one pharmacy was forced to close – during a period when Illinois was facing a shortage of pharmacists.[22] Yet when challenged, Illinois could not identify "a single person who was ever unable to obtain emergency contraception because of a religious objection," nor could it "provide any evidence that anyone was having difficulties finding willing sellers of over-the-counter Plan B, either at pharmacies or over the internet."[23] Thus, a rule intended to protect women seeking access to emergency contraceptives resulted in less access to health care for everyone.

Abortion is another core example. For over forty years federal law has prevented hospitals from coercing nurses, doctors, and other health care providers into taking part in abortions against their will.[24] When the Accreditation Council for Graduate Medical Education made abortion a mandatory part of all obstetrics training programs in the 1990s, Congress ordered federal funds to continue to flow to all programs that lost accreditation over this issue.[25] Instead of allowing programs that train obstetricians to close, Congress created targeted exemptions. Twenty years later,

---

Anesthesiology, American Nurses Association, and the International Academy of Compounding Pharmacists).

[19] Some would go further and outright prohibit physician involvement in lethal injection. See Robert D. Truog, I. Glenn Cohen, & Mark A. Rockoff, *Physicians, Medical Ethics, and Execution by Lethal Injection*, 311 J. AM. MED. ASS'N 2375 (2014).

[20] *Morr-Fitz, Inc. v. Blagojevich*, No. 2005-CH-000495, 2011 WL 1338081 (Ill. Cir. Ct. 7th, April 5, 2011).

[21] Morr-Fitz, 2011 WL 1338081, at 2.

[22] Morr-Fitz, 2011 WL 1338081, at 1; see also Jim Ritter, Area nursing shortage keeps getting worse, Chi. Sun-Times, September 19, 2005 (noting that there were not enough pharmacists in the Chicago area).

[23] Morr-Fitz, 2011 WL 1338081, at 2.

[24] A 1973 provision to the Public Health Service Act – known as the "Church Amendment" – forbids hospitals that receive public health service funds from discriminating against employees or applicants whose "religious beliefs or moral convictions" prevent them from participating in abortion or sterilization procedures. 42 U.S.C. § 300a-7(b)-(e).

[25] See Accreditation Council for Graduate Medical Education, *ACGME Program Requirements for Graduate Medical Education in Obstetrics and Gynecology*, IV.A.6.d).(1) (2015), available at www.acgme.org/Portals/0/PFAssets/ProgramRequirements/220_obstetrics_and_gynecology_2016 .pdf [https://perma.cc/3ZHW-67XC]; 42 U.S.C. § 238n(b) (known as the Coats Amendment). The ACGME standards allow medical residents who have a "religious or moral objection" to abortion to

we can be glad that Congress protected conscientious objectors. The American Congress of Obstetricians and Gynecologists predicts a shortage of 9,000 ob-gyns by 2030 and 15,000 ob-gyns by 2050.[26] Pushing people with religious or conscientious objection to abortion out of the field altogether does not increase women's access to needed care.

As Holly Fernandez Lynch has observed, the list of foreseeable health care conflicts does not end there.[27] And developments like the advance of assisted reproductive technology and the legalization of euthanasia bring acute conflicts of conscience into fields like oncology and gerontology where they have not previously been widespread.[28]

Here's why this matters. Because of this long tradition of protecting conscientious objectors, religious people are not unnecessarily deterred from entering the field of medicine. And religious organizations are motivated to invest in health care ministries, confident that a change of administration or a hostile judge will not force them to choose between continuing their ministry or keeping their faith.

One reason the HHS Mandate provoked such widespread and sustained opposition from religious communities – including religious health care providers like the Little Sisters of the Poor – is that it is an assault on both of these background principles. The HHS Mandate – which distinguished between churches and other religious nonprofits like schools, hospitals, and nursing homes – failed to respect the principle that all nonprofit religious organizations have a deep interest in preserving the character of their religious communities. The HHS Mandate further required religious nonprofits that offered health plans to also authorize the provision of drugs that they believe end a new human life.[29] This is serious enough in its own right, but it is even more concerning when viewed together with contemporaneous efforts to impose surgical abortion mandates on churches and religious nonprofits in states

---

opt out of the required training, and forbid programs from requiring training in induced abortions. VI.A.6.d)(2).

[26] American Congress of Obstetricians and Gynecologists, 2014 *ACOG Workforce Fact Sheet: Florida*, available at www.acog.org/-/media/Departments/Government-Relations-and-Outreach/WF2011FL.pdf?dmc=1&ts=20150422T1117327900 [https://perma.cc/4N4E-CZDS].

[27] Holly Fernandez Lynch, *Conflicts of Conscience in Health Care: An Institutional Compromise* (2008) (euthanasia); See I. Glenn Cohen, Ch. 25, this volume (assisted reproductive technology).

[28] Id. at 26.

[29] This was not an idiosyncratic or unscientific view: the government agreed that four of the contraceptives required under the Mandate could operate by destroying newly-created human embryos. Hobby Lobby, 134 S. Ct. at 2775 (observing that the religious objectors "have a sincere religious belief that life begins at conception" and that "[t]hey therefore object on religious grounds to providing health insurance that covers methods of birth control that, as HHS acknowledges may result in the destruction of an embryo") (citing Brief for HHS in No. 13–354, at 9, n. 4) (internal citations omitted).

like California and New York.[30] As Robin Wilson has pointed out, in the face of pressure like this, some religious charities may find themselves forced to exercise the "nuclear option" and shut down their operations entirely.[31] This would be a loss for many third parties – not just their employees but also the communities they serve.

2. THE HHS MANDATE AND THE CURIOUS CASE OF THE VANISHING THIRD-PARTY HARMS

What happened during the HHS Mandate that allowed the contributions of religious health care providers – and the background principles that allow them to flourish – to become so obscured? One answer is the emergence of an old objection in a new form. In both rounds of the HHS Mandate battle, third-party harms were a major theme for the government and its defenders.[32] In *Hobby Lobby* in particular, the government argued that the existence of identifiable third parties who could be harmed (in this case, Hobby Lobby's employees) was an absolute bar to the Green family's request for a religious accommodation.[33] This argument is not new, but it has been consistently rejected by the courts. The Supreme Court has long held that the Free Exercise Clause permits and at times requires accommodations that could harm some third parties, including employees of religious organizations.[34] In part this is because the Court has taken a broad view of third-party harms – one that included not only employees, but also beneficiaries of faith-based care and civil society more generally.

By the time the Little Sisters of the Poor reached the Supreme Court in 2016, the government's third-party harm argument – which was squarely rejected by *Hobby Lobby*[35] – had shifted. The government conceded that it was willing to tolerate harms to small business employees, but would not countenance the exact same harms

---

[30] Compl., *Skyline Wesleyan Church v. Cal. Dep't of Managed Health Care*, No. 37-2016-00003936 (Cal. Super. Ct. San Diego Cnty. February 2, 2016); Compl., *Roman Catholic Diocese of Albany v. Vullo*, No. 02070-16 (N.Y. Sup. Ct. Albany Cnty. May 4, 2016).

[31] Robin Fretwell Wilson, Ch. 17, this volume.

[32] See, e.g., Pet. Br. at 30–1, *Burwell v. Hobby Lobby*, 134 S. Ct. 2751 (2014), 2014 WL 173486; Resp'ts Br. at 74–5, *Zubik v. Burwell*, No. 14–1418 (U.S. February 10, 2016) (asserting that the religious ministries' less-restrictive alternatives could have a detrimental effect on third parties); see also Nelson Tebbe & Micah Schwartzman, Ch. 15, this volume. But see Carl H. Esbeck, Third-Party Harms, Congressional Statutes Accommodating Religion, and the Establishment Clause (Univ. of Mo. Sch. of Law Legal Studies Paper Series, Research Paper No. 2015-10) (November 17, 2015), available at http://papers.ssrn.com/sol3/papers.cfm?abstract_id=2607277 (arguing that newly created statutory entitlements cannot be used to block religious accommodations that preserve the pre-statute status quo).

[33] Pet. Br., Hobby Lobby, 2014 WL 173486, at 41.

[34] This is discussed at greater length below.

[35] Hobby Lobby, 134 S. Ct. at 2781 n.37.

when religious groups were doing the requesting.[36] The Supreme Court's order in *Zubik* sidestepped this contradiction, observing that the government appeared able to accomplish its policy objectives without burdening religious consciences, and that it should do so.[37] But as discussed below, there are reasons to think that the HHS Mandate's effect on third parties was part of the Court's thinking – particularly when third parties are defined to include both people who work for the Little Sisters as well as the Sisters' patients and the millions of Americans whose faith motivates them to serve others on a daily basis.

A. Background Law

Third-party harm arguments, which are the focus of Sepinwall's chapter in this volume and are also discussed in several other chapters, are nothing new in religious liberty law. They are routinely raised by government officials in prisoner litigation, where the identifiable third parties usually include prison employees.[38] But where a constitutional right is involved, the Supreme Court has repeatedly declined to hold that third-party harms are by themselves dispositive.[39] This is not because the Court has always found the harm to third parties to be de minimis – in *Gillette*, the Court upheld a religious accommodation that resulted in sending others to war.[40] But the Court has held that, at times, constitutional rights must be protected notwithstanding potential harm to identifiable third parties.

Thus, for example, in the 1963 case *Sherbert v. Verner*, the Court held that the possibility of "spurious" unemployment claims was insufficient to defeat a Seventh-day Adventist's request for unemployment compensation after she was fired for refusing

---

[36] Resp'ts Br., Zubik, at 65 ("If a small employer elects not to provide health coverage (or if a large employer chooses to pay the tax rather than providing coverage), employees will ordinarily obtain coverage through a family member's employer, through an individual insurance policy purchased on an Exchange or directly from an insurer, or through Medicaid or another government program. All of those sources would include contraceptive coverage.").

[37] *Zubik v. Burwell*, 136 S. Ct. 1557, 1560 (2016) ("The Government has confirmed that the challenged procedures 'for employers with insured plans could be modified to operate in the manner posited in the Court's order while still ensuring that the affected women receive contraceptive coverage seamlessly, together with the rest of their health coverage.'") (quoting Supplemental Brief for Respondents 14–15).

[38] See, e.g., *Holt v. Hobbs*, 135 S. Ct. 853, 864 (2015) ("The Department suggests that requiring guards to search a prisoner's beard would pose a risk to the physical safety of a guard if a razor or needle was concealed in the beard.").

[39] See, e.g., *New York Times v. Sullivan*, 376 U.S. 254, 281 (1964) ("[O]ccasional injury to the reputations of individuals must yield to the public welfare, although at times such injury may be great.") (internal quotation omitted); see also *Snyder v. Phelps*, 562 U.S. 443 (2011) (hate speech), *Gertz v. Robert Welch*, 418 U.S. 323 (1974) (defamatory speech); *Ashcroft v. ACLU*, 542 U.S. 656 (2004) (obscene material on public library computers).

[40] *Gillette v. United States*, 401 U.S. 437, 449–53 (1971).

to work on her Sabbath, "[f]or even if the possibility of spurious claims did threaten to dilute the fund and disrupt the scheduling of work, it would plainly be incumbent upon the appellees to demonstrate that no alternative forms of regulation would combat such abuses without infringing First Amendment rights."[41] In 1979, the Court held that the National Labor Relations Board lacked jurisdiction over private religious schools, in part to "escape" the "serious First Amendment questions that would follow" if the Board interfered in the relationship between a religious school and its employees.[42] In 1987, the Court upheld the religious exemption in Title VII against the allegation that it "offend[ed] equal protection principles by giving less protection to the employees of religious employers than to the employees of secular employers."[43] The Court ruled in part on the ground that it had the "legitimate purpose of alleviating significant governmental interference with the ability of religious organizations to define and carry out their religious missions."[44] And in 2012, the Court held that the EEOC could not enforce the Americans with Disabilities Act against a church-run school, saying:

> Requiring a church to accept or retain an unwanted minister, or punishing a church for failing to do so ... interferes with the internal governance of the church ... By imposing an unwanted minister, the state infringes the Free Exercise Clause, which protects a religious group's right to shape its own faith and mission through its appointments. According the state the power to determine which individuals will minister to the faithful also violates the Establishment Clause, which prohibits government involvement in such ecclesiastical decisions.[45]

In each of these cases, the Supreme Court held that the Constitution permitted or required the government to accommodate a religious person or organization – even though the religious accommodation could adversely impact an identifiable third person. This, then, was the law as it stood when Hobby Lobby reached the Court.

B. Round 1: *Third Party Harms in* Hobby Lobby

In *Hobby Lobby*, the Solicitor General adopted a "maximalist" version of the third-party harm argument and asserted that RFRA did not even apply in situations where third parties like employees could be harmed by a religious exemption.[46] Hobby

---

[41] *Sherbert v. Verner*, 374 U.S. 398, 407 (1963).
[42] N.L.R.B., 440 U.S. at 504.
[43] Amos, 483 U.S. at 338.
[44] Id. at 339.
[45] Hosanna-Tabor, 132 S. Ct. at 706.
[46] Pet. Br., Hobby Lobby, 2014 WL 173486, at 30–1; Hobby Lobby, 134 S. Ct. at 2781 n.37 ("HHS appears to maintain that a plaintiff cannot prevail on a RFRA claim that seeks an exemption from a legal obligation requiring the plaintiff to confer benefits on third parties.").

Lobby agreed that the Court should weigh the harm that a requested exemption could cause to third parties, but argued that this harm should be considered as part of the strict scrutiny analysis.[47] The Supreme Court agreed with Hobby Lobby and rejected the government's argument. The Court said:

> [I]t could not reasonably be maintained that any burden on religious exercise ... is permissible under RFRA so long as the relevant legal obligation requires the religious adherent to confer a benefit on third parties. Otherwise, for example, the Government could decide that all supermarkets must sell alcohol for the convenience of customers (and thereby exclude Muslims with religious objections from owning supermarkets) ... By framing any Government regulation as benefiting a third party, the Government could turn all regulations into entitlements to which nobody could object on religious grounds, rendering RFRA meaningless.[48]

Responding to this footnote, Nelson Tebbe and Michah Schwartzman have argued that the Supreme Court has a baseline problem.[49] They assert that the baseline for evaluating third-party harms is the world as it is after a law has been passed. Carl Esbeck has argued that this is wrong – that the correct baseline is on the day before Congress imposed the new legal requirements.[50] That is consistent with the way that Congress dealt with religious accommodations in Title VII. Like the ACA, Title VII was a major expansion of federal power into an area where private employers traditionally had substantial freedom. Also like the ACA, Title VII both bestowed new legal rights on employees and made them privately enforceable. Yet, as already discussed, the religious exemptions to Title VII assumed that the baseline for religious organizations was freedom to hire co-religionists.

The baseline – the day before the ACA was enacted – was that, under federal law, employers were free to include or exclude contraceptives and emergency contraceptives from their health plans. The baseline was also that, unless there was a good reason, the government treated all religious nonprofits the same. And finally, the baseline was that the government did not force anyone to be involved in what they regarded as the taking of human life against their will. Against this background, the government's overreach is clear. And, as the Court recognized, the proper place to consider harm to third parties is under RFRA's compelling interest prong. The government's maximalist argument – that the existence of harm to third parties is by itself enough to block a requested religious accommodation – failed to carry the day.

---

[47] Resp'ts Br., Hobby Lobby, 134 S. Ct. 2751 (2014), 2014 WL 546899, at 57–9.
[48] Hobby Lobby, 134 S. Ct. at 2781 n.37.
[49] Richard Schragger, Micah Schwartzman, and Nelson Tebbe, "When Do Religious Accommodations Burden Others?" in *The Conscience Wars: Rethinking the Balance between Religion, Identity, and Equality* (Susanna Mancini & Michel Rosenfeld eds., forthcoming 2017).
[50] Esbeck, Third-Party Harms, supra note 31.

C. Round 2: Third-Party Harms in Little Sisters

By the time *Little Sisters of the Poor*, *Zubik*, and other HHS Mandate challenges involving religious ministries reached the Supreme Court, the government's argument about third-party harms had changed in response to *Hobby Lobby*. Now the government argued that the accommodation it offered to religious ministries – which relied on their health plans to distribute religiously objectionable services, but which shifted the cost of paying for those services to their benefit providers – was necessary to protect the interests of the women who worked for the ministries.[51] The government's principal objection was that it wanted women employees to be able to get cost-free contraceptives "seamlessly," from their regular doctors, and without filling out any additional paperwork.[52] The religious ministries objected to the government's scheme because it still relied exclusively on their health plans, effectively hijacking the plans they had created and using them to carry out religiously forbidden acts against their will.[53]

The religious ministries suggested many alternative ways for the government to accomplish its policy objectives without involving them.[54] They also pointed out that the government had completely abandoned its asserted interest in "seamless" contraceptive coverage for people covered by the 30% of large employer health plans that enjoy grandfathered status, for the 10 million people enrolled in the government health plan Tricare, and for the 34 million people who work for small businesses, many of which offer no health coverage at all.[55] The government nevertheless insisted that, while alternatives like plans offered on HealthCare.Gov were adequate for small business employees who had no employer coverage, seamless coverage was necessary for religious ministries.[56]

In a highly unusual move, as discussed in this volume's Introduction, the Supreme Court asked both sides to submit supplemental briefs to address whether "contraceptive coverage may be obtained by petitioners' employees through petitioners' insurance companies, but in a way that does not require any involvement of petitioners beyond their own decision to provide health insurance without contraceptive coverage to their employees."[57] The Little Sisters and other religious ministries answered "yes" and pointed to existing government programs that did just that.[58]

---

[51] Resp'ts Br. at 73–6, Zubik.
[52] Oral Arg. Tr. at 51–2, Zubik.
[53] Pets. Br. in Nos. 15–35, at 44, 49–53, Zubik, (January 4, 2016).
[54] Pets. Br. in Nos. 15–35, at 72–8, Zubik; Pets. Br. in Nos. 14–1418, at 72–82, Zubik, (January 4, 2016).
[55] Pets. Reply Br. in Nos. 15–35, et al., at 23–6, Zubik.
[56] Resp'ts Br. at 62, Zubik.
[57] Zubik Supp. Br. Order (March 29, 2016).
[58] Pets. Supp. Br. at 6–9, 23, Zubik (April 12, 2016).

The government also answered yes, albeit grudgingly and on the fourteenth page of its twenty-page brief.[59] As a result, a unanimous Supreme Court halted the government's fines, vacated the decisions below, and remanded to give both sides the opportunity to "arrive at an approach ... that accommodates petitioners' religious exercise while at the same time ensuring that women covered by petitioners' health plans 'receive full and equal health coverage, including contraceptive coverage.'"[60]

What of the third-party harm question? It is difficult to say, because the *Zubik* order specifically declined to rule on the parties' legal arguments.[61] Reading between the lines, however, it is hard to escape the conclusion that larger concerns about additional third party harms – beyond those identified by the government – were lurking in the background. As we have seen, half a century of Free Exercise caselaw has recognized that when the government uses its coercive power against religious organizations, something fundamental is lost. Nor is this view limited to the past. As recently as 2012, Justices Alito and Kagan wrote in their concurrence in *Hosanna-Tabor* that

> [T]he autonomy of religious groups, both here in the United States and abroad, has often served as a shield against oppressive civil laws. To safeguard this crucial autonomy, we have long recognized that the Religion Clauses protect a private sphere within which religious bodies are free to govern themselves in accordance with their own beliefs.[62]

Justice Kagan, who joined Justice Alito's concurrence in *Hosanna-Tabor*, did not join Justice Sotomayor's concurrence in *Zubik*.[63] Indeed, Justice Sotomayor's *Zubik* concurrence – which emphasized the freedom of lower courts to repeat their prior rulings – only garnered a single other vote (Justice Ginsburg); the other six justices did not join her on this point.[64] It seems reasonable to conclude that concern for "the autonomy of religious groups" and the ministries they run continues to animate a majority of the Court. This view is confirmed by cases like *Hosanna-Tabor*, which was a 9–0 decision holding that federal nondiscrimination law could not be used to force a religious school to retain a minister against its will.[65] *Hosanna-Tabor* showed that the entire Supreme Court was aware of the first background principle that allows religious health care to flourish – the ability to select likeminded leaders.

---

[59] Resp'ts Supp. Br. at 14, Zubik (April 12, 2016).
[60] Zubik, 578 U.S. ___ at 4.
[61] Id.
[62] Hosanna-Tabor, 132 S. Ct. at 712.
[63] Zubik, 136 S. Ct. at 1561 (Sotomayor, J., concurring).
[64] Id.
[65] Hosanna-Tabor, 132 S. Ct. at 702 ("Both Religion Clauses bar the government from interfering with the decision of a religious group to fire one of its ministers.").

During the *Hobby Lobby* argument, questions about requiring abortion coverage showed that Justice Kennedy and Chief Justice Roberts were attuned to the second background principle – that we are particularly sensitive to religious objections to the taking of human life.[66] Any comprehensive account of third-party harms will grapple with the harm caused by undermining these two background principles as well.

CONCLUSION

Delivering health care to the poor and underserved is an enormous job. The state does much and should do more. But private philanthropy – religious and secular – also plays a critical role. It is not so much "live and let live" as it is "all hands on deck."

Even if you believe religious health care providers are sometimes deeply misguided – even if you would like Seventh-day Adventist doctors to prescribe conventional drugs more often, Catholic medical schools to offer abortion training, or the Little Sisters to help hospice patients end their lives – would U.S. health care be better off if they were forced to leave the field altogether? That is the risk that is run each time the courts are asked to undermine the background principles that religious health care providers rely on. Rules allowing religious hiring or accommodating religious teaching on the taking of human life may seem anachronistic in the abstract, but for religious organizations they are a source of life. We should think long and hard before abandoning these principles – not just for the sake of religious health care providers, but also for the sake of the people they serve.

---

[66] Hobby Lobby Oral Arg. Tr. at 75–6.

4

Not Your Father's Religious Exemptions

The Contraceptive-Coverage Litigation and the Rights of Others

Gregory M. Lipper

Religious exemptions from neutral, generally applicable laws are permissible and appropriate, but only within reason. With few exceptions, related to core questions of church autonomy, religious accommodations should not harm others; that is the balance struck by the Religion Clauses in a diverse country built on church-state separation and devoted to the religious freedom of everyone. But the Supreme Court's ruling in favor of Hobby Lobby and its decision to keep alive challenges to the accommodation have unleashed a new era of free-exercise claims – in which courts entertain religious objections to other people's conduct (often related to sex and reproductive care) and in the process imperil the rights and benefits of others.

It wasn't supposed to be this way. James Madison stated, "I observe with particular pleasure the view you have taken of the immunity of Religion from civil jurisdiction, *in every case where it does not trespass on private rights* or the public peace."[1] Garden-variety religious exemptions – the right to wear a beard, use ceremonial peyote, or promptly bury a loved one – advance these values by relieving burdens on religious exercise without harming anyone else.

But the exemptions sought in the contraceptive-coverage cases, detailed in this volume's Introduction, have hijacked these principles. First, the Supreme Court in *Hobby Lobby* recognized a free-exercise right to restrict the benefits and thus to control behavior of others – requiring exemptions that deprive tens of thousands of women of important medical coverage. Second, the Court did so despite serious questions about the sincerity of many of the plaintiffs – whether their objections were purely political, rather than religious – and even though many of the plaintiffs' objections arose from factual mistakes about the way certain contraceptives work.

---

[1] Letter from James Madison to Edward Livingston (July 10, 1822), reprinted in 9 *The Writings of James Madison* 98, 100 (Gaillard Hunt ed. 1910) (emphasis added).

Finally, by entertaining and sustaining these claims, the Court has managed to harm both women's health and religious liberty: Women have lost access to essential reproductive care, and political support for religious accommodations will dwindle as religious liberty becomes associated with aggressive attempts to deprive others of their rights. This chapter takes up these concerns one-by-one.

1. "FIRST, DO NO HARM"

In determining whether to require religious exemptions from laws that are neutral and generally applicable, the courts have long sought to avoid harming others. In *Sherbert v. Verner*, the Supreme Court held that the Free Exercise Clause required a religious exemption because the requested exemption would not "abridge any other person's religious liberties."[2] But in *United States v. Lee*, the Court ruled that the same clause did not entitle an employer to a religious exemption from paying social-security taxes, because the requested exemption would have "impose[d] the employer's religious faith on the employees."[3] And in *Estate of Thornton v. Caldor*, the Court determined that the Establishment Clause barred a state from requiring employers to accommodate sabbatarians in all cases, no matter what the circumstances, because "the statute takes no account of the convenience or interests of the employer or those of other employees who do not observe a Sabbath."[4]

The Religious Freedom Restoration Act did not purport to abolish these limits – nor could it have done so without violating the Establishment Clause. Indeed, in rejecting an Establishment Clause challenge to the prison-related provisions of the Religious Land Use and Institutionalized Persons Act, which provides RFRA-like protections for inmates and land use, the Court reiterated that the Establishment Clause required prison officials to "take adequate account of the burdens a requested accommodation may impose on nonbeneficiaries."[5]

Before *Hobby Lobby*, the exceptions to this rule were few and far between – and involved core questions of church autonomy, such as the right to hire and fire ministers (as in *Hosanna-Tabor Evangelical Lutheran Church & School v. EEOC*[6]) and the right to hire coreligionists (as in *Corporation of the Presiding Bishop of the Church of Jesus Christ of Latter-Day Saints v. Amos*[7]). Yet outside this narrow context

---

[2] 374 U.S. 398, 409 (1963).
[3] 455 U.S. 252, 261 (1982).
[4] 472 U.S. 703, 709 (1985)
[5] *Cutter v. Wilkinson*, 544 U.S. 709, 720 (2005).
[6] 132 S. Ct. 694 (2012).
[7] 483 U.S. 327 (1987).

of core church hiring decisions, courts consistently rejected religious employers' attempts to win exemptions from laws protecting employees:

- The Supreme Court rejected a free-exercise challenge to laws requiring employers to pay Social Security taxes; as discussed earlier, the Court observed that "[g]ranting an exemption from social security taxes to an employer operates to impose the employer's religious faith on the employees."[8]
- The Supreme Court rejected free-exercise challenges to minimum wage and overtime requirements of the Fair Labor Standards Act, concluding that "[l]ike other employees covered by the Act, [the religious foundation's employees] are entitled to its full protection."[9]
- A federal appeals court refused to authorize religious exemptions to the law requiring equal pay for men and women, based on a religious school's belief that males were the "head of the house."[10]
- Another federal appeals court refused to allow a religious employer to withhold health insurance from married women, again based on the school's belief that men were the "head of the household."[11]

Under these decisions, employers' religious objections did not entitle them to withhold compensation (cash or otherwise), either generally or from women. Sure, the government could have, in theory, stepped in to provide the missing compensation to affected employees. But no matter: Even with the theoretical availability of government support, employees did not give up their right to full and fair compensation just because their employer objected on religious grounds to laws guaranteeing that compensation.

Yet in *Hobby Lobby*, the Court discarded these principles. It allowed for-profit corporations whose owners had religious objections to contraception to deprive their employees of required compensation.

The Court claimed that its decision would not harm affected employees, pointing to a purportedly less-restrictive alternative: the accommodation, offered to nonprofit organizations, through which the organization would object in writing and the government would, in response, arrange for the objector's insurance company or plan administrator to provide the coverage at no cost to either the objector or its employees.[12] But after invoking the accommodation as a less-restrictive alternative requiring an exemption from the underlying coverage requirement, the majority

---

[8] Lee, 455 U.S. at 261.
[9] *Tony & Susan Alamo Found. v. Sec'y of Labor*, 471 U.S. 290, 303–305, 306 (1985).
[10] *Dole v. Shenandoah Baptist Church*, 899 F.2d 1389, 1392, 1398 (4th Cir. 1990).
[11] *EEOC v. Fremont Christian Sch.*, 781 F.2d 1362, 1364, 1367–9 (9th Cir. 1986).
[12] *Burwell v. Hobby Lobby Stores*, 134 S. Ct. 2751, 2781–2 (2014).

declined to decide whether that accommodation "complies with RFRA for purposes of all religious claims."[13]

Thus, not only did the court block the contraceptive-coverage requirement against religious objectors, but the court left the legality of the fallback mechanism – designed to soften the blows caused by these objections – uncertain as well. And dozens of challenges to the accommodation remained.

For a while, it looked like the accommodation would survive these challenges. Eight of nine federal appeals courts rejected challenges to the accommodation brought by religious nonprofit organizations.[14] And there were good reasons for those decisions: Most importantly, the government needs the ability to protect those who would otherwise be harmed by an exemption, such as the one required by *Hobby Lobby*. It's one thing to refuse to cover contraceptives; it's quite another to block the government from arranging to cover your employees after you refuse to do so.

The results of a contrary rule, moreover, would be bizarre. Under the plaintiffs' logic, a substantial burden on religious exercise would arise from an exemption provided to a conscientious objector who opposed fighting in a war – on the theory that once the objector requested an exemption, the Army would select a replacement, thus making the objector complicit in sending someone to war. Indeed, in an oral argument, the lawyer for the University of Notre Dame, one of the challengers to the accommodation, agreed with this "fantastic suggestion."[15]

Similar responses undermine a variant of the objectors' argument: that they are forced to contract with insurance companies that are providing insurance coverage to their students and employees or that the government is "hijacking" their health plans to distribute contraceptives against their wills. These are fancy ways of saying that they object to the government's regulating or facilitating conduct by third parties. For example, federal law prohibits employment discrimination on the basis of sex; but even if a client has a religious objection to women working outside the home, that client's religious exercise is not substantially burdened by retaining a law firm that necessarily hires women. The accommodation is no more hijacking the objectors' health plans than the antidiscrimination law is hijacking objectors' law firms.[16]

---

[13] Id. at 2782.
[14] See generally Tim Jost, *Eleventh Circuit Upholds Religious Accommodation on Contraceptive Coverage*, Health Affairs Blog (February 19, 2016), available at http://healthaffairs.org/blog/2016/02/19/eleventh-circuit-upholds-religious-accommodation-on-contraceptive-coverage/ [https://perma.cc/YE6Z-J2CC] (discussing lower-court decisions).
[15] See *Univ. of Notre Dame v. Sebelius*, 743 F.3d 547, 556 (7th Cir. 2014).
[16] I elaborate on this in Gregory M. Lipper, *Zubik v. Burwell, Part 1: Why Paperwork Does Not Burden Religious Exercise*, Bill of Health (March 16, 2016), available at http://blogs.harvard.edu/billofhealth/2016/03/16/zubik-v-burwell-part-1-why-paperwork-does-not-burden-religious-exercise/ [https://perma.cc/5AC3-VL75].

But despite the solid legal basis for the lower courts' decisions, the hijacking argument appeared to persuade four justices on a divided eight-member Supreme Court.[17] And as discussed in this book's introduction, the Court apparently sought to avoid a 4–4 tie in such a high-profile case by avoiding reaching the merits — instead sending *Zubik v. Burwell* and its companion cases back to the lower courts for further consideration of the accommodation and yet more possible alternatives to the accommodation.[18]

The extent to which the objectors sought to control third-party arrangements became even clearer in the supplemental briefing that took place between oral argument and the Supreme Court's nondecision. The Court asked the parties to address a proposal, detailed in this volume's Introduction, contemplating that the objectors would inform their insurance companies that they didn't want to cover contraceptives and then insurance companies would, without further prompting, separately notify and provide coverage to the objectors' employees.

Although the objectors purported to accept that arrangement, they added several caveats – "separate health insurance policies" with "separate enrollment processes, insurance cards, payment sources, and communications streams." These proposed limits, if accepted, would have restricted how third-party insurance companies could provide contraceptive coverage to the affected women, in a manner that would have deprived women of the seamless coverage contemplated by the Affordable Care Act.[19] Even then, the objectors insisted that the Court need not and should not identify an alternative that definitely complied with RFRA – going so far as to mock the government for "pleading with the Court to resolve this case in a way that lays to rest all future RFRA objections to the mandate."[20] And even if the Trump administration and Sessions Justice Department somehow retain, enforce, and defend the contraceptive-coverage regulations and accommodation – outcomes on which I wouldn't bet – President Trump's nominee to the Supreme Court, Justice Neil Gorsuch, will almost certainly cast a fifth vote to enjoin them.

And so the cycle will continue: Demand an accommodation, use the accommodation to undermine the previous regulation, challenge the accommodation in

---

[17] See, e.g., Linda Greenhouse, *A Supreme Court Hijacking*, N.Y. Times (March 30, 2016), available at www.nytimes.com/2016/03/31/opinion/a-supreme-court-hijacking.html?_r=0 [http://nyti.ms/1SyVOBR].

[18] *Zubik v. Burwell*, 136 S. Ct. 1557, 1560 (2016) (per curiam).

[19] See Supplemental Brief for Petitioners at 6 (internal quotation marks omitted); see also, e.g., Gregory M. Lipper, *The Zubik Supplemental Briefs: The Objectors Push for Second-Class Coverage, With a Smile*, Bill of Health (April 13, 2016), available at http://blogs.harvard.edu/billofhealth/2016/04/13/the-zubik-supplemental-briefs-the-objectors-push-for-second-class-coverage-with-a-smile/ [https://perma.cc/E43H-QL2T].

[20] Supplemental Reply Brief for Petitioners at 10.

court, rinse, repeat. Women who want the contraceptive coverage to which they are entitled will remain in limbo.

2. DOUBTFUL SINCERITY MEETS DUBIOUS SCIENCE

Religious exemptions are limited not only by concerns about the rights and interests of others, but also by a more basic, threshold requirement: The asserted religious objections must be sincere. People seeking religious exemptions must in fact believe that complying with the challenged laws would interfere with their religious exercise.[21] When objectors raise a series of increasingly attenuated claims and refuse to take yes for an answer, it highlights the possibility that the asserted religious objections are insincere.

In the contraception cases, evidence of insincerity came not only from the nature of the claims themselves, but, as I describe below, also from the conduct and statements of the challengers and their lawyers – much of which suggested that the religious objections were manufactured substitutes for mere political or ideological objections to the contraceptive-coverage regulations.[22]

Other than in cases brought by prisoners, challenges to the sincerity of free-exercise claimants are rare; courts are understandably reluctant to examine the sincerity of claims merely because the asserted religious beliefs are obscure or unusual. But in these cases, there was good reason to doubt the challengers' sincerity, as many of them had previously covered the very drugs and devices at issue in the lawsuits. Most of these companies offered the same explanation: After the Obama administration announced the contraceptive coverage regulations, the company reviewed its health care plan and "discovered" that the company was covering contraceptives.[23]

Despite these eleventh-hour conversions, the government took the asserted objections at face value: perhaps because it was confident that courts would not sustain RFRA claims by for-profit corporations, perhaps because it feared backlash from calling the plaintiffs insincere. Yet by declining to challenge sincerity, the government passed up the opportunity to pursue factual discovery. Had the government pursued it, fact discovery might well have borne fruit: Given that these plaintiffs were for-profit corporations, they may well have had email trails evincing their actual motivations for suing.

---

[21] See generally Ben Adams & Cynthia Barmore, *Questioning Sincerity: The Role of the Courts After Hobby Lobby*, 67 Stan. L. Rev. Online 59 (2014), available at www.stanfordlawreview.org/online/questioning-sincerity-the-role-of-the-courts-after-hobby-lobby/ [https://perma.cc/3RB6-AHZL].
[22] I describe these sincerity issues in more detail in Gregory M. Lipper, *The Contraceptive Coverage Cases and the Problem of Politicized Free Exercise Lawsuits*, 4 U. Ill. L. Rev. 1331 (2016).
[23] See, e.g., id. at 1336 & nn. 25–6 (collecting cases).

The government deferred even to the most brazen plaintiffs. For instance, the CEO of Eden Foods stated that his company was challenging the coverage regulations because, "I don't care if the federal government is telling me to buy my employees Jack Daniel's or birth control. What gives them the right to tell me that I have to do that?"[24] The Sixth Circuit observed, in response, that the CEO's "'deeply held religious beliefs' more resembled a laissez-faire, anti-government screed."[25] And yet even after the Supreme Court held, as a matter of law, that RFRA required an accommodation for those companies with sincere religious objections to covering contraceptives, the government declined to raise as a defense that Eden Foods was insincere.

If anything, questions about sincerity became even more pronounced in the challenges to the accommodation. Some religious organizations, such as Georgetown University and the Catholic Health Association, accepted and even praised the accommodation.[26] When the Obama administration first announced it, the University of Notre Dame's president called the accommodation a "welcome step toward recognizing the freedom of religious institutions." Yet Notre Dame filed suit three months later to challenge it. (That lawsuit was dismissed as premature.) After HHS issued the final accommodation in July 2013, Notre Dame waited five months to renew its challenge, filing its new lawsuit just weeks before the regulations were set to take effect. The trial judge observed that "Notre Dame has in many ways created its own emergency, and I am left to wonder why."[27]

It so happens that before Notre Dame filed its second lawsuit in late 2013, the university had decided to take advantage of the accommodation, and had said so in its student brochure.[28] But in October 2013, a powerful alumni group wrote to Notre Dame's President and urged the University to bring a new lawsuit because of the

---

[24] Irin Carmon, *Eden Foods Doubles Down in Birth Control Flap*, Salon (April 15, 2013, 6:45 AM), available at www.salon.com/2013/04/15/eden_foods_ceo_digs_himself_deeper_in_birth_control_outrage/ [https://perma.cc/58VN-PG5K].

[25] *Eden Foods, Inc. v. Sebelius*, 733 F.3d 626, 629 n.3 (citation omitted), vacated sub nom., *Eden Foods, Inc. v. Burwell*, 134 S. Ct. 2902 (2014).

[26] See Bridgette Dunlap, *For It Before They Were Against It: Catholic Universities and Birth Control*, RH Reality Check (February 13, 2013, 9:23 PM), available at http://rhrealitycheck.org/article/2013/02/13/before-birth-control-before-they-were-against-it-when-georgetown-fordham-and-notre-dame-and-other-catholic-affiliated-schools-supported-access-to-contraception/ [https://perma.cc/8UJK-6T6N]; Julie Rovner, *White House Bends On Birth Control Requirement For Religious Groups*, NPR (February 10, 2012, 11:49 AM), available at www.npr.org/sections/health-shots/2012/02/10/146693907/white-house-bends-on-birth-control-requirement-for-religious-groups.

[27] *Univ. of Notre Dame v. Sebelius*, 988 F. Supp. 2d 912, 919 (N.D. Ind. 2013).

[28] Univ. of Notre Dame, *Open Enrollment Decision Guide* 14 (2014), available at http://hr.nd.edu/assets/80205/2014_decision_guide_final.pdf [https://perma.cc/98HB-2ST5] ("New: Contraceptive Coverage – Our third party administrator, Meritain Health, will be offering coverage for these services.").

university's "symbolic importance" to the lawsuits.[29] After Notre Dame sued and the court denied its requests for emergency relief, the university's President stated that its "complicity is not an evil so grave that we would compromise our conscience by going along" with the accommodation.[30] "I don't see this as a scandal," he said, "because we are not giving out contraceptives."[31] Yet although the intervenors (a pair of Notre Dame students whom I represented while a lawyer at Americans United for Separation of Church and State) will likely challenge Notre Dame's sincerity if the case ever returns to the trial court for factual discovery, the government again declined to pursue a sincerity defense.

Also telling have been the divergent reactions of certain plaintiffs, and their lawyers at conservative religious legal organizations, to (1) offers of additional accommodations by HHS, and (2) interim orders from the Supreme Court providing for similar accommodations.

The government's original accommodation required an objecting organization to complete a form and send it to its insurance provider or third-party administrator. When it issued interim orders in December 2013 and June 2014, the Supreme Court tweaked this requirement: Instead of sending a form to its insurance company or administrators, an objecting nonprofit organization could tell the government in writing "that it is a nonprofit organization that holds itself out as religious and has religious objections to providing coverage for contraceptive services ..."[32] The Court, however, also authorized the government to "rely[] on this notice, to the extent it considers necessary, to facilitate the provision of full contraceptive coverage under the Act."[33]

In response to the June 2014 order, the government expanded the accommodation to allow objectors to submit an alternate form of notice similar to the one devised by the Supreme Court. Under this alternative, an organization may opt out of covering contraceptives by notifying the government of its religious objection, the nature of its health plan, and the identity of its insurance provider or plan administrator.[34]

---

[29] Brief in Response of Intervenor-Respondent at 6, *Univ. of Notre Dame v. Burwell*, No. 15–812 (citing email from William H. Dempsey, Chairman, Sycamore Trust, to Rev. John I. Jenkins, President, Univ. of Notre Dame (October 26, 2013, 03:46 PM)), available at www.au.org/files/15-812_BIO-Intervenor.pdf [https://perma.cc/2B8K-28ZE].

[30] Matthew Archbold, *Notre Dame Alumni: Fr. Jenkins Comments on HHS Mandate "Startling,"* Catholic Educ. Daily (April 14, 2014), available at https://cardinalnewmansociety.org/notre-dame-alumni-fr-jenkins-comments-on-hhs-mandate-startling/ [https://perma.cc/3YGZ-2EF6].

[31] Id.

[32] See *Wheaton Coll. v. Burwell*, 134 S. Ct. 2806, 2807 (2014) (interim order); see also *Little Sisters of the Poor Home for the Aged, Denver, Colo. v. Sebelius*, 134 S. Ct. 1022 (2014) (interim order).

[33] *Wheaton*, 134 S. Ct. at 2807.

[34] Coverage of Certain Preventive Services Under the Affordable Care Act, 79 Fed. Reg. 51,092, 51,094–5 (August 27, 2014).

HHS finalized this alternative accommodation in July 2015 and extended it to closely held for-profit corporations such as Hobby Lobby.[35]

In short, both the Supreme Court and the government required objectors to notify either the government or their insurance company or third-party administrator. And in each case, the government retained the right to rely on this notice to arrange for the objectors' employees to receive contraceptive coverage from third-party insurance companies or plan administrators. If the objectors genuinely wanted accommodations to relieve actual burdens on religious exercise, we'd expect them to have reacted similarly to each set of decisions.

It was not to be. The Becket Fund for Religious Liberty, which represents many of the plaintiffs and whose lawyer has a chapter in this volume, touted the Supreme Court's *Wheaton College* order as "another important victory against the HHS Mandate ... protecting the College's right to carry out its religious mission free from crippling IRS fines."[36] Yet when describing the government's nearly identical new accommodation, the Becket Fund warned that "the government still won't give up on its quest to force nuns and other religious employers to distribute contraceptives."[37] It is difficult to believe that these anomalous responses reflected bona fide reactions to good-faith attempts to relieve genuine burdens on religious exercise. The responses suggested, instead, that the objectors and their lawyers were more concerned with scoring political points against the Obama administration.

Many of these possibly insincere challenges depend on dubious science as well, attempting to conflate contraception and abortion. Several of the objectors' lawyers claim that they are challenging an "abortion-pill mandate" and that their clients are seeking to avoid complicity in the taking of human life.[38] (The Becket Fund's Adéle Keim in her chapter on these cases, states that we should be "particularly sensitive to religious objections to the taking of human life" and analogizes contraception to both abortion and capital punishment.) Since neither surgical abortion nor the actual abortion pill must be covered under

---

[35] Coverage of Certain Preventive Services Under the Affordable Care Act, 80 Fed. Reg. 41,318, 41,318 (July 14, 2015) (final rules).

[36] Press Release, Becket Fund for Religious Liberty, *Supreme Court Grants Emergency Relief to Christian College* (July 3, 2014), available at www.becketfund.org/wheaton-scotus-victory/ [https://perma.cc/K4UJ-8MRF].

[37] Press Release, Becket Fund for Religious Liberty, *Administration Issues Final Contraceptive Mandate Rules in Defiance of Supreme Court* (July 10, 2015), available at www.becketfund.org/new-hhs-mandate-rules-defiance-supreme-court/ [https://perma.cc/HDN7-DM43].

[38] *Defeat the Abortion-Pill Mandate, Defend Religious Liberty*, ACLJ, available at http://aclj.org/obamacare/oppose-abortion-pill-mandate-defend-religious-liberty [https://perma.cc/P2BA-46WC]; *No One Should Be Forced to Pay for Another Person's Abortion*, Alliance Defending Freedom, available at www.adflegal.org/issues/sanctity-of-life/beginning-of-life/defending-those-who-defend-life/key-issues/obamacare/hhs-obamacare [https://perma.cc/8NTL-XMQE] ("Obamacare's abortion pill mandate").

the Affordable Care Act, the objectors have instead combined certain religious beliefs about pregnancy with a misunderstanding of how certain contraceptives actually prevent pregnancy.

Under the scientific definition, pregnancy doesn't begin until a fertilized egg has already implanted in the uterus. Some people's religious beliefs provide that life begins at the time of fertilization, even though only one-in-five fertilized eggs implant in the uterus. According to this belief, any drug or device that prevents a fertilized egg from implanting in the uterus performs an abortion. The objectors add that four methods of contraception at issue in these cases – two forms of emergency contraception, and two types of IUDs – prevent a fertilized egg from implanting in the uterus.

As it turns out, three of the four purported abortifacients prevent only fertilization and are incapable of stopping the implantation of a fertilized egg. A fourth, the copper IUD, can, in theory, prevent implantation, but it's rarely (if ever) used that way; in practice, it prevents fertilization, not implantation. In sum, none of the purported abortifacients actually cause abortion – even under the plaintiffs' broader definition.[39]

Nevertheless, the plaintiffs' contrary assertions – that certain covered contraceptives cause abortions – went unchallenged by the government, some of whose drug-labeling reflects an outdated understanding, and thus went unaddressed by the courts. This left a material gap in the analysis: although courts must defer to religious beliefs (in this case, that life begins when sperm fertilizes an egg), they need not defer to a scientific misunderstanding about whether certain contraceptives in fact prevent fertilized eggs from implanting in the uterus. Courts don't debate whether Jews are allowed to eat pork, but they would reject the claim that broccoli comes from a pig.

Conflating contraception and abortion affected more than rhetoric. Most evangelical Protestants accept birth control but oppose abortion.[40] Thus, moreover, the lawsuits brought by the non-Catholic plaintiffs – including Hobby Lobby and dozens of others – depend on the claim that IUDs and emergency contraception cause abortion. And their refusals to cover IUD in particular are especially damaging to women: IUDs are 20 times more effective than birth-control pills, but are also

---

[39] See generally Gregory M. Lipper, *Zubik v. Burwell, Part 3: Birth Control is not Abortion*, Bill of Health (March 19, 2016), available at http://blogs.harvard.edu/billofhealth/2016/03/19/zubik-v-burwell-part-3-birth-control-is-not-abortion/ [https://perma.cc/J3HG-4DGX].

[40] See, e.g., Jamelle Bouie, *God Does Not Regard the Fetus as a Soul*, Slate (March 25, 2014 2:34 PM), available at www.slate.com/articles/news_and_politics/politics/2014/03/hobby_lobby_and_contraception_how_conservative_evangelicals_went_from_not.html [https://perma.cc/L73Y-K2HN].

considerably more expensive – making insurance coverage for IUDs especially important.[41]

Legitimate free-exercise claims must be sincere and grounded in fact. Although courts should not be second-guessing plaintiffs' religious beliefs, they should be assessing whether the plaintiffs do in fact hold those beliefs and whether the challenged circumstances do in fact exist. By failing to address these points, despite red flags suggesting the need to do so, the government left the courts' consideration of the plaintiffs' challenges incomplete, and added an asterisk to what was already an unprecedented use of religious liberty to deprive others of their rights.

3. BAD FOR WOMEN AND RELIGION

Although the contraceptive-coverage cases are commonly understood to involve a clash between women's health and religious freedom, these cases will harm both women and religion.

The harm to women is apparent, but still worth discussing. As a result of the lawsuits and resulting decisions and orders, tens of thousands of women have lost, and risk continuing to lose, access to affordable contraception.[42] This is no small matter, given that the CDC has listed family planning as one of the 10 most important public-health advances of the twentieth century.[43] Expanded access to contraception reduces the rates of unintended pregnancy and abortion, both of which are still high.[44] And as discussed earlier, the most convenient and effective contraceptives are the most expensive; the IUD and related care, for example, costs up to $1,000.[45] In addition, every year rape causes approximately 25,000 pregnancies; increased used of emergency contraception could prevent up to 22,000 of these.[46] And by allowing

---

[41] Sarah Kliff, *Free Contraceptives Reduce Abortions, Unintended Pregnancies. Full Stop*, Washington Post (October 5, 2012), available at www.washingtonpost.com/news/wonk/wp/2012/10/05/free-contraceptives-reduce-abortions-unintended-pregnancies-full-stop/ [https://perma.cc/YRT6-KPJF].

[42] See generally Supplemental Brief of Respondents, *Zubik v. Burwell*, at 20.

[43] CDC, *Achievements in Public Health, 1900–1999: Family Planning*, 48 MMWR Weekly 1073 (December 3, 1999), available at www.cdc.gov/mmwr/preview/mmwrhtml/mm4847a1.htm [https://perma.cc/YR3Y-VXHR].

[44] Lawrence B. Finer & Mia R. Zolna, *Shifts in Intended and Unintended Pregnancies in the United States, 2001–8*, 104 Am. J. Pub. Health S43, available at www.guttmacher.org/sites/default/files/pdfs/pubs/journals/ajph.2013.301416.pdf [https://perma.cc/64CN-8YL3]; Lawrence B. Finer & Mia R. Zolna, *Unintended Pregnancy in the United States: Incidence and Disparities*, 2006, 84 Contraception 478 (2011), available at www.contraceptionjournal.org/article/S0010-7824(11)00472-0/abstract [https://perma.cc/7T8K-PVKB].

[45] IUD, Planned Parenthood, available at www.plannedparenthood.org/learn/birth-control/iud?utm_source=Tumblr&utm_medium=IUDcostquestion&utm_content=IUD&utm_campaign=healthtumblr [https://perma.cc/2ZKJ-ZFPR].

[46] Felicia H. Stewart, *Prevention of Pregnancy Resulting from Rape*, 19 Am. J. Preventive Med. 228 (2000), available at www.ajpmonline.org/article/S0749-3797(00)00243-9/abstract [https://perma.cc/D8DK-U5ER].

women to control whether and when to have kids, contraceptives expand opportunities for women to pursue education and professional advancement.[47] Finally, contraceptives can improve women's health and, for some women, preserve their fertility.[48]

Access to contraception is no less important for women who work or study at religiously affiliated institutions. Many religiously affiliated entities have religiously diverse students and staff. In any event, birth control is used regularly by Catholics and Protestants alike: 98.6 percent of sexually active Catholic women and 99 percent of sexually active Protestant women have used contraception.[49]

The objectors have sought to downplay the importance of the coverage regulations by claiming, inaccurately, that the regulations are spotty.[50] Keim obliges in her chapter, stating for instance that "30% of large employer health plans ... enjoy grandfathered status."[51] But the grandfathering provision is transitional and lasts only until a health plan changes its scope or price, as virtually all plans will do. None other than Keim's then-colleague at the Becket Fund admitted as much to the trial court in *Hobby Lobby*: "[J]ust because of economic realities, our plan has to shift over time. I mean, insurance plans, as everyone knows, shift over time."[52] In the meantime, most grandfathered plans already cover contraceptives, so most of the employees in grandfathered plans are receiving contraceptive coverage. And of course, transitional measures have populated most significant laws, such as the Americans with Disabilities Act – they hardly undermine the importance of the law's protections.[53]

Even further afield, Keim claims that millions of small employers are exempt, but that claim is misleading: If small employers offer coverage, it must include contraceptive; if they don't, then their employees may obtain subsidized coverage on the

---

[47] See, e.g., Claudia Goldin & Lawrence F. Katz, *Career and Marriage in the Age of the Pill*, 90 Amer. Econ. Ass'n Papers & Proceedings 461 (2000), available at http://scholar.harvard.edu/files/goldin/files/career_and_marriage_in_the_age_of_the_pill.pdf [https://perma.cc/7XJQ-KPAM].

[48] See, e.g., Jennifer J. Frost & Laura Duberstein Lindberg, *Reasons for Using Contraception: Perspectives of US Women Seeking Care at Specialized Family Planning Clinics*, 87 Contraception 465 (2013), available at www.contraceptionjournal.org/article/S0010-7824(12)00739-1/pdf [https://perma.cc/A7MD-DWUA]; Jessica D. Gipson et al., *The Effects of Unintended Pregnancy on Infant, Child, and Parental Health: A Review of the Literature*, 39 Stud. in Fam. Plan. 18 (2008), available at www.jstor.org/stable/20454434?seq=1#page_scan_tab_contents [https://perma.cc/32KJ-HXU5].

[49] Kimberly Daniels et al., *Contraceptive Methods Women Have Ever Used: United States, 1982–2010*, 62 Nat'l Health Stat. Reps. (February 14, 2013), available at www.cdc.gov/nchs/data/nhsr/nhsr062.pdf#x2013;2010%20[PDF%20-%20251%20KB]</a> [https://perma.cc/W4ZD-7W92].

[50] I address these arguments in more detail in Gregory M. Lipper, *Zubik v. Burwell, Part 5: These Exceptions are Unexceptional*, Bill of Health (March 22, 2016), available at http://blogs.harvard.edu/billofhealth/2016/03/22/zubik-v-burwell-part-5-these-exceptions-are-unexceptional/ [https://perma.cc/MCS4-5E9W].

[51] Ch. 3, this volume.

[52] *Hobby Lobby*, 134 S. Ct. at 2800 (Ginsburg, J., dissenting) (quoting trial-court hearing).

[53] See Argument Transcript at 60–2, *Sebelius v. Hobby Lobby Stores, Inc.*

exchanges, and that coverage will include seamless access to contraception. The objectors, conversely, want the right to provide coverage, thus preventing women from getting full, subsidized coverage on the exchanges, but to exclude critical items – contraceptives – from that coverage. Unlike everyone else, these employees are left with the proverbial half-pregnancy.

The resulting harm to women cannot be avoided through purportedly less-restrictive alternatives, including having the government (a) provide contraceptives or contraceptive-specific coverage to women directly, (b) offer grants to other entities that provide contraceptives, or (c) expand eligibility for programs that provide contraceptives to low-income women. These proposed alternatives would impose financial or logistical barriers on women, who would need to identify and register for yet another new program, perhaps see a different doctor for contraception-related care, and possibly pay out-of-pocket. By requiring women to jump through logistical hoops and incur additional costs, the proposed alternatives would reduce access to and use of contraceptives, as studies show that even minor barriers can dramatically reduce access.[54]

Even these inferior alternatives wouldn't grow on trees: Congress would have to enact them. Yet far from trying to expanding access to birth control, Congress has been trying to slash funding for it.[55] And many of the same groups fighting contraceptive-coverage regulations – including the U.S. Conference of Catholic Bishops – actually oppose government-funded contraceptives too.[56]

More broadly, free-exercise claims to withhold health care have no logical stopping point. People assert religious objections to a range of essential drugs and treatments – including blood transfusions, psychiatric care, hysterectomies, vaccinations, or drugs or surgical products that contain pig or cow products. Allowing *Hobby Lobby*-style claims to proceed could undermine the Affordable Care Act's efforts to ensure that Americans have access to essential preventive care.

But suppose, as the Supreme Court suggested in *Hobby Lobby* and as the Becket Fund's Keim hint at in her chapter, these other forms of treatment can somehow be distinguished from contraceptives. That shouldn't comfort us either: It would mean,

---

[54] See, e.g., Diana Greene Foster et al., *Number of Oral Contraceptive Pill Packages Dispensed and Subsequent Unintended Pregnancies*, 117 Obstetrics & Gynecology 566, 570 (2011); Aileen M. Gariepy et al., *The Impact of Out-of-Pocket Expense on IUD Utilization Among Women with Private Insurance*, 84 Contraception e39, e41 (2011), available at www.ncbi.nlm.nih.gov/pubmed/22078204 [https://perma.cc/TC44-YXQQ].

[55] Emily Crockett, *House GOP Tries to Eliminate Public Funding for Family Planning*, Rewire (June 16, 2016), available at https://rewire.news/article/2015/06/16/house-gop-tries-eliminate-public-funding-family-planning/ [https://perma.cc/XH4T-R8Z7].

[56] Nancy Frazier O'Brien, *Pro-Life Official: Catholic Contraceptive Report Misleading*, Nat'l Catholic Rep. (April 26, 2011), available at http://ncronline.org/news/faith-parish/pro-life-official-catholic-contraceptive-report-misleading [https://perma.cc/TZ93-K255].

once again, that women's health care would be treated as second-class care. In adding the Women's Health Amendment to the Act, Congress recognized that "women of childbearing age spen[t] 68 percent more in out-of-pocket health care costs than men," in part because "the cost of reproductive health care, including contraceptives, is significant, and it falls disproportionately on women." Privileging objections to reproductive care would erode this important progress towards equality.

In addition to harming women, these cases may harm religion as well. If large portions of the public come to view free-exercise claims as just another facet of political or cultural opposition to sexual autonomy, birth control, and other aspects of modern life, political support for religious accommodations will plummet. The broad coalition that supported RFRA has split, with many progressives who previously embraced RFRA now calling for reforms.[57] And with *Hobby Lobby* foreshadowing that some courts will grant yet more religious exemptions that strip others of their rights, support for religious accommodations will likely continue to decline.[58]

The contraceptive-coverage litigation poses other threats to religious liberty as well. Mirroring the arguments made by the challengers in court, the Becket Fund's Keim faults the coverage regulations for distinguishing "between churches and other religious non-profits ..." But if for-profit corporations and nonprofit organizations demand the same exemptions offered to houses of worship, then the numerous exemptions granted to these houses of worship could be at serious risk. For that reason, Professor Douglas Laycock, who has a chapter in this volume (and who supported Hobby Lobby in the Supreme Court) warned that the objectors' challenges to the accommodation pose "a mortal threat" to religious liberty: "If legislators and administrative agencies cannot enact a narrow religious exemption without it being expanded to become all-inclusive, many of them will not enact any religious exemptions at all."[59] That is one reason to reject the argument, advanced by the Becket Fund's Keim, that nonprofit organizations should receive even exemptions that harm others because otherwise they will stop providing social services.

---

[57] Louise Melling, *Op-Ed, ACLU: Why We Can No Longer Support the Federal "Religious Freedom" Law*, Washington Post (June 25, 2015), available at www.washingtonpost.com/opinions/congress-should-amend-the-abused-religious-freedom-restoration-act/2015/06/25/ee6aaa46-19d8-11e5-ab92-c75ae6ab94b5_story.html [https://perma.cc/RK43-C3JW].

[58] See, e.g., Howard Friedman, *Why Is Indiana's RFRA So Controversial? This Blogger's Analysis*, Religion Clause (March 30, 2015 9:05 PM), available at http://religionclause.blogspot.com/2015/03/why-is-indianas-rfra-so-controversial.html [https://perma.cc/QB3X-M54K].

[59] Douglas Laycock, *How the Little Sisters of the Poor Case Puts Religious Liberty at Risk*, Washington Post (March 20, 2016), www.washingtonpost.com/opinions/how-the-little-sisters-of-the-poor-put-religious-liberty-at-risk/2016/03/20/eaaa6a34-e4b4-11e5-a6f3-21ccdbc5f74e_story.html [https://perma.cc/Y83C-3SCM].

There are yet other reasons to avoid allowing religious service providers to receive exemptions that harm others. Doing so would undo decades' worth of free-exercise law and might authorize unconscionable harms to others. Would this rationale, for instance, require exemptions from laws prohibiting discrimination on the basis of race, as Bob Jones University unsuccessfully argued to the Supreme Court in the 1980s?[60] Or what about exemptions from rules requiring the reporting of sexual abuse? And what about when the requested exemption implicates the very service being provided – such as when religious service providers who are receiving federal grants withhold reproductive care from victims of human trafficking and sexual assault?[61]

Keim's rationale for allowing harm-imposing exemptions is also mismatched. Any of these harm-imposing exemptions would necessarily become available to religious organizations, regardless of whether or not they provide social services and no matter how many or how few people they help. Under *Hobby Lobby*, I should add, they would have to be made available to billion-dollar for-profit chains as well. And yet none of them would be available to the many secular organizations – health clinics, homeless shelters, legal-aid bureaus, and others – that also help those in need.

There may be a variety of ways for the government to encourage nonprofit organizations, both religious and secular, to serve the public; but allowing religious organizations to harm others because some of them help others would be haphazard. Perhaps even worse, this rationale would inevitably invite courts to scrutinize the quality and quantity of the services that the religious claimants provide to the public. Religious entities would pay for broader exemptions with deeper entanglement.

And for what? Religious organizations already receive a range of exemptions and accommodations, including exemptions authorized by RFRA. When it comes to the contraceptive-coverage regulations, religious organizations have received an accommodation that relieves them of the need to pay for or provide contraceptive coverage but that enables the government to ensure that their employees don't lose that coverage. Further exemptions would undermine not only RFRA, but also the First Amendment's Establishment Clause, which require balancing religious organizations' interests against those of others – including people with different beliefs who depend on laws protecting their health, safety, and equality.

---

[60] *Bob Jones Univ. v. United States*, 461 U.S. 574 (1983).
[61] *ACLU of Mass. v. Sebelius*, 821 F.Supp.2d 474 (D. Mass. 2012), vacated as moot, 705 F.3d 44 (1st Cir. 2013).

5

Recent Applications of the Supreme Court's Hands-Off Approach to Religious Doctrine

From Hosanna-Tabor *and* Holt *to* Hobby Lobby *and* Zubik

Samuel J. Levine

In each of the past four terms, the United States Supreme Court has decided a case with important implications for the interpretation and application of the Religion Clauses of the United States Constitution:[1] *Hosanna-Tabor Evangelical Lutheran Church & Sch. v. EEOC*,[2] *Burwell v. Hobby Lobby, Inc.*,[3] *Holt v. Hobbs*,[4] and, most recently, *Zubik v. Burwell*.[5] Although the Court's decisions in these cases addressed – and seemed to resolve – a number of questions central to Free Exercise and Establishment Clause jurisprudence, including recognition of the "ministerial exception" and religious rights of a corporate entity, the decisions left a number of questions unanswered, such as the contours of Free Exercise rights for prisoners and the definition of a religious minister. More dramatically – though anticlimactically – in *Zubik*, rather than ruling in favor of one of the parties, the Court issued an unusual per curiam opinion instructing the parties to work to find a way to resolve the matter.

This chapter suggests that the Supreme Court's inability to answer some of these questions, or even to resolve the controversy in *Zubik*, is rooted in the Court's continuing, and arguably expanding, hands-off approach to religious doctrine. The hands-off approach, developed in a series of landmark cases, precludes judges from engaging in a close evaluation of the religious nature of Free Exercise and Establishment Clause claims in deference to adherents' characterizations of the substance and significance of a religious practice or belief.[6] Although the Court

---

[1] See U.S. Const. amend. I ("Congress shall make no law respecting an establishment of religion, or prohibiting the free exercise thereof ...").
[2] 132 S. Ct. 694 (2012).
[3] 134 S. Ct. 2751 (2014).
[4] 135 S. Ct. 853 (2015).
[5] 136 S. Ct. 1557 (2016).
[6] See, e.g., *Lyng v. Nw. Indian Cemetery Protective Ass'n*, 485 U.S. 439, 458 (1988); *United States v. Lee*, 455 U.S. 252, 257 (1982); *Thomas v. Review Bd.*, 450 U.S. 707, 714 (1981); *Serbian E. Orthodox Diocese v. Milivojevich*, 426 U.S. 696, 721 (1976); *Presbyterian Church v. Mary Elizabeth Blue Hull Mem'l Presbyterian Church*, 393 U.S. 440, 451 (1969); *United States v. Ballard*, 322 U.S. 78, 87 (1944). See

has offered both constitutional and practical justifications for this deference, the hands-off approach has been subject to considerable criticism among legal scholars.[7] Indeed, notwithstanding sound policy considerations underlying the Court's attempts to prevent judges from evaluating the substance of religious doctrine,[8] the hands-off approach may bring about additional problems of its own.

First, conceptually, in its articulation of the hands-off approach, the Court has failed to clarify a number of descriptive and normative issues. Second, as applied, a hands-off approach that requires unquestioned deference to religious claims may impose unworkable burdens on the government, courts, and society as a whole.[9] Conversely, courts may respond by placing substantial limitations on the range of claims that qualify for religious protection.[10] Perhaps most basically, adjudicating cases under the Religion Clauses, the Religious Freedom Restoration Act (RFRA),[11] state RFRAs,[12] and the Religious Land Use and Institutionalized Persons Act (RLUIPA)[13] requires consideration of religious claims and, at times, may necessitate

---

also *Nat'Newl Spiritual Assembly of the Baha'is of U.S. Under Hereditary Guardianship, Inc. v. Nat'l Spiritual Assembly of Baha'is of U.S., Inc.*, 628 F.3d 837, 846 n.2 (7th Cir. 2010); *Tomic v. Catholic Diocese of Peoria*, 442 F.3d 1036, 1039 (7th Cir. 2006); *Symposium: The Supreme Court's Hands-Off Approach to Religious Doctrine*, 84 Notre Dame L. Rev. 793 (2009).

[7] See, e.g., Jared A. Goldstein, *Is There a "Religious Question" Doctrine? Judicial Authority to Examine Religious Practices and Beliefs*, 54 Cath. U. L. Rev. 497 (2005); Richard W. Garnett, *A Hands-Off Approach to Religious Doctrine: What Are We Talking About?*, 84 Notre Dame L. Rev. 837 (2009); Kent Greenawalt, *Hands Off! Civil Court Involvement in Conflicts over Religious Property*, 98 Colum. L. Rev. 1843 (1998); Samuel J. Levine, *A Critique of Hobby Lobby and the Supreme Court's Hands-Off Approach to Religion*, 91 Notre Dame L. Rev. Online 26 (2015) [hereinafter Levine, A Critique of Hobby Lobby]; Samuel J. Levine, *Hosanna-Tabor and Supreme Court Precedent: An Analysis of the Ministerial Exception in the Context of the Supreme Court's Hands-Off Approach to Religious Doctrine*, 106 Nw. U. L. Rev. Colloquy 120 (2011); Samuel J. Levine, *Rethinking the Supreme Court's Hands-Off Approach to Questions of Religious Practice and Belief*, 25 Fordham Urb. L.J. 85 (1997) [hereinafter Levine, Rethinking the Supreme Court's Hands-Off Approach]; Samuel J. Levine, *The Supreme Court's Hands-Off Approach to Religious Doctrine: An Introduction*, 84 Notre Dame L. Rev. 793 (2009); Christopher C. Lund, *Rethinking the "Religious Question" Doctrine*, 41 Pepp. L. Rev. 1013 (2014); William P. Marshall, *Smith, Ballard, and the Religious Inquiry Exception to the Criminal Law*, 44 Texas Tech L. Rev. 239 (2011); Priscilla J. Smith, *Who Decides Conscience? RFRA's Catch-22*, 22 J.L. & Pol'y 727 (2014).

[8] See, e.g., Garnett, supra note 7.

[9] See, e.g., Goldstein, supra note 7; Greenawalt, supra note 7; Levine, *Rethinking the Supreme Court's Hands-Off Approach*, supra note 7; Marshall, supra note 7.

[10] See Levine, *Rethinking the Supreme Court's Hands-Off Approach*, supra note 7. This dynamic seems to have led directly to the Supreme Court's landmark decision in the 1990 case, *Employment Division v. Smith*, which sharply curtailed the reach of Free Exercise protections. See Greenawalt, supra note 7, at 1906; Levine, *Rethinking the Supreme Court's Hands-Off Approach*, supra note 7, at 88; Marshall, supra note 7, at 255 n.124.

[11] 42 U.S.C. § 2000bb-1.

[12] See National Conference of State Legislatures, State Religious Freedom Restoration Acts (October 15, 2015), available at www.ncsl.org/research/civil-and-criminal-justice/state-rfra-statutes.aspx [https://perma.cc/SUV5-3KRG].

[13] 42 U.S.C. § 2000cc-1.

careful judicial examination of the substance and nature of religious doctrine. This chapter argues that the challenge of reconciling the dual goals of adjudicating cases involving religion and maintaining appropriate deference to the beliefs of religious adherents manifests itself in the somewhat unsatisfying and often contentious nature of the religious freedom decisions handed down by the Supreme Court over the last four terms.

1. THE SUPREME COURT'S HANDS-OFF APPROACH TO RELIGIOUS DOCTRINE: A BRIEF OVERVIEW

Under current Supreme Court jurisprudence, religious freedom claims may be considered under the Free Exercise Clause, RFRA, state RFRAs, and RLUIPA – all of which, by definition, pertain only to claims that are premised upon religious practice or belief.[14] Accordingly, as a threshold matter, a court must determine whether a claim is sincerely based in religious practice or belief before applying constitutional or statutory religious protections.[15]

Once a court has accepted the sincerity of a religious claim, the Court's hands-off approach to religious doctrine precludes several other forms of inquiry, which would touch upon an evaluation of the metaphysical truth underlying the claim. As a basic element of the hands-off approach – indeed, as a basic premise of religious freedom in the United States – the American legal system does not recognize or reject the metaphysical truth or validity of a particular religion or religious belief.[16] As a corollary, courts must grant legal protection to sincere religious claims regardless of the perception, among the court or other observers, that the claim is grounded in an unlikely or even bizarre form of religious practice.[17]

Building on these basic premises, the Court has expanded the scope of the hands-off approach to likewise preclude inquiry into the accuracy or consistency of a religious claim when two or more individuals profess adherence to the same religion but assert different views of that religion's beliefs or practices. As the Court

[14] This discussion draws upon an analysis in Levine, *A Critique of Hobby Lobby*, supra note 7.
[15] See, e.g., *Holt v. Hobbs*, 135 S. Ct. 853, 862 (2015). An additional area of complexity in religious freedom cases, beyond the scope of this chapter, relates to the legal definition of religion. Notably, the Supreme Court has never mapped out the precise elements necessary for a system of belief to qualify as a religion under constitutional and statutory provisions. See, e.g., Kent Greenawalt, *Religion as a Concept in Constitutional Law*, 72 Cal. L. Rev. 753 (1984); John O. Hayward, *Religious Pretenders in the Courts: Unmasking the Imposters*, 20 Trinity L. Rev. 24 (2014); Courtney Miller, "*Spiritual but Not Religious*": *Rethinking the Legal Definition of Religion*, 102 Va. L. Rev. 833 (2016); Eduardo Peñalver, Note, *The Concept of Religion*, 107 Yale L.J. 791 (1997); Note, *Toward a Constitutional Definition of Religion*, 91 Harv. L. Rev. 1056 (1978). But see Christopher L. Eisgruber & Lawrence G. Sager, *Does It Matter What Religion Is?*, 84 Notre Dame L. Rev. 807 (2009).
[16] See, e.g., *Emp't Div., Dep't of Human Res. of Or. v. Smith*, 494 U.S. 872, 887 (1990).
[17] See, e.g., *United States v. Ballard*, 322 U.S. 78, 86–7 (1944).

has repeatedly emphasized in the context of cases involving disputes over church property, personnel issues, and other areas of religious practice, judges have no role in adjudicating intrafaith differences of belief.[18]

It should be noted that, despite the conceptual distinction between sincerity and accuracy of a religious claim, in practice, judges may tend to question the sincerity of a religious belief that appears mistaken, insubstantial, or irrational, particularly when that belief is challenged by other self-declared co-religionists. Nevertheless, once a court has found that a religious adherent is sincere in asserting a claim as religious in nature, it must afford Free Exercise, RFRA, or RLUIPA protections, regardless of whether the belief is shared – or repudiated – by others professing adherence to the same religion.

Finally, both RFRA and RLUIPA include provisions that prohibit the government from imposing a substantial burden on the exercise of religion unless it demonstrates that "the application of the burden to the person ... is in furtherance of a compelling governmental interest; and ... is the least restrictive means of furthering that compelling governmental interest."[19] Notably, although the Court has held that the hands-off approach precludes judicial evaluation of the centrality of a practice or belief within a religious system, questions remain as to whether this deference extends to categorizing a religious burden as substantial.[20]

Indeed, although the compelling state interest/least restrictive means evaluation can be challenging, the Supreme Court has engaged in this form of strict scrutiny for many decades, in the context of RFRA,[21] RLUIPA,[22] and the Free Exercise Clause.[23] In contrast, however, there have been few, if any, Supreme Court cases interpreting and applying the contours of the form of "substantial burden" that triggers the compelling state interest/least restrictive means test.

The resolution of this question may have a critical, if not dispositive, effect on the outcome of a case. If the Supreme Court's hands-off approach precludes judicial inquiry into the nature and degree of the burden that a law imposes on religion, the claimant's assertion of substantial burden will trigger the compelling state interest/ least restrictive means test. Conversely, if courts have the authority to evaluate – and potentially reject – the claimant's assertion of substantial burden, the government

---

[18] See, e.g., *Holt v. Hobbs*, 135 S. Ct. 853, 863 (2015); *Lyng v. Nw. Indian Cemetery Protective Ass'n*, 485 U.S. 439, 457–8 (1988); *Presbyterian Church v. Mary Elizabeth Blue Hull Mem'l Presbyterian Church*, 393 U.S. 440, 449–51 (1969); *Serbian E. Orthodox Diocese v. Milivojevich*, 426 U.S. 696, 721 (1976); *Thomas v. Review Bd.*, 450 U.S. 707, 714 (1981).

[19] 42 U.S.C. § 2000bb; 42 U.S.C. § 2000cc.

[20] See, e.g., Ira C. Lupu, *Hobby Lobby and the Dubious Enterprise of Religious Exemptions*, 38 Harv. J.L. & Gender 35, 80–2 (2015).

[21] See, e.g., *Gonzales v. O Centro Espirita Beneficente Uniao do Vegetal*, 546 U.S. 418 (2006).

[22] See, e.g., *Cutter v. Wilkinson*, 544 U.S. 709 (2005).

[23] See, e.g., *Sherbert v. Verner*, 374 U.S. 398 (1963); *Wisconsin v. Yoder*, 406 U.S. 205 (1972).

may prevail without having to satisfy the relatively high compelling state interest/ least restrictive means standard.

2. APPLYING THE HANDS-OFF APPROACH

A. Hosanna-Tabor *and* Holt

In the 2012 case, *Hosanna-Tabor Evangelical Lutheran Church & Sch. v. EEOC*,[24] in a unanimous opinion authored by Chief Justice Roberts, the Supreme Court formally recognized the ministerial exception, holding that "[b]oth Religion Clauses bar the government from interfering with the decision of a religious group to fire one of its ministers."[25] A crucial section of the opinion relied heavily on landmark church property decisions in which the Supreme Court first established the hands-off approach, requiring judicial deference to the theological determinations of ecclesiastical tribunals.[26] The Court found that "[o]ur decisions in [church property disputes] confirm that it is impermissible for the government to contradict a church's determination of who can act as its ministers."[27] Similarly, it concluded, "[w]hen a minister who has been fired sues her church alleging that her termination was discriminatory, the First Amendment has struck the balance for us."[28]

Notwithstanding the Court's unanimous decision in *Hosanna-Tabor*, a number of questions remained unanswered.[29] Indeed, the Court arguably achieved unanimity precisely because it restricted the scope of its analysis, avoiding some of the more complex issues that may arise in further application of the ministerial exception. In turn, the Court's avoidance of these issues may stem, in part, from a desire to avoid a full consideration of the difficulties posed by a broad application of the hands-off approach.

For example, the majority did not provide a legal standard to determine whether a given employee of a religious organization would be categorized as a minister. Justice Thomas, however, authored a concurring opinion advocating a nearly categorical hands-off approach: "[T]he Religion Clauses require civil courts to apply the ministerial exception and to defer to a religious organization's good-faith understanding of who qualifies as its minister."[30] A more extensive concurrence, authored

---

[24] 132 S. Ct. 694 (2012).
[25] Id. at 702.
[26] See, e.g., *Serbian E. Orthodox Diocese v. Milivojevich*, 426 U.S. 696 (1976). See also Levine, *Rethinking the Supreme Court's Hands-Off Approach*, supra note 7; Greenawalt, supra note 7.
[27] Hosanna-Tabor, 132 S. Ct. at 704.
[28] Id. at 710.
[29] See, e.g., Christopher C. Lund, *Free Exercise Reconceived: The Logic and Limits of* Hosanna-Tabor, 108 Nw. U. L. Rev. 1183 (2014); Michael W. McConnell, *Reflections on* Hosanna-Tabor, 35 Harv. J.L. & Pub. Pol'y 821 (2012).
[30] Hosanna-Tabor, 132 S. Ct. at 710 (Thomas, J., concurring).

by Justice Alito and joined by Justice Kagan, suggested that "[i]f a religious group believes that the ability of... an employee to perform [various] key [religious] functions has been compromised, then the constitutional guarantee of religious freedom protects the group's right to remove the employee from his or her position."[31]

Despite the difference in degree, both concurring opinions advocate a considerable measure of deference to religious adherents. The majority's refusal to adopt either of these positions – or even to define "minister" – may reflect an underlying concern that a broadly applied hands-off approach would prove unworkable, insulating religious organizations from employment discrimination claims and various other disputes with employees.[32] The Court may be unable to arrive at a consensus with respect to the contours of the hands-off approach more generally, given its potentially wide-ranging ramifications.

In the 2015 case, *Holt v. Hobbs*,[33] in another unanimous decision (this time authored by Justice Alito), the Court applied a combination of RFRA and RLUIPA to consider the religious freedom claims of an inmate in state prison. It first resolved the threshold question by accepting the sincerity of the plaintiff's religious belief: "Here, the religious exercise at issue is the growing of a beard, which petitioner believes is a dictate of his religious faith, and the Department does not dispute the sincerity of petitioner's belief."[34] Somewhat curiously, the Court then seemed to find it necessary – or at least useful – to cite the amicus brief for "Islamic Law Scholars" in support of the proposition that "Petitioner's belief is by no means idiosyncratic."[35] Notably, however, under a basic tenet of the hands-off approach, courts are precluded from considering the extent to which a religious practice or belief is consistent with a mainstream religious tradition. In fact, as the Court immediately added, "even if [the petitioner's claim] were [idiosyncratic], the protection of RLUIPA, no less than the guarantee of the Free Exercise Clause, is 'not limited to beliefs which are shared by all of the members of a religious sect.'"[36]

The Court's willingness to characterize the prisoner's belief on the basis of a substantive theological study may demonstrate the abiding confusion over the distinction between the sincerity and the truth of a religious claim. More broadly, its analysis may demonstrate an abiding confusion – or discomfort – latent in the continued application of the hands-off approach to any religious claim, regardless

---

[31] Id. at 712 (Alito, J., concurring).
[32] For similar critiques of the ministerial exception, see, e.g., Frederick Mark Gedicks, *Narrative Pluralism and Doctrinal Incoherence in* Hosanna-Tabor, 64 Mercer L. Rev. 405 (2013); Leslie C. Griffin, *The Sins of* Hosanna-Tabor, 88 Ind. L.J. 981 (2013).
[33] 135 S. Ct. 853 (2015).
[34] Id. at 862.
[35] Id.
[36] Id. at 862–3 (citation omitted).

of how far removed from a mainstream religious tradition. In any event, the Court unanimously found that the grooming policy substantially burdened the inmate's religious exercise and did not satisfy the compelling state interest/least restrictive means standard.[37]

As in *Hosanna-Tabor*, although the Justices reached unanimity, the majority opinion again seemed to leave unanswered a number of difficult questions, likewise implicated by the hands-off approach, involving the precise contours of the extent to which prison officials must defer to inmates' religious claims.[38] Justice Sotomayor filed a separate concurring opinion emphasizing her concern that deference to inmates' religious claims should not undermine the deference accorded to prison officials' security interests: "I do not understand the Court's opinion to preclude deferring to prison officials' reasoning when that deference is due – that is, when prison officials offer a plausible explanation for their chosen policy that is supported by whatever evidence is reasonably available to them."[39]

B. Hobby Lobby *and* Zubik

In stark contrast to the somewhat limited scope of the decisions in *Hosanna-Tabor* and *Holt*, the 2014 case *Burwell v. Hobby Lobby* provided an opportunity for the Supreme Court to apply the hands-off approach in a more expansive manner, with ramifications not only for issues of religious freedom but also for such contentious matters as abortion rights and the legal status of corporations. Unsurprisingly, likewise in stark contrast to the unanimous holdings in *Hosanna-Tabor* and *Holt*, *Hobby Lobby* resulted in a sharply divided Court, appearing to reflect fundamental differences over the contours of the hands-off approach and the degree of deference it requires courts to accord to religious claims.[40]

In *Hobby Lobby*, the plaintiffs challenged the provisions of the Affordable Care Act ("ACA")[41] requiring employers to provide health insurance to employees that included access to certain forms of contraception.[42] Writing for the five-justice

---

[37] Id.
[38] See, e.g., *Incumaa v. Stirling*, 791 F.3d 517 (4th Cir. 2015); *Sessing v. Beard*, 2015 WL 3953501, at *1 (E.D. Ca. June 29, 2015).
[39] Hosanna-Tabor, 135 S. Ct. at 867 (Sotomayor, J., concurring). Similar concerns over broad applications of the hands-off approach in the prison context have been raised repeatedly since the adoption of RFRA. See Levine, *Rethinking the Supreme Court's Hands-Off Approach*, supra note 7, at 98–9 n.59. See also Marci Hamilton, *The Supreme Court's New Ruling on the Religious Land Use and Institutionalized Persons Act's Prison Provisions: Deferring Key Constitutional Questions*, FINDLAW (June 2, 2005), available at http://writ.news.findlaw.com/hamilton/20050602.html [https://perma.cc/Q3Y4-G2QR].
[40] This section draws upon an analysis in Levine, *A Critique of Hobby Lobby*, supra note 7.
[41] See Patient Protection and Affordable Care Act of 2010, 124 Stat. 119; 42 U.S.C. § 300gg–13(a)(4).
[42] See *Burwell v. Hobby Lobby, Inc.*, 134 S. Ct. 2751, 2777–9 (2014).

majority, Justice Alito provided a rather systematic – if somewhat formalistic – application of the elements of the hands-off approach. First, the opinion established that the plaintiffs had a "sincere religious belief that life begins at conception" and "object[ed] on religious grounds to providing health insurance that covers methods of birth control that ... may result in the destruction of an embryo."[43]

Second, consistent with the deference required by the hands-off approach, the majority accepted the plaintiffs' theological understanding of their religious beliefs: "providing the insurance coverage demanded by the ... regulations lies on the forbidden side of the line, and it is not for us to say that their religious beliefs are mistaken or insubstantial."[44] Indeed, the majority noted, the plaintiffs' claim "implicates a difficult and important question of religion and moral philosophy, namely, the circumstances under which it is wrong for a person to perform an act that is innocent in itself but that has the effect of enabling or facilitating the commission of an immoral act by another."[45] Thus, according to the majority, "[a]rrogating the authority to provide a binding national answer to this religious and philosophical question" would "in effect tell the plaintiffs that their beliefs are flawed."[46] Not surprisingly, therefore, affirming basic principles set forth as part of the Court's hands-off approach, the majority declared that "[f]or good reason, we have repeatedly refused to take such a step."[47]

The majority then applied the remaining prongs of RFRA, relying again on the hands-off approach to defer to the plaintiffs' depiction of a substantial burden on religious exercise.[48] Finally, the majority concluded that the provisions in the ACA did not constitute the least restrictive means of furthering a compelling governmental interest.[49]

Writing for the four dissenters, Justice Ginsburg agreed with the majority that the plaintiffs' "religious convictions regarding contraception are sincerely held."[50] In addition, the dissent adopted one of the basic elements of the hands-off approach to religious doctrine, citing Supreme Court precedent to establish that "courts are not to question where an individual 'dr[aws] the line' in defining which practices run afoul of her religious beliefs."[51]

Nevertheless, despite initially deferring to the plaintiffs' characterization of their religious beliefs, the dissent argued that the law would not impose a substantial

[43] Id. at 2774.
[44] Id. at 2779.
[45] Id. at 2778.
[46] Id.
[47] Id.
[48] Id.
[49] Id. at 2779–85. See also id. at 2785–7 (Kennedy, J., concurring).
[50] Id. at 2798 (Ginsburg, J., dissenting).
[51] Id. (citing *Thomas v. Review Bd.*, 450 U.S. 707, 715 (1981)) (alteration in original).

burden on religious practice, finding that the plaintiffs' claims, "however deeply held, do not suffice to sustain a RFRA claim. RFRA, properly understood, distinguishes between 'factual allegations that [plaintiffs'] beliefs are sincere and of a religious nature,' which a court must accept as true, and the 'legal conclusion ... that [plaintiffs'] religious exercise is substantially burdened,' an inquiry the court must undertake."[52] Therefore, the dissent reasoned, the plaintiffs' claim did not subject the ACA provisions to the compelling state interest/lease restrictive means test.

Thus, the crucial point of contention among the Justices in Hobby Lobby turned directly on the dissent's willingness to evaluate – and reject – the plaintiffs' characterization of the degree to which the law would burden their exercise of religion. As Justice Ginsburg expressly noted, the dissent was premised on "[u]ndertaking the inquiry that the Court forgoes," leading to the "conclu[sion] that the connection between the families' religious objections and the contraceptive coverage requirement is too attenuated to rank as substantial."[53] In short, Justice Ginsburg dissented in large part because her understanding and application of the hands-off approach was more limited than that of the majority.

Justice Ginsburg's dissent further critiqued the majority's formalistic acceptance of the hands-off approach on the grounds that it raises practical and policy concerns. Near the end of her dissent, Justice Ginsburg presented a virtual parade of horribles, involving scenarios which, she argued, the majority's holding would render difficult for the government to administer and for courts to adjudicate.[54] As commentators have long noted, notwithstanding sound policy considerations in favor of precluding judicial inquiry into the accuracy of theological claims, deferring to religious adherents may prove overly burdensome for governments and courts attempting to accommodate sincerely held religious beliefs.[55]

Among the questions left unresolved by the Supreme Court's holding in Hobby Lobby – many of which involve elements of the hands-off approach – issues revolving around the application of the "substantial burden" test may stand out as the most contentious. Although the majority in Hobby Lobby held that, under the facts of the case, the government regulation placed a substantial burden on the plaintiff's exercise of religion – a point strongly contested by the dissent – the majority did not provide more general guidance for delineating the extent to which judges must defer to a religious claimant's characterization of substantial burden on religious practice.

---

[52] Id. (citation omitted).
[53] Id. at 2799.
[54] Id. at 2804–5.
[55] See, e.g., Goldstein, supra note 7; Greenawalt, supra note 7; Levine, *Rethinking the Supreme Court's Hands-Off Approach*, supra note 7; Marshall, supra note 7.

Indeed, the lack of guidance in *Hobby Lobby* arguably engendered the division that has subsequently split appellate judges in cases involving religious nonprofit employers' objections to filing forms or entering into contracts that would result in contraceptive coverage by an outside provider. The splits in and among circuits often turn on the application of the hands-off approach to religious doctrine, particularly in the context of the substantial burden standard.[56]

For example, in a 2015 case, in which the Seventh Circuit Court of Appeals split 2-1, the majority noted that "[t]he core of the disagreement between the plaintiffs and the government lies in how we apply the substantial burden test."[57] The majority initially applied aspects of the Supreme Court's hands-off approach, acknowledging that "it is not our province to decide religious questions."[58] Nevertheless, the majority insisted that "whether the government has imposed a substantial burden on ... religious exercise is a legal determination. And we are not required to defer to the plaintiffs' beliefs about the operation of the law."[59] Instead, the majority found that "contraceptive coverage under the ACA results from federal law, not from any actions required by objectors under the accommodations" and, therefore, the regulations operated in a way that did not substantially burden the plaintiffs' exercise of religion.[60]

A dissenting judge took the majority to task for failing to adhere to the precedent set in *Hobby Lobby*. In Judge Manion's view, the "straightforward" application of *Hobby Lobby* leads to the conclusion that the provision at issue imposed a substantial burden on the plaintiff's religious exercise.[61] If so, he argued, the majority's refusal to apply *Hobby Lobby* in this manner stemmed from "balk[ing] at the idea that we must accept a person's assertion that a law burdens their religion. The court fears that such a rule will allow a person to escape any number of regulations ... unless the government can meet the strict scrutiny test laid down by RFRA."[62] Indeed, this concern was voiced by Justice Ginsburg and the other dissenters in *Hobby Lobby*, who likewise refused to defer to the plaintiffs' claim of substantial burden.

---

[56] Although in nearly all these cases, the courts of appeals have accepted the government's interpretation of "substantial burden," (see *Sharpe Holdings, Inc. v. U.S. Dep't of Health & Human Servs.*, 801 F.3d 927, 939–40 & n.11 (8th Cir. 2015) (citing cases)), in one case the court deferred to the religious adherent's sincerely held view of the burden imposed on religion (see id. at 941), while several other appellate judges have adopted similar positions in concurring and dissenting opinions (id. at 941–2 (citing cases)).

[57] *Grace Schools v. Burwell*, 801 F.3d 788, 803 (7th Cir. 2015).

[58] Id. at 804.

[59] Id.

[60] Id. at 805.

[61] Id. at 809 (Manion, J., dissenting).

[62] Id.

As such, according to Judge Manion's reasoning, the majority failed to adhere to the Supreme Court's hands-off approach to religious doctrine as developed in *Hobby Lobby*. In Judge Manion's words, "since the nonprofits said that they sincerely believe that the accommodation violates their religion *because* the accommodation makes them complicit in the provision of contraceptive services, the court has attacked their claim that the law makes them complicit."[63] In particular, he found, "acting as an expert theologian, the court holds that the accommodation's operation as understood by the court is not a substantial burden to the nonprofits' religious exercise."[64]

When these cases reached the Supreme Court in *Zubik v. Burwell*,[65] it might have been expected that, as in *Hobby Lobby*, the Court would remain divided, resulting again in expansive majority and dissenting opinions exploring religious objections to the ACA in considerable detail. Moreover, it might have been expected – or hoped – that the Court would take the opportunity to clarify the appropriate degree of deference that the hands-off approach requires in adjudicating a claim of substantial burden on religious exercise. Instead, the Court issued a unanimous per curiam opinion, instructing the parties to work to find a resolution to the case.[66]

There has been much speculation offering possible reasons for the unusual outcome in *Zubik*.[67] Some have suggested that, because Justice Scalia passed away before the case was decided, the Court was left with a 4–4 split, and the Justices preferred a unanimous judgment to an evenly divided decision. More specifically, perhaps the Court remains sharply divided over the contours of the application of the hands-off approach to the question of substantial burden.[68] Rather than issuing an inconclusive 4–4 decision that would have echoed the divisions among appellate court judges,[69] the Supreme Court opted for unanimity. Once again, that unanimity results not from reaching consensus on important issues, but rather from avoiding resolution of difficult issues raised by the hands-off approach.

Indeed, as in *Holt*, Justice Sotomayor joined the unanimous majority but found it necessary to write a separate concurring opinion, joined by Justice Ginsburg, emphasizing that the Court "expresses no view on 'the merits of the cases'" such

---

[63] Id.
[64] Id.
[65] 136 S. Ct. 1557 (2016).
[66] Id.
[67] See, e.g., www.scotusblog.com/case-files/cases/zubik-v-burwell/ [https://perma.cc/98X6-U4UD]; www.washingtonpost.com/news/volokh-conspiracy/wp/2016/05/17/prof-michael-mcconnell-on-zubik-v-burwell-yesterdays-supreme-court-rfra-contraceptive-decision/ [https://perma.cc/72EU-CMT3].
[68] See, generally, University of Illinois Law Review Online Spring 2016 Symposium, available at https://illinoislawreview.org/online/2016/ [https://perma.cc/3U9N-U3XT].
[69] See supra note 58.

as "'whether petitioners' religious exercise has been substantially burdened.'"[70] Accordingly, Justice Sotomayor cautioned, "[l]ower courts ... should not construe" the opinion "as [a] signal[] of where this Court stands."[71] Yet, while it may not be possible to predict where the Court stands as a whole, Justice Sotomayor seems to have signaled her own abiding concerns over applying a broadly deferential hands-off approach to the substantial burden test.

CONCLUSION

Courts and scholars have offered sound justifications for the Supreme Court's hands-off approach to questions of religious doctrine, grounded in constitutional principles of religious freedom as well as more general concerns over judicial competence and the role of judges. Nevertheless, as recent cases have illustrated, the hands-off approach raises concerns of its own, at times serving as a source of contention and confusion. The ongoing tensions and divisions among Justices and judges revolving around these issues may suggest a need for the Supreme Court to revisit and perhaps rethink the contours of the hands-off approach to achieve clarity for the future.

---

[70] Zubik, 136 S. Ct. at 1561 (Sotomayor, J., concurring).
[71] Id.

PART II

Law, Religion, and Health Care Institutions

Introduction

Christine Mitchell

There is hardly a person in the United States who is not near a health care facility whose name bears witness to its religious origin – Adventist Health, Lutheran General, Mount Sinai, New England Baptist, St. Joseph's Hospital, and legions more. While reliably precise figures are not available, recent estimates indicate that one-in-six hospital beds in the United States is in a Roman Catholic hospital system[1] and a significant percentage (though not as high as the oft-repeated 70 percent) of all health care services are provided by faith-based organizations in developing countries.[2]

The history of health care service by faith-based groups, especially to the underserved, is ancient and generally admirable. Yet religious values are not always widely shared in heterogeneous secular societies. Today, many patients as well as employees in Catholic hospitals do not necessarily share the views of the Roman Catholic faith regarding contraception, for example. Conversely, Orthodox Jewish patients in secular hospitals may not find support for their desire to continue life-extending interventions against the advice of their physician. How should the specific faith-based beliefs of owners, leaders, employees, and patients in religious health care organizations be handled when they are in disagreement with those who are neither like-minded believers nor adherents of that faith?

The chapters in Part II of this volume explore the implications of health care being delivered by faith-based organizations, with particular attention to Roman Catholic health care, largely because Catholic beliefs are so well-articulated and

---

[1] Julia Kaye et al., Health Care Denied: Patients and physicians speak out about Catholic hospitals and the threat to women's health and lives, American Civil Liberties Union 6 (2016), available at www.aclu.org/report/report-health-care-denied?redirect=report/health-care-denied [https://perma.cc/S28U-8TF8].

[2] Rose Calnin Kagawa et al., *The Scale of Faith Based Organization Participation in Health Service Delivery in Developing Countries: Systemic Review and Meta-Analysis*, PLoS ONE (2012), available at journals.plos.org/plosone/article?id=10.1371/journal.pone.0048457 [https://perma.cc/BGH9-WV9E].

because Catholic hospitals have such a comparatively large role in health care delivery in the United States.

One theme explored in the following chapters is the extent to which religiously based health care corporations should be legally protected in implementing religiously based decisions about services to be offered (or not), that is, in the exercise of a religiously informed corporate conscience. Sister Melanie Di Pietro, co-director of the Center for Religiously Affiliated Nonprofit Corporations at Seton Hall Law School, describes how Catholic health care institutions and systems provide health care in accordance with their religious mission based on *caritas* (love in action). In her view, the corporation is the legal structure within which *caritas* is carried out by individuals. Law that grants corporations the capacity to act, using the same processes as natural persons to think and make corporate decisions, she argues, should apply as well to faith-based corporate decisions that involve the exercise of religion.

Elizabeth Sepper, an associate professor of law at Washington University in St. Louis, traces the traditional justifications for institutional conscience protections that underlie religious exemptions from laws that contradict faith-based beliefs. Even if corporations might be said to have a conscience, historical legal protections for faith-based health facilities, she argues, fail to reflect the features of modern health care with its mega health systems and mix of secular and religious hospitals within them.

Ryan Meade, on the other hand, counters that corporations do not and cannot have a conscience – indeed there is no such thing as a *religious* conscience per se, he argues; rather, conscience is a unified concept. Corporations, he claims, do not have an intellect or will, which are necessary conditions for arriving at the kind of human judgment necessary for conscience. An attorney and director of Regulatory Compliance Studies at Loyola University Chicago School of Law, Meade believes corporate conscience is a misplaced metaphor in the law. Tracing the historical development of the concept of conscience, Meade instead argues that the language of conscience should be limited to persons if it is to retain its power.

A second theme of the following chapters relates to the practical implications for individuals of religiously based restrictions on health care services. Sepper, for example, shows how former Roman Catholic hospitals – through contracts related to sales, mergers, and vertical and horizontal integration in large health systems – have restricted health services and research related to contraception, assisted reproductive technology, embryonic stem cells and fetal tissue. Citing a variety of examples, she shows that the Ethical and Religious Directives for Catholic Health Care Services (1) restrict access and availability to services for non-Catholic patients in markets such as Washington state (where 50 percent of the hospitals are Catholic), and (2) legally continue to restrict services through "zombie" religious identities based on contracts negotiated by formerly Catholic hospitals sold to secular entities. In this way, religious restrictions become eternal, with implications both for staff employed there and for patients receiving health care. Sometimes patients do not realize that an institution's prior religious affiliation might still restrict which health care services are available, based on contracts negotiated when the corporation changed ownership, even though the facility's name may have changed and even though it may have become a for-profit corporation.

David M. Craig also addresses the implications for individuals of legal protections for religiously based requirements of Catholic health care institutions. Looking at the opinions in *Burwell v. Hobby Lobby*, he cites the importance of employees and patients as well as owners and leaders sharing the institution's religious mission. A professor of Religious Studies at Indiana University, Craig unpacks the idea of "mission integrity" which involves identifying and enacting religious beliefs through practices and structures – something that Catholic health care institutions do especially well in comparison to for-profit companies such as Hobby Lobby. Craig wonders whether casting religious freedom in health care delivery in terms of mission integrity might lead to respect for the consciences of key constituencies, including those who practice different religious faiths or none at all. Given the Roman Catholic church's explicit belief in and respect for the authority of individual conscience since the Second Vatican Council in the 1960s, he wonders whether Catholic hospitals might eventually come to exercise their religious mission in unexpected ways, perhaps by paying for employees' contraception coverage.

In summary, the chapters in this part explore the ethical and legal complexities of protecting the rights of health care corporations, whether in the form of individuals or metaphorical persons, to exercise religion. While explaining and challenging the importance of such protections, the authors also note the real and potential negative effects upon persons either receiving or delivering health care who do not necessarily share their institution's faith-based values. In reading these chapters, consider also whether the rights of persons in need of health care services, which might be restricted on religious grounds, are respected as well.

6

A Corporation's Exercise of Religion

A Practitioner's Experience

Melanie Di Pietro, S.C.

Religious health care corporations were founded as an exercise of the religious belief[1] of the founding Catholic congregations of religious sisters. From their founding, these corporations provided care to the community in accordance with their religious mission. The religious values sustaining their efforts have, in recent times, been challenged – not for what these providers do for the community's benefit, but for what procedures they refuse to do because of their religious beliefs, such as abortion and contraception. These "culture war" issues, the focus of Laycock's chapter in this volume, "are turning many Americans toward a very narrow understanding of religious liberty, and generating arguments that threaten religious liberty more generally."[2] Yet the social, political, and legal protection of religious liberty, in thought and practice, *necessarily* involves an understanding of the "exercise of religion" as understood by adherents of each of the "rich mosaic of religious faiths" that constitute the "American community."[3] The challenges from profit and nonprofit religious corporations seeking the Religious Freedom Restoration Act (RFRA)'s[4] protection from the requirement to provide contraceptive coverage through their employer health insurance plans[5] has fueled academic and judicial debate on the capacity of a corporation to exercise religion and the "dangerous doctrines of corporate conscience."[6]

---

[1] See generally Christopher J. Kauffman, *Ministry and Meaning: A Religious History of Catholic Health Care in the United States* (1995).
[2] Douglas Laycock, *Religious Liberty and the Culture Wars*, 2014 U. Ill. L. Rev. 839 (2014).
[3] *Burwell v. Hobby Lobby Stores, Inc.*, 134 S. Ct. 2751, 2785 (2014) (Kennedy, J., concurring) (quoting in part *Town of Greece v. Galloway*, 134 S. Ct. 1811, 1849 (2014) (Kagan, J., dissenting)).
[4] Religious Freedom Restoration Act, 42 U.S.C. § 2000bb-1 (a)–(b) (2012).
[5] 45 C.F.R. pt. 147.131 (b)(4)(2013); 78 Fed. Reg. 39874 (2013).
[6] Elizabeth Sepper, *Contraception and Birth of Corporate Conscience*, 22 Am. U.J. Gender Soc. Pol'y. & L. 304 (2014). This chapter does not address the relationship between corporate conscience and the exercise of religion or specific statutory definitions of person, leaving those issues to treatment in another forum.

The incapacity of a corporation to "exercise religion" has been argued as follows: corporations "do not pray, worship, observe sacraments and take other religiously motivated actions separate from the intentions and directions of individual actors ..."[7] Rather, religious organizations "exist to serve a community of believers ..."[8] In addition, the size and diversity of non-Catholic employees and clientele, along with the diminishing presence of Catholic sisters, are sometimes offered to support the dilution of the religious character of the religious nonprofit health care corporation.

The exercise of religion is more complex than these conclusions suggest on their face. This chapter describes an alternative perception. A Catholic health care corporation "exercises religion" because, in Roman Catholic theology, worship and sacrament are inseparable from service. This practical theology is implemented in the structure and operation of the corporation whose theology of mission is openness to "work in harmony with others" to serve persons wherever they are encountered.[9] The ministry of health care "in the name of the Church and in communion with the Church"[10] is not limited to Catholic sisters.

An inappropriately narrow definition may contribute to the "culture wars" by making religion itself another "partisan issue."[11] This chapter's limited scope and purpose is a description offered to open up the analysis of the "exercise of religion" by a corporation. Therefore, the chapter does not offer any proposed solution to specific religious liberty claims.

This chapter uses examples from a published case study of the SSM Health Care System[12] for several practical reasons. First, it is a historically documented example of a modern health care corporation's deliberations about its function as a large, multistate Catholic employer and provider. Second, the processes described predate the current "culture wars" and illustrate that religious identity and practice, then and now, is broader than self-interest of the religious body, or any one issue. Third, the hierarchical and magisterium[13] structure of the Roman Catholic Church facilitates

---

[7] *Conestoga Wood Specialties Corp. v. Sec'y of U.S. Dept. of Health and Human Services*, 724 F.3d 377, 385 (3d Cir. 2013) (citations omitted).

[8] Burwell, 134 S. Ct. at 2803 (Ginsburg, J., dissenting).

[9] Benedict XVI, *Encyclical Letter Deus Caritas Est* n.25, b.34 (2005) [hereinafter DCE], available at http://w2.vatican.va/content/benedict-xvi/en/encyclicals/documents/hf_ben-xvi_enc_20051225_deus-caritas-est.html [https://perma.cc/MYY7-BVDE]. An encyclical promulgated by the Pope expresses a teaching of the Church.

[10] 1983 Code of Canon Law, c.116.

[11] Thomas C. Berg, *Progressive Arguments for Religious Organizational Freedom: Reflections on the HHS Mandate*, 21 J. Contemp. Legal Issues 279 (2013).

[12] Melanie Di Pietro & Alison Sulentic, *SSM Health Care: The Integration of Catholic Social Thought Values in a Modern Health Care System*, 46 J. Cath. Legal Stud. 175 (2007).

[13] "Hierarchy" generally refers to the Pope, bishops, and priests. "Magisterium" is the teaching authority of the Church. See Catechism of the Catholic Church 2033–4 (1995).

the identification of the beliefs and practical application of Church teaching regarding ministry to the purpose, governance structure, and operations of a modern religious nonprofit health care corporation. This case study is supplemented by the current practices of several large Catholic health care systems.

The content and the processes used by other religious health care providers, of course, differ according to the theology and governance of the specific religious body. The corporation's capacity to "exercise religion" is fundamental to the protection of a specific claim for religious accommodation or exemption by a corporation. The purpose of this chapter, addressing corporate capacity only, is to show how general principles of the practical theology of the Roman Catholic Church are operative in each dimension of the corporation. The brevity of the chapter does not permit a detailed explication of each principle. Section 1 begins with a description of the incorporation of the practical theology of worship and sacrament in the Legal Purpose[14] and governance structure of the corporation. Section 2 offers a description of the nonprofit religious health care corporation's "exercise of religion", in its own right, through the same principles of law that enable any corporation to transact its business in its own right. Section 3 illustrates the actual references to Catholic Social Teaching used in corporate decision making[15] "in the ordinary course of business." This chapter concludes with an invitation to the reader to examine the potential role a broader understanding of the "exercise of religion" may have in contributing to the ultimate protection of the principle of religious liberty, as it plays out in the specific intersection of law, religion, and health care in nonprofit religious health care corporations.

1. RELIGIOUS PRINCIPLES INCORPORATED IN THE LEGAL PURPOSE AND GOVERNANCE OF THE CORPORATION

The corporation described herein is a public benefit charitable corporation[16] with a distinct religious identity and pluralism in its trustees, employees, funding, and service clientele. It has the capacity to exercise religion as "an artificial person, existing

---

[14] Legal Purpose is capitalized to include the exempt purpose and the mission. See Melanie Di Pietro, *Duty of Obedience: A Medieval Explanation of Modern Nonprofit Governance Accountability*, 46 Duq. L. Rev. 99 (2007); 1A William Meade Fletcher et al., Fletcher Cyclopedia of the Law of Private Corporations § 91, 139 (rev'd 2010).

[15] For description of Catholic Social Teaching, see Kenneth R. Himes, OFM, *On Questions and Answers in Catholic Social Teaching* (2013) and E.J. Dionne, Jr. "Bringing Catholic Social Thought (Back) to Life", in Larry Synder, *Think and Act Anew: How Poverty in America Affects Us All and What We Can Do About It* (2010). Dionne quoted a Baptist friend as telling her divinity school class that CST is a "carefully thought-through system of ideas that links charity, justice, social action and public policy." Id.

[16] 26 U.S.C. §501 (c)(3) (2012).

in contemplation of law, and endowed with certain powers and franchises which, though they must be exercised through the medium of its natural members, are yet considered as subsisting in the corporation itself, as distinctly as if it were a real personage."[17]

A. The Legal Purpose of the Corporate Actor Is to Provide Health Care, Not Just as a Professional Welfare Activity but as a Service of Charity

The corporation has the power to create its identity, internal governance structure, and decisional processes in accordance with state law. The Legal Purpose stated in the organizational documents of a Catholic health care provider often incorporates the terms "ministry" or "mission" for health care offered in accordance with the teachings of the Roman Catholic Church, as promulgated and interpreted by the local Bishop. Upon the filing and acceptance by the state of the Articles of Incorporation, the Legal Purpose establishes its religious identity, authorizes its purposes, and grants the powers necessary to fulfill its purposes in accordance with the state corporation law. The language of the Legal Purpose, though succinct in legal documents, is rich in theological meaning gleaned from religious teaching involving worship, sacrament, belief, and motivation, including the criteria for evaluating the integrity of the services of health care. The language conveys more than a licensed provider of a professional service.

The theological word "ministry," or "mission," is used to describe the specific service of health care in its fully human meaning – treatment, care, healing, both within the person and in the relationship between the person served and the community of persons providing the service. As an intensely human experience, cure, treatment, and palliative care all require more than technological expertise. In Roman Catholic Church theology, health care is included in its theological understanding of *caritas*, or love in action, the theological term for charity.[18] *Caritas*, like the theological understanding of the human person,[19] is richer than the legal meaning of charity. The work of *caritas* and the sanctity of the human person are not optional in Roman Catholic theology. The theology underlying the "mission of health care," the Legal Purpose of the corporation, involves the comprehensive understanding of the dignity of the human person and the work of *caritas*, as well as the Church's self-definition and its mission in the world. The Church defines itself as a visible society and a spiritual community – one complex reality.[20] This definition of itself as a

---

[17] *Trustees of Dartmouth Coll. v. Woodward*, 17 U.S. 518, 667 (1819).
[18] Id. at 19, 20, 25.
[19] Compendium of the Social Doctrine of the Church nn.108–10. (2009).
[20] Vatican Council II, *The Dogmatic Constitution and the Church*, in *Constitutions, Decrees, Declarations* (1995).

visible society will be illustrated in the governance structure of the corporation. Pope Emeritus Benedict XVI provides a succinct declaration of the teachings (or beliefs) of the Church in the context of organized charity and the inseparable relationship of worship and sacrament to service in the encyclical *Deus Caritas Est*, articulating the essential role of the ministry (service) of charity: "The Church's deepest nature is expressed in her three-fold responsibility: of proclaiming the word of God; celebrating the sacraments and exercising the ministry of charity (diakonia) ... For the Church, charity is not a kind of welfare activity which could equally be left to others, but is a part of her nature, an indispensable expression of her very being."[21] If the central act of worship for Catholics, the Mass or Eucharist, "does not pass over into the concrete practice of love [it] is intrinsically fragmented."[22] The intrinsic outward mission to the larger community is clear. Health care, a ministry of charity[23] extends beyond the members of the Church. The parable of the Good Samaritan remains as a standard which imposes universal love towards the needy whom we encounter, "by chance... whoever they may be."[24]

The important point to note in these excerpts is the essential and inseparable function of the ministry of charity from sacrament and worship. The provision of health care, in this religious context, is the exercise of the belief in the Word (Gospel) and celebration of the sacraments. For religious health care providers, the ministry of service, responsive to immediate need, is not merely a nice thing to do; rather, it is essential to the mission of the Church. The statement cannot be more explicit – that the celebration of the Mass without expression in charity is simply incomplete. On its face, the language of the challenged definition of religion does not appear to appreciate the practical theology expressed in this teaching. The challenged definition of religion closes any further inquiry into the possibilities of the "exercise of religion" in different types of corporations.

B. Internal Governance Structure: Practical Expression of Sacramental Theology

The use of Members and directors to govern the corporation, as authorized by state law, provides a mechanism for the practical expression of the visible structure of the Church, based upon its sacramental structure. Individual baptized persons (lay persons) act privately in their own name. Through the sacrament of ordination, priests and bishops act publicly in the name of the Church. Through the authority of the Church (ordained persons), a group of nonordained persons may be given the right

---

[21] Benedict XVI, supra note 9, at n.25a.
[22] Id. at n.14.
[23] Id. at n.31a.
[24] Id. at n.25b.

to act in the name of the church for a purpose (ministry) authorized by the Church. This group is called a "public juridic person" in Church law, and is a corporate body similar to an American corporation. Like the American corporation, the public juridic person acts through human persons, but the action is deemed to be that of the public juridic person itself. The congregation of religious sisters associated with the corporation is a public juridic person authorized to carry out a health care mission. Because it is entrusted with this ministry in the name of the Church, the leadership of the public juridic person act as Members in the corporation and have the powers usually reserved to Members in state nonprofit corporation statutes. These powers reserved to Members are useful to protect the structure and integrity of the health care corporation to act in a public manner in communion with the teaching of the Church.

Currently, as the membership of the founding Catholic congregations of religious sisters is changing, some may think that the religious identity of the health care corporation changes. It does not. Church law provides a mechanism for the ministry of health care entrusted to the founding Catholic congregation of religious sisters to be transferred to successor public juridic persons. The leadership of the successor public juridic person assumes the same legal position in the health care corporation as previously held by the leadership of the founding Catholic congregation of religious sisters. The Legal Purpose expressing the religious identity of the health care corporation and its governance structure in relationship to the Church structure for ministry remain the same.

C. *The Theological Reason for Reserved Powers*

State statutes providing for Members reserve some fundamental powers to Members and vest remaining authority in directors.[25] The Members of the Catholic health care corporation are limited to the leadership of the public juridic person because the Church entrusts to the public juridic person a health care mission for the public good. Given the ministry role of the public juridic person in the visible structure of the Church, the theological reason for each of the following powers is readily evident: to amend articles and bylaws; to appoint and remove the directors; to approve substantial debt or sale of substantial property of the corporation; and to approve fundamental reorganizations, including dissolution, and distribution of assets upon dissolution. In addition, involvement in the selection of the chief executive officer and statement of Mission Guidelines or philosophy are often reserved by the Members.

---

[25] See Model Nonprofit Corp. Act § 601, 602, 610 (2008) (Am. Bar Ass'n, amended 2008). See also 15 Pa. Cons. Stat. §§ 5504, 5721 (1988).

Without the public juridic person's leadership's control as Members, the directors could change the religious identity and governance of the corporation. The public juridic person would not have the appropriate corporate authority it needs to fulfill its ministry responsibilities in the Church structure. Since the chief executive officer is responsible for the operations and culture of the corporation and directors are responsible for the oversight of the operational religious integrity of the corporation, the Members retain the authority to participate in election or appointment to these positions. The approval of changes in the substantial assets of the corporation, or fundamental reorganizations changing the dedication or control of assets, is to monitor any substantive change of the control, dedication or disposition of charitable assets for the Legal Purpose of the corporation.

The Members may add a power not reserved in state law but useful for mission. The Member may issue Mission Guidelines. A guideline may communicate a specific ministry focus which the Members may require to be included in the strategic plan of the corporation. The significance of this example to religious exercise is twofold: one, for some of the founding congregations of religious sisters, a guideline such as a focus on maternal and child health may preserve the original work the Church entrusted to their congregation; two, as illustrated in Section 2 of this chapter, specific Church documents and events may be the incentive for a ministry focus. For example, the Bishop is responsible for "coordinating the work of charity"[26] in his diocese. Within the corporate structure, the Members may use a Guideline to require care for the underserved population and collaboration with others to achieve such a goal. The theological reason identified for who the Members are, and the ministry purpose for each of the reserved powers, illustrate the practical "exercise religion" in a corporation.

D. Pluralism of Directors/Employees

One of the impediments to the "exercise of religion" by a corporation cited by those limiting the definition of religious exercise to individuals is the diversity of stakeholders, including directors, employees, and clientele of the corporation. However, this diversity is part of the history[27] and teaching of the Catholic Church in terms of its ministry to the community, as explained in the discussion of the Legal Purpose. Engagement with others of all faiths and people of good will expresses principles

---

[26] Pope Benedict XVI, *Apostolic Letter, On the Service of Charity* (December 1 2012), available at w2.vatican.va/content/benedict-xvi/en/motu_proprio/documents/hf_ben-xvi_motu-proprio_20121111_caritas.html [https://perma.cc/AFK7-9ERB].

[27] Marion Amberg, *Mayo Clinic: The Franciscan Connection*, available at www.Americancatholic.org//messenger/Oct 2006/Feature2.asp; Mary Electra Boyle, *Mother Seton Sisters of Charity of Western Pennsylvania* 141-4 (1946); 2 The Sisters of Charity of Seton Hill, 191-3.

of subsidiarity and cooperation with others found in the theological and social teachings of the Church.[28] Pope Emeritus Benedict XVI has recently reaffirmed this goal: "Interior openness to the Catholic dimension of the Church cannot fail to dispose charity workers to work in harmony with other organizations in serving various forms of need, but in a way that respects what is distinctive about the service which Christ requested of his disciples."[29] Pope Emeritus Benedict XVI continues:

> Charity, furthermore, cannot be used as a means of engaging in what is nowadays considered proselytism. Love is free; it is not practiced as a way of achieving other ends. But this does not mean that charitable activity must somehow leave God and Christ aside. For it is always concerned with the whole man. Often the deepest cause of suffering is the very absence of God. Those who practice charity in the Church's name will never seek to impose the Church's faith upon others. They realize that a pure and generous love is the best witness to the God in whom we believe and by whom we are driven to love.[30]

While respectful adherence to the religious distinctiveness embodied in the Legal Purpose is required, a personal assent of belief in the religious faith of the provider is not a condition for working in harmony with or providing services to believers or nonbelievers. Engagement with others to give loving service is a matter of religious integrity. Professionalism in the relationships and the services and care rendered[31] is a matter of justice. To suggest, directly or indirectly, that collaboration with others, without requiring or imposing personal adherence to the religious identity of the corporation, or the absence of Catholic sisters, or professionalism demanded in modern medicine, dilute religious identity is to offer a construction of the religion at odds with the religion's own teachings.

2. THE PUBLIC CHARITABLE RELIGIOUS HEALTH CARE CORPORATION EXERCISES RELIGION IN ITS OWN RIGHT

The nonprofit religious health care corporation exercises religion, in its own right, through the same principles of law that enable any corporation to transact its business in its own right. The state's acceptance of the Articles of Incorporation grants the corporation the inherent capacity to exercise all powers necessary to fulfill its Legal Purpose. The religious identity of the corporation subsists in the corporation itself, "as distinctly as if it were a real personage."[32] The discussion of the "exercise of

---

[28] See *The Pastoral Constitution on the Church in the Modern World*, supra note 20. See also DCE, supra note 9, at nn.28b, 34.
[29] Benedict XVI, supra note 9, at n.34.
[30] Id. at n.31c.
[31] Id. at n.31a.
[32] *Trustees of Dartmouth Coll. v. Woodward*, 17 U.S. 518, 667 (1819).

religion," though in the context of secular for-profit corporations, frames the question as "whether a corporation can 'believe' at all."[33]

This chapter is too short to dissect the theological oversimplification of this limitation of religion even for persons. For the purpose of this chapter, it suffices to note that this limitation fails to recognize the multiple dimensions of religion and that "faith does have a cognitive dimension."[34] The human agents vested by law to exercise the Legal Purpose and powers of a corporation use their human intellect and judgment to apply the Good Samaritan standard, the characteristics of ministry including social and moral principles derived from the religious tradition of the corporation. Human intellect and judgment are components of corporate decision-making. State law establishes the fundamental process for human agents to make any and all binding corporate actions: namely, the action of human persons in a statutorily created decisional body, acting through statutorily defined processes like notice, a quorum, adequate information, deliberation by a collective body, and each member voting with care and loyalty to the corporation as defined by its purpose.[35] The definition of religion that this chapter challenges, in the opinion of this author, ignores both the religious identity subsisting in the corporation itself and the role of reason in applying the religious principles of the religious corporation.

The integration of the Church's public teaching required by the Legal Purpose and relevant to the exercise of the health care ministry of the corporation involves the same intellectual, reasoning and judgment processes involved in the application of law or accounting principles to business matters. When directors of a public charitable corporation make a corporate decision concerning the necessity and adequacy of filing the corporation's income information return or setting executive compensation,[36] they are looking to the law governing the status of the corporation, not to the law governing their personal financial information. Similarly, the directors of the nonprofit Catholic health care corporation apply the teachings of the Church to their management decisions, not the religious teachings determined by the majority vote of directors. A religious teaching, promulgated by the Church's teaching authority, may be an absolute prohibition or it may be a teaching that allows for differing application in specific factual situations. The corporation is exercising religion in its own right, according to the mandate in its Legal Purpose, not

---

[33] *Conestoga Wood Specialties Corp. v. Sec'y of U.S. Dep't of Health & Human Servs.*, 724 F.3d 377, 385 (3d Cir. 2013), rev'd and remanded sub nom. *Burwell v. Hobby Lobby Stores, Inc.*, 134 S. Ct. 2751 (2014) (quoting Briscoe, C.J., concurring in part and dissenting in part (*Hobby Lobby Stores, Inc. v. Sebelius*, 723 F.3d 1114, 1174 (10th Cir. 2013), aff'd sub nom. (citations omitted))

[34] John O'Donnell, "Faith," in *The New Dictionary of Theology* 382 (Joseph A. Komonchak et al. eds, 1990).

[35] See Model Nonprofit Corporation Act, supra note 26, at §7–8.

[36] 26 U.S.C. §§ 6033, 4948 (2012).

because it says so, but because the law grants corporations the capacity to fulfill their Legal Purpose through the medium of natural persons.[37]

3. "EXERCISE OF RELIGION" IN THE ORDINARY COURSE OF BUSINESS

Management integrates principles of Church teaching in business decisions in the "ordinary course of business." This requires knowledge of the religious meaning of the language used in mission statements and Church documents. The theological, philosophical, anthropological roots, and the religious tradition of the language is often richer than standard dictionary definitions. For example, the study of "social and structural sin" and "virtue" in the SSM case study cited in this chapter's introduction is related to Franciscan writings that provide the meaning for a "wholistic philosophy of health care which requires a pragmatic examination of corporate responsibility with regard to social sin and structural sin."[38] Many Catholic health care systems create management structures to frame the "right questions" for developing a corporate culture reflective of the mission "in the ordinary course of business." In the words of the late Dennis Brodeur, "People who do not attribute an internal ethic to medicine when examining relationships dictated by contemporary market realities will ask questions different from those who do."[39] The very questions of the ethics of certain procedures in a Catholic hospital or the Mission Guidelines on service to a given population are examples of the role of internal ethics and market realities in determining priorities for limited resources or potential joint ventures. Church documents such as the following are used "to frame the questions" that identify potential conflicts between values and market forces. The "framing of the question" necessarily includes the criteria of mission identity, not just economic terms. As noted in an example presented later, the mission may force the abandonment of an otherwise justifiable transaction if only economic interests framed the analysis of the transaction.

The ethics, mission effectiveness, or corporate responsibility departments (whatever the name) are often the management structure providing the education for directors and managers for the application of religious and moral teaching in "the ordinary course of business" in the internal operations of the corporation, as well as to the issues to be negotiated in joint ventures with other unrelated parties.

One example recorded in the SSM case study describes a session of hospital presidents, led by labor lawyers, the system ethicist, and a presenter of the Church's social

---

[37] See generally Trustees, 17 U.S. at 667.
[38] Di Pietro & Sulentic, supra note 12, at 178.
[39] Id. at 184.

teaching, working through a response to a petition for union representation in light of the law and the social teachings concerning work and workers. These teachings also provide a criteria for a living wage and the incentive to examine both the wages of employees as well as attention to compensation differentials within the corporation.[40] While management responses were hotly debated, two things emerged from the process. The comparative study, whether it be labor laws or comparative clinical and business ethics, creates an informed and common reference point for corporate decision-makers to continue to identify a religious value that needs to be reinforced in the culture and in provider decisions. The public declaration of adherence to religious values holds all levels of governance and management accountable, internally and externally.

The following examples are a composite from contemporary use of selected Church teachings in corporate decisions provided by practitioners.[41] For example, *A Pastoral Letter of the American Catholic Bishops*[42] and *The Ethical and Religious Directives for Catholic Health Care*[43] both published by the United States Conference of Catholic Bishops, provide the reference for Catholic health care's promotion of health care reform. These same documents serve as a frame of reference for diversity initiatives and programs to increase access to health care for disadvantaged populations as well as programs to lessen disparities in care. Increased efforts to provide and improve palliative care programs evolved from the spiritual and pastoral presentation stressing the person at the heart of health care at annual World Days of the Sick celebrated by both St. John Paul II and Pope Emeritus Benedict from 2004 to 2006. Environmental efforts within many organizations have been revitalized by *Laudato Si*, the encyclical on the environment promulgated by Pope Francis.[44] These are only illustrative of the scope of 125 years of Church Social Teachings used by management to inform corporate decisions that are in addition to extensive pastoral care programs addressing the needs of patients of many faiths.

Mergers, acquisitions, and joint ventures are complex market realities. Both parties approach the negotiations identifying their multiple economic, management, community, corporate culture, and political interests. In addition to these

---

[40] For summaries of Catholic Social Teaching, see Peter Henriot, SJ et al., *Catholic Social Teaching: Our Best Kept Secret* 33, 43, 120–30 (1992).

[41] Interview with Ron Hamel, President, SSM Health Ministries, formerly Senior Director, Ethicist, Catholic Health Association; and interview with Rachel Barina, System Manager of Ethics, SSM Health, St. Louis, Missouri.

[42] U.S. Conference of Catholic Bishops, *A Pastoral Letter of the American Catholic Bishops* (1981).

[43] U.S. Conference of Catholic Bishops, *The Ethical and Religious Directives for Catholic Health Care* (5th ed. 2009).

[44] Francis, *Encyclical Letter Laudato Si* (2015), available at http://w2.vatican.va/content/francesco/en/encyclicals/documents/papa-francesco_20150524_enciclica-laudato-si.html [https://perma.cc/N995-YADQ].

interests, the law of private contract, charitable trust, and health care influence the negotiations and ultimate outcomes. While life issues are essential to the Catholic party in negotiating joint ventures, often the non-Catholic party, having its own values and community culture, and for its own reasons, agrees on the life issues. The transaction is ultimately a business transaction, based on terms and conditions fully disclosed and freely negotiated. For example, a Catholic party, motivated by its religious heritage, may attempt to negotiate a criteria for the amount of charity care going forward; or a commitment to wellness or even to the continuation of a service provider in a specific geographical area. An otherwise economically promising joint venture may be declined if the partner is not willing to accept Medicare and Medicaid patients.[45] Any agreement that is reached between the parties reflects the satisfactory resolution of their interest and the transaction that the parties believe is good for the community.

CONCLUSION

This chapter has offered a description of the role of the practical theology of worship, sacrament and the social teaching of the Roman Catholic Church in the details of the corporate structure and operations of Catholic nonprofit health care corporations. In any analysis balancing the religious liberty claims of health care corporations, the starting point is critical. The description of the intentional infusion of the concretely articulated principles of the theology of worship, sacrament, and the derivative moral and ethical principles of Church teaching into every facet of the modern Catholic health care corporate structure and operation is offered as a context to re-examine the narrow construct of religion as limited to internal recesses of the mind and heart or personal feelings and beliefs of individuals only. While the description of religion challenged in this chapter has been in the context of for-profit corporations, the "exercise of religion," needs to be reexamined as the discussion of health, law, and religion continues. Focusing on the fundamentals of corporate law, the effect of the Legal Purpose, the established standards for corporate decision making, and actual management practices as described in this chapter, this author finds it difficult to accept the suggestion that the same law granting to any corporation the capacity to act, and the same processes of thinking and judgment of natural persons authorized by corporate law to effect binding corporate decisions in any legal, accounting or public relations matter, are not equally effective in the "exercise of religion" in corporate decision making as illustrated in this chapter.

---

[45] Telephone interview with Sister Mary Jean Ryan, founding president of SSM Health Care (February 10, 2016).

Health care corporations founded and operated by the many religious denominations that are part of the American civic sector were not, and are not, a romantic endeavor based on emotions and feelings or self-interest of the religious body. The ultimate protection of all parties and constitutional principles will not be served unless, in any conflict, legislators, scholars and judges seek an "adequate legal framework"[46] that appropriately balances all legitimate interests in accordance with American principles of law. The adequacy of the legal framework depends on the question: whether the understanding of the "exercise of religion" is sufficiently inclusive of the beliefs of adherents of religious traditions operating health care corporations.

---

[46] Compendium, supra note 20, at n.418.

7

The Natural Person as the Limiting Principle for Conscience

Can a Corporation Have a Conscience If It Doesn't Have an Intellect and Will?

Ryan Meade

The current political, legal, and popular discussion of health care providers refusing to provide certain controversial services is often cast in the language of conscience. Although there seems to be universal consensus in the United States that conscience is worth protecting in some fashion under the law, there is little consensus on when to protect it. The debate runs into even less consensus when the language of conscience is applied to corporations. Adding another twist, current debates on conscience are consumed by questions about when the state will retreat in favor of exercise of religion. The American tendency to equate conscience and religion is a peculiar angle on conscience, since religion plays no role in the classical understanding of conscience.

Most recently, the popular press deemed *Burwell v. Hobby Lobby Stores, Inc.* to be about conscience, when it really was not. The Supreme Court's majority, concurrence, and dissent did not use the term "conscience" in a way germane to how any of the opinions approached the contraceptive mandate.[1] The justices kept their focus on the question of *exercise of religion*, not on conscience, despite the political and media discussion of the case using the language of conscience.[2] It seemed lost on

---

[1] 134 S. Ct. 2751 (2014). The justices use the term "conscience" seven times in the course of 95 pages. Most of these usages are quotes or references to failed proposed legislation colloquially called a "conscience amendment." Only one use of the term "conscience" comes close to the approach in popular discussion; this is when Justice Alito, writing the opinion of the Court, refers to the 1972 Church Amendment (42 U.S.C. § 300a-7(b)) as allowing an entity to not "engage in activities to which they object on grounds of conscience." Id. at 2773. His use of "grounds of conscience" is out-of-place with the rest of his opinion, which focuses on "exercise of religion."

[2] See Hobby Lobby 134 S. Ct. 2751. For a small sampling of representative popular reports on the Hobby Lobby case emphasizing "conscience" despite the careful language of the justices' opinions in the

The author wishes to thank Kristin Myers, JD, LLM for her invaluable research assistance and Nicholas Weil, JD, LLM for his helpful comments.

the commentariat that, at the federal level, the law does not yet recognize that a corporation has a conscience. A handful of federal laws recognize that fictional persons can have religious beliefs and moral convictions,[3] but this differs from conscience.

If we value the notion of conscience, then we must speak about it precisely and meaningfully. A serious look at conscience must start with an analysis of what conscience is. It must also disentangle religion from conscience-talk. If language that describes the exercise of religion remains collapsed into conscience-talk, then the advance of a corporate conscience doctrine (and a corollary dilution in the meaning of conscience) is inevitable. I want to focus on conscience and not exercise of religion, but in the context of the current debates there seems to be no way around dealing with the former without wading into the latter.

To stave off the rise of corporate conscience, I propose a limiting principle to conscience language: the natural person. My argument that there can be no such thing as a corporate conscience hinges on recovering a more precise understanding of conscience than is in use today, and requires a distinction between exercise of religion and conscience. More specifically, I propose that, in looking deeply at the classical understanding of conscience, we will see that conscience is an act of judgment that requires a mind (intellect and will) and although religious belief may inform judgment it is only one input to the act of judging facts. The act of applying moral principles to particular facts is a uniquely human act that requires an intellect and will. Corporations[4] lack conscience because they lack a literal mind (intellect and will). While it is possible for a collection of individuals to pool their judgments and move the corporation to "act," this is different from how an individual human mind functions. A corporate conscience is at best a metaphor; and as I will discuss, we must be very careful about anchoring the law of the corporate form in metaphor. The corporate form lends itself to being described with human attributes that are analogical (sharing a common literal feature with humans) but at the point that anthropomorphization is merely metaphor it is best to tread carefully, lest we lose

---

case, see James Taranto, *The Corporate Conscience*, The Wall Street Journal (June 30, 2014), available at www.wsj.com/articles/best-of-the-web-today-the-corporate-conscience-1404158831 [https://perma.cc/QT2H-J9PL]; *Obamacare and Religious liberty: A corporate conscience?*, The Economist (October 2013), available at www.economist.com/blogs/democracyinamerica/2013/10/obamacare-and-religious-liberty [https://perma.cc/ZFB9-M9JE].

[3] See 42 USC § 300a-7; 42 USC § 238n; 42 USC § 1395w-22(j)(3)(B); 42 USC § 1396u-2(b)(3); 22 USC § 7631(d).

[4] This chapter uses the term "corporation" to refer to any entity or association granted standing under law as if it were an individual natural person. Though existing in a somewhat limited way under Roman law, fictional personality burgeoned in Medieval legal theory. For a general discussion of the personality principle under Roman law (deciding a case "as if" the party were a citizen), see Andrew M. Riggsby, *Roman Law and the Legal World of the Romans* 215–17 (2010). See also Boudewijn Bouckaert, *Corporate Personality: Myth, Fiction or Reality?* 25 Isr. L. Rev. 156 (1991) for a discussion of personality during the Middle Ages.

sight of the importance of that attribute. Conscience is a unique attribute of humanity of which no resemblance can be seen in the corporate form.

Although the law has not gone to the point of according corporations a conscience, I join others in worrying that we are seeing the "birth of corporate conscience."[5] My concern is based on the use of language, not on a public policy objection to allowing corporate persons exemptions or accommodations. I am concerned with what I perceive as an erroneous understanding of conscience, exacerbated by the discussion occurring on whether to extend conscience-talk to business organizations.[6] Conscience-talk must be limited in application to humans and not attributed to corporate personality. We must recover the language of conscience in order to preserve its important role in ethical and legal discussions.

1. RECOVERING THE CLASSICAL NOTION OF CONSCIENCE

When contemporary conscience-talk metaphorically ascribes conscience to a corporation, it fails to bring along a deep analysis of how humans think through moral decisions. Too often, conscience is cast merely as a conviction or ethical stand without appreciating the process of reaching a moral viewpoint. It is this human process which corporations cannot replicate. The classical notion of conscience focuses heavily on conscience as an act, rather than conscience as a thing. This act requires the central powers of the human mind, namely, the intellect and the will.

The concept of conscience is often described as a voice, a feeling, a visceral instinct grounding a conviction, or a sense of right and wrong.[7] In a religious context, it sometimes is seen as a moral doctrine illumined through faith or the teaching of a religious authority, whether sacred scripture or a religious body. All these conceptions of conscience end up in the same place: a conviction that a person has an interior compulsion to do or not to do something. These fuzzy descriptions of conscience and the characterization of conscience as atomistically private threaten to render conscience a purely subjective thing.

The classical, pre-Enlightenment understanding of conscience brings a rigor to the language of conscience that this contemporary discussion lacks.[8] Essential to the

---

[5] For a discussion critical of corporate conscience from a different perspective, see Elizabeth Sepper, *Contraception and the Birth of Corporate Conscience*, 22 Am. U.J. Gender Soc. Pol'y & L. 303 (2014).

[6] For discussions explicitly advocating a theory of corporate conscience, see James D. Nelson, *Conscience, Incorporated*, Mich St. L. Rev. 1565 (2013); Mia Mahmuder Rahim, *Raising Corporate Social Responsibility – The "Legitimacy" Approach*, 9 Macquarie J. Bus. L. 102 (2012).

[7] For a discussion of challenges in how to define conscience, see Nadia N. Sawicki, *The Hollow Promise of Freedom of Conscience*, 33 Cardozo L. Rev. 1389, 1394–1400 (2012).

[8] In an effort to make a distinction between classical and modern discussion of conscience, I set the dividing line roughly with the Enlightenment. However, this is not without significant caveats. The most important post-medieval thinker on conscience, Immanuel Kant, sets out a framework for conscience that is more consistent with the classical view of conscience than others of his time.

classical view of conscience is that conscience is not a thing, a voice, or a power of the mind – rather, conscience is an act. Conceiving conscience as an act first took shape in the Stoics[9] and was brought to its fullest articulation in the Middle Ages by Thomas Aquinas.[10]

For Aquinas and the scholastics of the late Medieval and early Renaissance periods, conscience is a judgment. Specifically, conscience is the application of knowledge to particular facts.[11] Conscience occurs when a human person applies moral principles to particular facts to judge a situation right or wrong.

Aquinas' commentary on conscience is the zenith of philosophically dissecting the mechanics of judgment. In developing his critique of judgment, Aquinas builds on Aristotle's philosophy of the mind. Aristotle did not have an explicit theory of conscience, but his philosophy of the mind provides the foundation for Aquinas to name a mental judgment as conscience. In this classical conception of mind, the process of judging (applying principles to facts) involves what are termed the intellect and will,[12] two distinctly human attributes. The process of judgment is not visceral or instinctive; it is reflective and deliberate. Whether principles are derived from deductive or inductive reasoning or primarily based on accepting authority to form premises, an elementary character of humanity is the reflective application of principles to facts.[13] Reasoning at its most fundamental parses experiences (facts) and applies principles (universals) to those facts. One essential feature that distinguishes humans from the rest of the world is that we judge. When a human acts, the person has judged an activity and believes an activity to be good or bad.

In exploring the classical notion of conscience, I am giving only the highest-level sketch of the dominant pre-Enlightenment philosophy of mind. My point is to underscore that conscience is not a visceral instinct or an unreflective duty, and least of all something nonrational, but rather is a distinctly rational act.

Without belaboring the intricacies of this theory, I will briefly set out the process of conscience. At a very high level, the intellect is the power of the mind that accumulates knowledge and understanding.[14] The intellect deliberates. The will is the human appetite for the good and inclines the human to the good or to avoid the

---

[9] Timothy C. Potts, *Conscience in Medieval Philosophy* 2 (1980).
[10] See 1 Thomas Aquinas, *Summa Theologiae I*, q. 79, aa. 12–13 (1981) [hereinafter *ST*]; Thomas Aquinas, *Questiones Disputate de Veritate*, qq. 16–17 [hereinafter *QDdV*].
[11] "The application of knowledge to something is accomplished through an act." Aquinas, *ST*, at I, q. 79, a. 13. See also Aquinas, *QDdV*, at q. 17, a. 1 ("Conscience seems to be an act, for it is said to accuse and excuse. But one is not accused or excused unless he is actually considering something. Therefore, conscience is an act.").
[12] Although Aristotle specifically posed a notion of the intellect, his treatment of the will is subtler. See Anthony Kenny, *Aristotle's Theory of the Will*, Ch. 8 (1979).
[13] Aristotle, "Nicomachean Ethics," in *The Complete Works of Aristotle* 1098a (Jonathan Barnes ed., 1984).
[14] Aquinas, *ST*, at I, q. 79.

bad.[15] After the intellect applies knowledge to a fact to determine whether a state of affairs is good or bad, the intellect presents its conclusion to the will. The will moves the human to comply with the judgment of the intellect as to whether something is good or bad. This philosophy of mind is built on an epistemology that posits that the human person obtains knowledge through sense impressions and abstracts universals from the particular things that are impressed upon the person.[16] Moral principles are universals abstracted from particular experiences. The accumulation of the experience of these universals in the intellect is the acquisition of knowledge. The mind stores and uses this accumulated knowledge in repetitive interaction with the world.

In operation, the process of judgment takes the following form. When a state of affairs p is presented to the intellect, the accumulated experience of the intellect interacts with the presentation of p to make a judgment of p. It is possible for the intellect to not reach a conclusion of whether p is good or bad, but it is impossible, under this theory, for the intellect to not try to make a judgment. In the absence of a conclusion, the intellect searches for more information.

To illustrate this, take a very simple example of a physician needing to decide what to do about a patient not responding to a particular dose of medication while suffering debilitating side effects. The physician must decide, at minimum, whether to recommend increasing the dose to a level that is possibly more effective (that likely exacerbates complications) or abandoning the drug altogether. The physician applies various principles to facts. The physician uses professional experience and stored clinical knowledge to assess the patient's presentation. The physician will likely apply principles, such as avoiding side effects resulting in long-term damage equal to or greater than the untreated condition. Unique facts, such as the patient's strong desire to mitigate painful side effects, may inform the application of principles. The physician will reach a conclusion and make a recommendation. This is not merely the application of scientific data to a situation, but the mental act of ethical decision making. Only a human can perform this process.

As human persons interact with the world, they process experiences and refine conscience through these repetitive interactions. Conscience as a form of life settles in to how we fit into and act in the world.

2. RELIGION AS ONE OF MANY INPUTS TO CONSCIENCE

The contemporary discussion of conscience is cast strongly in religious terms. Conscience as an interior act of ethical decision making, however, allows us to disentangle conscience from religion. The striking aspect of Aquinas' formulation of

[15] Aquinas, *ST*, at I-II, q. 8, a. 1.
[16] Anthony Kenny, *Aquinas on Mind* (1993).

conscience discussed earlier is that it does not rely in any way on religious conviction or principles. It relies solely on the reasoning process.

This brings us to why there is no religious conscience per se. The popular discussion of conscience, particularly in the wake of *Hobby Lobby*, seems to suggest that there is something unique about a so-called "religious conscience." While religion can be an important input for a person's judgment process in that religion may provide a grounding for some of the principles a person applies to facts, religion is just one input among many. The human act of conscience works the same way no matter inputs on principles an individual draws from.

When the classical approach to conscience interacts with religious conviction, the act of conscience does not leave its grounding in the deliberation of the intellect and the movement of the will. The intellect builds up its principles in many ways. Some are basic "first things" and some are the logical extension of first things. Other inputs are experiences that are based on a preponderance of evidence even if not quite understood, and still others are based simply on authority. The only way to talk strictly of a religious conscience is if we assert that a person applies to facts certain principles that are assented to purely on the basis of religious authority. Operationally, this is no different than if a person were to accept on authority some principle based on a scientist's authority. The scientist or the cleric may come to a conclusion of their respective principles in different ways, but nothing prohibits the "believer" from assenting to the scientist or cleric's principles based not on evidence but on trust. I have never been to the moon, but I accept on authority that others have been there and confirmed that it is not made of cheese. We may disagree on which authorities to accept, but once a person accepts a principle and applies it, then they exercise their reasoning powers and engage in rational thought. Judgment must utilize those principles that the intellect has accepted or assented to; it can use nothing else.

The discussion of religious conscience in the wake of Hobby Lobby has taken the conversation on conscience down a rabbit hole, further away from the classical understanding of conscience. When the discussion about the act of judgment (conscience) is discussed in terms of visceral feelings of right or wrong, rather than applications of universals to particulars, it is one move away from a proper understanding of conscience. When religious motivations for those visceral feelings are given some type of pride of place, it formalizes a misunderstanding about conscience as being anchored outside of the reasoning process. The notion of a "religious conscience" seems to reduce conscience down to a laundry list of a religion's doctrines and magisterial teachings. This is shortchanging conscience.

Religion is of critical importance to the believer but is a trifling matter to the act of conscience. We might refer to a "religious conscience," but in so doing we simply mean an act of conscience situated in principles based on religious sources important to a particular person. Conscience cannot be said to be religious any more than it can be said to be irreligious.

3. CAN WE SPEAK OF A CORPORATION HAVING A CONSCIENCE?

Now that we have set out the idea of conscience as an act and attempted to set aside the distracting question of a "religious conscience," I would like to return to the corporate form. The corporate form is an arena where anthropomorphic attributes are ascribed to a fictional person, but not all human attributes can be predicated of corporations in the same way. There are some human attributes that are the same as those of a fictional person, such as legal standing to sue (the corporation sues in court the same way a human sues in court). There are other human attributes that the corporation has in similarity to humans, enough to use a term robustly, but how the attribute in the corporation plays out slightly different than it plays out in a human (the corporation speaks when it publishes something under its corporate name in similar way a human speaks when the human publishes under their name, though the corporation may be speaking as the result of a multitude of humans developing and crafting the document, whereas the individual human speaks as a singular individual). Still other human attributes might be described of a corporation in a way that the description in no way is meant to apply even small similitude, but is merely a convenient term for communicating an idea (a holding company may be referred to as a "parent" of its subsidiaries and this in no way implies parenthood in the human sense). The law employs different modes of speaking about the corporate form having human attributes.

If we were to assert that there is a corporate conscience, which mode of speaking would we be using? If conscience is predicated of a corporation, is it more like standing in a court to sue, speaking, or parenthood? It seems to be more like parenthood than the others. Parenthood as a metaphorical term for a collection of business organizations "related" to each other would never be confused with human parenthood. The use of the metaphor to the corporate form is benign because corporate parenthood could never be confused for human parenthood. But what of a metaphorical corporate conscience? When conscience is already confused in the popular discussion, metaphorical use of the notion of conscience risks undermining the understanding of conscience even further.

These three modes of speaking about human attributes of the corporate form correspond to a traditional distinction among descriptors: univocal, analogical, and metaphorical.

A univocal term involves an attribute that can be applied to two things in an identical way; the two things have the same nature allowing for identical description. Both nursing homes and ambulance companies are said to be "health care organizations," although nursing homes and ambulance companies differ greatly in other attributes. In the case of A and B, both are said to have an X factor that is identical. When speaking of X in A, we are speaking of the same form of X in B.

An analogical term involves imperfect likeness even though there is not perfect identity. Thomas Aquinas' structure of analogical reasoning is a hallmark of discussing analogy.[17] For Aquinas, analogy is seen as proportionate equivalence,[18] in the sense that when speaking of A and B there is a characteristic (X) that is in both in a way that is equivalent though not identical. This characteristic may be in A as X and in B as X', but there is sufficient equivalence between X and X' that we can speak about them as X with the same term. However, when X' in B no longer can be meaningfully equivalent to X in A, then X' ceases to have useful equivalence to X in A and we cannot learn from X in A to understand X' in B. At that point, X' and X do not share enough in common to meaningfully refer to them both as X. To the extent we insist on continuing to refer to X' as X, it is only a metaphorical comparison to X in A. It may be better at this point to start referring to X' as Y.

Metaphor is a representation of something to which there is a likeness, but it is not meant to be literal. A person is not X in a literal way, but can be said to be X to get a conceptual sense of a particular person. For example, "nurses are the heart of the hospital." No one assumes this line is literally speaking of hearts. But what if the law began to regulate the nurses as if they were in-transit hearts for transplantation? That is an absurd question because treating metaphor literally often leads to absurdity. Metaphor conveys an idea, but stops there. Metaphor is a rhetorical device to convey concepts in an explicitly nonliteral way. Law needs to address states of affairs in as literal a rendering as possible in order to avoid confusion. If law uses metaphor to regulate activity it is using rhetorical devices to regulate behavior. This opens the law to imprecision at best, absurdity at worst. Applying metaphorical human attributes to the corporate form must be done sparingly and only when the metaphor could never be confused with the real thing.

Assuming the reader can stipulate that corporations do not literally have a conscience as I have described conscience, is it possible to speak metaphorically of a corporation having a conscience? If a corporation does not have a human conscience, then any reference to corporate conscience must be a metaphor. Even if our common parlance casually refers to corporate conscience when an organization issues a policy statement, can the law meaningfully grapple with and regulate something that is merely a metaphor?

The psychology I presented here is unique to a human being and cannot be said to exist in a corporation, and so the notion of a corporate mind is not a univocal term

---

[17] Aquinas, *ST*, at I, q. 13.
[18] Ralph McInerny, *Aquinas & Analogy* (1996).

to human mind. A corporate mind is not an analogical descriptor either because there is no base commonality of anything like an intellect or will in a corporation. To speak of a corporate mind is left to the default position of a metaphor, which by its definition involves the use of two things that have no literal similitude.[19] In saying that a corporation does not have a mind it follows that it does not have a conscience, since having a mind is essential for the act of conscience.

Thinking involves activity that cannot be replicated outside of humans: namely, abstraction of universals from particulars, accumulations of principles, and the reapplication of those principles to new facts. Only humans can do this. To speak of a corporate psychology necessarily devolves to particular humans thinking, acting, and moving the corporation.

Asserting conscience is to assert not only the human thought process, but a detailed process of judgment that cannot be replicated by the corporate structure. A corporation can assert a position on an issue, but that is either the vote of a collection of people or some agent's conclusion that is adopted by the corporate structure. A corporation stating that it wants to improve the environment may be the corporate policy of the organization but it is not every time the judgment of a single human intellect and will. Conscience is an act deep in the interior of the individual human mind.

The only way to speak of a corporate conscience is metaphorically, and this is unhelpful in describing a space of negative rights for a business organization. It reinforces the already dangerous fuzziness of conscience-talk in contemporary discourse.

The mental intricacies of the act of judging cannot be meaningfully applied to corporate personality. However, an objection might be raised: a corporation is made up of a collection of human persons, and the leadership (at a minimum, the governing body) can collectively apply principles to facts, so doesn't this approximate a human person's judgment? Can't this approximate conscience? No, it cannot be the locus of corporate conscience precisely because a corporation is a collection of individuals, and a collective cannot approximate a mind. The human person is a unity that applies principles for a singular motivation of doing good. The collection of decisions or votes of a board to move a corporation to "act" cannot be said in any way to be a unity, for there is a disparity of intellects involved. A key and central feature of the human person is its interior unity. A disparity of intellects goes too far and endangers the very concept of conscience.

---

[19] For an insightful lecture discussing the role of analogy and metaphor, including the limits of using metaphor, see Anthony Kenny, "Humanism versus Anthropomorphism" (2014) available at www.humanephilosophy.com/single-post/2014/11/21/HPPIRC-Seminar-Sir-Anthony-Kenny-Humanism-versus-Anthropomorphism. I am in debt to this lecture for inspiring the initial spark for this chapter.

Any human attribute that cannot be ascribed to the corporate form in univocal or analogical ways should not be attributed to the corporate form unless it is clear that the term is not being used in any way as it is used for the human attribute. There is very little room for metaphor in written law. Metaphorical attributes render the law unclear and threaten nonsense when the base literal matter is already confused. Understanding conscience is already in a precarious state today, as evidenced by the discussion of *Hobby Lobby*. It should be further diluted by metaphorically ascribing the corporate form a conscience.

CONCLUSION

When we recover the classical notion of conscience, we see that a metaphorical attribution of conscience to corporations fails because conscience is not a thing or end result of a vote but is the uniquely human operation of the mind engaged in moral decision making. The popular discussion of conscience in the wake of *Hobby Lobby* needs adjustment, both in anchoring conscience in humans and also disentangling conscience from distracting discussions of religion.

Whether a corporation can be said to have a conscience is a question of whether there can be any meaningful analogical or univocal attribution of the central functions of the human mind – the intellect and will – to the corporate personality. If conscience is an interior human act (i.e., a mental act), as I propose, then any other thing said to be engaged in conscience must have a mind. A corporation cannot exercise conscience, because it does not have an intellect and will. When we treat conscience as divorced from human psychology and say that a fictional person can have a conscience, we undermine a critical and unique feature of the natural person. To say a corporation has a conscience is to speak metaphorically about human attributes, and metaphor can offer little foundation to law.

That being said, it is not inappropriate to attribute some characteristics of the human person to the fictional corporate person. Justice itself would be at serious risk if we did not apply some of these attributes. But there is a danger of going too far. The danger is not so much in creating injustices in the workings of the corporation in civil society but in diminishing the centrality of human persons in civil society. If human persons are placed on a level playing field with all fictional persons, whether corporations, the state, associations or other bodies, then humans are merely one of many things in society. If a collection of things are equal and said to have the same attributes, then Attribute-X logically could be regulated, manipulated, or eviscerated, in the same manner across all things said to have Attribute-X? But certain attributes belong only to human persons in their individuality. Conscience, I propose, is one attribute that cannot be applied to any other real or fictional thing in civil society. Conscience is the domain of the human person. It is a singularly human act.

8

Contracting Religion

Elizabeth Sepper

DeKalb Community Hospital in Tennessee was founded as a secular facility in 1969. In 1995, it was purchased by Baptist Hospital of Nashville. It became religious and was renamed Baptist DeKalb Hospital. In 2002, it was again sold, this time to Catholic Ascension, and became Catholic.[1] Four years later, secular owners took it over. But an affiliation with Capella Healthcare resulted in Catholic restrictions being imposed.[2] Today, its name – Saint Thomas DeKalb Hospital – reflects the Catholic religion that prohibits the performance of abortions and sterilizations in the facility.[3]

As the example of DeKalb hospital demonstrates, religious compliance in health care increasingly arises through commercial transactions, rather than association of individuals or pursuit of charitable goals. Through contract, as Section 1 of this chapter shows, individuals and institutions may come to comply with religious beliefs, which they otherwise may not share, and to impose religious restrictions on medical care. At the vertical level, providers who hold different or no religious beliefs can become subject to religious restrictions through contractual commitments. At the horizontal level, secular hospitals may follow the religion-based position of their health care partners as a condition of commercial transaction.

Private law also can render religious restrictions on reproductive and end-of-life care perpetual. As Section 2 explains, provisions in sales contracts and restrictive covenants in deeds have limited health care after religious hospitals have been sold. Health care continues to be restricted for religious reasons, even as the hospitals lose the affiliation with a religious body or the attachment to founders, directors, or employees that made them religious.

---

[1] Melanie Evans, *Ascending in Healthcare*, Modern Healthcare, May 14, 2007.
[2] *Saint Thomas to Partner with DeKalb Community Hospital*, WJLE (TN), December 8, 2011, www.wjle.com/news/2011/saint-thomas-partner-dekalb-community-hospital.
[3] Saint Thomas DeKalb Hospital, About Us, www.sthealth.com/Locations/Saint-Thomas-DeKalb-Hospital/About-Us.

As Section 3 argues, traditional conceptions of what religious health care institutions are – and thus their prevalence – have not kept pace with the changing health care marketplace and the degree to which it has allowed the "contracting of religion." As Section 4 contends, contracting for religion restricts space for religious exercise by individuals and institutions of other faiths. It obscures the degree to which health care access is impeded, as religious restrictions spread into institutions far removed from the designated religious, nonprofit hospital.

Although many faith traditions engage in health care delivery,[4] this chapter focuses on Catholic health care due to the comprehensiveness of its restrictions on care and the market share of its facilities. The Ethical and Religious Directives for Catholic Health Care Services (ERDs) restrict assisted reproductive technology, treatments derived from fetal tissue or embryonic stem cells, contraception, condoms, sterilization, and abortion.[5] They also limit end-of-life care, allowing the use or withdrawal of artificial life support only to the extent that it is not contrary to Catholic teaching.[6] The ERDs constrain information delivered to patients to "morally acceptable alternatives."[7] Moreover, Catholic restrictions apply widely. In a market where approximately seventy percent of hospitals are nonprofit, Catholic health care systems are four of the five largest nonprofit systems.[8] Although we lack data on the number of hospitals complying with Catholic doctrine due to affiliation or after sale, officially designated Catholic hospitals constitute 16 percent of the national market[9] and represent nearly half of hospitals in Washington and one-third in another eight states.[10]

1. CONTRACTING COMPLIANCE WITH RELIGIOUS PRECEPTS

Private law has played a significant role in expanding the universe of providers that conform to Catholic positions in health care. Through contract, religious restrictions routinely extend to individuals and entities that otherwise would not refuse

---

[4] See, e.g., Susan Berke Fogel & Lourdes A. Rivera, *Saving Roe Is Not Enough: When Religion Controls Healthcare*, 31 Fordham Urb. L.J. 725, 732–34 (2004).
[5] United States Conference of Catholic Bishops, *Ethical and Religious Directives for Catholic Health Care Services* 38–41, 45, 48, 52, 53, & 66 (5th ed. 2009), available at www.usccb.org/issues-and-action/human-life-and-dignity/health-care/upload/Ethical-Religious-Directives-Catholic-Health-Care-Services-fifth-edition-2009.pdf [https://perma.cc/C6R3-GLG4].
[6] Id. at 24, 59.
[7] Id. at 27.
[8] Catholic health care has 1,400 long-term and other health facilities and about 600 hospitals. *Facts & Statistics: Catholic Health Care in the United States*, Catholic Health Ass'n of the U.S., available at www.chausa.org/about/about/facts-statistics [https://perma.cc/EZ9B-NWS5] (last updated January 2016).
[9] Id.
[10] Massoud Hayoun, *Catholic Hospital Mergers Threaten Women's Health, Activists Say*, Al Jazeera America (January 30, 2014), available at http://america.aljazeera.com/articles/2014/1/30/catholic-hospitalsthreateningwomensreproductivehealthactivistssa.html [https://perma.cc/6PVR-BJ38].

such services. Vertical integration has resulted in binding individual providers to Catholic doctrine through contract.[11] Horizontal integration – mergers, joint ventures, or partnerships – frequently generates compliance with Catholic restrictions in facilities considered secular, affiliated with other faiths, or operated as public hospitals.

Within religious health care facilities including Catholic hospitals, lay people who profess a wide array of beliefs deliver care to patients and oversee operation of modern health care facilities. Contract serves as the mechanism by which compliance with religious restrictions is secured. Office space leases, admitting privilege agreements, employment contracts, and physician group-purchase agreements require health care providers to abide by Catholic restrictions on patient care. Refusal to agree to the ERDs results in loss of admitting privileges or employment.[12]

Restrictions affect a significant proportion of physicians. Forty-three percent of physicians report having practiced in an officially designated religious institution over the course of their careers, a large number of which had institutional policies of refusal.[13] As vertical integration has surged and fewer health care providers remain independent of a hospital or health care system, providers increasingly enter into contracts that commit them to religious-based rules. Simultaneously, horizontal integration subjects many more providers and patients to the reach of religious restrictions.

Over the past twenty-five years, Catholic health care systems have increased in size and scope.[14] In the 1990s, they began to merge or affiliate with non-Catholic hospitals as a wave of consolidation swept the nation.[15] In the 2010s, the Affordable Care Act is fueling another round of consolidation,[16] with some predicting that twenty percent of hospitals will merge within five years.[17]

---

[11] Physicians for Reprod. Choice & Health & MergerWatch, *Mergers and You: The Physicians' Guide to Religious Hospital Mergers* 4–5 (2001), available at www.prch.org/files/Mergers%20and%20You%20The%20Physicians%20Guide%20to%20Religious%20Hospital%20Mergers_0.pdf [https://perma.cc/FM4B-HM4U].

[12] *Watkins v. Mercy Med. Ctr.*, 520 F.2d 894, 895 (9th Cir. 1975); see also Lois Uttley & Ronnie Pawelko, *No Strings Attached: Public Funding of Religiously-Sponsored Hospitals in the United States* 32 (2002).

[13] Debra B. Stulberg et al., *Religious Hospitals and Primary Care Physicians: Conflicts Over Policies for Patient Care*, 25 J. Gen. Internal Med. 725, 727 (2010).

[14] ACLU & MergerWatch, *Miscarriage of Medicine: The Growth of Catholic Hospitals and the Threat to Reproductive Health Care*, 4 (December 2013), available at www.aclu.org/sites/default/files/assets/growth-of-catholic-hospitals-2013.pdf [https://perma.cc/KZ6C-LB3R].

[15] Carol S. Weisman et al., *The Implications of Affiliations Between Catholic and Non-Catholic Health Care Organizations for Availability of Reproductive Health Services*, Women's Health Issues, May/June 1999, at 121, 126–7.

[16] Leemore Dafny, *Hospital Industry Consolidation – Still More to Come?*, 370 New Eng. J. Med. 198 (2014).

[17] Julie Creswell & Reed Abelson, *New Laws and Rising Costs Create a Surge of Supersizing Hospitals*, N.Y. Times (August 12, 2013), available at www.nytimes.com/2013/08/13/business/bigger-hospitals-may-lead-to-bigger-bills-for-patients.html?pagewanted=all&_r=1 [https://perma.cc/9D6E-PS5Y].

In full-asset mergers or acquisitions by Catholic health care systems, the purchased hospital may become officially designated as Catholic.[18] It will have a sponsoring religious order, provide Catholic pastoral services, and require all health care providers to comply with Catholic restrictions. Now-Catholic hospitals, nonetheless, frequently appear outwardly indistinguishable from their former selves. Catholic restrictions must be followed in "St. Luke's Episcopal Health System" and "Jewish Hospital."[19] More troubling, however, is that after a merger, hospitals sometimes retain their secular identities but abide by religious restrictions.[20]

Affiliation as opposed to asset acquisition often results in application of Catholic directives.[21] Joint ventures, partnerships, management agreements, or lease agreements typically mean that each health care corporation maintains its own identity. Nonetheless, across these affiliations, health care facilities have agreed to Catholic religious restrictions on care.

When Catholic and secular facilities form nominally secular partnerships, restrictions may be imposed systemwide. For example, in the mid-1990s, secular Elliot Hospital entered into a partnership called Optima Health with Catholic Medical Center in Manchester, New Hampshire. Despite promises to doctors that all treatments would continue, Optima banned abortions in order to comply with the directives.[22] Similarly, nonsectarian Bayfront Medical Center in St. Petersburg, Florida, came to follow the ERDs through its involvement in a regional consortium. Because two Catholic hospitals participated in the consortium, the other six hospitals had to ban abortion and sterilizations and permit a nun to review their end-of-life policies.[23]

Affiliations between religious hospitals similarly generate compliance with Catholic norms. For example, Hoag Presbyterian Hospital in Newport Beach, California, entered into an affiliation agreement with St. Joseph Health System to integrate care across their hospitals.[24] The transaction purported to maintain their separate faith

---

[18] Weisman et al., supra note 15, at 125 (providing examples).
[19] ACLU & MergerWatch, supra note 14, at 8, 16.
[20] Carol M. Ostrom, *Hospitals' Proposed Affiliation with Catholic Systems Opposed*, Seattle Times (April 27, 2013), available at www.seattletimes.com/seattle-news/hospitalsrsquo-proposed-affiliation-with-catholic-systems-opposed/ [https://perma.cc/9H4X-VDTM].
[21] ACLU & MergerWatch, supra note 14, at 16.
[22] Alison Manolovici Cody, *Success in New Jersey: Using the Charitable Trust Doctrine to Preserve Women's Reproductive Services When Hospitals Become Catholic*, 57 N.Y.U. Ann. Surv. Am. L. 323, 344–5 (2000).
[23] Wes Allison & Bryan Gilmer, *Bayfront to Leave BayCare*, St. Petersburg Times (October 24, 2000), available at www.sptimes.com/News/102400/TampaBay/Bayfront_to_leave_Bay.shtml [https://perma.cc/R9Q7-HV6L].
[24] Jill Cowan, *Hoag Hospital Can Refuse Elective Abortions, State Rules*, L.A. Times (April 4, 2014), available at www.latimes.com/local/lanow/la-me-ln-hoag-abortions-20140404-story.html [https://perma.cc/M327-Y5CW].

identities. Shortly thereafter, however, Hoag announced a halt to nontherapeutic abortions, citing low demand.[25] Subsequent reports showed that the partnership required restriction of reproductive care.[26] Similarly, when three Baptist hospitals in Nashville affiliated with St. Thomas hospitals, the parties committed to "respect and preserve the heritage, mission and values of both faith-based organizations."[27] Yet, Baptist hospitals agreed to offer only medical services "consistent with Catholic canonical law."[28] For eleven years, "Baptist Hospital" operated under the ERDs.[29]

Public hospitals also have adopted religious restrictions when they affiliated with a Catholic entity.[30] In Austin, for example, a Catholic hospital entered into a lease and management contract with Brackenridge, the public hospital primarily responsible for the city's indigent care. The agreement made clear that Brackenridge would retain ownership and the facility would not be identified as Catholic.[31] Nonetheless, it required the public hospital to turn away women seeking emergency contraception and refer them to a public clinic instead.[32]

2. PERPETUAL RESTRICTIONS ON HEALTH CARE

Catholic health care systems have acted not only as buyers but as sellers, transferring hospitals to secular (and frequently for-profit) owners. Yet, as hospitals have been sold, provisions in asset purchase agreements and restrictive covenants in deeds have maintained religious restrictions. Sometimes, institutions lose their religious identity but continue compliance with religious rules. In other instances, they keep a religious affiliation even though their ownership is not religious, they operate as for-profits, and/or religious orders no longer play a role.

Asset purchase agreements frequently incorporate the ERDs. After a sale, the now-secular hospital continues to prohibit provision of, referral for, or counseling about

---

[25] Id.
[26] Id.
[27] Nicki Pendleton Wood, *Letter Confirms Baptist Planned Sale to St. Thomas and Ascension Health*, Nashville Post (May 7, 2001), available at www.nashvillepost.com/business/health-care/article/20447395/letter-confirms-baptist-planned-sale-to-st-thomas-and-ascension-health [https://perma.cc/YCP8-XDBR].
[28] Id.
[29] *St. Thomas Health Renaming Baptist, Other Hospitals*, WSMV News (July 11, 2013), available at www.wsmv.com/story/22812676/st-thomas-expected-to-rename [https://perma.cc/7CYN-Q2SD].
[30] ACLU & MergerWatch, supra note 14, at 16; Aaron Corvin, *ACLU Says Faith-Based Hospitals Jeopardize Reproductive, End-of-Life Care*, Columbian (March 24, 2013), available at www.columbian.com/news/2013/mar/24/ACLU-faith-based-hospitals-jeopardize-care/ [https://perma.cc/623L-J9MU].
[31] Barbra Mann Wall, *Conflict and Compromise: Catholic and Public Hospital Partnerships*, 18 Nursing Hist. Rev. 100, 101 (2010).
[32] Id. at 110–11.

certain reproductive or end-of-life services.[33] Such terms are generally enforceable, like any other contract term.[34] They often call for decades or an eternity of compliance in the formerly Catholic facilities.[35]

Catholic sellers typically are unwilling to negotiate a sale without some commitment to restrictions from buyers.[36] The buyers may have no religious or moral objection to these health services, but may agree to the provisions for a number of economic reasons. The religious name may have some perceived value, or commitment to maintaining restrictions may reduce the sales price. Buyers also may embrace religious compliance to break into a new market.[37] Indeed, some for-profit systems actively market themselves as willing to enforce religious doctrine in formerly Catholic facilities.[38]

In a relatively new phenomenon,[39] for-profit buyers have agreed to not only continue Catholic restrictions but also form a peculiar new institution – the for-profit, investor-owned Catholic hospital.[40] As the *Wall Street Journal* wrote, describing the purchase of six-hospital Caritas Christi Health Care by for-profit Cerberus Capital Management, "Catholic nuns, meet your new owners: A three-headed dog from hell."[41] Although their owner is a for-profit private equity firm, the Caritas Christi hospitals maintain not only compliance with the ERDs, but also official designation as Catholic.[42] The purchase agreement provides for oversight of religious compliance by the Catholic hierarchy and includes a $25-million liquidated damages clause, which applies if the buyer violates its religion-based obligations.

---

[33] Cinda Becker, *Pennsylvania Pacts*, Modern Healthcare (November 19, 2007), at 17 (reporting one such example).

[34] Catholics for a Free Choice, *Merger Trends 2001: Reproductive Health Care in Catholic Settings* 12 (2002), available at www.catholicsforchoice.org/topics/healthcare/documents/2001mergertrends.pdf [https://perma.cc/V9KW-7NTZ]; MergerWatch, *Fighting Religious Health Restrictions: Preventing the Continuation of Restrictions When Religious Hospitals Are Sold* 3 (2004), available at http://static1.1.sqspcdn.com/static/f/816571/11352513/1300824208687/bp_for_profits.pdf?token=YkA%2Bvltoy WUnvQjI6DTamKmbNDA%3D [https://perma.cc/2DDD-4TK2].

[35] MergerWatch, supra note 34, at 10 (reporting that sale required adherence to the Directives for 30 years); id. at 5 ("According to Richard Fiske of Tenet Healthcare, most of the Tenet agreements with Catholic hospitals continue the Directives in perpetuity.").

[36] Spencer L. Durland, *Note, the Case Against Institutional Conscience*, 86 Notre Dame L. Rev. 1655, 1665 (2011).

[37] Melanie Evans, *Exiting Two States*, Modern Healthcare (May 9, 2011), at 16.

[38] Fogel & Rivera, supra note 4, at 31.

[39] Lisa C. Ikemoto, *When A Hospital Becomes Catholic*, 47 Mercer L. Rev. 1087, 1097–8 (1996).

[40] Lisa Wangsness, *Worcester's For-Profit St. Vincent May Offer Peek at Boston Hospital's Future*, Boston Globe (April 28, 2010), available at www.telegram.com/article/20100428/NEWS/100429713 [https://perma.cc/T3PQ-V86L].

[41] Gregory Corcoran, *In Hospital Deal, How Much Is a Catholic Identity Worth? Just 3%*, Wall St. Journal: Deal Journal (June 24, 2010, 5:11 PM), available at http://blogs.wsj.com/deals/2010/06/24/in-hospital-deal-how-much-is-a-catholic-identity-worth-just-3/ [https://perma.cc/89L7-JATZ].

[42] Id.

Sales agreements also may purport to require future owners to restrict reproductive and end-of-life care. For example, in purchasing Queen of Angels/Hollywood Presbyterian Medical Center in Los Angeles, Tenet agreed to abide by the ERDs from 1998 to 2018 and to ensure any subsequent owners also commit to follow the directives until 2018.[43] Sales of land and office buildings have included restrictive covenants in deeds that seek to forever prohibit the use of the property for sterilization, abortion, or assisted suicide.[44]

While information is difficult to obtain, several examples suggest religious compliance endures in formerly Catholic-owned hospitals even after subsequent sales. For example, having purchased two St. Louis-area hospitals in 2001, Tenet negotiated with the subsequent buyer to preserve adherence to the ERDs.[45] Similarly, Tennova, a now-secular hospital system in Tennessee, maintained religious compliance as it switched from secular nonprofit to for-profit ownership.[46] Even where contract terms do not so require, path dependence may mean continued limits on services. Once a hospital ceases providing reproductive and end-of-life care services to comply with religious doctrine, it may not restore them.

3. CONFOUNDING TRADITIONAL ACCOUNTS OF RELIGIOUS HEALTH CARE

In academic and political discourse, the religious hospital has long been treated as the exemplar of religious flourishing in commerce. Traditional accounts of religious institutionalism – rooted in association and church mission – however, have not kept pace with the changing health care market. Contract institutes compliance with religious rules across a variety of health care institutions in a way that confounds analogies to associations and to churches. In particular, sales agreements perpetuate religious restrictions long after the traditional markers of religious institutional identity fade.

Traditional accounts of religious institutions take two forms. The first analogizes to a voluntary association. Individuals, as the argument goes, come together to further their moral convictions. Institutions then "become vehicles for individuals to realize their own values and identities."[47] They ensure that individuals can live out

---

[43] MergerWatch, supra note 34, at 4–5.
[44] Id. at 3.
[45] Judith Vandewater, *Tenet Sells 2 St. Louis-Area Community Hospitals*, St. Louis Post-Dispatch (November 30, 2004).
[46] Stephanie Bouchard, *HMA Aims to Acquire Seven Hospitals*, Healthcare Finance (May 3, 2011), available at www.healthcarefinancenews.com/news/hma-aims-acquire-seven-hospitals [https://perma.cc/8RLK-WTST].
[47] Suzanne Davis & Paul Lansing, *When Two Fundamental Rights Collide at the Pharmacy: The Struggle to Balance the Consumer's Right to Access Contraception and the Pharmacist's Right of Conscience*, 12 DePaul J. Health Care L. 67, 100 (2009).

their conception of the good life in community with others, disassociate themselves from acts or individuals of whom they disapprove, and agree on institutional norms that reinforce their own convictions.

The second theory primarily analogizes the hospital to a church and emphasizes the institution rather than the individuals. On this view, an institution makes moral judgments and strives to maintain its religious identity as embodied in its mission statement and policies.[48] Although one might make a broad claim that all health care corporations have moral agency and devotion to mission, scholars frequently default to the position that religious nonprofit health care is special due to its connection to a church's religious mission.[49] Courts similarly suggest that sectarian hospitals might be unique.[50] The health care enterprise constitutes a mechanism for fulfilling the goals of a church itself.

Whether to safeguard the value of moral association or church mission, both accounts conclude that the secular state should grant religious health care institutions some freedom to define the scope of the care they provide. The primary manifestation of these theories in law is conscience legislation, which allows hospitals to refuse to provide certain procedures, most frequently abortion, end-of-life care, and sterilization, with the stated purpose of protecting conscience.[51] Although hospitals are under no legal obligation to offer any specific set of services, health care providers have longstanding legal duties not to abandon a patient, to treat them in accordance with acceptable standards of medical practice, to inform them of treatments and their risks and benefits, and to refer them for services they are not able to provide.[52] State conscience laws can exempt institutions from these requirements as well as from their statutory duties to stabilize or treat patients suffering from emergency conditions or in active labor,[53] to ensure rape survivors access to emergency contraception,[54] to offer counseling to terminally ill patients about available palliative

---

[48] Kathleen M. Boozang, *Deciding the Fate of Religious Hospitals in the Emerging Health Care Market*, 31 Hous. L. Rev. 1429, 1505–8 (1995).

[49] Kent Greenawalt, *Objections in Conscience to Medical Procedures: Does Religion Make a Difference?*, 2006 U. Ill. L. Rev. 799, 824 (2006); Ana Smith Iltis, *Institutional Integrity in Roman Catholic Health Care Institutions*, 7 Christian Bioethics 95, 98–102 (2001).

[50] See, e.g., *Valley Hosp. Ass'n v. Mat-Su Coal. for Choice*, 948 P.2d 963, 972 (Alaska 1997).

[51] 42 U.S.C. § 300a-7(b) (2000).

[52] 61 Am. Jur. 2d Physicians, Surgeons, Etc. § 121 n.5–7 (2016); see also Maxine M. Harrington, *The Ever-Expanding Health Care Conscience Clause: The Quest for Immunity in the Struggle Between Professional Duties and Moral Beliefs*, 34 Fla. St. U. L. Rev. 779, 804, 822 (2007).

[53] State laws, however, cannot exempt hospitals from the federal Emergency Medical Treatment and Active Labor Act, 42 U.S.C. § 1395 (1986).

[54] Cal. Penal Code § 13823.11(e)(1) (West 2009); 410 Ill. Comp. Stat. 70/2.2 (2002); Ohio Rev. Code Ann. § 2907.29 (West 2003); N.M. Stat. Ann. § 24-10D-3 (West 2010); N.Y. Pub. Health Law § 2805-p (McKinney 2007); S.C. Code Ann. § 16-3-1350(B) (2002); Wash. Rev. Code § 70.41.350(1)(c) (2003); see also Guttmacher Institute, *State Policies in Brief: Emergency Contraception* (March 1,

care,[55] and to honor advance directives. Although many conscience statutes protect any hospital that refuses to deliver care, more specific statutes require ethical, moral, or religious grounds for refusal.

The use of private law raises a number of difficult questions for these theories. First, what does it mean for a health care institution to have a *religious* identity? In commerce, what distinguishes religious from nonreligious entities? Are health care entities bound by contract to religious institutions? As the Supreme Court has embraced broad autonomy for religious institutions[56] and recognized for-profit entities as able to exercise religion,[57] the question of institutional religious identity in commerce has become more significant. Previously, one might have deferred to the Catholic Church as to which institutions were Catholic. All Catholic hospitals were considered part of a charitable mission of the Church and were, by definition, nonprofit (that is, charitable) institutions. Today, however, facilities may reflect Catholic doctrine even when they further no charitable mission, are repudiated by the Church, or are owned in no part by Catholic entities. Others – including public and investor-owned entities – are acknowledged to be secular, but nonetheless follow Catholic religious restrictions.

Second, can the analogy to voluntary associations survive industrywide contracting for religious compliance? In the early days of Catholic health care, orders primarily of religious women provided nursing care and served as administrators. Today, religious orders remain formally linked to health care, as hospitals require sponsorship from a religious order (or diocese) in order to be designated as Catholic. But orders have little-to-no patient interaction and sponsor "systems in markets in which they no longer have – or never did have – an active presence."[58]

The perpetuation of religion in sales challenges the associational view in particular. Once the founders are no longer involved, the religious orders have disaffiliated, and a secular corporation owns a facility, who constitutes the corporation? In the absence of an association – however defined – of religious people, how can religious belief and sincerity of faith be assessed? The application of religious restrictions within and to health care institutions today demonstrates that stakeholders assume religious identity or obey religious principles not as a matter of shared faith, but in conformity to contract. This use of contract suggests that these organizations do not function like voluntary associations, which unite people by shared religious belief. Instead, employees are induced to abide by restrictions through economic transaction and with contracts backed by threat of civil action.

2016), available at www.guttmacher.org/sites/default/files/pdfs/spibs/spib_EC.pdf [https://perma.cc/85LX-EDYQ].

[55] See, e.g., N.Y. Pub. Health Law § 2997-c (McKinney 2011).
[56] *Hosanna-Tabor Evangelical Lutheran Church & School v. EEOC*, 132 S. Ct. 694, 699 (2012).
[57] *Burwell v. Hobby Lobby Stores, Inc.*, 134 S. Ct. 2751, 2775 (2014).
[58] Lawrence E. Singer, *Does Mission Matter?*, 6 Hous. J. Health L. & Pol'y 347, 347 (2006).

Finally, can a contractual obligation constitute a religious mission? Under the mission-oriented theory, one might endorse contracts binding non-Catholic individuals and entities as furthering the Church's mission. From a Catholic hospital's perspective, contract works to protect the institution from complicity in the act of a third party. No hospital itself performs abortions or provides emergency contraception. Instead, through contract, it seeks to avoid complicity in procedures that medical staff might otherwise perform. The use of contract in health care, however, raises the specter of complicity without end. In tying sales to compliance with ERDs, Catholic health care systems claim an objection to acts remote in time and distance, in institutions to which they have no ties or financial interest, and by individuals over whom they have no oversight. The stickiness of religious compliance thus muddies the meaning of religious identity for the mission-oriented theory as well.

4. RISKS TO ACCESS AND RELIGIOUS EXERCISE

Contracted-for religion limits space for other religious viewpoints in health care. It risks religious restrictions spreading like contagion across the marketplace to the detriment of access to medical care.

The spread of religious compliance through contract narrows space for religious exercise in several ways. First, one religious perspective becomes overrepresented. The level of refusal does not reflect the beliefs of the constituents of the organization or of providers as a whole. Consider, for example, that just counting those officially designated as Catholic, sixteen percent of hospitals prohibit artificial insemination and in vitro fertilization, but fewer than 5 percent of ob-gyns object to performing those procedures.[59]

Second, contracting for religion creates new conflicts over conscientious belief between providers who seek to deliver care and institutions that limit care. Such disputes may be common. Twenty percent of physicians who practice at religious hospitals[60] and 52 percent of ob-gyns who work in Catholic hospitals report conflicts over religion-based policies.[61] Empirical studies show that such disagreement exists regardless of whether the organization unites believers of a particular faith.[62] The rates of conflict of a Catholic physician and a non-Catholic physician with a Catholic hospital are approximately the same. A lack of transparency in

---

[59] Ryan E. Lawrence et al., *Obstetrician-Gynecologists' Beliefs about Assisted Reproductive Technologies*, 116 Obstetrics & Gynecology 127, 127 (2010).

[60] Because some religious hospitals do not impose restrictions, this number may understate the occurrence of conflicts between physicians and refusing hospitals. Stulberg et al., supra note 13, at 727.

[61] Debra B. Stulberg et al., *Obstetrician–Gynecologists, Religious Institutions, and Conflicts Regarding Patient Care Policies*, 207 Am. J. Obstetrics & Gynecology 73.e1, 73.e4 (2012).

[62] Stulberg et al., supra note 13, at 728.

Catholic/non-Catholic transactions also undermines the notion that providers voluntarily embrace Catholic restrictions. In many sales of Catholic hospitals to secular corporations, terms go undisclosed.[63]

Permitting religiously restricted care, moreover, has a significant effect on patients' access to health care – reproductive and end-of-life care in particular. Due to mergers, nearly half of hospital markets are highly concentrated (uncompetitive) and none is highly competitive.[64] Given the market share of official and unofficial Catholic institutions, a patient in the U.S. health care market is likely to encounter major medical institutions with religiously restricted care. Almost one-third of official Catholic hospitals are in rural areas.[65] Some enjoy "a practical, but not state-enforced, monopoly on obstetrical services."[66]

Contracting for religion may play a significant, but unknown, role in limiting care. The spread of restrictions and their application to nonobjecting partner institutions suggest that access to contested care (abortion in particular) may be more limited than we previously thought. If we only look at Catholic institutions, we may undercount the reach of religious restrictions.

As hospitals merge and affiliate with one another, determining whether a hospital adheres to Catholic ERDs becomes difficult for potential patients or employees. As a rule, hospitals do not advertise the services they prohibit. Once sold to a secular buyer, formerly Catholic hospitals may no longer retain any outward sign of religiosity, though they continue to restrict care. Although hospitals officially linked to the Catholic Church through sponsorship agreements appear on official rosters of Catholic hospitals, the other hospitals that comply with religious restrictions through partnerships or following sales go unidentified.

The health care experience demands skepticism of claims that legislative conscience exemptions for abortion, sterilization and other services are merely ways to protect religious and conscientious beliefs. In health care, private law has worked to limit medical care in facilities that are not religious, and by providers that have no individual moral or religious objection to providing necessary medical care. Conscience exemptions for such institutions seem to undermine societal interests in religious liberty and health care access – in the absence of a countervailing interest in any person's associational interests or any church's autonomy.

Under such circumstances, decision-makers may reconsider the institutional conscience exemptions that authorize hospitals to withhold abortions, sterilizations,

---

[63] Joe Carlson, *Offering Salvation: Ascension, Equity Firm Forge Deal They Say Could Save Catholic Hospitals*, Modern Healthcare (February 21, 2011), at 6.
[64] David M. Cutler & Fiona Scott Morton, *Hospitals, Market Share, and Consolidation*, 310 JAMA 1964, 1966 (2013).
[65] Singer, supra note 58, at 376–7.
[66] *Ham v. Holy Rosary Hosp.*, 529 P.2d 361, 376 (Mont. 1974).

and end-of-life care. They might merely require disclosure of the procedures that an institution will not allow, as a number of end-of-life statutes provide.[67] State attorneys general could more closely scrutinize affiliations, as well as nonprofit conversions, to identify and avert limits on care. New legislation – such as that in California – could prohibit contract terms that continue religious restrictions after a hospital is sold.[68] The framework of existing conscience legislation also might be altered so as to balance conscience and medical care. Although bioethicists have long called for consideration of patient access in the form of referrals, emergency care, and alternative access, statutes typically ignore such concerns. Alternatively, these statutes could more tightly define those institutions eligible for conscience protections. In so doing, they would avoid the many questions raised by contracting for religion and ensure that exemptions do not stay in place as institutions change ownership and corporate form.

CONCLUSION

In *Burwell v. Hobby Lobby*, the Supreme Court dismissed the possibility that corporate religious identity might spread throughout the corporate world.[69] It opined that "the idea that unrelated shareholders – including institutional investors with their own set of stakeholders – would agree to run a corporation under the same religious beliefs seems improbable."[70] It suggested that "corporate giants" and publicly traded corporations would be unlikely to assert RFRA claims.[71]

The experience of religious organizations in health care shows the contrary. People who hold different or no religious beliefs become subject to religious restrictions. Secular and for-profit institutions assume a religious mantle. Religious restrictions on health care continue, even as hospitals are sold.

---

[67] See, e.g., Alaska Stat. § 13.52.060(e) (2009).
[68] Cal. Corp. Code § 5917.5 (West 2014).
[69] *Burwell v. Hobby Lobby Stores, Inc.*, 134 S. Ct. 2751, 2769 (2014).
[70] Id. at 2774.
[71] Id.

9

Mission Integrity Matters

Balancing Catholic Health Care Values and Public Mandates

David M. Craig

In the controversy around the Department of Health and Human Services' (HHS) rules on contraceptive benefits coverage, one remarkable fact has gone largely unnoticed. Neither the Catholic Health Association (CHA) nor any of its member health care organizations joined the legal challenges to the contraceptive mandate. This accommodating approach to HHS' accommodation deserves attention as a counter-example to liberal and conservative narratives about law, religion, and health care in the United States. In this chapter, I explore the case of Catholic health care nonprofits, drawing on a qualitative study of mission and values that I conducted at religious health care organizations across the country.[1] I argue that the individual religious belief standard presumed in *Burwell v. Hobby Lobby*,[2] introduced in this volume's Introduction and discussed in many of its chapters, is an incoherent basis for judging organizational religious exercise. A better standard is needed, given the extensive reliance on religious nonprofit health care organizations in the United States.

The argument moves in three steps. First, I demonstrate that the majority and dissenting opinions in *Hobby Lobby* both rely on an individual religious belief standard as opposed to an alternative standard of organizational religious mission integrity. A mission integrity standard bases organizational religious exercise on the degree to which an organization's stated religious mission and values have been integrated into its operations. This standard more accurately reflects how organizations exercise religion through cooperative practices instead of through individuals' beliefs. Second, I turn to another policy arena where law, religion, and health care have collided – the 1969 community benefit standard. Under this rule, the Internal Revenue Service mandates that nonprofit hospitals have to provide uncompensated care, effectively requiring religious nonprofit hospitals to define their values in particular

---

[1] Study 0506-65B was approved by the Indiana University–Purdue University Indianapolis Institutional Review Board.
[2] 134 S. Ct. 2751 (2014).

ways. Yet the federal government has taken an accommodating approach to this public mandate, and Catholic hospitals have been accommodating in turn. As a result, governmental interests have been advanced while reserving significant latitude for organizational religious freedom. I close by applying a mission integrity standard to *Hobby Lobby* and *Zubik v. Burwell*.[3] Religious nonprofits are better candidates for free exercise protections than for-profit corporations, though religious service providers would also face some restrictions on their religious freedom.

1. RELIGIOUS BELIEF OR MISSION INTEGRITY?: RETHINKING ORGANIZATIONAL RELIGIOUS EXERCISE

Political liberals sometimes invoke two popular distinctions to set limits around religious freedom. The stricter principle separates belief from practice. The idea is that individuals are free to affirm any religious beliefs, but they should restrict the practice of their beliefs to private worship, often with fellow congregants. The more flexible distinction permits some public expression of religious practice so long as it does not impose specific religious beliefs on the broader public.[4]

Catholic health care organizations do not conform to either distinction. They are not communities of coreligionists affirming private beliefs. In addition, practicing Catholic values in health care directly affects employees, patients, and the public as Catholic health care organizations use their mission and values to govern certain treatment choices by physicians and nurses, guide employee orientation and evaluations, and structure the delivery of care.

One issue here is the difference between belief and practice. Catholic hospitals do not simply affirm and express beliefs. Instead, they practice beliefs that have been translated into mission and values statements. Another issue is that Catholic health care organizations cannot practice their mission and values without participation from their employees, including those with a different faith or none at all. Simply put, mission-driven nonprofits enact – or impose – their mission and values through cooperative practices. This crucial point is obscured by the objection from secular liberals that HHS' accommodation permits, as if for the first time, some religious organizations to impose their beliefs on employees who do not share the view that the sanctity of human life begins at conception.

---

[3] 136 S. Ct. 1557 (2016).
[4] These popular views are reflected in two Supreme Court decisions. *Reynolds v. United States* protected "mere opinion" from legislative power, while naming "social duties" and "good order" as reasons to restrict religious "action." 98 U.S. 145, 164 (1878). *Cantwell v. Connecticut* subjected religious conduct "to regulation for the protection of society," though "the power to regulate must be so exercised as not ... unduly to infringe the protected freedom." 310 U.S. 296, 304 (1940). See also Kent Greenawalt, *Religion and the Constitution*, vol. 1 28–9 (2009).

Neither the majority nor the dissenting opinions in *Hobby Lobby* attend to the dynamics of this cooperative practice of religious mission. Instead, they each ground organizational religious exercise in a test of unanimity in individuals' religious beliefs. In Justice Samuel Alito's majority opinion, a fundamental question is which types of organization, if any, qualify as "persons" under the 1993 Religious Freedom Restoration Act (RFRA). Do only religious nonprofits qualify for protection, or do for-profit corporations also qualify? He frames the issue as an either/or. Either *only* "natural persons" – that is, human beings – can exercise religion, or *both* "natural persons" and *all* "artificial persons" – that is, corporations – can exercise religion. Since HHS concedes that religious nonprofit corporations enjoy free exercise rights, Alito asks, what distinguishes them from for-profit corporations claiming these rights?[5]

Alito finds no difference between the two types of artificial persons, but interestingly, his argument revolves around the free exercise rights of natural persons. Individuals may choose to associate for religious purposes, so, according to Alito, any association of individual believers expressly acting on shared religious beliefs can claim free exercise rights under RFRA. Alito cites Justice Ruth Bader Ginsburg's suggestion in her dissent that "nonprofit corporations are special because furthering their religious 'autonomy ... often furthers individual religious freedom as well.' But," he continues, "this principle applies equally to for-profit corporations: Furthering their religious freedom also 'furthers individual religious freedom.'"[6] In Alito's reading of the facts, the owners of Hobby Lobby, Mardel, and Conestoga Wood chose to associate through the for-profit corporate form as one expression of their religious beliefs. Moreover, bringing religion into their work life testifies to the sincerity of their beliefs. Most importantly, the owners affirm the same beliefs, as illustrated by the members of the Green family, who own Hobby Lobby and Mardel, all signing a pledge to "run the businesses in accordance with the family's religious beliefs and to use the family assets to support Christian ministries."[7] This test of unanimity in individuals' religious beliefs provides a clear standard for organizational religious exercise and limits the number of for-profit corporations able to claim free exercise.

Alito's reasoning applies an individualistic methodology to organizations. For individuals, the scope of religious exercise is set by the content of a person's religious beliefs. When individuals associate for religious purposes, however, the scope of religious exercise is determined by a Venn diagram of their overlapping beliefs. As a result, free exercise protection must be extended to closely held for-profit

---

[5] Hobby Lobby, 134 S. Ct. at 2768–9.
[6] Id. at 2769.
[7] Id. at 2765–6.

corporations where the associated individual owners are unanimous in their religious beliefs.

Alito's reasoning is odd. What constitutes religious exercise by an artificial person is unanimity in the religious beliefs of natural persons. If consensus among individuals' religious beliefs is the legal test, then the greater this overlap, the more substantial an organization's religious exercise is. As the overlap narrows, an organization's religious freedom dissipates, regardless of the sincerity of individual members' beliefs. Notice that "sincere" religious belief has subtly changed from individual profession to group agreement. So, presumably, if a Reform rabbi, an Evangelical pastor, and a Muslim imam owned a closely held for-profit corporation, their disparate theological beliefs would grant the organization few, if any, grounds for claiming religious exercise. They would not each be able to claim organizational religious freedom for their respective religious beliefs. Instead, the same judgment would seem to apply here that Alito applies to publicly owned corporations: "the idea that unrelated shareholders – including institutional investors with their own set of stakeholders – would agree to run a corporation under the same religious beliefs seems improbable."[8] What matters for Alito is overlap among the religious beliefs of the controlling parties, not the full range of religious beliefs professed by the people who own, let alone work for, a corporation.

Turning to Ginsburg's dissent, she argues that nothing in Supreme Court precedent or the legislative history of RFRA suggests that for-profit corporations have free exercise rights. Less clear in her argument, however, is how religious nonprofits and for-profit corporations differ. Ginsburg grants that "churches and other nonprofit religion-based organizations" have free exercise protections. As already noted by Alito, she quotes approvingly from Justice William Brennan's concurrence in *Corporation of Presiding Bishop of Church of Jesus Christ of Latter-day Saints v. Amos*: "'For many individuals, religious activity derives meaning in large measure from participation in a larger religious community,' and 'furtherance of the autonomy of religious organizations often furthers individual religious freedom as well.'"[9] The omitted lines between the two excerpts are telling. Brennan interjects that "[a religious] community represents an ongoing tradition of shared beliefs, an organic entity not reducible to a mere aggregation of individuals." Importantly, a religious community defines itself by "determining that certain activities are in furtherance of [its] religious mission."[10] Brennan's analysis does not stop at private beliefs shared by individuals. Religious mission is defined through the activities that join community members. Yet Ginsburg also falls back on an individualistic

---

[8] Id. at 2774.
[9] Id. at 2794 (Ginsburg, J., dissenting) (citing *Corp. of Presiding Bishop of Church of Jesus Christ of Latter-day Saints v. Amos*, 483 U.S. 327 (1987) (Brennan, J., concurring))
[10] *Amos*, 483 U.S. at 327 (Brennan, J., concurring).

methodology, arguing that organizational religious exercise requires all of the members of an organization to be unanimous in their religious beliefs. In her words, "Religious organizations exist to foster the interests of persons subscribing to the same religious faith. Not so of for-profit corporations. Workers who sustain the operations of those corporations commonly are not drawn from one religious community."[11] While it is true that the employees of Hobby Lobby and Conestoga Wood are not from the same religious community, neither are the employees of Catholic health care organizations.

Ginsburg's reasoning fails to address Alito's question about the line between religious nonprofits and for-profit corporations. A few generations ago, Catholic hospitals might have been described using her language of a "community of believers" that exists "to foster the interests of persons subscribing to the same religious faith." The religious orders of nuns who founded Catholic hospitals also staffed and administered them throughout much of the twentieth century. Today's Catholic health care organizations remain a healing ministry of the Church, and they celebrate their founding sisters. But they are no longer imbued with the nuns' living presence that guided daily practice and governed operating structures.[12] Nevertheless, although lay leaders have taken charge, mission and values are still structured into operations and expected of employees. Governance is top-down, but disagreement is possible for employees willing to challenge the leadership's understanding of mission and values.

Religious mission in Catholic health care is reducible neither to Ginsburg's community of believers nor to Alito's leadership team of believing associates. Errant in both accounts is the premise that unanimity in individuals' religious beliefs is the substance of an organization's religious exercise.[13] Ginsburg would require this unanimity to pervade an organization, making it hard to see how most religious hospitals, universities, or social service agencies could claim religious exercise, contrary to her concession. Alito allows this unanimity to be confined to management. Thus, he leaps from the inclusive observation that "an established body of law specifies the rights and obligations of the *people* (including shareholders, officers, and employees) who are associated with a corporation" to the exclusive conclusion that "protecting the free-exercise rights of corporations like Hobby Lobby, Conestoga, and Mardel protects the religious liberty of the humans who own and control those

---

[11] Hobby Lobby, 134 S. Ct. at 2795 (Ginsburg, J., dissenting).
[12] Kevin Sack, *Nuns, a 'Dying Breed,' Fade from Leadership Roles at Catholic Hospitals*, N.Y. Times (August 21, 2011), at A12.
[13] Both justices overlook the dissent of Mary Beck Briscoe, Chief Judge of the Tenth Circuit Court of Appeals, who criticizes the "unanimity of belief" standard in *Hobby Lobby v. Sebelius*, 723 F.3d 1114, 1173 (2013) (Briscoe, C.J., dissenting).

companies."[14] "All of the people" boils down to just the owners. Whether construed broadly or narrowly, a standard of unanimous individual religious belief ignores how organizations exercise religion by implementing their mission and values throughout their operating practices and structures.

Consider how Catholic health care organizations structure the value of respect for human life into their operations. The Ethical and Religious Directives of Catholic Health Care Services (ERDs) instruct Catholic providers on the impermissibility of fertility treatments, surrogacy, abortion, sterilization, and contraception.[15] Catholic hospitals do not deliver these services, and those restrictions are known to employees and patients. More important than which services are prohibited, however, is the systemic imprint of this value on Catholic health care organizations. Respect for human life is one of their core values, all of which are introduced to new employees, posted on facility walls, and assessed in annual job evaluations.[16] In terms of employee training, the value of respect for human life primarily motivates the reverence and compassion that are due to patients through everyday gestures and attitudes. Efforts to cultivate this healing ministry are frequent topics in various organizational practices, such as value reflections at department meetings, sacred stories in hospital newsletters, mission dialogues, and training retreats. The practical breadth of this value enables leaders and employees to buy in, even if they do not personally affirm Catholic teachings forbidding specific medical procedures. Otherwise Ethical and Religious Directive 9 would be untenable: "Employees of a Catholic health care institution must respect and uphold the religious mission of the institution and adhere to these Directives. They should maintain professional standards and promote the institution's commitment to human dignity and the common good."[17]

Under a mission integrity standard, courts would assess the sincerity of the violated religious belief or value by reviewing evidence of its integration into the organization's practices and structures. Catholic health care organizations have integrated their religious value of respect for human life throughout their operations, which is why HHS' contraceptive mandate should have accommodated them from the outset.

---

[14] Hobby Lobby, 134 S. Ct. at 2768.
[15] U.S. Conference of Catholic Bishops (USCCB), *Ethical and Religious Directives for Catholic Health Care Services* 25–8 (5th ed., 2009).
[16] For example, a poster from Providence Health illustrates the value of respect with the biblical text, "All people have been created in the image of God (Genesis 1:27)." In the background a young female caregiver radiates her compassion with a beaming smile, as she places her hand on the shoulder of a grey-haired patient clothed in that iconic sign of vulnerability, a hospital robe. See *Providence is Calling: Mission and Core Values*, available at www.providenceiscalling.jobs/mission-core-values/ [https://perma.cc/EP7Z-VRAK] (last visited June 27, 2016).
[17] USCCB, supra note 15, at 13.

2. ARTICULATING COMMUNITY BENEFITS: RELIGIOUS EMPLOYERS VERSUS ELIGIBLE INSTITUTIONS

Respect for human life is only one religious value that Catholic hospitals have integrated into their operations. Directive 9 above cites the common good as another primary commitment, and this value has been central to a second debate around law, religion, and health care. To keep their tax-exempt status, nonprofit hospitals have to provide "community benefits." Critics of religious hospitals have argued that they should be required to commit a minimum percentage of their revenues to uncompensated care for patients who cannot pay their bills.[18] Catholic health care nonprofits have resisted these charity care mandates·as meddling in their religious mission.

A brief look at this debate is instructive for two reasons. First, it highlights the policy risks for U.S. health care if public mandates are implemented without accommodating mission-driven religious nonprofits. Second, it challenges the claim that Catholic health care nonprofits are a direct extension of the bishops' understanding of Catholic values. Catholic hospitals work in a middle ground between Catholic teachings, on the one hand, and public policy expectations and competitive market forces, on the other hand. While churches, temples, and mosques can operate with a largely settled religious mission, religious nonprofit service organizations must articulate their mission in response to multiple constituencies inside and outside the organization.

In the principled language of the ERDs, Catholic hospitals' charitable work should serve "the biblical mandate to care for the poor" and also "contribute to the common good."[19] In practice, meeting both goals simultaneously has been challenging and has required ongoing dialogue inside Catholic health care organizations. The Illinois State Supreme Court case of *Provena Covenant Medical Center v. Director of Revenue* (2010) illustrates the tensions that can arise between these two Catholic values of serving the poor and promoting the common good in the context of community benefit mandates.

The case began with the Champaign County Board of Review denying a property tax exemption claimed by Provena Covenant Medical Center (PCMC) in 2002. This denial was affirmed by the Illinois Department of Revenue, and the Illinois State Supreme Court ultimately ruled in favor of the Department in 2010. Although a state case, and thus subject to the Illinois State Constitution's more stringent standard – that "the property at issue is used exclusively for a charitable purpose" – the

---

[18] Jack Hanson, *Are We Getting Our Money's Worth? Charity Care, Community Benefits, and Tax Exemption at Nonprofit Hospitals*, 17 Loyola Consumer L. Rev. 399–404 (2005); see also S. Comm. on Fin. Minority Staff, 110th Cong., *Tax-Exempt Hospitals: Discussion Draft* 2 (July 2007).

[19] USCCB, supra note 15, at 10.

court's analysis of religious mission is instructive.[20] Notably, the court distinguished religious beliefs from mission-driven operations. In the majority's ruling, "Religious purpose is not determined solely by the professed motives or beliefs of the property's owner. A court must also take into account the facts and circumstances regarding how the property is actually used."[21] On this basis, the court found that, despite PCMC's (unadvertised) charity care policy, "both the number of uninsured patients receiving free or discounted care and the dollar value of the care they received were *de minimis*."[22]

Between the start of this case and the State Supreme Court's decision, CHA published revised community benefits guidelines that effectively agreed with the court's challenge to PCMC's definition of charity care. In the new guidelines, charity care included only free and reduced care for uninsured and underinsured patients, and financial losses on charity care must be calculated using hospital costs instead of charges. On both points, PCMC's old policies fell short of CHA's clarification of Catholic values.[23]

At the same time, however, CHA's guidelines placed the value of serving the poor within a common good framework. Specifically, Catholic hospitals were encouraged to conduct two "community-building activities": (1) facilitating local stakeholder coalitions to advise hospitals on community health needs and (2) partnering with other service providers to improve health outcomes for poor and vulnerable populations.[24] By confining charitable mission to "service to and advocacy for ... the poor[,] the uninsured and the underinsured," the *Provena* majority ignored a fundamental tension in Catholic health care mission.[25] On the one hand, mandating higher levels of charity care requires Catholic hospitals to lose more money delivering uncompensated care in expensive emergency departments and acute care settings. On the other hand, improving low-income patients' health through preventive care and chronic disease management demands capital investment to build integrated health care networks outside of hospitals. In short, losing money on charity care – service to the poor – strips resources away from the more promising delivery of integrated care in community settings – service to the poor *and* common good.

There are several lessons here. First, the mission and values of religious nonprofit service providers sometimes evolve in response to public policy. Second,

---

[20] *Provena Covenant Med. Ctr. v. Dep't of Revenue*, 236 Ill. 2d 368, 384 (2010).
[21] Id. at 409.
[22] Id. at 412.
[23] Catholic Health Ass'n (CHA), *A Guide for Planning and Reporting Community Benefit* (1st ed. 2005) at 31. The guidelines partly agree with Provena Covenant's accounting methods, such as including losses on patients in means-tested programs like Medicaid.
[24] Id. at 31–3.
[25] Provena, 236 Ill. 2d at 399.

policy makers and judges are in the position of potentially denying or distorting an organization's religious values, and they should exercise due caution. Finally, while PCMC had to catch up to CHA's guidelines, imposing an inflexible charity care mandate means sacrificing both the autonomy of religious hospitals and the prospect of better health care for underserved populations encouraged by this new articulation of Catholic values.

I use the word "articulate" in two senses – a verbal sense of speaking values into greater clarity through mission dialogue, and a practical sense of implementing values throughout an organization's operations. Religious mission means little without systemic implementation. An articulated mission is analogous to an articulated limb that has a specific structure related to its operations. This structure facilitates certain movements as characteristic of the limb's functions. The range of motion comes with limits, too, some of which are inherent in the structure and some of which are due to external forces and constraints. CHA and its member hospitals have articulated a Catholic approach to community benefits by building accounting and delivery structures that combined their values of common good and service to the poor.

By contrast, there are religious organizations with settled missions. Churches, temples, and mosques, along with their auxiliaries and denominational bodies, can presuppose a settled mission because their members assent to a common doctrine. HHS defines such organizations as "religious employers" and distinguishes them from "eligible institutions" such as Catholic hospitals. HHS initially defined religious employers as follows: "(1) Has the inculcation of religious values as its purpose; (2) primarily employs persons who share its religious tenets; (3) primarily serves persons who share its religious tenets."[26] Understandably, many religious groups, including CHA, objected strenuously that this definition implied that they cared about shared worship to the exclusion of community service.[27] For many congregations, worship and service are joint expressions of members' religious practice of a living, if largely settled, mission.

Reading between the lines of HHS' definition, it focuses on unity in religious values and tenets. Such religious unity suggests a defensible distinction between religious employers and eligible institutions. Religious employers can count on their mission being settled and, more importantly, its being settled by representative leaders when questions arise. Eligible institutions, however, must be responsive to diverse constituencies as they articulate and rearticulate their religious mission and values.

[26] 76 Fed. Reg. 46623 (Aug 3, 2011).
[27] USCCB, *Comments on Interim Final Rules on Preventive Services* 19–20 (2011); CHA, *Interim Final Rule Defining Religious Employer Exception* 5 (2011); and Stanley W. Carlson-Thies, *Which Religious Organizations Count as Religious?: The Religious Employer Exemption of the Health Insurance Law's Contraceptives Mandate*, 13 Engage 58–60 (2012).

In general, religious nonprofit service organizations have articulated missions, not settled missions. Religious schools, universities, and social service agencies may not face the same level of government scrutiny as religious hospitals, but they engage with multiple constituencies. Indeed, sometimes these organizations negotiate their values with outside groups and external forces. In Catholic health care, mission dialogues can be lively sites of internal disagreement. Catholic hospitals have had to negotiate their mission in response to the communities they are required to benefit and to public policy structures and market forces that lie outside their control. Acknowledging that mission may be articulated by insiders and negotiated with outsiders underscores how far a religious nonprofit may have to go in living out its mission as a faithful servant and steward in civil society. It also explains why Catholic health care organizations have sometimes departed from their bishops – for example, in supporting the Affordable Care Act (ACA),[28] accepting HHS' accommodation, and, in some organizations, adopting same-sex spousal benefits[29] – despite the bishops' claims to definitively settle Catholic values.

I have written elsewhere that the "social good" of U.S. health care is deeply reliant on private-public partnerships and religious heath care nonprofits play a vital role in advancing national health care priorities.[30] U.S. health care is not organized as a public good, so law cannot be the only means of advancing governmental interests. With community benefits policy, the dance of accommodation between public mandates and Catholic values has nudged health care toward prevention and chronic disease management for vulnerable populations and helped inject these priorities into the ACA. Although religious values and governmental interests clash more directly in the contraceptive mandate, the awkward dance of accommodation between HHS and CHA promises that Catholic health care organizations will be more supportive of the ACA's other policy goals while accepting that women's health and gender equity are being also served.

3. APPLYING A MISSION INTEGRITY STANDARD

This chapter has argued for a mission integrity standard as a better test of organizational religious exercise. I have also indicated how Catholic health care providers articulate and even negotiate their religious mission in response to public mandates. But how would this standard apply to the more intractable disputes represented by *Hobby Lobby* and *Zubik v. Burwell*?

---

[28] Helene Cooper, *Nuns Back Bill Amid Broad Rift Over Whether It Limits Abortion Enough*, N.Y. Times (March 20, 2010), at A10.

[29] Joan Frawley Desmond, *Spousal Benefits for Same-Sex Partners at Catholic Universities and Hospitals*, Nat'l Cath. Reg. (October 20, 2014).

[30] David M. Craig, *Health Care as a Social Good* 85–90 (2014).

The *Zubik* challenge is more germane to Catholic hospitals. The petitioners argued that taking any action that triggered contraceptive benefits involved them in violating their religious beliefs, even if the benefits were arranged and paid for by a third party. Their objection was stated cogently by the original district court decision in *Zubik v. Sebelius*. In the court's opinion, the Bishops of Erie and Pittsburgh faced a schizophrenic situation because their dioceses (religious employers) were exempt from the contraceptive mandate but their diocesan charities and schools (eligible institutions) were only granted accommodation. HHS' dual regulatory scheme "allows the *same* members of the *same* religion to completely adhere to their religious beliefs at times (when the 'exemption' applies), while other times, forces them to violate those beliefs (when the 'accommodation' applies)." Further, the court added, the bishops "must personally take at least three affirmative actions (sign a self-certification form,[31] compile a list of employees, and provide these to an insurer or [third-party administrator])."[32]

When organizational religious exercise is framed in terms of individuals' religious beliefs, HHS regulations do seem schizophrenic in their consequences. As courts have often stated, they cannot parse the theological subtleties of people's sincere religious beliefs.[33] So Bishop David Zubik's beliefs are accepted as sincere, and given the hefty fines for noncompliance under the contraceptive mandate, religious exercise is judged to be substantially burdened, even though only minimal action (self-certification) and distant involvement (employee choices about health benefits) are at stake.

But when organizational religious exercise is understood instead in terms of mission integrity, it matters whether the mission is controlled through settled doctrine interpreted by authoritative leaders or the mission is articulated through cooperative practices that depend on buy-in from outsiders to the faith. The application of doctrine looks different in the second instance even in Catholic tradition. Tom Judge, a Catholic chaplain at Depaul University, has observed that, since the Second Vatican Council in the 1960s, the Catholic belief in respect for human dignity has been allied with the belief in freedom of conscience. Under Catholic doctrine, human beings are created to grow into loving God, but respecting human dignity warrants people's freedom to follow their own understanding. So people who practice different religions, or none at all, have authority over their conscience.[34] This theological rationale opens the door for any employee – from the director of human resources

---

[31] By the time *Zubik v. Burwell* reached the Supreme Court, as described in this volume's Introduction, the only necessary action was self-certification of religious objections to HHS.
[32] *Zubik v. Sebelius*, 983 F. Supp. 2d 576, 605 (W.D. Pa. 2013) (emphasis in original).
[33] See, e.g., *Burwell v. Hobby Lobby*, 134 S. Ct. 2751, 2777–8 (2014).
[34] Tom Judge, *A Catholic Perspective on the Department of Health and Human Services Mandate concerning Contraception*, 15 DePaul J. Health Care L. 43 (2013).

to workers needing contraceptive benefits coverage – to certify an eligible Catholic institution's religious objections, thereby triggering contraceptive coverage. In this scenario, no individual has to violate sincere personal religious beliefs about contraception or abortion. More generally, when an employee voluntarily signs a form that requires an outside entity to provide contraceptive benefits and relieves her employer of paying penalties, there is no substantial burden on the organization's operating practices or its integrated value of respect for human life. Under a mission integrity standard, the Supreme Court would affirm that HHS' accommodation does not burden the religious exercise of eligible institutions, especially given the government's compelling interests in women's health and gender equity. If, however, the court's proposed compromise in their May 2016 per curiam opinion had succeeded in guaranteeing contraceptive benefits to employees without the necessity of any certification by eligible institutions, then I would have supported this new step in the dance of accommodation between religious values and public mandates.

Turning to *Hobby Lobby*, it appears that the major rulings in favor of for-profit corporate religious exercise recognize the importance of religious mission and values. The opinions quote Hobby Lobby's and Mardel's statements of purpose[35] as well as Conestoga Wood's vision and values.[36] They cite the first two corporations' practices of closing stores on Sundays, buying newspaper ads proclaiming "Jesus as Lord and Savior," funding ministries in the United States and abroad and not promoting alcohol use or sales in any way.[37] Yet nothing in the record demonstrates that Hobby Lobby, Mardel, or Conestoga Wood had integrated the value of respect for human life into their operations prior to the ACA. After declaring the corporations to be religious, the rulings turn on the owners' stated religious beliefs that certain contraceptives are abortifacients.[38]

Under a mission integrity standard, the religious belief or value in question has to be exercised through business practices in which constituencies other than the owners participate.[39] Space does not permit me to elaborate specific tests of mission integration, but courts would look to corporate practices in employee training and benefits, consumer marketing, philanthropic activities, or other public services. Catholic health care organizations integrate their religious mission and values in all of these operating areas. The same may be true of some for-profit corporations, and I acknowledge that for-profit corporations could exercise religion through mission integration. If, however, a corporation claims to exercise a religious belief but

---

[35] *Hobby Lobby v. Sebelius*, 723 F.3d 1114, 1121 (2014).
[36] Hobby Lobby, 134 S. Ct. at 2770.
[37] Sebelius, 723 F.3d at 1121.
[38] Hobby Lobby, 134 S. Ct. at 2775.
[39] My thinking here is influenced by Ronald J. Colombo, *The Naked Private Square*, 51 Hous. L. Rev. 53, 80 (2013).

provides no evidence of having implemented it in operating practices, then the claim should receive no credence, regardless of how sincerely individual leaders raising the objection holds to their religious beliefs on the matter. Deference to the religious beliefs of an individual – or a group of high-ranking individuals – ignores how religious organizations operate in the absence of a settled mission to which all members assent. These organizations must explicitly name and enact their religious mission and values to ensure that employees, clients, and customers can choose to participate or dissent. Given the record of facts in *Hobby Lobby*, the Supreme Court should have denied these corporations' free exercise claims against the contraceptive mandate or, possibly, remanded the case for further fact-finding.

Liberals and conservatives stress the novelty of recent cases around the contraceptive mandate. For liberals, organizational religious freedom is newly expansive. For conservatives, public mandates are newly intrusive on free exercise. In this complex cultural time, the case of Catholic health care offers a track record of accommodation in which religious nonprofits retain their autonomy as mission-driven religious organizations while adjusting their operations and mollifying certain objections to governmental interests. Navigating these tensions requires avoiding both blanket dismissal of organizational religious exercise where not all of the members share religious beliefs as well as total deference to the religious beliefs of individual leaders. A mission integrity standard focuses attention where organizations do or do not exercise religion. This standard will require courts to assess the sincerity of religious mission as they have largely refused to do with individuals' religious beliefs. Accurate and nuanced tests of mission integrity should be developed, ones that acknowledge employee participation in and public benefit from religious mission while preventing the silencing of employees' interests. We will strike better balances by looking to the ongoing efforts of eligible institutions to build operating practices and structures that leaders and employees can both live out and live with together.

PART III

Law, Religion, and Health Insurance

Introduction

Marc A. Rodwin

Contemporary disputes involving law, religion, and health insurance arise in part due to competing conceptions of the role of the state, religious institutions, and the private sector in the provision of health care services. There is controversy over answering these key questions: How should the collective financing of health services be organized? Who should be responsible for providing health services? Should health care for the poor be provided through private charities? Should medical care for those who are not indigent be financed through mutual self-aid, or should employers provide health care for their employees as a fringe benefit of employment? Should the government be responsible for providing health to the public at large?

The collective financing of health care has been organized using at least six distinct models. These include:

1) as a form of charity organized as part of a religious mission;
2) as a form of charity organized by a secular organization;
3) as voluntary mutual self-aid organized and financed by individuals and private associations;
4) as a fringe benefit that employers confer upon employees;
5) as a government responsibility and function;
6) as a private good sold in markets.

Today, Americans generally conceive of health care as services that they obtain either through employment or self-purchase, sometimes with assistance from the state. However, institutions that provide medical care and conceptions about who should be responsible for providing medical services have evolved over time, as can be seen from reviewing the evolution of hospitals in France and other European countries. This history reveals not only tensions between the state, religion, and insurance, but also the rich and complex interactions between them.

In medieval Europe, as part of its charitable mission, the Catholic Church took responsibility for caring for groups that society had largely abandoned (the indigent, the aged, infirm, mentally incompetent, vagabonds) in what were called Houses of God, or hospitals. As part of their charity, hospitals also provided medical care to their residents. Reformers in the eighteenth century suggested that hospitals should be devoted exclusively to providing medical services and that they should not be used to supply housing and other services for the poor; however, it was not until the French revolution that hospitals were transformed into medical institutions. The French revolution also changed hospitals from religious institutions into organizations that were mainly owned, financed, and operated by the state. The postrevolutionary government made providing hospital services a government responsibility, although religious and secular organizations continued to operate some of the hospitals. Initially, state-owned hospitals were exclusively for the poor; only in the late nineteenth and early twentieth centuries were hospitals allowed to serve the middle class, which previously received medical services from practitioners in private practice.[1]

In the same period as France expanded access to hospitals to the middle class, it also developed other ways to supply medical care outside of hospitals. These included using mutual self-aid societies to finance health care, supplying medical care as a benefit of employment, and providing medical care through government-operated or regulated insurance programs. This history reveals that religious institutions, private insurance organizations, employers, and the state have jockeyed to control the health economy and define what services should be provided and to whom.

Fast-forward to debates in the United States today. One of the challenges of implementing the Affordable Care Act (ACA) involves accommodating the interests of religious employers while advancing the state's interest in providing health services and maintaining the interests of individuals receiving those services. Some employers and individuals object on religious grounds to certain aspects of the ACA and would therefore like to be exempt from the ACA's legal requirements. For example, religious nonprofits and schools objected to being required to include certain contraception as part of their health benefits.

The chapters in this part examine two types of problems that arise due to the ACA imposing a tax on individuals who do not purchase insurance (which applies only if more than 50 of the firm's full-time employees purchase health insurance on their own and receive government subsidies) and on employers who do not provide insurance to their full-time employees. The chapter by Rachel E. Sachs examines

---

[1] Marc A. Rodwin, *Conflicts of Interest and the Future of Medicine: The United States, France, and Japan* ch. 2 (2011).

accommodations for employees who object to other aspects of traditional insurance and who want to participate in an alternative arrangement to finance medical expenses. The chapter by Holly Fernandez Lynch and Gregory Curfman examines accommodations for employers who object on religious grounds to abortion and certain contraception and therefore do not want to pay for or facilitate the provision of such services.

The Affordable Care Act also accommodates the interests of individuals who do not want to purchase standard health insurance policies. The ACA generally obliges individuals to pay a tax if they do not purchase insurance that covers essential health benefits; however, it provides several exemptions. Rachel Sachs examines the religious exemption for individuals who participate in health care-sharing ministries (HCSMs), which offer a way for faith-based communities to finance the medical costs of members without a formal insurance contract or other legal obligations. HCSMs also allow participants to choose what sorts of expenses they want to help pay for.

At first blush, the idea of HCSM appears novel and an aberration from health insurance as we know it today. However, the idea reflects mutual self-aid approaches which were used to finance medical care in the nineteenth and early twentieth centuries, and also the tradition of religious institutions organizing the delivery of health services. The growth of HCSMs reveals that society can draw on ideas and approaches developed long ago as it explores new ways to finance medical care.

Sachs analyzes the ACA's compromise between alternative models of health insurance based on social solidarity, actuarial fairness, and personal responsibility. She shows that HCSMs strike a different balance between these insurance models to the balance struck under standard ACA insurance. Furthermore, she suggests that there is value in promoting pluralism in insurance models and that HCSMs are a natural experiment that scholars should continue to evaluate to improve upon the existing models of health insurance.

Holly Fernandez Lynch and Gregory Curfman examine recent efforts to accommodate the religious beliefs of employers who object to paying for contraception or abortion as well as the way the Supreme Court addressed these disputes in *Hobby Lobby v. Burwell* and *Zubick et al. v. Burwell*. They provide context for understanding these cases by tracing the development of employer-sponsored insurance. They also show that employer sponsorship entails employer influence, if not control, over what benefits insurance covers, thereby giving employers a place in the bedrooms of their employees and generating ideological conflict. Lynch and Curfman argue that these features of employer-sponsored insurance create problems that outweigh its benefits. They suggest that it would be preferable to develop another way to provide insurance to the public, though still acknowledging that employer-sponsored insurance is likely to continue into the foreseeable future.

There are two aspects of these disputes over what insurance covers that I want to highlight. First, we should look critically at the employers' claim that they should decide what services are covered because it is their money that pays for the insurance. Does the money belong to employers or does it really belong to employees? Standard economic analysis shows that employers treat employee benefits as part of total employee compensation and maintains that employers reduce salaries paid to their employees to make up for any health or other employee benefits that they provide. Employees often prefer to obtain some of their compensation in the form of health insurance benefits because the cost of the insurance premium is not counted towards their taxable income. If the money paid for health insurance is functionally part of the employee's compensation, why should employers have any more say on how employees use those funds than they do in how employees spend their salaries?

Second, we should remember that religious employers would not need accommodations if we did not choose to finance a substantial share of health care spending by having the state subsidize private health insurance that employers purchase on behalf of their employees. This issue does not arise when the government finances health insurance directly as it does through Medicare and Medicaid, government programs for the elderly, people with permanent disabilities, and qualifying individuals who are poor. When Congress decided to expand health insurance in 2010, it could have avoided subsidizing the employer's purchasing of private insurance and instead relied entirely on expanding Medicaid or Medicare eligibility, or by creating a new federal program that directly financed medical care. In fact, there were proposals to create a public insurance option as an alternative to expanding private insurance. As Lynch and Curfman make clear, accommodation for religious employers also ceases to be an issue when the state subsidizes insurance that individuals purchase on their own.

10

Religious Exemptions to the Individual Mandate

Health Care Sharing Ministries and the Affordable Care Act

Rachel E. Sachs

Scholars, policy makers, and courts have devoted an enormous amount of attention to the Affordable Care Act's (ACA) individual mandate. By contrast, relatively little scholarship has focused on the exceptions to the individual mandate, which carve out three broad categories of people from its requirement to maintain minimum essential coverage:[1] individuals who are not lawfully present in the United States, incarcerated individuals, and those with particular religious convictions.[2] This chapter will focus on the religious exemption[3] and in particular its application to members of health care sharing ministries (HCSMs).[4] HCSMs have been mentioned only infrequently in the academic literature,[5] but they are fascinating case studies through which to explore a range of scholarly questions about health law and policy, including those that go to the very core of our health insurance system.

This chapter proceeds as follows. Section 1 provides a detailed explanation of health care sharing ministries, considering their role within the ACA and their practical functioning, in terms of their membership, covered care, and reimbursement. Section 2 then takes a broader view, considering the ways in which the ministries themselves reflect the ideals of health insurance embodied in the ACA. Because the ministries reflect a different balance between conceptions of health insurance than the ACA, they present a natural experiment, allowing scholars to consider the efficacy and importance of different theories of insurance. Although whether this

---

[1] The Act also contains separate exemptions from the tax imposed for failure to obtain minimum coverage, exempting certain low-income groups, members of Indian tribes, and those with only brief coverage gaps. 26 U.S.C.A. § 5000A(e) (2012).
[2] 26 U.S.C.A. § 5000A(a), (d)(2), (3), (4) (2012).
[3] Id. at § 5000A(d)(2).
[4] Id. at § 5000A(d)(2)(B).
[5] The most detailed analyses typically focus on how courts do and should apply insurance law to HCSMs. See generally, e.g., Benjamin Boyd, *Health Care Sharing Ministries: Scam or Solution?*, 26 J.L. & Health 219 (2013).

experiment succeeds or fails remains to be seen, this chapter concludes with some thoughts on potential avenues for further research in this area.

1. THE ROLE OF HEALTH CARE SHARING MINISTRIES IN THE ACA

The ACA exempts individuals who are members of HCSMs from the individual mandate. Essentially, HCSMs are structures in which members of particular religious groups share each other's medical bills rather than purchase traditional insurance. More technically, the Act defines an HCSM as an organization

- (I) which is described in section 501(c)(3) and is exempt from taxation under section 501(a),
- (II) members of which share a common set of ethical or religious beliefs and share medical expenses among members in accordance with those beliefs and without regard to the State in which a member resides or is employed,
- (III) members of which retain membership even after they develop a medical condition,
- (IV) which (or a predecessor of which) has been in existence at all times since December 31, 1999, and medical expenses of its members have been shared continuously and without interruption since at least December 31, 1999, and
- (V) which conducts an annual audit which is performed by an independent certified public accounting firm in accordance with generally accepted accounting principles and which is made available to the public upon request.[6]

At present, the vast majority of all ministry members belong to one of just three HCSMs: Medi-Share/Christian Care Ministry, Christian Healthcare Ministries, and Samaritan Ministries International.[7] Moreover, clause IV prevents the formation of new HCSMs, effectively limiting the reach of the exemption to HCSMs currently in existence. If any of these entities ceases to operate, another cannot be formed to take its place, and as such it is conceivable that there will be a functional end date to this exemption. This is not mere speculation. Prior instances of mismanagement and fraud have led to court-ordered receiverships for ministries,[8] events which may

---

[6] 26 U.S.C.A. § 5000A(d)(2)(B).

[7] Timothy Stoltzfus Jost, *Loopholes in the Affordable Care Act: Regulatory Gaps and Border Crossing Techniques and How to Address Them*, 5 St. Louis U. J. Health L. & Pol'y 27, 43 (2011); Robin Fretwell Wilson, *The Calculus of Accommodation: Contraception, Abortion, Same-Sex Marriage, and Other Clashes Between Religion and the State*, 53 B.C. L. Rev. 1417, 1501 (2012).

[8] In 2000, the predecessor to Christian Healthcare Ministries was placed into receivership and it was discovered that former officials had defrauded the organization of roughly $15 million. Sandra G. Boodman, *Seeking Divine Protection*, Washington Post (October 25, 2005).

have inspired clause V, requiring an annual independent audit that is made publicly available.

Clauses II and III provide the substantive core of the HCSM exemption. They stipulate that such ministries must "share medical expenses among members" and require HCSMs to retain members "even after they develop a medical condition," but they leave all other aspects of membership, coverage, and reimbursement unspecified. If HCSMs were regulated in the same way as insurance companies, these issues would be easily explicated by reference to the ACA or state laws. However, thirty states explicitly create safe harbors for HCSMs from being regulated as insurance companies.[9] The HCSMs themselves often note on their promotional material and websites that they are not insurance companies and that the product they sell is not insurance.[10]

It is, therefore, important to understand how HCSMs work in practice. Although the details of the existing HCSMs differ, their essential structure is the same. Members make regular monthly contributions to their ministry based on family size and age.[11] When members incur medical expenses, they may submit their bills to their HCSM. If the HCSM deems the bills eligible for sharing, it will either transfer funds to the member itself or will facilitate the transfer from other members.[12]

Although on the surface HCSMs closely resemble insurance companies in their method of operation, at each of these three stages – membership, care coverage, and reimbursement – HCSMs differ from traditional insurance companies. First, HCSMs limit their membership. Each ministry requires that its members attest to their belief in central tenets of Christianity[13] and also adhere to healthy, biblical lifestyles. In particular, members may not use tobacco or illegal drugs, may consume alcohol only in moderation, and may not engage in sexual intercourse outside of marriage.[14]

Second, the ministries differ from insurers as to the services which are eligible for sharing, and to what extent. Medi-Share and Samaritan Ministries both categorically exclude from sharing certain medical services that are indicators of non-biblical

---

[9] Alliance of Health Care Sharing Ministries, *State Info* (2016), available at www.healthcaresharing.org/Newstateinfo/ [https://perma.cc/6QGS-FAVA].

[10] Most pages of Medi-Share's Program Guidelines document state "Medi-Share is not insurance." Medi-Share, *Program Guidelines & Frequently Asked Questions* 2 (2015).

[11] Jost, supra note 7, at 43.

[12] See generally Alliance of Health Care Sharing Ministries, *What is Health Care Sharing?* (2015), available at www.healthcaresharing.org/Newhcsm/ [https://perma.cc/R9CA-SRHQ].

[13] Citizens' Council on Health Care, *Medical Sharing Ministries – A Comparison Chart* 3 (2010); see also Alliance of Health Care Sharing Ministries, *Health Care Sharing Ministries – Comparison Chart* 3 (2013).

[14] Alliance of Health Care Sharing Ministries, supra note 13, at 3. Historically, Medi-Share has engaged in health underwriting, meaning that some particularly sick individuals were not eligible for coverage at all. Jost, supra note 7, at 43.

lifestyles, including abortion, contraception, injuries resulting from the abuse of drugs and alcohol, and sexually transmitted diseases, unless acquired "innocently."[15] Medi-Share goes further in its enumerated categories, explicitly excluding sharing for "maternity expenses for children conceived out of wedlock."[16]

Both ministries also exclude routine and preventive care, including physicals, vaccinations, and screening tests like mammograms or colonoscopies.[17] Screening tests may, however, be covered when used for diagnostic purposes, such as if a colonoscopy is conducted to investigate observed symptoms.[18] Medi-Share also categorically exempts mental health care, including both psychiatric and psychological services,[19] while Samaritan excludes all psychological services but covers a small amount of psychiatric care.[20] Both ministries impose strict limits on most other categories of coverage, including phased-in limits on coverage of pre-existing conditions.[21]

Third, HCSMs differ strongly from insurance companies on the subject of reimbursement. The ministries are careful not to say that any particular treatment is *reimbursable* or that its members submit *claims*.[22] Instead, they say that a treatment is *eligible for sharing*, such that members' medical bills will be published for other members to fill. None of the ministries guarantee the coverage of a particular (or even any) medical expense. Unlike insurance companies, HCSMs are not required to maintain reserves.[23] Thus, it is possible that the amount published for sharing in any given month will exceed the contributions made.[24] Each organization, therefore, has contingency plans for what would happen in such a case, such as by prorating available funds so that each shared bill is paid partially.[25]

---

[15] Medi-Share, supra note 10, at 35–6; Samaritan Ministries, *Guidelines for Health Care Sharing* 26, 31 (2016).

[16] Medi-Share, supra note 10, at 35. Each of these carve-outs has exceptions, as described infra. Id. Further, the fact that Samaritan does not explicitly exempt these categories does not mean it would share them. Samaritan "retains the discretion to not share [other treatments that violate Biblical principles] ... even though not listed below." Samaritan Ministries, supra note 15, at 31.

[17] Medi-Share, supra note 10, at 36–7; Samaritan Ministries, supra note 15, at 27, 32.

[18] Samaritan Ministries, supra note 15, at 27.

[19] Medi-Share, supra note 10, at 35.

[20] Samaritan Ministries, supra note 15, at 30.

[21] Medi-Share, supra note 10, at 30; Samaritan Ministries, supra note 15, at 23. Both organizations profess to have no annual or lifetime coverage limits. Medi-Share, supra note 10, at 25; Samaritan Ministries, supra note 15, at 10. However, the limits they impose on individual categories of coverage may create de facto limits.

[22] Medi-Share, supra note 10, at 8 ("Members do not file claims, nor does the ministry handle claims because we are not an insurance company. 'Claim' literally means that you have a right to someone else's money; remember, Christian Care Ministry does not pay your medical bills with its money.").

[23] Jost, supra note 7, at 44.

[24] Wilson, supra note 7, at 1501.

[25] Samaritan Ministries, supra note 15, at 22.

Yet with this potential financial insecurity comes membership in a community. Rather than receiving a check from an insurer, Samaritan members with eligible medical bills receive checks from other ministry members, often with notes or cards attached.[26] Members of Medi-Share receive a check directly from their ministry, but they also receive letters from other members wishing them well.[27] HCSMs feel personal and supportive in a way that insurance does not.

This chapter is too brief to fully consider all the interesting aspects of HCSMs, and so in the space remaining I want to analyze HCSMs as compared to the broader purposes and structure of the ACA. In some ways, HCSMs balance two primary models of health insurance in a manner that closely resembles the ACA's own choices between these models. Yet in other ways HCSMs reflect a different combination of motivations underlying these models, in a manner that may lead either to their flourishing or to their eventual disappearance.

2. SITUATING HEALTH CARE SHARING MINISTRIES AGAINST THE PURPOSES OF THE ACA

Scholars of health law and health insurance often characterize societal choices to adopt particular health insurance programs along a continuum ranging from social solidarity to actuarial fairness.[28] These two models of insurance allocate financial risk very differently between insured individuals. An insurance system hewing closely to a strong version of social solidarity would pool risk across a broad population such that healthy citizens subsidize the costs of insurance for sicker ones.[29] The idea is that "we are all in this together, and no one should be abandoned."[30] Historically, the United States has lagged behind other Western nations in adopting health insurance embodying the ideals of social solidarity,[31] although programs like

---

[26] See, e.g., Michelle Andrews, *Some Church Groups Form Sharing Ministries to Cover Members' Medical Costs*, Kaiser Health News (April 25, 2011); JoNel Aleccia, *Christian Co-Ops Swap Burden of Medical Bills*, NBCNews.com (April 14, 2010), available at www.nbcnews.com/id/36473470/ns/health-health_care/t/Newchristian-co-ops-swap-burden-medical-bills/#.VSgbUtzF_To [https://perma.cc/J45N-D3UE].

[27] See, e.g., Boodman, supra note 8.

[28] Deborah A. Stone, *The Struggle for the Soul of Health Insurance*, 18 J. Health Pol. Pol'y & L. 287, 290 (1993); see also Sara Rosenbaum, *Insurance Discrimination on the Basis of Health Status: An Overview of Discrimination Practices, Federal Law, and Federal Reform Options*, 37 J.L. Med. & Ethics 103, 105 (2009); Wendy K. Mariner, *Social Solidarity and Personal Responsibility in Health Reform*, 14 Conn. Ins. L.J. 199, 205 (2008).

[29] Stone, supra, at 292. Risk-pooling of this type is more technically referred to as community rating, Rosenbaum, supra, at 105, which may be engaged in to a greater or lesser degree.

[30] Mariner, supra note 28, at 205; see also Rosenbaum, supra note 28, at 105.

[31] See, e.g., Timothy Stoltzfus Jost, *Why Can't We Do What They Do? National Health Reform Abroad*, 32 J.L. Med. & Ethics 433, 433–4 (2004); id. at 438; John V. Jacobi, *The Ends of Health Insurance*, 30 U.C. Davis L. Rev. 311, 314 (1997); Stone, supra note 28, at 289–90.

Medicaid or other laws like the Emergency Medical Treatment and Active Labor Act[32] or Genetic Information Nondiscrimination Act[33] appear to be motivated by such thinking.

Alternatively, an insurance system strongly embodying the goal of actuarial fairness would charge different prices to individuals based on the expected value of insurance to that person.[34] Healthy individuals who do not appear to be at risk for particular conditions would be charged lower prices than would sick individuals or those at risk for developing a range of conditions and, therefore, for consuming greater amounts of health care. Prior to the passage of the ACA, the practice of medical underwriting often prevented these latter individuals from obtaining insurance. Even if they were permitted to enroll, pre-existing condition exclusions or extremely high premiums might dissuade them from doing so.[35]

Professor Tom Baker has argued that the ACA embodies several elements of the social solidarity model, largely (though not entirely) rejecting the actuarial fairness model.[36] The ACA reflects the ideals of social solidarity in two primary ways. First, it expands the population of people with insurance, adding more (and often healthier) people into the risk pool. Part of this expansion is accomplished by broadening the Medicaid-eligible population to include able-bodied adults for the first time, recognizing "a national entitlement to health care for all of the poor"[37] and moving away from a fragmented system, primarily targeted toward the "deserving poor," to a more universal system.[38] Another significant part of this expansion is accomplished through the individual mandate. Second, the ACA strongly limits the ability of insurers in the individual market to vary their prices on the basis of factors affecting health status.[39]

The ACA does retain some elements of the actuarial fairness model.[40] Most notably, although the ACA *limits* insurers' ability to impose community rating on premiums, it does not *eliminate* it. The Act permits the prices charged to the oldest groups in a pool to be up to three times those charged to the youngest, and tobacco users may be charged one-and-a-half times more than non-users.[41]

---

[32] Nicholas Bagley & Jill R. Horwitz, *Why It's Called the Affordable Care Act*, 110 Mich. L. Rev. First Impressions 1, 3 (2011).
[33] Rosenbaum, supra note 28, at 111.
[34] Tom Baker, *Health Insurance, Risk, and Responsibility After the Patient Protection and Affordable Care Act*, 159 U. Pa. L. Rev. 1577, 1597–98 (2011); Stone, supra note 28, at 293–4.
[35] Stone, supra note 28, at 306; Rosenbaum, supra note 28, at 105.
[36] Baker, supra note 34, at 1579–80, 1601; see also, e.g., Allison K. Hoffman, *Three Models of Health Insurance: The Conceptual Pluralism of the Patient Protection and Affordable Care Act*, 159 U. Pa. L. Rev. 1873, 1876, 1887–8 (2011).
[37] Baker, supra note 34, at 1584.
[38] Nicole Huberfeld, *The Universality of Medicaid at Fifty*, 15 Yale J. Health Pol'y L. & Ethics 67, 70 (2015).
[39] Baker, supra note 34, at 1589.
[40] Id. at 1601.
[41] Id. at 1589–90.

In Baker's view, the ACA also adds another actuarial fairness element to "the new health care social contract": the "responsibility to be as healthy as you can."[42] Although this responsibility is not explicit in the Act, several ACA provisions embody its aims. For instance, the ACA eliminates all cost-sharing for a range of preventive services in an effort to increase consumption thereof.[43] Further, it permits a variety of rewards to be offered for participation in wellness programs.[44] These rewards may be quite substantial, including a rebate on premiums of up to 30 percent.[45] In practice, wellness initiatives may replicate some of the effects of the actuarial fairness model, as healthier individuals receive rebates and sicker individuals do not.

In many ways, HCSMs embody key elements of both the social solidarity model and the newly emphasized responsibility for one's own health. The social solidarity case for HCSMs is clear: participation in an HCSM is based around membership in a particular religious faith, and HCSMs are built on ideals of community and support, much like the mutual aid societies that were prevalent historically.[46] HCSMs further take steps to cultivate relationships among their members, as an ailing member would receive not only a check from the ministry, but also letters of support from other members. And, like the ACA, HCSMs employ only minimal community rating, as monthly contributions are based only on family size and age. Admittedly, HCSMs may undermine the social solidarity embodied in the ACA by taking people out of that broader risk pool. But HCSMs themselves embody this goal on a smaller scale.

HCSMs also embody the goal of individual responsibility, although not in precisely the same ways as the ACA. As noted above, HCSMs do not generally permit preventive care services to be shared, and they do not have formal wellness programs in the sense in which the ACA contemplates them. However, they often have similar structures in place. Members of Medi-Share who have particular conditions or a high probability of developing those conditions may be required to participate in the "Restore Program," in which the member works with a Health Coach to achieve health goals. The penalty for failing to achieve these goals may be termination of membership.[47] More explicitly, as a condition of membership, Samaritan requires an agreement "to practice good health measures."[48]

---

[42] Id. at 1580; see also Mariner, supra note 28, at 213.
[43] Baker, supra note 34, at 1602; Kaiser Family Foundation, *Preventive Services Covered by Private Health Plans Under the Affordable Care Act* (2014), available at http://kff.org/health-reform/fact-sheet/preventive-services-covered-by-private-health-plans/ [https://perma.cc/UG7T-JN5Z].
[44] Baker, supra note 34, at 1603.
[45] Id.
[46] See generally, e.g., Brian J. Glenn, *Understanding Mutual Benefit Societies at the Turn of the Twentieth Century*, 26 J. Health Pol. Pol'y & L. 638 (2001); see also Jacobi, supra note 31, at 315–16; Timothy Stoltzfus Jost, *A Mutual Aid Society?*, 42 Hastings Ctr. Rep. 14, 14–16 (2012).
[47] Medi-Share, supra note 10, at 14.
[48] Samaritan Ministries, supra note 15, at 15.

In some ways, therefore, we should understand HCSMs as microcosms of the ACA, choosing different policy instruments but still striving for the same goals as the broader Act. Yet in other ways this discussion is incomplete. Social solidarity, actuarial fairness, and personal responsibility can tell us an enormous amount about how to design individual insurance systems. But they do not clearly resolve disputes about the reasons we might adopt a health insurance system in the first place. To this end, Professor Allison Hoffman has offered three theories of health insurance, each of which aims to address a different type of risk:

> The first theory posits that the primary goal of health insurance is to mitigate the risk of harms to health; insurance design prioritizes funding care – both preventive and remedial – to maintain or promote health. I call this the "Health Promotion" theory of health insurance. The second theory posits that the primary goal of health insurance is to mitigate harms to wealth; that is, insurance should be designed in a way that medical costs are covered when they threaten financial security. I call this theory the "Financial Security" theory of health insurance. The third theory posits that health insurance should prioritize coverage of medical costs that result from unavoidable harms, which are more the result of bad brute luck than of individual behavior. Accordingly, I call it the "Brute Luck" theory of insurance.[49]

In Hoffman's view, the ACA embodies all three theories simultaneously. The Health Promotion theory explains the ACA's requirement that insurance plans cover recommended preventive services like colonoscopies[50] or annual flu shots[51] with no cost-sharing, even though they are not "risks" or due to luck.[52] The Financial Security theory is responsible for the many ways in which the ACA limits individual exposure to the financial shocks of health care, removing lifetime coverage caps and cabining annual out-of-pocket maximum amounts.[53] And the Brute Luck theory, which in many ways is analogous to the actuarial fairness and personal responsibility models, underlies the Act's fondness for wellness programs.[54]

Hoffman considers and examines the conflicts between these theories and the way they play out in the ACA. For instance, the ACA's coverage of certain preventive services without cost-sharing embodies the Health Promotion theory but is

---

[49] Hoffman, supra note 36, at 1888 (2011) (footnotes omitted). We might view these theories as overlapping with the social solidarity and actuarial fairness models, but they are not coextensive.

[50] American Cancer Society, *Recommendations for Colorectal Cancer Early Detection* (2015), available at www.cancer.org/cancer/colonandrectumcancer/moreinformation/colonandrectumcancerearlydetection/colorectal-cancer-early-detection-acs-recommendations [https://perma.cc/T535-RRX7].

[51] Centers for Disease Control, *Key Facts About Seasonal Flu Vaccine* (2015), available at www.cdc.gov/Newflu/Newprotect/Newkeyfacts.htm [https://perma.cc/RJ7Q-L3VA].

[52] Hoffman, supra note 36, at 1890, 1904–5.

[53] Id. at 1914, 1918.

[54] Id. at 1934–5.

inconsistent with both the Financial Security and Brute Luck theories.[55] Although these theories create tensions within the Act itself, Hoffman suggests that the ACA's broader conceptual pluralism may be key to its stability.[56] Because the American people do not share a single vision of what insurance is for, a law with elements of each vision might have superior staying power when compared to a more theoretically coherent but less broadly appealing statute.

We might then be concerned about the HCSM model, which eschews the main elements of the Health Promotion theory and adopts a few elements of the Financial Security theory, but in the end skews far more toward the Brute Luck theory. HCSMs' decisions not to share preventive services and to limit or prevent sharing for many of the ACA's Essential Health Benefits distance them sharply from the Health Promotion theory. HCSMs do adopt elements of the Financial Security Model, in the structure of their members' deductible-like payments[57] and lack of a formal lifetime cap on coverage. However, the fact that the ministries do not technically provide insurance means that they cannot provide financial security to the same extent as a regulated insurer. The ACA sought to protect individuals from the financial shocks of an unexpected illness,[58] and HCSM members do not take full advantage of that protection. Even though they may be aware of their exposure,[59] the financial burdens faced by some members of these ministries might be cause for concern.[60]

HCSMs approximate the Brute Luck model more closely than does the ACA. In addition to refusing coverage for preventive services, both Medi-Share and Samaritan limit or prevent sharing for conditions or events that are thought to be attributable to the member. Both refuse to share injuries resulting from car accidents involving abuse of alcohol or illegal drugs or drag-racing.[61] Both ministries' exemptions from sharing for the treatment of sexually transmitted diseases and Medi-Share's for "maternity expenses for children conceived out of wedlock"[62] also fall into this category, as these exemptions have further carve-outs for involuntarily

---

[55] Id. at 1941; see also Mariner, supra note 28, at 209.
[56] Hoffman, supra note 36, at 1953.
[57] While the ministries do not refer to the amounts members must pay before the ministry shares their expenses as deductibles, the payments perform the same function. Medi-Share requires that members pay an Annual Household Portion out of pocket before their bills become eligible for sharing. The Annual Household Portion is capped at $10,000 but can be as low as $500. Medi-Share, supra note 10, at 7. Samaritan, by contrast, will not share bills for a particular illness which total less than $300, on the idea that members can handle these bills themselves. Samaritan Ministries, supra note 15, at 9, 21.
[58] See 42 U.S.C.A. § 18091(2)(A) (2010).
[59] Cf. Jost, supra note 7, at 41.
[60] See, e.g., Wilson, supra note 7, at 1501–2.
[61] Medi-Share, supra note 10, at 43; Samaritan Ministries, supra note 15, at 31.
[62] Medi-Share, supra note 10, at 35.

imposed burdens.[63] A sexually transmitted disease acquired through a blood transfusion or work-related needle stick, or an out-of-wedlock pregnancy resulting from rape, would be eligible for sharing.[64]

This imbalance of theories might result in instability and attrition for the HCSMs. The Health Promotion ideas that insurance should cover certain essential health benefits and be prohibited from denying coverage for pre-existing conditions are exceedingly popular.[65] If health care prices continue to rise, ministry members may find that traditional insurance is their only way to access such services. An individual experiencing a health shock not eligible for sharing, such as the onset of a mental health condition or an out-of-wedlock pregnancy,[66] might leave her ministry and enroll in another plan to obtain needed care.[67] If the attrition is significant, HCSMs may combine with each other to ensure that they have the ability to spread risk sufficiently. The ACA's grandfather clause means that no new ministries could take their place.

This story is not inevitable. As Hoffman notes, "conceptual pluralism may serve as a kind of legislative experiment, setting up a structure where three different ideas are simultaneously road-tested for effectiveness and popularity."[68] Health Promotion may be far less effective and popular than we believe, in which case the HCSMs might flourish. The nearly six-fold increase in HCSM membership in the last few years alone provides evidence for this possibility.[69]

But the potential for instability is something to watch going forward, as it may be hastened or forestalled by states' regulatory choices. Massachusetts, for example, has a religious exemption to its individual mandate requirement.[70] This exemption appears to be targeted at Christian Scientists,[71] because if exempted individuals "receive medical health care," they must pay not only their medical bills but also the penalty associated with their failure to obtain coverage.[72] Imposing an analogous

---

[63] Hoffman, supra note 36, at 1926.

[64] Medi-Share, supra note 10, at 35; Samaritan Ministries, supra note 15, at 26.

[65] See, e.g., Kaiser Family Foundation, *Health Tracking Poll* (March 20, 2013), available at http://kff.org/health-reform/poll-finding/march-2013-tracking-poll/ [https://perma.cc/E6QL-7M4W].

[66] Since 40% of all births in the United States are to unmarried women (Centers for Disease Control, *Unmarried Childbearing* (2015), available at www.cdc.gov/Newnchs/Newfastats/Newunmarried-childbearing.htm [https://perma.cc/4KKZ-4N55]), this likely happens with some regularity.

[67] Because attrition from an HCSM is not a qualifying event, such individuals may need to wait for open enrollment. Alternatively, some women may qualify for Medicaid upon pregnancy, since every state provides such coverage to women even above the poverty line.

[68] Hoffman, supra note 36, at 1953-4.

[69] See infra text accompanying notes 74-5.

[70] Mass. Gen. Laws Ann. ch. 111M, § 3 (West).

[71] Maura Reynolds, *Health Bills Allow Some Religious Exemption*, CQ Politics (August 3, 2009), available at www.nbcnews.com/id/32267628/ns/politicscq_%20politics/t/health-bills-allow-some-religious-exemption/#.VTAhMNzF_Tp [https://perma.cc/73B3-JB2W].

[72] Mass. Gen. Laws Ann. ch. 111M, § 3 (West).

penalty on HCSM members – for instance, a penalty triggered if the member sought care for which they could not pay within a specified time frame, suggesting that sharing is not available – might discourage some would-be members from joining.

CONCLUSION

Although HCSMs have existed for decades, the ACA brought these organizations into the national spotlight by exempting their members from the individual mandate. At a broad level, the HCSMs similarly advance the goals of social solidarity and personal responsibility embodied in the ACA. But their particular coverage systems reflect a different balance of ideas about the purpose of health insurance, in a way that may create instability in the model. Yet they may also serve as a natural experiment, allowing scholars to consider the efficacy and importance of the Health Promotion theory of insurance.

Further research might focus on testing empirical predictions about these ministries. One avenue of research would explore the effect of HCSMs on states' individual insurance markets. Those joining HCSMs are likely to be healthier than the general population purchasing insurance on the individual exchanges.[73] Their choice to opt out and join an HCSM may have small but real adverse selection effects on those markets. In 2011, Professor Tim Jost predicted that HCSM membership "is unlikely to become large enough to undermine ACA risk pooling," due to the small number of HCSM members at that time – just 100,000 nationwide.[74] But the Alliance of Health Care Sharing Ministries now suggests that over 580,000 Americans are members of HCSMs.[75] In some states, ministries might have enough members to disrupt the functioning of the exchanges.[76]

Other research might study the amount of out-of-pocket expenses incurred by ministry members as compared to those of the general population or consider the effect of HCSM solidarity on health outcomes. In any case, such research will surely be illuminating.

---

[73] This hypothesis is informed by their eligibility requirements. HCSMs can reject particularly sick individuals, and a population with no tobacco use and minimal alcohol use is likely to be healthier than the general population.
[74] Jost, supra note 7, at 43–4.
[75] Alliance of Health Care Sharing Ministries, *What is Health Care Sharing?* (2016), available at www.healthcaresharing.org/Newhcsm/ [https://perma.cc/R9CA-SRHQ].
[76] As far as I am aware, the ministries do not make public the number of members they serve in each state. However, an April 2014 news article suggested that just one HCSM, Medi-Share, had nearly 7,000 members in California, 8,500 in Texas, 6,000 in Florida, and nearly 5,000 in Colorado. Kate Shellnutt & Kate Tracy, *Obamacare's Bump: More Christians Now Sharing Health Care Costs*, Christianity Today (April 4, 2014). These numbers have likely increased since then, and other HCSMs may also be responsible for significant populations.

11

Bosses in the Bedroom

Religious Employers and the Future of Employer-Sponsored Health Care

Holly Fernandez Lynch and Gregory Curfman

The United States is a nation founded on religious freedom. Every elementary school child learns about the Mayflower pilgrims and their quest to avoid religious persecution, but these pilgrims were also seeking economic opportunity in a new land.[1] As the country developed, principles of religious freedom were embedded in our Constitution's First Amendment to ensure the freedom of all Americans to worship as they wish and live in accordance with their religious beliefs, while simultaneously avoiding marginalization and preserving opportunities to participate in society as fully engaged citizens. More recently, this constitutional commitment to religious freedom has been buttressed through "religious freedom restoration acts" (RFRAs) passed at both the federal and state levels in response to fears of waning protection.

Like the pilgrims, today's religious believers also seek to combine religious freedom with economic opportunity. They launch and grow secular companies, hire employees of different faiths, and provide goods and services locally, nationally, and internationally, looking to make a living and profit in the marketplace while adhering to their religious beliefs. Other religious believers also seek engagement with their broader communities through nonprofit endeavors that may be related to their religious missions of education or caring for others, but that employ and serve those with different beliefs. In each of these contexts, the question arises: what should we do when religious employers object to broadly applicable legal requirements for reasons based on their religious beliefs that may not be shared by their employees or customers?

As described in this volume's introduction, this question has been the subject of dozens of lawsuits in response to the Obama era federal regulatory requirement stemming from the Patient Protection and Affordable Care Act (ACA) that employers of a certain size offer their employees health care coverage that includes free

---

[1] William Bradford, *Of Plymouth Plantation 1620–1647* (Francis Murphy ed. 1981).

access to contraceptives.[2] Employers objecting to this requirement – or to the various legal accommodations – argue that their rights to religious freedom deserve robust protection even when they are engaged in the economic sphere. Others, however, raise significant concerns about the burdens that such robust protections may impose on employees with different views.

This chapter uses the controversy over mandated contraceptive coverage in employer health plans as a jumping-off point to do two things: (1) evaluate the proper scope of religion in the workplace – not among employees, but rather employers; and (2) assess the implications for employers' role in their employees' health care more generally, via employer-sponsored health insurance. Notably, each of these goals is possible and remains important regardless of the ultimate fate of the contraceptive coverage mandate in a post-Obama administration. We argue that the federal Religious Freedom Restoration Act (RFRA), when properly construed, is capable of facilitating an appropriate balance between the religious beliefs of employers and their employees. However, what these conflicts over contraceptives coverage demonstrate is yet another reason to view the current system of relying heavily on employer-based health insurance as deeply flawed.

More specifically, even as strong supporters of women's reproductive freedom, we maintain that employers legally need not – and ethically should not – always be required to check their religious beliefs at the door. Instead, we argue that society should support and even encourage "employers with a conscience" in a wide range of circumstances, although not without exception. The problem, in our view, is not the extension of statutory protections of religious freedom to for-profit employers or even extension of such protections to complicity rather than direct action. Instead, the unique contribution of this chapter, beyond contextualizing the reasons why it is often important to support religious employers in the secular sphere, is to highlight a heretofore-overlooked problem that the contraceptive coverage cases have laid bare. These cases have been substantially debated in terms of religious freedom and reproductive rights, but in our view, one of their most important features is demonstration of a serious difficulty associated with relying on a system of employer-sponsored health insurance: namely, that the system, by its very nature, opens the door for bosses to enter their workers' bedrooms, and other private decision-making spaces. Nonetheless, we recognize that regardless of whether Democrats or Republicans lead the way, the American system appears unwilling to abandon employer-sponsored health insurance altogether, and in fact, seems to be moving in the opposite direction.

[2] Ctr. for Consumer Info. & Ins. Oversight, *Fact Sheet: Women's Preventive Services Coverage, Non-Profit Religious Organizations, and Closely-Held For-Profit Entities* (2015), available at www.cms.gov/CCIIO/Resources/Fact-Sheets-and-FAQs/womens-preven-02012013.html [https://perma.cc/M7LZ-Z2LA].

1. THE IMPORTANCE OF PROTECTING RELIGION, EVEN IN BUSINESS

A. *The Extent of Appropriate Compromise*

The public response to the litany of cases challenging the contraceptives coverage mandate and the associated accommodations offered by the Obama administration (exemplified by the cases culminating in *Hobby Lobby v. Burwell* and *Zubik et al. v. Burwell*) suggested that religious liberty is in a zero-sum game with women's reproductive freedoms. We think that is wrong. It is possible to advance both religious liberty and reproductive autonomy simultaneously by insisting that religious freedom be infringed *only when absolutely necessary* given the impact of accommodation on third parties. When properly construed, we argue that this is precisely the balance set forth by the federal RFRA, at least in those many cases where the government's compelling interest coincides with the relevant interests of third parties.[3]

As described in the introduction to this volume, RFRA provides that the government "may substantially burden a person's exercise of religion only if it demonstrates that application of the burden to the person – (1) is in furtherance of a compelling governmental interest; and (2) is the least restrictive means of furthering that compelling governmental interest."[4] Thus, even though these two criteria set a very high standard of review, the law does not provide *absolute* protection of religious freedom, nor does it allow government interests to be pursued by *any* means.

With regard to the latter concern, even if we are convinced that the government can articulate a compelling interest in facilitating women's access to contraceptives[5] – as we are[6] – we need not insist that employers abide by the mandate despite their

---

[3] As Professor Sepinwall rightly points out in her chapter of this volume, RFRA protects third parties only when their interests happen to coincide with the government's, as RFRA focuses exclusively on whether the government has a compelling interest and does not directly call for consideration of third-party interests in their own right. We agree that RFRA could be strengthened in this regard, but in the context of the contraceptives coverage mandate, the interests of the government and relevant third parties align since the mandate was specifically intended to benefit women.

[4] 42 U.S.C. §2000bb-1(b).

[5] Laurie Sobel and Alina Salganicoff, Kaiser Family Foundation, *Contraceptive Coverage at the Supreme Court Zubik v. Burwell: Does the Law Accommodate or Burden Nonprofits' Religious Beliefs?* (March 21, 2016), available at http://kff.org/womens-health-policy/issue-brief/contraceptive-coverage-at-the-supreme-court-zubik-v-burwell-does-the-law-accommodate-or-burden-nonprofits-religious-beliefs/ [https://perma.cc/FJE5-WR7T].

[6] Without a doubt, the mandate does not close all gaps in access, but the government need not completely resolve a problem in order to demonstrate a compelling interest; moving incrementally toward improvement should be sufficient. The contraceptives coverage mandate does just that, in two big steps: equalizing the burden of family planning by removing costs that previously fell disproportionately on women, and making contraceptives accessible to women who could previously not afford them. See *Final Rule: Coverage of Certain Preventive Services Under the Affordable Care Act*, 78 Fed. Reg. 39870, 39872–73 (July 2, 2013) (describing the government's compelling interest).

religious objections because there is a way to achieve the very same goal without doing so. Namely, the government could offer (and ultimately did offer) all relevant employers with religious objections an accommodation by which the objecting employer somehow notifies the government of its objection[7] such that the health insurer or third-party administrator can step in to facilitate seamless access to free contraceptives for female employees and beneficiaries without the employer's involvement.[8] In other words, there is an "out" that avoids having to legally evaluate whether one's religious beliefs are in fact violated (as when courts distinguish between complicity and direct action), "how bad" the violation of religious beliefs actually is for the believer, how consistent the religious objection is with the objector's other beliefs or behaviors, or how accurate the religious belief is in the face of scientific and medical facts. These are issues that the law should not delve into – courts do not question the validity of religious beliefs, for the obvious reason that one of religion's defining features is that it is not amenable to demands for proof or reason, and while assessing sincerity is fair game, sincerely held religious beliefs need not always demand perfect consistency in behavior.[9] Importantly, respecting these features of religion, and calling for protection when compromise is available, does not suggest any animosity or indifference to women's reproductive freedoms. Whenever both interests can be accommodated, why should we force one to lose?

Nonetheless, when both interests cannot be accommodated, one must cede. Then and only then it is appropriate to expect that religious believers comport with generally applicable legal requirements as a condition of broader societal inclusion. Again, this is precisely what RFRA requires. Thus, employers may still take issue with any accommodation that falls short of *completely* absolving them of complicity in objectionable services and behavior – for example, because providing any notice of their objection "triggers" provision of contraceptives and/or because they view the provision of contraceptives within the same insurance plans as unacceptable "hijacking" of those plans.[10] But they are not entitled to anything further because there is no less-restrictive alternative that would provide seamless access to contraceptives.[11]

---

[7] This was the compromise established in response to *Hobby Lobby*, but it is possible that explicit notice from the religious objector is not needed, so long as the insurer or third-party administrator is somehow made aware of the need to step in.

[8] Ctr. for Consumer Info. & Ins. Oversight, supra note 2.

[9] Ben Adams and Cynthia Barmore, *Questioning Sincerity: The Role of the Courts After Hobby Lobby*, 67 Stan. L. Rev. Online 59 (2014), available at www.stanfordlawreview.org/online/questioning-sincerity [https://perma.cc/N3PF-7Z6Y].

[10] Greg Lipper, *Zubik v. Burwell, Part 1: Why Paperwork Does Not Burden Religious Exercise*, Bill of Health Blog (March 16, 2016), available at http://blogs.harvard.edu/billofhealth/2016/03/16/zubik-v-burwell-part-1-why-paperwork-does-not-burden-religious-exercise/ [https://perma.cc/4LKF-SY2Z].

[11] In returning the *Zubik* line of cases to the circuit courts rather than deciding them on the merits, the Supreme Court did not require that the government concede accomplishment of its ultimate goal of providing seamless contraceptives coverage. Instead, it simply acknowledged that *if* further

This is not to question the validity or sincerity of the objectors' claims, but rather to acknowledge them while maintaining that they must nonetheless give way in some contexts.

As discussed in the Supreme Court's *Hobby Lobby* opinion, some have suggested that the government could cover contraceptives directly when an employer objects,[12] and as part of a universal government health care system, that could make sense. But our country has repeatedly rejected such approaches, and maintained an essential role for employers, as discussed below. More importantly, there are critical questions about what limiting principle might apply if government rescue were to count as an available alternative in the RFRA analysis.[13] Should the possibility of the government stepping in really be considered every time religious believers object to general requirements that impact others? In that case, RFRA's balancing test would quickly devolve into an easy win for religious believers, as the government almost always could take the responsibility on itself. Although RFRA was indeed intended to offer broad protection, that would go too far.

In this vein, it is important to recognize that, at times, compromise will not be possible. For example, in the *Hobby Lobby* dissent, four justices worried about other types of employer objections extending beyond contraceptives to blood transfusions, antidepressants, medications derived from pigs, and vaccinations, as well as possibly opening the door to religious discrimination against the LGBT community and others in the workplace.[14] These are indeed frightening prospects, but RFRA stands against them. In each of these examples, in order for the coverage refusal or other discrimination to be permitted, there would have to be either no compelling government interest to the contrary or some less-restrictive alternative to achieving that interest. However, ensuring affordable access to each of the health measures listed earlier could almost certainly qualify as a compelling interest, given that death or other serious health consequences could ensue from lack thereof. And the government also has an indisputable and compelling interest in protecting equality of opportunity in the workplace for all employees. Moreover, the alternative of having insurers step in to cover other potentially objectionable health care services,

---

compromise was available, it ought to be pursued. 136 S.Ct. at 1560. Such compromise has not been forthcoming, however. U.S. Dep't of Labor, Employee Benefits Security Administration, FAQs About Affordable Care Act Implementation Part 36, Jan. 9, 2017, www.dol.gov/sites/default/files/ebsa/about-ebsa/our-activities/resource-center/faqs/aca-part-36.pdf (noting, as of the end of the Obama administration, that "no feasible approach has been identified at this time that would resolve the concerns of religious objectors, while still ensuring that the affected women receive full and equal health coverage, including contraceptive coverage . . .").

[12] *Burwell v. Hobby Lobby Stores, Inc.*, 134 S.Ct. 2751, 2780–81 (2014).
[13] Id. at 2802–3 (Ginsburg, J., dissenting).
[14] Id. at 2804–5.

as they have been called upon in the context of contraceptives coverage, would not be available for nonpreventative interventions because coverage would not be cost-neutral for insurers. More importantly, there is no alternative to outright and absolute prohibition of discrimination against individuals that would be capable of similarly avoiding the dignitary harms they might face if discriminated against.[15] Accordingly, case-by-case analysis would likely demonstrate that third-party burdens must trump religious objection in these scenarios, too.

B. Why Compromise?

It is sometimes suggested that religious individuals who object to the requirements that would be imposed on them in the public sphere should simply stay out of it. They should not own businesses, employ others, or do anything that could potentially impact those with different views and beliefs. Indeed, part of the consternation over the *Hobby Lobby* opinion had to do with whether religious believers ought to be permitted to take advantage of the benefits of the corporate form, which protects individual owners from liability, while simultaneously being able to exercise their individual rights.[16] But again, if we *are* able to accommodate religious beliefs – held by individuals or corporations, whether they are seeking profit or acting philanthropically – without damage to third parties, on what basis would we justifiably not do so?

Suggesting that religious individuals simply keep to themselves as a matter of course, as many opponents of the *Hobby Lobby* decision seem wont to do, denies the importance of religious freedom to our country, as well as the importance to religious believers of being able to fully engage with their communities, and indeed, to thrive economically while adhering to their deeply held values. This is not to say that religious believers will never have to make sacrifices or choose between their beliefs and their outward engagement; indeed, we explained our view of the extent of appropriate compromise above. But the choice between religious beliefs and community participation should not be imposed unnecessarily. Thus, accommodation of employers' religious objections should not be viewed as an example of judicial overreach or indifference to the rights of others, but rather the sort of compromise we *ought* to seek in a nation that values diversity and tolerance.

---

[15] Although some view objection to contraceptives coverage as discriminatory against women, it is more appropriately characterized as an objection to a service than objection to the particular individual seeking it. We do recognize, of course, the potential for disparate impact nonetheless.

[16] Amy Sepinwall, *Corporate Piety and Impropriety: Hobby Lobby's Extension of RFRA Rights to the For-Profit Corporation*, 5 Harv. Bus. L. Rev. 173 (2015).

C. Don't We Want Businesses with a Conscience?

It is also important to point out that, in many cases, we should not want a blanket rule that forces or encourages religious business owners to check their beliefs at the door. Indeed, some individuals may start businesses precisely to advance their religious calling to help others, and the business need not be nonprofit to achieve that goal. Hobby Lobby offers a compelling example: founded as a family business "based on biblical principles, including integrity, service to others and giving to those in need," the company is closed on Sundays to "allow employees time for worship and to spend time with their family," donates more than ten percent of its annual income to charity (including many religious causes), and has implemented a generous minimum wage (more than 90 percent above the federal minimum) for full-time hourly employees.[17] The company employs 28,000 people. Should we have excluded this family from the business world, just to avoid the possibility of religious conflict?

More generally, it is interesting to contrast the outcry in some corners about the *Hobby Lobby* result (and subsequent litigation) against the frequent and intensifying calls for corporate social responsibility, often from the same corners. We increasingly demand that companies do more than advance profits at all costs, but rather expect them to engage with their workers, suppliers, customers, the environment, and society generally in a respectful and responsible way – and, in particular, to avoid complicity with immoral or illegal behavior. In other words, we look for corporations with a conscience.[18] Certainly, secular companies are able to achieve this goal, and many have taken the step of filing as "benefit corporations," but religious roots and obligations may be particularly supportive. At the very least, it is appropriate to recognize that if businesses are "to be responsible for their actions, they must be treated as having some moral agency."[19]

On what basis could we legitimately tell companies that they should act in accordance with their conscience in one domain (e.g., demanding safe and fair working conditions from all suppliers), but not another? Surely it is insufficient to say that exercise of corporate conscience is acceptable only when "we" agree with the

---

[17] Hobby Lobby Stores, Inc., *Hobby Lobby Marks 40 Years of Helping Families Celebrate Life*, (2010), available at www.hobbylobby.com/assets/pdf/40years/40years.pdf?CFID=31425203&CFTOKEN=d e8c412765fef896-5CC08E10-A7F4-7F8F-0F83600018DA8A69 [https://perma.cc/SU3L-26W5]; The Becket Fund for Religious Liberty, *Hobby Lobby Media Information and Fact Sheet*, available at www.becketfund.org/hobbylobbyfactsheet/ [https://perma.cc/KU7X-UMVF].

[18] Jeffrey Stinson, *More States Encourage "Companies with a Conscience,"* Pew Charitable Trusts: Stateline (December 2, 2014), available at www.pewtrusts.org/en/research-and-analysis/blogs/stateline/2014/12/2/more-states-encourage-companies-with-a-conscience [https://perma.cc/6QMR-KEEM].

[19] Mary Ann Glendon, *Free Businesses to Act with Conscience*, Boston Globe (December 8, 2013), available at www.bostonglobe.com/opinion/2013/12/08/should-business-have-conscience/cK606 G6dwrWeRJjk1uPVYM/story.html.

direction and outcome, or only when the conscientious views are nonreligious. Perhaps the difference is that conscientious corporations are viewed as protecting others or important social goods, whereas religious objectors are viewed as intrusive and imposing in the workplace setting. However, it is important to remember, and will be discussed further later, that we have enabled a system that explicitly calls on employers to be involved in their employees' health care.

The point here is not to suggest that companies owned by religious owners are *more* suited or able to act in accordance with the principles of corporate social responsibility per se, but rather only to point out that we do not, in fact, expect employers to be *amoral*, nor would we necessarily want them to be. Businesses and other organizations with a conscience are generally something to be desired. And once we recognize that employers (in both individual and corporate capacities) *can* have a conscience, we must also recognize their organizational convictions, even if we disagree with their content – so long as third parties are not inappropriately burdened, as explained earlier.

Certainly, it is not possible to make a blanket statement that allowing religion into the employment or corporate space is a good thing. Indeed, sometimes – as when religious beliefs call for discrimination against certain groups, for example, or otherwise have unavoidable negative consequences on third parties – this combination is problematic and to be avoided. But it also would be unwise to bar religion from the business world completely, both for religious believers and the rest of society.

2. THE PROBLEM OF EMPLOYER-SPONSORED HEALTH INSURANCE

So far, we have argued that RFRA, when properly construed, offers a reasonable balance between religious liberty and the interests of others, the Obama administration offered an appropriate accommodation for those employers opposed to the contraceptives coverage mandate, and these employer objections fit within the existing paradigm of corporate conscience. All that said, we agree with many others that bosses have no place in their employees' bedrooms.[20] The problem, however, is that we have put them there,[21] by establishing employer-sponsored health insurance

---

[20] Note that the problem is not just a matter of religious employers, as some nonreligious employers have even raised secular objections to the contraceptives coverage mandate. See, e.g., *March for Life v. Burwell*, 128 F.Supp.2d 116 (D.D.C. 2015); *Real Alternatives, Inc. v. Burwell*, – F.Supp.3d – (M.D. Pa. 2015) WL 8481987. Thus, there are likely to be other sources of conflict between employees and employers on the scope of covered services.

[21] Amy Sepinwall, *Can a Corporation Have a Conscience?*, Washington Post (March 21, 2014), available at www.washingtonpost.com/opinions/can-a-corporation-have-a-conscience/2014/03/21/95ifd6b4-af76-11e3-a49e-76adc9210f19_story.html [https://perma.cc/Y8HJ-JFCS]; Stuart M. Butler, *Bye-Bye Employer Sponsored Health Insurance*, JAMA Forum (August 6, 2014), available at newsatjama.jama.com/2014/08/06/jama-forum-bye-bye-employer-sponsored-health-insurance/ [https://perma.cc/53VP-PH3T]; Paul Waldman, *Hobby Lobby Decision Shows We Need to Get Rid of the Employer-Based*

as the main system by which 155 million Americans – over half of the nonelderly population – obtain their health insurance.[22]

If employer-sponsored health insurance creates these religious conflicts and results in such strange bedfellows, should we move to a different model altogether? Probably yes, with this being one reason among many. Indeed, the winds may be slowly changing. But for now, the current approach has some important benefits, and, perhaps more importantly, there seems to be insufficient political will for fundamental change.

A. A Brief History of Employer-Sponsored Health Insurance

How did we get here? During World War II, strict wage and price controls were put in place by the federal government to control inflation and regulate the allocation of manufactured goods to promote the war effort. In contrast to wages, benefits – including health insurance provided by employers – were not subject to regulation, which allowed employers to offer generous health benefits in lieu of wage increases to attract the best employees.[23] The exclusion of health benefits from wage controls was a first major step in cementing employer-sponsored health insurance as part of our national landscape.

A second important step was taken in 1954 with the passage of the Internal Revenue Code. Section 106 of the code clearly spells out that contributions for the purchase of health insurance made by employers and their employees are exempt from federal income taxes (and as stipulated in another section of the Code, from payroll taxes as well). Thus, given this strong financial incentive, employer-sponsored health insurance became even more entrenched as a fixture in American society, since similar tax breaks are not available to individuals outside the context of employment-sponsored health insurance.[24]

More recently, the Affordable Care Act further secured employer-sponsored health insurance through its Employer Shared Responsibility Provision (commonly referred to as the "employer mandate"), which became fully active in 2016. This provision stipulates that employers with fifty or more full-time employees must

---

Health Insurance System, Washington Post: Plum Line Blog (June 30, 2014), available at www.washingtonpost.com/blogs/plum-line/wp/2014/06/30/hobby-lobby-shows-that-we-need-to-get-rid-of-the-employer-based-health-insurance-system/ [https://perma.cc/L6PH-48PP].

[22] Congressional Budget Office, *Federal Subsidies for Health Insurance Coverage for People Under Age 65: 2016 to 2026*, 4 (2016), available at www.cbo.gov/sites/default/files/114th-congress-2015–2016/reports/51385-HealthInsuranceBaseline_OneCol.pdf [https://perma.cc/3EZX-JTDV].

[23] Waldman, supra note 21.

[24] Blaine Saito, Note, *The Value of Health and Wealth: Economic Theory, Administration, and Valuation Methods for Capping the Employer Sponsored Insurance Tax Exemption*, 48 Harv. J. on Legis. 235 (2011).

provide health insurance benefits to their employees or pay a fine; thus, employers, along with government, insurers, and individuals, must share in the responsibility of providing health insurance to all Americans. Whether the ACA and its mandates will survive Republican threats of repeal is uncertain as of Spring 2017 when this volume went to press, but elimination of the employer mandate would by no means eliminate employer-sponsored health insurance; instead, it would simply remove one of many factors that supports the continuation of this American tradition.

B. The Drawbacks and Benefits of Employer-Sponsored Health Insurance

In addition to laying the groundwork for employer control over health care, opening the door to religious (or other) conflicts when employers oppose various medical services, there are a variety of other problems with our current system of employer-sponsored health insurance. Falling short of comprehensive analysis, these include at least the following.[25]

First, when health insurance coverage is treated as a "benefit," it is more likely to be viewed as a privilege instead of a right or entitlement, as it is often viewed in other countries. This perception may make it politically difficult to achieve more comprehensive coverage in the United States, even recognizing the progress that has been made in expanding the government safety net and building the Exchange market under the ACA. Moreover, this approach may allow responsibility to be shifted to employers and individuals for a right that is arguably part of the government's responsibility to its citizens.

Another concern is that rising health care costs combined with employer-sponsored coverage can result in stagnant pay, since employees ultimately pay for their employer-sponsored coverage in the form of lower wages or reduced benefits in other areas.[26] In other words, no matter what, employees are still paying – which makes the possibility of religious conflict resulting in coverage restrictions even more troublesome. However, employees may not always understand this, and the perception that someone else is paying for their health care coverage may result in overuse and waste in the system.[27]

There are also problems with the tax exemption for both employer and employee contributions toward health insurance coverage. First, the exemption is regressive,

---

[25] Honerman provides more extensive analysis. See Brian Honerman, *Employer-Based Health Care – All Cons, No Pros*, O'Neill Inst. Blog (April 17, 2014), available at www.oneillinstituteblog.org/employer-based-health-care-cons-pros/ [https://perma.cc/R7BR-CBCM].

[26] Butler, supra note 21; Uwe E. Reinhardt, *Is Employer-Based Health Insurance Worth Saving?*, N.Y. Times: Economix Blog (May 22, 2009), available at http://economix.blogs.nytimes.com/2009/05/22/is-employer-based-health-insurance-worth-saving/?_r=1 [https://perma.cc/S5MN-NQAC].

[27] Butler, supra note 21.

benefiting the highest-paid employees the most, since they are generally in the highest tax brackets and have the highest-cost health care coverage. Relatively little of the tax-break benefits lower-paid workers.[28] And second, the tax exemption is quite costly – as of 2010, it was calculated to reduce federal and state tax revenues by $260 billion per year, making it the government's third-largest expenditure on health care, after Medicare ($400 billion) and Medicaid ($300 billion).[29] Furthermore, the tax exemption does not apply to persons buying health insurance in the individual market, which raises a question about a fundamental lack of fairness in our health insurance system.

Another problem with an employer-based system is that when employers are involved in coverage, they gain a legitimate interest in employee health and may take efforts to reduce coverage costs. On the one hand, this may be a feature, rather than a bug, as discussed later. On the other, it may feel intrusive or violative of privacy when employers attempt to impose employee wellness programs or other cost-reducing mechanisms.[30]

Finally, when employers self-insure, as nearly two-thirds of U.S. employers do, this results in a system in which health risks are pooled based on an individual's employer rather than the general population (or some other grouping). In self-insuring for health care, employers assume the financial risk, since the risk pool consists only of their own employees. However, there is nothing to suggest that this is the optimal way to group risk.[31] Indeed, for a small employer, it may cause disastrous increases in premiums if even one employee becomes gravely ill. Also, self-insurance may incentivize employers to "cherry-pick" healthy employees and to discriminate against others through the application of onerous employee wellness programs. Self-insurance causes an additional problem in regard to ERISA (Employee Retirement Income Security Act) preemption. Although self-insured health plans are subject to preemption of certain state insurance laws, commercial health insurance plans are not. Thus, two employees in the same state may or may not be under state insurance regulation based on whether or not their firm self-insures.

Despite these problems, among others, the current system does have some advantages. Most workers are satisfied with the benefits they have now, only one in five

---

[28] Id.
[29] Jonathan Gruber, *The Tax Exclusion for Employer-Sponsored Health Insurance* (Nat'l Bureau of Econ. Research, Working Paper No. 15766, 2010), available at www.nber.org/papers/w15766.pdf [https://perma.cc/S3NL-M59N].
[30] See Dan Munro, *Does Hobby Lobby Signal the End of Employer Sponsored Health Insurance?*, Forbes (July 6, 2014), available at www.forbes.com/sites/danmunro/2014/07/06/does-hobby-lobby-signal-the-end-of-employer-sponsored-health-insurance/ [https://perma.cc/7SJG-KH2E]; Kristin Madison, *Employer Wellness Incentives, the ACA, and the ADA: Reconciling Policy Objectives*, 51 Willamette L. Rev. 407 (2015).
[31] Honerman, supra note 25.

would surrender some health benefits for higher wages, and most feel confident that their employers or unions have selected the best available health plans.[32] Moreover, a sizable minority of employees lack confidence in their ability to choose the best plan if their employer stopped offering coverage, even if they were provided an objective rating system.[33] The place of employment provides a convenient locus for obtaining group health insurance, allowing negotiation for lower premiums and lower prices for individual health services. Perhaps because of this, health benefits remain an important mechanism by which employers may compete with one another for the best employees.[34] In addition, large employers are able to effectively negotiate lower premiums with insurance companies because they have enough employees to reduce their actuarial risks. Finally, employer-sponsored health insurance gives employers a strong incentive to care about their employees' health, though when employees change jobs frequently the incentive is to focus more on short-term than long-term health. When done with appropriate sensitivity, employee wellness plans may offer important mechanisms to improve individual health and health outcomes. Thus, while employer involvement in health insurance is not all bad, it is essential to recognize that many of its benefits would also be achievable in other ways, such that they do not provide strong or lasting support for the status quo.[35]

C. The Political Realities of Change

A variety of alternatives to employer-sponsored health insurance have been suggested over the years, but complete elimination of employer involvement seems unlikely, at least for now. On the plus side, there have been several promising steps in the right direction. For example, the ACA made substantial headway toward a parallel system of nonemployer coverage via insurance exchanges and expanded government coverage – and indeed, fewer small and medium-sized companies have been offering coverage in recent years,[36] although that trend has been stabilizing. With the fate of the ACA now hanging in the balance, there is uncertainty whether

---

[32] Paul Fronstin and Ruth Helman, *Views on Employment-Based Health Benefits: Findings from the 2014 Health and Voluntary Workplace Benefits Survey*, 36(2) EBRI Notes (2015), available at http://papers.ssrn.com/sol3/papers.cfm?abstract_id=2567820## [https://perma.cc/C25T-6UJ3].

[33] Id. Of course, many employers still offer plan choice, but have narrowed down available options from which employees may select, which may ease decision making.

[34] Reed Abelson, *Despite Fears, Affordable Care Act Has Not Uprooted Employer Coverage*, N.Y. Times (April 4, 2016), available at www.nytimes.com/2016/04/05/business/employers-keep-health-insurance-despite-affordable-care-act.html [http://nyti.ms/236xShG].

[35] Honerman, supra note 25.

[36] Peter Ubel, *Obamacare and the End of Employer-Based Health Insurance*, Forbes (November 14, 2013), available at www.forbes.com/sites/peterubel/2013/11/14/obamacare-and-the-end-of-employer-based-health-insurance/ [https://perma.cc/R2W4-QLVZ].

the exchanges will permanently remain as an alternative to employer-sponsored insurance. Furthermore, even if the exchanges do survive, several large insurers have already eliminated their policies on many of the insurance exchanges, pointing to inadequate financial return.[37] Thus, there is considerable instability in the exchange markets, which will need to be carefully monitored and may soon require intervention if the exchanges are to survive.

Nonetheless, there appears to be insufficient political will for a full-scale revolution that would eliminate employer involvement in health insurance entirely. On this front, the best evidence is the ACA's entrenchment of the employer-sponsored system via the employer mandate, although the mandate could be overturned with a repeal of parts or all of the ACA. Moreover, while the ACA's so-called "Cadillac tax" – a large excise tax to be levied on employers offering the most expensive employee health plans – was intended to reduce health care usage and costs by encouraging employers to offer plans that are cost-effective and engage employees in cost-sharing, potentially rendering employer coverage less attractive to all parties, its implementation has been delayed to 2020, and there is strong bipartisan support for outright repeal.[38] Some newly proposed "repeal and replace" legislation would delay the implementation of the "Cadillac tax" until 2024.

Ultimately, the exchanges have not been an enticing alternative for workers.[39] Even though the premiums may be affordable (due to subsidies or otherwise), the deductibles and out-of-pocket drug expenses on many "silver" plans offered on the exchanges are so high that some covered individuals or families are hesitant to use the insurance. In addition, the subsidies made available for low-income consumers were declared unconstitutional by a lower court. The Obama administration appealed, but with the election of Donald Trump, the House may simply settle the case.[40] Furthermore, the provider networks for some policies on the exchanges may be so narrow that insured persons may find that their own doctors are "out of network" and do not accept their insurance plan.[41]

[37] Cynthia Fox and Ashley Semanskee, *Preliminary Data on Insurer Exits and Entrants in 2017 Affordable Care Act Marketplaces*, Kaiser Family Foundation (August 28, 2016), available at http://kff.org/health-reform/issue-brief/preliminary-data-on-insurer-exits-and-entrants-in-2017-affordable-care-act-marketplaces.

[38] Amy Goldstein, *Congress to Delay ACA's 'Cadillac' Tax on Pricey Health Plans Until 2020*, Washington Post (December 16, 2015), available at www.washingtonpost.com/national/health-science/cadillac-tax-and-two-other-aca-taxes-part-of-budget-deal-on-hill/2015/12/16/e2b01ff8-a365-11e5-ad3f-991ce3374e23_story.html [https://perma.cc/T7BP-8WRA].

[39] Abelson, supra note 34.

[40] Timothy Jost, Rapid Developments in *House v. Burwell*. Health Affairs Blog. http://healthaffairs.org/blog/2016/12/29/rapid-developments-in-house-v-burwell/

[41] Elisabeth Rosenthal, *We Don't Take Obamacare*, N.Y. Times (May 14, 2016), available at www.nytimes.com/2016/05/15/sunday-review/sorry-we-dont-take-obamacare.html?_r=0 [http://nyti.ms/27nbtw8].

The 2016 Democratic presidential candidates both pushed for further health care reform beyond the ACA, but only Bernie Sanders campaigned for a true single-payer national health care program. His proposal faced significant scrutiny, however, as being unworkable in terms of cost projections[42] and, more generally, politically infeasible. Furthermore, a single-payer system considered by the State of Vermont has been shelved because the plan proved far too expensive to implement. Hillary Clinton proposed a more modest approach, including allowing people the opportunity to buy into Medicare before reaching the current age of eligibility (i.e., adopting a "public option"), while leaving a substantial role for employer-sponsored plans, among other choices.[43] Some Republicans, too, have expressed concern that health insurance is too closely tied to employment, creating problems when people are laid off, fired, or quit. However, their solution is to introduce further flexibility and options, while recognizing that "[e]mployer sponsored insurance is a critical part of our health care system and must be protected."[44] Even among harsh critics of the ACA, there has been almost no debate about employer coverage.[45]

These political winds, along with deep entrenchment of the current system, have led some experts to estimate that employers will remain the source of coverage for most Americans for at least the next decade.[46] Dramatic changes in the economy, the labor market, or health care costs could change this trajectory, but so far, there has been no political compulsion to change.[47] Thus, despite the many flaws in this system, it appears that bosses will still have an entry point into the bedroom for the foreseeable future.

CONCLUSION

The various religious objections to the ACA's contraceptives coverage mandate highlight the need for reasonable compromise between those who seek to exercise their religious beliefs in the public economic sphere and those who stand to

---

[42] Urban Institute, *The Sanders Single-Payer Health Care Plan: The Effect on National Health Expenditures and Federal and Private Spending* (May 9, 2016), available at www.urban.org/research/publication/sanders-single-payer-health-care-plan-effect-national-health-expenditures-and-federal-and-private-spending [https://perma.cc/QGZ9-CGYA].

[43] Sahil Kapur, *Clinton Calls for Health-Care Public Option, Medicare Buy-In*, Bloomberg Politics (May 9, 2016), available at www.bloomberg.com/politics/trackers/2016-05-09/in-virginia-clinton-calls-for-health-care-public-option-medicare-buy-in [https://perma.cc/2VVF-MH9E].

[44] Hearing on "Health Care Solutions: Increasing Patient Choice and Plan Innovation," Subcommittee on Health, 114th Cong. (2016) (statement of Hon. Joe Pitts), available at http://energycommerce.house.gov/sites/republicans.energycommerce.house.gov/files/documents/114/hearings/health/HHRG-114-IF14-MState-P000373-20160511.pdf [https://perma.cc/PCZ6-7ZSJ].

[45] Abelson, supra note 34.

[46] Id.

[47] Id.

be impacted by such exercise. We suggest that RFRA is capable of achieving that compromise, when properly understood and applied; here, it is appropriate to offer religious employers some accommodation so long as women seeking contraceptives are still able to achieve seamless access, as contemplated by the mandate itself. At its core, however, this conflict highlights a fundamental problem with employer-sponsored health insurance. We believe that, despite its potential advantages, employer-sponsored health insurance has unintended consequences that outweigh its benefits, and it is time to consider a move to a different system of health insurance for employed persons. Until such time as we remove employers as the principal providers of health benefits for employed Americans, we can expect such ideological conflicts to continue to complicate the employer–employee relationship.

PART IV

Professional Responsibilities, Religion, and Health Care

Introduction

Holly Fernandez Lynch

Health care professionals may have conscientious objections (religious or otherwise) to the legally permissible medical services their patients seek in a wide variety of circumstances. Most commonly, they object to the provision of certain reproductive services, but end-of-life care is also an area fraught with the potential for ethical conflict between patients and providers, as are others. What should the law demand in these contexts, how should professions self-regulate their members, and what should patients expect? These issues are the subject of the chapters in this part.

While the law often provides robust protection to conscientious objectors in the health care context, the extent of legal protection varies from state to state with regard to the type and scope of services that may be refused and to whom, and with regard to the protections available to patients seeking access. Such "conscience clauses" are sometimes met with support, recognizing that health care professionals have a claim to personal integrity that is not abandoned by joining a profession. But they are also frequently met with opposition on the ground that objecting professionals are putting their own interests before those of their patients. Indeed, one response to conscientious refusal by health care professionals is the suggestion that they should simply leave the profession and find something else to do.

In the chapters that follow, Claudia E. Haupt and Nadia N. Sawicki present two different, but related, models for addressing the problem. First, Haupt suggests that certain conscientious objectors may actually place themselves *outside* of the profession, as "external outliers." As such, their refusals (or deviations) render them subject to malpractice claims for violating the standard of care set by the profession. Sawicki does not take things so far, but does argue for conscientious objectors to at least be required to disclose the nature and scope of their objections to patients upfront, as part of the informed consent process. Failure to do so, on Sawicki's account, would result in common law liability for negligent informed consent. Thus, Sawicki calls for objectors to disclose the manner in which they may diverge from their profession, while allowing the objection to stand, whereas Haupt suggests that at least certain types of objectors (depending on their reasons) may not be part of their proclaimed profession at all, arguing that such objections should not be legally accommodated. In both cases, however, objectors would have responsibilities beyond the status quo in order to avoid liability.

Haupt helpfully recognizes that professions are not monolithic; there may be disagreement within them, short of conscientious objection. Thus, she notes that, within professional knowledge communities, professionals will engage in reasonable debate about appropriate practice. So long as these debates are within the *shared* terms of the professional knowledge community – using shared methodologies and reasons – they are appropriate, in her view. For example, clinicians may disagree about whether there is sufficient scientific evidence to alter the prevailing standard of care, such that some clinicians will be "internal outliers," on Haupt's terms, compared to the profession's mainstream. But these internal outliers remain part of the profession, indeed an important part that can push the profession toward appropriate change over time. In contrast, external outliers deviate from the profession's mainstream for religious or other reasons that are not part of knowledge community's shared terms of engagement. Accordingly, Haupt suggests they ought not be accommodated.

There are at least two potential concerns with this approach. First, although Haupt recognizes that the shared terms of professional knowledge communities may include ethical or value judgments (rather than only judgments about scientific fact), it is unclear why some value judgments are acceptable when espoused by a professional group rather than by individual professionals. Her answer lies in whether the judgments stem from shared reasons, but that cannot be sufficient, since religious reasons may also be shared by at least some others in the knowledge community. What Haupt means is something more specific – not simply shared reasons, but rather *sharable*, or public, reasons – reasons that anyone in the community could engage with and debate. This is a key distinction from religious reasons, which are not "public" in the sense of being a matter of belief rather than argument.

If we take Haupt's point to be one about requiring public reasons in order for deviation from the profession's mainstream knowledge community to be acceptable, then we are left to conclude that those with other reasons really should find something else to do with themselves, since they cannot comport with the profession's requirements. Although Haupt would not be alone in this approach, it reveals a second concern, which is that the solution goes too far. Why not treat conscientious objectors as subspecialists, rather than outside the profession entirely? Already, not every member of a professional community provides every service within the profession's regulated monopoly; medical specialties are a perfect reflection of that fact. Even within particular medical specialties, clinicians may focus on a certain type of patient or service in which they have particular expertise or interest. Thus, it seems appropriate to allow them to specialize further based on their conscientious beliefs while staying within the realm of the profession – at least in some circumstances. If a gynecologist could provide superior service to patients in most areas, for example, it seems unnecessary to push her entirely out of the profession simply because her religious objection to abortion is not a public reason.

In this regard, Sawicki's approach seems helpful. Disclosure of clinicians' conscientious objections when patients are deciding whether to engage their services or seek an alternative has the potential to accommodate both the needs of patients and the interests of objectors. Moreover, it is quite similar to a clinician's disclosure of a particular subspecialization – "I am unable to perform that type of surgery because I focus on this type" is similar to "I am unable to perform that gynecological service because I focus on this type." Further, it is plausible that some patients may even *prefer* a professional who is unwilling to provide certain services; patients who share the conscientious objection may appreciate the option to match with a like-minded provider.

As Sawicki notes, however, objecting professionals must be willing at least to disclose their limitations and the alternatives they are unwilling to provide in order for patients to make a fully informed choice. Some objectors may argue that disclosure renders them complicit in facilitating or enabling the very thing to which they object, but that sacrifice may indeed be a non-negotiable aspect of membership in the profession.

Of course, disclosure alone will not solve the problem of conscientious objection by professionals. For one thing, it does nothing to ensure patients' access to professional services, which they may be otherwise unable to obtain. Professions as a whole have a responsibility to ensure such access, and that responsibility may sometimes fall on individual professionals. This is most notably the case, for example, when a patient is facing an emergency or could not otherwise seek alternative care.

A simple disclosure requirement also fails to place any limitations on the grounds for a clinician's objection. While Haupt would define those limits as grounds that could be accepted within the shared knowledge community, other reasonable limits could include accepting objections to a particular service while rejecting objections to (or judgments about) the sort of person who is requesting the service. Already, civil rights laws protect patients against invidious discrimination, such that they ought to be viewed as critical companions to laws and policies protecting provider conscience.

Ultimately, the question at hand is how to define the range of services that comprise a profession, or a professional specialty. Both Haupt and Sawicki recognize that not every health care professional must provide every service, but Haupt would allow only those deviations based on shared or sharable reasons, whereas Sawicki posits that deviations should be protected from tort liability only if disclosed in a reasonable fashion to patients. Either approach is preferable to the status quo in many states in which conscientious objectors enjoy near-blanket protection without regard to the impact on those to whom their profession has taken on a social obligation – namely, patients.

12

Religious Outliers

Professional Knowledge Communities, Individual Conscience Claims, and the Availability of Professional Services to the Public

Claudia E. Haupt

Clients typically consult professionals because they want to access the useful body of knowledge which professionals possess in order to solve an individual problem. To achieve that goal, the client depends on accurate and comprehensive professional advice. But professionals sometimes depart from, or do not deploy, their full range of professional knowledge. The professional might have a political, philosophical, or religious disagreement with their profession: your therapist believes homosexuality is sinful and ought to be remedied by conversion therapy;[1] your pharmacist considers abortion a grave moral wrong and some forms of birth control to be abortifacients.[2] Or she might have a scientific disagreement with the profession: your doctor thinks marijuana is medically beneficial;[3] perhaps she finds mammograms useless.[4] What are justifications for departure from core professional knowledge? And how should the law treat these manifestations of a professional's outlier status?

---

[1] See Pickup v. Brown, 740 F.3d 1208 (9th Cir. 2013) (upholding California conversion therapy law against Free Speech challenge), cert. denied 134 S.Ct. 2871 (2014); *Welch v. Brown*, 834 F.3d 1041 (9th Cir. 2016) (upholding California conversion therapy law against Free Exercise and Establishment Clause challenge); *King v. Christie*, 767 F.3d 216 (3d Cir. 2014) (upholding New Jersey conversion therapy law against Free Speech and Free Exercise challenge).

[2] See *Stormans v. Wiesman*, 794 F.3d 1064, 1071 (9th Cir. 2015) (upholding Washington's requirement that pharmacies dispense all available prescription medications), cert. denied, 136 S. Ct. 2433 (2016). .

[3] See *Conant v. Walters*, 309 F.3d 629 (9th Cir. 2002).

[4] See, e.g., Gina Kolata, *Vast Study Casts Doubts on Value of Mammograms*, N.Y. Times, February 12, 2014, available at http://nyti.ms/1eSbFcm [https://perma.cc/6CRP-YL4T] (reporting on Mette Kalager, Hans-Olov Adami & Michael Bretthauer, *Editorial, Too Much Mammography*, Brit. Med. J. (2014); Anthony Miller, Claus Wall, Cornelia J. Baines, Ping Sun, Teresa To & Steven A. Narod, *Twenty Five Year Follow-up for Breast Cancer Incidence and Mortality of the Canadian National Breast Screening Study: Randomised Screening Trial*, Brit. Med. J. (2014)).

I have argued elsewhere that the professions are best understood as knowledge communities, that is, communities whose main reason for existing is the generation and dissemination of knowledge.[5] This chapter conceptualizes conscience claims of professionals as claims of outliers that may place them outside of their professional knowledge communities. For purposes of this chapter, I will limit my inquiry specifically to the religiously based outlier status of professionals providing health services. This chapter analyzes the tension among individual conscience claims, professional duties, and the availability of professional services to the public. Closer consideration of stakeholders' duties to one another permits a normative reevaluation of such claims. Understanding the professions as knowledge communities and investigating professionals' attendant duties sheds new light on these tensions and points toward a conceptual solution.

I suggest that, to the extent that a professional's outlier status is grounded in disagreement based on shared notions of validity, departure from the knowledge community's insights must be permissible. Indeed, dynamic development and refinement of professional insights will often depend on such divergent assessments. Take the medical marijuana example. While advising patients on its medical benefits was once considered an outlier position, increased research has led to more mainstream acceptance of its therapeutic qualities. The knowledge community, in other words, is actively revising what it considers good advice by reinterpreting its shared knowledge basis and employing a shared methodology to do so. However, outlier status based on exogenous reasons – for the purposes of this chapter, particularly religious reasons – undermines the status of the professional as a member of the knowledge community that is founded in shared notions of validity and common ways of knowing and reasoning. The pharmacist who refuses to advise on the availability of certain forms of birth control does so based on a personal religious belief that is not the result of a reinterpretation of shared professional knowledge by means of a shared methodology.

My task herein is to explain and defend this distinction in light of the expectations toward professionals. These are the expectations of the knowledge community to which the professional belongs, as well as of the client they serve and to whom they owe a fiduciary duty. It will be the reasonable expectation of the knowledge community that the individual professional accurately communicates their knowledge to the client.[6] Correspondingly, the client seeking professional advice reasonably

---

[5] Claudia E. Haupt, *Professional Speech*, 125 Yale L.J. 1238, 1241 (2016).

[6] There is another dimension that I subsume under the knowledge community's expectations of the individual professional, but that others have identified separately as the expectation of the professional: "[r]easonable belief about what a job entails is one measure of whether refusals of conscience should be protected." Kent Greenawalt, *Refusals of Conscience: What Are They and When Should They Be Accommodated?* 9 Ave Maria L. Rev. 47, 55 (2010). Professor Greenawalt points out that nurses

may expect that they will receive competent and comprehensive professional advice in accordance with the profession's insights. In other words, the client expects that they will access the entire body of knowledge that constitutes the state of the art in the field. The normative corollary can be found in the law of professional malpractice where the standard of care against which the professional's advice is measured is determined by the profession itself: exercise of the profession according to the degree and skill of a well-qualified professional. The knowledge community thus determines the benchmark against which the individual professional's liability is assessed.

The first section of this chapter introduces the concept of knowledge communities, focusing the analysis on knowledge communities as providers of professional services. The second section takes a normative view of the duties of a professional and justifications for departure from professional norms within and outside of knowledge communities. It specifically focuses on religious justifications as the basis for professional advice.

Outliers within knowledge communities – "internal outliers" – whose disagreement is based on alternative assessments within the range of the profession's shared ways of knowing and reasoning are part of the knowledge community. Their advice constitutes good professional advice so long as it reflects defensible findings based on the profession's agreed-upon standards for evaluating professional knowledge. But outliers whose disagreement is premised on rejecting the shared way of knowing and reasoning due to external, including religious, beliefs – "external outliers" – place themselves outside the knowledge community.

1. PROFESSIONAL KNOWLEDGE COMMUNITIES

The professions, I suggest, are best thought of as knowledge communities. Not all occupations are considered professions; historically, the three paradigmatic learned professions were law, medicine, and the clergy.[7] I explicitly exclude the clergy from this discussion, and focus specifically on the health professions.[8] To be sure, the

---

trained at a time when abortion was illegal would not reasonably expect to be called upon to assist in such a procedure. That is certainly true. Under my theory of the professions as knowledge communities, however, the job of the individual professional entails whatever the knowledge community defines it to be, even if its scope changes over time.

[7] See, e.g., Walter Gellhorn, *The Abuse of Occupational Licensing*, 44 U. Chi. L. Rev. 6, 7 (1976); Maxwell J. Mehlman, *Professional Power and the Standard of Care in Medicine*, 44 Ariz. St. L.J. 1165, 1225 (2012).

[8] Aside from the protection of religious speech otherwise afforded by the Free Exercise Clause of the First Amendment, it seems problematic to fit the clergy into the knowledge community concept, particularly across denominations. Exclusive claims to ultimate truth will be difficult to reconcile with

concept of "profession" itself is contested. But its most relevant defining feature for the present purposes – and one generally shared among the numerous and varying definitions – is the knowledge-based character of the professions.[9] Individual professionals "may differ in their individual judgments about particular issues, [but] their role as professionals traditionally implies their subscription to a body of knowledge that is shared among their peers."[10] The individual professional thus serves as the conduit between the knowledge community and the client.

A. Professionals as Members of Knowledge Communities

The term "knowledge communities" describes a network of individuals who share common knowledge and experience as a result of training and practice.[11] These individuals solve similar problems by drawing on a shared reservoir of knowledge. Their common understandings allow for the generation and exchange of insights within the knowledge community. Given the shared knowledge and understandings of this knowledge, members of knowledge communities have shared notions of validity, intersubjective understanding, and a common way of knowing and reasoning. Within the discourse of the profession, the acceptance of professional insights will depend on the rules established by the profession. Scientific insights, for example, will be subjected to peer review and hypotheses will be subjected to the process of falsification. Professional standards are generated by testing insights within the discourse of the knowledge community. The current state of the art provides the foundation of the professional's advice (though current debates within the field may influence what counts as a defensible professional position).[12] The knowledge community, moreover, shares certain norms and values that constitute their professional norms.[13] The relationship between the knowledge community and the individual professional, thus, is defined by their common knowledge.

It is critical to recognize that this does not mean that knowledge communities are monolithic. But the shared notions of validity limit the range of opinions that may be considered valid within the profession. Professionals may depart from the core of professional knowledge so long as their departure is still justified by reference to the shared knowledge basis. With respect to the advice-giving function of

---

a knowledge community's underlying shared notions of validity and a common way of knowing and reasoning.

[9] See Haupt, supra note 5, at 10–12 (discussing various definitions of "profession" offered in the literature and the centrality of knowledge as a defining feature).

[10] Daniel Halberstam, *Commercial Speech, Professional Speech, and the Constitutional Status of Social Institutions*, 147 U. Pa. L. Rev. 771, 772 (1999).

[11] Haupt, supra note 5, at 11–12.

[12] Id. at 32.

[13] Id. at 12.

professionals, this significantly distinguishes professional speech from other types of speech, where the truth is considered "just another opinion."[14] The fundamental question addressed throughout this chapter is what justifications underlie valid professional opinions.

Multiple links tie the individual professional back to the knowledge community. The professional "is understood to be acting under a commitment to the ethical and intellectual principles governing the profession and is not thought of as free to challenge the mode of discourse or the norms of the profession while remaining within the parameters of the professional discussion."[15] The malpractice liability scheme likewise assumes this connection in imposing the profession's standard of care on the individual professional. Professionals may be held liable for "unprofessional" advice, that is, advice that fails accurately to communicate the knowledge community's insights. In order to achieve fair results under this scheme, professionals may be held liable only under a standard that is exclusively determined by the profession.

Knowledge communities have specialized expertise, based on shared understandings of their field's knowledge; they have a fundamental interest in not having the state (or anyone else, for that matter) corrupt or distort what amounts to the state of the art in the respective field.[16] But where knowledge communities – and, by extension, individual professionals – do not possess such specialized knowledge or competence, such deference is not required. The knowledge community has a superior understanding of issues directly related to its core knowledge. But no amount of specialized training, for instance, by itself makes a professional more competent to render general value judgments on moral issues unrelated or only tangentially related to professional insights. For example, professional determinations based on medical expertise can be made regarding the total and irreversible cessation of all brain functions ("brain death") and its diagnostic criteria. However, it is a value judgment whether this medical diagnosis constitutes the end of life of the individual; this is a matter with ethical, philosophical, and religious dimensions beyond medical expertise.[17]

Finally, it is worth noting that many professionals are not solo practitioners, but, rather, work within various institutional settings. Their obligations to their profession

---

[14] Paul Horwitz, *First Amendment Institutions* 248 (2012) (internal quotation marks omitted).
[15] Halberstam, supra note 10, at 834.
[16] See id. at 773.
[17] See, e.g., Walter F. Haupt & Wolfram Höfling, *Diagnosis of brain death: medical and legal aspects with special reference to the German Transplantation Law (TPG)*, 70 Fortschritte der Neurologie und Psychiatrie 583 (2002) (discussing "the clinical signs of total and irreversible cessation of brain function" and noting that "individuals having suffered brain death still possess the protection of their personal human rights according to the German constitution since it cannot be conclusively demonstrated that total loss of brain function alone constitutes the cessation of life in the sense of the German constitution."). See also Thaddeus Mason Pope's chapter in this volume.

may clash with their obligations to their institutional employer. The entities in which professionals are embedded can be governmental or private, religious or secular. Depending on these variables, professionals will be pulled in different directions regarding the content of their advice. But the First Amendment should protect professionals who resist those forces to guard their professional advice against outside interference.[18] Professionals' primary allegiances ought to be to their patients on the one hand and their knowledge community on the other. They are the conduits through which the knowledge community's insights are transmitted to the client.

B. *The Scope of Professional Knowledge*

Knowledge communities, to reiterate, are not monolithic; tort law has long acknowledged this fact. Professional malpractice liability holds the individual professional to follow the standards of the profession. It ensures that the professional's advice accurately communicates the knowledge community's insights within the professional–client relationship. On the flip side, "unprofessional" advice is unprotected. Robert Post explains the connection between malpractice liability and professional knowledge as follows:

> [M]alpractice law outside of public discourse rigorously polices the authority of disciplinary knowledge. It underwrites the competence of experts. Doctors, dentists, lawyers, or architects who offer what authoritative professional standards would regard as incompetent advice to their clients face strict legal regulation. In such contexts, law stands as a surety for the disciplinary truth of expert pronouncements. By guaranteeing that clients can plan to rely on expert professional judgment, law endows such communication with the status of knowledge.[19]

But this is only true if the knowledge community can decide for itself, free from outside interference, what "disciplinary truth" is. The determinative standard of care is exercise of the profession according to the degree and skill of a well-qualified professional. A lawyer "must exercise the competence and diligence normally exercised by lawyers in similar circumstances."[20] Likewise, "[a] doctor commits malpractice when he treats a patient in a way that deviates from the norms established by the medical profession."[21] It is thus the knowledge community that determines

---

[18] Since the First Amendment only protects against government interference with speech, its protections will not be available when a nongovernmental employer imposes limitations that may conflict with a professional's knowledge community. Providing less-than-comprehensive advice due to limitations imposed by the employer may still be actionable, however, under a tort regime that recognizes a duty to disclose such limitations. See Nadia N. Sawicki's chapter in this volume.

[19] Robert C. Post, *Democracy, Expertise, and Academic Freedom: A First Amendment Jurisprudence for the Modern State* 44–45 (2012).

[20] Restatement (Third) of the Law Governing Lawyers § 52(1) (2000).

[21] Alex Stein, *Toward a Theory of Medical Malpractice*, 97 Iowa L. Rev. 1201, 1209 (2012).

the standard of care. Moreover, only the knowledge community's specific insights matter. Deference is thus awarded to the core knowledge, not to peripheral interests such as those that are purely economic and not based on professional expertise.[22]

With respect to informed consent requirements, similarly, the knowledge community's standard limits the extent to which a physician may depart from the knowledge community's insights.[23] This is because "the scope of disclosure is bound only by what is material to medical, as opposed to non-medical, interests. Cabining the information that physicians must disclose to that which is material to patients' *medical* decisions avoids holding physicians accountable for matters that go beyond their expertise."[24] Again, it is the knowledge community's professional knowledge that circumscribes the relevant information.[25] And it is therefore necessary to keep the knowledge community's information-formation process free from outside interference.

Of course, professional associations have held, at one point or another, positions they now consider erroneous or outdated. For instance, the American Medical Association was at the forefront of the campaign to criminalize abortion in the nineteenth century.[26] The American Psychological Association did not declassify homosexuality as a mental disorder until 1973.[27] But the professions themselves should determine their positions.[28] In assuming, changing, or updating these positions, the knowledge communities use professional standards.

2. JUSTIFICATIONS FOR OUTLIER STATUS

This section investigates what constitutes an appropriate basis for justifying a professional's outlier status. It considers the interests of professionals and knowledge communities, and client expectations toward them. The point of departure is the

---

[22] Id. at 1243 ("Rules that the profession is authorized to make need to utilize medical knowledge to diagnose and cure patients. Those rules consequently must be based on medical reasons. Courts scrutinize those reasons for minimal plausibility to make sure that the profession's rules are not blatantly unsafe to patients. Furthermore, the profession has no exclusive authority to base its rules of patient treatment upon reasons extraneous to medicine. Correspondingly, courts fully scrutinize the profession's non-medical reasons and decisions.").

[23] See also Sawicki, supra note 18.

[24] Sonia M. Suter, *The Politics of Information: Informed Consent in Abortion and End-of-Life Decision Making*, 39 Am. J.L. & Med. 7, 15 (2013) (emphasis in original).

[25] See id. 15–16 (explaining that "the law is reluctant to intrude too much into the medical decision-making process. Courts struggle to strike a balance that promotes autonomy while preserving some element of professional discretion for physicians.").

[26] See Reva B. Siegel, *The New Politics of Abortion: An Equality Analysis of Woman-Protective Abortion Restrictions*, 2007 U. Ill. L. Rev. 991, 1000–02 (2007); Reva Siegel, *Reasoning from the Body: A Historical Perspective on Abortion Regulation and Questions of Equal Protection*, 44 Stan. L. Rev. 261, 280–318 (1992).

[27] Horwitz, supra note 14, at 251 n.51.

[28] Cf. id. (pointing out that the American Psychological Association declassified homosexuality "not as a result of legal pressure but in response to changing professional views and broader social norms.").

concept of the professions as knowledge communities, and especially the notion of a shared knowledge basis. For all valid outlier claims, consequently, reference to the shared knowledge basis is necessary. Scientific disagreement within the knowledge community will be based on individual professionals' divergent interpretation of the shared knowledge. The advice-giving function of the individual professional is thus linked to the range of defensible opinions within the knowledge community. If, however, the advice is based on an assessment of the knowledge based on exogenous reasons – and, for the present purposes, in particular on religious reasons – the professional places himself outside of the knowledge community. We might think of professionals in the first scenario as *internal outliers*, that is, internal to the knowledge community, and in the second scenario as *external outliers*, that is, placing themselves outside the knowledge community.

A. Internal Outliers and Shared Knowledge Justifications

Internal outliers share the knowledge community's notions of validity, methodology, and intersubjective understanding. But their results deviate from the "mainstream." Yet, their outlier status is based on the application of the agreed-upon methods to the same data, only to reach divergent results. Ultimately, outlier status is thus grounded in the same set of professional insights. This is the key to understanding that knowledge communities are not monolithic. The same data, whatever it might be for the respective field, often may be interpreted in multiple and varying ways. As a matter of tort liability, the resulting professional advice, consequently, is "good" professional advice falling within the range of defensible professional knowledge.[29]

Different assessments of shared knowledge, if valid under the agreed-upon methodology, will produce good professional advice, even if it departs from the mainstream. But if the assessment of the shared knowledge is faulty or based on methodological errors – as, for example, in the discredited and subsequently retracted study linking certain vaccines to autism[30] – it will not result in defensible professional advice because it falls outside the defensible range of valid professional insights. Thus, internal outliers can produce good or bad professional advice. (The range of advice is represented in Figure 12.1.)

There is more to be said about the range of defensible professional knowledge and how the boundaries are best determined.[31] Given the focus on religious outliers

---

[29] Haupt, supra note 5, at 41–2.
[30] AJ Wakefield et al., RETRACTED: *Ileal-Lymphoid-Nodular Hyperplasia, Non-specific Colitis, and Pervasive Developmental Disorder in Children*, 351 The Lancet 637 (1998). See also The Editors of the Lancet, *Retraction – Ileal-Lymphoid-Nodular Hyperplasia, Non-specific Colitis, and Pervasive Developmental Disorder in Children*, 375 The Lancet 445 (2010).
[31] I further investigate these issues in Claudia E. Haupt, *Unprofessional Advice*, 19 U. Pa. J. Const. L. ___ (forthcoming 2017).

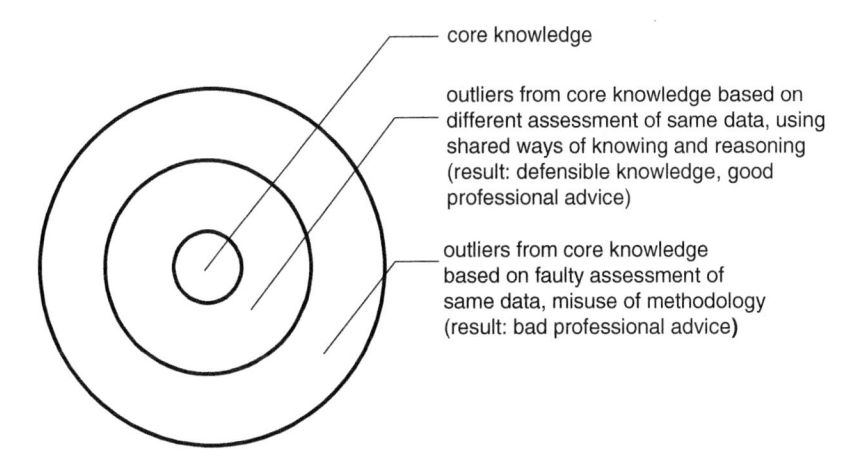

FIGURE 12.1 Internal Outliers (within the Knowledge Community)

here, the insight that there is a range of defensible knowledge that produces outliers within the knowledge community shall suffice.

B. *External Outliers and Religious Justifications*

External outliers base their divergence from professional consensus on exogenous reasons; often, their disagreement will be religiously motivated. But motivation and justification do not necessarily align. Outliers who justify their departure from professional knowledge in terms exogenous to professional discourse – such as religious outliers – must be distinguished from outliers who may have a religious disagreement with the profession, but who nonetheless purport to share the knowledge basis of the profession in promoting their views. The few remaining proponents of conversion therapy, for example, may have a religious disagreement with the knowledge community,[32] yet they ostensibly make their argument in terms of the shared knowledge basis.[33]

Whereas internal outliers' divergent assessments of shared knowledge can produce a range of valid professional opinions, external outliers' exogenous

---

[32] See, e.g., Benjamin Kaufman, *Why NARTH? The American Psychiatric Association's Destructive and Blind Pursuit of Political Correctness*, 14 Regent U.L. Rev. 423 (2002) ("When people are discriminated against on the basis of their religious beliefs or denied help that they believe is in their best interests, they need an advocate to defend their rights.").

[33] Id. (explicitly invoking the methodology of the profession: "Concerned that professional organizations and publications in the mental health field have fallen under the control of those who would use them to forward social constructionist theories, political agendas, and advocacy research, NARTH has fought for a return to established theoretical approaches, solid research, therapy that puts the patient first, and freedom to discuss, debate, and disagree.").

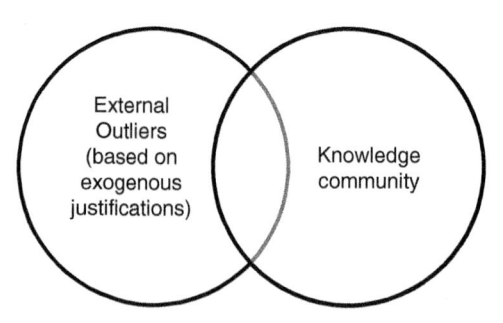

FIGURE 12.2 External Outliers

justifications for departure from the professional standards will generally place them outside of the knowledge community. It is useful to interrogate expectations toward professionals along two axes: the relationship between the knowledge community and the individual professional, and the professional–client relationship. My focus here will be on exogenous justifications, and in particular religious justifications, for outlier status.

i. The Relationship Between the Knowledge Community and the Professional
With respect to the professional's advice-giving function, the knowledge community's interest lies in having individual professionals render accurate, comprehensive advice. Correspondingly, the individual professional has an autonomy interest in communicating the message according to the standards of the profession to which she belongs.[34] It is this bond that is destroyed when professionals place themselves outside the knowledge community for exogenous reasons. In reciprocal fashion, the individual professional's interest lies in preserving the integrity of the knowledge community's insights just as the knowledge community's interest lies in having the individual professional communicate its insights correctly.

In light of these reciprocal interests, the knowledge community is the appropriate site for conscience-formation and negotiation of accommodation within the profession.[35] (In Figure 12.2, such justifications for departure from the professional standard would be located in the intersection.) There is a recognized concept of

---

[34] Haupt, supra note 5, at 1272.
[35] While I focus here on religious justifications for outlier status, I do not want to imply that only religious justifications will constitute an appropriate basis for negotiating the accommodation of conscience-based departures from professional knowledge. I am inclined to follow Kent Greenawalt's suggestion that "rights of conscience for individuals not to participate in health-care services should be formulated in terms that are not limited to religion." Greenawalt, supra note 6, at 53. The crucial point, however, is that the site of negotiation is located within the knowledge community.

"professional conscience."[36] The key here is that it is internal to the knowledge community. Elizabeth Sepper notes that "physicians' conscientious judgments must be rooted in shared professional norms." Resulting "conflicts manifest themselves between a patient's values and the values of the profession as a whole, rather than one doctor's values."[37] While there is no claim to superior competence regarding value judgments per se, the knowledge community is able to assess value judgments in light of their shared knowledge. Within its internal discourse, it can assess the effect of value judgments on professional knowledge and advice-giving by the individual professional. This tracks Sepper's observation that "each physician must seek to maintain professional integrity, not only personal beliefs. One's fellow physicians serve as a – or perhaps the – referent moral community."[38] As a result, justifications for outlier status should originate within professional norms and ethics.

A critic might object that this understanding places the membership in a profession above other constitutive aspects of a professional's identity. I do not mean to suggest that all other aspects of a professional's identity are secondary, and this is particularly true for the professional's religious beliefs. But the focus here is on the role of knowledge communities and the role of the advice-giving individual professional within the professional–client relationship. In this position as conduit between the knowledge community and the client, within the professional–client relationship, the individual rendering professional advice is a professional first.

The approach suggested here, while institutionalizing professional knowledge within the knowledge community, departs from other proposals that focus on institutional providers of health services. Some suggest that a sensible dividing line for allocating conscience exceptions might be drawn between nonreligious and religiously affiliated hospitals.[39] A possible defense of this line of reasoning "may arise from a sense that religious organizations are fundamental entities independent of the state, something that is not true about most nonreligious organizations created for providing services such as health care."[40] This distinction is plausible. But the view proposed here shifts the institutional focus to the professional's knowledge community as the site of conscience formation within the profession. Therefore, as long as a professional renders professional services, regardless of the institutional setting in which these services are provided (a religiously affiliated hospital or a nonreligious institution), she would be primarily bound by the ethics of her profession. As in the case of the individual professional, the professional rendering advice

---

[36] See, e.g., Elizabeth Sepper, *Doctoring Discrimination in the Same-Sex Marriage Debates*, 89 Ind. L.J. 703, 730–5 (2014) (discussing formation of professional conscience within medicine).
[37] Id. at 734.
[38] Id. at 735.
[39] See, e.g., Greenawalt, supra note 6, at 53.
[40] Id.

is a professional first. Consequently, the individual professional also has an interest in acting according to the tenets of her profession in relation to the institutional employer.[41]

ii. The Professional–Client Relationship

The professional–client relationship is typically characterized by an asymmetry of knowledge; the client seeks the professional's advice precisely because of this asymmetry. The very reason the professional's advice is valuable to the client is thus predicated on the knowledge the professional possesses and the client lacks.[42] The client's interests are only served if the professional communicates information that is accurate (under the knowledge community's current assessment), reliable, and personally tailored to the specific situation of the listener. To bridge the knowledge gap, and to ensure the protection of the client's decisional autonomy interests, the professional has to communicate all information necessary to make an informed decision to the client.[43] As Nadia Sawicki points out in this volume, "[w]hen patients seek health care services without knowing that the scope of available services is limited by an objecting provider or institution, those patients may be harmed in a variety of ways."[44] Viewed through a lens of public reason from the perspective of the client, the client's expectation is that the professional will not operate based on justifications that are not shared by the profession.

If the patient does not receive full information, she may not know what is being withheld, or even that any information is being withheld.[45] Furthermore, the client does not know what is contested professional knowledge and what is not. She may encounter a professional who, for religious reasons, will not provide advice on certain treatment options or medications. But the justification for these omissions will not be based on professional knowledge. In the spirit of public reason, the client must reasonably be able to expect that professional advice will be based upon reasons internal to the knowledge community rather than individual, exogenous justifications for departure.

Could this information deficit be cured by disclosure? The advice-giving professional could tell the client that the advice she dispenses is limited. Sawicki anchors

---

[41] See generally Elizabeth Sepper, *Taking Conscience Seriously*, 98 Va. L. Rev. 1501 (2012).
[42] See, e.g., *King v. Christie*, 767 F.3d 216, 232 (3d Cir. 2014) ("Licensed professionals, through their education and training, have access to a corpus of specialized knowledge that their clients usually do not. Indeed, the value of the professional's services stems largely from her ability to apply this specialized knowledge to a client's individual circumstances.").
[43] Haupt, supra note 5, at 29. The same point applies within the framework of informed consent doctrine, see Sawicki, supra note 18.
[44] Sawicki, supra note 18.
[45] See, e.g., Jill Morrison & Micole Allekotte, *Duty First: Towards Patient-Centered Care and Limitations on the Right to Refuse for Moral, Religious or Ethical Reasons*, 9 Ave Maria L. Rev. 141, 148–9 (2010).

such a requirement within the context of the informed consent doctrine.[46] The state might require that any professional whose advice departs from the knowledge community's insights due to exogenous justifications provide such a disclosure.[47] In principle, such disclosure will inform the client of the limited scope of professional advice. However, in practice, there is a significant filtering problem. Imagine a doctor informing a patient that, due to his faith, he will dispense only advice that is consistent with his faith. Even if the patient is of the same faith, it is at least questionable whether it will be obvious to her which advice is left out. Just as professional knowledge communities are not monolithic, faith communities are not monolithic. But even if disclosure puts the client on notice, the dissenting professional is still not communicating the full range of professional knowledge. Thus, a disclosure regime only partially cures the problem.

CONCLUSION

Conceptualizing the professions as knowledge communities provides a useful perspective. There are more nuances along the way, but, in the first instance, this is a helpful way to think about the relationship among professionals, knowledge communities, and their relationship to clients. Applied to the First Amendment context, this perspective gives guidance on a variety of issues, ranging from First Amendment protection of professional speech to religious accommodations of professionals' outlier status.

To the extent that the knowledge community decides that an individual professional's assessment is encompassed by the range of defensible professional knowledge, state regulation should mirror this. In the context of professional malpractice, such advice will be considered good professional advice. But to the extent that individual professionals depart from the insights of the knowledge community beyond what it considers within the scope of defensible professional knowledge, their advice will not be considered good professional advice. This chapter suggests that the dividing line reflects the common knowledge basis and shared notions of validity. The law thus should not accommodate objections to providing comprehensive and accurate professional advice by external outliers who do not share the common knowledge basis and engage in the same ways of knowing and reasoning, and who base their professional advice on extraneous justifications. This does not mean that

---

[46] Sawicki, supra note 18 (arguing that "the legal doctrine of informed consent is broad enough to encompass a duty to disclose conscience-based limitations on practice.").

[47] See, e.g., *Evergreen Ass'n, Inc. v. City of New York*, 740 F.3d 233 (2d Cir. 2014) (upholding certain mandatory disclosures for crisis pregnancy centers). See generally Caroline Mala Corbin, *Compelled Disclosures*, 65 Ala. L. Rev. 1277, 1340–51 (2014) (discussing compelled disclosures in crisis pregnancy centers).

the professional is prohibited from voicing his own opinion in public discourse, whether religious or secular. The free speech and free exercise clauses of the First Amendment provide robust protection of that right. But the professional will speak as an individual in those instances, not as an advice-giving member of the profession within the professional–client relationship.

13

A Common Law Duty to Disclose Conscience-Based Limitations on Medical Practice

Nadia N. Sawicki

Legal and ethical doctrines of informed consent require that physicians disclose to their patients material information about the treatment options that may be medically appropriate for them. And although the fact that a physician has religious or conscience-based limitations on the types of treatments he is willing to provide certainly seems material to a patient's understanding of her treatment options, American courts have not yet had the opportunity to consider whether such information falls within the scope of the common law informed consent disclosure duty. As a result, patients seeking treatment from providers with conscientious limitations on care[1] (or by providers who practice within institutions that impose such limitations) may lack the information necessary to exercise their right to decide what care to receive and from whom, and may consequently suffer serious health consequences.

In this chapter, I argue that the legal doctrine of informed consent is broad enough to encompass a duty to disclose conscience-based limitations on practice. Common law precedent in some jurisdictions has imposed upon physicians a duty to disclose personal characteristics that may affect the risks of treatment or the patient's choice of providers, as well as personal (typically financial) conflicts that may affect the physician's medical judgment. In cases where personal beliefs or institutional limitations restrict the types of treatments a provider can offer to his patients, both of these concerns are implicated.

Judicial recognition of a common law duty to disclose conscience-based limitations on practice would benefit patients by allowing them to recover damages when they are injured as a result of a physician's failure to timely disclose a medically appropriate treatment option that he (or the treatment facility) opposes on conscience grounds, and would encourage providers to be more forthright about their limitations on practice. Commentators have long argued that physicians have an

---

[1] Limitations on medical practice may be motivated by either religious or nonreligious conscience-based beliefs; the analysis herein applies to both.

ethical obligation to disclose their conscientious objections to patients;[2] this chapter proposes that there may be an enforceable legal obligation as well.

1. SCOPE OF THE PROBLEM

Many health care providers – both individual and institutional – maintain deeply held religious or conscientious commitments that prohibit them from offering certain forms of medical treatment.[3] In the context of reproductive care, for example, providers may express objections to contraception, emergency contraception, abortion, tubal ligation, or prenatal genetic testing. Other providers may object to treatments in the end-of-life care context, such as withholding or withdrawal of life-sustaining treatment, the provision of futile care, palliative sedation, or physician aid-in-dying (in those states where it is legal). Some health care providers may also object on complicity grounds to less direct forms of cooperation, such as providing factual information about controversial medical treatments.

A wide spectrum of federal and state laws give legal protection to providers and institutions with conscientious objections to treatment, particularly in the abortion context.[4] However, legal protections for refusal to provide information are less

---

[2] See, e.g., Armand H. Matheny Antommaria, *Conscientious Objection in Clinical Practice: Notice, Informed Consent, Referral, and Emergency Treatment*, 9 Ave Maria L. Rev. 81 (2010–11); T.A. Cavanaugh, *Professional Conscientious Objection in Medicine with Attention to Referral*, 9 Ave Maria L. Rev. 189 (2010–11); Patrick A. Tully, *Morally Objectionable Options: Informed Consent and Physician Integrity*, 8 Nat'l Cath. Bioethics Quarterly 491, 491–504 (2008); Rosalind Ekman Ladd, *Some Reflections on Conscience*, Am. J. Bioethics (19 December 2007), at 32; Edmund D. Pellegrino, *Value Neutrality, Moral Integrity, and the Physician*, 28 J.L. Med. & Ethics 78 (2000); Sylvia A. Law, *Silent No More: Physicians' Legal and Ethical Obligations to Patients Seeking Abortions*, 21 N.Y.U. Rev. L. & Soc. Change 279, 304 (1994). See also Am. Med. Ass'n, Opinion 1.1.7, Physician Exercise of Conscience, *Code of Medical Ethics* (Chicago, Ill.: American Medical Association, 2016) (requiring that physicians disclose to potential patients any interventions they cannot in good conscience provide).

[3] This chapter focuses exclusively on objections to medical treatments that are both (i) legal and (ii) within the legally acceptable standard of care (and thus medically appropriate) in the context of a given patient condition. The disclosure duties proposed herein would apply only to providers who a reasonable patient might expect to offer information or access to the treatment in question (for example, a gerontologist would not be required to disclose his conscientious objection to emergency contraception, but would likely be required to disclose his opposition to palliative sedation at the end of life). For more detail on these limitations, see Nadia N. Sawicki, *Mandating Disclosure of Conscience-Based Limitations on Medical Practice*, 42 Am. J. L. & Med. 85, 89–91 (legality and standard of care), 105 (provider context) (2016).

[4] Applicable federal laws include the Church Amendment, 42 U.S.C. §300a-7 (protecting providers and institutions with religious or moral objections to sterilization or abortion); the Weldon Amendment, Pub. L. 114–113, Consolidated Appropriations Act, Sec. 507(d) of Title V of Division H (protecting providers and institutions that refuse to provide, pay for, or refer for abortions); 42 U.S.C. §238n (protecting providers and institutions that refuse to provide, train in, or refer for abortions); 42 U.S.C. §18113 (protecting providers and institutions that refuse to participate in assisted suicide); and 18 U.S.C.

well-established than for refusal to provide controversial care directly – only some broadly drafted state conscience laws protect providers from liability if they claim a conscientious objection to the provision of medical information about controversial treatments.[5]

Evidence suggests that providers and institutions whose clinical practices are limited for reasons of conscience often fail to make patients aware of these limitations. A 2000 public opinion survey, for example, found that many patients are unaware that religiously affiliated health care facilities, by virtue of their religious commitments, are limited in the treatments they able to offer.[6] Forty-five percent of women surveyed said that they *would expect to receive* "medical services or procedures that are contrary to Catholic religious beliefs" if they went to a Catholic hospital, and an additional 23 percent said that they *did not know* whether to expect such services.[7] Of the 32 percent of women surveyed who *did expect* Catholic hospitals to limit access to treatment, many failed to accurately identify the types of treatments that might be restricted on the basis of religious teachings.[8] A recent *New York Times* article about hospital mergers provides further evidence of this gap in patient knowledge, concluding that when secular hospitals affiliate with Catholic health care institutions, "[t]he restrictions [on care] at any given hospital may not be clear."[9] Given that a substantial portion of American health care is provided at Catholic or Catholic-affiliated health care institutions, these figures are worthy of concern.

Even outside religiously affiliated health care facilities, limitations on the provision of controversial services are often not obvious, even to the providers practicing within those facilities. In a 2010 survey of obstetricians and gynecologists, many respondents reported that practice restrictions on the provision of abortion were not

---

§3597 (protecting providers with religious or moral objections to participation in capital punishment). See also Thaddeus Mason Pope, *Legal Briefing: Conscience Clauses and Conscientious Refusal*, 21 J. Clinical Ethics 163 (2010) (describing state and federal conscience laws in a variety of contexts).

[5] Laws that protect health care providers who refuse to "recommend," "counsel," "suggest," "advise," or "provide information" about controversial procedures include La. Rev. Stat. Ann. 40:1299.31; S.C. Code Ann. § 44-41-50(a) and (b); 745 Ill. Comp. Stat. Ann. 70/6; Mo. Ann. Stat. § 197.032; Mont. Code Ann. § 50-20-111(2); Or. Rev. Stat. Ann. § 435.485(1); Colo. Rev. Stat. Ann. 25-6-102(9); Ark. Code. Ann. 20-16-304(5); Fla. Stat. Ann. 381.0051(5). However, given the varying interpretations of these terms, it can be difficult to discern precisely what kind of behavior is protected by law.

[6] *Religion, Reproductive Health and Access to Services: A National Survey of Women* (Belden Russonello & Stewart, April 2000) (survey of 1,000 women over 18).

[7] Id. at 13.

[8] While 62% expected limitations on access to abortion and 42% expected limited access to birth control, only 6% identified the morning-after pill as a restricted service, 3% identified sterilization, and 1% identified physician aid-in-dying. Id. at 14.

[9] Reed Abelson, *Catholic Hospitals Expand, Religious Strings Attached*, N.Y. Times (February 20, 2012), available at www.nytimes.com/2012/02/21/health/policy/growth-of-catholic-hospitals-may-limit-access-to-reproductive-care.html [https://perma.cc/JRC7-XQQ2].

made clear to them at the time of their hiring.[10] These implicit and explicit institutional practice restrictions, according to the study's authors, were grounded not only in ideological opposition, but also "fear [of] loss of business due to the stigma and controversy that may surround abortion provision[.]"[11] If a physician choosing to join a health care practice is unaware of institutional limitations on reproductive services within that practice, surely patients are in no better position to discover this information.

When patients seek health care services without knowing that the scope of available services is limited by an objecting provider or institution, those patients may be harmed in a variety of ways. At the most basic level, a patient choosing among different providers is harmed when information about the services those providers do or do not offer is not made available to her. A patient receiving care from a provider who objects on grounds of conscience to a specific form of treatment may never be aware that such a treatment exists, that the treatment might be medically appropriate, or that it is available from other providers without conscience-based limitations on practice. Delays in accessing care as a result of a provider or institution's conscientious refusal to provide information or services can range from mere inconvenience to serious adverse health outcomes, particularly in the reproductive care setting.

In the context of emergency contraceptives that need to be taken within 72 hours of unprotected intercourse to be effective, a provider's refusal to recommend emergency contraception as an option (or a pharmacist's refusal to dispense it) may make it impossible for a woman to avoid unintended pregnancy. For patients seeking abortions in states that restrict access to second- and third-trimester abortions, time is of the essence, and a refusing provider or one who declines to provide relevant information about the availability of abortion can mean the difference between the woman being able to legally obtain an abortion or not. In Catholic hospitals that oppose sterilization on religious grounds, women undergoing cesarean deliveries cannot schedule a concurrent tubal ligation; but because many women choosing to deliver at Catholic hospitals may not know about this limitation,[12] they are subject to increased risks of medical complications associated with a second surgery at a later date and with a different physician.[13]

---

[10] Lori Freedman et al., *Obstacles to the Integration of Abortion into Obstetrics and Gynecology Practice*, 42 Persp. Sexual & Reprod. Health 146, 148–9 (2010) (qualitative interviews with 30 obstetricians and gynecologists).

[11] Id. at 150.

[12] See generally Reed Abelson, *Catholic Hospitals Expand, Religious Strings Attached*, N.Y. Times (February. 20, 2012), at A1 (discussing restrictions on care, including tubal ligation, at Catholic hospitals and their affiliates).

[13] See, e.g., Debra B. Stulberg et al., *Tubal Ligation in Catholic Hospitals: A Qualitative Study of Ob-gyns' Experiences*, 90 Contraception 422 (2014) (surveying physicians at Catholic hospitals that

Finally, for women with miscarriages or life-threatening pregnancies, an objecting provider or one who fails to accurately describe the scope of medical options can result in life-threatening complications. According to a report by the National Women's Law Center, when unstable patients are miscarrying, "immediate uterine evacuation reduces the patient's risk of complications, including blood loss, hemorrhage, infection, and the loss of future fertility," and delays in treatment may result in "unnecessary blood transfusions, risk of infection, hysterectomy or even death."[14] Many physicians working in Catholic-owned hospitals report that hospital policies on miscarriage management have interfered with their medical judgment in cases where termination of pregnancy or uterine evacuation is considered the medical standard of care.[15] Patients who are unaware of these institutional policies may, therefore, be harmed if they choose to seek obstetric care at a Catholic hospital rather than a secular one.[16]

To cite just one example,[17] consider the case of Tamesha Means, a pregnant woman whose water broke at 18 weeks and was sent home twice from the hospital without being informed that her pregnancy was not viable and that the best medical option would be to induce labor and terminate the pregnancy.[18] While Ms. Means was waiting to be discharged, she developed an acute infection resulting from the premature rupture of her amniotic membranes, and delivered a breech baby that

> prohibit simultaneous cesarean delivery and tubal ligation, requiring patients to undergo "unnecessary subsequent surgery" and be put at risk of later unwanted pregnancy).

[14] Nat'l Women's Law Ctr., Below the Radar: Health Care Providers' Religious Refusals Can Endanger Pregnant Women's Lives and Health (Jan 2011).

[15] Id. at 2; Angel M. Foster, Amanda Dennis, & Fiona Smith, *Do Religious Restrictions Influence Ectopic Pregnancy Management? A National Qualitative Study*, 21 Women's Health Issues 104 (2011); Lori R. Freedman, Uta Landy, and Jody Steinauer, *When There's a Heartbeat: Miscarriage Management in Catholic-Owned Hospitals*, 98 Am. J. Pub. Health 1774 (2008).

[16] Dr. Jacob M. Appel, a physician, attorney, and bioethicist, recently wrote,

> [a]t the present moment, as a physician, I would not feel comfortable with a woman I cared about seeking obstetric services at a Catholic hospital ... From this point forward, I will tell my pregnant patients, in all but the most emergent and high-risk circumstances, to instruct any ambulance that picks them up to avoid Catholic hospitals.

> Jacob M. Appel, *After St. Joseph's: Are Women Still Safe in Catholic Hospitals?*, Huffington Post (May 16, 2010), available at www.huffingtonpost.com/jacob-m-appel/after-st-josephs-are-wome_b_578086.html [https://perma.cc/LDH2-A2BJ].

[17] For other examples in the media, see Sawicki, supra note 3, at 96.

[18] Compl., *Means v. U.S. Conference of Catholic Bishops*, No. 2:13-cv-14916 (E.D. Mich. Nov. 29, 2013) (hereinafter Means Complaint). Means' lawsuit, which was brought against the U.S Conference of Catholic Bishops and the Catholic Health Ministries (rather than against the hospital or providers), was dismissed for lack of personal jurisdiction and failure to state a claim. Op., Means (E.D. Mich. June 30, 2015). The court held that the doctrine of ecclesiastical abstention prohibited adjudication of the claim, but noted that Means could pursue a remedy against the health care providers for medical negligence. Id.

survived less than three hours. In her complaint, Ms. Means alleged that the hospital's failure to inform her of her medical options was a violation of the medical standard of care, causing her serious injuries, including severe pain, increased medical risk during delivery, and emotional trauma. Additional lawsuits against Catholic health care institutions are pending on similar grounds – in October 2015, for example, the ACLU filed suit against Trinity Health Corporation, one of the largest Catholic health care systems in the United States, for its practices in treating miscarrying patients.[19] The lawsuit alleges that Trinity violated EMTALA and the Rehabilitation Act when it refused to terminate the pregnancies of five women whose amniotic sacs had broken prematurely, and who consequently suffered sepsis, hemorrhaging, life-threatening infections, and severe pain.

2. INFORMED CONSENT DOCTRINE

Patients suffer consequences like those just described because there is currently no well-established legal duty on the part of providers or institutions to disclose the nature of their conscientious objections, the limitations on the types of treatment they provide, or the fact that their discussion of medical options may exclude treatment options that other providers would consider medically appropriate. With very limited exceptions,[20] federal and state conscience laws do not impose such disclosure obligations. And there have, to date, been no judicial decisions resolving the issue of whether providers who fail to disclose that their scope of practice is restricted as a result of their conscientious beliefs might be subject to tort liability.[21] However, a careful examination of the common law doctrine of informed consent suggests that – at least in some jurisdictions – a patient injured by her provider's nondisclosure would have a viable claim for tort recovery.

The physician's legal duty to obtain informed consent has been well-established since the 1960s and '70s. To prevail in a typical informed consent action, a patient must demonstrate that (1) her physician breached a duty to disclose a material risk associated with a medical procedure; (2) a reasonable patient would more likely than not have made a different medical decision had she known of the undisclosed risk; (3) the patient suffered a compensable injury as a result of her decision; and (4) the patient's injury was in fact caused by the undisclosed risk.

---

[19] Compl., *ACLU v. Trinity Health*, Case No. 15-cv-12611 (E.D. Mich. October 1, 2015).
[20] See Sawicki, supra note 3, at 103-4 (discussing the federal Patient Self-Determination Act and state laws requiring health care facilities to disclose end-of-life care policies).
[21] One court has allowed a malpractice claim to proceed against a hospital that failed (for unspecified reasons) to provide information about emergency contraception to a rape victim. See *Brownfield v. Daniel Freeman Marina Hospital*, 208 Cal. App. 3d. 405 (Cal. Ct. App. 1989).

Although the scope of the physician's duty to disclose varies depending on the state in which he practices,[22] courts in all jurisdictions have effectively agreed on a set of disclosures considered material to an informed medical decision: this includes information about the patient's diagnosis and prognosis; about the proposed treatment and its risks and benefits; about alternative treatments and their risks and benefits; and about the risks and benefits of taking no action (hereafter referred to as the "standard risk-and-benefit disclosure").

Historically, the standard risk-and-benefit disclosure has included only *medical* information relevant to the patient's treatment decision.[23] In recent years, however, some courts and legislatures have expanded the disclosure duty to include facts beyond those traditionally designated as medically material – such as information about the physician's personal characteristics and financial conflicts of interest, information about social support resources available to patients, and information reflecting social or moral judgments. In those cases where courts have expanded informed consent disclosure requirements beyond purely medical facts, two common justifications are offered. First, courts have recognized that a physician's personal characteristics may be material to a patient's decision to seek treatment from another provider, particularly where those characteristics increase the risk of negative medical outcomes for the patient. Second, some courts have held that physicians have an obligation to disclose conflicts of interest, unknown to the patient, that may affect their medical judgment or treatment recommendations. In the case of physicians whose religious or conscientious convictions cause them to limit their scope of practice or the types of medical treatments they will recommend, both justifications are implicated.

A. Physician Characteristics, Medical Risks, and Treatment Alternatives

Under the standard risk-and-benefit disclosure, physicians are required to discuss not only the treatments they recommend, but also the availability (and risks and benefits) of alternative treatments. Accordingly, some courts have held that the common law informed consent duty requires disclosure of physician-specific information – such as information about the provider's experience, physical limitations, or personal history – when it is material to the patient's evaluation of treatment alternatives. Where a physician's conscientious beliefs preclude him from offering treatments that other providers might deem medically appropriate, the common law

---

[22] Jurisdictions are evenly divided between a patient-based standard and a physician-based standard for identifying the information that must be disclosed as part of the informed consent process. Barry Furrow et al., *Health Law* (Second Edition) (West, 2000), at 314.

[23] See generally Nadia N. Sawicki, *Modernizing Informed Consent: Expanding the Boundaries of Materiality*, 2016 U. Ill. L. Rev. 821 (2016).

duty to disclose the existence of medically appropriate alternatives would seem to require – at the very least – a disclosure that alternative treatments not offered by the patient's physician might be available elsewhere.

In *Johnson v. Kokemoor*, the most prominent case supporting disclosure of physician-specific characteristics, a patient who was rendered quadriplegic after surgery brought an informed consent claim on the grounds that her physician, Dr. Kokemoor, "failed ... to divulge the extent of his experience in performing this type of operation [basilar bifurcation aneurysm surgery]."[24] A jury found for the patient after the trial court admitted evidence that Dr. Kokemoor failed to accurately disclose how often he had performed this procedure, and failed to discuss the comparative risks of seeking treatment from a more experienced surgeon. The Wisconsin Supreme Court upheld the trial court's decision to admit this evidence, holding that "a reasonable person in the plaintiff's position would have considered such information material in making an intelligent and informed decision about the surgery."[25] The court emphasized that Wisconsin's common law doctrine of informed consent requires disclosure of "all of the viable [treatment] alternatives," and framed the issue of Dr. Kokemoor's experience as relevant to the patient's evaluation of alternative treatments.[26]

Courts in other states have also held that information about a provider's experience may need to be disclosed where those facts suggest that there might be an increased risk of injury or that the patient's interests might be better served by seeking care from another provider.[27] In *Barriocanal v. Gibbs*, for example, the Delaware Supreme Court held that the trial court erred in excluding evidence that the physician failed to inform his patient of his lack of recent experience performing aneurysm surgery, and of the option of having the surgery at a teaching hospital instead.[28] The court described the information about the physician's qualifications as going "'to the very heart' of the plaintiff's [informed consent] case" given the Delaware informed consent law's requirement that health care providers disclose "the risks and alternatives to treatment or diagnosis which a reasonable patient would consider material to the decision whether or not to undergo the treatment or diagnosis."[29]

[24] *Johnson v. Kokemoor*, 545 N.W.2d 495, 497 (Wis. 1996).
[25] Id. at 505.
[26] Id. at 498.
[27] See, e.g., *DeGenarro v. Tandon*, 873 A.2d 191 (Conn. App. 2005) (holding that provider's lack of experience with dental equipment must be disclosed if it adds to the risk of the procedure); *Barriocanal v. Gibbs*, 697 A.2d 1169 (Del.1997). See also *Goldberg v. Boone*, 912 A.2d 698 (MD 2006) (holding that the jury must determine whether the availability of a more experienced surgeon was material for the purposes of informed consent); *Wlosinski v. Cohn*, 713 N.W. 2d 16, 20, n. 1 (Ct. App. Mich. 2005) (rejecting an expanded disclosure duty, but limiting its holding to "statistical data ... and other background information that has no concrete bearing on the actual risks of a given procedure.").
[28] *Barriocanal v. Gibbs*, 697 A.2d 1169 (Del.1997).
[29] Id. at 1173.

Courts have also suggested that physicians have a duty to disclose other personal characteristics where those characteristics might increase the risk of patient harm. For example, a surgeon may be required to share information about his own health status if it could negatively affect his performance in the operating room.[30] Likewise, while the common law doctrine of informed consent does not generally require that a physician disclose a history of substance abuse, courts have suggested that there may be a duty to disclose such a history where the physician's treatment of the patient actually occurs under the influence of drugs or alcohol, or otherwise results in conduct falling below the standard of care – again, recognizing that a personal characteristic about the physician may translate into a medically material risk for the patient.[31]

That said, many courts consider disclosure of a physician's personal characteristics – even those that increase medical risks to patients – to be outside the traditional scope of informed consent, as they speak to risks that are provider-dependent rather than "inherent in the treatment."[32] However, because the ultimate goal of the consent process is to protect patients' rights to evaluate the medical risks and benefits of various treatments, the more reasonable interpretation of informed consent doctrine would require disclosure of physician-specific characteristics that are likely to change the medical risks associated with a given treatment. Where a physician's personal beliefs or conscience-based limitations on practice affect the possible physiological risks of receiving treatment from that provider, disclosure would be well within the requirements of the standard medical risk-and-benefit disclosure.

In addition to potentially increasing the risk of medical harm to patients, a physician's conscience-based limitations on practice clearly implicate the requirement that physicians disclose medically appropriate treatment alternatives as part of the informed consent process. As noted above, some state conscience laws appear to

[30] See, e.g., *Hawk v. Chattanooga Orthopaedic Grp.*, 45 S.W.3d 24 (Tenn. Ct. App. 2000) (allowing informed consent claim where surgeon failed to inform patient of a disabling hand condition). See also *Slutzki v. Grabenstetter*, 2002 WL 31114657 (Iowa Ct. App. 2002) (unpublished) (finding that surgeon had no duty to disclose that she suffered from a herniated disc where that condition was not aggravated by the position of the operating table); *May v. Cusick*, 630 N.W.2d 277 (Wisc. App. 2001) (unpublished) (finding no duty to disclose history of stroke where there was no evidence that physician suffered residual effects that would constitute a material risk).

[31] See, e.g., *Hidding v. Williams*, 578 So.2d 1192 (La. App. 1991) (upholding trial court's finding that failure to disclose chronic alcohol use was a breach of the informed consent duty, where the physician "abused alcohol at the time of [plaintiff's] surgery," and an expert testified that a physician suffering from alcohol dependence should disclose this fact); *Williams v. Booker*, 310 Ga. App. 209, 211–12 (Ga. App. 2012) (holding that a physician's history of addiction is relevant in a malpractice case where the addiction "translates into conduct falling below the applicable standard of care[.]'"). See also *Mau v. Wisconsin Patients Compensation Fund*, 668 N.W.2d 562 (Wisc. App. 2003) (unpublished) (denying an informed consent claim where a doctor with a history of substance abuse had not been using drugs recently, and was not operating under the influence at the time of the operation).

[32] See Sawicki, supra note 3, at 114; Sawicki, supra note 23, at 832, 845-6.

override this common law duty by insulating physicians from tort liability if they choose not to provide patients with medical information about specific treatments they consider morally objectionable. However, these conscience laws do not negate a patient's common law right to know that alternative treatments do exist. As I have argued elsewhere, the common law obligation to inform patients about treatment alternatives would seem to require – even in states with the strongest conscience protections – that a physician disclose (even in the most general terms) the fact that there exist other medically appropriate treatment alternatives beyond those that he chooses to offer.[33] Under this limited disclosure model, the provider would be required to reveal that while an objectionable intervention exists (by either referencing the intervention by name, or by speaking generally), it is not available due to the provider's or institution's conscientious objection.

Thus, inasmuch as a physician's conscientious or religious beliefs and concomitant limitations on practice may increase the risk of medical harm to patients, or eliminate treatment options that might be available to the patient elsewhere, such information ought to be disclosed. Even under conservative interpretations of common law informed consent doctrine, knowledge of these limitations would certainly be medically material when the patient is choosing between various treatment options and providers.

B. Physician Interests Affecting Medical Judgment

Some courts have also concluded that physicians have a common law duty to disclose facts about their personal interests where those interests are likely to affect their medical judgment or treatment recommendations. These cases typically arise in the context of financial conflicts. In *Moore v. Regents of the University of California*, for example, the California Supreme Court considered a suit against a physician who provided ongoing treatment to a patient without disclosing that he had financial incentives to develop and sell a lucrative cell line derived from the patient's tissue. The court held that, in order to satisfy the duty of informed consent, a physician "must ... disclose personal interests unrelated to the patient's health, whether research or economic, that may affect his medical judgment."[34] Similarly, a Minnesota appellate court in another financial conflict case described a physician's failure to disclose a drug kickback scheme as "a classic informed consent issue," writing that it is "well accepted that patients deserve medical opinions about treatment plans and referrals unsullied by conflicting motives."[35] And while courts have

---

[33] Sawicki, supra note 3, at 102–106.
[34] *Moore v. Regents of the Univ. of Cal.*, 793 P.2d 479, 485 (Cal. 1990).
[35] *DAB v. Brown*, 570 N.W.2d 168, 170–71 (Minn. Ct App 1997).

generally been unreceptive to financial conflict of interest cases when framed as fiduciary duty claims, they have recognized that such suits can proceed on informed consent, traditional malpractice, or other grounds.[36]

Many commentators in health law and ethics support the expansion of common law disclosure duties to include personal interests beyond financial ones.[37] Howard Brody, for example, advocates for a "transparency model" of informed consent, in which disclosure is adequate only if "the physician's basic thinking has been rendered transparent to the patient."[38] Rather than requiring a standardized disclosure of risks and benefits, the physician would instead be required to explain her decision-making process and the factors she considered in making a recommendation. This conversation would certainly include discussion of the medical risks and benefits of various treatments, but would likely also include some nonmedical information, such as factors personal to the treating physician that would affect the treatment options offered.

When a physician's religious or conscientious beliefs impact her practice and treatment recommendations, being transparent about those influences on medical judgment would be consistent with the principles of informed consent. And to the extent that some courts have recognized that physicians have a duty to disclose financial conflicts of interest and other "personal interests ... that may affect ... medical judgment," disclosure of deeply held conscientious beliefs that affect a physician's medical judgment and treatment recommendations would be a natural extension of this reasoning.

CONCLUSION

The argument that a physician's failure to disclose his conscience-based limitations on practice might be a violation of the legal duty to obtain informed consent is one that has not yet been tested in the courts. And while the precedents described earlier

---

[36] See Sawicki, supra note 3, at 109–10 (discussing *Neade v. Portes*, 739 N.E.2d. 496 (Ill. 2000) and others).

[37] See, e.g., Mark G. Kuczewski, *Talking About Spirituality in the Clinical Setting: Can Being Professional Require Being Personal?*, Am. J. Bioethics (10 July 2007), at 4, 9 (arguing that clinicians, in the informed consent process, should "make clear the values that are guiding their recommendations," referring to cultural and spiritual values); Francoise Baylis & Jocelyn Downie, *Professional Recommendations: Disclosing Facts and Values*, 27 J. Med. Ethics 20, 21 (2001) (arguing that physicians' duty to render their reasoning transparent requires disclosure of both "factual-informational details and value judgments"); Marjorie Maguire Shultz, *From Informed Consent to Patient Choice: A New Protected Interest*, 95 Yale L.J. 219, 274 (1985) (noting that "decisions made in a climate of conflicting values or judgments are every bit as consequential as those made when there are [financial] conflicts of interest").

[38] Howard Brody, *Transparency: Informed Consent in Primary Care*, Hastings Ctr. Rep. (September–October 1989), at 5, 7.

would support such a conclusion, it is worth recognizing some jurisdictions still maintain an extremely narrow view of the scope of informed consent disclosure.[39] Thus, not every situation of nondisclosure of conscientious objection would be captured by a common law disclosure duty. That said, many commentators agree that the legal duty of disclosure should be expanded to include some nonmedical information, and the recent trend towards expansion of informed consent duties in some jurisdictions suggests that this may be the direction in which American common law is headed.

However, expanding the scope of informed consent duties and imposing tort liability on providers who fail to disclose their conscientious limitations on practice is not the only solution. As a practical matter, perhaps a better way of ensuring that patients are aware when they enter bounded treatment relationships is to impose a statutory disclosure duty on *institutions* that employ physicians with conscientious limitations on practice, or that maintain institutional limitations on practice grounded in religious commitments.[40] This option would ease concerns about expanding individual providers' liability, particularly in cases where the limitations are institutional and not personal.

In the absence of a movement for statutory change, however, it is worth considering the possibility of using common law informed consent principles to establish such a disclosure duty. Informed consent doctrine is the foundational mechanism through which American common law implements and enforces ethical principles of patient autonomy, and is thus an appropriate remedy for patients who are injured as a result of a physician's nondisclosure of his conscience-based limitations on medical practice.

---

[39] See Sawicki, supra note 3, at 114, n.142 (limitations of medical materiality) and 105, n. 89 (limitations based on the type of medical intervention offered). Note that while jurisdictions that follow a physician-based standard of disclosure may be viewed as less likely to accept an expansion of the common law duty, even states with physician-based standards rely on patient-centered language in explaining the concept of materiality. Sawicki, supra note 23, at 835-6.

[40] See generally Sawicki, supra note 3, at 126–27; Nadia N. Sawicki, *Religious Hospitals and Patient Choice*, Hastings Ctr. Rep. (November-December 2016).

PART V

The Impact of Religious Objections on the Health and Health Care of Others

Introduction

Richard H. Fallon Jr.

The topic of The Impact of Religious Objections on the Health and Health Care of Others involves a tangle of statutory and constitutional issues as well as pressing concerns of legal policy and fairness. The largest swathe of legal issues arises at the intersection of the Affordable Care Act (ACA) and the Religious Freedom Restoration Act (RFRA). Under the ACA, covered employers must provide health care benefits to their employees. But RFRA creates an exception for parties for whom compliance would constitute a substantial burden on religious freedom unless the government can demonstrate that not excusing them is "the least restrictive" means of promoting a "compelling" interest. From both a legal and a policy perspective, highly fraught issues emerge when recognition of a legally mandated accommodation for religious objectors – sparing them the need to provide or cooperate with the provision of coverage for contraceptives – would harm women's interests in obtaining health care.

To answer the resulting questions requires interpretations of both the ACA (and its surrounding regulations) and RFRA. Barely in the background, however, stand possible commands and prohibitions issuing from the Establishment Clause. So do practical considerations of fairness, respect for conscience, and public policy in protecting women's health. My principal aim in this short introduction will be to frame some of the relevant issues and identify some connections among them.

The first question involves when an employer can claim that compliance with a statutory directive to furnish health care or facilitate the government in ensuring its availability would constitute a substantial burden on religious freedom. In *Hobby Lobby*,[1] the Supreme Court determined that a statutory obligation to fund access to contraceptives can rise to the level of a substantial burden. But it is a further question whether, and if so when, an employer can claim a substantial burden if

[1] *Burwell v. Hobby Lobby Stores, Inc.*, 134 S. Ct. 2751 (2014).

required to take other, lesser steps that the employer claims would render him, her, or it "complicit" in religiously forbidden activities.

In her chapter in this part, *Conscientious Objection, Complicity, and Accommodation*, Amy J. Sepinwall argues for giving great weight to a religious objector's subjective sense of complicity when identifying substantial burdens.[2] There is a deep connection, she argues, between the claims of conscience and people's sense of self. People can feel conscientiously obliged to avoid implication in wrongs "to which they bear only a tenuous connection." And in accommodating claims of conscience, there is no plausible alternative to allowing each individual to report what his or her conscience dictates, Sepinwall writes.

This is a powerful point, in response to which I would offer just one observation. For better or for worse, the Supreme Court insists that standing to claim legal rights depends on injury and that what counts as injury has a factual element for which psychic distress will not suffice.[3] If the Court adheres to this position (as it has for approaching fifty years), lines would need to be drawn on some basis between senses of complicity that are sufficiently objectively reasonable to underlie claims of injury and purely psychological senses of complicity that are not.

A second main issue in contemporary debates is whether third-party burdens matter to the narrow tailoring inquiry. We can begin by identifying relatively polar positions. One view would be that a governmental mandate cannot constitute the least restrictive means of promoting compelling governmental ends if it imposes any cognizable burdens on third parties. At the other pole would be the view that the law – including the Establishment Clause – is utterly indifferent to third-party burdens: it may forbid the imposition of some burdens on directly regulated parties (such as, for example, through mandates that employers undertake expensive measures to accommodate their employees' wish to practice their religions), but it is unconcerned with burdens on nonregulated third parties.

Professor Sepinwall appears equivocal at several points but concludes her summary of current law by writing that "the doctrine does not require courts to attend to third-party interests." In her view, this state of affairs is "deeply troubling." In response, she proposes that the government should bear a duty to make a good faith effort to alert third parties affected by a lawsuit seeking an exemption, and then should fund those third parties' legal representation.

In their chapter, entitled *How Much May Religious Accommodations Burden Others?*, Professors Nelson Tebbe, Micah Schwartzman, and Richard Schragger also seek to carve out a middle position.[4] Although they maintain that "[a]n absolute

---

[2] Ch. 14, this volume.
[3] See, e.g., *Spokeo, Inc. v. Robins*, 136 S. Ct. 1540, 1547–9 (2016); Richard H. Fallon, Jr., *The Fragmentation of Standing*, 93 Tex. L. Rev. 1061, 1066–7 (2015).
[4] Ch. 15, this volume.

bar on third-party harms would generate absurd results," they insist that it would be equally absurd to conclude that the imposition of excessively large harms would not violate the Establishment Clause. Seeking a golden mean, they argue for adaptation of the "undue hardship" test that courts have used to measure the limits of Title VII's demand that employers make "reasonable" accommodations for religiously motivated employees.

The attractiveness of this position depends on the desirability of context-sensitive standards – such as an "undue hardship" test – in comparison with hard-edged rules that would either permit no burdens or ignore all possible burdens on third parties. Tebbe, Schwartzman, and Schragger locate themselves decisively both in the pro-standards camp and in a cohort that seeks a substantive middle ground in protecting religious conscience, enforcing the Establishment Clause, and protecting women's health.

Robin Fretwell Wilson's chapter, *Unpacking the Relationship Between Conscience and Access*, also aspires to finding a middle ground, but with a focus on policy issues rather than issues of legal interpretation.[5] Her main example involves religious exemptions for doctors and hospitals that object to performing abortions. Based on an informative examination of differently structured, complete or partial exemptions for religious objectors, Professor Wilson groups them into three categories. Some have the effect of impeding women's access to abortion. But some exemption policies, she argues, actually improve the public's overall access to health care since, without them, some service-providers would exit the health care field altogether. And some partial or qualified exemptions, in her estimation, turn out to be "access-neutral," because nonobjecting care providers are almost always available.

Professor Wilson's survey leaves her hopeful about the availability of win-win solutions, or at least the avoidance of zero-sum games in which protection for claims of religious conscience results in burdens on women seeking health care, or vice versa. Accordingly, she lauds the Supreme Court's decision in *Zubik v. Burwell*, in which "the Court gave an over-arching instruction: agree on how religious organizations can 'do nothing more than contract for a plan that does not include coverage for some or all forms of contraception,' while women receive seamless 'cost-free contraceptive coverage from the same insurance company.'"[6] As Wilson recognizes, "the parties' differences may yet prove unbridgeable," but she appears optimistic.

Looking beyond *Zubik*, how hopeful ought she, and others who seek a middle ground in the collision between claims to religious freedom and claims of untrammeled access to health care, to be? Mary Anne Case's chapter, entitled *A Patchwork*

---

[5] Ch. 17, this volume.
[6] *Zubik v. Burwell*, 136 S. Ct. 1557, 1560 (2016).

Array of Theocratic Fiefdoms?" RFRA Claims against the ACA's Contraception Mandate as Examples of the New Feudalism, suggests that optimism would be misplaced.[7]

Professor Case aims less to participate in narrowly legal or specific policy debates than to frame issues in broad historical and sociological context. For anyone who has watched the evolution of debates about the accommodation of religious views for the past several decades (or more), it could not be plainer that the framing of legal and policy issues has shifted dramatically. Traditionally, "conservative" jurists disfavored demands for religious accommodation under the Free Exercise Clause. By contrast, liberals worried that denials of accommodation would result in cruel burdens on religious minorities. In recent decades, the political valence of demands for religious accommodation has shifted. Conservative jurists largely favor a broad construction of RFRA's accommodation mandate. By contrast, liberals worry about harm to third parties if employers can deny health care coverage to women wanting access to contraception and if religiously motivated individuals can deny services to same-sex couples.

Professor Case provocatively weighs in on these issues by characterizing the closely held corporations and nonprofit religious organizations that claim exemptions under RFRA as seeking quasi-feudal privileges and near sovereignty over use of their property. With her eye fixed squarely on women who are threatened with loss of contraception coverage under the ACA, she fears the advent of a "new patriarchy." Professor Case's analysis vividly exemplifies the stakes as they appear from one side in what partisans view as a culture war. The other side, of course, views the central issue as involving religious freedom.

The fight over contraception and exemption mandates vividly exemplifies the likely significance of Supreme Court nominations and confirmations in shaping the future of the law in this fraught area. We may also wonder whether shifting cultural and political currents will open middle ground or foreclose the possibility of compromise.

---

[7] Ch. 16, this volume.

14

Conscientious Objection, Complicity, and Accommodation

Amy J. Sepinwall

Burwell v. Hobby Lobby Stores, Inc.[1] inaugurated an unprecedented deference to religious challenges to secular laws,[2] which *Zubik v. Burwell* neither retrenched nor replaced.[3] On the Court's highly deferential stance, complicity claims seem to know no bounds: just so long as the objector thinks himself complicit in an act his religion opposes, the Court will conclude that the challenged legal requirement substantially burdens his religious exercise.[4] The result is a set of exemptions or Court-imposed negotiations based on assertions of complicity that many courts and commentators find far-fetched, and perhaps even fantastical.[5]

---

[1] 134 S Ct 2751 (2014).
[2] See, e.g., Micah Schwartzman, Richard Schragger & Nelson Tebbe, *The New Law of Religion*, Slate (July 3, 2014), available at www.slate.com/articles/news_and_politics/jurisprudence/2014/07/after_hobby_lobby_there_is_only_rfra_and_that_s_all_you_need.html [https://perma.cc/S7GV-GWDG].
[3] *Zubik v. Burwell*, 578 U.S. ____ (2016). See, e.g., Amy J. Sepinwall, *Burdening "Substantial Burdens,"* 2016 U. Ill. L. Rev. Online 43, 44 & n. 4, available at https://illinoislawreview.org/wp-content/uploads/2016/05/Sepinwall.pdf [https://perma.cc/39QQ-MQHF] (explaining why it is fair to think that a majority of the Justices would have found a substantial burden).
[4] Cf. Elizabeth Sepper, Substantiating the Burdens of Compliance, 2016 U. Ill. L. Rev. Online 61, available at https://illinoislawreview.org/wp-content/uploads/2016/05/Sepper.pdf [https://perma.cc/RC4C-ZJ3J].
[5] See, e.g., *Priests for Life v. U.S. Dep't of Health and Human Servs.*, 772 F.3d 229, 249 (D.C. Cir. 2014) (referring to the burden the contraceptive mandate's accommodation process imposed as "de minimis"); Patrick J. McNulty & Adam D. Zenor, *Corporate Free Exercise of Religion and the Interpretation of Congressional Intent: Where Will It End?*, 39 S. Ill. U.L.J. 475, 508–509 (2015). Cf. *Eden Foods, Inc. v. Sebelius*, 733 F.3d 626, 629 n. 3, cert. granted, judgment vacated sub nom. *Eden Foods, Inc. v. Burwell*, 134 S. Ct. 2902 (2014). Some commentators consider the religious nonprofits' claims to be not earnest fantasy so much as disingenuous moves in the current round of the culture

I am grateful to Elizabeth Sepper for extremely helpful comments, and to the Wharton Dean's Office for research funding supporting this work. Parts of the chapter – indicated below – reproduce with permission portions of Amy J. Sepinwall, *Conscience and Complicity: Assessing Pleas for Religious Exemptions in Hobby Lobby's Wake*, 82 U. Chi. L. Rev. 1897 (2015) and Amy J. Sepinwall, *Burdening "Substantial Burdens,"* 2016 U. Ill. L. Rev. Online 43.

Nonetheless, I think these complicity claims justifiable, and I seek to defend them in Section 1. But I also urge a more extensive inquiry into the burdens of an exemption than what doctrine currently requires. In particular, I argue that courts should balance the burden to the religious adherent (RA) of complying with the law against the burdens third parties would incur were the RA to be granted an exemption. Although some jurists and scholars condemn *Hobby Lobby* precisely because it ignores third-party costs,[6] the doctrine does not currently require courts to attend to these costs. RFRA weighs the *government's* interest in compliance with the challenged legal requirement. But the government's interest need not coincide with the interests of third parties, as I argue in Section 2. And, where their interests do not coincide, RFRA's test might permit an exemption that nonetheless has significant costs for third parties. In Section 3, I propose a test that would provide the requisite balancing.

1. THE CONTRACEPTIVE MANDATE'S SUBSTANTIAL BURDENS

The complicity claims in *Hobby Lobby* and *Zubik* are not obvious. We do not think employers are implicated in the goods or services employees purchase with their salaries. So why think, as the Hobby Lobby owners contend, that they are implicated in goods or services their employees access through other parts of their compensation packages? The *Zubik* challenges are perhaps even more difficult to appreciate. How can employers become complicit in contraceptive use through the process of registering their *objections* to the contraceptive mandate? Nonetheless, I think that, with some elucidation, these claims have merit. I seek to supply that elucidation here.

The first thing to note is that accurately assessing the merits and strength of a complicity claim necessarily requires appeal to the objector's felt sense of implication. I do not claim that the inquiry should begin and end with this subjective element. It is but one input courts should consider in determining whether the burden the objector adduces is "substantial."[7] The remaining elements, I explain, are objective and within a court's purview to measure. But unlike other theorists who argue that, in determining the substantiality of a religious burden, courts should eschew

---

wars. See, e.g., Mary Anne Case, *Why "Live-and-Let-Live" Is Not A Viable Solution to the Difficult Problems of Religious Accommodation in the Age of Sexual Civil Rights*, 88 S. Cal. L. Rev. 463, 471–2 (2015); Douglas NeJaime & Reva B. Siegel, *Conscience Wars: Complicity-Based Conscience Claims in Religion and Politics*, 124 Yale L. J. 2516, 2542–54 (2015). While I find their concerns convincing – and deeply troubling – I bracket them here.

[6] See infra Section 2.
[7] Amy J. Sepinwall, *Complicitous Compliance* (manuscript on file with author).

any appeal to the objector's own sense of complicity,[8] I think we cannot escape that appeal if we are to track the meaning and relevance of conscientious objection in the first place.

Doctrine and professional codes of ethics allow for conscientious exemptions because of the connection between conscience and our sense of self.[9] These sources recognize the importance of protecting individuals from the confrontation with conscience that arises when one is made to act contrary to one's most foundational, identity-defining convictions. Thus we allow physicians who oppose the death penalty to abstain not only from administering lethal drugs but even from doing something that "would assist, supervise, or contribute to the ability of another individual to directly cause the death of the condemned."[10] By the same token, in the event of a military draft, we exempt pacifists not only from combat but also from military service that would be far-removed from the theater of war. Our rationale for affording these exemptions is a recognition that it would be deeply violative of a person's sense of self were she to be compelled to do something that she believes contrary to her conscience, *even if the causal difference she were to make is quite minor* (as it would be, for example, if the pacifist were put on kitchen duty on a military base that trained soldiers for combat, but was not housing actual combatants in the war).

Moreover, even if the objector operates with a more capacious sense of implication than we find in law or our own moral lives, we typically see this as cause for admiration. For example, we praise the person who cares greatly about not contributing to environmental degradation and so goes above the call of duty when it comes to reducing their carbon footprint. Or we laud the person who worries about sweatshop labor and so chooses to buy clothing only from stores adhering to fair labor standards. Even if *we* are not so conscientious – indeed, even if we believe that we are not morally required to reduce our carbon footprint or practice enlightened consumerism to the extent that these conscientious individuals do – we do not respond to their efforts by trying to convince them that they have misapprehended their moral responsibility. We do not say to them, "you know, you play so little a causal role in pollution/sweatshop labor, that you really aren't complicit in the practices you abhor so there's no reason for you to impose on yourself the limits you do."

---

[8] See, e.g., Abner S. Greene, *A Secular Test for a Secular Statute*, 2016 Ill. L. Rev. 34, 36, available at https://illinoislawreview.org/wp-content/uploads/2016/05/Greene.pdf [https://perma.cc/TD6X-W7ZG].

[9] Amy J. Sepinwall, *Conscience and Complicity: Assessing Pleas for Religious Exemptions in Hobby Lobby's Wake*, 82 U. Chi. L. Rev. 1897 (2015).

[10] American Medical Association, Opinion 2.06, AMA Code of Ethics (last updated June 2000), available at www.ama-assn.org//ama/pub/physician-resources/medical-ethics/code-medical-ethics/opinion206.page [https://perma.cc/BXJ6-5VQN].

Instead, we respect and honor the fact that they embrace and act on such rigorous standards, oftentimes at a material cost to themselves.

The point here is twofold: first, it is generally a good thing that people take themselves to be implicated in wrongs to which they bear only a tenuous causal connection. Their felt sense of implication prompts them to live their lives with greater care for the effects of their actions on others. Second, in matters of conscience, we generally allow each individual to determine for themself what acts, and what relationship to those acts, will put her conscience on the line. Each of us has to live with our conscience, so it is up to each of us to determine for ourselves when our conscience will be implicated or injured as a result of our own or others' acts. In other words, the very meaning and role of conscience for us is subjective. If we care that the law protects conscience, then we should care that the law tracks a subjective sense of complicity.

Now, the foregoing argument turns on a blanket approval of heightened conscientiousness. But one might think matters are more complicated. In particular, one might think that we should distinguish between (1) conscientious conduct that goes *above and beyond* the call of duty (for example, more care for the environment than duty requires) and (2) conscientious conduct that would have the RA do *less* than his legal duty requires (for example, by declining to fulfill the statutory obligation to subsidize contraception).[11] The former might well be praiseworthy. But why should we admire the latter, let alone think it justifies an exemption from the legal obligation in question?

In response, notice that all conscientious exemptions function to release the objector from a legal duty he would otherwise bear. In other words, all conscientious exemptions would have the RA do less than his legal duty requires. Perhaps, then, the distinction between exceeding one's duty and not living up to one's duty is meant to be relevant only in the special case where we face a tenuous complicity claim. The worry would then be better cashed out in this way: "We don't care how attenuated your complicity claim is if you are going to do at least as much as you should. But if heeding your conscience requires that you do less than what you should, then you had better be *significantly* implicated in the conduct you deem wrong; otherwise, no exemption for you." But phrased in that way, the worry seems to do no more than restate the claim that strength of causal connection matters. I have argued, by contrast, that strength of causal connection should not matter. Again, we do and should care about how complicity will feel to the objector, and the objector's subjective sense of complicity need not take proximity into account.

Applying these insights to *Hobby Lobby*, we can see a reason to reject the view that the owners' connection to their employees' contraceptive use is too attenuated

---

[11] I am grateful to Elizabeth Sepper for raising this objection.

to make the owners complicit.[12] Instead, we should recognize that whether the contraceptive mandate renders an employer complicit turns only on whether the employer feels strongly that subsidizing contraception would deeply offend their conscience.

But what about the *Zubik* petitioners? One might reasonably contend that their concern about complicity is so off the mark as to not warrant any credence at all.[13] Indeed, I have raised what I take to be knock-down objections to each of the petitioners' arguments.[14] In particular, I rebut the petitioners' arguments that the accommodation process has them facilitate contraceptive use.

But I do think there is a convincing justification for their position (albeit not one they articulate): the accommodation process involves the petitioners in the *ratification* of a wrong, which is a wrong in itself. One ratifies a wrong when one fails to condemn that wrong. Mere extrication is not enough to avoid ratification; instead, one must make clear that the whole scheme to which one objects is morally flawed. To see this, consider two different ways pacifists responded to the draft during the Vietnam War. The military allowed for conscientious objection, so some pacifists who did not want to fight simply availed themselves of the military's opt-out process. But other protestors took the further – and illegal – step of burning their draft cards. Why? Because registering as a conscientious objector in the established way would have legitimated the overall scheme; it would have had the pacifist treat the war in Vietnam as a matter over which reasonable minds could disagree and not as the morally repugnant affair these protesters took it to be. In short, burning a draft card was, for them, an effort to avoid the wrong of ratification.

In refusing to go along with the government's process for opting out of the contraceptive mandate, the *Zubik* petitioners might be seen in a similar vein. For them, contraceptive use is so grave a moral wrong that they cannot simply allow the government to release them from the mandate but then have the government go on, business as usual, to supply contraception. The *Zubik* petitioners "object to objecting"[15] because, were they not to do so, they would be legitimating the overall contraceptive delivery scheme; they would be guilty of the wrong of ratification. Understood in this way, the *Zubik* petitioners' concern might well count as a substantial burden.

Now, to be perfectly clear, these sympathetic reconstructions of the complicity claims in *Hobby Lobby* and *Zubik* do not in and of themselves entail that the objectors in those cases ought to have prevailed on the merits. Even where a substantial

---

[12] See, e.g., Kent Greenawalt, *Hobby Lobby: Its Flawed Interpretive Techniques and Standards of Application*, 115 Colum. L. Rev. Sidebar 153, 168 (2015); Greene, supra note 7.
[13] See supra note 6.
[14] Sepinwall, supra note 2.
[15] Transcript of Oral Argument at 13, line 13, *Zubik v. Burwell*, 578 U.S. ___ (2016) (No. 14–1418) (argued March 23, 2016).

burden exists, RFRA compels courts to weigh the burden on the religious adherent against interests in compliance with the challenged legal requirement. I turn now to an interrogation of RFRA's strict scrutiny test to see if it is sufficiently protective of the interests at stake.

2. MISSING THIRD PARTIES: A TROUBLING OVERSIGHT

In her *Hobby Lobby* dissent, Justice Ginsburg rails against the majority's position in significant part because, according to her, the Court impermissibly overlooks the costs of an accommodation to third parties[16] – there, the "thousands of women employed by Hobby Lobby and Conestoga or dependents of persons those corporations employ."[17] Many scholars agree that the doctrine requires courts to take third parties' interests into account, and they contend that *Hobby Lobby* went wrong in failing to do so.[18]

I share the view that third-party interests should factor into a court's decision to grant or deny a religious exemption. But, as I argue here, I do not believe that the doctrine does in fact attend to third-party interests in the ways it should. In particular, the doctrine gestures to third parties only in dicta. Further, whatever the doctrine does say in support of third-party interests gives little clue about *how* these interests should figure in, as well as about *how much* they should figure in.[19] To establish these claims, I address three doctrines and one procedural mechanism that *appear* to protect third-party interests. I argue that none is ultimately up to the task.

A. *The Compelling-Interest Prong of RFRA*

Under RFRA, once the challenger has established a substantial burden, the government is asked to adduce the compelling interest that the challenged requirement is designed to serve.[20] Sometimes, the government's interest aligns or overlaps with the

---

[16] See Hobby Lobby, 134 S Ct at 2787 (Ginsburg dissenting). In *Conscience and Complicity*, I offer a lengthy analysis of the cases Justice Ginsburg invokes in support of her proposition that the Court is required to weigh third-party burdens. I argue that the case law does not in fact support that proposition. See supra note 8 at 168–72.

[17] Hobby Lobby, 134 S Ct at 2787 (Ginsburg dissenting).

[18] See, e.g., Frederick Mark Gedicks & Rebecca G. Van Tassell, *RFRA Exemptions from the Contraception Mandate: An Unconstitutional Accommodation of Religion*, 49 Harv CR– CL L. Rev. 343, 356–72 (2014); Micah Schwartzman & Nelson Tebbe, *Obamacare and Religion and Arguing off the Wall*, Slate (November 25, 2013, 2:32 PM), available at www.slate.com/articles/news_and_politics/jurisprudence/2013/11/obamacare_birth_control_mandate_lawsuit_how_a_radical_argument_went_mainstream.html [https://perma.cc/C9XW-67UP]. But see Kara Loewentheil, *When Free Exercise Is a Burden: Protecting "Third Parties" in Religious Accommodation Law*, 62 Drake L. Rev. 433, 438.

[19] See Loewentheil, supra note 17 at 474; id. at 438 (making a similar claim).

[20] See 42 USC § 2000bb-1.

interests of third parties who will be affected by an exemption from the challenged legal requirement. This was largely true in the contraceptive mandate cases, where the government's aim was to promote women's health, and it was women who risked being burdened if courts released religious employers from having to comply with the mandate. But in other cases, the government's interest diverges from that of third parties and, when it does, the government need not press both its own interest as well as the interests of the affected third parties. For example, consider a religious adherent who objects to a military draft because he believes homosexuality is evil and, in the wake of the Don't Ask, Don't Tell Repeal Act of 2010,[21] would find it too offensive to his values to serve alongside individuals who are openly gay. The legal requirement he challenges – his conscription – is motivated by an interest in national security. This may be compelling enough in its own right to deny the objector an exemption. But if it is not (if, say, there are enough potential conscripts without drafting the objecting religious adherent), the government cannot defend conscripting him on the ground that his exemption denigrates gays and lesbians. For ensuring the dignity of gays and lesbians is not the interest the conscription program is designed to serve. It is in this sense, then, that the compelling interest test does not necessarily position the government to defend third-party interests. Instead, that test may leave third parties out in the cold.

B. The Establishment Clause

Some commentators look to the Establishment Clause to protect third parties from a religious exemption that would otherwise burden them. Thus, for example, Frederick Gedicks and Rebecca Van Tassell contend that "the Court condemns permissive accommodations on Establishment Clause grounds when the accommodations impose significant burdens on third parties who do not believe or participate in the accommodated practice."[22] Even assuming that their contention is correct,[23] it does not guarantee third-party protection in all cases. For example, there may be cases in which an exemption does not result in an Establishment Clause violation, and yet third parties do have genuine cause to feel that their interests have been

---

[21] Pub L. No. 111–321, 124 Stat 3515, codified as 10 USC § 654.

[22] Gedicks & Van Tassell, supra note 17. See also Martin S. Lederman, *Reconstructing RFRA: The Contested Legacy of Religious Freedom Restoration*, Yale L.J. Forum, 433–7 (March 16, 2016); Frederick Mark Gedicks & Andrew Koppelman, *Invisible Women: Why an Exemption for Hobby Lobby Would Violate the Establishment Clause*, 67 Vand. L. Rev. En Banc 51, 54 (2014); Hobby Lobby, 134 S Ct at 2802 n 25 (Ginsburg dissenting).

[23] I offer a close reading of the relevant caselaw in *Conscience and Complicity*, supra note 8 at 1968 & n. 259, in an effort to argue that the cases do not in fact support an interpretation of the Establishment Clause that would offer robust protection to third parties in their own right.

sacrificed. One of *Hobby Lobby*'s progeny bears out just this problem: in *March for Life v. Burwell*,[24] a federal district court granted an exemption from the contraceptive mandate on secular moral grounds. The court found that the Equal Protection Clause could not countenance treating religious and secular objections to the contraceptive mandate separately. *March for Life* did not then involve government support of religion, and so there could not have been an Establishment Clause violation. But the concerns for the women covered by *March for Life*'s insurance plan stand independent of whether the exemption conflicts with the Establishment Clause. More generally, the Establishment Clause will be of no avail in any case where an exemption is granted on secular moral grounds.

C. *Cutter's Accounting for Third-Party Costs*

Cutter v. Wilkinson,[25] a case involving prison inmates who challenged the prison's denial of religious accommodations, contains what is perhaps the most succinct statement that third-party harms matter: "[p]roperly applying [federal religious freedom laws], courts must take adequate account of the burdens a requested accommodation may impose on nonbeneficiaries."[26] This is powerful language, all the more so because Justice Alito quoted it in a footnote in the *Hobby Lobby* majority opinion.[27] One might then think, contrary to what I have argued, that the settled view of the Court is that third-party costs matter.[28]

Yet, even if the Court has adopted the view that it must "take adequate account" of third-party costs, this would hardly establish that the Court is committed to protecting third parties. What will count as having taken "adequate account" of third-party interests? How much weight must these interests be given for a court's accounting to have been "adequate"? And what does giving them their due weight entail? Is it enough for a court merely to note that the exemption will impose burdens on third parties? Or does the statement mean that, when courts do recognize that third parties will be burdened, they should seek to arrive at an alternative accommodation? Or should they deny the accommodation altogether? *Cutter* itself provides no answers to these questions, because the Court found that "nonbeneficiaries" would not be harmed by the requested accommodation.

---

[24] 128 F.Supp.3d 116 (2015).
[25] 544 US 709 (2005).
[26] *Cutter*, 544 US at 720.
[27] See *Hobby Lobby*, 134 S. Ct. at 2781 n 37.
[28] I am grateful to Professors Koppelman and Schwartzman, each of whom urged this language upon me.

The *Hobby Lobby* majority arrived at the same conclusion with respect to the third parties there, given the availability of alternative arrangements for providing contraception.[29] Third parties should not have to rely on so precarious a statement of what the law requires.

D. Third-Party Intervention

Even if one agrees that neither RFRA nor the Establishment Clause straightforwardly contemplates third-party interests, one might think that the concern about overlooking third parties is mitigated by the possibility that they will seek to intervene in the case and bring their interests before the court in that way.[30] But it would be foolhardy to rely on this mechanism alone. For one thing, possibly affected third parties must seek a court's permission to be heard, and the court has discretion to grant or deny the intervention.[31] For another, while the contraceptive-mandate cases received a lot of publicity – and so readily put third parties on notice that their rights were subject to abrogation – other cases seeking religious exemptions may not be so prominent. Third parties cannot be counted on to know that their interests are at stake. Finally, it is unfair for third parties to incur litigation costs to protect their interests when they are not specially responsible for the law the RAs challenge.

E. Summary

In short, the doctrine does not require courts to attend to third-party interests; nor does it facilitate third parties in getting their interests before the court. This oversight is deeply troubling because every complicity claim stands to affect third parties. By its nature, complicity arises only in light of one party's contribution to another's conduct.[32] To avoid complicity, the would-be contributor might seek an exemption from having to make the contribution. (For example, a religious employer might seek an exemption from having to subsidize his employees' contraception.) But if a court grants the exemption, then the putative beneficiary is left without a contribution that she may have been expecting (and, in the contraceptive-mandate cases, correctly believes is her statutory right). Given that a complicity claim pits the interests of a religious adherent against those of the third parties in whose conduct the RA claims he will be complicit, it is crucial that courts attend to third-party interests.

---

[29] Hobby Lobby, 134 S Ct at 2781 n 37.
[30] See, e.g., *University of Notre Dame v. Sebelius*, 743 F3d 547, 558–9 (7th Cir 2014).
[31] See FRCP 24(b).
[32] See NeJaime & Siegel, supra note 4 at 2566.

3. BALANCING CONCERNS FOR COMPLICITY AGAINST THIRD-PARTY COSTS

We have seen that claims of complicity should be treated with great deference. At the same time, whether these claims should yield an exemption should depend, in significant part, on whether third parties would incur an undue burden as a result. Current doctrine does not mandate rigorous consideration of third-party burdens. In this section, I articulate a test that stands to correct this oversight.[33] The elements of this test aim not to replace but to add to RFRA's current strict scrutiny test, which contemplates the government's own interests.

So: how should courts weigh deference to religion against third-party costs? Assume that a court has determined that the challenged law imposes a substantial burden on the objector. And assume further that the government has failed to meet its burden under strict scrutiny: it cannot establish that the challenged law protects a compelling interest in the least restrictive way. Under the current doctrine, the religious objector would then prevail in his bid for an exemption. The element I add here, however, blocks that automatic outcome. Instead, on my proposal, the court must then consider the costs of an exemption on third parties.

To that end, courts should conceive of a spectrum of costs that an exemption could impose on third parties, and that spectrum should contain a threshold. The threshold marks the boundary between permissible and impermissible third-party costs; costs beyond the boundary impose an unjust burden on third parties. But just where should this threshold be located on the spectrum? I submit that this is a matter for democratic deliberation. As a society, we must decide how important respect for religion is and, correspondingly, how great the costs we should be willing to impose on third parties for the sake of respecting religious observance.

Although we have yet to undertake those deliberations, we can already note a couple of ancillary considerations. First, the government should seek to minimize occasions for conflict between religious beliefs and third-party interests. Second, when granting an exemption would implicate third-party interests, courts and the government must work to ensure that these interests are raised and adequately defended.

This brings us to a piece of doctrinal revision, which provides a means for third parties to have their interests represented in court. The government bears an obligation to assess whether a requested exemption would impose costs on third parties. When the government determines that it would, the government must make a good-faith effort to alert the relevant third parties to the proceedings. For example,

---

[33] Micah Schwartzman, *Conscience, Speech, and Money*, 97 Va. L. Rev. 317, 346–54 (2011) (also advocating a balancing test in cases of conscientious objection but including only the objector's and the government's interests in the test, not those of third parties).

the government might take out advertisements in national news sources (paper and electronic) or contact a representative advocacy group (for example, National Abortion and Reproductive Rights Action League, in the case of the contraceptive mandate).

Further, the government – which is to say, taxpayers – should fund the third parties' legal representation. As a society, we should be willing to incur some costs in exchange for protecting religious freedom. But these costs should be shared equally among us. We would impermissibly chill requests for religious exemptions were we to require the objectors to pay for third parties' legal representation. And requiring third parties to fully fund their efforts to protect themselves would expose them to a disproportionate burden even if they were to prevail. Accordingly, the government should have to subsidize third parties' legal costs on behalf of us all.[34]

It is important to note that third parties should be given an opportunity to represent their own interests, even if these appear fully to overlap with the government's interest in the legal requirement. In *Zubik*, for example, the government defended the existing accommodation process as being the least restrictive way to ensure "seamless" contraceptive coverage at no cost to the women covered by the religious nonprofits' insurance plans.[35] One would think that the government's arguments capture what is at stake for the plans' female beneficiaries. But the government sometimes uses paternalistic – even demeaning – language to justify the need to make contraceptive access easy for women.[36] Allowing women to voice the need in their own words would likely obviate this concern.

Finally, it will not be sufficient to contact only the third parties most immediately affected by the case – for example, the beneficiaries of the insurance scheme who would be impacted by an exemption. If the religious objectors succeed, then other employers with the same objection may well be permitted to deny their beneficiaries the challenged coverage. As such, the government should bear an obligation to contact one or more organizations that can represent the interests of all potentially affected third parties. And there is a separate reason to notify an advocacy organization, rather than the potentially affected employees themselves: as Professors Micah Schwartzman and Nelson Tebbe have compellingly argued with respect to *Hobby Lobby*, "employees are (understandably) reluctant to come forward against their employers, even though their constitutional claim is strong and even though they

---

[34] For that matter, we might decide that parties who succeed in securing a conscientious exemption should have their legal fees reimbursed, too, or at least that we should offer reimbursement to those plaintiffs who can show financial hardship. If conscience is worth protecting, then we might not want the ability to pay to stand as a barrier to those with legitimate claims.
[35] Brief for Respondents at 27–8, *Zubik v. Burwell*, 2135 S. Ct. 1544 (2016) (No. 14–1418).
[36] I elaborate on this point in Sepinwall, supra note 2 at 51–2.

have a lot to lose if the case goes the wrong way."[37] Their concerns would arise in any employer's challenge to some workplace regulation.

CONCLUSION

Many scholars oppose the deferential stance I advocate here on the ground that too much deference will require the government to defend any and every challenged law under a test that is strict in theory and, all too often, fatal in fact.[38] I agree that deference might well increase the government's burden. But it need not increase the government's failure rate. Requiring courts to balance a religious exemption against not only the government's interest but also the relevant third parties' interests lends heft – necessary and significant heft – to the secular side of the scale. We can afford deference to religion, but only because and to the extent that we attend to third parties' interests too.

---

[37] Schwartzman & Tebbe, supra note 17.
[38] For the view that *Hobby Lobby* significantly ratcheted up the government's burden, see, for example, Frederick Mark Gedicks, *"Substantial" Burdens: How Courts May (and Why They Must) Judge Burdens of Religion Under RFRA*, 85 GEO. WASH. L. REV. 94, 149 n.241 (2017) Sepper, supra note 3 at 61. Cf. Lederman, supra note 21 at 440–1 (arguing that *Hobby Lobby* opened the door to this revolutionary reconstruction of RFRA but that it did not compel that result).

15

How Much May Religious Accommodations Burden Others?

Nelson Tebbe, Micah Schwartzman, and Richard Schragger

In considering contemporary conflicts between the values of religious freedom and equality, a mediating principle has proved to be important—namely, the rule that when the government grants religious accommodations, it must avoid harm to others. Normally, when the government lifts regulatory burdens on religious actors, any associated costs fall on the government or on the public. But accommodating religious citizens sometimes entails costs to other private citizens. And when that happens, the government may run up against constitutional limits. The rule against third-party harm, as it has come to be known, holds that the government cannot accommodate religious citizens if that means harming other private citizens. In this Chapter, we address the limits of this principle: how much harm to others is enough to defeat a religious accommodation?

Here is the doctrinal background. In cases concerning both the Establishment Clause and the Free Exercise Clause, the Supreme Court has held that government may not accommodate religious citizens if that means shifting burdens to other private citizens. The Court has explained that "[t]he First Amendment ... gives no one the right to insist that, in pursuit of their own interests, others must conform their conduct to his own religious necessities."[1] As we have argued elsewhere,[2] the

---

[1] *Estate of Thornton v. Caldor, Inc.*, 472 U.S. 703, 710 (1985). *Caldor* was decided under the Establishment Clause. For a free exercise decision rejecting a claim to an exemption because of harm to others, see *United States v. Lee*, 455 U.S. 252, 261 (1982).

[2] See, e.g., Micah Schwartzman, Richard Schragger, & Nelson Tebbe, *Hobby Lobby and the Establishment Clause, Part III: Reconciling Amos and Cutter*, Balkinization (December 9, 2013), available at http://balkin.blogspot.com/2013/12/hobby-lobby-and-establishment-clause_9.html [https://perma.cc/X8B5-82Y3].

We thank William McDavid and Steven Bovino for excellent research assistance. For comments, we thank Michael Dorf, James Nelson, Elizabeth Sepper, and participants at the Annual Law and Religion Roundtable, Cardozo Law School, and Cornell Law School.

government may not force some private citizens to bear costs associated with the religious observances of other private citizens.

More recently, the rule against third-party harms[3] has been implicated in conflicts over provisions protecting reproductive freedom for women, marriage equality, and civil rights for LGBT citizens. For example, the Court in *Burwell v. Hobby Lobby Stores, Inc.* granted a religious accommodation to a business corporation that objected to the contraception mandate imposed by the Obama Administration under the Affordable Care Act (ACA).[4] That dispute had obvious ramifications for the freedom and equality of the company's female employees and for the female dependents of its male employees.[5] Similarly, the Court's decision in *Zubik v. Burwell* may well affect the employees of religious nonprofits.[6] And conflicts between religious freedom and LGBT rights have become familiar, including in the important context of health care.[7]

Critics of the principle of avoiding harm to others have developed several objections. Here, we focus on the criticism that third-party harms cannot *always* render religious accommodations unconstitutional, because many such exemptions have negative effects on others.[8] An absolute bar on third-party harms would generate absurd results by making virtually all religious exemptions impermissible, despite the fact that thousands of these provisions exist in federal and state law. According to

---

[3] These other citizens are commonly referred to as third parties to distinguish them from the government and the religious claimants.
[4] 134 S.Ct. 2751 (2014).
[5] See Elizabeth Sepper, *Free Exercise Lochnerism*, 115 Colum. L. Rev. 1453, 1456–7 (2015).
[6] *Zubik v. Burwell*, 136 S.Ct. 1557 (2016) (vacating lower court opinions and remanding to circuit courts); see Nelson Tebbe, Micah Schwartzman, & Richard Schragger, Zubik *and the Demands of Justice*, Scotusblog (May 16, 2016), available at www.scotusblog.com/2016/05/symposium-zubik-and-the-demands-of-justice/ [https://perma.cc/5G69-T7TM]. Whether *Zubik* affects third parties depends on how events unfold not only in the Court but also in Congress and the White House, as the Introduction to this volume describes in detail.
[7] For a detailed treatment of contemporary conflicts between religious freedom and equality law, including a defense of the principle of avoiding harm to others, see Nelson Tebbe, *Religious Freedom in an Egalitarian Age* 49–70 (Harvard University Press, 2017). In subsequent work, we plan to explore further the normative principles that justify the third-party harm doctrine, including the scope of those principles and whether they apply to accommodations that extend to nonbelievers – for example, conscientious objection to military conscription, as illustrated by *United States v. Seeger*, 380 U.S. 163 (1965), and *Welsh v. United States*, 398 U.S. 333 (1970).Some of the conflicts between LGBT rights and religious freedom, including in the context of health care, are explored in other parts of this volume, especially chapters 18, 19, and 25.
[8] For a discussion of other objections, including an argument about how to determine the proper baseline for measuring third-party harms, see Richard Schragger, Micah Schwartzman, & Nelson Tebbe, "When Do Religious Accommodations Burden Others?," in *The Conscience Wars: Rethinking the Balance between Religion, Identity, and Equality* (Susanna Mancini & Michel Rosenfeld eds., forthcoming 2017).

this objection, such an extreme rule would cut against both established precedents and the considered convictions of many Americans.

In responding to this objection, we acknowledge that there are some situations in which the harm to religious freedom is so significant, and the countervailing burden on others so slight, that accommodations ought to be upheld despite some harm to third parties. Below, we give examples supporting that conviction. But if the principle of avoiding harm to others is not absolute, that raises a crucial question: *how much* burden-shifting to third parties is constitutionally permissible? In other words, once it has been established that a third party has suffered some kind of burden as a consequence of a religious accommodation, how much of a burden is too much?

Our answer is that a promising model can be found in employment discrimination law. Title VII, the main federal statute prohibiting discrimination against workers, contains a provision that requires employers to provide reasonable accommodations for the religious observances of their workers.[9] But there are limits. Title VII does not require employers to accommodate religious employees where doing so would impose "undue hardship" on the employer.[10] In other words, federal civil rights law protects religious freedom by extending religious exemptions from workplace rules, but not if that would harm third parties – or, more precisely, *not if it would harm them too much*.

In this chapter, we argue that "undue hardship" provides an attractive and workable standard for limiting harms to third parties. This standard helps to answer the objection that a rule against third party harms would prohibit all religious accommodations. And it does so by drawing on decades of experience in the federal courts, which have applied the undue hardship standard against the background of serious Establishment Clause concerns and have reached results that are generally sensible. Extrapolating from the employment context, we look to the undue hardship standard for needed guidance in other areas involving claims for religious accommodations that have harmful effects on others.

1. TWO VERSIONS OF THE OBJECTION

The constitutional principle of avoiding third-party harms has met with significant resistance.[11] In this chapter, we address one of the main criticisms, which is that

---

[9] 42 U.S.C. s 2000e(j).
[10] Id.
[11] See, e.g., Kevin Walsh, *Did Justice Ginsburg endorse the Establishment Clause third-party burdens argument in Holt v. Hobbs?*, Mirror of Justice (January 21, 2015), available at http://mirrorofjustice.blogs.com/mirrorofjustice/2015/01/did-justice-ginsburg-endorse-the-establishment-clause-third-party-burdens-argument-in-holt-v-hobbs-.html [https://perma.cc/8DYY-ZGBE]; Richard W. Garnett, *Accommodation, Establishment, and Freedom of Religion*, 67 Vand. L. Rev. En Banc 39, 45 (2014).

the principle threatens to undermine all, or nearly all, religious accommodations. There are actually two versions of this objection. The first is that a bar on third-party harms cannot possibly be the rule, since religious exemptions invariably shift harm onto third parties. If many religious accommodations are permissible, and if they necessarily entail harms to others, then it cannot be the case that the law forbids accommodations that impose such harms.[12]

We reject this argument because it rests on a false premise – namely, that *all* religious accommodations burden third parties.[13] In fact, some existing accommodations do not shift harms onto others in ways that raise constitutional concerns. Consider *Holt v. Hobbs*, a recent Supreme Court decision.[14] A Muslim inmate wished to grow a half-inch beard for religious reasons, despite prison rules prohibiting facial hair. The Court ruled in his favor under the Religious Land Use and Institutionalized Persons Act (RLUIPA),[15] and rightly so. Accommodating the inmate had no negative effects for the prison or other inmates, according to all the available evidence.[16] And that case is not anomalous. Several of the Title VII cases that we review later in the chapter also involve religious accommodations that do not affect employers, unions, or other employees.[17] It is simply not the case that religious accommodations always shift burdens to others.[18]

A second, milder version of the objection is more powerful. According to this argument, there are at least *some* religious accommodations that ought to be upheld even though they externalize costs. In those cases, the religious freedom interest is significant and the effect on other citizens is relatively minor.

---

[12] For an argument that approaches this one, even if it stops short of the strongest version, see Marc O. DeGirolami, *Holt v. Hobbs and the Third-Party-Harm Establishment Clause Theory*, Mirror of Justice (October 27, 2014), available at http://mirrorofjustice.blogs.com/mirrorofjustice/2014/10/where-has-the-establishment-clause-third-party-harm-argument-gone.html [https://perma.cc/7MRY-VSR9]; Marc O. DeGirolami, *Free Exercise by Moonlight*, 53 San Diego L. Rev. 105, 143 (2016).

[13] See, e.g., Marc O. DeGirolami, *On the Claim that Exemptions from the Mandate Violate the Establishment Clause*, Mirror of Justice (December 5, 2013), available at http://mirrorofjustice.blogs.com/mirrorofjustice/2013/12/exemptions-from-the-mandate-do-not-violate-the-establishment-clause.html [https://perma.cc/5QPM-BKG6] ("all exemptions burden third parties in one way or another"); DeGirolami, *Holt v. Hobbs and the Third-Party-Harm Establishment Clause Theory*, supra note 12 ("Virtually all accommodations impose harms or burdens of some kinds on others, though both the nature and the degree of the harms will vary.").

[14] 135 S.Ct. 853 (2015).

[15] 42 U.S.C. § 2000cc et seq.

[16] Justice Ginsburg, joined by Justice Sotomayor, concurred in *Holt* precisely on the ground that in that case, unlike in Hobby Lobby, third-party harms were not involved. 135 S.Ct. at 867 (Ginsburg, J., concurring).

[17] See infra Section 3.

[18] See Micah Schwartzman, Richard Schragger, & Nelson Tebbe, *Holt v. Hobbs and Third Party Harms*, Balkinization (January 22, 2015), available at http://balkin.blogspot.com/2015/01/holt-v-hobbs-and-third-party-harms.html [https://perma.cc/D5A4-28SF].

We think this point is correct. Consider an example, which we take from Christopher Lund.[19] Mary Stinemetz was suffering from a debilitating disease and required a liver transplant to save her life.[20] Liver transplants in cases like hers were considered safe and effective and were covered by her insurance policy. The difficulty was that Stinemetz was a Jehovah's Witness who was opposed to blood transfusions on religious grounds. While "bloodless liver transplants" were medically approved and were offered at a hospital in a neighboring state, the insurance company refused to pay to transfer her there. Stinemetz eventually won her court case,[21] but her victory came too late. She was no longer medically eligible for the transplant, and she eventually died of her disease.[22]

In the actual case, Stinemetz was covered by Medicaid, so there were no third parties – the dispute was between her and the government.[23] But consider a hypothetical variation in which she is covered by private insurance. Suppose, further, that government regulations allow the insurer to refuse to pay for her transfer, even though the transfer costs are modest. Now, in this example, Stinemetz claims a religious exemption from those regulations. Under such circumstances, in which interference with Stinemetz's free exercise is serious and the costs to the insurance company are modest, we do not believe that the principle of avoiding harm to third parties prevents an accommodation.

This example shows that the rule against shifting harm onto third parties must have limits. But our intuition about the correct resolution of the hypothetical Stinemetz case does not tell us anything about the *degree* of harm to others that should be tolerated before the Free Exercise Clause or the Establishment Clause is violated. How much harm to others is permissible?

2. UNDUE HARDSHIP AND THE ESTABLISHMENT CLAUSE

We propose "undue hardship" as an attractive and workable standard for determining how much harm to others can be tolerated before a religious accommodation becomes impermissible.[24] Although courts have applied this standard in the context of employment law, it can provide useful guidance in other areas as well. In

---

[19] Christopher C. Lund, "Keeping Hobby Lobby in Perspective," in *The Rise of Corporate Religious Liberty* 290 (Micah Schwartzman et al. eds., 2016).
[20] *Stinemetz v. Kansas Health Policy Authority*, 252 P. 3d 141, 155–6 (Kan. App. 2011).
[21] Id.
[22] Lund, supra note 19, at 290.
[23] Stinemetz, 252 P.3d at 143.
[24] For another proposal, which we find promising, see Frederick Mark Gedicks & Rebecca Van Tassell, "Of Burdens and Baselines: Hobby Lobby's Puzzling Footnote 37," in *The Rise of Corporate Religious Liberty* 337 (Micah Schwartzman et al. eds., 2016). Gedicks and Van Tassell argue that third-party harms are impermissible if they are "material" or significant enough that others would take them into

this section, we argue that the Supreme Court has interpreted the standard against the background of Establishment Clause concerns, and that lower courts have uniformly understood it to be consistent with the Constitution. In the next section, we argue further that the undue hardship standard has generated outcomes that balance the interests of religious believers and third parties in a manner that is generally reasonable and defensible.

Recall that Title VII requires employers to "reasonably accommodate" religious practitioners, unless doing so would result in "undue hardship on the conduct of the employer's business."[25] The Supreme Court interpreted this requirement in *Trans World Airlines, Inc. v. Hardison*.[26] Larry Hardison worked for the airline TWA. He was also a member of the Worldwide Church of God and he believed that his faith required him to observe the Sabbath on Saturdays. Hardison asked for Saturdays off, but the airline was unable to accommodate him.

Part of the difficulty was that TWA had a collective bargaining agreement that apportioned days off from work according to a seniority system. Hardison did not have sufficient seniority to avoid working on Saturdays. Moreover, the airline was unable to find him another position within the company or to find workers who would voluntarily swap days off. After Hardison was terminated, he sued.

The question in *Hardison* was what constitutes undue hardship on the employer, and specifically whether TWA was required to modify the seniority system.[27] The Court held that requiring TWA and the union to depart from the seniority system would constitute an undue hardship.[28] Allowing Hardison to take Saturdays off would mean that other employees could not, even though they were senior to him. And those senior employees had a right to their preferences under the contract. "[T]o give Hardison Saturdays off," the Court explained, "TWA would have had to deprive another employee of his shift preference at least in part because he did not adhere to a religion that observed the Saturday Sabbath."[29] And that, the Court

---

account in determining their response. An advantage of this standard is that it is familiar from other areas of law, but a drawback is that materiality might preclude accommodations that should nevertheless be permissible, such as the one in our hypothetical Stinemetz scenario. Our difference with Gedicks and Van Tassell on this point should not overshadow our more fundamental agreement that the third-party harm doctrine should be limited and that plausible standards for drawing that boundary are available.

[25] 42 U.S.C. s 2000e(j); Pub. L. 92–261, § 2, Mar. 24, 1972, 86 Stat. 103. Awkwardly, Congress passed the new provision as an amendment to Title VII's definition of religion: "The term 'religion' includes all aspects of religious observance and practice, as well as belief, unless an employer demonstrates that he is unable to reasonably accommodate to an employee's or prospective employee's religious observance or practice without undue hardship on the conduct of the employer's business."

[26] 432 U.S. 63, 73–4 (1977).

[27] Id.

[28] Id. at 77.

[29] Id. at 81.

concluded, was not required by Title VII. In a key passage, the Court explained that "[i]t would be anomalous to conclude that by 'reasonable accommodation' Congress meant that an employer must deny the shift and job preference of some employees, as well as deprive them of their contractual rights, in order to accommodate or prefer the religious needs of others."[30] Although the Court explicitly declined to reach the Establishment Clause issue in *Hardison*, its reasoning was consistent with the principle of avoiding harm to others.[31]

Importantly, the Court also offered a standard for resolving future conflicts between religious employees and the interests of others. It explained that an "undue hardship" exists if an employer is required "to bear more than a de minimis cost" to accommodate an observant employee. Addressing a suggestion that TWA could replace Hardison with supervisory personnel from other departments or pay other employees premium wages to work on Saturdays, the Court explained that both of these would involve impermissible costs:

> To require TWA to bear more than a de minimis cost in order to give Hardison Saturdays off is an undue hardship. Like abandonment of the seniority system, to require TWA to bear additional costs when no such costs are incurred to give other employees the days off that they want would involve unequal treatment of employees on the basis of their religion... While incurring extra costs to secure a replacement for Hardison might remove the necessity of compelling another employee to work involuntarily in Hardison's place, it would not change the fact that the privilege of having Saturdays off would be allocated according to religious beliefs.[32]

The upshot is that shifting costs in order to accommodate religious beliefs – or having privileges "allocated according to religious beliefs," in the Court's language – is not required when the burdens are more than de minimis.

Although the Court did not reach the Establishment Clause question in *Hardison*, it ruled against a background of serious constitutional concerns. TWA and the union had argued repeatedly that accommodating Hardison would violate the Establishment Clause.[33] Moreover, those arguments had been accepted below. The district court reasoned that Title VII would run up against constitutional questions if

---

[30] Id.
[31] Id. at 70 ("Because we agree with petitioners that their conduct was not a violation of Title VII, we need not reach the other questions presented [including the Establishment Clause issue].")
[32] Id. at 84. Marci Hamilton adopts the de minimis standard for limiting religious accommodations under the Establishment Clause. Marci A. Hamilton, *God vs. the Gavel: Religion and the Rule of Law* 275 (2005).
[33] *Hardison*, 432 U.S. at 70 ("In separate petitions for certiorari TWA and IAM contended that adequate steps had been taken to accommodate Hardison's religious observances and that to construe the statute to require further efforts at accommodation would create an establishment of religion contrary to the First Amendment of the Constitution.").

it required TWA and the union to go further to accommodate Hardison.[34] The court of appeals acknowledged the argument, too.[35] In some real sense, then, the Supreme Court could avoid the Establishment Clause question only because of how it interpreted the undue hardship standard.

Dissenting from the Court's decision, Justice Marshall also noted that "important constitutional questions would be posed by interpreting the law to compel employers (or fellow employees) to incur substantial costs to aid the religious observer."[36] Justice Marshall, joined by Justice Brennan, thought that the Court could have allowed the employer to incur somewhat greater expense in order to accommodate Hardison without implicating the Constitution. So he dissented from the Court's interpretation of undue hardship as defeating religious accommodations that resulted in anything more than de minimis cost to the employer. Nevertheless, he recognized that "[t]he Court's interpretation of the statute, by effectively nullifying it, has the singular advantage of making consideration of petitioners' constitutional challenge unnecessary."[37]

After *Hardison*, lower courts have appreciated that the Justices' interpretation of the undue hardship standard avoids potential difficulties under the Establishment Clause. One court read *Hardison* to articulate a constitutional rule,[38] whereas other courts have noticed a relationship of consistency. For example, the California Supreme Court ruled that its religious accommodation requirement, which it interpreted like the one in Title VII, did not violate the Establishment Clause, in part because it did not require the employer to expend funds or favor religious employees.[39] While the California court did not hold that this interpretation of the statute was *required* by the Establishment Clause, it did reason that, interpreted this way, the statute was *consistent* with it. Similarly, the Ninth Circuit upheld Title

---

[34] *Hardison v. Trans World Airlines*, 375 F. Supp. 877, 883 (W.D. Mo. 1974).

[35] *Hardison v. Trans World Airlines, Inc.*, 527 F.2d 33, 43 (8th Cir. 1975) ("The view that it is constitutionally impermissible for a government to enforce accommodation of religious beliefs in a manner which results in privileges not available to a nonbeliever, or which result in inconvenience to the nonbeliever, is not without articulate support.").

[36] Id. at 90 (Marshall, J., dissenting).

[37] Id. at 89. Other scholars have recognized the constitutional dimensions of *Hardison*. For example, Carl Esbeck has said that "The Supreme Court did not reach the claim that § 2000e(j) was in violation of the Establishment Clause ... albeit the prospect of such a ruling likely influenced the Court's interpretation of what was required to show 'undue hardship.'" Carl H. Esbeck, *Third-Party Harms, Congressional Statutes Accommodating Religion, and the Establishment Clause*, at 8 (2015), available at http://ssrn.com/abstract=2607277 [https://perma.cc/VH5Y-TS2U].

[38] See *Turpen v. Missouri-Kansas-Texas R. Co.*, 736 F.2d 1022, 1026 (5th Cir. 1984) ("As the Supreme Court recognized in the leading case construing the scope of the employer's duty, [Hardison,] courts must balance the prohibitions of the Establishment Clause of state-mandated favoritism in employment on the basis of religion and the respect for 'bona fide' seniority systems built into the statutory scheme of Title VII against Congress' intent in § 701(j) to correct discrimination on the basis of religion.").

[39] *Rankins v. Comm'n on Prof'l Competence*, 593 P.2d 852, 858–9 (Cal. 1979).

VII's religious accommodation provision against an Establishment Clause challenge.[40] In particular, it held that requiring employers to accommodate employees' religious practices under the *Hardison* standard did not amount to an impermissible establishment, even if it resulted in the imposition of some small cost on other employees.[41] Other circuit courts have come to the same conclusion.[42]

In sum, Title VII as interpreted by the Supreme Court does not require imposing more than de minimis costs on employers or other employees, and it satisfies the principle against shifting harm onto others. Whether or not the Court's interpretation of the undue hardship standard is required by nonestablishment, it certainly is consistent with the constitutional rule.

3. UNDUE HARDSHIP IN THE LOWER COURTS

Applying the undue hardship rule in light of *Hardison*, lower courts have had the latitude to reach sensible results. Even though the Supreme Court's de minimis interpretation of the undue hardship standard sounds uncompromising, it has, in fact, been applied in ways that are more balanced. Courts have required employers to accommodate some employees even where doing so would result in some cost to others. Moreover, they have developed a body of case law that can provide helpful guidance for resolving disputes about harmful accommodations more generally.

In this section, we differentiate among three types of cases. First, courts sometimes rule in favor of religious employees because accommodating them would have virtually no effect on anyone else. Second, and most commonly, the employee's claim is denied because it would impermissibly burden the employer, the union, or other employees. Third – and the category in which we are most interested – courts sometimes require an accommodation even though it would mean harming others in a way that does not constitute undue hardship. In these cases, some adverse impacts on third parties are tolerated.

A. No Effect

Several courts have required religious accommodations because there was *no* impact on the employer or other employees. For example, in *Protos v. Volkswagen of America*, the Third Circuit ruled in favor of a Sabbatarian in an opinion by Judge

---

[40] *Tooley v. Martin-Marietta Corp.*, 648 F.2d 1239, 1245–6 (9th Cir. 1981).
[41] Id. at 1246 ("A religious accommodation does not violate the Establishment Clause merely because it can be construed in some abstract way as placing an inappreciable but inevitable burden on those not accommodated.").
[42] See, e.g., Turpen, 736 F.2d at 1026; *McDaniel v. Essex Int'l, Inc.*, 696 F.2d 34, 36–7 (6th Cir. 1982); *Nottelson v. Smith Steel Workers*, 643 F.2d 445 (7th Cir. 1981); *Protos v. Volkswagen of Am., Inc.*, 797 F.2d 129, 136 (3d Cir. 1986); *E.E.O.C. v. Ithaca Indus., Inc.*, 849 F.2d 116, 119 (4th Cir. 1988).

Adams (who was well known for his opinions on religious freedom).[43] Angeline Protos, like Hardison, worked under a collective bargaining agreement that apportioned days off according to a seniority system, and she had insufficient seniority to be absent every Saturday. But there was one important difference between the cases: Volkswagen maintained a group of roving employees to cover absences. Those employees were numerous enough to cover for Protos, and they were not paid a premium. On those facts, the district court found that accommodating her was virtually costless to the company, the union, and other employees.[44]

Other courts similarly have found for observant workers in situations where exempting them would be costless.[45] In particular, where a Sabbatarian can be accommodated through voluntary shift swaps without impairing the business's functions, courts have found either no cost whatsoever or that any cost is de minimis.[46] While some of these cases do not reach the undue hardship question, holding instead that voluntary shift swaps constitute a reasonable accommodation by the employer, they are consistent with the rule that requiring an employer to do *more* than arrange or allow voluntary shift swaps can constitute undue hardship.[47]

Thinking back to Section 1, these cases also show that it is inaccurate to say that religious accommodations always entail third-party harms. The real question, then, is the one we address in this chapter: not whether there is a principle of avoiding harm to others, but how much burden-shifting defeats a religious accommodation under that rule. The next two categories of cases explain how lower courts have approached that question in applying the undue hardship standard.

B. Undue Hardship

In the majority of cases applying the *Hardison* standard, federal courts have found that exempting an observant employee from workplace requirements would impose an undue hardship on the employer, the union, or other employees. In those situations, courts have held that Title VII was not violated by the employer. They have stressed that the undue hardship inquiry is context-specific, taking into account both

---

[43] Protos, 797 F.2d at 135. Among other influential opinions, Judge Adams wrote a concurrence in *Malnak v. Yogi*, 592 F.2d 197, 200–15 (3rd Cir. 1979) and the opinion in *Africa v. Pennsylvania*, 662 F.2d 1025 (3d Cir. 1981).
[44] Protos, 797 F.2d at 134–5 (deferring to the district court's factual findings).
[45] See, e.g., Brown v. Gen. Motors Corp., 601 F.2d 956 (8th Cir. 1979) (ruling for the plaintiff on facts similar to those in Protos).
[46] See, e.g., Davis v. Fort Bend Cty., 765 F.3d 480, 489 (5th Cir. 2014); Beadle v. Hillsborough Cty. Sheriff's Dep't, 29 F.3d 589, 593 (11th Cir. 1994).
[47] *Eversley v. MBank Dallas*, 843 F.2d 172, 176 (5th Cir. 1988); *Morrissette-Brown v. Mobile Infirmary Med. Ctr.*, 506 F.3d 1317, 1322 (11th Cir. 2007).

the fact and the magnitude of alleged costs.[48] Monetary and nonmonetary costs on employers and other employees also figure into their analysis.[49]

Cases in which courts find an undue hardship are common and include many different scenarios: where other workers would be subject to involuntary shift swaps despite a contract, as in *Hardison* itself;[50] where other employees would have to take on additional work;[51] where the employer would suffer a loss of efficiency or would have to pay additional wages;[52] and where the accommodation would result in disruption of work routines and a loss of morale.[53] Situations where accommodations are defeated because of effects on other private citizens are numerous and varied.

C. Harm to Others that Falls Short of Undue Hardship

Although the undue hardship standard is exacting, not all burden shifting is impermissible. Cases falling into this third and final category are crucial, because they demonstrate that the undue hardship standard allows for a range of accommodations – even though undue hardship is interpreted strictly by the Supreme Court to mean anything more than de minimis harm to third parties. This leeway allows courts to extend relief where the burden on religion is great compared to the effects on others, although they do not articulate their task as involving balancing or the exercise of judicial discretion. Judges believe that Congress struck the balance, and that they are merely applying its standard in particular cases.

A leading case is *Tooley v. Martin-Marietta Corp.*, which concerns union dues.[54] Herman Tooley was a Seventh Day Adventist who believed that it was sinful to support organized labor by paying union dues. His workplace, however, had a collective bargaining agreement that required all workers, including those who declined to become members, to contribute to the union. He asked for a religious accommodation under Title VII, and he offered to donate an equivalent amount to a mutually agreeable charity. The court ruled in his favor.

Notably, Tooley's accommodation was not devoid of effects on others. In particular, it deprived the union of dues that it otherwise would have received from him. So the question was whether that cost to a third party should have defeated the exemption because it imposed an undue hardship on the union, understood as anything

---

[48] See, e.g., *Webb v. City of Philadelphia*, 562 F.3d 256, 260 (3rd Cir. 2009); *Anderson v. General Dynamics*, 589 F.2d 397, 400 (9th Cir. 1978); *Tooley v. Martin-Marietta Corp.*, 648 F.2d 1239, 1243 (5th Cir. 1981).
[49] See Webb, 562 F.3d at 260; *Brener v. Diagnostic Ctr. Hosp.*, 671 F.2d 141, 147 (5th Cir. 1982).
[50] *Trans World Airlines, Inc. v. Hardison*, 432 U.S. 63, 79 (1977).
[51] See *Bruff v. N. Mississippi Health Servs., Inc.*, 244 F.3d 495 (5th Cir. 2001).
[52] See Hardison, 432 U.S. at 84; *Mann v. Frank*, 7 F.3d 1365, 1370 (8th Cir. 1993).
[53] See *Brener v. Diagnostic Ctr. Hosp.*, 671 F.2d 141, 147 (5th Cir. 1982).
[54] 648 F.2d 1239, 1243 (5th Cir. 1981).

more than a de minimis cost. The Ninth Circuit responded that even though the union would be deprived of dues, "[t]he substituted charity provision is consistent with the balancing of interests promoted by" Title VII's religious accommodation provision.[55] It reasoned that the union had enjoyed surplus reserves for the previous three years. And even though Tooley was not alone – there were three other workers who also objected to paying union dues on religious grounds – the reserves exceeded the dues that would be lost by accommodating the four employees.[56] Although an accommodation that deprived the union of funds necessary for its maintenance or operation could constitute an undue hardship, that circumstance was not present.[57]

Moreover, the court considered not just the effect on the union and the employer, but also on other employees. In particular, workers could complain that the accommodation allowed Seventh-day Adventists to support a charity of their choice, whereas they were required to give that money to the union even if they too would have preferred to donate it to another worthy cause.[58] The Ninth Circuit determined that this consequence, while real, was not serious enough to defeat the accommodation. It held that the accommodation did not advantage observant employees "in a manner so substantial and direct that it" should be denied.[59]

Finally, the *Tooley* court considered the precise concern we have been tracking, namely that the accommodation benefits religious employees "at the expense of their co-workers" in violation of the Establishment Clause.[60] In response, it held that "[a] religious accommodation does not violate the Establishment Clause merely because it" has the effect of "placing an inappreciable but inevitable burden on those not accommodated."[61] In sum, a religious accommodation that did shift some costs to third parties nevertheless was permissible because it did not impose an undue hardship on them – and it satisfied the Establishment Clause despite its burden on others.[62]

Other courts have come to similar conclusions in other situations. In *Crider v. University of Tennessee*, the Sixth Circuit emphasized that "grumbling" by other employees is not sufficient to defeat a religious accommodation, and that "undue hardship is something greater than hardship."[63] In that case, a Sabbatarian asked for

---

[55] Id. at 1242.
[56] Id. at 1243.
[57] Id. at 1243–4; see also *O'Brien v. City of Springfield*, 319 F. Supp. 2d 90, 109 (D. Mass. 2003).
[58] Tooley, 648 F.2d at 1246.
[59] Id.
[60] Id.
[61] Id.
[62] See also *Burns v. S. Pac. Transp. Co.*, 589 F.2d 403, 407 (9th Cir. 1978).
[63] *Crider v. Univ. of Tennessee, Knoxville*, 492 F. App'x 609, 613 (6th Cir. 2012) (quoting *Draper v. United States Pipe and Foundry Co.*, 527 F.2d 515, 520 (6th Cir.1975)); see also id. at 614 (noting that *Draper*, although decided before *TWA v. Hardison*, survives that opinion); *Anderson v. General Dynamics*

an accommodation, even though it would have meant requiring other employees to work on Saturdays against their wishes. Unlike in *Hardison*, where a collective bargaining agreement gave employees a right to certain days off in accordance with a seniority system, in *Crider*, requiring other employees to cover for the Sabbatarian did not result in the loss of a contractual right, though it might have resulted in "grumbling."[64] After all, workers could be subject to weekend assignments for any number of reasons – being asked to work on a Saturday to accommodate the religious observance of a coworker did not *necessarily* present an unusual inconvenience. Whether it did was a question of fact. The Sixth Circuit therefore remanded, explaining that if the employer could show consequences more significant than dissatisfaction by other workers, it might be able to satisfy the undue hardship standard.[65]

A different sort of cost was found to be acceptable in *E.E.O.C. v. Townley*.[66] Jake and Helen Townley ran a company according to the tenets of their Christian faith. As part of their mission, they required all workers to attend weekly devotional services.[67] When Louis Pelvas objected because he was an atheist, his supervisor reiterated that attendance was required, but also told Pelvas that he could sleep or read the newspaper during the services. In litigation, the Townleys argued that exempting Pelvas would impose "spiritual costs" on them and on other workers. The court rejected that argument and ruled for Pelvas. It held that spiritual costs, though cognizable,[68] must affect the conduct of the business in order to count as an undue hardship.[69] But it also said that even when spiritual costs were considered on their own terms, they did not amount to an undue hardship under the facts. At most, the

---

Convair Aerospace Division, 589 F.2d 397 (1978). But cf. *Brener v. Diagnostic Ctr. Hosp.*, 671 F.2d 141, 147 (5th Cir. 1982) (holding that requiring other employees to swap shifts in order to accommodate plaintiff did not result in mere "grumbling" and was an undue hardship).

[64] *Crider*, 492 F. App'x. at 615. Still other courts have endorsed the view that mere differential treatment of other employees cannot be enough to defeat a religious accommodation. See, e.g., *Brown v. Gen. Motors Corp.*, 601 F.2d 956, 961 (8th Cir. 1979)

[65] Notably, the *Crider* court also said that costs to other employees do not count in the undue hardship analysis, only detrimental effects on the employer's business – which could incorporate harm to employees if it caused those employees to quit, for instance. This holding is inconsistent with *Hardison*, where a major consideration was the impact on other workers' rights under the seniority system. It also conflicts with decisions in other circuits, which take into account harms to other employees. See, e.g., *Balint v. Carson City, Nev.*, 180 F.3d 1047, 1054 (9th Cir. 1999); *Townley*, 859 F.2d at 616; *Protos v. Volkswagen of Am., Inc.*, 797 F.2d 129, 134–5 (3d Cir. 1986). We therefore reject this aspect of *Crider* as a model for limiting the third-party harm doctrine. Harms to all third parties should count. Nevertheless, *Crider* presents an example of how a court might, in an unusual case, find that accommodating a religious citizen harms other private citizens, but not too much.

[66] *E.E.O.C. v. Townley Engineering & Mfg. Co.*, 859 F.2d 610 (1988).

[67] Id. at 611–12.

[68] Id. at 615 ("We acknowledge that spiritual costs can exist.").

[69] Id.

court said, exempting Pelvas would have "slightly reduced" the "ease with which [the company] spread its word to its employees," but that was not enough.[70]

Consider finally *McDaniel v. Essex International, Inc.*[71] Doris McDaniel was a Seventh-day Adventist who, like Hardison, objected to supporting the union. Unlike Hardison, however, she offered to pay the portion of dues necessary for collective bargaining and to donate an amount equivalent to the remainder to a mutually agreeable charity.[72] After the union refused to even consider this offer and demanded that McDaniel be fired, the employer terminated her. The Sixth Circuit ruled for McDaniel, holding that the only burden on the company was the cost of litigating its dispute with the union. A difference from *Hardison* was that accommodating McDaniel need not have affected other employees at all.[73] Under those circumstances, although the employer "was placed in a difficult position," the burden on it did not amount to undue hardship.[74]

Overall, then, the undue hardship standard, as interpreted by the Supreme Court, tracks the concern with religious accommodations that shift harms to other private citizens, and it provides both a standard and a set of precedents that sensibly limit application of the principle in situations where the costs to others are slight. In many cases, religious accommodations that shift burdens will be inappropriate, but there will be other situations where burden-shifting is reasonable and where harms to others, though perhaps material, are disproportionately small compared to the benefits to religious freedom from accommodations.

CONCLUSION

Under the approach we have outlined in this chapter, Mary Stinemetz would have won her case.[75] Even if, in our hypothetical scenario, granting an accommodation would have imposed costs on her insurance company, those costs would not have been sufficient to defeat her claim. The undue hardship test, as best understood, allows religious accommodations that relieve serious burdens on religion but impose slight costs on others. Both as a normative matter and as an account of what lower

---

[70] Id. at 616.
[71] 696 F.2d 34 (6th Cir. 1982).
[72] Id. at 38.
[73] Id. at 37–8.
[74] Id. at 38 ("The only hardship which Essex points to is the necessity to litigate a dispute with the union for failing to discharge the plaintiff. Of course, its submission to the union's demand for the plaintiff's discharge embroiled Essex in litigation which has now lasted nearly ten years.").
[75] See supra note 24 (citing *Stinemetz v. Kansas Health Policy Authority*, 252 P. 3d 141, 155–6 (Kan. App. 2011)).

courts are actually doing, this is the most appealing interpretation of the test for whether a third-party harm prevents the government from accommodating religion.

Regardless of whether or not the undue hardship standard is accepted as the best model, the crucial conceptual point is that government accommodation of religious practices must avoid harm to others. That is a bedrock tenet of the law governing religious freedom in our country. Like other constitutional principles, however, the doctrine of avoiding harms to third parties is not absolute. And, as recent litigation has again made clear, defining its limits is essential to our broader understanding of the First Amendment.

16

"A Patchwork Array of Theocratic Fiefdoms?"* RFRA Claims Against the ACA's Contraception Mandate as Examples of the New Feudalism

Mary Anne Case

The new millennium in the United States is, somewhat surprisingly, becoming a time in which an individual's legal rights, including rights of access to goods and services in the health care context, may turn out to be increasingly, rather than decreasingly, a function of his or her hierarchical attachments, such as those to a state, employer, church, or family. The Affordable Care Act (ACA) is a paradigm example of this phenomenon, which I have termed the new feudalism.[1] As with the old feudalism, an individual may have some choice of to whom or what to become attached and may be subject to multiple overlords, but it is one's network of overlords, rather than an undifferentiated, impersonal free market, let alone a market so regulated as to give all equal access regardless of attachments, which, in important respects, determines an individual's access to rights, goods, and services. Thus, to

---

* *Autocam Corp. v. Sebelius*, No. 12–cv–1096, 2012 WL 6845677 at *7 (W.D.Mich. December 24, 2012) (observing that the rule proposed by the ACA contraception mandate objectors "would paralyze the normal process of governing, and threaten to replace a generally uniform pattern of economic and social regulation with a patchwork array of theocratic fiefdoms"). This paper forms part of a larger project on the new feudalism, first presented as the keynote lecture at Tulane Law School's November 2014 Forum on the Future of Law and Inequality.

[1] Others have earlier used this term in contexts having some family resemblance to the very recent phenomena I am describing. See, e.g., Robert Reich, *The New Property*, 73 Yale L. J. 733, 768–73 (1963). Reich sees the philosophy behind such benefits cases as *Flemming v. Nestor*, 363 U.S. 603 (1960) (authorizing termination of old-age benefits to an alien deported from the U.S. for Communist Party membership) as "resemb[ling that] of feudal tenure" in that "wealth is held conditionally, the conditions being ones which seek to ensure the fulfillment of obligations imposed by the state." Id. at 769. These cases have, according to him, "more than a suggestion of the condition of fealty demanded in olden times." Id. at 770. Although Reich does note as feudal elements in the domains he analyzes that "there is a merging of public and private" and "the sovereign power is shared with large private interests," id. at 770, his principal emphasis in analyzing "the distribution and use of wealth in such a way as to create and maintain dependence" is on the way in which this is seen to further "the interest of the state or society or the lord paramount," id. My own emphasis, by contrast, will be not on the state as lord paramount, but on something more akin to subinfeudation, on the interests of the secular and religious corporate bodies and individuals who now claim a share of quasi-sovereign power.

determine what health insurance options are legally available to an individual and at what price, one must now follow a path through that individual's employer, family members, and state of residence.[2]

Four sets of cases concerning the logic and limits of the ACA's new feudalism have already reached the Supreme Court. In two, the relevant feudatories were the states, such that these cases can also be said to concern the old federalism. This chapter will concentrate on the other two sets of ACA challenges to have reached the Supreme Court, each a Religious Freedom Restoration Act (RFRA) challenge to the ACA's contraception mandate, one set brought by closely held for-profit corporations under the caption *Burwell v. Hobby Lobby Stores*,[3] and the other brought under the caption *Zubik v. Burwell* by religious nonprofits, most affiliated with a church, but none so fully integrated with any church as to qualify for the exemption from the contraception mandate the Obama administration extended to "churches, their integrated auxiliaries, and conventions or associations of churches," as well as to the "exclusively religious activities of any religious order."[4] Both are discussed in greater depth in this volume's Introduction and in many of the chapters in this volume. This chapter will argue that among the best ways in which to understand the claims being made in these cases is using frameworks from the pre-modern past, including the freedom of the church, cuius regio eius religio, and patriarchal power, each of which has elements of a claim of sovereignty.

1. THE NEW FEUDALISM AND THE OLD FEDERALISM

Whatever the fate of the ACA itself, the questions of federalism posed by it have new, perhaps increasing relevance as the Trump administration and the Republican Congress on the one hand seek to move back to an older model of block grants or per capita allotments for programs like Medicaid and on the other threaten to clamp down on states who announce their divergence from certain federal policies. Thus, the framework of the two Supreme Court ACA cases raising claims on behalf of states will remain significant.

As a result of the first of these cases, *National Federation of Independent Businesses (NFIB) v. Sebelius*, whether a nonelderly, nondisabled indigent person with no insurance through an employer or family member can receive health care through Medicaid became a function of the decision made by his or her state to either accept or reject the federal government's conditional offer of increased

---

[2] Employer-sponsored health insurance for employees and their dependents has been a peculiar feature of the U.S. health care system since the mid-twentieth century, but only with the passage of the ACA did it take on the characteristics of a legal mandate. For further discussion, see Holly Fernandez Lynch & Gregory Curfman, Ch. 11, this volume.
[3] 134 S. Ct. 2751 (2014).
[4] 26 U.S.C. § 6033(a)(3)(A)(i) & (iii); 45 C.F.R. § 147.131(a).

Medicaid funding.[5] Gradually, in the years since the NFIB decision, approximately two-thirds of the states, often through a unilateral decision by the state's governor, have accepted the ACA's Medicaid expansion conditions; but one-third continue to refuse,[6] leaving their citizens unable to access these benefits. As a result of the second decision, *King v. Burwell*, citizens of all states remain eligible for potential federal subsidies for the purchase of private insurance regardless of whether their home state established its own exchange or instead relied on the federal exchange to serve the state's citizens. Had the plaintiffs in *King v. Burwell* prevailed, those ineligible for Medicaid or employer-based insurance could only have potentially qualified for subsidies if their state in fact established its own exchange; now, although the policies available still will be state-based, it will not be state of residence but only income level and lack of availability of insurance through an employer or family member that will determine eligibility for subsidies. Because neither of these two ACA cases centrally implicates religion,[7] this chapter will not discuss them further, although it will be useful to keep them, as well as the general structure of the ACA, in mind as the chapter proceeds.

2. THE RELIGIOUS NONPROFITS AND THE FREEDOM OF THE CHURCH

The claims at stake in RFRA objections to the contraception mandate have been cogently characterized by both supporters and opponents as sounding in autonomy and freedom of contract.[8] In this chapter I want to highlight the extent to which they are also property claims, verging on claims of sovereignty.

---

[5] *Nat'l Fed'n of Indep. Bus. v. Sebelius*, 132 S. Ct. 2566 (2012) (NFIB).

[6] See The Henry J. Kaiser Foundation, *Current Status of State Medicaid Expansion Decisions* (July 7, 2016), available at http://kff.org/health-reform/slide/current-status-of-the-medicaid-expansion-decision/ [https://perma.cc/2MS5-S8ZL].

[7] Given the emphasis of the chapter on corporate as distinguished from individual rights, it is, however, worth noting that, although the Supreme Court did not discuss them in NFIB or any other case to date, there were individual challenges to the ACA's individual mandate brought under the Religious Freedom Restoration Act, all unsuccessful. Thus, for example, plaintiffs Edward Lee and Susan Seven-Sky were denied an exemption from the individual mandate notwithstanding their RFRA claim of "a sincerely held religious belief that God will provide for [their] physical, spiritual, and financial well-being" such that "[b]eing forced to buy health insurance conflicts with [their] religious faith because [they] believe that [they] would be indicating that [they] need a backup plan and [are] not really sure whether God will, in fact, provide for [their] needs." *Mead v. Holder*, 766 F.Supp.2d 16, 43 (D.D.C. 2011), aff'd sub. *Seven-Sky v. Holder*, 661 F.3d 1 (D.C. Cir. 2011) (quoting complaint). The D.C. federal courts found this to be no "more than a de minimis burden on their Christian faith" and hence unredressable under RFRA, especially since 1) the plaintiffs intended to pay the tax rather than purchase insurance and 2) they had expressed no objection to other social welfare taxes such as social security. Id.

[8] For an exposition by an opponent, see, e.g., Elizabeth Sepper, *Free Exercise Lochnerism*, 115 Colum. L. Rev. 1453 (2015).

I will begin by examining the claims of the Zubik plaintiffs, including those of the mediagenic Little Sisters of the Poor. Perhaps not until oral argument at the Supreme Court was it made clear to most observers that these plaintiffs were not just asking to be relieved of the obligation to sign a form opting out of the contraception mandate. They were instead arguing that nothing tangible or intangible that they could possibly be seen to control, no part of "*their* plan infrastructure,"[9] nothing that was "theirs," could be allowed a role in providing the objected-to contraceptives.[10] As the opening page of Archbishop Zubik's brief put it, their religious objections extended to any "actions that cause the objectionable coverage to be delivered to *Petitioners' own* employees and students by *Petitioners' own* insurance companies in connection with *Petitioners' own* health plans."[11] The involvement of any aspect of what was "theirs" in the delivery of contraceptives to "their" women was an impermissible burden, according to the plaintiffs. Thus, no aspect of "their" health plan, conceptualized as a thing over which they exercised dominion, must play any role in providing contraception to "their" female affiliates, who should not be allowed to obtain contraception tied in any way to that affiliation.

Claims that the government was seeking to "hijack"[12] and "commandeer"[13] the Zubik plaintiffs' health plans are noteworthy. The word "commandeer," when used before the Supreme Court, has echoes of contestation over sovereignty, associated as it is with disputes concerning the limits of federal power over the apparatus of the sovereign states.[14] But hijack refers to property, as Paul Clement's oral argument on behalf of the Little Sisters made clear. Acknowledging that a "health plan is somewhat intangible," Clement suggested

> if you put this in more tangible terms, ... if the consequence of us filing the form was that they would come in to one of the Little Sisters homes [for the aged] and set up shop in a room, they could pay us rent, it wouldn't cost us a thing. And then they operated a Title X clinic out of our homes? I think everyone would

---

[9] Brief for Petitioners at 51, *E. Tex. Baptist Univ. v. Burwell*, Nos. 15–35, 15–105, 15–119, & 15–191 (U.S. January 4, 2016) (emphasis in original).

[10] See, e.g., id. at 14 (objecting that "the mandated 'payments for contraception services' are inextricably tied to the eligible organization's health plan").

[11] Id. at 1 (emphasis added).

[12] See, e.g., id. at 53 ("[T]here is no need to hijack the delivery plans of religious non-profits as the delivery vehicle.").

[13] See Reply Brief for Petitioners at 34, *Zubik v. Burwell*, Nos. 14–1418, 14–1453 & 14–1505 (U.S. March 11, 2016) ("The Government likewise argues that any alternative other than commandeering Petitioners' health plans would impose 'logistical and administrative hurdles.'").

[14] See, e.g., NFIB, 132 S. Ct. at 2602 (discussing cases in which the Court "str[uck] down federal legislation that commandeers a State's legislative or administrative apparatus for federal purposes"). Cf. *Printz v. United States*, 521 U.S. 898 (1997) (striking down portions of the Brady Bill that, in the Court's view, commandeered the services of state law enforcement officials).

understand that, of course, we are complicit in the coverage that's provided on our premises.[15]

This argument seemed to resonate with several of the Justices, but, particularly in context, it should, for the following reasons, have been counterproductive to the plaintiffs' aims: What Clement seems to be describing is akin to an eminent domain proceeding against the Little Sisters – a portion of their property is taken for the public use of operating a Title X clinic and they are paid just compensation in the form of rent. There is substantial doubt over whether the Religious Land Use and Institutionalized Persons Act (RLUIPA) can offer a defense to eminent domain.[16] Nor are religious owners of property otherwise immune from takings, especially if their objection to the taking is not the religious significance of the property to them, but the religiously objectionable use to which the government intends to put it. Moreover, rather than being an absurd hypothetical, the scenario Clement describes might, specifically with respect to access to contraception, turn out to be a feasible less restrictive alternative under RFRA. The government might in future, for example, consider using eminent domain to take over space in a Catholic health care facility in which medical goods and services that the facility objects to providing might conveniently be made available.

It is unsurprising that Justices Roberts and Alito are the ones who, at oral argument, most clearly grasped and ran with the broad claims to dominion over intangible property raised by the religious organizations in Zubik, because these two are the authors, respectively, of the majority and a concurring opinion in Hosanna Tabor,[17] a case that extended constitutional protections unprecedented in American law to religious organizations.[18] Indeed, Chief Justice Roberts begins his novel corporatist history of the religion clauses in Hosanna Tabor with Magna Carta's guarantee that "the English church shall be free, and shall have its rights undiminished and

---

[15] Transcript of Oral Argument at 20, *Zubik v. Burwell*, No. 14–1418 (U.S. March 23, 2016). One source for Clement's analogy may be the Brief of Thirteen Law Professors as Amici Curiae in Support of Petitioners, *Zubik v. Burwell*, Nos. 14–1418, 14–1453, 14–1505, 15–35, 15–105, 15–119, 15–191 (U.S. January 11, 2016).

[16] For discussion, see Christopher Serkin & Nelson Tebbe, *Condemning Religion: RLUIPA and the Politics of Eminent Domain*, 85 Notre Dame L. Rev. 1 (2009). Because Serkin and Tebbe "conceptualize RLUIPA as a prophylaxis against intentional discrimination," id. at 2–3, their views as to its limits may have less traction in the vastly expanded accommodation environment post-Hobby Lobby.

[17] *Hosanna-Tabor Evangelical Lutheran Church & Sch. v. Equal Emp't Opportunity Comm'n*, 132 S. Ct. 694 (2012).

[18] For further discussion, see Mary Anne Case, *Citizens of the City of God United? The Confused Premises and Radical Implications of Hosanna Tabor* (unpublished manuscript) (on file with the author). For evidence that religious institutions were under much tighter control by secular law in earlier times in the United States, see generally Sarah Barringer Gordon, *The First Disestablishment: Limits on Church Power and Property Before the Civil War*, 162 U. Pa. L. Rev. 307 (2014).

its liberties unimpaired,"[19] giving new energy to those scholars committed to an American version of what they call "the freedom of the church."[20]

While invoking Magna Carta puts the development of corporate religious liberty squarely in a feudal context, an American example of guarantees made to religious organizations might be even more apropos when discussing accommodations to the contraception mandate. Expositions of the history and meaning of American religious freedom are replete with references to Thomas Jefferson's letter to the Danbury Baptists, which contains (as the Constitution itself does not) reference to "building a wall of separation between Church & State."[21] In the age of Hosanna Tabor, Hobby Lobby, and Zubik, when a long history of U.S. government solicitude for individual religious liberty such as that Jefferson expressed to the Danbury Baptists[22] is being supplemented with new solicitude for corporate religious liberty, another of Jefferson's letters has new relevance.[23] Replying in 1804, shortly after the Louisiana Purchase, to the Nuns of the Order of St. Ursula at New Orleans, Jefferson assured them:

> I have received, holy sisters, the letter you have written me wherein you express anxiety for the property vested in your institution by the former governments of Louisiana. [T]he principles of the constitution and government of the United states are a sure guarantee to you that it will be preserved to you sacred and inviolate, and that your institution will be permitted to govern itself according to it[s] own voluntary rules, without interference from the civil authority. [W]hatever diversity of shade may appear in the religious opinions of our fellow citizens, the charitable objects of your institution cannot be indifferent to any; and it's furtherance of the

[19] Hosanna-Tabor, 132 S. Ct. at 702 (quoting the first clause of Magna Carta).
[20] See particularly the work of Rick Garnett and Steven Smith, such as their respective chapters in *The Rise of Corporate Religious Liberty* (Zoe Robinson, Chad Flanders & Micah Schwartzman eds., Oxford University Press 2015). In the same volume, see Robin West's "Freedom of the Church and our Endangered Civil Rights: Exiting the Social Contract" for a critique of this claimed "right of churches and church-affiliated institutions, not just individuals, to be exempt on grounds of institutional religious liberty from some otherwise binding legal obligations," id. at text accompanying note 119.
[21] Thomas Jefferson, *Letter to the Danbury Baptists* (January 1, 1802), available at www.loc.gov/loc/lcib/9806/danpre.html [https://perma.cc/V2TR-9MDF].
[22] Although Jefferson's letter is addressed, not to an individual, but to "a committee of the Danbury Baptist association," it stresses that "religion is a matter which lies solely between Man & his God, that he owes account to none other for his faith or his worship." Id.
[23] Interestingly, Jefferson's Letter to the Ursuline Nuns, infra note 25, is not mentioned in Roberts's Hosanna-Tabor opinion. It did, however, feature prominently in the comments another nun, head of the Catholic Health Association of the United States, submitted to the Department of Health and Human Services objecting to the Interim Final Rule defining Religious Employer Exception for Group Health Plans and Health Insurance Issuers Relating to Coverage of Preventive Services under the Patient Protection and Affordable Care Act. See letter of Sr. Carol Keehan, DC, Catholic Health Ass'n, *Comments on Religious Employer Exceptions to Preventive Services* (September 22, 2011), available at www.chausa.org/Pages/Advocacy/Issues/Faith-based_and_Ethical_Concerns/ [https://perma.cc/28XV-E7R5].

wholesome purposes of society, by training up it's younger members in the way they should go, cannot fail to ensure it the patronage of the government it is under. [B]e assured it will meet all the protection which my office can give it.[24]

Although, on one level, Hosanna Tabor has breathed new life into the proposition that "the principles of the constitution ... guarantee... that [a religious] institution will be permitted to govern itself according to it[s] own voluntary rules, without interference from the civil authority," on another, Jefferson's assurances that "the property vested in [such an] institution ... will be preserved to [it] sacred and inviolate" may sound to those litigating the ACA cases uncomfortably close to Barack Obama's infamous assurance that "if you like your health care plan, you'll be able to keep your health care plan."[25]

Putting Jefferson's letter in historical context mitigates against overreading its promises. Both the nuns' anxiety and Jefferson's response to it should be seen in the context of French revolutionary decrees putting all the property of the Church at the disposal of the nation on November 2, 1789 and dissolving all religious orders on February 13, 1790. In looking for traces of the new feudalism, it is important to remember that there is nothing in U.S. history like the night of August 4, 1789, when the French revolutionaries abolished all feudal privileges, leaving no intermediate institutions between the individual and the state. On the contrary, as commentators from Burke to Tocqueville observed, the United States has always recognized and valued intermediate institutions.

The intermediate institutions central to the new feudalism are, however, closer to those Tocqueville would have associated with dangerous inequalities of wealth and power in the old regime – the institutional Catholic Church and the hereditary aristocracy – than they are to the voluntary associations he found so valuable to the early American republic. The victory in Hobby Lobby went to corporations wholly owned by multiple generations of a single family, not to any whose shares were publicly traded.[26] And more democratically organized intermediate institutions, such as the labor union, have had much less success before the Supreme Court in recent years than hierarchical churches and family corporations.[27] The Supreme Court is

---

[24] Thomas Jefferson, *Letter to Ursuline Nuns of New Orleans* (13 July 1804), available at http://rotunda.upress.virginia.edu/founders/default.xqy?keys=FOEA-print-04-01-02-0068 [https://perma.cc/5HH2-WKKU].

[25] See Politifact, *Obama: "If you like your health care plan, you'll be able to keep your health care plan"* (2016), available at www.politifact.com/obama-like-health-care-keep/ [https://perma.cc/99AA-M7JL].

[26] The Court in *Burwell v. Hobby Lobby Stores, Inc.* (Hobby Lobby) posited that "numerous practical restraints would likely prevent" a public corporation from ever asserting a RFRA claim, although it imposed no "practical constraints" whatsoever on a family-owned corporation's assertion of religious beliefs. 134 S.Ct. 2751, 2774 (2014).

[27] This may be most clear when a labor union is in direct conflict with either the hierarchical church or the family. See *Nat'l Labor Relations Bd. v. Catholic Bishops*, 440 U.S. 490 (1979) (holding that, to avoid First Amendment problems with encroaching on the autonomy of the church, the NLRA

thus on a trajectory to reverse or stall a centuries-long trend toward abolition of the feudal privileges of religious and family corporations, as it puts more quasi-sovereign power within reach of such bodies. Indeed, as the next section will discuss, the Supreme Court's interpretation of RFRA comes close to turning the heads of family corporations like the Greens into divine right sovereigns, whose will, so long as it can be derived from their religious convictions, can have some of the force of law.[28]

3. THE FOR-PROFIT CORPORATIONS AND *CUIUS REGIO EIUS RELIGIO*

In contrast to the religious nonprofits, the for-profit ACA accommodation plaintiffs are much less systematically committed either to religious exercise generally or to opposing contraception and abortion in particular. In making this observation, I am not focusing on the for-profit character of these closely held corporations, but simply observing that, as it happens, the nonprofits who sued are almost all explicitly affiliated with an organized religion that has long set its face against abortion or against contraception more generally and these nonprofits have long incorporated tenets of that religion, including but by no means limited to matters covered by the contraception mandate, in their governing documents and their prior corporate behavior.[29] Thus, no one who enrolls in or is employed by Notre Dame or Wheaton College, no one who is employed by or cared for by the Little Sisters, can fail to be aware in advance of, or to be affected in day-to-day interactions by, the organization's commitment to exercising a particular set of religious commitments.

By contrast, from all that appears in their litigation materials, the same is far from true of the particular closely held for-profit corporations who sued to avoid the application to them of the ACA contraception mandate. Many, including Hobby Lobby itself, had been so unconcerned with their complicity in the delivery of contraceptives that they had not even noticed that their insurance companies had long provided contraception coverage to their employees, and they scrambled to change their plans only after the passage of the ACA, as discussed in greater depth in Greg Lipper's chapter in this volume.[30] Most did not mention religious commitments in

---

should not be interpreted as extending its protections to employees of church-run schools); *Harris v. Quinn*, 134 S. Ct. 2618 (2014) (holding that mother paid by the state to care for her disabled son need not pay a "fair share" fee to the union that negotiates payment terms with the state).

[28] Cf. Carl Schmitt, *Political Theology: Four Chapters on the Concept of Sovereignty* (trans. George Schwab 2005) ("Sovereign is he who decides on the exception.").

[29] The exceptions to some extent reinforce the rule – unaffiliated with a religion, they are wholly and explicitly committed to opposing abortion; it is, indeed, their raison d'etre. See, e.g., *March for Life v. Burwell*, 128 F.Supp.3d 116, 122 (D.D.C.) (deciding an equal protection challenge by "non-profit, non-religious pro-life organization" seeking same accommodation offered to religious organizations).

[30] See Gregory M. Lipper, Ch. 4.

their corporate documents before the passage of the ACA, and even afterwards most cited few, if any, other religiously motivated corporate behaviors besides those at issue in the litigation.[31]

Nevertheless, a majority of the Supreme Court deferred completely to the claims of these corporations and their owners, demanding neither consistency nor clarity, nor any compensatory bearing of burdens; and affording these corporations and their owners an astonishing amount of control over the way in which they fulfilled both their civil and their claimed religious obligations.[32] The Court went so far as to say that, because the Hobby Lobby plaintiffs "have religious reasons for providing health-insurance coverage for their employees,"[33] the legally available option of dropping health care coverage for their employees entirely so as to avoid any obligation to include contraception insurance need not be considered as a viable alternative to the accommodations demanded.

The Court invoked the pre-RFRA constitutional case of *Thomas v. Review Board* for the proposition that it was foreclosed from questioning any aspect of the plaintiffs' religious convictions beyond their sincerity.[34] Thomas, however, did sacrifice something for his religious convictions – his job, for which unemployment insurance was far from full compensation. By contrast, the corporate objectors to the contraception mandate, so long as they had property and power over others, need do no more than announce their religious preferences for RFRA to be mobilized to shape the law around them.[35]

The Supreme Court's insistence that "protecting the free-exercise rights of corporations like Hobby Lobby ... protects the religious liberty of the humans who own and control those companies"[36] has echoes of another accommodation to the religious preferences of the powerful, the 1555 Peace of Augsburg's *cuius regio eius*

---

[31] Hobby Lobby, which closed on Sundays, declined to sell products related to alcohol consumption and placed advertisements with religious messages, see Hobby Lobby, 134 S.Ct. at 2766, was on the high end of corporate religious activity among the more than four score plaintiff corporations.

[32] As I have previously observed, this is one of many current examples of a religious accommodation claim in which "religiously motivated opponents of sexual rights seem to want to have their cake, eat it too, and shove it down [opponents'] throats." See Mary Anne Case, *Why "Live-And-Let-Live" Is Not a Viable Solution to the Difficult Problems of Religious Accommodation in the Age of Sexual Civil Rights*, 88 U.S.C. L. Rev. 463, 471 (2015).

[33] Hobby Lobby, 134 S.Ct. at 2777.

[34] See *Thomas v. Review Bd. of Ind. Emp't Sec. Div.*, 450 U.S. 707, 716 (1981).

[35] As Greg Lipper's chapter in this volume illustrates, some who were nevertheless accommodated did not even bother to frame their objections as sincerely religious, but rather as what the Sixth Circuit called "a laissez-faire, anti-government screed." See *Eden Foods, Inc. v. Sebelius*, 733 F.3d 626, 629 n.3 (citation omitted), vacated sub nom., *Eden Foods, Inc. v. Burwell*, 134 S. Ct. 2902 (2014) (discussed in Lipper, supra note 30).

[36] Hobby Lobby, 134 S.Ct. at 2768. In other words, the golden rule is: he who has the gold makes the rules.

religio, which gave to those who "own[ed] and control[led]" a territory the ability to determine the faith its inhabitants must conform to.[37]

Just as feudal tenure and its faith-based successor *cuius regio* produced "a patchwork array of theocratic fiefdoms," so the domain over which the Green family exercises its sway and may now live out its faith is not a geographically contiguous territory, but extends to physical properties (stores and warehouses) in multiple states, plus an intangible network of corporate entities and contracts it has with employees and suppliers (including the suppliers of health insurance to those employees). The subordinate persons within these domains, unless they exercise a right of exit, are now, with little prior notice and whatever their own faith commitments, subject to the religious commitments of the Greens as those commitments from moment to moment may evolve.[38]

4. THE NEW PATRIARCHY

The new feudalism has a frightening amount in common with the old domestic relations,[39] as the litigation of religious objectors to the contraception mandate makes plain.[40] Thus, for example, in its cert. petition, Notre Dame University insists:

> Just as a Mormon might refuse to hire a caterer that insisted on serving alcohol to his wedding guests, or a Jew might refuse to hire a caterer determined to serve pork at his son's bar mitzvah, it violates Notre Dame's religious beliefs to hire or maintain a relationship with any third party that will provide contraceptive coverage to its plan beneficiaries.[41]

---

[37] See, e.g., Benjamin J. Kaplan, *Divided by Faith: Religious Conflict and the Practice of Toleration in Early Modern Europe* p. 103 ff. (describing how *cuius regio* worked to "tur[n] religious choice into an attribute of sovereignty" for rulers).

[38] Elizabeth Sepper, Ch. 8, this volume, describes a similar feudal patchwork as it applies to Catholic health care, but with fewer possibilities for the hospitals, doctors, and patients involved to exit.

[39] Scholarly discussions of twentieth-century corporate experiments with benefit schemes for employees seem to shift seamlessly between analogies to the patriarchal family and to the feudal estate. See, e.g., Nikki Mandel, *The Corporation as Family; the Gendering of Corporate Welfare 1890–1930* (2004); Sanford M. Jacoby, *Modern Manors: Welfare Capitalism since the New Deal* (1997).

[40] Cf. Susan Frelich Appleton, *The Forgotten Family Law of Eisenstadt v. Baird*. 28 Yale Journal of Law and Feminism 1, 31 (2016). Appleton notes Hobby Lobby's kinship with classic substantive due process cases *Meyer v. Nebraska* and *Pierce v. Society of Sisters*, saying: "Hobby Lobby treats the corporate entity and its employees as family. In effect, the corporation, occupying the role of parent, successfully objected to a law that 'standardizes' the treatment of employees, who occupy the place of children, and prevents the transmission of chosen 'family values' to them."

[41] *Univ. of Notre Dame v. Burwell*, 2014 U.S. Briefs 392 at 817 (cert. petition). Cf. *Marsh v. Alabama*, 326 U. S. 501, 506 (1946) (rejecting as violative of First Amendment free speech protections the claim, with respect to a company town, that "the corporation's right to control the inhabitants of Chickasaw is coextensive with the right of a homeowner to regulate the conduct of his guests").

Famously, of course, the Anglo-American law of domestic relations historically encompassed not only Husband and Wife, Parent and Child, but Guardian and Ward, Master and Servant, giving the master of the household patriarchal power over all his dependents. In the late nineteenth-century aftermath of slave emancipation, relations between masters and servants emerged from the domestic sphere and the domain of status into that of contract and wage labor.[42] And in the late twentieth-century aftermath of civil rights protests and women's liberation, universities ceased to be seen as standing in loco parentis to their students.[43] Notre Dame's analogizing of its employees and students to persons invited by a patriarch to a family gathering and therefore served only what the patriarch wishes to provide in accordance with his religious beliefs is therefore strikingly inappropriate for the twenty-first century.

Children are now presumed emancipated upon reaching the age of majority and even minors may access contraception without parental consent.[44] In perhaps the most extreme attempt to use RFRA literally to re-establish patriarchy, however, Missouri legislator Paul Wieland sued to block his daughters – two of whom are adults but under age 26, and thus still covered under the ACA by his employee health care plan – from using that plan to access contraception to which he, their father, has a religious objection.[45] His attorney told a federal appeals court that Wieland and his wife "stand in the same shoes" as Hobby Lobby, and Hobby Lobby's "employees are to Hobby Lobby what the daughters are to Paul and Teresa Wieland."[46] Astonishingly, the federal courts have now accepted this argument, and authorized Wieland's insurance provider, itself an arm of the state of Missouri, to make a contraception-free insurance policy available to him (and, therefore, his adult daughters).[47]

---

[42] See generally, e.g., Amy Dru Stanley, *From Bondage to Contract: Wage Labor, Marriage and the Market in the Age of Slave Emancipation* (1998). Cf. *Dred Scott v. Sanford*, 60 U.S. 393, 527 (Catron, J, concurring) (saying that, to the slaveholder, his "slaves [are] parts of his family in name and in fact" as well as his property).

[43] See, e.g., Phillip Lee, *The Curious Life of* In Loco Parentis *at American Universities*, 8 Higher Education in Review 65, 72–6.

[44] For an overview of state laws on access, see, e.g., Guttmacher Institute, *Minors Access to Contraceptive Services* (September 1, 2016), available at www.guttmacher.org/sites/default/files/pdfs/spibs/spib_MACS.pdf [https://perma.cc/A95Q-YEES].

[45] *Wieland v. U.S. Dep't. of Health & Human Servs.*, 978 F. Supp. 2d 1008, 1010 (E.D. Mo. 2013), vacated, 793 F.3d 949 (8th Cir. 2015).

[46] ThinkProgress, *The Strange Case Of A Father Who Sued The Obama Administration To Keep His Daughters From Getting Birth Control* (September 11, 2014), available at https://thinkprogress.org/the-strange-case-of-a-father-who-sued-the-obama-administration-to-keep-his-daughters-from-getting-8a2e0d611703#.ecmgi6ti1 [https://perma.cc/9QEZ-KAY3].

[47] See generally *Weiland v. U.S. Dep't of Health & Human Servs.*, No. 4:13-cv-01577-JCH, 2016 WL 3924118 (E.D. Mo. July 21, 2016).

While it remains to be seen how any of these cases will be definitively resolved, it would be a profound irony if the final result of RFRA's application were to be that the ACA's contraception mandate, designed to serve the compelling governmental interest of improving the liberty and equality of women, instead presents new risks of sending them on the road back to feudal serfdom and patriarchal domination under the control of their religiously motivated employers, educators, or parents.

17

Unpacking the Relationship Between Conscience and Access

Robin Fretwell Wilson

Many people reflexively accept or reject health care conscience protections. Those prizing religious freedom argue that conscience protections ensure that religious believers can both take jobs in medicine and act consonant with their faith.[1] This group sometimes gives short shrift to concerns about access to needed medical services.[2] On the other side, advocates for reproductive rights sometimes see access concerns as so overriding that no religious convictions should ever be accommodated, even when there would not be an impact on access.[3]

Both accounts are too simplistic. A more nuanced account would divide conscience clauses into those that are access-expanding, access-neutral, or access-contracting and ask what characteristics make a conscience clause a threat to access, a wash for access, or, counter-intuitively, access-preserving.

This chapter provides that more nuanced account. It shows that it is possible to balance conscience and access, in at least some cases, by using common-sense devices, such as notice, parity rules, protections conditioned on not causing harm, and thickened duties to transfer pregnant women in distress. This chapter recognizes, however, that some protections jeopardize access more than others – for example, federal efforts to insulate conscience against encroachment by state authorities with "super conscience clauses" effectively hobble efforts to be more responsive to access concerns.

In a civil society, we should strive to maximize conscience protections without jeopardizing access. As the U.S. Supreme Court's remand in *Zubik v. Burwell*[4]

---

[1] E.g., Matthew S. Bowman & Christopher P. Schandevel, *The Harmony Between Professional Conscience Rights and Patients' Right of Access*, 6 Phoenix L. Rev. 31 (2012).

[2] See, e.g., Adam Sonfield, *New Refusal Clauses Shatter Balance Between Provider "Conscience," Patient Needs*, Guttmacher Rep. on Pub. Pol'y (August 2004), at 1, 2–3, available at www.guttmacher.org/pubs/tgr/07/3/gr070301.pdf [https://perma.cc/R62U-QGDR].

[3] See Julian Savulescu, *Conscientious Objection in Medicine*, 332 British Med. J. 294, 297 (2006) ("[V]alues and conscience ... should not influence the care an individual doctor offers" because "'value-driven medicine' [opens] a Pandora's box of idiosyncratic, bigoted, discriminatory medicine.").

[4] 136 S. Ct. 1557 (2016).

reminds us, realizing reproductive access without encroaching on conscience is achievable.

1. ACCESS-PRESERVING PROTECTIONS

Although counter-intuitive, giving individual providers and institutions the flexibility to follow their convictions when deciding what services to offer can promote access to contested services. Consider Congress' inaugural health care conscience clause, the Church Amendment. Shortly after *Roe v. Wade*,[5] Congress clarified that receiving federal hospital construction funds did not compel objecting institutions to provide abortions.[6] Congress also protected individual physicians from losing staff privileges or suffering other "discrimination" for doing abortions *or* refusing to do them. This equal-opportunity conscience protection reveals that conscience protections need not imperil access.[7]

Reproductive rights advocates are right that "the risk of imposition on those who do not share the objector's beliefs is especially great when an employer, hospital, health plan, pharmacy, or other corporate entity seeks an exemption."[8] Institutional providers pose a special challenge for access because institutions control large swaths of the market. Catholic hospitals care for one-sixth of all U.S. patients;[9] many possess monopoly power,[10] as others in this volume note. In some communities, a Catholic hospital is the sole hospital, a phenomenon sure to increase as Catholic health systems acquire other non-Catholic health systems.[11]

---

[5] 410 U.S. 113 (1973).
[6] 42 U.S.C. § 300a-7(c)(1).
[7] See Jody Feder, Cong. Research Serv., RS21428, *The History and Effect of Abortion Conscience Clause Laws* 5 (2005).
[8] Catherine Weiss, Director, ACLU Reproductive Freedom Project, Testimony on Refusal Clauses in the Reproductive Health Context Before the House Energy and Commerce Committee Health Subcommittee (July 11, 2002), available at www.aclu.org/reproductive-freedom/testimony-aclu-reproductive-freedom-project-director-catherine-weiss-refusal-cl [https://perma.cc/4GR8-VUQQ].
[9] U.S. Conference of Catholic Bishops, *Catholic Health Care, Social Services and Humanitarian Aid*, available at www.usccb.org/about/media-relations/backgrounders/health-care-social-service-humanitarian-aid.cfm [https://perma.cc/QU2Z-UVCL] (645 Catholic hospitals serve 87,972,910 patients annually).
[10] See Lori R. Freedman & Debra B. Stulberg, *Conflicts in Care for Obstetric Complications in Catholic Hospitals*, 4 AJOB Primary Research 1, 2 (2013); Reed Abelson, *Catholic Hospitals Expand, Religious Strings Attached*, N.Y. Times (February 20, 2012), available at www.nytimes.com/2012/02/21/health/policy/growth-of-catholic-hospitals-may-limit-access-to-reproductive-care.html [http://nyti.ms/18GUdaD].
[11] See id; Nina Martin, *Catholic Hospitals Grow, and With Them Questions of Care Pro Publica* (October 17, 2013), available at www.propublica.org/article/catholic-hospitals-grow-and-with-them-questions-of-care [https://perma.cc/GQ7X-NXE9].

An absolute right to refuse to provide a contested service can impede the public's ability to receive services, especially if few others are willing to perform the service in the immediate area.[12] Respect for conscience should never allow a provider to be in a "blocking position,"[13] which is far more likely with large regional hospitals than with individual providers.

Yet, evaluating whether conscience protections jeopardize access is complex. Consider the Church Amendment's protections for objecting institutions. In the months preceding *Roe* and the Church Amendment, a federal district court enjoined a private, nonprofit hospital from barring physicians from performing tubal ligations on patients.[14]

The decisions sparked a "striking outcry."[15] A Catholic bishop threatened "civil disobedience" – raising the "real and present danger that ... religious hospitals, if coerced into performing ... abortions or sterilizations contrary to their religious precepts, will simply eliminate their obstetrics department."[16] Faced with "the possibility that medical facilities may be forced to reject Federal support or to close obstetrical operations," Congress could not "see the gains in such a policy."[17]

In Congress' estimation, protecting conscience would not erase access: because a "majority of the hospitals [were] publicly owned ... no area ... would be without a hospital within a reasonable commuting distance which would perform abortion or sterilization procedures. Moreover, in an emergency situation – life or death type – no [hospital], religious or not, would deny such services."[18] In Congress' predictive judgment, conscience protection yielded more access by women to needed services, not less.

Figure 17.1 depicts how our reflexive suppositions about the impact on access can diverge from reality. For example, one assumes that institutional exemptions wipe access, placing them on the far left of a spectrum between no access and full access. Yet, the Church Amendment preserved *some* access by avoiding the wholesale closure of ob-gyn departments, moving it closer to the center of Figure 17.1.

---

[12] See, e.g., *State Policies in Brief: Refusing to Provide Health Services*, Guttmacher Inst. (November 1, 2014), available at www.guttmacher.org/statecenter/spibs/spib_RPHS.pdf [https://perma.cc/P3E5-C79J]; see generally Robin Fretwell Wilson, "The Erupting Clash Between Religion and the State over Contraception, Sterilization, and Abortion," in *Religious Freedom in America: Constitutional Traditions and New Horizons* (Allen Hertzke ed., 2014).

[13] Robin Fretwell Wilson, *The Calculus of Accommodation: Contraception, Abortion, Same-Sex Marriage, and Other Clashes Between Religion and the State*, 53 B.C. L. Rev. 1417, 1449 n.109 (2012). Time constraints also impact whether a provider acts as a "choke point." See Flynn and Wilson, infra note 30.

[14] *Taylor v. St. Vincent's Hospital*, 369 F. Supp. 948 (D. Mont. 1973).

[15] 119 CONG. REC. 9595 (1973) (statement of Sen. Frank Church).

[16] Id. Elsewhere, Senator Church describes as a "real and present danger that many of these religious hospitals, if coerced into performing operations for abortions or sterilizations contrary to their religious precepts, will simply eliminate their obstetrics department" Id. at 9600.

[17] Id. at 9596 (statement of Sen. Adlai Stevenson).

[18] Id.

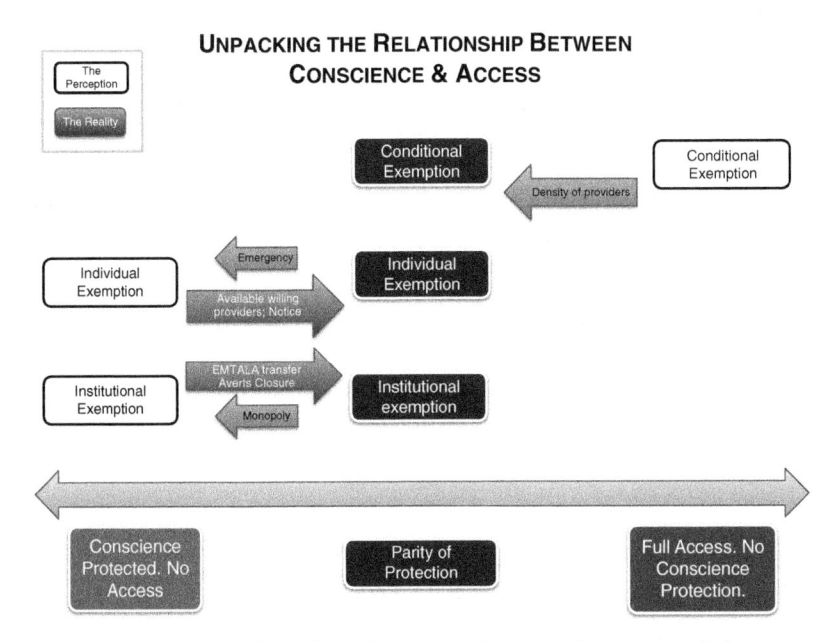

FIGURE 17.1 Unpacking the Relationship Between Conscience & Access

Threats of closure must be weighed carefully. Before the Obama Administration made significant concessions for religious nonprofits objecting to the contraceptive coverage mandate,[19] religious leaders like then-Archbishop of Chicago Cardinal George ominously warned that "unless something changes," the Archdiocese's directory listing "Catholic hospitals and health care institutions ... will be blank."[20] In Phoenix, a Catholic church stripped Arizona's largest hospital of its Catholic affiliation after the hospital terminated an eleven-week pregnancy to save the mother's life (the facility did not close).[21] In other contexts, religious objectors have acted on promises to close.[22]

---

[19] Coverage of Preventive Services Under the ACA, 77 Fed. Reg. 8725, 8728 (February 15, 2012).
[20] Francis Cardinal George, *What Are You Going to Give Up This Lent?*, Catholic New World (February 26, 2012), available at www.catholicnewworld.com/cnwonline/2012/0226/cardinal.aspx.
[21] Ed Pilkington, *US Catholic Hospital's Ties to Church Cut Over Abortion That Saved Mother*, Guardian, (December 22, 2010), available at www.theguardian.com/world/2010/dec/22/us-catholic-bishop-hospital-abortion [https://perma.cc/RV2W-W7J7]. Hospitals have unilaterally decided to de-affiliated after being barred from performing abortions. See Lois Uttley et al., *Miscarriage of Medicine: The Growth of Catholic Hospitals and the Threat to Reproductive Health Care*, MergerWatch 14 (2013), available at www.aclu.org/files/assets/growth-of-catholic-hospitals-2013.pdf [https://perma.cc/88JX-LSC2].
[22] See William Wan, *Same-Sex Marriage Leads Catholic Charities to Adjust Benefits*, Washington Post, March 2, 2010, available at www.washingtonpost.com/wp-dyn/content/article/2010/03/01/AR2010030103345.html [https://perma.cc/2FSA-MQ3T].

Threats should not alone be dispositive. When evaluating closure risk, legislators and regulatory bodies would be wise to consider existing market share, market concentration, the scarcity of other providers, the likelihood that the owner would sell a facility or that the government or a private buyer would acquire the facility before any shut-down, predicted transition time, and the likelihood that the objector would bend to civil strictures rather than close. They should also evaluate whether objectors would be loath to shed more lucrative health care enterprises.[23] Catholic hospitals have dissolved consolidated hospital operations and pulled the plug on mergers when pressed to provide abortions.[24]

With Catholic-affiliated hospitals accounting for a sizeable chunk of inpatient admissions nationally, policymakers may well be unwilling to engage in a high-stakes game of chicken. Legislatures, not institutions, should make these judgments after extensive hearings. While testimony can be slanted in favor of particular outcomes, supporters of reproductive rights are just as powerful as institutional objectors, ensuring a full airing of the question. Furthermore, well-informed legislators are capable of weighing and balancing plural interests.

Conscience protections can also enhance or preserve access by guaranteeing conscience in both directions.[25] The Church Amendment protected all moral or religious beliefs "about abortion," placing the decision to provide abortions or to refuse to do abortions beyond the reach of "discrimination" by institutional actors, like religious hospitals. Physicians remain an important, if small, component of access to needed services as well, challenging the simplistic account that individual conscience protections necessarily threaten access.[26]

2. ACCESS-NEUTRAL EXEMPTIONS

Conscience protections can burden patients.[27] But better information and conditional exemptions may alleviate that burden. Recognizing this, legislatures granting

---

[23] Kelly M. Doran et al., *Housing as Health Care – New York's Boundary-Crossing Experiment*, 369 New England J. Med. 2374 (2013).

[24] Francis J. Butler, *Will Charity Laws Close Catholic Hospitals?* America, October 29, 2001, available at http://americamagazine.org/issue/348/article/will-charity-laws-close-catholic-hospitals [https://perma.cc/U2XU-VH6Z].

[25] See J. Stuart Adams & Robin Fretwell Wilson, *Protecting Religious Liberty Requires Protections for All*, Cornerstone (April 30, 2015), available at http://berkleycenter.georgetown.edu/cornerstone/rfra-in-indiana-and-beyond/responses/protecting-religious-liberty-requires-protections-for-all [https://perma.cc/NM33-UKMU] (discussing two-way speech protections).

[26] Rachel K. Jones & Jenna Jerman, *Abortion Incidence and Service Availability in the United States*, 2011, Persp. on Sexual and Reprod. Health, March 2011, available at www.guttmacher.org/pubs/journals/psrh.46e0414.pdf [https://perma.cc/Q9CH-NTAP].

[27] See Kyung Song, *Olympia Women Complain After Pharmacies Refuse Prescriptions*, Seattle Times (August 1, 2006), available at http://community.seattletimes.nwsource.com/archive/?date=20060801&slug=pharmacy01m [https://perma.cc/E9TJ-28UG].

unqualified rights to object have incorporated notice requirements. Some abortion conscience clauses require objecting institutions to prominently display a notice.[28] Over time, which institutions offer contested services may seep into public consciousness.[29] Of course, notice has limited benefit for urgent services, like some reproductive decisions.[30] While notice is not a complete solution, conscience protections work best when they eliminate "search costs."[31] Moreover, thickened transfer duties may avoid hard decisions about which life to save, as Section 4 explains.

States utilize this approach with end-of-life care, as well as abortion. Oregon and Washington permit institutions to restrict physicians working within their four walls from "practicing life-ending procedures ... if notice is given."[32] Patients and physicians wanting greater flexibility can admit patients elsewhere. Notice-based refusals are crucial for Catholic facilities that abide by Ethical and Religious Directives for Catholic Health Care Services (ERDs).[33] Of course, if a provider will not respect a patient's do-not-resuscitate order, the patient may be resuscitated against her will – making transfer to appropriate caretakers critical, as Section 4 explains.

Notice requirements reduce hardships not just to the public, but to institutions offering a contested service. Requiring objecting employees to disclose objections in writing allows institutions to staff around objectors.[34] Feasibility will depend on the number of likely objectors and willing providers, hours of service, staffing arrangements, and how often patients seek specific services.

Because the refusal happens internally, the public is not impacted. Disclosure *ex ante* serves an important screening function, too, separating individuals with deeply felt objections from those who are more ambivalent.

---

[28] Neb. Rev. Stat. § 28–337 (2016); see also Or. Rev. Stat. § 435.475 (2016); Cal. Health & Safety Code § 123420(c) (2016); Adam Sonfield, *Provider Refusal and Access to Reproductive Health Services: Approaching a New Balance*, 11 Guttmacher Policy Review 2, 2 (Spring 2008), available at www.guttmacher.org/pubs/gpr/11/2/gpr110202.pdf [https://perma.cc/EW4B-ZHQ3].

[29] Barbara B. Hagerty, *Nun Excommunicated for Allowing Abortion*, National Public Radio (May 19, 2010).

[30] Cameron Flynn & Robin Fretwell Wilson, *When States Regulate Emergency Contraceptives Like Abortion, What Should Guide Disclosure?*, J.L. Med. & Ethics 72, 72 (Spring 2015).

[31] See Nathan J. Diament et al., *Comments Submitted to the U.S. Department of Health and Human Services with Regard to the Proposed Rescission of the "Conscience Regulation" Relating to Healthcare Workers and Certain Healthcare Services* 4 n.11 (April 7, 2009), available at http://law.wlu.edu/faculty/facultydocuments/wilsonr/HHSLetterFinal.pdf [https://perma.cc/92SG-AMHL].

[32] Wash. Rev. Code § 70.245.190 (2016); Or. Rev. Stat. § 127.885 (2016).

[33] U.S. Conference of Catholic Bishops, *Ethical and Religious Directives for Catholic Health Care Services* 27 (5th ed. 2009), available at www.usccb.org/issues-and-action/human-life-and-dignity/health-care/upload/Ethical-Religious-Directives-Catholic-Health-Care-Services-fifth-edition-2009.pdf [https://perma.cc/4J8R-H2GM]. Roughly half of Catholic facilities follow the directives on sterilization.

[34] Thoughtful staffing arrangements can ensure access. See infra notes 41–3; 54–6.

"Consistent fact-based transparency" benefits the public directly, "blunt[ing] the effect" of denials.[35] For instance, information "about whether ... a plan covers abortion would benefit all consumers – those seeking a plan that includes abortion coverage [and] those seeking a plan that excludes it."[36] Granted, insurance plans are complicated and hard to decipher and some employers do not offer abortion in any plan. But where employers offer a menu of options, notice enhances awareness and allows informed choice.

The sudden reversal by major medical centers of "long-standing polic[ies] exempting employees who refuse[d] [to help with abortions] religious or moral objections,"[37] shows that some institutions can staff around objectors without compromising access. Mount Sinai Hospital staffed around nurse Cathy Cenzon-DeCarlo's religious objections to assisting with abortion without friction for years.[38] In 2009, Cenzon-DeCarlo's supervisor threatened her with termination and "patient abandonment" charges if she refused to assist with a twenty-two-week abortion.[39] Cenzon-DeCarlo says her superior could have assisted with the abortion, which required "surgery within 6 hours;" the hospital said it had no "replacement and ... the patient's life was at risk."[40]

Mount Sinai ultimately agreed with the U.S. Department of Health and Human Services (HHS), which enforces federal conscience protections, to resume the prior arrangement.[41] It affirmed the "legal right of any individual to refuse to participate" in abortion procedures, regardless of emergency or elective status. Under Mount Sinai's "alternative coverage" process, supervisors consult a list of willing

---

[35] Press Release, (July 17, 2014), available at www.ag.ny.gov/press-release/ag-schneiderman-proposes-bill-blunt-effect-supreme-courts-hobby-lobby-decision-new [https://perma.cc/8XPK-J9A8]; 2015 N.Y. Assembly Bill 182. See also Wendy Chavkin et al., *Conscientious Objection and Refusal to Provide Reproductive Healthcare: A White Paper Examining Prevalence, Health Consequences, and Policy Responses*, 123 Int'l. J. of Gynecology & Obstetrics S41, table 1 (2013).

[36] Kinsey Hasstedt, *Abortion Coverage Under the Affordable Care Act: The Laws Tell Only Half the Story*, 17 Guttmacher Pol'y Rev. 15, 15 (Winter 2014), available at www.guttmacher.org/pubs/gpr/17/1/gpr170115.pdf [https://perma.cc/9XJ9-EZQA].

[37] Rob Stein, *New Jersey Nurses Charge Religious Discrimination over Hospital Abortion Policy*, Washington Post (November 27, 2011), available at www.washingtonpost.com/national/health-science/new-jersey-nurses-charge-religious-discrimination-over-hospital-abortion-policy/2011/11/15/gIQAydgm2N_story.html [https://perma.cc/U53B-PG94].

[38] *Cenzon-DeCarlo v. Mount Sinai Hosp.*, No. 09-3120, 2010 WL 169485, at *1 (E.D.N.Y. January 15, 2010), aff'd, 626 F.3d 695 (2d Cir. 2010).

[39] Memorandum in Support of Motion for Preliminary Injunction at 1, 6, Cenzon-DeCarlo, 2010 WL 169485 (No. 09-3120), available at www.adfmedia.org/files/Cenzon-DeCarloPIbrief.pdf [https://perma.cc/YZ3N-SDX4].

[40] Id., at 4, 8; Carpo Affidavit ¶¶ 7, 11, *Cenzon-DeCarlo v. Mount Sinai Hosp.*, No. 10237-10 (N.Y. Sup. Ct. February 7, 2011).

[41] The Mount Sinai Hosp., N.Y., *Nursing Clinical and Administrative Manual* 4 (2011), available at www.adfmedia.org/files/MtSinaiPolicy.pdf [https://perma.cc/7HU4-F9PG].

providers after an objection.[42] This may increase costs if objectors represent a significant fraction of all providers or serve on thinly staffed units. Nonetheless, the fact that Mount Sinai staffed around Cenzon-DeCarlo for years – and agreed to resume that arrangement – suggests that religious objection need not imperil access. Maintaining lists of willing providers helps avoid win-lose scenarios.[43]

Some states pair the right to refuse with a duty to refer, fusing religious objection to the public's interest.[44] Some medical organizations back this approach.[45] Obviously, when services are elective and not time-sensitive, a duty to refer preserves access without sacrificing religious freedom.[46]

Another approach cabins the right to refuse when unacceptable outcomes would result. For instance, Iowa limits the right of private hospitals to object to performing or assisting with an abortion unless "necessary to save the life of a mother."[47] Maryland withdraws the right to object to performing abortions when refusal would cause "death

[42] Id. Mount Sinai agreed to train employees and prohibit discrimination based on abortion objections. Letter from Linda C. Colón, Reg'l Manager, Office of the Sec'y, U.S. Dep't of Health & Human Servs., to Matthew S. Bowman, Attorney, Alliance Defending Freedom, and David Reich, Interim President, Mount Sinai Hospital 2–3 (February 1, 2013), available at www.adfmedia.org/files/Cenzon-DeCarloHHSfindings.pdf [https://perma.cc/2L4U-5L7P].

[43] Id., at 3. Citing cases like *Shelton v. Univ. of Med. & Dentistry of N.J.*, 223 F.3d 220, 228 (3d Cir. 2000), some contend that all objections, even those that can be staffed around, represent a "[lapse] in medical professionalism," making courts "appropriately intolerant" of objectors. See Weiss Testimony, supra note 8. In Shelton, the court found a public hospital reasonably accommodated a Pentecostal nurse opposed to assisting with emergency abortions by offering transfer at the same pay and benefits to another unit providing no "religiously untenable" services – a transfer Shelton refused. Shelton, 223 F.3d at 220, 226. That refusal ultimately doomed Shelton's claim, not the court's "intolerance" of religious objectors.

[44] North Carolina Board of Pharmacy, *Pharmacist FAQs: Frequently Asked Questions for Pharmacists on Conscience Clause*, available at www.ncbop.org/faqs/Pharmacist/faq_ConscienceClause.htm [https://perma.cc/C79T-LLYG]; *Plan B Availability OTC Raises Logistical and Administrative Challenges*, 35 Nat'l Ass'n of Boards of Pharmacy Newsletter 1, 2 (November–December 2006), available at www.nabp.net/publications/assets/NovDec06NABP.pdf [https://perma.cc/KD4F-RXFQ]. Some express the duty to refer as a "professional obligation to take appropriate steps to avoid ... abandoning or neglecting a patient." Letter from Lawrence H. Mokhiber, Executive Secretary, New York State Board of Pharmacy, to Supervising Pharmacists, Re: Policy Guideline Concerning Matters of Conscience (November 18, 2005), available at www.op.nysed.gov/prof/pharm/pharmconscienceguideline.htm [https://perma.cc/3K43-4CJB].

[45] ACOG Committee on Ethics, *The Limits of Conscientious Refusal in Reproductive Medicine*, Opinion 385, at 1 (November 2007), available at www.acog.org/Resources_And_Publications/Committee_Opinions/Committee_on_Ethics/The_Limits_of_Conscientious_Refusal_in_Reproductive_Medicine [https://perma.cc/CU69-RMYU] ("Physicians and other health care providers have the duty to refer patients in a timely manner to other providers if they do not feel that they can in conscience provide the standard reproductive services.").

[46] Information about willing providers is needed to prevent patients from wasting time "searching" for nonobjecting providers. Although objectors may resist on complicity grounds, requiring professionals to provide accurate information should be non-negotiable. Rebecca Dresser, *Professionals, Conformity, and Conscience*, 35 Hastings Center Rep. 9 (2005).

[47] Iowa Code Ann. § 146.1 (West 2016); see also Mo. Ann. Stat. §§ 188.205, 188.210, 188.215 (West 2016).

or serious physical [or] long-lasting injury to the patient" or when it would be "contrary to the standards of medical care."[48] South Carolina distinguishes between public and private hospitals; the latter may refuse to "permit their facilities to be utilized for the performance of abortions," but cannot "refuse an emergency admittance."[49] Each approach honors religious objections up to a certain point.

Qualifying conscience protections by substantial – not imagined – hardship to the public avoids the need to default to an absolutist, for-the-patient-to-win-the-objector-must-lose posture. It also preserves the ability of people of faith to work in medicine, expanding choice for patients who value pro-life providers.[50]

Consider the 2011 lawsuit against the University of Medicine and Dentistry of New Jersey (UMDNJ), alleging that hospital staff "repeatedly [told objecting nurses] ... that they must assist abortions or ... be terminated."[51] Notwithstanding federal and state conscience protections,[52] when a nurse "reiterated her religious objections," UMDNJ staff replied that UMDNJ has "'no regard for religious beliefs' of nurses ... 'everyone on this floor is required to do [abortions],' [and] 'no patients can be refused by any nurse.'"[53] Following a temporary injunction, the parties agreed that, except when the mother's life is at risk and there are no other nonobjecting staff available to assist, objecting nurses will not have to assist with abortions.[54] In emergencies, their "only involvement ... would be to care for the patient until such time as a nonobjecting person can get there to take over the care."[55] The settlement effectively converts the absolute right to say no under the Church Amendment and parallel state laws[56] – whatever the costs to patients – into a right qualified by hardship to patients. Refashioned, the objector's right to refuse ends where a patient's life is at risk and no one else can perform the needed service.

Those who prioritize conscience over access see conditional exemptions as encroaching on their rights – in Figure 17.1's terms, that the conditional exemption

---

[48] Md. Code Ann., Health–Gen. § 20-214 (West 2016).
[49] S.C. Code Ann. § 44-41-40 (2016).
[50] Bowman, supra note 1.
[51] Verified Complaint at 7–8, *Danquah v. Univ. of Med. & Dentistry of N.J.*, No. 2:11-cv-06377 (D.N.J. October 31, 2011), Life News, available at www.lifenews.com/wp-content/uploads/2011/11/newjerseynursesabortion.pdf [https://perma.cc/M34M-MRJZ].
[52] See N.J. Stat. Ann. § 2A:65A-1 (West 2016) (unqualified right to refuse).
[53] Id. at 7–9.
[54] Transcript of Proceedings at 5–6, Danquah, No. 2:11-cv-06377, (D.N.J. October 31, 2011), ADF Media, available at www.adfmedia.org/files/DanquahSettlementTranscripts.pdf [https://perma.cc/3ZKK-AZKH].
[55] Id. at 5–6. Judge Linares "retain[ed] jurisdiction" to ensure the agreement's terms "are in fact followed." Id. at 5.
[56] Robin Fretwell Wilson, "Matters of Conscience: Lessons for Same-Sex Marriage from the Healthcare Context," in *Same-Sex Marriage and Religious Liberty: Emerging Conflicts appendix* (Douglas Laycock, Anthony R. Picarello, Jr., & Robin Fretwell Wilson eds, 2008) (collecting statutes).

provides no insulation for conscience. But by limiting the nurses' involvement generally to maintaining the patient's status quo, we avoid forcing the resignation of providers who can serve other patients and provide other services. In every instance but the most dire, conditional exemptions preserve the ability of health care providers to stay in their profession.

3. ACCESS-FREEZING "SUPER CONSCIENCE CLAUSES"

Perhaps the greatest challenge to access is "super conscience clauses" like the Weldon Amendment. The Weldon Amendment strips federal agencies and state or local governments of specified funds if they "subject any institutional or individual health care entity to discrimination [for refusing to] provide, pay for, provide coverage of, or refer for abortions" – putting aside cases of rape, incest, or life-threatening pregnancy.[57]

The Weldon Amendment resulted from the push-and-pull of advocates' increasingly creative testing of the limits of conscience protections.[58] For instance, although the Church Amendment protected physicians from punishment for refusing to do abortions, nothing prevented accreditors from later requiring all accredited medical schools to train students to perform abortions. In 1996, Congress enacted the Coates-Snow Amendment to block that move.[59]

Recognizing that effective conscience protections must regulate at every level of government, Congress began attaching the Weldon Amendment to budget riders in 2004. The Weldon Amendment erects an unqualified right to object by threatening to defund governmental bodies that might otherwise place greater emphasis on access. California, for example, risks $90 billion in federal funds if it impermissibly penalizes entities that refuse to carry out or cover abortions.[60] In effect, Congress blocked state and local counterparts from placing duties on objecting providers that undercut the thick conscience protections Congress has instituted.

While super conscience clauses have the virtue of shutting down end-runs and effectively providing a stable social understanding of when one's right to refuse begins and

---

[57] Pub. L. No. 108–447, § 508(a), (d)(1); Pub. L. No. 109–49, § 508(a), (d)(1). See I. Glenn Cohen, *Are All Abortions Equal? Should There Be Exceptions to the Criminalization of Abortion for Rape and Incest?*, 43 J.L. Med. & Ethics 87 (2014), for a critique of these exemptions.

[58] Judith C. Gallagher, *Protecting the Other Right to Choose: The Hyde-Weldon Amendment*, 5 Ave Maria L. Rev. 527 (2007).

[59] 42 U.S.C. § 238n ("health care entit[ies]," including "postgraduate physician training program[s]" receiving federal financial assistance, cannot be penalized for "refus[ing] to provide abortion").

[60] Bob Egelko, *Abortion Foes Threaten Suit that May Cut State's Federal Funds: Threatened legal action puts federal funds at risk*, SFGate (August 25, 2014), available at www.sfgate.com/news/article/Abortion-foes-threaten-suit-that-may-cut-state-s-5709487.php. State challenges have failed. See, e.g., *California v. United States*, 2008 WL 744840 (N.D. Cal. 2008).

ends, they frustrate efforts by state and local actors to assess the impact of conscience protections on access and to recalibrate accordingly. Recently, California required health plans to cover elective abortions, including late-term abortions. After religious employers objected, HHS issued a nonaction letter because religious employers, rather than the issuing insurance companies, had objected.[61] Although it is unclear whether the Obama Administration's choice to issue a nonaction letter meshes with Congress' intent,[62] or will continue as policy under the Trump Administration, threatening state and local governments with a massive loss of funding nonetheless means that other governments cannot easily revisit federal policy decisions.

Thus, super conscience clauses can harm patients by concretizing policy decisions and making them largely immune from changing facts and circumstances. Despite medical advances, "pregnancy is not a risk-free life event, particularly for many women with chronic medical conditions."[63] When Congress enacted the Patient Protection and Affordable Care Act (ACA),[64] it gave health plans discretion to cover abortion as part of the essential health benefits.[65] States could enact laws to ban *all* abortion coverage by health plans offered through state-established exchanges, as some states did,[66] but states need not ban abortion coverage.

California chose *to require* health plans to affirmatively "treat maternity services and legal abortion neutrally."[67] That decision precipitated both the complaint to HHS and a federal lawsuit under the Weldon Amendment to force California to allow insurers to offer plans to religious employers that exclude elective abortion; plaintiffs say California in the past has authorized plans covering a subset of all abortions, namely for cases of rape, incest, and risk to a mother's life.[68] The Weldon

[61] Jocelyn Samuels, Director, Office of Civil Rights, Department of Health and Human Services, to Catherine W. Short et al. (June 21, 2016), ADF Media, available at www.adfmedia.org/files/CDMHCInvestigationClosureLetter.pdf [https://perma.cc/G4WP-V69V].
[62] The Weldon Amendment nowhere explicitly requires a covered individual or institutional entity to object, and so may indirectly protect employers' moral objections.
[63] Jennifer Haberkorn, *Experts Split from Walsh on Abortion*, Politico (October 19, 2012), www.politico.com/story/2012/10/medical-experts-say-abortions-still-needed-despite-advances-082640 [https://perma.cc/MMV4-E3ND].
[64] Patient Protection and Affordable Care Act, Pub. L. No. 111–148, 124 Stat. 119 (2010), amended by Health Care and Education Reconciliation Act of 2010, Pub. L. No. 111–52, 124 Stat. 1029 through May 1, 2010,
[65] ACA Sec. 1303(b)(1)(A)(ii); 42 U.S.C. §18023.
[66] Id.; Alina Salganicoff et al., *Coverage for Abortion Services in Medicaid, Marketplace Plans and Private Plans*, Kaiser Family Foundation Issue Brief (January 2016), available at http://files.kff.org/attachment/issue-brief-coverage-for-abortion-services-in-medicaid-marketplace-plans-and-private-plans [https://perma.cc/JN3S-UMPN].
[67] Tracy Seipel, *California Reverses Position on Health Insurance Abortion Coverage*, Mercury News (August 22, 2014), available at www.mercurynews.com/health/ci_26387230/state-reverses-position-health-insurance-abortion-coverage [https://perma.cc/3UNN-FVFR].
[68] Complaint for Declaratory and Injunctive Relief and Nominal Damages, *Skyline Wesleyan Church v. California Department of Managed Health Care*, No. 37-2016-00003936 (Cal. Super. Ct. February 4, 2016) at 66–7.

Amendment, religious employers contend, requires California to permit insurers to offer plans that cover no abortions.

In refusing to grant California a quick win, a federal district court observed that "the parties may wish to investigate whether they can come to an arrangement that will meet the needs of all stakeholders,"[69] citing *Zubik*.

While a system of individualized exemptions may work, one-off rules may be in tension with California's asserted compelling interest in mandating coverage by all insurers in the state. If the Weldon Amendment applies, California cannot act on its judgment that women need unfettered access. Thus, super conscience clauses block access in ways that ordinary conscience clauses do not.

4. DEVELOPING EARLIER DECISION POINTS

As pressure mounts to scrap conscience protections,[70] objecting hospitals need to develop ways to abide by their faith tenets *without* putting women at risk. The ERDs "prohibit health service providers from taking 'direct' action against the embryo."[71] While the Catholic principle of double effect permits physicians to act to save a patient's life, even it means hastening a fetus's death, that consequence cannot be "directly willed," and the precipitating act must be "morally acceptable."[72]

Far too often, however, "[b]ecause the fetus [is] still alive, [treating physicians] wouldn't intervene."[73] The experience for women awaiting treatment can be

---

[69] *Skyline Wesleyan Church v. California Department of Managed Health Care*, Case 3:16-cv-00501 (S.D. Cal. June 20, 2016), slip op. at 8, n.2 (citing *Zubik v. Burwell*, 136 S. Ct. 1557, 1560 (2016)).

[70] Robert Pear, A Bush Rule on Providers of Abortion is Revised, N.Y. Times (February 18, 2011), available at www.nytimes.com/2011/02/19/health/policy/19health.html?_r=0 [http://nyti.ms/1ObETX1]; 2016 Democratic Party Platform Draft (July 1, 2016), available at https://demconvention.com/wp-content/uploads/2016/07/2016-DEMOCRATIC-PARTY-PLATFORM-DRAFT-7.1.16.pdf [https://perma.cc/Q2ZS-AVWV] ("We will continue to oppose – and seek to overturn – federal and state laws and policies that impede a woman's access to abortion, including by repealing the Hyde Amendment.").

[71] Angel M. Foster et al., *Assessing Hospital Policies & Practices Regarding Ectopic Pregnancy & Miscarriage Management National Women's Law Center* (2015) at 4, available at https://nwlc.org/wp-content/uploads/2015/08/ibis_rh_-_nwlc_qualitative_study_report.pdf [https://perma.cc/RXM8-WGNK].

[72] See *The Principle of Double Effect*, Catholics United for the Faith (1997), available at www.cuf.org/FileDownloads/doubleeffect.pdf [https://perma.cc/VD4F-9N3D]. See also George Weigel, *Clarifying "Double Effect,"* First Things (February 23, 2011), available at www.firstthings.com/web-exclusives/2011/02/clarifying-ldquodouble-effectrdquo; David F. Kelly et al., *Contemporary Catholic Health Care Ethics* 108, 109 (2013) (abortions permissible if the "directly intended effect is the preservation or restoration of the mother's health").

[73] Lori R. Freedman et al., *When There's a Heartbeat: Miscarriage Management in Catholic-Owned Hospitals*, 98 Am. J. Pub. Health 1774, 1776–7 (2008), available at www.ncbi.nlm.nih.gov/pmc/articles/PMC2636458/ [https://perma.cc/7T7Q-9EQR].

horrific, and, if sepsis develops, life-threatening.[74] For pregnant women at objecting hospitals, the principal problem stems from delay: the hospital does not act soon enough when an ectopic pregnancy, miscarriage, or other condition necessitates an emergency abortion.[75]

Recently, the American Civil Liberties Union sued to force objecting institutions to transfer patients or treat them under the federal Emergency Medical Treatment and Labor Act (EMTALA).[76] Enacted in 1986, EMTALA requires hospitals to treat, stabilize, or transfer patients in active labor.[77]

A number of Catholic hospitals proactively transfer pregnant women in distress, as scholars have shown:

> Catholic hospital ethics committees advised their physicians to transfer patients to another provider for the specific purpose of obtaining an abortion. In these cases, the woman's health or life was threatened by her pregnancy, and the Catholic ethics committees did not want to allow her to experience irreversible harm.[78]

If hospitals cannot treat a patient, they should aggressively work, first, to avoid being the facility that admits a patient the facility has reason to believe it cannot serve and, second, to transfer women needing abortions at the earliest indication of distress. Hospitals already place themselves on "drive-by" status when overwhelmed, and sometimes divert patients for selective reasons, too.[79]

---

[74] Molly Redden, *Abortion Ban Linked to Dangerous Miscarriages at Catholic Hospital, Report Claims*, Guardian (February 18, 2016), available at www.theguardian.com/us-news/2016/feb/18/michigan-catholic-hospital-women-miscarriage-abortion-mercy-health-partners [https://perma.cc/7NUX-8STN].

[75] See, e.g., Foster, supra note 71, at 4; Frances W. Casey et al., *Elective Abortion*, Medscape (February 29, 2016), available at http://emedicine.medscape.com/article/252560-overview; Kim Painter, *Doctors Say Abortions Do Sometimes Save Women's Lives*, USA Today (October 22, 2012), available at www.usatoday.com/story/news/nation/2012/10/19/abortion-mother-life-walsh/1644839/ [https://perma.cc/C7WJ-7RQJ].

[76] *Amended Complaint, ACLU v. Trinity Health Corp.*, Case No. 15-cv-12611 (October 1, 2015), ADF Media, available at www.adfmedia.org/files/TrinityHealthComplaint.pdf [https://perma.cc/UPS6-FHD9]; Candice Williams, *Mich. Health System Sued for Emergency Abortion Policy*, Detroit News (October 1, 2015), available at www.detroitnews.com/story/news/local/wayne-county/2015/10/01/mich-health-system-sued-emergency-abortion-policy/73172420/ [https://perma.cc/EA4A-MFN7]. The suit failed for lack of standing. *American Civil Liberties Union v. Trinity Health Corporation*, 15-cv-12611 (E.D. Mich. 2016), ADF Media, available at www.adfmedia.org/files/TrinityHealthDismissal.pdf [https://perma.cc/VC7W-4S94].

[77] See 42 U.S.C. § 1395dd.

[78] Freedman & Stulberg, supra note 10, at 8. See also Angel M. Foster, *Do Religious Restrictions Influence Ectopic Pregnancy Management?, A National Qualitative Study*, 21 Women's Health Issues 104, 104 (2011), available at www.ncbi.nlm.nih.gov/pubmed/21353977 [https://perma.cc/3D8K-APZ8].

[79] Emergency Med. Servs. Comm. of the Am. Coll. of Emergency Physicians, *Guidelines for Ambulance Diversion* (October 1999), available at www.acep.org/Clinical--Practice-Management/Guidelines-for-Ambulance-Diversion-2147470413/ [https://perma.cc/DX69-T5FC].

Some may wonder whether a hospital would assert complicity-based claims not to transfer a patient in order to prevent abortion.[80] To my knowledge, no religious institution has ever asserted such a claim.[81] But even if one was asserted, EMTALA imposes a duty to treat or transfer, without room for religious exceptions. Nor should there be any exception. If a hospital cannot treat a distressed patient, then it must let others treat her. Trapping a woman in a hospital that cannot render needed medical attention is not acceptable.

With evidence-based medicine,[82] it should be possible to develop protocols for transferring patients upon arrival to the optimal provider or even to route patients directly to the best site for their needs. Of course, distances will matter, as will the receiving institution's expertise.[83] Further, transferring patients is not a cure-all. Some "patients of limited means cannot realistically access care" at the receiving hospital for insurance or financial reasons.[84] Transferring facilities should assist patients to be billed in-network by the receiving facility if the transfer was necessitated by the transferring facility's faith tenets, not the patient's desires. Likewise, regulators, like state attorneys general overseeing the merger of Catholic hospitals, could require transferring facilities to make the transfer a financial wash for patients.

Although lawsuits pressing EMTALA claims have thus far proven unsuccessful,[85] that religious conscience can come at such high costs to women means that holding onto conscience protections will become increasingly difficult. In a range of contexts, advocates are pushing back.[86] Thickened duties to transfer patients before a crisis may necessitate some changes to practice.[87] But protecting women remains the surest way to protect the objecting hospital's own ability to operate according to its faith tenets.[88]

---

[80] Ethical Directive 70 expressly prohibits Catholic health care organizations from engaging in immediate material cooperation in actions like abortion.
[81] However, a Chicago ambulance driver refused to transport a patient for an abortion. Rob Stein, *Medical Crisis of Conscience*, Washington Post (July 16, 2006), available at www.washingtonpost.com/wp-dyn/content/article/2006/07/15/AR2006071500846.html [https://perma.cc/PVB8-NV3J]. See supra Section 2 (discussing feasibility of staffing around individual objectors).
[82] See generally Pierre L. Young & Leigh Anne Olsen, *The Healthcare Imperative: Lowering Costs and Improving Outcomes* (2010).
[83] ACOG Committee on Ethics, supra note 45. Transfers may better serve women who are miscarrying because religiously affiliated hospitals generally tend to be small community hospitals. Harry A. Sultz & Kristina M. Young, *Health Care USA: Understanding Its Organization and Delivery* 75–6 (Katey Birtcher & Tracey Chapman, 6th ed. 2009).
[84] Freedman & Stulberg, supra note 10, at 8.
[85] *American Civil Liberties Union v. Trinity Health Corporation*, 15-cv-12611 (E.D. Mich. 2016), ADF Media, available at www.adfmedia.org/files/TrinityHealthDismissal.pdf [https://perma.cc/G3BU-2ER4] (dismissed for lack of standing).
[86] See Do No Harm Act, H.R. 5272, 114th Cong. (2015).
[87] Foster, supra note 78, at 104.
[88] Catholic scholars are exploring whether the principle of double effect allows a greater range of treatment options, such as "hospital within hospital" arrangements or other partnerships to provide

5. LESSONS FROM ZUBIK

In what is arguably the most heated debate in recent decades over the limits of religious conscience[89] – claims to be exempt from the contraceptive coverage mandate – the U.S. Supreme Court in *Zubik* sent the parties back to the appeals courts with instructions to mediate their differences.[90] As is discussed in greater depth in this volume's Introduction and many other chapters, the Obama Administration crafted an accommodation that shifted the obligation to provide contraceptive coverage from objecting nonprofits to another entity, giving women needed access, without hassle and without cost.[91] Until the *per curiam* opinion, the protracted litigation over whether the government had accommodated religious nonprofits *enough* had taken on the winner-takes-all-quality animating conscience debates.[92]

Sensing room to remove objecting nonprofits from the equation without sacrificing needed access, the Court gave an overarching instruction: agree on how religious organizations can "do nothing more than contract for a plan that does not include coverage for some or all forms of contraception," while women receive seamless "cost-free contraceptive coverage from the same insurance company."[93] Although the parties' differences may yet prove unbridgeable,[94] and many chapters in this volume criticize the opinion, the spirit of *Zubik* is clear: in a pluralistic society, we should embrace creative fixes that preserve as much religious freedom as possible while allowing social progress. As Professor Michael McConnell said: "the Supreme Court demonstrated that even in these contentious times it can find

---

emergency abortions. Monica Sloboda, *The High Cost of Merging with a Religiously-Controlled Hospital*, 16 Berkeley Women's L.J. 140, 144 (2001); see Kelly, supra note 72, at 287.

[89] See Ethan Bronner, *A Flood of Suits Fights Coverage of Birth Control*, N.Y. Times, January 26, 2013, available at www.nytimes.com/2013/01/27/health/religious-groups-and-employers-battle-contraception-mandate.html [http://nyti.ms/1Ap7n3I].

[90] Richard W. Garnett, *The Future of Accommodation*, SCOTUSblog (May 17, 2016), available at www.scotusblog.com/2016/05/symposium-the-future-of-accommodation/ [https://perma.cc/AC4N-UEQJ].

[91] See Richard Wolf, *Obama Tweaks Birth Control Rule*, USA Today (February 10, 2012), available at http://content.usatoday.com/communities/theoval/post/2012/02/source-obama-to-change-birth-control-rule/1#.V2h9WLgrLD4 [https://perma.cc/5WWX-KC6N].

[92] The Court's supplemental briefing asked whether "contraceptive coverage may be obtained by petitioners' employees through petitioners' insurance companies, [without] involvement of petitioners beyond their own decision to provide health insurance without contraceptive coverage to their employees." Order Requesting Supplemental Briefing in *Zubik v. Burwell*, 577 U.S. at 1.

[93] *Zubik v. Burwell*, 136 S. Ct. 1557 (2016), slip op. at 3.

[94] See Kelsey Dallas, *Supreme Court Sends Birth Control Mandate Challenge Back to Lower Courts*, Deseret News (May 16, 2016), available at www.deseretnews.com/article/865654385/Supreme-Court-sends-birth-control-mandate-challenge-back-to-lower-courts.html?pg=all [https://perma.cc/68M4-APH6].

solutions to practical problems on the basis of reasonable accommodation."[95] For "reasonable people of good will," the primary hurdle to "protect[ing] religious freedom without sacrificing the democratic will" may be our own suppositions that each comes at the expense of the other.

CONCLUSION

Whether and how conscience protections affect access is a difficult question. The impact on access depends on the specific contours of conscience protections themselves and on external constraints, such as whether objecting providers will exit the market. In the end, continued protection for the religious convictions of health care providers will depend on consciously reconciling those protections with the needs of patients.

---

[95] Eugene Volokh, *Prof. Michael McConnell on Zubik v. Burwell*, Washington Post (May 17, 2016), available at www.washingtonpost.com/news/volokh-conspiracy/wp/2016/05/17/prof-michael-mcconnell-on-zubik-v-burwell-yesterdays-supreme-court-rfra-contraceptive-decision/ [https://perma.cc/X5KS-8PXU].

PART VI

A Case Study – Religious Beliefs and the Health of the LGBT Community

Introduction

Noa Ben-Asher

Views on homosexuality have shifted dramatically in the last five decades. But for some individuals and groups, many of whom identify with an organized religion, the growing acceptance of homosexuality has triggered conflict. In 1975, the American Psychological Association (APA) resolved that "homosexuality per se implies no impairment in judgment, stability, reliability, or general social or vocational capabilities."[1] By 2015, the Supreme Court held that "same-sex couples may exercise the fundamental right to marry in all States."[2] The chapters in this part explore legal struggles that arise when mental health professionals with negative views on homosexuality operate within progressive-liberal medical and legal spheres that have mostly rejected their views. Susan J. Stabile's chapter focuses on whether a graduate student training for a counseling profession, who objects to homosexuality, should be able to opt out of counseling LGBTQ individuals. Craig J. Konnoth's chapter explores therapists' claims that legal prohibitions on sexual orientation-change efforts (SOCE) violate their religious freedom.

At least two related themes are prominent in these chapters. The first has to do with the potential or real harm that a mental health professional's objection to homosexuality may have on third parties (mostly patients or potential patients). The second involves whether and how accommodating a mental health professional's religious objection to homosexuality could result in the establishment of religion, prohibited by the US Constitution.

It is a basic liberal premise that an individual should be free to behave according to their beliefs so long they do not harm others.[3] The two chapters share the premise

---

[1] Am. Psychol. Ass'n, *Introduction, Practice Guidelines for LGB Clients Guidelines for Psychological Practice with Lesbian, Gay, and Bisexual Clients*, (2012), available at www.apa.org/pubs/journals/features/amp-a0024659.pdf [https://perma.cc/D3MA-EYCX].
[2] *Obergefell v. Hodges*, 135 S. Ct. 2071 (2015).
[3] See generally John Stewart Mill, *On Liberty* (1859).

that enabling a mental health professional or student to act on his or her rejection of homosexuality may, at times, be harmful to LGBTQ patients. Konnoth's chapter operates under the assumption that SOCE are harmful to (at the very least) those on whom they are attempted, and that the liberal state is therefore justified in banning these practices.[4] This harm-based rejection of SOCE is consistent with the American Counseling Association position that conversion therapy is a religious practice that has no convincing evidence of effectiveness,[5] and with APA guidelines that question the effectiveness of efforts to change sexual orientation. Popular culture also widely manifests this understanding of SOCE as harmful to LGBTQ individuals.[6]

In the educational context discussed in Stabile's chapter, identifying the harm when a student requests accommodation of her negative views on homosexuality is more difficult. Referring an LGBTQ individual to another therapist seems significantly less harmful than active conversion therapy on a patient. Stabile points out that "there is no evidence of a shortage of counselors available to counsel gays and lesbians,"[7] and that counselors "'appear to assume that referring is always an option when working with clients.'"[8] Nonetheless Stabile observes that discriminatory referral practices could be harmful. In particular, where referral occurs in the middle of counseling, "a gay or lesbian who may have already faced difficulties related to his or her sexual orientation ... may 'be emotionally harmed by the psychologist making a referral, interpreting that action to be yet another form of rejection similar to' the rejection at the hands of family and friends."[9] Beyond potential harm to specific individuals, she discusses concerns that open-mindedness toward difference is part of counseling field and that "adequate training should include making sure students can counsel outside of their comfort zones."[10]

Stabile concludes that the religious views of counselors should be accommodated while protecting the interests of patients. She attempts to strike a balance of accommodating religious objections of counselors while not violating the no-harm principle. She concedes that sometimes protection of LGBTQ patients

---

[4] It is arguable that there SOCE also impose a serious dignitary harm to the wider group of LGBTQ individuals and allies.
[5] See Joy S. Whitman et al., *Am. Counseling Ass'n ACA in the News: Ethical Issues Related to Conversion or Reparative Therapy* (January 16, 2013).
[6] See, e.g., *But I'm a Cheerleader* (Ignite Entertainment 1999) (a comic satire about conversion therapy for gender and sexual nonconforming youth); *Anderson Cooper 360: The Sissy Boy Experiment* (June 7–9, 2011) (a CNN documentary film about failed gender and sexual orientation therapy in the 1970s that led to the suicide of the individual on which it was attempted).
[7] Susan J. Stabile, Ch. 18, at 11.
[8] Id. at 8 (quoting Michele P. Ford & Susan S. Hendrick, *Therapists' Sexual Values for Self and Clients: Implications for Practice and Training*, 34 Prof. Psychol.: Res. & Prac. 80 (2003)).
[9] Id. at 9–10.
[10] Id. at 10.

will require "some limitation on the ability of such a person to counsel others. For example, where a high school has a single counselor available for students, giving that position to someone who is not capable of counseling certain groups of people is inimical to the interests of the client."[11] In sum, when examined side-by-side, the two chapters seem to share the premise that determining *how much* accommodation religious objections to homosexuality deserve requires a careful and specific assessment of the harm principle.

The second theme that arises from these chapters is whether accommodating a therapist's religious views of homosexuality can be viewed as a prohibited establishment of religion. Konnoth's illuminating account of the history of sexual orientation therapy *as a form of religious practice* leads him to the persuasive conclusion that

> the religious basis of SOCE suggests another line of defense for states that enact prohibitions on these practices ... even assuming that the therapists' speech at issue receives a high degree of scrutiny as some judges have claimed, the state can assert a compelling interest in prohibiting SOCE – preventing religious establishment.[12]

As Konnoth explains,

> the state would argue that the state action at issue is not a ban on speech per se. Rather, it is a denial of a state-provided resource – a license – that facilitates private speech. Denying state resources for religious purposes prevents religious establishment, which is a compelling purpose that satisfies First Amendment Scrutiny.[13]

If indeed SOCE is a religious practice (and not a medical one) as the plaintiff therapist in *Welch v. Brown* acknowledged,[14] providing a state license for this religious practice may indeed be viewed as establishment of religion.

While not addressing the issue directly, Stabile does not seem to view state licensing of individuals who reject homosexuality as problematic under the Establishment Clause per se. Stabile argues that accommodating religious objection of a student to homosexuality is appropriate where the interests of patients can be protected. As a rule, she argues, they should not be deprived of a license to practice.

The difference between these two chapters on the establishment question is not as stark as it may seem. Konnoth's chapter focuses on SOCE, which, he argues, are themselves a form of religious ministry. His argument, based on historical analysis, is essentially that state prohibition of *the practice* itself should be viewed as a bar on the establishment of evangelical Christianity in the United States. By contrast, Stabile's chapter is not about any particular religious practice: it is about referral of

---

[11] Id.
[12] Craig J. Konnoth, Ch. 19, at 8.
[13] Id. at 8–9.
[14] 907 F. Supp. 2d 1102, 1105 (E.D. Cal. 2012).

patients to other therapists due to religious objection to homosexuality. Accordingly, for Stabile, state licensing of therapists with religious objection to homosexuality is not in-and-of-itself a problematic establishment of religion. But, rather, an example of healthy religious pluralism.

At a broader level, the chapters in this part reflect an interesting moment in the relation of medical science to religion/morality. Up until the 1970s, the psychiatric evaluation of homosexuality was in line with the religious/moral one. Homosexuality was viewed as a mental illness *and* a moral/religious failing. But since then, an ongoing rift has formed between the medical professions and some moral/religious convictions on the question of homosexuality. The chapters in this part reflect an aversion of a professional field (psychiatry) that is modern, scientific, experiment-based to ideas that seem to belong elsewhere: religion and morality. Together, they nicely illustrate how the harm principle and the Establishment Clause offer scholars and lawmakers conceptual tools to urge this inevitable divorce between medical science and religion, at least on the question of homosexuality.

18

Religious Convictions About Homosexuality and the Training of Counseling Professionals

How Should We Treat Religious-Based Opposition to Counseling About Same-Sex Relationships?

Susan J. Stabile

Despite the increasing acceptance of same-sex relationships, many Americans oppose such relationships on religious grounds. The Catholic Church views homosexual inclinations as disordered, and homosexual acts as sinful, as do some other Christian denominations. Although not everyone follows their church's lead on this issue, many do, putting them at odds with the way law and society now view same-sex relationships.

Tension between increasing normalization of same-sex relationships and religious-based opposition thereto has arisen in a variety of settings. One such area relates to the training of students planning to enter counseling professions. How should graduate schools training students to become psychologists, social workers, or counselors deal with students who object on religious grounds to counseling gays and lesbians about their relationships, or at all? Can the religious objections of such students be accommodated, and if so, how?

Although these questions implicate freedom of speech and religion, I am less concerned with the constitutional analysis than with the question of the extent to which a graduate student's religious-based opposition to counseling homosexuals can or should be accommodated. My thesis here is that the religious convictions of those who wish to enter the counseling professions can be respected while still safeguarding the interest of those seeking counseling, and those convictions should be protected.

1. LEGAL CHALLENGES TO GRADUATE COUNSELING PROGRAMS

A. *The* Ward *and* Keeton *Cases*

Several courts have addressed clashes between curricular requirements and a student's opposition to same-sex relationships on religious grounds.

Ward v. Polite involved a well-performing student in Eastern Michigan University's graduate-level counseling degree program.[1] During the course of her studies, Julea Ward frequently said that her Christian faith would prevent her from affirming a client's same-sex relationship or extramarital heterosexual relationships. The final stages of her counseling program included a practicum in which students counseled actual clients. Learning that one of her assigned clients was gay, Ward sought permission to either refer the client to another student or begin counseling with the option of making a referral later if relationship issues arose during counseling sessions. Although the university initially granted that permission, it subsequently commenced a disciplinary hearing against Ward, resulting in her expulsion from the program.

When Ward sued, the federal district court granted the University's motion for summary judgment, relying on the broad deference given to universities in curricular determinations.[2] The court also referenced the school's incorporation into its academic policies of the Code of Ethics of the American Counseling Association (ACA), which provides that counselors may not impose their own values on clients. The court recognized that Ward would likely encounter gay students as a high school counselor (her desired profession) and that she did not have a right to interfere with a curriculum designed to adequately train her to practice her profession.[3]

On appeal, the Sixth Circuit reversed the district court's grant of summary judgment.[4] Despite the great latitude granted to educational institutions regarding their curricular decisions, the court believed that a reasonable jury could conclude that Ward was expelled from the program because of speech or faith-based animus. That neither the ACA Code of Ethics nor the school's own policy prohibited values-based referrals, combined with certain statements of university officials, was sufficient to "permit the inference that Ward's religious beliefs motivated their actions."[5] The case was ultimately settled.[6]

Keeton v. Anderson-Wiley involved a counseling student at Augusta State University (ASU).[7] Jennifer Keeton told professors and classmates that, based on her religious beliefs, she would try to convert clients she counseled from homosexual to heterosexual. In response, the university demanded that she engage in a remediation program, which Keeton initially agreed to, but then refused to complete. ASU

---

[1] 667 F.3d 727 (6th Cir. 2012).
[2] *Ward v. Wilbanks*, 2010 U.S. Dist. LEXIS 127038 (E.D. Mich., July 26, 2010).
[3] 2010 U.S. Dist. LEXIS 127038, at *35–7.
[4] *Ward v. Polite*, 667 F.3d 727 (6th Cir. 2012).
[5] Id. at 738.
[6] Nick DeSantis, *Eastern Michigan U. Settles Counseling Student's Lawsuit for $75,000*, Chronicle of Higher Education, December 11, 2012.
[7] 664 F.3d 865 (11th Cir. 2011).

found that she demonstrated an intention to violate the prohibition in the ACA Code of Ethics (which ASU had adopted as part of school policy) against imposing counselor values on clients and discriminating against homosexual clients. Keeton sued; the federal district court denied her motion for a preliminary injunction, concluding that the remediation plan was viewpoint-neutral and not in response to her religious views,[8] a denial upheld by the Eleventh Circuit.[9]

Ward and *Keeton* broadly stand for the proposition that "the even-handed enforcement of a neutral policy is likely to steer clear of the First Amendment's free-speech and free-exercise protections."[10] As a matter of constitutional law, a school may adopt a policy against referrals on all grounds, including religiously based opposition to counseling homosexuals. Presumably, it could also adopt a limited referral policy to cover exigencies such as illness. It may also discipline students for failing to comply with generally applicable curricular requirements and an applicable code of ethics.[11]

B. Existing and Proposed Legislation

Several states either have enacted or proposed legislation addressing religious-based opposition to counseling on particular issues. For example, Arizona passed legislation in 2011 providing that

> A university or community college shall not discipline or discriminate against a student in a counseling, social work or psychology program because the student refuses to counsel a client about goals that conflict with the student's sincerely held religious belief if the student consults with the supervising instructor or professor to determine the proper course of action to avoid harm to the client.[12]

In response to the *Ward* decision, in June 2012, the Michigan House passed the Julea Ward Freedom of Conscience Act, providing in relevant part that an educational institution may not

> discipline or discriminate against a student in a counseling, social work, or psychology program because the student refuses to counsel or serve a client as to goals that conflict with a sincerely held religious belief or moral conviction of the student,

---

[8] 733 F Supp. 1368, 1381 (S.D. Ga. 2010).
[9] *Keeton v. Anderson-Wiley*, 664 F.3d 865 (11th Cir. 2011). On remand, the court granted defendants' motion to dismiss.
[10] *Ward v. Polite*, 667 F.3d 727, 741 (6th Cir. 2012).
[11] A complaint was recently filed against Missouri State University (MSU) alleging facts similar to those in *Ward* and *Keeton*. Plaintiff Andrew Cash alleged that he was ordered to discontinue his internship required for his M.S. in Counseling from MSU because of his religious views regarding counseling same-sex couples on relationship issues. *Cash v. Hofherr et al.*, 2016-CV-03155-MDH (W.D. Mo. April 19, 2016). No further action has been taken in the case.
[12] Ariz. Rev. Stat. § 15–1862(E) (Ariz. 2012).

if the student refers the client to a counselor who will provide the counseling services.[13]

For some, such legislation represents an important protection of religious freedom; for others, it puts the interests of the therapist over the needs of the client.

2. VIEW OF THE COUNSELING PROFESSION AND ITS IMPACT ON TRAINING PROGRAMS

A. *The Profession*

Historically, homosexuality was viewed as a form of mental illness, with the result that counseling was aimed at curing or managing a disease.[14] Today, however, no major American medical health professional association holds that view.[15] In 1975, the American Psychological Association (APA) resolved that "homosexuality per se implies no impairment in judgment, stability, reliability, or general social or vocational capabilities."[16] In 2009, it went further, affirming that same-sex attractions, feelings, and behaviors "are normal and positive variations of human sexuality regardless of sexual orientation identity."[17]

As a result of this changed view, the counseling professions[18] have moved toward "affirmative counseling" – counseling "that celebrates and advocates the authenticity and integrity of lesbian, gay and bisexual persons and their relationships.[19] This includes helping clients to accept their orientation and to cope with any stigmatization resulting therefrom.[20]

---

[13] H.R. 5040, 2012 Leg., Reg. Sess. (Mich. 2012). Legislation proposed in 2012 in Virginia is even broader, providing that no institution of higher learning may discriminate in any way against a student who "refuses to perform academic coursework or any other degree requirement on the grounds that it would force him to violate a sincerely held religious belief." H.R. 1207, 2012 Leg., Reg. Sess. (Va. 2012).

[14] Katie Godfrey et al., *Essential Components of Curricula for Preparing Therapists to Work Effectively with Lesbian, Gay, and Bisexual Clients: A Delphi Study*, 32 J. Marital & Fam. Therapy 491, 492 (2006).

[15] Marianne Schneider Corey & Gerald Corey, *Becoming a Helper* 226 (5th ed. 2007).

[16] Am. Psychological Ass'n, *Introduction, Practice Guidelines for LGB Clients Guidelines for Psychological Practice with Lesbian, Gay, and Bisexual Clients* (2012), available at www.apa.org/pubs/journals/features/amp-a0024659.pdf [https://perma.cc/D3MA-EYCX].

[17] Id. at 121.

[18] As the language of the legislation referenced in Section 1.B. suggests, there are at least three different counseling professions: professional counselors, psychologists and social workers, each with a somewhat different emphasis. For a general introduction to the mental health professions, see Michael R. Espina, *An Introduction to the Mental Health Professions*, 26 Pa. Law. 40 (2004).

[19] Frank R. Dillon & Roger L. Worthington, *The Lesbian, Gay, and Bisexual Affirmative Counseling Self-Efficacy Inventory (LGB-CSI): Development, Validation, and Training Implications*, 50 J. Counseling Psychol. 235, 236 (2003).

[20] Margaret S. Schneider & Bob Tremble, *Training Service Providers to Work with Gay or Lesbian Adolescents: A Workshop*, 65 J. Counseling & Dev. 98 (1986).

The APA treats religious objections to homosexuality as a form of prejudice based on religious beliefs. Its 2007 Resolution on Religious, Religion-Based and/or Religion-Derived Prejudice "condemns prejudice ... derived from or based on religious or spiritual belief" and includes as an example negative attitudes toward "those who are not exclusively heterosexual."[21] The document instructs that psychologists must avoid allowing "bias from their own spiritual, religious, or nonreligious beliefs" to take precedence over "professional practice and standards or scientific findings."[22]

Consistent with that view, the counseling professions oppose conversion or reparative therapy that aims to change a patient's sexual orientation. The ACA passed a resolution in 1999 stating that it does not endorse reparative therapy to "cure" homosexuality (since there is no mental disorder to be cured).[23] The ACA views conversion therapy as a religious, not psychological, practice, and one that lacks convincing evidence of effectiveness.[24] The APA Guidelines similarly question the effectiveness of efforts to change sexual orientation.[25]

B. Graduate Counseling Education

It is inevitable that counselors will have certain values and biases that conflict with those of their clients. "The belief that psychologists can be completely objective and value-free is no longer the predominant perspective in the field of psychology. Rather, it is now accepted that psychologists have values and that these values are infused throughout their professional work."[26]

One goal of education is to help prospective counselors to recognize their biases and the influences of their personal beliefs[27] and to learn how to manage differences between their values and the values of their clients. Because a good counseling relationship requires that clients feel accepted, part of professional training is ensuring that counselors will be able to respect people whose personal beliefs may be wildly

---

[21] Resolution, American Psychological Association Council of Representatives, *Resolution on Religious, Religion-Based and/or Religion-Derived Prejudice* (August 16, 2007).

[22] Id.

[23] Joy S. Whitman et al., *ACA in the News: Ethical Issues Related to Conversion or Reparative Therapy*, Am. Counseling Ass'n (May 22, 2006), available at www.counseling.org/pressroom/newsreleases.aspx?AGuid=b68aba97-2f08-40c2-a400-0630765f72f4 [https://perma.cc/7PU3-VD8K].

[24] Id.

[25] Am. Psychological Ass'n., *Guidelines for Psychological Practice with Lesbian, Gay, and Bisexual Clients*, Guideline 3. 67 Am. Psychol. 10, 14, January 2012.

[26] Megan Shiles, *Discriminatory Referrals: Uncovering a Potential Ethical Dilemma Facing Practitioners*, 19 Ethics & Behav. 142, 142 (2009). See also Marianne Schneider Corey & Gerald Corey, *Becoming a Helper* 222 (5th ed. 2007).

[27] On the issue of addressing biases, see John E. Pachankis & Marvin R. Goldfried, *Clinical Issues in Working with Lesbian, Gay, and Bisexual Clients*, 41 Psychotherapy: Theory, Res., Prac., Training 227 (2004).

at odds with their own and to affirm the client even where the counselor does not affirm some of the client's beliefs.[28]

In recent years, training has been viewed to be particularly important with respect to biases related to sexuality because they fall into a category of biases and values – those relating to morality, ethics and lifestyle – that are more likely than others to impact the counseling relationship.[29] Thus, "national organizations for therapists have begun to call attention to the importance of training therapists to work with LGB clients,"[30] including by providing opportunities for prospective counselors "to confront and to address their homophobia and heterosexist biases."[31]

The accreditation standards for the counseling professions reflect this view. The APA's Accreditation Policies and Procedures require that teaching programs demonstrate respect for and understanding of "cultural and individual diversity," a term that includes sexual orientation.[32] Similarly the Accreditation Policy and Standards of the Council of Social Work Education's Commission on Accreditation requires that social workers "gain sufficient self-awareness to eliminate the influence of personal biases and values in working with diverse groups" and includes sexual orientation as one dimension of diversity.[33] Such standards reflect the conviction that students should be trained to deal with diverse groups in ways that respect those groups.

3. ADDRESSING THE CONFLICT

Tolerance, respect, and nondiscrimination include tolerance and respect for different religious views and a commitment to avoid discrimination on the basis of such views. Thus, I resist concluding that no one whose religious-based opposition to homosexuality prevents them from counseling gays or lesbians or counseling them about their relationships can be a counselor. The question is whether – or to what extent – that opposition can be tolerated in the profession and/or in the training process. Can the religious convictions of students training in the counseling professions be accommodated while ensuring they receive adequate training? Can religious

---

[28] "To be respectful of a person does not entail fully embracing his or her moral system." Steven M. Donaldson, *Counselor Bias in Working with Gay Men and Lesbians: A Commentary on Barret and Barzan*, 42 Counseling & Values 88 (1998).

[29] Sherry Cormier & Paula S. Nurius, *Interviewing and Change Strategies for Helpers: Fundamental Skills and Cognitive Behavioral Interventions* 22 (Brookes/Coles 5th ed. 2003).

[30] Godfrey, supra note 22 at 491.

[31] Id. at 492.

[32] Am. Psychological Ass'n, *Guideline and Principles for Accreditation of Programs in Professional Psychology* 6 (2013), available at www.apa.org/ed/accreditation/about/policies/guiding-principles.pdf [https://perma.cc/82M6-Z54C].

[33] Council on Social Work Education, *Advanced Social Work Practice in Clinical Social Work, Educational Policy* 2.1.4, available at www.cswe.org/File.aspx?id=26685 [https://perma.cc/N9AW-PU6B].

convictions against homosexuality be tolerated in the practice of the counseling professions?

A. Affirmation vs. Neutrality

As Judge Sutton observed in *Ward*, standards of the counseling profession "(1) do not require a Muslim counselor to tell a Jewish client that his religious beliefs are correct if the conversation takes a turn in that direction, and (2) do not require an atheist counselor to tell a person of faith that there is a God if the client is wrestling with faith-based issues."[34]

The issue is more complicated here. Because the counseling professions have taken the position that the appropriate way to counsel homosexuals is an "affirmative counseling" approach that requires the celebration and acceptance of "the authenticity and integrity" of homosexual relationships, what is asked of a counselor is not merely to remain neutral, but to affirm such relationships as authentic relationships to be celebrated.

Religious-based opposition to counseling is sometimes expressed not as a refusal to counsel gays per se but as refusal to counsel about homosexual relationships, to provide assistance in improving a homosexual relationship, or to otherwise appear to affirm or condone a homosexual behavior.[35] In other words, adherents of religious faiths who view homosexual relationships as "sinful" feel unable to counsel homosexuals about their relationships in the way the profession has determined is appropriate. That was Julea Ward's issue: she realized she would be unable to "affirm" a client's homosexual relationship (or any extramarital sexual relationship).[36]

While as a general rule, counselors may need to recognize the influence of their personal beliefs and learn to manage differences between their values and their clients' values, not all differences in values are the same. I may value independence more than money, but that doesn't render me unable to counsel someone for whom money is a primary objective. Or, someone who has never been exposed to someone of another ethnicity may have work to do to overcome certain prejudices born of ignorance, but doing so does not strike at the heart of their identity and most fundamental beliefs. Those examples are enormously different from thinking someone can affirm that which they believe to be sinful. Neutrality might be possible.

---

[34] *Ward v. Polite*, 667 F.3d 727 (6th Cir. 2012).
[35] For example, in *Bruff v. North Mississippi Health Services, Inc.*, plaintiff had no objection per se to counseling homosexuals, but sought to be excused from "actively helping people involved in the homosexual lifestyle to have a better relationship with their homosexual partners." 244 F.3d 495, 497 (5th Cir. 2001).
[36] 667 F.3d 727, 729 (6th Cir. 2012).

Affirmation is not. The question then becomes whether the ability to refer clients is a viable way to deal with religious conflicts.

B. Use of Referrals

The ethical rules of the counseling professions permit referrals.[37] Indeed, "when a psychologist is uncomfortable working with a client's presenting concern, it may be in the client's best interest to refer him or her with the understanding that the psychologist is not competent to work with that client."[38] There are two separate questions with respect to referrals in the current context: the issue of referrals by a counseling professional and the wisdom of allowing referrals as part of the educational process.

i. The Issue of Referrals in the Profession

Referrals, including those due to a conflict over sexual values, are not uncommon in the counseling professions.[39] Counselors "appear to assume that referring is always an option when working with clients"[40] and that "difficulty in working with some clients does not, in itself, imply incompetence."[41]

Some, however, are more hesitant about the use of referrals. For example, although not disputing that there may be situations where referral is in a client's interest, Megan Shiles expresses concern for what she terms discriminatory referral practices.[42] The referral of a patient on the grounds such as race, disability, ethnicity or sexual orientation – without consultation, supervision, or exhaustion of all other possibilities – constitutes, in Shiles' opinion, unfair discrimination in violation of APA standards.

In contrast, Joseph Horton observes:

> Sometimes a personal bias, religious, or otherwise, would prevent a counselor from providing the high quality, neutral service that fully respects the client and the client's right to self-determination. For example, I once heard a person who does marital therapy say that he did not counsel couples when the husband was

---

[37] See, e.g., Am. Psychological Ass'n, *Ethical Principles of Psychologists and Code of Conduct Standard* 2.01(b) (2010), available at www.apa.org/ethics/code/index.aspx?item=5 [https://perma.cc/QGT9-9VRK].

[38] Shiles, supra note 26 at 143.

[39] Michele P. Ford & Susan S. Hendrick, *Therapists' Sexual Values for Self and Clients: Implications for Practice and Training*, 34 Prof. Psychol.: Res. & Prac. 80 (2003) (reporting study findings that 40% of therapists had referred clients because of conflicts over sexual values).

[40] Id. at 146.

[41] Shiles, supra note 26 at 148 (citing Theodore P. Remley & Barbara P. Herlihy, "Professional Practice in a Multicultural Society," in *Ethical, Legal, and Professional Issues in Counseling* 159 (2d ed. 2007)).

[42] Shiles, supra note 26.

physically abusive. The therapist believed that his strong negative feelings about abusive husbands would prevent him from counseling such couples well. The ethical approach for counselors in these situations is to refer clients to a therapist who will better meet their needs. To demand that counselors always be neutral regardless of their biases and convictions is to demand superhuman abilities.[43]

In a situation like Julea Ward's, Horton argues that referral is an act that "treat[s] homosexual clients with integrity and respect for their right of self-determination."[44]

On the one hand, "if referrals are acceptable, including for many nonreligious-based reasons, [a school] can't deny someone who has a religion-based need to refer."[45] On the other, there is reason to be cautious about referrals in this context.

It is one thing to refuse to take on a client when one believes oneself incapable of counseling effectively. It is another to do what Julea Ward suggested when she learned she had been assigned a client who was homosexual – to begin counseling with the option of making a referral later if relationship issues arise during counseling.

As Ward's suggestion reveals, issues relating to one's sexuality or sexual relationships may not present in the initial encounter. The agenda on day one of a counseling relationship may be very different from the agenda four-to-five months into the relationship. A client may come in seeking counseling for depression or job-related troubles and, only after some time, turn to discussion of a same-sex attraction or relationship. This is particularly likely in the case of a client who is not comfortable with his or her sexuality (who may not even have come out when counseling began).

Extricating oneself from an ongoing relationship is very different from not entering the relationship on in the first place. Referral in the midst of a counseling relationship risks harming the client. It may be particularly harmful in the case of a gay or lesbian who may have already faced difficulties related to his or her sexual orientation. Such a patient may "be emotionally harmed by the psychologist making a referral, interpreting that action to be yet another form of rejection similar to" the rejection at the hands of family and friends.[46]

---

[43] Joseph J. Horton, *Homosexuality, Religion and Counseling*, Mens News Daily, (September 22, 2010), available at www.mensnewsdaily.com/2010/09/22/homosexuality-religion-and-counseling/ [https://perma.cc/J4YK-2KP8].

[44] Id.

[45] Mark Oppenheimer, *A Counselor's Convictions Put her on Trial*, N.Y. Times (February 3, 2012), available at www.nytimes.com/2012/02/04/us/when-counseling-and-conviction-collide-beliefs.html [https://perma.cc/2J9K-NH9F]. See also *College Student Counselor Can Refer Homosexual Clients, Court Rules*, Christian Post (January 27, 2012), available at www.christianpost.com/new/college-student-counselor-can-defer-homosexual-clients-court-rules-68130/ [https://perma.cc/4F4Y-88DR] ("Counselors refer clients elsewhere all the time for personal, financial, or ethical reasons, and referrals for religious reasons should be treated no differently.").

[46] Shiles, supra note 26 at 152 (citing *Bruff v. North Mississippi Health Services, Inc.*, 244 F.3d 495 (5th Cir. 2001) and Mary A. Hermann & Barbara Richter Herlihy, *Legal and Ethical Implications of Refusing to Counsel Homosexual Clients*, 84 J. Counseling & Dev. 414 (2006)).

The risks – in this context and others –suggest that referrals should be used sparingly. Indeed, the APA Standard on Personal Problems and Conflicts implies as much: "referral should serve as the last resort action taken by psychologist."[47]

ii. The Wisdom of Referrals as Part of the Education Process

Whatever one thinks about referrals by professional counselors, allowing referrals as part of the education process presents a separate question. One could believe there are circumstances where a professional counselor is justified in referring a patient whom she believes she would have difficulty counseling, but still view student referrals during a practicum as inappropriate.

Part of the education of counselors is helping them determine if counseling is the right field for them. I begin with that observation because many believe that "[i]f a counselor's values were so strong that he or she could not counsel clients who held differing beliefs, we would be concerned that the counselor is not well suited for the counseling profession."[48] Shiles interprets the APA's standards as suggesting that "the psychologist's inflexible rules regarding who he will or will not work with will prevent him from practicing competently."[49] If one cannot be open toward those with different views and lifestyles, counseling may not be the right field.

Identifying and learning how to deal with one's biases is thus an important part of the educational process, suggesting there is educational value in giving someone the opportunity to deal with the very person they would have difficulty counseling in a supervised practicum setting, so that they learn how to manage the difficulty. To excuse the person from the very case that may be the most problematic for her means she is not getting training where it may be most needed.[50] Thus, even if one can function well in the profession (e.g., by referrals), there is a good argument that adequate training should include making sure students can counsel outside of their comfort zones.

But there is a tension here. Julea Ward knew her position and her views on homosexuality – a position at odds with the view of her profession. The profession sees her as having a bias or prejudice that should be changed. In discussing the issue, Katie Godfrey and her co-authors speak of efforts to have students clarify, evaluate, and "potentially chang[e] their own biases, prejudices, and values."[51] If the goal of training is to get a student to change her view of homosexuality, to learn to celebrate

---

[47] Id. at 151 (citing Gerald Corey et al., "Values and the Helping Relationship," in *Issues and Ethics in the Helping Professions* (2d ed. 2007)).

[48] Shiles, supra note 26 (citing Theodore P. Remley & Barbara P. Herlihy, "Professional Practice in a Multicultural Society," in *Ethical, Legal, and Professional Issues in Counseling* 159 (2d ed. 2007)).

[49] Shiles, supra note 26, at 150.

[50] Id. at 148.

[51] Godfrey, supra note 26 at 500.

homosexual relationships as authentic, is that really likely to happen in the case of a strong, religious-based opposition to homosexuality? It is one thing to say there is value in learning to deal with people with different values, but another to try to effectuate a change in a deeply held religious view. If such a change is not likely, the benefit of disallowing a referral in the educational process seems virtually nonexistent.

C. Protecting the Interests of the Patient

I think it is a safe conclusion that the educational process for counselors must accept that students with religious-based opposition to homosexuality cannot be trained out of that opposition, and that the practicum process cannot succeed in forcing such students to affirmatively counsel gays about their relationships. The issue, then, is whether the interests of patients can be protected in a way that also respects the religious beliefs of counselors. If so, there is reason to provide conscience protection for such students as part of the educational process. Let me suggest two possibilities.

i. Limited Certification

That some counselors may not feel comfortable counseling homosexuals about their relationships does not create an access issue. There is no evidence of a shortage of counselors available to counsel LGBT patients. Concerns about access thus do not warrant requiring every counselor has to counsel homosexuals about their relationships.

Saying that those with religious-based opposition to homosexuality should not be excluded from the counseling professions, however, does not mean there are not situations where protecting the interests of patients requires some limitation on the ability of such a person to counsel others. For example, where a high school has a single counselor available for students, giving that position to someone who is not capable of counseling certain groups of people is inimical to the interests of the client. In fact, Julea Ward wanted to counsel high school students and went back for her degree after teaching high school for several years.[52]

That raises the question of whether balancing the interests of counselor and patients might be achieved by educational institutions granting some kind of limited certification that would certify that certain graduates are qualified to practice in certain settings but not others. If one believes that counselors should be trained to be able to work with people of all kinds, a limited certificate may seem suboptimal.

---

[52] 667 F.3d 727, 730 (6th Cir. 2012); Peter Schmidt, *Federal Judge Upholds Dismissal of Counseling Student Who Balked at Treating Gay Clients*, Chronicle of Higher Education (July 27, 2010), available at http://chronicle.com/article/Judge-Upholds-Dismissal-of/123704/ [https://perma.cc/PR72-7WND].

In addition, it would not guarantee that issues won't arise that make it difficult for a counselor to counsel in accordance with the norms of the profession. Imagine, for instance, a limited license counselor in a Mormon school presented with a Mormon youth struggling with his sexual identity. Nonetheless, a limited certificate may offer a way to balance the competing interests by keeping the counselor out of settings where harm can be foreseen; it may be the best that can be achieved.

ii. Disclosure

Another possibility is requiring that a therapist disclose to patients any issues the counselor believes she is unable to address in a counseling relationship, allowing the patient to decide whether to proceed in the relationship. As one commentator observed, "[b]ias cannot be avoided. The harm is being unaware of our biases and thus being unable to discuss them with our clients in an open and nonjudgmental manner so that they can make full use of their autonomy and decide for themselves.[53]

This approach is only possible when the therapist is practicing in an area where there is sufficient access to other therapists. From the point of view of the patient, there is still some risk of rejection, as in the case of referrals. And disclosure may lose a counselor as many heterosexual patients as homosexual ones. Nonetheless, allowing the parties go in with an understanding of the possibilities and limitations of the relationship may offer a way to protect both the counselor's religious convictions and the patient's wellbeing.

CONCLUSION

This discussion is a subset of the much broader question of our society's ability to tolerate unpopular religious views. The increasing acceptance of same-sex relationships as a normal and positive means of expression of sexuality has tended to produce a lack of tolerance toward those whose religious beliefs lead them to a different view of such relationships.

It may be that some people should not be counselors. It is not the job of a counselor to tell people what they should or should not do. Rather, counselors help facilitate processing by individual clients, helping them look at all sides and make their own decisions, and must be able to respect people outside of their own belief system.

However, tolerance and religious freedom, as well as the needs of patients who themselves have religious opposition to same-sex relationships, mean that it is

---

[53] Steven M. Donaldson, *Counselor Bias in Working with Gay Men and Lesbians: A Commentary on Barret and Barzan*, 42 Counseling & Values 88 (1998).

important that we do not impose unnecessary barriers to the ability of those with religious-based opposition to homosexuality to practice in the counseling professions. Limited certification and disclosure offer two possible ways of respecting the religious views of those who wish to enter the counseling professions without doing damage to the primary objective of an educational institution of training counselors in a manner that protects the interests of those who seek counseling.

19

Reclaiming Biopolitics

Religion and Psychiatry in the Sexual Orientation Change Therapy Cases and the Establishment Clause Defense

Craig J. Konnoth

In *Pickup v. Brown*, *Welch v. Brown*, and *King v. Christie*, plaintiffs challenged laws prohibiting mental health professionals from engaging in sexual orientation change efforts (SOCE) within the scope of their licenses.[1] They argued (inter alia) that the laws violated their speech rights by prohibiting them from engaging in certain talk therapies, and interfered with their free exercise of religion.[2] The Ninth and Third Circuits held that the behavior involved in these cases was either (a) not protected speech,[3] or (b) speech subject to a lesser degree of protection, which the state had a sufficient interest in preventing.[4]

In future cases, however, these arguments may not prove enough. The scope of speech protected under the First Amendment has expanded in recent years. In several cases, courts have held that various kinds of speech in medical contexts receive constitutional protection.[5] Future courts may therefore conclude that talk therapy constitutes fully protected constitutional speech.

---

[1] See *Pickup v. Brown*, 740 F.3d 1208 (9th Cir. 2014); *King v. Governor of the State of N.J.*, 767 F.3d 216 (3d Cir. 2014). There is some dispute as to whether the states' bans were restricted to the scope of the professionals' licenses. The courts appeared to be satisfied that this was the case.

[2] See *King v. Christie*, 981 F. Supp. 2d 296, 305 (D.N.J. 2013); *Welch v. Brown*, 907 F. Supp. 2d 1102, 1105 (E.D. Cal. 2012); *Pickup v. Brown*, 42 F. Supp. 3d 1347 (E.D. Cal. 2012), aff'd, 728 F.3d 1042 (9th Cir. 2013), and aff'd, 740 F.3d at 1208.

[3] See Pickup, 740 F.3d at 1231 (concluding that any effect of the ban on free-speech was merely incidental).

[4] See King, 767 F.3d at 224. I myself am inclined to the Ninth Circuit's approach.

[5] See, e.g., *Sorrell v. IMS Health Inc.*, 564 U.S. 552 (2011) (finding the prohibition regarding pharmaceutical marketing data invalid under First Amendment); *United States v. Caronia*, 703 F.3d 149, 152 (2d Cir. 2012) (holding that forbidding off-label uses raises First Amendment concerns).

Thanks are owed to Rick Mula for excellent research and proofing assistance. The author was involved in defending the California law at issue in the cases discussed in this chapter as a Deputy Solicitor General in the California Department of Justice. The views here are his own and do not draw on work product from the litigation.

To address that eventuality, I explore the pedigree of the therapies that undergird SOCE. I show that SOCE is best understood as a form of religious ministry. States can therefore argue that permitting SOCE within the scope of state-issued medical licenses would endorse those practices and undermine the states' compelling interest in preventing religious establishment. While this argument is not unassailable, I believe it would ultimately withstand scrutiny.

1. THE NATURE OF CHRISTIAN COUNSELING

A. *The Secular Victory*

In 1935, Bertrand Russell outlined five areas in which religious and scientific narratives were in conflict. In order from the most "remote" from human life to the "nearest," the two paradigms presented rivaling explanations of "the heavens ... the earth ... life ... the human body, and last of all ... the human mind."[6] While he concluded that scientific explanations had prevailed over religious teachings in nearly all these areas, Russell found that religion still claimed explanatory power over the human mind, as psychology was "only just beginning to be scientific."[7] By mid-century, however, the monopoly over the human mind was being "passed from the religious pastorate to various medical and quasi-medical professions: psychiatry, neurology, social work, and clinical psychology."[8]

According to prominent thinkers, most notably Michel Foucault, these professions assert control over the human mind in ways that are more technical and all-encompassing than religious approaches. The religious model operates in terms of discrete acts. Each act is evaluated by itself – a good act merits reward; a bad one, penance. The medical model, however, operates at the level of profiles rather than specific acts. In so doing, it takes into consideration the totality of a person's acts and behavior, and even her family history.[9] The individual is imbued with an identity

---

[6] Bertrand Russell, Religion and Science 49 (1997).
[7] Id. at 143.
[8] See, e.g., David A. Powlison, *Competent to Counsel? The History of a Conservative Protestant Anti-Psychiatry Movement* 41–2 (January 1 1996) (unpublished Ph.D. dissertation, University of Pennsylvania) (on file with author); Russell, supra note 6, at 18 ("Pastoral counseling was supplanted by secular psychotherapy in large part."); E. Brooks Holifield, *A History of Pastoral Care in America: From Salvation to Self-Realization* 261–9 (2005).
[9] Foucault makes this point most forcefully in Michel Foucault, Psychiatric Power: Lectures at the Collège De France 1973–1974 (Arnold I. Davidson ed., Graham Burchell trans., 2006); Michel Foucault, *Madness and Civilization* (Richard Howard trans., 1988); see also Michel Foucault, *History of Sexuality: An Introduction* 65 (Robert Hurley trans., 1990). Although this volume focuses on sexuality – which is the focus of this paper – his approach is largely of a part with his broader work on psychiatry and psychoses in general.

based on this totalistic diagnosis. This identity is used as a baseline to evaluate all of the individual's past and present behavior, and often seeks to predict their future.

The all-encompassing power the professions exert in relation to the individual is heightened because of their technical mode of operation. In the religious context, the sinner himself recognizes, and then confesses, the sin. But in psychiatry, the patient knows nothing. They must confess to the therapist everything, providing a wide-ranging catalogue of all their behavior.[10] And the questioner determines whether and what kind of problem exists – he is the "master of truth itself."[11]

Finally, religious control generally operates in specialized, religious contexts. But psychiatric methods "spread into other institutions" including the school, the prison, the army, and even the family.[12] Mental assessment is no longer "localiz[ed]" to specific contexts and to specific bad acts, but spread to "a whole series of relationships: children and parents, students and educators, patients and psychiatrists, delinquents and experts."[13]

B. Reclaiming Counseling

i. The Evangelical Revival

Both Catholic and mainline (as opposed to evangelical) Protestant religious figures were aware of the threat psychology posed to their earlier monopoly and sought to co-opt the potential power of the new science towards religious ends.[14] In the mid-1930s, a prominent Southern Baptist Theological Seminary scholar sought to "capture psychology for Christ."[15] Similarly, the newly formed Chicago Society of Catholic Psychologists sought "the integration of ... psychology with the principles of ... the Catholic Church."[16]

But these efforts were largely unsuccessful. As a substantive matter, pastoral counseling relied on scientific rather than religious perspectives for its intellectual content.[17] Rogerian methods (a form of talk therapy) dominated the work of the most prominent pastoral thinkers of this period.[18] In turn, they explicitly rejected attempts to integrate scriptural teachings into psychological theory. One

---

[10] See Foucault, History of Sexuality, supra note 9, at 66.
[11] Id. at 66–7.
[12] See Foucault, Psychiatric Power, supra note 9, at 85, 189.
[13] Id.
[14] See generally Robert Kugelmann, *Psychology and Catholicism: Contested Boundaries* (2013).
[15] Holifield, supra note 8, at 227. Note that the Seminary itself would be better characterized as non-fundamentalist during this period. See generally William A. Mueller, *A History of Southern Baptist Theological Seminary* (1959).
[16] Kugelmann, supra note 14, at 272.
[17] See Powlison, supra note 8, at 46.
[18] Id. at 275, 278, 281–2, 300.

prominent Protestant counselor for example, cautioned that one should not "moralize, generalize ... or direct" the patient; another criticized the use of the Bible as "as a symbol of authority."[19] On the Catholic side, sixty members of the American Catholic Psychology Association suggested that the 1968 papal encyclical regarding birth control "rested on a false psychology of man."[20]

Even as the attempts of mainstream Protestants and Catholics to develop a distinctively religious brand of mental health languished, evangelical Protestants began their own efforts. Before World War II, the evangelical movement was largely isolationist and outspokenly rejected psychological approaches.[21] In the 1950s and 1960s, however, the evangelical movement began turning away from isolationism and engaged more with American culture.[22] This brought the movement face-to-face with the sciences, including psychology.[23] In the 1970s, prominent evangelical institutions started schools and journals designed to train counselors to engage in mental health practice from a religious perspective.[24] Books designed for a lay audience sought to integrate psychological approaches within broader evangelical worldviews.[25] And numerous entities, both non- and for-profit, set up programs that engaged in counseling from an evangelical perspective for those seeking mental health assistance.[26]

There remained the danger, however, that evangelical psychology, like the mainline Protestant and Catholic efforts before it, would secularize. This fear was not illusory. Early on the in the movement, certain offshoots of evangelical psychology such as the Fuller seminary, and the Christian Association for Psychological Studies (CAPS), with its *Journal of Psychology and Christianity*, went precisely in this direction.[27] In the 1970s, the future of evangelical psychology was unclear.

In 1970, Jay Adams, the founder of Biblical Counseling movement, published his magnum opus, *Competent to Counsel*. Adams accused evangelicals who relied on psychotherapeutic methods of secular goals.[28] Adams sought to professionalize

---

[19] Donald Capps, *Biblical Approaches to Pastoral Counseling* 19–20 (2003).
[20] Kugelmann, supra note 14, at 293.
[21] Id. at 50; David Harrington Watt, *A Transforming Faith: Explorations of Twentieth-Century American Evangelicalism* 139–43 (1991).
[22] See Holifield, supra note 8, at 12.
[23] See generally George Marsden, *Reforming Fundamentalism: Fuller Seminary and the New Evangelicalism* (1995).
[24] See Powlison, supra note 8, at 233–9 (describing the steps that led to the creation of Fuller Theological Seminary graduate school of psychology (1965)); Marsden, supra note 23, at 142 (citing Rosemead Sch. Prof. Psychol. (1968) and J. Psychol. & Theology (1973)).
[25] Id. (discussing James Dobson's book, *Dare to Discipline* (1970)).
[26] Id. (discussing Focus on the Family, the New Life Treatment Centers, and the Minirth Meier, and Rapha treatment centers).
[27] Id. at 352; Capps, supra note 19.
[28] Powlison, supra note 8, at 4.

biblical counseling in order to go toe-to-toe with evangelical psychologists. He created the National Association of Nouthetic Counselors, and instituted a program for training, education, and accreditation with four levels of membership, including a professoriate at the highest level.[29]

Although Biblical counseling practices only became relatively popular in the 1990s, Adams's work was widely read in the 1970s and 1980s, and helped move the fundamentalist counseling movement further to the right.[30] First, Adams's message resonated among pastors, on whom evangelical psychologists relied for client referrals. Pastors had traditionally used "prayer and bible verse prescription" to help alleviate the crises of their congregants. Adams' antimedical, biblical approach validated these traditional methods with a system and a "science."[31] As one Baptist minister observed, *Competent to Counsel* meant that he was "no longer counseling as a wallowing Rogerian."[32] Further, pastors became increasingly concerned by the perceived secularization of some evangelical psychologists, such as members of CAPS. To defend their legitimacy in the eyes of the pastors and distance themselves from CAPS, evangelical psychologists had to reaffirm their commitment to scripture over psychological orthodoxy in explicitly religious terms.[33]

But in the face of the growing secularization of some of their colleagues, Adams also genuinely pricked the consciences of many leading evangelical psychologists.[34] Adams was generally disliked because of his confrontational style. Nonetheless, Gary Collins, later head of the American Association of Christian Counselors, admitted that, despite their many differences, "Adams argues convincingly that ... much that has been called Christian counseling must be rejected" as incompatible with scripture.[35] Larry Crabb, another immensely influential counselor in the 1980s and 1990s, who had a great antipathy towards Adams, nonetheless agreed "that the counseling processes ... must be thoroughly reconceptualized from a biblical foundation."[36] Adams was recognized, and received an award as one of the fathers of Christian Counseling at the First International Congress on Christian Counseling in 1988.[37]

Ultimately, Adams framed the debate in biblical rather than psychological terms. This meant that evangelical psychologists had to turn to scripture rather than science

[29] Id. at 120.
[30] Id. at 100, 89.
[31] Id. at 107.
[32] Id. at 99; 106–107.
[33] Id. at 299.
[34] Id. at 368, 89.
[35] Gary R. Collins, *How to Be a People Helper* 168 (1995).
[36] Larry Crabb, *Basic Principles of Biblical Counseling: Meeting Counseling Needs Through the Local Church* 49 (1975).
[37] Id.

to justify their work. "[V]alue and stigma hinged on how one's views comported with the yardstick of divinely spoken canon."[38] Evangelical psychologists were forced to justify psychological methods based on the Bible.

In so doing, they argued that the Bible permitted such study of nature as God's "second book" of revelation.[39] They also framed their criticism of Adams in biblical terms. For example, they claimed that Adams' form of counseling focused on the problems of sinning, rather than being sinned against, and promoted a "legalistic, works-oriented" doctrine rather than one of grace.[40] Evangelical psychologists therefore situated the shibboleth for their work in scripture rather than science.

By focusing on Adams' critique of counseling in particular, I do not mean to downplay the influence of more general fundamentalist theological currents that helped move and maintain fundamentalist pastors on the right.[41] But the debates with Adams both anchor and demonstrate the priorities of evangelical psychology. What is clear was that, by the late 1980s, most evangelical psychotherapists had become far more explicitly conservative in their theology and ethics.[42] The ultimate lodestone of psychological practice became scriptural prescription rather than the scientific method.

ii. Religious Aims, Psychotherapeutic Methods

The theological shift of the 1980s in evangelical counseling proved lasting. The American Association of Christian Counselors (AACC) continues to define "Christian counseling as a unique and case-based form of Christian discipleship, assisting the church in its call to bring believers to maturity in the lifelong process of sanctification – of growing to maturity in Christ."[43] AACC remains the umbrella organization for fundamentalist counselors, with the support of the leading lights of the movement, including Crabb and Focus on the Family. It was a plaintiff in both the *Pickup* and *King* cases.[44]

Nonetheless, although their goals are religious, the *methods* these therapists use remained psychotherapeutic in nature, demanding an all-encompassing analysis of human life. One counselor explains the distinction between religious and medical methods. "[I]f a client admits hitting his wife, a priest will focus on confession" of that particular act; "[a] counselor, in contrast, might focus on helping the client explore

---

[38] Powlison, supra note 8, at 303.
[39] Id. at 308.
[40] John Carter, *Towards a Biblical Model of Counseling*, 8 J. Psychol. & Theology 45, 47 (1980); Powlison, supra note 8, at 322.
[41] See, e.g., Marsden, supra note 23, at 162–7.
[42] Powlison, supra note 8, at 373.
[43] *About Us*, American Association of Christian Counselors, available at www.aacc.net/about-us/ [https://perma.cc/F3UV-G3B9] (last visited February 6, 2015).
[44] Id.

his anger about being abused himself as a child, his misconceptions about gender roles and his current struggles for control in his marriage. The priest focuses on the immediate problem, whereas the counselor looks for ... context."[45] "[A] priest," counselors are told, "reduc[ed] complex emotional problems to simple formulas of personal sin."[46] By contrast, counselors go beyond the sinful act, and require patients to document "unconscious wishes, [and] inner sinful patterns," which then are used to create an entire profile or identity.[47] Therapists prefer long-term relationships between therapists and clients, rather than sometimes one-time encounters between a particular priest and confessant.[48] The goal is not merely "chang[ing] behavior." Rather, therapists suggested "sift[ing] through the morass of sin in [a] person's life"[49] to understand "the development of pathology."[50]

The chapter on homosexuality in Gary Collins's classic textbook exemplifies the combination of totalistic psychotherapeutic methods in the service of religious goals. Collins explains that the "Bible [i]s the standard against which all psychology must be tested and [i]s the written Word of God with which all valid counseling must agree."[51] Collins begins his chapter by observing that "in every Bible passage that mentions homosexuality, it is mentioned negatively. It seems likely, therefore, that erotic homosexual acts are wrong."[52] Accordingly, condoning and helping adjustment to homosexual behavior is never a viable option. Rather, the counselor must "[e]ncourage behavior change."[53]

But these religious goals are achieved through psychotherapeutic methods. A counselor cannot, like a priest, simply tell his clients to drive out their impure and lustful thoughts. Rather, she must inquire into the patient's "worship, work, family, recreation, time management, exercise, and rest."[54] The goal is for the counselee to "[b]reak with ... gay friendships" and "avoid people, publications, and situations" that remind the person of his old lifestyle. This, in turn, results in "a genuine grief process" that the counselor must help address.[55] A counseling approach therefore gives to the Christian counselor a greater degree of control than mere pastoral advice.

---

[45] Id. at 169.
[46] Mark R. McMinn, *Psychology, Theology, and Spirituality in Christian Counseling* 166 (1996).
[47] Powlison, supra note 8, at 314.
[48] Id. at 127.
[49] James A. Oakland et al., *An Analysis and Critique of Jay Adam's Theory of Counseling*, 28 J. Am. Sci. Affiliation 101, 107 (1976).
[50] Bruce Narramore, *The Concept of Responsibility in Psychopathology and Psychotherapy*, 13 J. Psychol. & Theology 91, 95 (1985).
[51] Id. at 43.
[52] Collins, supra note 35, at 381.
[53] Id. at 392.
[54] Id.
[55] Id. at 392.

Reliance on scientific discourse also boosted the legitimacy of evangelicalism itself. As Aziza Ahmed has pointed out, reliance on scientific discourse has characterized conservative Christian discourse in the abortion context.[56] Intelligent design theories similarly seek to wrest from the control of science a monopoly regarding the explanations for the origins of the universe and life.[57] In the same way, as psychology became part of the American social fabric, "[a]ligning themselves with an increasingly powerful impulse in American culture ... bolstered the ... authority and prestige" of fundamentalist leaders.[58]

But unlike conservative abortion medicine and intelligent design theory, fundamentalist psychology is turned inward in its religious focus. In theory, the "scientific" arguments against abortion are analytically independent of scripture-based antiabortion arguments. Intelligent design theory, similarly, does not necessarily depend on specific scriptural precepts. But evangelical psychology takes scriptural orthodoxy as its guiding principle. The relevant analysis for constitutional purposes, therefore, should turn on sexual orientation change efforts (SOCE) as a religious, rather than a medical, activity.

2. THE ESTABLISHMENT CLAUSE DEFENSE AND THE LIMITS OF PSYCHIATRIC PRACTICE

As this history suggests, SOCE, like all evangelical counseling, is quintessentially a form of religious practice. The Welch plaintiffs acknowledged as much, arguing that prohibiting SOCE burdened the free exercise of religion: SOCE, they explain, is a form of "religious ministry;"[59] and part of the "care for the congregation."[60] Upon remand (after losing their free-speech claims on appeal), the plaintiffs continued to press their free exercise claim, and emphasized the "religious nature of the therapy" by the "work of the Holy Spirit."[61] "Christian counseling begins with specific biblical principles rather than secular theories."[62]

Similarly, although other plaintiffs attempted to downplay the religious nature of their activities, organizations such as the AACC (one of the plaintiffs) prioritize

---

[56] Frank Pasquale et al., *Panel on Science and Democracy, Public Health in the Shadow of the First Amendment Conference at Yale Law School* (October 18 2014).
[57] Cf. supra note 6 and accompanying text.
[58] Watt, supra note 21, at 146.
[59] Memorandum in Support of Preliminary Injunction at 8, *Welch v. Brown*, 907 F. Supp. 2d 1102 (E.D. Cal. 2012) (No. 12-CV-02484).
[60] Id. at 9.
[61] Supplemental Brief at 4, *Welch v. Brown*, 907 F. Supp. 2d 1102 (E.D. Cal. 2012) (No. 12-CV-02484) (entered October 8, 2014).
[62] *Minister Tools and Resources*, Family Counseling Services, available at www.fcssandiego.com/tools.html [https://perma.cc/Z5MY-HL8E] (last visited February 6, 2015).

biblical guidance above evidence-based methods, as noted earlier. Ronald Newman, one of the two individual plaintiffs in *King*, explains on the website of the Christian counseling organization that he began that its members "encourage and support one another in our service to Jesus Christ through the ministry and/or vocation of Christian counseling, as well as to cooperate in serving the body of Christ and the community at large."[63]

This religious basis of SOCE suggests another line of defense for states that enact prohibitions on these practices. The Ninth and Third Circuits held that psychotherapy is not fully protected speech for First Amendment purposes. But even assuming that the therapists' speech at issue receives a high degree of scrutiny as some judges have claimed,[64] the state can assert a compelling interest in prohibiting SOCE – preventing religious establishment. The state would argue that the state action at issue is not a *ban* on speech per se. Rather, it is a denial of a state-provided resource – a license – that facilitates private speech. Denying state resources for religious purposes prevents religious establishment, which is a compelling purpose that satisfies First Amendment scrutiny.

The Supreme Court has recognized that the State may deny access to a limited, state-created forum in order to prevent religious establishment under certain circumstances. In *Rosenberger v. University of Virginia*, the state denied funding to religious student newspapers though it provided subsidies to other newspapers.[65] In *Good New Club v. Milford*, the school denied religious clubs access to school facilities that were available to other student clubs.[66] In each of these cases, the Court acknowledged that where the State provides resources to entities with religious goals, it retains a compelling interest in avoiding religious establishment. That is, it is important that the state not be seen as itself endorsing any particular religion.

SOCE litigation falls within this line of cases. A license is a "privilege ... entitling the licensee to do something that he or she would not be entitled to do without the license."[67] It gives the holder the ability to engage in speech within a specific

---

[63] *About the Christian Counseling Consortium of S.J.*, Christian Counseling Consortium, available at http://christiancounselingsj.webs.com/ [https://perma.cc/YCG4-C3UP] (last visited February 6, 2015).
[64] *Pickup v. Brown*, 740 F.3d 1208, 1215 (9th Cir. 2014) (O'Scannlain J., dissenting from denial of en banc rehearing); *Welch v. Brown*, 907 F. Supp. 2d 1102 (E.D. Cal. 2012).
[65] 515 U.S. 819, 847–8 (1995).
[66] 533 U.S. 98, 113–14, 120 (2001); see also *Lamb's Chapel v. Ctr. Moriches Union Free Sch. Dist.*, 508 U.S. 384, 395–6 (1993) (holding that State could not grant after-hours access to school premises to secular groups but deny the same to religious groups). An alternative approach is for the states to claim that any licensed speech constitutes government speech which it may control at its discretion. Cf. *Walker v. Texas Division*, 576 U.S. 1 (2015). For reasons I cannot here discuss, I believe that that approach will not succeed.
[67] 51 Am. Jur. 2d Licenses and Permits § 1 (2015).

state-sanctioned therapeutic relationship. The government, therefore, creates a forum in which it has a compelling interest in avoiding religious establishment.

However, asserting an interest in avoiding establishment is not enough. In *Good News Club*, as in the other cases, a majority of the Court rejected the Establishment defense on what appear to be two grounds. First, it noted that in neither case would the government be seen as the *speaker* of the message. Government aid went to a huge variety of nonreligious groups with very different messages and viewpoints. Accordingly, there was "no realistic danger that the community would think that the [government] was endorsing religion."[68] Second, precisely because of the range of content and viewpoints involved, the *message* would not be seen as religion-supportive. Rather, the message sent would be that the government provided "aid ... to a broad range of groups ... without regard to ... religion."[69] Since the speaker would not be seen as the government and the support would not be seen as endorsing religion, the government had no anti-establishment interest.

But the case for an Establishment Clause interest is far more robust with SOCE. First, a license is a form of state endorsement. It is a state "imprimatur" of the person engaged in the practice; it demonstrates "public trust [in]... those with proven qualifications."[70] Licenses to engage in therapy in California, for example, are prominently entitled "State of California, Board of Behavioral Sciences." The certificate has the Great Seal of the state, and the signatures of the chairperson and executive officer of the Board. The license notes that the board has issued the license to the licensee pursuant to state law.[71] Accordingly, a license is more akin to state endorsement than the fora created in the other cases.

Second, any exemption sends a message endorsing religion. Unlike the school funding or public forum cases, the medical licensure regime does not allow a large variety of groups in – it allows only the licensing of forms of medical practice. Any exemption for religion then would be unique. Religious ministry alone, of all other nonmedical practices, would be given special dispensation. Hence, the state may more plausibly claim an establishment interest.

Yet the state's case is not invulnerable. Plaintiffs will point out that analogous arguments have failed. In *Good News Club*, for example, the dissent also argued that the religious and nonreligious groups were engaging in different kinds of behavior. Other groups whose activities had been permitted engaged in "mere discussion of a subject." But plaintiffs engaged in "worship" rather than a discussion.[72] The

---

[68] Good News Club, 533 U.S. at 113 (citations omitted) (relying in part on the Lemon test). The Court followed similar reasoning in Rosenberger. Id. at 99.
[69] Id. at 115 (citations omitted).
[70] 51 Am. Jur. 2d Licenses and Permits § 15 (2015).
[71] Sample certificate on file with author.
[72] Good News Club, 533 U.S. at 138 (Souter, J., dissenting).

majority responded that worship was both discussion and conduct: it could "also be characterized properly as the teaching of morals and character development from a particular viewpoint."[73] Similarly, here, plaintiffs may argue that what they seek is *both* a religious ministry and a medical treatment, designed to prevent disease – at least as they understand it.

This argument is not without merit. Indeed, it points to fundamental limitations in our understanding of psychology itself. Is psychotherapeutic practice so clearly defined that religious goals must fall outside its purview? Is its practice defined by its methods – which evangelical psychologists adopt – or by secular, "scientific" goals?

Consider the DSM V, which outlines mental health disorders and their treatments. The DSM V does not define the limits of mental health practice. Rather, it defines diagnostic criteria and disorders. "The diagnostic criteria," it tells us, "identify symptoms, behaviors, cognitive functions, personality traits, physical signs, syndrome, combinations, and durations that require clinical expertise to differentiate from normal life variation and transient responses to stress."[74] The symptoms and so on are defined as such, in other words, only because they are not part of "normal life." In turn, "[t]he boundaries between normality and pathology vary across cultures for specific types of behaviors ... Hence, the level at which an experience becomes problematic or pathological will differ."[75] In other words, whether something is a symptom of a mental health disorder or not depends heavily on cultural norms.

Turning to the definition of "mental disorder," we find that it is:

> [A] syndrome characterized by clinically significant disturbance in an individual's cognition, emotion regulation, or behavior that reflects a dysfunction in the psychological, biological, or developmental processes underlying mental functioning. Mental disorders are usually associated with significant distress or disability in social, occupational, or other important activities.... [s]ocially deviant behavior (e.g., political, religious, or sexual) ...are not mental disorders unless the deviance...results from a dysfunction in the individual, as described above.[76]

Now, we are told that religiously "deviant behavior" is not a disorder as a general matter – but it *can* be a disorder if it results from a "dysfunction." The dysfunction in turn may be associated with a disability with respect to "social ... or other important activities." Importance (and disability for that matter), however, is surely in the eye of the beholder. In other words, even if we agree that the goal of psychiatric practice is to apply "diagnostic criteria" to rid a patient of "disorders," we do not agree

---

[73] Id. at 111 (majority opinion).
[74] *Diagnostic and Statistical Manual of Mental Disorders* 5 (5th ed. 2013).
[75] Id. at 14.
[76] Id. at 20.

on much. To some large extent, each of those terms may be culturally, and even religiously, defined.

This chapter is, of course, not the place to grapple with cultural relativism in psychiatric practice. Suffice it to say that this relativism does present a challenge to an establishment argument, but not, I think, an insurmountable one. In *Good News Club*, the instructional fora were created for "instruction in any branch of ... learning" and "social, civic and recreational meetings and entertainment."[77] Reasonable minds could see religious proselytizing as falling within this category, so granting religious entities access to the fora would not be seen as giving a special preference to religion.

For courts to follow the path of *Good News Club*, they would have to hold that religious ministry could, in fact, constitute medical practice. This, as I have argued, is not an outlandish claim. But I do not believe that courts are ready to elide the distinction between religion and medicine as a legal matter. Cultural norms from Russell's day until today continue to present religion and science as mutually exclusive for the most part. And as a practical matter, acknowledging multiple subjective approaches to medical practice from many different viewpoints – as many as the student newspapers in *Rosenberger* or clubs in *Good News Club* – could undermine the standard setting that is important to medical practice and malpractice law. It is therefore unlikely that courts will blur the line between religion and medicine.

CONCLUSION

State regulation is increasingly being subject to First Amendment challenge. Seeking to limit the reach of what counts as protected speech is not enough. It is also important to articulate the interests that underlie the state's ability to regulate speech in the medical context at least. An Establishment Clause argument helps articulate one such important interest. However, to the extent psychologists themselves seek to limit the viability of religious forms of therapy as legitimate medical practice, they may wish to sharpen their definition of mental health practice. Such steps would strengthen the state's hand in any First Amendment challenges.

---

[77] Good News Club, 533 U.S. at 102.

PART VII

Accounting for Patients' Religious Beliefs

Introduction

Robert D. Truog

The four chapters in this part cover a range of intriguing issues related to the legal and ethical deference we should accord to religious beliefs. In this introduction I will reflect on some of the key themes addressed by these authors.

Thaddeus Mason Pope and Teneille R. Brown take up, respectively, religious objections to the determination of death by neurological criteria ("brain death"), and decisions to refuse to provide certain treatments to patients on the grounds that to do so would be futile. Although these topics may appear to be categorically distinct, they actually share overlapping features. Despite the seeming endless controversies over what constitutes futile treatment,[1] most would agree that it is self-evident that providing medical treatment to a dead person is futile. Since patients diagnosed as brain-dead are considered legally dead, brain death is currently the one, and only, medical condition in the United States where medical treatments are deemed legally futile. Yet, both concepts remain controversial, as I elaborate below.

Pope addresses the thorny topic of legal exemptions and accommodations around brain death that are accorded based on religious views. But there is an important difference between deference to religious beliefs around the diagnosis of brain death and other types of religious exceptions. Consider, for example, Jonathan F. Will's discussion in this part of decisions to refuse blood transfusions for minors on religious grounds by Jehovah's Witness patients and families. In these cases, an authoritative medical opinion exists that the patient is at high risk of death unless blood transfusions are administered. Situations like these represent a true conflict between medical ethics (the duty of physicians to save lives when possible) and a religious conviction (the belief that acceptance of a blood transfusion will be punished by eternal damnation).

---

[1] Cheryl J. Misak, Douglas B. White, & Robert D. Truog, *Medical Futility: A New Look at an Old Problem*, 146(6) Chest 1667 (2014).

The situation with brain death is strikingly different from the Jehovah's Witness example, however, in two important ways, one legal and one metaphysical. Legally, in the United States the diagnosis of brain death requires "the irreversible cessation of all functions of the entire brain, including the brainstem." Yet, a large and uncontroversial literature shows that the actual medical tests required to diagnose brain death fail to examine at least several critical functions, such as hormonal regulation of salt and water balance and maintenance of body temperature, and that these functions persist in many patients who fulfill the standard medical criteria.[2] Hence, the standard tests required to diagnose brain death do not assure that the requirements of the law are fulfilled.

The second issue is metaphysical. As Pope explains, "the law limits itself to identifying the physiological standards that should be used by the medical profession to ascertain when an individual has died. The law does not try to say what death actually 'is.'" The medical criteria for diagnosing brain death were designed to identify brain-injured patients who will never regain consciousness nor breathe on their own. But there is no obvious reason for believing that these two characteristics constitute the death of the individual.[3] While many people would choose not to live in a state of irreversible unconsciousness, others believe that life of any sort is sacred and should be supported, and there is nothing illogical or incoherent about such a view.

All of which leaves me somewhat perplexed about Pope's conclusions. He argues in favor of religious accommodation to objections to brain death, but limited to continuation of life support for an additional day or two in deference to a patient or family's religious convictions. He cautions against expanding wholesale exemptions to the diagnosis of brain death, as is the case in New Jersey, at least until we have more empirical data about the consequences of doing so. Yet, if the diagnosis of brain death can be challenged not only on religious grounds, but also on whether the medical criteria are legally sufficient and whether they cohere with a uniform metaphysical understanding of what it means to be dead, then it would seem that these objections are grounded in deep questions of both law and principle, and deserve a more substantial response than the cursory respect of a brief delay in making the diagnosis. Indeed, his position would probably not require any changes in the law at all, given that almost all hospitals are, in fact, willing to delay the diagnosis for a couple of days, simply as an act of compassion for a grieving family.

Teneille Brown provides a scholarly analysis of whether federal and state Religious Freedom Restoration Acts would legally prohibit clinicians from unilaterally withholding or withdrawing life-sustaining treatments deemed to be futile. I find her analysis quite convincing (and reassuring) that this is *not* the case. Among several

---

[2] Robert D. Truog, *Is It Time to Abandon Brain Death?*, 27(1) Hastings Center Report 29 (1997).
[3] Franklin G. Miller & Robert D. Truog, *Death, Dying, and Organ Transplantation* (2012).

arguments that Brown offers to support her position, she believes that one of the strongest is the state's interest in protecting professional autonomy and ethics. She writes, "Requiring that physicians comply with what they feel is medically ineffective, or worse – torture – would violate the providers' freedoms."

I suggest that this claim, while fundamentally sound, needs to be unpacked and placed in context. On one hand, studies document serious problems with burnout from the moral distress that clinicians experience from providing treatments that they believe to be futile.[4] On the other hand, in many cases the family members who are at the bedside, observing and experiencing exactly the same situation as the clinicians, do not see the treatments as undignified or as a source of suffering, but rather as exactly what they believe the patient would have wanted. Indeed, it is not uncommon for these patients to have living wills explicitly expressing their desire to receive such treatment. Furthermore, concerns about "torture" can be mitigated by the use of analgesics and sedatives to virtually assure that the patient is not experiencing any pain.

For these reasons, a recent consensus document, endorsed by all the major physician and nursing critical care societies in North America and Europe, has advocated a somewhat different justification to support unilateral limitations of life-sustaining treatments.[5] This justification does not rely primarily on an appeal to the autonomy and ethics of the profession, but rather on a fair process that seeks an "all things considered" judgment, made on a case by case basis, reflecting societal as well as professional norms, the availability of resources, and so forth, to make a determination about whether continued use of life support is appropriate.

Jonathan Will explores questions of religion and decision making for minors through the paradigmatic case of how the religious beliefs of Jehovah's Witnesses impact decision making for minors around blood transfusions. Beginning with the assumption that patients under the age of majority are presumed to be legally incompetent to make medical decisions on their own behalf, he explores when this presumption may be successfully rebutted under the mature minor doctrine. Will recognizes that "[p]erfect voluntariness is an unrealistic ideal, but the question is whether the minor's decision is 'voluntary enough to be protected from paternalistic interferences.'"

This question is particularly complex in the case of children of Jehovah's Witness families, where a decision to accept a transfusion will result in immediate excommunication from the fellowship of the faith and a belief in eternal condemnation

---

[4] Ellen Elpern, Barbara Covert, & Ruth Kleinpell, *Moral Distress of Staff Nurses in a Medical Intensive Care Unit*, 14(6) Am. J. Critical Care 523 (2005).

[5] Gabriel T. Bosslet et al., *An Official ATS/AACN/ACCP/ESICM/SCCM Policy Statement: Responding to Requests for Potentially Inappropriate Treatments in Intensive Care Units*, 191(11) Am. J. Respiratory Critical Care Med. 1318 (2015).

in the eyes of God. Furthermore, the religion holds independent thinking to be sinful and disloyal to God. How does one decide when the judgment of the minor is, in fact, mature and consistent with autonomous beliefs? Jonathan Will counsels us, wisely in my view, to approach these decisions very cautiously and with careful consideration of all of the developmental and psychological issues at play. At the end of the day, the decision often falls to a judge, who must weigh all of the evidence and make a decision. In one case from my own experience, involving a 15-year-old who had adopted the religion of his Jehovah's Witness girlfriend against the will of his parents, a judge personally came to our hospital and spent over an hour with the young man, alone in his hospital room, before reaching the judgment that he was competent to refuse blood transfusions in the treatment of his leukemia. Fortunately, the young man survived despite not receiving blood which otherwise would have been given.

Finally, Abbas Rattani and Jemel Amin Derbali present a wonderful discussion about how we should think about criminality in the context of religious extremism and mental illness. The crux of the problem, as I understand it, is how do we differentiate between criminal acts that arise from the religious views of a rational actor, versus those that arise from mental illness? The authors provide a number of excellent insights and guidelines to help in sorting out these distinctions, but also develop a sub-theme that deserves special emphasis.

Rattani and Derbali point out the strong role that social norms play in our assessment of religious ideation. In particular, extremist views espoused by religions with which we are more familiar are generally viewed with greater sympathy than others. In our current environment, where even mainstream Muslim beliefs are often demonized, this point is worthy of special consideration.

20

Brain Death Rejected

Expanding Legal Duties to Accommodate Religious Objections

Thaddeus Mason Pope

The determination of death by neurological criteria (DDNC or "brain death") has been legally established, for decades, as death in all U.S. jurisdictions and in most other developed countries.[1] It is supported by a "durable worldwide consensus."[2] Moreover, the consequences of DDNC are clear. Once a patient is determined dead, clinicians typically discontinue physiological support. In short, DDNC is a "hard clinical endpoint" where technological interventions reach the limits of required or accepted medical practice.[3]

Despite this legal consensus, hospitals continue to grapple with a significant (and growing) number of conflicts. Some families do not accept DDNC as death and want clinicians to continue physiological support. While some of these disputes are due to misunderstanding or diagnostic mistrust, many are religiously based.[4] Today, only four U.S. states legally require hospitals to "accommodate" families with religious objections to DDNC. In this chapter, I argue that other states should enact similar accommodation requirements.

Given the legal status of DDNC, clinicians typically have no duty to continue physiological support after DDNC. But this rule presents a profound problem for patients with religious objections to DDNC. For these individuals, the denial of physiological support after DDNC violates fundamental values. Indeed, hospitals

---

[1] J.L. Bernat, *The Whole-Brain Concept of Death Remains Optimum Public Policy*, 34 J. L. Med. & Ethics 35–43 (2006); E.F.M. Wijdicks, *Brain Death Worldwide: Accepted Fact but No Global Consensus*, 58 Neurology 20–5 (2002); D. Gardiner et al., *International Perspective on the Diagnosis of Death*, 108 British J. Anaesthesia i14–i28 (2012).
[2] J.L. Bernat, *The Definition and Criterion of Death*, 118 Handbook Clinical Neurology 419–35 (2013).
[3] M.J. Clarke, M.S. Remtema, & K.M. Swetz, *Beyond Transplantation: Considering Brain Death as a Hard Clinical Endpoint*, 14 Am. J. Bioethics 43–5 (2014).
[4] See generally Thaddeus M. Pope, *Brain Death Forsaken: Growing Conflict and New Legal Challenges*, 37 J. Leg. Med. (forthcoming 2017); Thaddeus M. Pope, *Legal Briefing: Brain Death and Total Brain Failure*, 25 J. Clinical Ethics 245–57 (2014); Christopher M. Burkle & Thaddeus M. Pope, *Brain Death: Legal Obligations and the Courts*, 35 Seminars Clinical Neurology 174–9 (2015).

often refuse to accommodate religious objections to DDNC. I concede that granting a complete exemption to DDNC may be problematic. Instead, I argue that all states should enact "reasonable accommodation" laws, requiring a brief period of continued ventilator support.

1. LEGAL STATUS OF DETERMINING DEATH BY NEUROLOGICAL CRITERIA (DDNC)

Every U.S. state has enacted the Uniform Determination of Death Act, or a nearly identical statute.[5] The UDDA provides that death may be determined by the application of either of two alternative standards: (1) "irreversible cessation of circulatory and respiratory function" or (2) "irreversible cessation of all functions of the entire brain, including the brain stem."[6]

The latter standard is also known as the determination of death by neurological criteria (DDNC). The satisfaction of *either* standard is sufficient to determine death. So, if cessation of all brain function is confirmed, then the patient may be declared dead, despite ongoing cardiopulmonary functions maintained by artificial ventilation or pharmacological support.

2. CLINICIAN DUTIES TO "TREAT" END AFTER DDNC

Once a patient is determined dead, clinicians typically discontinue physiological support. Once death is determined, there is no longer a duty to treat. This is well established both in appellate case law[7] and in medical practice.[8] Once dead, the patient is no longer a patient.[9] The hospital is no longer in a treatment relationship with a patient; it is instead the custodian of a corpse.[10] Indeed, to continue "treatment" could constitute abuse of the newly dead.[11]

But there are three situations in which hospitals continue physiological support after DDNC. First, if the patient is an organ donor, support is continued until the transplant. Second, if the patient is pregnant, support may be continued until delivery. Sometimes this is at the family's request, and sometimes it is legally required.[12]

---

[5] See Pope, supra note 4.
[6] 12 U.L.A. 589 (1980).
[7] See Pope, supra note 4 (collecting citations).
[8] Id.
[9] Id.
[10] R.D. Miller, *Problems in Health Care Law* 765–75 (2006).
[11] See, e.g., *Range v. Douglas*, 763 F.3d 573 (6th Cir. 2014); J.A. Anderson, L.W. Vernaglia, & S.P. Morrigan, *Refusal of Brain Death Diagnosis: The Health Lawyer's Perspective*, 9 JONAS Health Care L., Ethics & Reg. 90–2 (2007).
[12] See, e.g., Pope, supra note 4.

Third, organ-sustaining measures might be continued to accommodate religious objections.[13] Below, I focus on this third exception.[14]

3. MILLIONS OF AMERICANS HAVE RELIGIOUS OBJECTIONS TO DDNC

While most major religions in the world accept DDNC as death, several religions (or at least certain sects of these religions) object to DDNC.[15] These include Japanese Shinto as well as some (but not all) Orthodox Jews, Native Americans, Buddhists, and Muslims.[16] Approximately six million Americans are affiliated with one of these religions.[17]

For the adherents of these religions, the imposition of a "brain death" standard violates strongly held beliefs about the meaning of death.[18] These individuals believe that death can be determined only by the total cessation of cardiac and respiratory activity (regardless of whether such activity is artificially sustained). Even Teneille Brown, who argues against accommodating "miracles" in the next chapter of this volume, concedes that denial of life support can occur in "life and death situations of tremendous spiritual and religious significance."

Drafters of the UDDA and analogous state laws were careful to address only the "determination" of death and not the "definition" of death.[19] That is, the law limits itself to identifying the physiological standards that should be used by the medical

---

[13] Hospitals also accommodate nonreligious objections. See infra note 21.
[14] Families object not only to discontinuing physiological support but also to the performance of the brain death exam itself. See, e.g., *VCU Health System Authority v. Lawson*, No. 160968 (Va. June 27, 2016) (petition for review from Richmond City No. CL162358); *Pierce v. Loma Linda University Medical Center*, No. DS1609831 (Bernardino County Sup. Ct., Cal. June 7, 2016) (petition for TRO).
[15] See generally Eelco Wijdicks, Brain Death 69–79 (2d ed. 2011); E.F.M. Wijdicks, *Brain Death*, 118 Handbook Clinical Neurology 191–203 (2013); A. Earl Walker, Cerebral Death 139–42 (3d ed. 1985).
[16] See generally Robert M. Veatch & Lainie F. Ross, Transplantation Ethics 105–106 (2d ed. 2015); Jeffrey M. Singh & Mark Bernstein, *Brain Death*, Neurosurgical Ethics in Practice: Value-based Medicine 109, 115 (A. Ammar, M. Bernstein eds., 2015). See also Andrew C. Miller, *Opinions on the Legitimacy of Brain Death amongst Sunni and Shi'a Scholars*, 55 J. Religion & Health 394 (2016); R.S. Olick et al., *Accommodating Religious and Moral Objections to Neurological Death*, 20 J. Clinical Ethics 183–90 (2009). R.S. Olick, *Brain Death, Religious Freedom, and Public Policy: New Jersey's Landmark Legislative Initiative*, 1 Kennedy Institute Ethics J. 275–88 (1991); Kenneth Shuster, "When Has the Grim Reaper Finished Reaping?" *How Embracing One Religion's View of Death Can Influence Acceptance of the Uniform Determination of Death Act*, 30 Touro L. Rev. 655 (2014); N. Berlinger, B. Jennings & S.M. Wolf, The Hastings Center Guidelines for Decisions on Life-Sustaining Treatment and Care Near the End of Life 107 (2013).
[17] Pew Forum on Religion and Public Life, *U.S. Religious Landscape Survey Religious Affiliation: Diverse and Dynamic* (2008).
[18] I do not distinguish deeply held moral beliefs from religious beliefs regarding DDNC.
[19] Cf. Uniform Law Commission, Determination of Death Act Summary, available at uniformlaws.org/ActSummary.aspx?title=Determination of Death Act.

profession to ascertain when an individual has died. The law does not try to say what death actually "is." It does not attempt to answer the bigger philosophical and theological question of what is so essential to human life that, when it is lost, the individual should be considered dead.[20] But since DDNC results in stopping physiological support, the law still implicates these philosophical and theological questions.

4. LEGAL REQUIREMENTS TO ACCOMMODATE RELIGIOUS OBJECTIONS

Many health care facilities across the country *voluntarily* offer a short-term accommodation as a compassionate measure to help the family cope with the patient's death.[21] But in only four states is the duty to accommodate *mandated* by law.[22] Statutes and regulations in California, Illinois, New Jersey, and New York explicitly and specifically require hospitals to "accommodate" families asserting religious objections on the patient's behalf after a patient is declared dead by neurological criteria.[23] New Jersey's accommodation mandate is the broadest (and is effectively an exemption). New York and California have less expansive requirements. Illinois' requirement is the weakest.

---

[20] New York State Department of Health and New York State Task Force on Life and the Law, The Determination of Death 11 (1986).
[21] See generally D.D. Ayeh et al., *Physicians' Opinions About Accommodating Religiously Based Requests for Continued Life Sustaining Treatment*, 51 J. Pain & Symptom Mgmt. 971 (2016); Anne L. Flamm et al., *Family Members' Requests to Extend Physiologic Support after Declaration of Brain Death: A Case Series Analysis and Proposed Guidelines for Clinical Management*, 25 J. Clinical Ethics 222–37 (2014); *Dority v. Superior Court of San Bernardino County*, 193 Cal. Rptr. 288, 289 (Cal. Ct. App. 1983); L.R. Frankel & C.J. Randle Jr., "Complexities in the Management of a Brain-Dead Child," in *Ethical Dilemmas in Pediatrics: Cases and Commentaries* 135, 137 (L.R. Frankel et al. eds. 2005); M.J. Edens et al., *Neonatal Ethics: Development of a Consultative Group*, 86 Pediatrics 944–9 (1990); R. Gustaitis, *Right to Refuse Life-Sustaining Treatment*, 81 Pediatrics 317–21 (1988). Some have persuasively argued for such accommodation. See R.A. Burt, *The Medical Futility Debate: Patient Choice, Physician Obligation, and End-of-Life Care*, 5 J. Palliative Med. 249–54 (2004).
[22] As explained by Teneille Brown in this volume, accommodation may also be required under state religious freedom restoration acts. While no state RFRA has yet been applied to the DDNC context, the federal RFRA was applied in an analogous context. A federal court interpreted RFRA to require the state to accommodate a religious objection to an otherwise required autopsy. *Yang v. Sturner*, 728 F. Supp. 845 (D.R.I. 1990).
[23] The primary means of accommodation is through continued ventilator support. Other accommodations include the opportunity to transfer. See, e.g., *Winkfield v. Children's Hospital & Research Center at Oakland*, No. 13-CV-05993-SBA (N.D. Cal. January 6, 2014) (status report reporting settlement and transfer); In re Koochin, No. 043901708 (3rd Jud. Dist. Ct., Salt Lake Cty., Utah October 27, 2004) (six-year-old boy transferred home); *Brain-Dead Florida Girl Will Be Sent Home on Life Support*, N.Y. Times (February 19, 1994) (13-year-old girl transferred home); Flamm et al., supra note 21.

A. New Jersey: Indefinite Accommodation

In 1991, New Jersey enacted the New Jersey Declaration of Death Act.[24] As in every other state, this statute provides that an individual who has "sustained irreversible cessation of all functions of the entire brain, including the brain stem, shall be declared dead."[25] But in contrast to every other state, the statute includes a unique categorical exception.[26] When triggered, this exception amounts to an indefinite duty to accommodate a religious objection to DDNC.

Specifically, the New Jersey Declaration of Death Act provides that the death of an individual shall *not* be declared upon the basis of neurological criteria "when the licensed physician authorized to declare death, has reason to believe ... that such a declaration would violate the personal religious beliefs of the individual."[27]

While the statute does not define what qualifies as a legitimate religious belief, statutory interpretation would likely be guided by extensive constitutional analysis of this question. The threshold under the First Amendment is low.[28] Therefore, the New Jersey statute probably also includes "moral" objections, nontheistic beliefs which are sincerely held. This interpretation is implied by the broad definition of "religion" under Title VII of the Civil Rights Act of 1964.[29]

Consequently, it seems that upon the assertion of any plausible religious claim, in New Jersey death shall be declared "solely upon the basis of cardio-respiratory criteria." On the other hand, New Jersey providers and courts have rejected accommodation requirements without evidence that the patient herself held the religious beliefs.[30]

In short, if the patient has religious objections to DDNC and those objections are made known to clinicians, then the patient may not be declared dead until the complete irreversible cessation of her circulatory and respiratory functions. If the family does not consent to stop ventilator support, then under New Jersey law the patient may not be legally dead for a significant period of time after the determination of total brain failure.

---

[24] P.W. Armstrong & R.S. Olick, *Innovative Legislative Initiatives: The New Jersey Declaration of Death Act and Advance Directives for Health Care Acts*, 16(1) Seton Hall Legislative J. 177–97 (1992); Olick, supra note 16.

[25] N.J. Rev. Stat. § 26:6A-3.

[26] This is due in part because New Jersey has a large Jewish population. M.A. Grodin, *Religious Exemptions: Brain Death and Jewish Law*, 36 J. Church & State 357–72 (1994); Olick et al., supra note 16.

[27] N.J. Rev. Stat. § 26:6A-5; N.J. Admin. Code § 13:35-6A.6.

[28] *Employment Division v. Smith*, 494 E.S. 872, 887 (1990); *United States v. Meyers*, 906 F. Supp. 1494, 1499 (D. Wyo. 1995).

[29] 29 C.F.R. § 1605.1.

[30] *Life Support Is Removed After a Court Order*, N.Y. Times (February 20, 1998).

In other words, the New Jersey statute grants objecting individuals an "exemption" or "loophole" from the generally accepted standards for determining death. The New Jersey statute requires "indefinite accommodation" of religious objections by health care providers.[31] This law is unique in changing the patient's life/death status. One consequence is that the same person could be legally dead in Pennsylvania, yet, by merely crossing the Delaware River, still be legally alive in New Jersey.

B. New York: Reasonable Accommodation

New York judicially recognized DDNC in 1984.[32] In 1986, the New York State Task Force on Life and the Law recommended that the Department of Health recognize this standard.[33] And in 1987, the NYDOH adopted the Task Force's recommendation in administrative regulations.[34] But the NYDOH did more than formally recognize DDNC. It also required hospitals to accommodate religious or moral objections to DDNC.

In 2011, the NYDOH clarified its regulation. Specifically, the NYDOH confirmed that the New York accommodation requirement is not a categorical exception like the New Jersey accommodation requirement. Religious or moral objections to DDNC cannot change one's life/death status. Instead, New York hospitals must merely "establish written procedures for the reasonable accommodation of the individual's religious or moral objections to use of the brain death standard" when such an objection has been expressed by the patient or surrogate.[35]

In New York, the duty of accommodation is far less demanding than in New Jersey. The NYDOH leaves hospitals substantial discretion in designing their accommodation policies. Under the regulation, policies "may" include specific accommodations, such as "the continuation of artificial respiration under certain circumstances, as well as guidance on limits to the duration of the accommodation."[36] One major New York hospital provides up to 72 hours.[37] Policies "may" also provide guidance on "the use of other resources, such as clergy members, ethics committees, palliative care clinicians, bereavement counselors, and conflict mediators to address objections or concerns."[38]

---

[31] See Flamm et al., supra note 21.
[32] *People v. Eulo*, 63 N.Y.2d 341 (N.Y. Ct. App. 1984).
[33] New York State Task Force on Life & the Law, supra note 20.
[34] 10 N.Y.C.R.R. § 400.16 (1987).
[35] New York State Department of Health and New York State Task Force on Life & the Law, *Guidelines for Determining Brain Death* (November 2011), available at www.health.ny.gov/professionals/hospital_administrator/letters/2011/brain_death_guidelines.pdf [https://perma.cc/MUE4-V6WH].
[36] Id., at 4.
[37] New York City Health and Hospital Corporation, *Corporate Brain Death Policy*, available at http://thaddeuspope.com/braindeath.html [https://perma.cc/V2P2-3BE5].
[38] NY Guidelines, supra note 35, at 4.

C. California: Reasonable Accommodation

California recognized DDNC when it adopted the Uniform Determination of Death Act in 1982.[39] But, in 2009, a new California statute expanded the obligations of hospitals with respect to patients declared dead on the basis of neurological criteria.[40] California does not carve out a categorical exception like New Jersey. But, in two respects, the California duty of accommodation is broader and more expansive.

First, both New Jersey and New York require accommodation of *only* religious or moral objections. Indeed, the NYDOH specifically addresses objections to the DDNC based either upon psychological denial that death has occurred or upon an alleged inadequacy of the brain death determination. The NYDOH confirms that since such objections are not based upon the individual's moral or religious beliefs, reasonable accommodation is not required in such circumstances.[41]

In contrast, California requires accommodation of ***all types*** of objections. The California statute requires that general acute care hospitals adopt a policy for providing family with a "reasonably brief period of accommodation" after DDNC.

But while broad in the types of objections covered (e.g., religious, moral, psychological), the California duty of accommodation is limited in several material respects. It requires maintenance of only one type physiological support and only for one specific and objectively attainable purpose. First, during the "reasonably brief period of accommodation," a hospital is required to continue only previously ordered cardiopulmonary support. No other medical interventions are required. Second, the "brief period" is narrowly defined as only "an amount of time afforded to gather family or next of kin at the patient's bedside."[42] This usually entails an accommodation under 24 hours in duration.[43] Some hospitals permit up to 36 hours.[44]

The second respect in which the California duty of accommodation is broader (at least than that in New York) concerns religious objections. If the patient's legally

---

[39] Cal. Health & Safety Code §§ 7180–1.
[40] Cal. Health & Safety Code § 1254.4(a).
[41] However, hospital staff should demonstrate sensitivity to these concerns and consider using similar resources to help family members accept the determination and fact of death. Among other interventions, family presence during DDNC improves understanding without an adverse impact on psychological wellbeing. I. Tawil et al., *Family Presence during Brain Death Evaluation: A Randomized Controlled Trial*, 42(4) Critical Care Med. 934–42 (2014).
[42] Cal. Health & Safety Code § 1254.4(b).
[43] See, e.g., Flamm et al., supra note 21; New York City Health and Hospital Corporation, supra note 37; Southern California Bioethics Committee Consortium, Survey (2015).
[44] Cedars Sinai Medical Center, FAQs: AB2565: *The Accommodation of Brain Death Act*, available at www.cedars-sinai.edu/Patients/Programs-and-Services/Healthcare-Ethics-/Documents/2565-FAQs-NEW-PDF-158326.pdf [https://perma.cc/39GF-U93V]; *Winkfield v. Children's Hospital Oakland*, No. 4:13-CV-05993-SBA (N.D. Cal. 20 December 2013) (Opposition to Proposed TRO and Injunctive Relief) (noting that CHO has considered 2–3 days a reasonable accommodation in DDNC cases over the past 10 years).

recognized health care decision maker, family, or next-of-kin voices any special religious or cultural practices and concerns, the hospital must make "reasonable efforts to accommodate those religious and cultural practices and concerns." The legislative history suggests that the intended accommodations include permitting rituals such as herbal applications and washings.[45]

This duty of religious/cultural accommodation is broader than California's general duty of accommodation.[46] And it is broader than the NYDOH duty of moral or religious accommodation. For example, the hospital must accommodate not only the patient's, but also the family's, objections. But it is unclear exactly how much is required. The only guidance in the statute states, "in determining what is reasonable, a hospital shall consider the needs of other patients and prospective patients in urgent need of care."[47]

D. Illinois: Take into Account

Illinois recognized DDNC in 1983.[48] In 2007, Illinois amended its hospital-licensing act to include an accommodation requirement.[49] The statute provides: "Every hospital must adopt policies and procedures to allow health care professionals, in documenting a patient's time of death at the hospital, to take into account the patient's religious beliefs concerning the patient's time of death."[50]

While prima facie similar to accommodation requirements in other states, the Illinois language is distinctly weaker. Like California and New York, the statute delegates to hospitals discretion in defining the accommodation by directing that they "adopt policies and procedures." But the Illinois statute imposes no specific accommodation requirement. It uses permissive instead of mandatory language. The hospital's policies and procedures need only "allow" health care professionals to "take into account" the patient's religious beliefs concerning the patient's time of death.

Take, for example, the policy at the University of Illinois-Chicago. It provides: "After the patient is declared dead, life support mechanisms **should** be

---

[45] Wijdicks, supra note 15, at 209–10.
[46] Dix v. Superior Court, 53 Cal.3d 442, 459 (1991) ("[W]e avoid statutory constructions that render particular provisions superfluous or unnecessary.").
[47] Cal. Health & Safety Code § 1254.4(d). In both the McMath and Lopez cases the hospitals argued that accommodating dead patients would adversely impact the ability to serve other patients with a better prospect for benefit. Relatedly, justice arguments are increasingly common in the futility context. See, e.g., T.N. Huynh et al., *The Opportunity Cost of Futile Treatment in the ICU*, 42 Critical Care Med. 1977–82 (2014).
[48] In re Haymer, 450 N.E.2d 940 (Ill. App. 1983).
[49] Ill. Pub. Act No. 095-0181.
[50] 210 ILCS 85/6.23.

removed..."[51] This seems to appropriately "allow" a physician to "take into account" the patient's religion and continue physiological support after DDNC. This leaves accommodation to the discretion of individual clinicians.

On the other hand, by permitting a deviation in "documenting" a patient's time of death, the statute may actually operate more like the law in New Jersey than the laws in New York or California. In other words, instead of mandating certain duties after DDNC, it may permit clinicians to declare death later than the time of DDNC.

5. HOSPITALS DO NOT ALWAYS ACCOMMODATE RELIGIOUS OBJECTIONS TO DDNC

California, Illinois, New Jersey, and New York have significant populations of objecting religions.[52] But these are not the only states in which individuals have asserted religious objections to DDNC. Without a legal mandate, requests for accommodation are more commonly denied.[53] Here are just three examples.

Shahida Virk was declared dead in Michigan. Her husband and his religious leader asked for accommodation, explaining that removal of physiological support "would constitute murder in the Islamic faith."[54] But the hospital denied the request. An appellate court later affirmed the dismissal of the family's tort and contract claims because the hospital had "no duty to accommodate or give preferential treatment."[55]

Similarly, Motl Brody was declared dead in Washington, D.C. His Orthodox Jewish parents objected to DDNC and asked for continued physiological support, but the hospital refused. The parents were unable to obtain a court order.[56]

Finally, in Massachusetts, Cho Fook Cheng was declared dead. But Cheng's family refused to let doctors stop physiological support. They said that their belief as Buddhists was that Cheng's beating heart meant his spirit and consciousness were

---

[51] University of Illinois Medical Center, *Determination of Neurologic Death in Adults and Children* (April 2010), available at http://thaddeuspope.com/images/U_Illinois_Chicago_neurodeath.pdf [https://perma.cc/3SGJ-FL5F] (emphasis added).

[52] See Olick, supra note 16.

[53] Ariane Lewis et al., *Prolonging Support after Brain Death when Families Ask for More*, 24 Neurocritical Care 481 (2016). See also Chaim David Zwiebel, *Accommodating Religious Objections to Brain Death: Legal Considerations*, 17 J. Halacha & Contemp. Soc'y 49, 50 (1989) ("[I]nformal accommodation is by no means universal."). On the other hand, courts usually grant temporary restraining orders preserving the status quo until more evidence can be gathered and presented to adjudicate the claims. T.M. Pope, *Involuntary Passive Euthanasia in U.S. Courts: Reassessing the Judicial Treatment of Medical Futility Cases*, 9 Marquette Elder's Advisor 229–68 (2008).

[54] *Virk v. Detroit Receiving Hosp.*, No. 180621, 1996 WL 33348748, at *1 (Mich. Ct. App. October 25, 1996) (unpublished).

[55] Id.

[56] In re Motl Brody, No. 1:08-CV-01898 (HHK) (D.D.C. 2008).

not ready to move on.[57] But the hospital went to court to get an order allowing its clinicians to stop physiological support.

6. HOSPITALS SHOULD BE REQUIRED TO ACCOMMODATE RELIGIOUS OBJECTIONS TO DDNC

States have a significant interest in a uniform standard for the determination of death.[58] But this interest is not weighty enough to justify not accommodating those with religious objections. Opponents argue that practical considerations make accommodation "unworkable."[59] But their arguments are not compelling. Even Teneille Brown concedes, in her chapter herein, that a short accommodation period would not materially impede compelling state interests.

A. *Five Reasons to Accommodate Religious Objections*

For five reasons, uniformity will not be undone by a brief period of reasonable accommodation. First, accommodation already works in four populous states. Second, it affects very few cases. Third, because of its limited duration and scope, accommodation would work equally well in other states. Fourth, accommodation is not analogous to wholesale exemption. Fifth, DDNC is a more fragmented and contested concept today than it was when other states enacted their religious accommodation requirements.

1. **Accommodation already works in four populous states.** Perhaps the best evidence in support of accommodating religious objections to DDNC is the positive track record in the four states that already require it. New York has required accommodation of religious objections since 1986. New Jersey has required accommodation since 1991. And Illinois and California have required it for nearly ten years. In none of these four states have any deleterious consequences (material or otherwise) been reported.

2. **Expanding accommodation impacts very few cases.** Accommodation requirements affect a very small population. Only 30 percent of U.S. deaths occur in

---

[57] Megan Tench, After Buddhist Dies, Legal Battle Continues, Boston Globe, December 3, 2006.
[58] See, e.g., President's Commission for the Study of Ethical Problems in Medicine and Biomedical and Behavioral Research, *Defining Death: Medical, Legal, and Ethical Issues in the Determination of Death* (1981); New Jersey Commission on Legal and Ethical Problems in the Delivery of Health Care, *The New Jersey Advance Directives for Health Care and Declaration of Death Acts Statutes, Commentaries and Analyses* 86–9 (1991).
[59] New York State Task Force, supra note 20, at 12; Veatch and Ross, supra note 16 at 112 (referring to "policy chaos").

a hospital.[60] Less than 1 percent of these hospital deaths are by DDNC.[61] Since those with religious objections comprise only 2 percent of the U.S. population, only 0.006 percent of deaths might involve an accommodation.[62] Since there are 2.5 million annual deaths, that is just 150 cases nationwide in a year. Most of those are in the four states that already legally mandate accommodation. These four states comprise one-fourth of the U.S. population and an even higher percentage of the objecting religions. Therefore, the net marginal impact of expanding accommodation would be minimal.

3. **Accommodation is limited in duration and type.** Furthermore, even for this small subset of cases, accommodation is not disruptive. It is limited in both duration and type.[63] As implemented in California, Illinois, and New York, the accommodation is for only a limited time; hospitals usually continue physiological support for just 24 hours,[64] and that physiological support is normally limited to mechanical ventilation. It does not include vasopressors, hormones, or antibiotics. Moreover, not even mechanical ventilation is required if the hospital resources are needed for a living patient.

4. **Accommodation is not exemption.** Some have argued that accommodation would be unworkable because people's objections "range on a spectrum."[65] Indeed, some prominent scholars have argued for permitting people to "opt in" to being determined dead on a "higher brain death" standard.[66] But no state has actually done that. New Jersey permits an "opt out," and even that retains a single standard (cardiopulmonary) that is already universally accepted.

The unworkability objection applies only to the type of expansive accommodation seen in New Jersey. Only New Jersey grants a complete exemption from DDNC, and only New Jersey requires insurance coverage after DDNC. In contrast, accommodation laws in California, Illinois, and New York do not change the individual's life/death status. Unlike New Jersey, these laws preserve

---

[60] CDC National Center for Health Statistics, *Trends in Inpatient Hospital Deaths: National Hospital Discharge Survey, 2000–10*, NCHS Data Brief No. 118 (March 2013), available at www.cdc.gov/nchs/data/databriefs/db118.htm [https://perma.cc/NHG9-8HWE].

[61] L.A. Siminoff, *Families' Understanding of Brain Death*, 13 Progress Transplantation 218–24 (2003) (estimating only 50 DDNC per million).

[62] Pew Forum on Religion and Public Life, *U.S. Religious Landscape Survey Religious Affiliation: Diverse and Dynamic* (2008).

[63] Cf. Martin L. Smith & Anne L. Flamm, *Accommodating Religious Beliefs in the ICU: A Narrative Account of a Disputed Death*, 1 Narrative Inquiries Bioethics 55–64 (2011).

[64] See Lewis et al., supra note 53.

[65] New York State Task Force, supra note 20, at 12.

[66] See Veatch & Ross, supra note 16.

the uniformity of the determination of death, and instead only change hospital duties after DDNC, recognizing plurality and diversity by allowing a brief period of accommodation.[67]

5. **Value-laden nature of brain death.** While DDNC is widely accepted, it has never been universally supported. It has been described as "at once well settled and persistently unresolved."[68] For decades, DDNC has been subjected to persuasive criticisms and serious concerns.[69] Central to these criticisms and concerns is the fact that the bodies of individuals determined dead by neurological criteria still do many of the things done by living organisms. For example, these "brain dead" bodies can still heal wounds, fight infections, mount a stress response to surgical incisions, and even gestate a fetus.[70] In 2008, these theoretical and practical problems were acknowledged but ultimately dismissed by the President's Council on Bioethics.[71]

But more recently, these long-standing disagreements over DDNC's validity have been reignited. Controversies over DDNC have "taken on new life in medical, ethical, and public debate."[72] For example, the Supreme Court of Nevada seriously questioned whether standard medical assessments of DDNC satisfy the legal standard for death.[73] As currently implemented, DDNC does not literally measure the cessation of "all" functions of the "entire" brain. Instead, the medical profession has decided that the cessation of only some functions is sufficient. Other lawsuits even more directly attack generally accepted medical criteria for DDNC.[74]

In short, DDNC is increasingly seen as a contested value judgment rather than as a scientific, objective truth. Since there is no way to adjudicate the "correctness" of competing moral or religious judgments, the case for accommodating those with alternative values becomes more compelling.[75]

---

[67] Geoffrey Miller, *Reexamining the Origins and Application of DDNC*, 13 J. Bioethics Inquiry 27 (2016).
[68] Alexander M. Capron, *Brain Death: Well Settled, Yet Still Unresolved*, 344 New Eng. J. Med 1244 (2001).
[69] See Pope, supra note 1.
[70] D.A. Shewmon, *Constructing the Death Elephant: A Synthetic Paradigm Shift for the Definition, Criteria, and Tests for Death*, 35 J. Med & Phil. 223 (2010).
[71] President's Council on Bioethics, *Controversies in the Determination of Death* 6 (2008).
[72] S.H. Johnson, *Death, State by State*, 44 Hastings Center Rep. 9–10 (2014).
[73] Thaddeus M. Pope, *Legal Standards for Brain Death*, 13 J. Bioethical Inquiry 173 (2016).
[74] See, e.g., *Winkfield v. Rosen*, No. RG15760730 (Alameda County Sup. Ct., Cal. 2016); *Fonseca v. Kaiser Permanente*, No. 2:16-cv-00889- KJM-EFB (E.D. Cal. 2016).
[75] Veatch & Ross, supra note 16, at 42, 105, 119.

B. Accommodation vs. Exemption

Some commentators have argued that these five reasons justify more than just a limited accommodation. They contend that these considerations support a wholesale exemption from DDNC, as in New Jersey. While this argument has significant weight, it is not clearly dispositive.

First, expanding exemption would impede state interests in uniformity far more than mere accommodation. Second, we must more carefully assess prior experience with exemption before making such a drastic move. While New Jersey has served as the laboratory, its outcomes have not been reported or assessed. We need more evidence before copying that model.

Third, it would be anomalous to require clinicians to indefinitely accommodate religious objections to DDNC when we do not require them to indefinitely accommodate religious objections in more common, less-drastic medical situations when the family's claims are stronger (such as family-clinician conflicts over continuing dialysis for patients in a persistent vegetative state). For the sake of consistency, if we permit a religious opt-out for brain death, then we should also allow a religious opt-out from medical futility rules and policies. But the consequences of extending clinician duties this far are uncertain.

In short, although the case for accommodation is clear, the case for exemption requires more empirical substantiation. Proponents may be correct that the ethical case for exemption may be just as strong as the case for reasonable accommodation. But the legal case must also consider the practical consequences. These still remain unknown and potentially hazardous.

CONCLUSION

The state's interests in the uniform legal recognition of DDNC are not sufficiently weighty to justify compelling those with contrary religious beliefs to accept determinations of death on these grounds. But only four states strike a minimally appropriate balance in requiring hospitals to accommodate religious objections to DDNC. Other states should follow their lead and enact laws mandating hospitals to *reasonably* accommodate such objections without necessarily fully exempting them.

21

Accommodating Miracles

Medical Futility and Religious Free Exercise

Teneille R. Brown

The term "medical futility" covers any request for treatment that is considered inappropriate because it "merely preserves permanent unconsciousness or cannot end dependence on intensive medical care."[1] The case of Baby Rena from the early 1990s provides an early example of this concept. Baby Rena was HIV+ and had respiratory distress and cardiac failure. She had excessive cerebral spinal fluid in her brain, kidney dysfunction, needed a ventilator to breathe, and required constant sedation. The treating physician felt that keeping Rena on the ventilator was inhumane and medically futile, and suggested withdrawal. A Christian couple who intended to foster Baby Rena prayed for a miracle in the face of her failing health, and were adamant that her care "be motivated by a spiritual sense of obedience to God."[2] Baby Rena ultimately died on a ventilator after receiving cardio-pulmonary resuscitation. The intended foster mother was "stunned," as her faith held that health was there for anyone who would just claim it through prayer.[3]

Since the popularized case of Baby Rena, religiously motivated appeals for clinically unjustified interventions have not subsided. The family of Bobbi Kristina Brown, daughter of Bobbi Brown and Whitney Houston, "asked friends and fans to pray for a miracle" in early 2015 after she nearly drowned in a bathtub and was rendered unconscious.[4] She died after being kept on a ventilator for almost six months.

---

[1] Lawrence J. Schneiderman, Nancy S. Jecker, and Albert R. Jonsen, *Medical Futility: Its Meaning and Ethical Implications* 112 Annals Intern Med. 949, 949 (1990).
[2] David Smolin, *Praying for Baby Rena: Religious Liberty, Medical Futility, and Miracles*, 25 Seton Hall L. Rev. 960, 962–4 (1995)
[3] Id.
[4] Kent Sepkowitz, For Bobbi Kristina Brown, *Science and the Miraculous Don't Have to Be At Odds*, Daily Beast (February 11, 2015), available at www.thedailybeast.com/articles/2015/02/11/for-bobbi-kristina-brown-science-and-the-miraculous-don-t-have-to-be-at-odds.html?via=newsletter&source=DDAfternoon [https://perma.cc/A93H-AAPP]; CBS/AP, *Bobbi Kristina Brown's Cause of Death Revealed*, CBS News (March 4, 2016 at 7:35 AM), www.cbsnews.com/news/bobbi-kristina-brown-cause-of-death-revealed/ [https://perma.cc/6FJ9-QDDU].

The 2013 case of Jahi McMath presents another tragic standoff between surrogates claiming belief in religious miracles and secular hospital staff. Jahi was an Oakland teenager who went into cardiac arrest after a routine tonsillectomy to alleviate sleep apnea. After being placed on a ventilator, the hospital staff declared Jahi brain-dead and initiated withdrawal of artificial support. Jahi's mother insisted that as long as Jahi's heart was beating, God could work a miracle. Unlike the Baby Rena case, this conflict actually went before a judge. The judge ruled that the ventilator could be withdrawn if Jahi's family could not find an alternative facility that would provide her care.[5] Jahi's family received permission to remove Jahi from Oakland Children's Hospital, and, as of December of 2015, Jahi's family was still caring for her in a "home environment" in New Jersey.

This was a crucial move, for reasons described by Thaddeus Pope in the preceding chapter of this volume. In part to accommodate the orthodox Jewish community, New Jersey legislators passed a statute that allows a religious exemption from declaring a brain-dead individual legally dead if "such a declaration would violate the personal religious beliefs of the individual."[6] In these cases, patients who are brain-dead but able to breathe with the assistance of a ventilator may be considered legally alive in New Jersey. However, the exemption is technically only available to those whose religious beliefs dictate that the ability to breathe is the only relevant criteria for declaring someone dead. Presumably Jahi's parents believe that Jahi's personal religious beliefs are consistent with this exception, but we have no evidence of this. Jahi has remained on a ventilator for the last two years with no reported signs of improvement; she is still brain-dead.[7]

Another woeful futility case involves two-year-old Israel Stinson, who went into cardiac arrest during treatment for asthma.[8] Three physicians confirmed that the child was brain-dead and, consistent with California state law, decided to withdraw the artificial support. As of May 2016, the family was challenging the withdrawal in federal court. Among other claims, Israel's family argues that California's statutory

---

[5] CBS/AP, *Jahi McMath's Family Hopes for Miracle After Judge Rules Life Support Can be Removed*, CBS News (December 25, 2013 at 10:06 AM), available at www.cbsnews.com/news/brain-dead-teens-family-hopes-for-miracle-after-judge-rules-life-support-can-be-removed/ [https://perma.cc/3RFT-H8DP].

[6] N.J. Stat. Ann. § 26:6A-5 (West 2016).

[7] *Family Continues Legal Battle to Have Brain-Dead Girl Declared Alive*, CBS News (December 24, 2015 at 12:29 PM), available at www.cbsnews.com/news/family-continues-legal-battle-to-have-brain-dead-girl-declared-alive/ [https://perma.cc/45R2-R3RQ]; see also Kristen Bender, Jahi McMath, *Girl Declared Brain Dead after Tonsillectomy, Still on a Ventilator One Year Later*, Huffington Post (December 12, 2014), available at www.huffingtonpost.com/2014/12/12/jahi-mcmath-_n_6313166.html

[8] Ray Sanchez, *California Family Fights to Keep 2-Year-Old Son on Ventilator*, CNN (May 12, 2016), available at www.cnn.com/2016/05/12/health/california-israel-stinson-case/index.html [https://perma.cc/YH94-2PHD].

brain death criteria are not consistent with their Christian beliefs and violate their religious freedom. Israel's mother has said, "I know you're going to come out of this, baby, whenever you're ready – when God sees ready."[9] While this case challenges the constitutionality of brain death criteria, discussed in Pope's chapter, it implicates similar religious freedom concerns as traditional futility cases.

Given how surprising the clinical outcomes were in the latter three cases, they may be outliers. The surrogates might have been in shock regarding their loved one's prognoses, and unable to come to grips with the fact that they would never return to the way they were. Additionally, while the patients' families appeal to God or religious freedom, racial factors or distrust of the providers or hospital may also play a role.[10]

These four cases represent very private moments that became heartbreaking public spectacles. Often, however, these scenarios play out in the quiet of long-term care facilities or intensive care units, without any legal battles or media buzz. As more patients are kept alive through artificial means, medical futility cases will increase, and the role of religion will vary. Religions provide different guidance on principles such as suffering, impermanence, the role of consciousness, the definition of death, and whether God could intervene to perform a miracle. Medical futility may be challenged on scientific grounds as well. Physicians may disagree about whether a patient could return to a life that is acceptable to her, or even whether the patient's current state is acceptable. Different religious and medical perspectives inevitably confuse any clinical standard of futility.[11] Even so, in many cases, health care providers do agree that continuing aggressive treatments may not be clinically or ethically justified.

1. MEDICAL FUTILITY STATUTES IMMUNIZE PROVIDERS WHO WITHDRAW TREATMENT

To address the problem of families requesting that "everything be done,"[12] when the provider thinks that further treatment is medically inappropriate, the majority of

---

[9] Linsey Bever, "*God is telling me not to let go*": *A Mother Fights to Keep Her 2-Year-Old on Life Support*, Washington Post (May 6, 2016), available at www.washingtonpost.com/news/to-your-health/wp/2016/05/06/god-is-telling-me-not-to-let-go-a-mother-fights-to-keep-her-2-year-old-on-life-support/ [https://perma.cc/YC75-2FKN].

[10] As Robert Truog points out, "[f]utility cases most commonly involve patients and families from the more marginalized and disadvantaged segments of our society. These are families who have lived on the outskirts of our healthcare system, and who have frequently been denied or perceive that they have been denied, care that is beneficial." Robert D. Truog, *Medical Futility*, 25 Ga. St. U.L. Rev. 985, 988 (2009).

[11] Mohamed Rady & Joseph Verheidje, *The Determination of Quality of Life and Medical Futility in Disorders of Consciousness: Reinterpreting the Moral Code of Islam*, 15 Am. J. of Bioethics 14, 14 (2015); Tuck Wai Chan and Desley Hegney, Buddhism and Medical Futility, Bioethical Inquiry, DOI: 10.1007/s11673-012-9392-9 (2012).

[12] Lawrence Schneiderman & Nancy Jecker, *Wrong Medicine: Doctors, Patients, and Futile Treatment* 40 (1995).

states have passed so-called medical futility statutes.[13] These statutes are intended to provide physicians immunity from negligence claims if they unilaterally refuse to offer futile treatment, so long as particular statutory safeguards are met.[14] Some statutes do not specifically mention the term "futility," and instead just indicate that if a provider chooses for reasons of "conscience" not to provide life-sustaining care, she can do so.[15]

2. DO MEDICAL FUTILITY STATUTES VIOLATE STATE RELIGIOUS FREEDOM RESTORATION ACTS?

A. Is the Religious Practice Substantially Burdened?

This chapter will ask one question: whether such medical futility statutes might violate the right to free exercise of religion. As described in the introduction to this volume, the prevailing federal constitutional standard governing religious free exercise after the 1990 case of *Department of Human Resources v. Smith* holds that neutral laws of general applicability will not violate the First Amendment's Free Exercise clause.[16] Medical futility statutes easily satisfy this standard because the statutes apply regardless of the patient's stated reasons for wanting futile treatments; in other words, they are generally applicable and religiously neutral. Once the First Amendment does not appear to be violated, we turn to the more robust protection offered by the Religious Freedom Restoration Acts (RFRAs), federal and state, which were passed in response to *Smith*. Right from the start, we can do away with the federal RFRA because the medical futility statutes are passed by states.[17] State RFRAs therefore provide the only potential means for a religious freedom claim in this context.

---

[13] Thaddeus Pope, *Medical Futility Statutes: No Safe Harbor to Unilaterally Refuse Life-Sustaining Treatment*, 75 Tenn. L. Rev. 1 (2007).

[14] Id. The withdrawal is almost never *truly* unilateral, as the clinical team consults repeatedly with family, social workers, and others before aggressively advocating for removal of futile treatments. Even so, the term reflects that the provider may terminate treatments when the patient does not consent, subject to a jury's determination that the withdrawal was "reasonable" or satisfied the "standard of care." This statutory language often subjects physicians to the very fears of negligence liability that the statutes are intended to eliminate. See Cheryl Misak, Douglas White, & Robert Truog, *Medical Futility: a New Look at an Old Problem*, 146 CHEST 1667 (2014) (reframing the futility discussion from the typical lens of a unilateral withdrawal, and instead suggesting that "medical decisions are never made unilaterally... [but] are made in the context of an implicit and evolving social contract among patients, physicians, and societies at large.")

[15] Utah Code Ann. § 75-2a-115 (West).

[16] *Employment Div., Dept. of Human Res. of Oregon v. Smith*, 494 U.S. 872, 872 (1990).

[17] *City of Boerne v. Flores*, 521 U.S. 507, 508 (1997) ("Although Congress certainly can enact legislation enforcing the constitutional right to the free exercise of religion, see, e.g., *Cantwell v. Connecticut*,

RFRAs have been passed by 21 states,[18] all modeled on the federal law and requiring strict scrutiny when a state law burdens the exercise of religion. There are significant differences between states in terms of the threshold burden on religion that is required and whether there are areas where the law does not apply. Regardless of the differences, however, the *Smith* case remains the constitutional floor for protecting free exercise under the First Amendment.[19] States are allowed to create greater protections, which most of the RFRAs do, but they cannot protect religious free exercise less than the *Smith* standard (i.e., permitting intentional religious discrimination).

State courts have struggled to interpret their state RFRAs.[20] Quite puzzlingly, some courts have equated the strict scrutiny standard from their RFRA with the rational basis scrutiny of *Smith*, and others have interpreted their RFRA to provide less protection than *Smith*.[21] State RFRAs were intended to revert to the more exacting standards of the pre-*Smith* First Amendment era, so the states' interests in burdening religious believers need to be compelling. To invoke most state RFRAs, the plaintiff needs to show that the governmental action places a "substantial burden" on the plaintiff's exercise of a sincere religious belief.[22] Only if it does must the state interest in the law be narrowly tailored to further a compelling state interest; thus, the threshold definition of "burden" under the state RFRAs is quite important.

Some states (such as Alabama, Connecticut, Florida, Illinois, New Mexico, Rhode Island, South Carolina, and Texas) have not included a statutory definition of "substantial burden" in their RFRAs, whereas four state legislatures did define this term. Arizona's definition appears the broadest, as it states, "the term substantially burden is intended solely to ensure that this article is not triggered by trivial, technical or de minimis infractions."[23] Idaho and Oklahoma's RFRAs state that to substantially burden religious exercise is merely to "inhibit or curtail religiously motivated practices."[24] One may quibble with whether these definitions comply with standard

---

its § 5 power 'to enforce' is only preventive or 'remedial.' The Amendment's design and § 5's text are inconsistent with any suggestion that Congress has the power to decree the substance of the Amendment's restrictions on the States." (internal citations omitted)).

[18] Sixteen states introduced legislation in 2015 regarding the creation of, or alteration to, a state religious freedom law. See 2015 State Religious Freedom Restoration Legislation, National Conference on State Legislatures (September 3, 2015), available at www.ncsl.org/research/civil-and-criminal-justice/2015-state-rfra-legislation.aspx [https://perma.cc/E4W8-U9QX]; 42 U.S.C.A. § 2000bb-1 (2014).

[19] Christopher C. Lund, *Religious Liberty After Gonzales: A Look at State RFRAs*, 55 S.D. L. Rev. 466, 493 (2010).

[20] Id. at 485–6.

[21] Id.

[22] James A. Hanson, *Missouri's Religious Freedom Restoration Act: A New Approach to the Cause of Conscience*, 69 Mo. L. Rev. 853, 857 (2004).

[23] Ariz. Rev. Stat. Ann. Section 41–1493.01 (2015).

[24] James W. Wright Jr., *Making State Religious Freedom Restoration Amendments Effective*, 61 Ala. L. Rev. 425, 433–4 (2010).

notions of a "substantial burden," as a very minor incursion on religious exercise would require strict scrutiny in Arizona, Idaho, and Oklahoma. Pennsylvania's statutory definition is the most detailed in this respect, and includes any act that

(1) Significantly constrains or inhibits conduct or expression mandated by a person's sincerely held religious beliefs.
(2) Significantly curtails a person's ability to express adherence to the person's religious faith.
(3) Denies a person a reasonable opportunity to engage in activities which are fundamental to the person's religion.
(4) Compels conduct or expression which violates a specific tenet of a person's religious faith.[25]

Given that there are 21 state RFRAs, there is not sufficient space to interpret each statute individually here.[26] However, let us apply a few definitions of "substantial burden" to the medical futility cases at hand. Because no medical futility statute prohibits the patient or family from praying for a miracle, before the patient needs treatment, while the patient is receiving treatment, and even when providers consider the care futile, one characterization of the burden could find that state medical futility statutes *impose no substantial burden on religious exercise*. Under one reading of the Pennsylvania statute, no one is denied a reasonable opportunity to pray, nor is their ability to pray significantly curtailed. The question is whether the family should be allowed to pray under a specific set of conditions – namely, while the patient is being supported by artificial life support.

The denial of additional time to pray for a miracle might meet the threshold statutory definition of "burden" under Idaho or Oklahoma's RFRAs, as the denial of life support while the patient prays for a miracle could be said to "inhibit or curtail religiously motivated practices." Under Arizona's definition of a burden, the denial of life support could also likely not be considered a trivial infraction of religious free exercise, given that these are often life and death situations of tremendous spiritual and religious significance. This expansive view of religious liberty certainly "encroaches" on the rights of others; namely, the rights of the providers not to be required to provide futile care at the expense of other patients who might need their services.[27] In the states where it *could* be found that the denial of futile

---

[25] 71 PA. Stat. Ann. §2403 (West 2015).
[26] Jason Goldman, *Religious Freedom: Why States Are Unconstitutionally Burdening Their Own Citizens As They "Lower" the Burden*, 2015 Cardozo L. Rev. de novo 57, 69 (2015) (describing the different conceptions of "burden" under state RFRAs).
[27] "When initially enacted, the Conscience Clauses protected recipients of federal funds and their staffs from being required to participate in abortion or sterilization procedures that conflicted with the providers' religious or moral beliefs. One year later, Congress expanded the Conscience Clauses to

treatment results in a burden of religious exercise that triggers the state's RFRA, the state would then need to demonstrate that the medical futility laws are narrowly tailored to advance a compelling state interest.

B. Is There a Compelling State Interest Being Furthered by Futility Statutes?

Although the states employ different thresholds for what counts as a sufficient burden, each requires that the state advance a compelling interest in the legislation.[28] When determining whether a state's interest is compelling, the courts in most states have said they look to First Amendment jurisprudence. Thus, the compelling interest inquiry would resemble that under the *Smith* and pre-*Smith* decisions, discussed earlier.

While "only those interests of the highest order and those not otherwise served can overbalance legitimate claims to the free exercise of religion,"[29] the medical futility statutes could handily clear this hurdle. The states' compelling interests in prohibiting religious exemptions from medical futility statutes are:

1) difficulty distinguishing the potentially abundant religiously insincere from sincere claims,
2) the need for a principled and generally applicable basis for terminating potentially indefinite life support,
3) respecting provider autonomy,
4) respecting physician's reputation and integrity by reinforcing the line between healing and harming,
5) insulating professional medical standards from religious or any other nonmedical requests,
6) preserving scarce resources in the event of an epidemic or other public health need.

Any of these could satisfy strict scrutiny, and some already have. In the context of physician-assisted suicide and abortions, both Congress and the Supreme Court have recognized the need to protect the autonomy and religious beliefs of health care

---

permit a health care provider to refuse to perform any health service or research that conflicts with personal religious or moral beliefs." Kathleen M. Boozang, *Deciding the Fate of Religious Hospitals in the Emerging Health Care Market*, 31 Hous. L. Rev. 1429, 1481–2 (1995); see also 42 U.S.C. 300a-7(d); Lynn D. Wardle, *Protecting the Rights of Conscience of Health Care Providers*, J. Legal Med., 177, 177 (1993). Kathleen M. Boozang, *Deciding the Fate of Religious Hospitals in the Emerging Health Care Market*, 31 Hous. L. Rev. 1429, 1516 (1995).

[28] Lund, supra note 19, at 478.
[29] *Wisconsin v. Yoder*, 406 U.S. 205, 215, 92 S.Ct. 1526, 32 L.Ed.2d 15 (1972).

providers.[30] The Church Amendment, which was passed by Congress in 1973, clarified that the receipt of federal Medicare funds would not provide a basis for mandating a health care provider "to perform or assist in the performance of any sterilization procedure or abortion if his performance or assistance in the performance of such procedure or abortion would be contrary to his religious beliefs or moral convictions."[31] It also provided that no "entity" could be compelled to "make its facilities available for the performance of any sterilization procedure or abortion if [such] performance ... is prohibited by the entity on the basis of religious beliefs or moral convictions."[32] In the context of the Hyde Amendment, the protection of a physician's freedom of speech and religion were "clearly a compelling state interest."[33] Several states then enacted other health care refusal laws. These laws did not just exempt providers from performing abortions or sterilizations, but were expanded to include other practices that the provider might consider immoral, such as futile treatments.[34]

The state's interest in maintaining a distinction between physicians' duties to heal rather than harm is also compelling, and has been identified as such in the context of physician-assisted suicide.[35] Providers worry that administering futile treatments might be torturing patients without any medical benefit, as the patient may be heavily sedated or physically restrained in order to keep the breathing or feeding tube in place. Forcing providers to administer medically ineffective treatment that might cause great discomfort blurs the line between healing and harming. This provides a second compelling state interest in denying a religious exemption to medical futility laws.

Even the staunchest religious freedom supporters recognize that public health and safety concerns present compelling state interests.[36] During the last swine flu outbreak, hospitals were at capacity with their ventilators, and states did not have policies in place for how to best allocate these scarce resources. Public health authorities developed guidelines on the proper rationing of ventilators in the event

---

[30] See *Washington v. Glucksberg*, 521 U.S. 702, 731 (1997).
[31] 42 U.S.C. 300a-7(b)(1) (2015).
[32] 42 U.S.C. 300a-7(b)(2)(A) (2015).
[33] Leora Eisenstadt, *Separation of Church and Hospital: Strategies to Protect Pro-Choice Physicians in Religiously Affiliated Hospitals*, 15 Yale J.L. & Feminism 135, 167 (2003).
[34] Douglas Nejaime & Reva B. Siegel, *Conscience Wars: Complicity-Based Conscience Claims in Religion and Politics*, 124 Yale L.J. 2516, 2538 (2015).
[35] "The State also has an interest in protecting the integrity and ethics of the medical profession ... physician-assisted suicide could, it is argued, undermine the trust that is essential to the doctor-patient relationship by blurring the time-honored line between healing and harming." *Washington v. Glucksberg*, 521 U.S. 702, 731, 117 S. Ct. 2258, 2273, 138 L. Ed. 2d 772 (1997).
[36] "The National Council of Churches ... have suggested that religious practices be restricted only when they threaten 'public health and safety.'" James E. Ryan, *Smith and the Religious Freedom Restoration Act: An Iconoclastic Assessment*, 78 Va. L. Rev. 1407, 1442 (1992).

of another flu epidemic.[37] If religious patients could commandeer the use of the ventilator indefinitely through state RFRAs, this could thwart public health efforts. This presents another robust and compelling state interest in denying a religious exemption to medical futility laws, at least in certain conditions, in order to keep ventilators available to others.

In addition to these professional autonomy and public health compelling interests, the state has an interest in preventing "an administrative problem of such magnitude" as to render the religious exemptions unworkable.[38] In the context of medical futility statutes, the state's interest here is exceedingly strong. The basis for this interest is the inability to distinguish between sincere and insincere religious requests. For example, in the case of Jahi McMath, was it a sincere belief in miracles that led her mother to transfer her to New Jersey, or an inability to confront her child's unexpected and sudden brain death? How could a court decide whether this belief was sincere or merely convenient? A state's interest may become compelling when viewed in the aggregate, even if it might not be as compelling when viewed through one specific claim.[39] However, the state should question whether the marginal interest is compelling in denying *this particular type of exemption* to this class as opposed to its global state interest in passing the statute as it applies to everyone.[40]

C. Are the Statutes the Least Restrictive Means to Further These Compelling Interests?

Even though any of these state interests in rejecting religious claims to continue futile treatment could be considered compelling, their pursuit may only be through the least restrictive means necessary. The Seventh Circuit reminded us in the context of the Affordable Care Act's mandatory contraception coverage, "[s]trict scrutiny requires ... a close "fit" – between the governmental interest and the means chosen

---

[37] One problem identified by North Carolina's department of health was that in the event of a flu epidemic, there would not be enough ventilators: "During the worst week of an extreme global epidemic, demand could outstrip the state's supply of these devices by more than 300 percent, federal computer models indicate." Jim Nesbitt, *N.C. Arms Against Threat of Flu Pandemic*, N.C. News & Observer (December 3, 2006 at 12:30 AM), available at www.ncprogress.org/PDF/120306-newsobserver_com_NC_arms_against_threat_of_flu_pandemic.pdf [https://perma.cc/64AB-VK8C]; see also New York State Health Department Press Release, *New York State Health Department Seeks Public Engagement on Ventilator Allocation Guidelines* (August 23, 2007), 2007 WLNR 16489484 (2015); Sheri Fink, ProPublica, *Preparing for a Pandemic, State Health Departments Struggle With Rationing Decisions* (October 24, 2009), 2009 WLNR 29869288 (2015);

[38] *Sherbert v. Verner*, 374 U.S. 398, 408–409 (1963).

[39] William P. Marshall, *In Defense of Smith and Free Exercise Revisionism*, 58 U. Chi. L. Rev. 308, 312 (1991).

[40] *Burwell v. Hobby Lobby Stores, Inc.*, 134 S. Ct. 2751, 2779 (2014) (quoting *Gonzales v. O Centro Espirita Beneficente Uniado do Vegetal*, 546 U.S. 418, 431, 126 S.Ct. 1211, 163 L.Ed.2d 1017 (2006)).

to further that interest... There are many ways to promote public health and gender equality, almost all of them less burdensome on religious liberty ..."[41] As applied to medical futility statutes and the state's public health interest, there are indeed other ways the state could control against the inability to ration life-sustaining devices in the event of an epidemic. Specifically, the state could suspend medical futility statutes if a public health emergency is declared, but not before. Therefore, a medical futility statute that applies in noncrisis situations may not be considered the least restrictive necessary. States would need to advance another compelling interest to ensure that the statute passes strict scrutiny.

A better source for upholding medical futility statutes is the state's interest in professional autonomy and ethics. Requiring that physicians comply with what they feel is medically ineffective treatment, or worse, torture, would violate the providers' freedoms. The only way to minimize the impact on those seeking exemptions while still respecting providers' autonomy would be to offer patients or their families an opportunity to find an alternative facility or provider that would agree to provide the futile care (as Jahi McMath's family did in the case described above). It may be that a medical futility statute must have this sort of notice and opportunity to transfer the patient in order to satisfy strict scrutiny as the least restrictive means necessary. Courts would need to determine just how much time should be given to the family to effectuate a transfer in order for the statute to survive a constitutional challenge. In any event, the objecting providers or facility should not have a duty to find a transfer or help find a facility that would treat the patient. If the treatment that is required is truly medically futile, it would be imprudent to require objecting providers and facilities to assist in a transfer to a facility that is presumably offering substandard, or medically ineffective, care. The provider's autonomy is likely not excessively infringed if she must give the family a week or two's notice and opportunity to transfer before terminating futile treatments. But once a reasonable amount of time is given to the family so that they can attempt to find a transfer facility, there is nothing more the original facility could force the provider to do without violating her sense of professional ethics and autonomy.

The state's interest in managing the administrative burden of potential RFRA claims in turn bolsters the "least restrictive" prong of strict scrutiny. As Thomas Berg explains, "[t]he threat of cumulative exemptions comes not only from other sincere religious objectors, but from other persons who could feign the same objection to get the benefits of exemption."[42] Further, the text of the First Amendment constrains any deep scrutiny into desperate patients who might try to "game" the system because the state

---

[41] *Korte v. Sebelius*, 735 F.3d 654, 686 (7th Cir. 2013).
[42] Thomas C. Berg, *What Hath Congress Wrought? An Interpretive Guide to the Religious Freedom Restoration Act*, 39 Vill. L. Rev. 1, 41 (1994).

cannot inquire too closely into whether the belief is legitimate, heartfelt, or even shared with other members of the same faith.[43] Given that many people find religion and God near the end of their lives, and particularly in response to medical crisis, limiting the exemptions to a manageable number would be impossible. Here, the analysis of whether the interest is compelling dovetails with the question of whether the statute is the least restrictive means necessary. The fact that there is no way to more narrowly tailor the statute to protect religious freedoms renders the interest in categorical nonexemption to medical futility statutes compelling and also the least restrictive means necessary. Any patient could request that they be provided indefinite life support on religious grounds, and there would be no principled basis for later terminating this support.

There are no alternatives to indefinitely providing futile treatments. The only potential concession, though not an alternative, is to grant these individuals a certain amount of time to pray for a miracle or come to terms with their loved one's imminent (or already legally declared) death, which most providers and some futility statutes already do. There must be some principled limit on the amount of time a patient or his surrogate could mandate clinically futile care. The medical standard of care provides this principled limit. Any other standard introduces an arbitrary limit that is impossible to defend, and creates its own potential for unfair discrimination.

Refusing religious exemptions for medical futility statutes can be contrasted with the Supreme Court cases where exemptions were granted. For example, the exemptions from working on the Sabbath are not likely to overwhelm employers or employee benefit programs as a minority of religions celebrate a Saturday Sabbath and others will choose to work on that day. In those contexts, the fear of numerous (even feigned) religious exemptions does not render exemptions unworkable. There *is* potential for high school students to request not to finish high school on religious grounds, such as those made by the Old Order Amish in *Yoder*. However, either the Supreme Court was not concerned that these exemptions would overwhelm the states or they felt that in that particular case the Old Order Amish had demonstrated sufficient sincerity and vocational alternatives.[44] Either way, respected religious freedom scholars such as Douglas Laycock agree that "the number of potential claims

---

[43] See *Welsh v. United States*, 398 U.S. 333, 339 (1970); *United States v. Seeger*, 380 U.S. 163, 176 (1965); *Thomas v. Review Bd. of Indiana Employment Sec. Div.*, 450 U.S. 707, 716 (1981).

[44] This concern seems to have been implicit in Justice White's concurring opinion in *Yoder*: "This would be a very different case for me if respondents' claim were that their religion forbade their children from attending any school at any time and from complying in any way with the educational standards set by the State." 406 U.S. at 238. However, Justice Douglas's dissenting opinion emphasizes his perceived irrelevance of this sort of inquiry: "[T]he emphasis of the Court on the 'law and order' record of this Amish group of people is quite irrelevant. A religion is a religion irrespective of what the misdemeanor or felony records of its members might be." Id. at 247.

is relevant to assessing the government's interest ... if the government has a compelling interest in denying exemption to the whole group of similarly situated objectors, it also has a compelling interest in denying exemption to each one of them."[45]

CONCLUSION

In conclusion, when it comes to avoiding exceptions for religious beliefs to medical futility statutes, there are at least three state interests that are compelling and the least restrictive means necessary. These are: a) respect for the professional autonomy of physicians, b) the need to distinguish harming patients from healing them, and c) the need to manage the administrative burden of numerous claims. Given the multiple compelling state interests in denying a religious exemption in medical futility cases and the inability to accommodate religious believers without exposing hospitals and providers to an unlimited conscription of services, it seems unlikely that a petitioner would prevail on state RFRA grounds. As the medical futility statutes likely satisfy the strict scrutiny required of the state RFRAs, they also satisfy the lesser-included rational basis test required of the First Amendment. Religious patients claiming that medical futility statutes violate their free exercise will have a very difficult time prevailing. Even so, this only answers the legal questions.

When physicians concern themselves chiefly with the legal ramifications, they lose sight of important ethical dimensions. Whereas the courts are not allowed to inquire into whether a patient's personal religious belief is genuine or shared with members of their faith, this is precisely what a chaplain or social worker should do. Outside of the domain of constitutional law, one medical scholar claimed that "[c]laims about miracles may ... be subjected to scrutiny according to the criteria of the patient's faith. Faith is, in this sense, public and not private. Judging the authenticity of patients' or families' claims about miracles therefore involves examining such claims in light of the deposit of faith of the person's own religious tradition."[46] Knowing whether the patient shares these beliefs with members of her faith is useful in ruling out denial or negative psychological coping. In cases where a patient's family begs for more time for a miracle to occur, it may be that they are simply unprepared for death and expressing this in terms of needing a divine intervention. Focusing initially on the ethical dimensions allows providers to ask the pressing spiritual questions that would not be encouraged under a purely legal analysis. If possible, terminal patients should be asked early on about the kind of death that they want. Questions such as "what sort of life would be worth living for you?" and "what

---

[45] Douglas Laycock, *RFRA, Congress, and the Ratchet*, 56 Mont. L. Rev. 145, 148 (1995).
[46] Daniel Sulmasy, *Distinguishing Denial From Authentic Faith in Miracles: A Clinical-Pastoral Approach*, 100 S. Med. J. 1268, 1268 (2007).

sort of life would not be worth living?" may help elicit these preferences. Asking these questions could obviate future requests for futile treatment. However, if the time comes and the patient or his surrogates express belief in divine intervention, then they should be asked "what would a miracle look like?" and "what would it mean if God did *not* grant this miracle?" Religious scholars of various denominations and from different cultural backgrounds assert that God is not a magician, and if the patient or his family cannot ultimately dispose themselves to the divine will, then they are likely in denial.[47] Efforts to educate providers on the importance of spiritual end-of-life care should disambiguate the legal from the ethical, and emphasize the ethical importance of asking these spiritual questions that are foreign to the law.

---

[47] Id. at 1270.

22

Putting the Insanity Defense on Trial

Understanding Criminality in the Context of Religion and Mental Illness

Abbas Rattani and Jemel Amin Derbali

> When Muslims or people in the Middle East commit violence it's immediately Islam. Islam. It's bad. A white person can write a Christian manifesto, shoot hundreds of people with a submachine gun, have a bomb in his car, and it's bad parenting. He's mentally unstable. He went off his meds. Why can't I be mentally unstable? Why can't Muslims ever be mentally – I want to be mentally unstable! I would love to be mentally unstable!
>
> – Aasif Mandvi, 2015 Radio and Television Correspondents' Dinner; C-SPAN, March 26, 2015

As public health and legal scholarship increasingly consider the interface between mental illness and the criminal justice system, questions pertaining to the intersection of mental illness, religious extremism, and culpability continue to remain both complex and unanswered. This chapter will discuss mental health issues that are particularly difficult to assess, given their confluence with religious beliefs – which, at times, may blur current understandings of delusional disordered thinking. We also consider the question of who is counted as mentally ill within the criminal justice system and how current mechanisms distinguish between delusions, personality disorders, and overvalued beliefs in assessing culpability.

Nidal Hasan, a 39-year-old U.S. Army psychiatrist, shot and killed 13 on a military base. In his defense, he admitted to waging "jihad" because the U.S. was at war with Islam. Before the shooting, people who knew Hasan were concerned with his behavior that they variously described as "disconnected, aloof, paranoid, belligerent, and schizoid." He was sentenced to death.

Acknowledgments: Keith G. Meador, MD, ThM, MPH, Kimberly Brown, PhD, Stephen A McLeod-Bryant, MD, and John L Miller, JD provided helpful suggestions on a conference presentation version of this manuscript. Daniel Zwerdling, *Walter Reed Officials Asker: Was Hasan Psychotic?*,

Carlos Bledsoe, 23-year old man, opened fire on military recruiters, claiming he was also waging jihad against the U.S. His father described his growing religious extremism as corresponding with Bledsoe going "out of his mind," and his lawyers argued that he was suffering from delusion.[1] He pled guilty and was sentenced to life in prison.

Rezwan Ferdaus pled guilty to plotting an attack on the Capitol and Pentagon with an FBI informant. An FBI agent admitted that Ferdaus told him that he was depressed, and had anxiety and "intrusive thoughts" in the month leading up to the plot.[2] Ferdaus is serving a 17-year sentence.[3]

Mohammad Reza Taheri-azar, after attempting a mass homicide at the University of North Carolina at Chapel Hill, immediately called the police on himself and confessed to the act, claiming his actions were part of his religious right to "avenge the deaths of Muslims worldwide."[4] While being found competent to stand trial and convicted, a more recent evaluation raised concerns that he may have had an undiagnosed psychiatric illness.[5]

In Canada, Chiheb Essagheir was convicted of plotting an attack with another person on the national train system. At sentencing, it became clear through a series of courtroom outbursts and psychiatric evaluations that Essagheir was possibly suffering from psychosis and schizophrenia. He was judged competent to stand trial and sentenced to life in prison.[6]

These cases represent a pattern and reflect a challenging profile of criminal actors at the intersection of delusion and religious belief, a profile that will serve as a reference point for our investigation into the issues at stake in this chapter. In each case,

National Public Radio (November 11, 2009, 2:54 PM), available at www.npr.org/templates/story/story.php?storyId=120313570 [https://perma.cc/65CD-2RGW].

[1] Stephanie Simon, *Attack Suspect Battles Own Lawyers*, The Wall Street Journal (July 19, 2011), available at www.wsj.com/articles/SB10001424052702304567604576454382530634642 [https://perma.cc/4FWJ-JTZK].

[2] The Associated Press, *Massachusetts Man, Razwan Ferdaus, Sentenced to 17 Years in Terror Plot*, MASSLive (November 1, 2012, 2:25 PM), available at www.masslive.com/news/index.ssf/2012/11massachusetts_man_rezwan_ferda_1.html [https://perma.cc/W9E8-W8B3].

[3] Jess Bidgood, *Massachusetts Man Gets 17 Years in Terrorist Plot*, N.Y. Times (November 2, 2012), available at www.nytimes.com/2012/11/02/us/rezwan-ferdaus-of-massachusetts-gets-17-years-in-terrorist-plot.html [https://perma.cc/AM4R-WZYE].

[4] Pit Pandemonium, *Alumnus Drives Through Pit in Act to "Avenge Muslim Deaths,"* Daily Tar Heel (March 6, 2006).

[5] Jessica Rocha, Samiha Khanna, Jane Stancill, *Suspect Says He Meant to Kill: The Man Accused of Injuring 9 at UNC-CH is Calm in Court, Says He'll Represent Himself*, News & Observer (March 7, 2006); Bradley Saacks, *Pit Driver: "I Am Genuinely Sorry" for 2006 Rampage*, Daily Tar Heel (March 2, 2016).

[6] Richard Warnica, *Via Terror Plot Sentencing Ends with Lawyer Urging Judge to Hospitalize Chiheb Esseghaier*, National Post (September 4, 2015, 10:03 PM), available at http://news.nationalpost.com/toronto/via-terror-plot-sentencing-ends-with-lawyer-urging-judge-to-hospitalize-chiheb-esseghaier [https://perma.cc/22BR-VACM].

the person exhibited increasingly troubling behavior, reflecting growing mental instability to those around them that coincided with increasingly extreme socio-religious beliefs. This extremism isolated them from their religious communities that rejected these positions, even as they were able to largely function normally in their daily lives. Their criminal actions, while committed alone or in very small groups, were motivated by reference to a grand apocalyptic war between "Islam" and "the West" that brought them into ideological, if not strategic, allegiance with larger global extremist groups.

As is clear from the profile these cases suggest, there is a real difficulty in distinguishing normal religious beliefs from delusional ones, which introduces new questions of culpability and the need for further probing. To what extent should the justice system assess mental health in determining the culpability of individuals who commit acts of violence if their actions are influenced by delusional beliefs, personality disorders, or predisposing mental vulnerabilities? Does the law's consideration of culpability fairly account for mental illness in cases motivated by religious extremism? How are mental illness and religiosity differentiated in assessing wrongdoing when a defendant claims to be operating within his or her own conceived religious/moral frameworks? Fairness infuses these questions, motivated by the belief that ensuring appropriate protections for mentally ill actors requires a concerted investigation into how individuals conceive of their actions.

We argue that more exacting consideration should be given to the mental state of defendants in cases where religion is used as a primary motivator of criminality, as it may be indicative of an underlying issue in appreciating right and wrong. We are not arguing that every religious extremist suffers from mental illness, but rather that more exacting tools are needed for considering cases in which the line between belief and delusion is especially hard to distinguish. Such consideration is in the interest of fairness, but could also help point a way forward for preventing such violence by properly containing and treating those that may be prone to extremism before they act.

We frame our argument by reviewing a few examples of psychiatric issues (e.g., religious delusion, personality disorder) that blur the line between normal and abnormal. Next, we examine current mechanisms for addressing such mental health concerns in U.S. federal courts and their deficiencies in these cases. Finally, we discuss the case of biased assessment of culpability within the courts as it relates to the religious beliefs of underrepresented religious groups. This chapter aims to expand the preliminary work on religious extremism, wrongdoing,[7] and how the law accounts for mental illness as a mitigating factor in determining culpability.

---

[7] See generally Marian Lim, *The Sanity of Faith: What Religious Fundamentalism Teaches About the Insanity Defense and the First Amendment*, 17 New Crim. L. Rev. 252 (2014).

1. CHALLENGES IN PSYCHIATRIC DIAGNOSIS

How do we begin to understand crimes committed in the name of religion or God? How do we account for the complex interplay between "normal" religiosity and varying degrees of psychopathy? This interplay is further complicated when we consider the fact that, within the case of delusions, sociocultural and environmental variables influence how we categorize what we define as "normal" versus pathological.[8]

The preceding cases delineate a popular caricature of Muslim actors as rational, sane actors carrying out religious injunctions. The individual does not seem to exhibit any bizarre, odd or overtly psychotic symptoms, nor is their function impaired (e.g., they can retain employment). Furthermore, their actions make sense within the context of their belief. However, the confusion arises in determining whether the held belief is indicative of a delusional disorder or represents normal thinking. One could argue, diagnostically, that the actors in the aforementioned cases suffer from delusional disorder. Noteworthy is the juxtaposition of their beliefs falling outside the most conservative interpretations of the broader Islamic belief system, indicating the role sociocultural norms play in grading the delusional nature of one's belief.

For the purposes of this chapter, we will focus on delusional and personality disorder. The Diagnostic and Statistical Manual of Mental Disorders defines delusional disorder as a persistent, false belief system with a specific theme lasting more than a month; characterized by the absence of other psychotic symptoms (e.g., hallucinations), behavior that is not obviously strange or bizarre (apart from the behavior related to the delusion), and the ability to function generally without impairment. Additionally, personality disorder is characterized by a maladaptive, inflexibly pervasive pattern of behavior leading to subjective stress. Oftentimes, the person is unaware of the behavior and is impossible to convince otherwise. Examples of personality disorders include schizoid (recluse, detached, emotionless), antisocial (disregard towards the rights of others), and paranoid (distrustful, leery, hypervigilant).[9]

Religious extremism (often incorrectly conflated with religious fundamentalism),[10] on the other hand, is defined herein as a one-dimensional focus and ascription to strict, exclusivist interpretations of religious doctrine. Characteristically, religious extremists wield literalist readings of scripture as rhetorical justification or motivation towards the pursuit of a secondary objective or cause. Exclusivist and dualistic language can be used by groups to situate the actor in an "us" versus "them" context, wherein the actor is in the morally right position, carrying out a set of behaviors that are seen as just from their vantage point. Thus, societal "wrongdoing" is

---

[8] See generally American Psychiatric Association, *Diagnostic and Statistical Manual of Mental Disorders* (5th ed. 2013).
[9] See id.
[10] See generally Lim, supra note 8.

normalized as morally right within particular environmental and social contexts by certain actors.

Viewed together, determining what distinguishes delusional from extremist thinking becomes challenging. In both conditions, actors believe that they are operating in accordance with their belief systems and are unlikely to view their beliefs as "wrong." Once actors inhabit this cognitive space, how do we then distinguish their cognitive appreciation of their behaviors, especially if their own understanding of wrongdoing is situated in a different conception of justice? It is not the case that these individuals admit their actions are immoral or wrong; on the contrary, they view themselves as moral exemplars – charged with the divine duty of restoring justice to the world. In the context of personality disorders or delusional disorder, for example, convincing patients otherwise is nearly impossible – they remain egosyntonic.

Moreover, instead of viewing psychoses as categories of normal versus abnormal, we recognize that symptoms of delusion and personality disorder exist on a continuum.[11] Behavior is shaped by one's context, life events, environment, and unknown factors; as such, various actions should be examined, probed, and evaluated with full attention to these influencing factors, symptoms, and signs.[12] One's mental state and understanding of reality influence one's behavior and it is important to view persons holistically – not simply by the crime committed.

It should be made clear again that we are not suggesting religious extremists inherently suffer from personality or delusional disorder, but we do argue that religious extremism may obfuscate underlying cognitive issues. Thus, determining whether or not an actor appreciates the nature of his actions, though difficult, is necessary for justice. Moreover, we contend that consideration should be given to the psychiatric and psychological vulnerabilities driving maladaptive behavior and criminality by religiously motivated actors.

A. Diagnosis and the Identification of Norms

The social acceptability of a belief may be one approach to determining whether an idea is delusional or normal. For example, if we evaluate the religious ideas of the profiles cited earlier against their community's or broader understandings of an Islamic belief system, we can appreciate the delusional nature of their apocalyptic ideas of establishing Islamic rule. And when confronted by fellow Muslims, these

---

[11] See American Psychiatric Association, Diagnostic and Statistical Manual of Mental Disorders (5th ed. 2013), Randy Borum, *Psychological Vulnerabilities and Propensities for Involvement in Violent Extremism*, 32 Behav. Sci. & L. 286 (2014), Rachel Pechey & Peter Halligan, *The Prevalence of Delusion-Like Beliefs Relative to Sociocultural Beliefs in the General Population*, 44 Psychopathology 106 (2011).

[12] See Borum, supra note 12.

actors are capable of recognizing that their beliefs are unwelcome and uncommon, while still maintaining the validity and righteousness of their own beliefs.

However, the social acceptability of a belief can be relative, and this is often the point of contention when evaluating normalcy. It could be argued that these extreme beliefs are common among certain fundamentalist or extremist fringe factions of Islam, and although these beliefs may not be widely held by Muslims, they are, nonetheless, arguably held by an (albeit small) group of religious extremists. Although it is clear that religious extremist groups such as Al-Qaeda or Daesh (i.e., ISIS) hold beliefs that are vastly under representative of the majority of the global Muslim population,[13] the nature and quality of their beliefs make it difficult to distinguish who among the religious extremist actors are afflicted with particular psychopathies. Tangentially, if psychiatry is concerned primarily with the mental status of an individual, how then do we evaluate extremist group beliefs, especially when one group's "extreme" beliefs is another group's normal?[14] To what extent does religious extremism shroud the various degrees of psychopathy by offering behavioral outlets?

With conditions like personality-disorder, actors may appreciate differences in right- and wrongdoing more generally, but may still be resistant to recognizing their own behaviors as wrong. They may even admit to committing crimes with minimal or absent affect. In all of the preceding cases, the defendants admitted to their criminal actions and, in cases that went to trial, the defendants actively rejected suggestions of pleading insanity. Given the general lack of familiarity with minority religious doctrines (e.g., Islam) and the persistence of Islamophobia, juries may not qualitatively appreciate underlying psychiatric issues. With the clinical community still wrestling with the difficulties of differentiating between overvalued beliefs and identifying the ways in which religious ideation influence mental health, how can we expect courts to be adequately equipped to probe these questions? The language used by actors can influence or implicitly bias how we come to perceive their actions, and a lack of familiarity with normalcy (especially in the context of contentious religious beliefs) or appreciation for psychopathy can further make the culpability determination challenging.

Noteworthy are the cases, like those cases cited earlier, of the lone actor who may not be affiliated with any particular extremist group, but whose delusions adopt a similar rhetorical quality to extremist practitioners – making it additionally complex to disentangle normal from disorder on the psychopathy spectrum. In the

---

[13] See Pew Forum on Religion & Public Life, *Muslim Americans: No Signs of Growth in Alienation or Support for Extremism* (2011).

[14] Ironically, the extremist fringe group Al-Qaeda declared their counterpart Daesh as being "too extreme" for them. See Krishnadev Calamur, *ISIS: An Islamist Group Too Extreme Even for Al-Qaida*, National Public Radio (June 13, 2014, 3:46 PM), available at www.npr.org/blogs/thetwo-way/2014/06/13/321665375/isis-an-islamist-group-too-extreme-even-for-al-qaida [https://perma.cc/WRS2-WSKK].

earlier profiles, the actors situated themselves in the rhetoric of religious extremism prior to the attack and, often, during the legal process, showing an understanding of their actions while also claiming they were morally just and in accordance to their religious belief system.[15] As noted in these examples, the polarizing language of extremist religious doctrines often obfuscates an appreciable gauge of underlying psychiatric issues.

2. ISSUES OF LEGAL CULPABILITY

Courts are not well equipped to address questions of mental health and culpability in religiously motivated criminal cases. Courts can only consider questions of mental health and culpability in the context of the insanity defense. However, the insanity defense is not an appropriate mechanism for these types of cases, even when there are legitimate concerns regarding the effects of mental illness on the criminal actions of religiously inspired actors.

Under federal law, insanity is an affirmative defense that requires a defendant to prove that he, "as a result of a severe mental disease or defect, was unable to appreciate the nature and quality or the wrongfulness of his acts."[16] The Insanity Defense Reform Act of 1984 circumscribed a court's consideration of a defendant's mental health as a defense, limiting it to cases in which an insanity defense has been raised: "Through the Act, Congress intended to prohibit the presentation of evidence of mental disease or defect, short of insanity, to excuse conduct."[17] Therefore, if a defendant cannot come close to meeting this restrictive definition of insanity, his mental health cannot be raised at trial. However, even if a defendant can hope to meet these standards, the nature of religious extremism cases makes them especially poorly suited for application of the insanity defense because of the specific definition of insanity used, the procedure by which the defense is raised, and implicit biases of participants in the legal process.

A. *Insanity Standard*

Insanity is a total defense to a crime, meaning that if successful, the defendant is considered not guilty, period. The definition of insanity has two major prongs; first, a defendant must have a "severe mental disease or defect."[18] In defining a severe

---

[15] See Jessica Rocha, Samiha Khanna, & Jane Stancill, *Suspect Says He Meant to Kill: The Man Accused of Injuring 9 at UNC-CH is Calm in Court, Says He'll Represent Himself*, News & Observer, March 7, 2006.
[16] 18 U.S.C. § 17 (2012).
[17] Id.; see also *United States v. Westcott*, 83 F.3d 1354, 1358 (11th Cir. 1996).
[18] 18 U.S.C. § 17 (2012).

mental disease or defect: "proof [of] mental disorder is not enough."[19] Instead, a defendant must prove that the disorder is severe and affected the defendant *at the time of the crime*.[20] The second prong is that a defendant, as a result of this severe mental defect, must have been unable to appreciate the wrongfulness of his actions at the time of the crime.[21] A failure to appreciate wrongfulness often comes from the nature of the psychopathy, defined as "the belief of a state of supposed facts that do not exist, and which no rational person would believe."[22]

The federal insanity law does not define "wrongfulness," leaving some ambiguity in how this is applied practically. Courts interpreting the law have determined that wrongfulness should generally be defined with respect to moral wrongfulness, not legal wrongfulness.[23] Moral wrongfulness is defined objectively with reference to the community rather than subjectively with reference to the defendant.[24] *United States v. Ewing* further notes: "[W]rongfulness for purposes of the federal insanity defense statute is defined by reference to objective societal or public standards of moral wrongfulness, not the defendant's subjective personal standards of moral wrongfulness."[25]

This objective definition of assessing knowledge of wrongfulness precludes many religiously inspired/motivated defendants. Those who use consequentialist or divine command theoretical frameworks to morally account for their actions often hold a characteristically delusional belief that their actions are morally commanded and justified under religious principles – and that they are doing the work of God. While the universal wrongfulness of their actions is clear, defendants often do not appreciate that their actions are morally wrongful unto themselves. However, they do recognize that their actions are wrongful when compared to the community around them. Since defendants' actions are often predicated on apocalyptical frameworks, the fact of deviation from a communal definition of morality is often what supports the subjective delusion of moral rightness in the first place. Therefore, without a more subjective definition of wrongfulness or a more flexible definition of the community by which an objective standard is applied, such defendants will never meet the definition of insanity.

Furthermore, this definition of culpability, being focused on the mental state of the defendant at the time of the crime, does not account for the unique situation of

---

[19] *United States v. Schlater*, F. 3d 1251, 1257 (7th Cir. 1996).
[20] See id.
[21] 18 U.S.C. § 17 (2012).
[22] *Knight v. Edwards*, 153 Tex. 170, 175, 264 S.W.2d 692, 695 (1954).
[23] See *United States v. Ewing*, 494 F.3d 607, 622 (7th Cir. 2007).
[24] See id.
[25] Id.

the actor whose act can be validated by extremist groups. In essence, a defendant's delusions may fit right in with extremist moral positions that share the same descriptive religious language – giving criminal actions a moral purpose and validation. Within the determination of legal insanity, an emphasis is placed on one's cognitive processes and nature of mental illness, suggesting that one's actions are to be examined in the context of one's mental state. Theoretically, the law is designed to hold individuals accountable for their wrongdoing based on their voluntary and knowing participation in the crime, and intentionality in criminality is crucial in the determination of culpability. However, it may be inappropriate to apply the same standards of culpability in the case of wrongdoing committed by actors with some underlying psychopathy and sane, rational actors simply executing religious injunctions.

B. Raising the Insanity Defense

The burden is on the defendant to prove the elements of the insanity defense.[26] However, many defendants in these cases simply refuse to plead insanity.[27] Instead, their sustained belief in the rightness of their actions leads them to refuse to admit that they have any delusions or personality maladaptations, even if their mental state influenced their criminal actions.[28] A judge may decide that an obviously delusional defendant is not competent to stand trial, and not competent to decide whether to accept an insanity defense,[29] but in every preceding case in which it was raised, the actor was deemed competent.

Multiple cases have highlighted the difficulty of applying criminal insanity to religiously justified criminal actions. Nidal Malik Hasan, described in the examples at the start of this chapter, refused to offer an insanity defense despite serious questions about his mental state at the time of his criminal acts, dismissed his attorneys, and admitted to the killings, saying only that he was a soldier who had decided to "switch sides" in what he thought was an American war against Islam.[30] Carlos Bledsoe also refused to offer an insanity defense and complained of pressure to plead

---

[26] 18 U.S.C. § 17 (2012).

[27] See. e.g., Manny Fernandez, *Major is Arraigned in Fort Hood Killings*, N.Y. Times (July 20, 2011), available at www.nytimes.com/2011/07/21/us/21hood.html?_r=0 [https://perma.cc/MAQ5-HX47].

[28] See e.g., Daniel Zwerdling, *Walter Reed Officials Asked: Was Hasan Psychotic?*, National Public Radio (November 11, 2009), available at www.npr.org/templates/story/story.php?storyId=120313570 [https://perma.cc/S9VT-MCEP].

[29] See *Dusky v. United States*, 362 U.S. 402, 402, 80 S.Ct. 788, 789, 4 L.Ed.2d 824 (1960).

[30] Billy Kenber, *Nidal Hasan Sentenced to Death for Fort Hood Shooting Rampage*, The Washington Post (August 28, 2013), available at www.washingtonpost.com/world/national-security/nidal-hasan-sentenced-to-death-for-fort-hood-shooting-rampage/2013/08/28/aad28de2-0ffa-11e3-bdf6-e4fc677d94a1_story.html [https://perma.cc/Y4T9-NC6E].

insanity: "I wasn't insane or post-traumatic ... [The killing was] justified according to Islamic laws and the Islamic religion."[31] Similarly, Chiheb Essagheir berated and spat at his court-appointed attorney in court when the attorney attempted to argue that he suffered from mental illness.[32] He, too, was deemed competent.[33] If defendants refuse to acknowledge their underlying psychiatric issues (which is unlikely given the conditions of the pathology), courts cannot sincerely probe the questions of culpability.

C. Bias in Assessing Culpability: The Case of Islamophobia

The question of assessing culpability in the context of crimes perpetrated by defendants citing religious motivations, as is the case in the preceding profiles, is further complicated by bias and pervasive unfamiliarity with minority religious ideologies. The process of raising an insanity defense in court, and the actor's inherent susceptibility to human opinion, makes these questions salient. While psychological experts or forensic psychiatrists are asked to present evidence, a judge decides whether a defendant meets a minimal burden to present the insanity defense at trial.[34] If so, a jury decides whether the defendant meets the definition of insanity and can therefore qualify as criminally culpable for his or her actions.[35] Each of these human actors has significant influence in the process of assessing fitness and culpability.

For our purpose, we focus our attention on Islamophobia and the powerful role the media plays in inundating and reinforcing dubious prejudicial associations, providing suspect definitions, and inappropriately suggesting relationships between religious groups and crime.[36] In the case of Islam, Muslims are frequently depicted

---

[31] James Dao, *Man Claims Terror Ties in Little Rock Shooting*, N.Y. Times (January 21, 2010), available at www.nytimes.com/2010/01/22/us/22littlerock.html?ref=global-home [https://perma.cc/7H4X-8S5N]. A judge may decide that a mentally ill defendant is not competent to stand trial, but this is procedural and does not address the question of criminal culpability.

[32] Diana Mehta, *Man convicted in Via terror plot spits at lawyers when court hears he's mentally ill*, CTV News (September 2, 2015), available at www.ctvnews.ca/canada/man-convicted-in-via-terror-plot-spits-at-lawyers-when-court-hears-he-s-mentally-ill-1.2544265 [https://perma.cc/PFC7-AC48].

[33] Richard Warnica, *Would-be Terrorist Chiheb Esseghaier Is Clearly Insane, But Should That Even Matter in Court?*, National Post (August 28, 2015), available at http://news.nationalpost.com/news/canada/would-be-terrorist-chiheb-esseghaier-is-clearly-insane-but-should-that-even-matter-in-court [https://perma.cc/TZJ5-N7W2].

[34] 18 U.S.C. § 17(b) (2012).

[35] See *United States v. Brawner*, 471 F. 2d 969, 983 (D.C. Cir. 1972)

[36] See generally Edward W. Said, *Covering Islam: How the Media and the Experts Determine How We See the Rest of the World* (1981); Ian Palmer, *Terrorism, Suicide Bombing, Fear and Mental Health*, 19 Int'l Rev. Psychiatry 289 (2007); Media Tenor. *Coverage of American Muslims gets worse: Muslims framed mostly as criminals. News Analysis of U.S. TV news and international business papers 2007-2013* (2013); available at http://us.mediatenor.com/en/library/speeches/260/coverage-of-american-muslims-gets-worse; Max Fischer, *It's not just Fox News: Islamophobia on*

as violent, and Islam is depicted as a religion wherein violence is an acceptable and moral form of retribution or law enforcement.[37] These messages have the effect of influencing our discernment between normal and pathological. In the examples we have reviewed thus far, it is clear that a *prima facie* evaluation of these actors' motivations seem plausible and sane, arguably as a product of how we have come to depict and caricaturize Muslims. Moreover, the nonbizarre nature of delusions and the ability of such actors to continue to function socially is largely contextualized in relationship to the little we seem to know about Muslims and the presentation of mental illness.

Once these mischaracterizations enter the social consciousness and become normalized, they in turn affect how we view abnormal thought processes. As one study by O'Connor and Vandenberg noted, "conventionality is a major factor influencing both clinicians' and non-clinicians' assessment of the pathology of religious belief."[38] The study further noted that in clinically untrained assessments of religious beliefs and psychosis, "social norms play an important role in the assessment of religious ideation."[39]

Additionally, mental health professionals may also possess their own bias in determining pathology.[40] In another study by O'Connor and Vandenberg, mental health professionals were assessed for their ability to decide whether or not a religious belief was essential to a religious tradition, and whether it would result in a threat to harm others.[41] Unfamiliar religious beliefs were considered more pathological in comparison to more mainstream beliefs ($p<0.01$); Nation of Islam had significantly higher pathology and harm ratings compared to Mormon and Catholic ($p<0.05$), with Mormon scoring higher for both ratings compared to Catholic ($p<0.05$).[42] Even when beliefs were presented without any religious affiliation, less mainstream beliefs were also evaluated as pathological. The researchers concluded that clinicians considered "beliefs associated with Nation of Islam very differently than Catholic or Mormon beliefs," potentially because of a lack of familiarity or awareness of content of these beliefs.[43] This highlights the challenge that courts have

---

cable news is out of control, Vox (January 13, 2015), available at www.vox.com/2014/10/8/6918485/the-overt-islamophobia-on-american-tv-news-is-out-of-control.

[37] Media Tenor, *Coverage of American Muslims gets worse*; Fischer, *It's not just Fox News*.

[38] Shawn O'Connor & Brian Vandenberg, *Differentiating Psychosis and Faith: The Role of Social Norms and Religious Extremism*, 13 Mental Health, Religion & Culture 171 (2010).

[39] Id.

[40] See Shimon Waldfogel & Stacey Meadows, *Religious Issues in the Capacity Evaluation*, 18 Gen. Hosp. Psychiatry 173 (1996).

[41] See generally Shawn O'Connor & Brian Vandenberg, *Psychosis or Faith? Clinicians' Assessment of Religious Beliefs*, 73 J. Consulting & Clinical Psychol. 610 (2005).

[42] Id.

[43] Id.

in distinguishing between delusion and religious belief, especially when dealing with a nonmajoritarian religion. Moreover, this arguably reflects an overcorrecting in determining psychopathology, especially in the backdrop of Islamophobia and general unfamiliarity with the accepted parameters of the Islamic belief system. These findings have serious implications in the criminal justice system, emphasizing how unfamiliarity may lead to inappropriate assessments and evaluations of belief systems.

It is not entirely unusual, then, that with the hyper-misattributions in the media of Islam and violence, crimes couched in this religious rhetoric would be evaluated differently from those couched in mainstream Christian beliefs. Therefore, we posit that a court is less likely to appropriately assess and probe psychiatric issues in cases involving Islam. In the case of Chihab Essagheir, when his attorney attempted to argue that he was mentally ill, the judge "expressed concern with the fact two 'secular' psychiatrists had come to such conclusions about an obviously religious man."[44]

Furthermore, since delusional disorder is characterized by nonovertly bizarre behavior which can subjectively be evaluated by juries, an actor's fixed and persistent religiously themed delusion will likely be overlooked and considered normal for a Muslim defendant. Actors with personality disorder will appear egosyntonic and defiantly resistant to treatment or any insinuations that they may be mentally ill. Thus, providing a positive defense of insanity among these actors will be unlikely. The tendency toward implicit bias in turn will affect how these actors are considered in assessing culpability in the courts.

CONCLUSION

Determining culpability among religious defendants may be especially challenging when their maladaptive behaviors or thoughts are related to an underlying mental issue. Appropriate consideration and deliberation is necessary to fairly assess the actor's awareness of wrongdoing and his level of responsibility in the context of the law. Because these people are found in the criminal system, courts are by necessity the sites for asking these questions. However, our criminal justice system is ill equipped to properly consider mental illness as a mitigating factor in determining individual culpability for crimes.[45] Attempts in Europe to rehabilitate young people returning from fighting with militants abroad show the potential of rehabilitation as

---

[44] Warnica, supra note 7.
[45] While the insanity defense is deficient as a mechanism for addressing mental health, sentencing and the doctrine of diminished capacity has the potential to be a more powerful site for courts to address these concerns in cases of religious extremism and violence.

opposed to criminal punishment to solve the threat posed by these individuals.[46] In the United States, halfway-houses and counseling have served as an experimental option.[47] Alternatives to addressing similar populations within the legal system need to be explored further.[48]

This chapter is largely exploratory in raising questions of bias, the psychiatric and psychological nature of individuals and groups respectively, and moral culpability and decision-making capacity of individuals in the context of the law and the insanity defense. More empirical research is necessary to illuminate the role of personal bias toward particular religious groups in affecting sentencing and forensic mental health evaluations, as well as the development of better metrics and diagnostic tools for mental illness. Additionally, work must be done to consider how the criminal justice system can better address questions of culpability in cases of religion and mental health. Finally, future work should address the unique challenges posed by Islamophobia when assessing mental illness and culpability. As our understanding of mental health evolves, so too should the law.

---

[46] See Bharati Naik, Atika Shubert, & Nick Thompson, *Denmark Offers Some Foreign Fighters Rehab Without Jail Time – But Will it Work?*, CNN (October 28, 2014, 11:25 AM), available at www.cnn.com/2014/10/28/world/europe/denmark-syria-deradicalization-program/ [https://perma.cc/Z9SX-5T38].

[47] See Dina Temple-Raston, *A Model for De-Radicalization in Minneapolis*, National Public Radio (February 19, 2015, 4:05 PM), available at www.npr.org/2015/02/19/387554218/a-model-for-de-radicalization-in-minneapolis [https://perma.cc/P77Q-5U9H].

[48] See, e.g., Hanna Pickard, *Choice, Deliberation, Violence: Mental Capacity and Criminal Responsibility in Personality Disorder*, 40 Int'l J.L. & Psychiatry 15 (2015); Hanna Pickard & Nicola Lacey, *From the Consulting Room to the Court Room: Taking the Clinical Model of Responsibility without Blame into the Legal Realm*, 33 Oxford J. Legal Stud. 1 (2013); Hanna Pickard, *Responsibility without Blame: Therapy, Philosophy, Law*, 213 Prison Service J. 10 (2014).

23

Religion as a Controlling Interference in Medical Decision Making by Minors

Jonathan F. Will

There is an ongoing debate about whether certain adolescents ought to have the right to make medical decisions for themselves. This issue becomes more complicated when the adolescent's refusal of treatment would lead to their death, and that complexity is heightened when the adolescent's decision is based on religious beliefs.[1]

In the context of adolescent refusal of life-saving medical treatment, these issues arise because of several general aspects of the law. First, the law presumes that those over the age of eighteen may make decisions for themselves, whereas those seventeen and under may not.[2] Second, parents have a constitutional right to make decisions on behalf of their minor children.[3] Third, this parental right has limits; parents are not permitted to imperil the lives of their children.[4] Finally, in situations in which a parent may not refuse life-saving medical treatment on behalf of the child, families have asserted that the decision is being made by a minor mature enough to have their own decision respected.

This chapter addresses how religion might serve as a controlling interference that prevents autonomous choice by the adolescent purporting to make the medical decision. Section 1 provides a brief background on the law and ethics of medical decision making on behalf of and by minors. Section 2 offers examples of minors refusing life-saving treatment based on asserted religious beliefs. It also highlights the potential that these minors are unduly influenced by family or religious leaders (or both), and that the current legal landscape inadequately addresses these

---

[1] Jonathan F. Will, *My God My Choice: The Mature Minor Doctrine and Adolescent Refusal of Life-Saving or Sustaining Medical Treatment Based Upon Religious Beliefs*, 22 J. Contemp. Health L. & Pol'y 233 (2006).
[2] Rhonda Gay Hartman, *Adolescent Decisional Autonomy for Medical Care: Physician Perceptions and Practices*, 8 U. Chi. L. Sch. Roundtable 87, 88 (2001).
[3] *Troxel v. Granville*, 530 U.S. 57, 65–6 (2000).
[4] *Prince v. Massachusetts*, 321 U.S. 158, 170 (1944).

concerns. Finally, Section 3 offers a path forward in assessing the voluntariness of religious refusals made by minors.

I do not suggest that all minors asserting religious objections should be forced to receive treatment against their expressed wishes. Indeed, the mature minor doctrine serves a valuable role in respecting the autonomy of certain adolescents. I conclude, however, that the presumption that those under the age of eighteen are incompetent should be preserved. And where states permit minors to rebut this presumption, medical professionals and the State itself must be vigilant in determining whether the minor's choice reflects a decision made free from controlling interference. It just so happens that this concern is often amplified in the context of religious refusals.

1. MEDICAL DECISION MAKING ON BEHALF OF AND BY MINORS

The United States Supreme Court has held that those aged seventeen and under are presumed to lack the "maturity, experience, and capacity for judgment required to make life's difficult decisions."[5] The Court elaborated, "most children, even in adolescence, simply are not able to make sound judgments concerning many decisions, including their need for medical care or treatment."[6]

Instead, in most circumstances the law empowers parents or guardians to make these decisions on behalf of minors. The justification for this framework "rests on a presumption that parents possess what a child lacks in maturity, experience, and capacity for judgment" and that "natural bonds of affection lead parents to act in the best interests of their children."[7]

Although parents are given wide latitude to make medical decisions for their minor children, there are exceptions. For instance, while parents may refuse a life-saving blood transfusion for themselves based on religious beliefs, the Supreme Court makes clear, "it does not follow they are free ... to make martyrs of their children."[8] In such a case the State would step in as *parens patriae* to order the treatment.

There are situations in which certain minors are empowered to make medical decisions without parental involvement. Many states permit minors to consent to treatment for sexually transmitted infections, drug or alcohol dependency, and physical or sexual abuse.[9] Minors may also be given decision-making authority based on

---

[5] *Parham v. J.R.*, 442 U.S. 584, 602 (1979).
[6] Id. at 603.
[7] Id. at 602.
[8] Prince, 321 U.S. at 170.
[9] Kimberly M. Mutcherson, *Whose Body is it Anyway? An Updated Model of Healthcare Decision-making Rights for Adolescents*, 14 Cornell J.L. & Pub. Pol'y 251 (2006); Rhonda Gay Hartman, *Coming of Age: Devising Legislation for Adolescent Decision-Making*, 28 Am. J.L. & Med. 409, 421–2 (2002).

social status such as graduating from high school, joining the military, getting married, or having children of their own.[10] Notably, these treatment and status exceptions do not necessarily involve a determination that the minors in question possess a greater level of maturity than their adolescent counterparts.[11]

An assessment of adolescent maturity may be utilized in the context of abortion, however. The Supreme Court has held that a minor may bypass parental consent upon a showing that either she is mature enough to make the decision for herself or, regardless of her maturity, that that abortion would be in her best interests.[12] Although the Court has never extended this judicial bypass mechanism to other areas of medical decision making, it reflects a willingness to entertain an assessment of the decision making capacity of those under the age of majority. Through the mature minor doctrine, some states have taken up this mantle.

The mature minor doctrine is founded on the premise that certain minors possess the requisite capacity to make autonomous decisions, deserving of respect as such. Those supporting the doctrine point to studies performed beginning in the late 1970s and early 1980s indicating that the competence of certain, but not all, older adolescents is on par with young adults.[13] One researcher in particular highlighted a "specific concern about the degree of parental influence acting as a coercive force" that would negate the voluntariness of the minor's decision.[14] Any assessment would necessarily be context-specific.

States adopting the mature-minor doctrine typically do not eliminate the presumption of incompetence; rather, they create a framework in which minors may rebut the presumption.[15] The Supreme Court of Tennessee provided one of the most oft-cited formulations of the standard for rebutting adolescent incompetence:

> whether a minor has the capacity to consent to medical treatment depends upon the age, ability, experience, education, training, and degree of maturity or judgment obtained by the minor, as well as upon the conduct and demeanor of the minor at the time of the incident involved. Moreover, the totality of the circumstances, the nature of the treatment and its risks or probable consequences, and the minor's ability to appreciate the risks and consequences are to be considered.[16]

---

[10] Id.
[11] Hartman, supra note 2, at 422.
[12] *Belloti v. Baird*, 443 U.S. 622, 643–4 (1979).
[13] Hartman, supra note 2, at 96–8.
[14] David G. Scherer, *The Capacities of Minors to Exercise Voluntariness in Medical Treatment Decisions*, 15 Law & Hum. Behav. 431, 434–5 (1991).
[15] Cf. Mutcherson, supra note 9, at 303 (arguing in favor of a presumption of competence for older adolescents).
[16] *Cardwell v. Bechtol*, 724 S.W. 2d 739, 748 (1987).

To be consistent with the foundational bioethical principle, minors meeting this standard ought to have their autonomous decisions respected.[17]

Embracing patient autonomy is to accept that patients are owed respect "for their ability to make reasoned choices that are their own and that others may or may not share."[18] Physicians may not share the beliefs of Jehovah's Witnesses that lead the latter to refuse life-saving blood transfusions.[19] But we acknowledge that patients are in a better position to determine what "they believe will best promote their own well-being" and that physical health is not the only value (or even the most important value) that is given consideration.[20]

Importantly, respecting autonomy presupposes that the patient's ultimate decision is made free from controlling interferences.[21] And although interference and influence are inevitable, the decisions of autonomous agents are not controlled by third parties; they "are governed by a self-conception developed over time in relation to cultural and social experiences."[22]

In practice, attributes of autonomous persons go hand-in-hand with standards of competence, with each featuring a certain level of cognitive skill and independence of judgment.[23] Adults are presumed to possess the capacity necessary to make independent decisions in line with their self-conceived notion of well-being. Therefore, adults are vested with the authority to control their medical treatment. When minors seek to rebut their presumed incompetence, however, they have the burden to establish that the asserted decision is in line with their own self-conceived sense of well-being.

Minors develop such a self-conception through the filter of experiences shaped by their parents or guardians. This includes religious upbringing, which is considered "one of the core aspects of parenting."[24] Section 2 now explores adolescent refusal of life-saving medical treatment based on the religious beliefs instilled by parents and religious leaders in the context of respecting patient autonomy.

---

[17] See, e.g., Tom L. Beauchamp & James F. Childress, *Principles of Biomedical Ethics* 99–140 (6th ed. 2009). The authors acknowledge critiques of traditional views of autonomy, most notably by feminist scholars who emphasize notions of "relational autonomy," but those critiques support rather discount the importance of ensuring that decisions are made free from the controlling interference of others.

[18] Edmund D. Pellegrino & David C. Thomasma, *The Virtues in Medical Practice* 21 (1993).

[19] Jehovah's Witnesses interpret several Biblical passages as forbidding the consumption of blood, which they view to include blood transfusions. See *The Jehovah's Witness Tradition: Religious Beliefs and Health Care Decisions* (Edwin R. Dubose et al. eds, 2001).

[20] Allen E. Buchanan & Dan W. Brock, *Deciding for Others: The Ethics of Surrogate Decision Making* 30 (1989).

[21] Ruth R. Faden & Tom L. Beauchamp, *A History and Theory of Informed Consent* 256 (1986).

[22] Will, supra note 1, at 242.

[23] Beauchamp & Childress, supra note 17, at 113–14.

[24] Emily Buss, *What Does Frieda Yoder Believe?* 2 U. Pa. J. Const. L. 53, 54 (1999); *Wisconsin v. Yoder*, 406 U.S. 205, 214 (1971).

2. RELIGIOUS REFUSALS, INFLUENCE, AND CAUSE FOR CONCERN

A. Dennis Lindberg

Dennis was diagnosed in 2007 with acute lymphocytic leukemia shortly after his fourteenth birthday. He began chemotherapy with an estimated 70–75 percent chance of survival, but both he and his legal guardian (a Jehovah's Witness) refused the blood transfusions necessary to treat the severe anemia resulting from the chemo.[25] Without the blood transfusions his condition deteriorated rapidly rendering him unconscious.

As discussed in Section 1, Dennis's guardian, his aunt, could not refuse the blood transfusions for him, given the life-threatening consequences of doing so. A Washington State judge, against the protests of his parents (who had given up custody due to prior drug abuse), determined that Dennis was mature enough to make the decision for himself.[26] Without speaking to Dennis, the judge stated, "I don't believe Dennis's decision is the result of any coercion. He is mature and understands the consequences of his decision."[27] His opinion indicated, "I don't think Dennis is trying to commit suicide. This isn't something Dennis just came upon, and he believes with the transfusion he would be unclean and unworthy."[28] Dennis died three weeks after his initial diagnosis, and less than one year after being baptized into the Jehovah's Witness faith.[29]

Despite the consequences, it is important not to discount the nature of the beliefs behind the refusal of treatment. Some Jehovah's Witnesses compare forced blood transfusions to rape[30] believing if they receive blood it will sever their relationship with the church and with God, thereby forfeiting a chance at eternal life.[31] By refusing blood transfusions, a Jehovah's Witness is expressing a view that her sense of spiritual well-being is more important than physical well-being.[32] Surely if autonomy is to be respected, we must honor such decisions regardless of whether we share the person's underlying beliefs.[33] But such respect is only due where the patient is competent and was able to make the decision free from controlling interference.

---

[25] Rita Swan, *Boy Dies After Refusing Blood*, Child, Inc., 1–2 (2007), available at http://childrenshealthcare.org/wp-content/uploads/2010/10/2007-04-fnl.pdf.
[26] *Boy Who Refused Blood Transfusion Dies*, CBS News (November 30, 2007, 8:23 AM), available at www.cbsnews.com/news/boy-who-refused-blood-transfusion-dies/.
[27] Id.
[28] Id. at 3–4.
[29] Swan, supra note 25, at 1.
[30] In re E.G., 515 N.E.2d 286, 289 (Ill. App. Ct. 1987).
[31] See *The Jehovah's Witness Tradition*, supra note 19, at 6.
[32] Pellegrino & Thomasma, supra note 18, at 58.
[33] Beauchamp & Childress, supra note 17, at 102.

While we presume both an adult's competence and ability to make decisions independently, even in states adopting the mature minor doctrine, such minors would have to prove it.[34] This analysis must take into account both the minor's general capacity to think independently and the level of influence confronted in the given circumstance. Dennis Lindberg's situation offers insight.

There is no real question that Dennis's aunt and the religious leaders surrounding his hospital bed felt that they were acting in his best spiritual interests. They argued that it was necessary to keep nonbelievers away from him so as not to test his faith.[35] The aunt described attempts by his grandmother or friends from school to reach out to him as "Satan's greatest test."[36] As his condition became more perilous, the religious circle tightened around him. How, if at all, does this inform an assessment of Dennis's status as an autonomous agent whose independent decisions are deserving of respect?

B. Religion and Independent Thinking

Certain aspects of the Jehovah's Witness faith are of particular import in this regard. Dr. Osamu Muramoto wrote a series of essays in the *Journal of Medical Ethics* outlining his concerns regarding the religion's blood policy. The church's governing body, the Watch Tower Bible and Tract Society (WTS), through its official magazine *The Watchtower*, admonishes adherents to "avoid independent thinking," and instead to abide unquestioningly to the tenets of the faith prescribed by WTS.[37] Muramoto writes that "free thought and decision-making are prohibited for JWs," and he conveys the message of a former WTS leader who wrote that independent thinking is viewed as "sinful, an indication of disloyalty to God and his appointed 'channel.'"[38] Entire websites exist where former members support each other and convey similar messages.[39]

---

[34] If an eighteen-year-old Jehovah's Witness (born and raised within the religion) refused a blood transfusion, this might raise a red flag for a treating physician. But because of the legal presumptions in place, the physician would have the burden to prove to a court that this young adult's decision was unduly influenced and should not be respected.

[35] Swan, supra note 25, at 4–7.

[36] Id. at 7.

[37] Osamu Muramoto, *Bioethics of the Refusal of Blood by Jehovah's Witnesses: Part 1. Should Bioethical Deliberation Consider Dissidents' Views?*, 24 J. Med. Ethics 223, 225 (1998) [hereinafter Muramoto Part 1].

[38] Id. at 225.

[39] See, e.g., *Ten Years After Leaving the Jehovah's Witness Religion*, JW Struggle, available at www.jwstruggle.com/2014/01/ten-years-after-leaving-the-jehovahs-witness-religion/ [https://perma.cc/9UWE-3EK2] (last visited March 6, 2015); Jehovah's Witness Recovery, www.jehovahswitnessrecovery.com/ (last visited March 6, 2015).

Sinful as it may be to adherents of the faith, independent thinking is a hallmark of autonomous agents. Adults may make an autonomous decision to forego future expression of autonomy by joining the organization (or remaining within it) and submitting to its authority – thereby calling us to honor their subsequent refusal of blood transfusions. But children of the organization do not have that luxury.

Instead, they are brought up in an environment that is not conducive to developing their skills as independent thinkers. As Kimberly Mutcherson notes, "children come to develop capacities for decision-making and for exercising liberties through guidance and practice."[40] Yet, these children may be deprived of that practice. This is particularly troubling when coupled with the potentially coercive impact adults can have on children and the sometimes perilous consequences of submitting to that influence in the context of refusing medical treatment.

For a decision to be deserving of respect as autonomous it must be free from controlling interference. Muramoto describes situations where patients agreed to blood transfusions, only to change their minds after confronting organizational pressure.[41] But external influence is unavoidable and not always problematic. After all, patients routinely consult family members before deciding on a course of treatment. It is ultimately a question of degree with influence coming in three basic flavors: persuasion, manipulation, and coercion.

C. Types of Influence

Persuasion, in the sense of appeal to reason, does not prevent autonomous authorization.[42] Coercion, on the other hand, exists where a party presents a credible threat of harm (physical, psychological, or social) that forces another person to act in a way so as to avoid that harm,[43] and is never permissible.

It is less clear when manipulation crosses the line into undue inducement, where manipulation is defined broadly to encompass any influence that goes beyond persuasion but falls short of coercion.[44] Influence becomes progressively less permissible where used to displace "a person's self-directed course of action,"[45] or where it alters a person's ability to reason about alternatives.[46] The behavior of parents and/or

---

[40] Mutcherson, supra note 9, at 289.
[41] Osamu Muramoto, *Bioethics of the Refusal of Blood by Jehovah's Witnesses: Part 3. A Proposal for a Don't Ask Don't Tell Policy*, 25 J. Med. Ethics 463, 465 (1998).
[42] Faden & Beauchamp, supra note 21, at 347.
[43] Id. at 339.
[44] Id. at 354.
[45] Beauchamp & Childress, supra note 17, at 133.
[46] Emily A. Largent & Holly Fernandez Lynch, *Paying Research Participants: Regulatory Uncertainty, Conceptual Confusion, and a Path Forward* (2016) (forthcoming, Yale J. Health L., Pol'y, & Ethics, January 2017).

religious leaders may not be coercive yet may be sufficiently manipulative – particularly given the vulnerable state of certain minors – so as to prevent an autonomous decision. This could be true even where the minor otherwise possesses the capacity to understand the treatment decision in question.

For instance, penalties for disobeying WTS teachings are severe. Such individuals are disfellowshipped; they are "spiritually cut off from the congregation; the former spiritual ties [are] completely severed," including with members of the person's family.[47] Marci Hamilton recounts the feeling of former members that "the threat of being thrown out of [the organization] and shunned from them is one powerful enough [to keep victims of abuse silent when told to do so by the organization]."[48] Such loss of family and friends was described by one individual as a "fate worse than death."[49]

One man (now 66) referred to himself as a "brainwashed boy [who] acceded to what was his father's will" when describing his own decision, at seventeen, to refuse a blood transfusion that led to the loss of his leg.[50] Another adolescent Jehovah's Witness complained of "shunning, information control, behavior control, and brainwashing."[51] These types of influences could well be tantamount to coercion or impermissible manipulation (thus preventing autonomous choice), but the analysis is necessarily context specific and dependent on the impact such behavior has on the adolescent decision maker.

Even Kent Greenawalt, who suggests that most sixteen-year-olds have developed independent thoughts about religion, acknowledges that the analysis should not focus on "most"; rather, the analysis must consider teenagers whose parents have nontraditional views regarding medical treatment who may exert impermissible influence.[52] Indeed, other commentators indicate that children living in deeply religious homes are "constrained ... by a continuing relationship of dependency and the limited opportunity [they] have enjoyed to widen [their] horizons."[53] Buchanan and Brock write that if children do not truly believe that the decision is theirs to

[47] Muramoto Part 1, supra note 37, at 224.
[48] Marci A. Hamilton, *God vs. The Gavel* 25 (2005) (internal citation omitted).
[49] Juliet Guicon & Ian Mitchell, *Medical Emergencies in Children of Orthodox Jehovah's Witness Families: Three Recent Legal Cases, Ethical Issues and Proposals for Management*, 11 Paediatric Child Health 655, 656 (2006).
[50] See Eglintonpc, *Blood. My story*, Jehovah's Witness Recovery (December 20, 2014, 5:22 AM), available at www.jehovahswitnessrecovery.com/forum/viewtopic.php?f=18&t=22178&sid=9446019c7b5f7152428 ea134a6e9b6cc.
[51] See Ska8erboi, *Thoughts of a 17 Year Old*, Facts about Jehovah's Witnesses, http://jwfacts.com/watchtower/experiences/sk8erboi.php (last visited March 7, 2015).
[52] Kent Greenawalt, *Objections in Conscience to Medical Procedures: Does Religion Make a Difference*, 2006 U. Ill. L. Rev. 799, 813–14, n.58 (2006).
[53] Margaret Brazier & Caroline Bridge, "*Coercion or Caring: Analysing Adolescent Autonomy*," in *Children, Medicine and the Law* 486 (Michael Freeman, ed. 2005).

make, "they will not resist attempts by others to impose those others' choices on them."[54] Further, children (particularly those aged fifteen and younger) often "do not assert themselves well against authority figures."[55] A minor's expressed decision to refuse life-saving treatment should not be honored unless it was reached free from controlling interference from parents, religious leaders, or otherwise.

As a Jehovah's Witness, Dennis Lindberg may well have been taught to avoid independent thinking. Given that adolescents are particularly susceptible to peer pressure, Dennis may not have been acting as maturely and independently as the judge held. In fairness, the judge was operating in the absence of well-established guidance for dealing with such situations. There are very few cases in the United States dealing with the mature minor doctrine, and far fewer in the context of religious refusals of life-saving medical treatment.[56] Even taken together, they offer little insight.

D. An Undeveloped Body of Law

It is important to acknowledge the broad legal protections offered to those asserting religious motivations in the area of Free Exercise jurisprudence.[57] Given the constitutional magnitude of protecting religious beliefs, courts have been hesitant to look behind those beliefs to determine whether impermissible harm is taking place. Hamilton writes that such courts often feel "backed into a corner" when confronting First Amendment challenges.[58] But the deference and/or sensitivity that judges give to religious beliefs should not obscure the role that the medical professionals and courts must play in this context, which is to determine whether the minor in question ought to be empowered to make the decision at hand.[59]

The most relevant case in the United States saw three levels of the judiciary in Illinois weighing in when Ernestine Gregory, aged seventeen years, six months, refused a life-saving blood transfusion. The trial court ordered the treatment, expressing concern (though without elaboration) that "outward appearances and expressed beliefs often do not reflect the individual's true wishes."[60] The intermediate appellate court showed deference to religion like that described by Hamilton. It determined that Ernestine was mature (without mention of the concerns discussed earlier regarding undue influence), and emphasized the "paramount importance of

---

[54] Buchanan & Brock, supra note 20, at 223.
[55] Id.
[56] See Will, supra note 1, at 263–83 (discussing less than a dozen relevant cases). More recent examples include In re Cassandra C., 316 Conn. 476 (Conn. 2015) and In re Hauser, No. JV-09-068, 2009 WL 1421504 (Minn. Dist. Ct. May 14, 2009)).
[57] See Hamilton, supra note 48.
[58] Id. at 26.
[59] Guicon & Mitchell, supra note 49, at 655.
[60] In re E.G., 515 N.E.2d 286, 293 (Ill. App. Ct. 1988) (McNamara, J. dissenting).

religious freedom in the history of our nation."[61] The Illinois Supreme Court officially adopted the mature-minor doctrine, but its analysis focused almost exclusively on the medical aspect of the decision, intentionally avoiding the constitutional question of whether minors like Ernestine have a First Amendment right that would support her decision to refuse medical treatment.[62]

Courts in Canada, where the age of consent is sixteen, have also handled such situations and appear more sensitive to the issues raised in this chapter. In one case involving an adolescent's refusal of a blood transfusion, the court considered the behavior of those surrounding the patient and determined that "the undue influence put [on the minor] in the last few weeks [took] away her ability to make an informed choice."[63] More specifically, the court noted that the adolescent was given incorrect information and believed that she could survive without the transfusion.[64] In another case the court determined that a thirteen-year-old Jehovah's Witness "was not capable of refusing consent because he was deeply influenced by his father, whom he always obeyed without question."[65]

More recently, the Supreme Court of Canada heard a case involving a fourteen-year-old (AC) who refused blood transfusions.[66] Although AC denied being pressured by her parents, the majority of Canada's high court expressed uncertainty as to how probing the psychiatric inquiry really was. The Court felt that where the refusal of treatment carries a high risk of death, "a careful and comprehensive evaluation of the maturity of the adolescent will necessarily have to be undertaken to determine whether his or her decision is a genuinely independent one." While the Court did not announce a formulaic approach, it suggested that judges ought to consider "whether the adolescent's views are stable and a true reflection of his or her core values and beliefs" as well as "the potential impact of the adolescent's lifestyle, family relationships and broader social affiliations on his or her ability to exercise independent judgment."[67] This is a step in the right direction, and courts in the United States would be wise to follow a similar path.

3. IDENTIFYING NONCONTROLLED DECISIONS AND SUBSTANTIAL AUTONOMY: A PATH FORWARD

It will undoubtedly be difficult to determine whether a given minor's decision has been unduly influenced. Faden and Beauchamp, while admitting to no definitive

---

[61] Id. at 290.
[62] In re E.G., 549 N.E.2d 322, 327–8 (Ill. 1989).
[63] Guicon & Mitchell, supra note 49, at 657.
[64] Id.
[65] Re Dueck (1999), 171 D.L.R. 4th 761 (Can. Sask. Q.B.).
[66] A.C. v. Manitoba (Director of Child and Family), [2009] 2 S.C.R. 181 (Can.).
[67] Id. at par. 96.

criteria for making the assessment, speak of impermissible influences as those that render "an action less than substantially noncontrolled and therefore outside the territory of influences compatible with substantially autonomous acts."[68] Perfect voluntariness is an unrealistic ideal, but the question is whether the minor's decision is "voluntary enough to be protected from paternalistic interferences."[69]

Relying heavily on the work of Joel Feinberg, Buchanan and Brock suggest that those assessing the voluntariness with which a decision is made be mindful of coercion, duress, or even more subtle manipulation.[70] The task is to distinguish influences that are "compatible with substantial autonomy from influences that are not,"[71] and in many cases it will not be obvious; it will "require experienced judgment and extensive knowledge of the situation" and of the minor in question.[72] To that end, emergency situations would need to be handled differently than nonemergencies.

Where analysis cannot be performed due to emergent circumstances, life-saving treatment should be given to stabilize the minor even if the parents convey that the minor had previously expressed views regarding the refusal of treatment. Jehovah's Witness minors may carry cards refusing emergency blood transfusions, but such cards should be disregarded.

In nonemergent circumstances medical professionals should be vigilant in assessing whether the risk of undue influence is present. Because individuals respond differently to external stimuli, each situation demands careful analysis of the extent to which the minor is capable of resisting such influence and remaining sufficiently independent. As with determining competency more generally, assessing the independence with which a decision is made "is in essence a commonsense judgment about the adequacy of the patient's decision-making abilities for the decision task at hand."[73]

Those making the assessment should do so without giving deference to the religious nature of the decision, and without giving undue weight to the parents' agreement with the minor's purported decision. To avoid improper influence from the medical professionals themselves, a neutral party (psychiatrist, social worker, or ethics consultant) should consult with the minor privately, in the absence of family members and religious leaders.[74] If the parents or religious leaders resist, judicial intervention may be necessary.

---

[68] Faden & Beauchamp, supra note 21, at 259.
[69] Buchanan & Brock, supra note 20, at 43.
[70] Id. at 42–3.
[71] Faden & Beauchamp, supra note 21, at 337.
[72] Id. at 373.
[73] Buchanan & Brock, supra note 20, at 81–2.
[74] Osamu Muramoto, *Bioethics of the Refusal of Blood by Jehovah's Witnesses: Part 2. A Novel Approach Based on Rational Non-Interventional Paternalism*, 24 J. Med. Ethics 295, 298 (1998) [hereinafter Muramoto Part 2].

The consultant should be cognizant of the stressful nature of the situation and that it is not sufficient to take the minors' words at face value. A single question, such as "do you feel pressured," would not be sufficient, as the minor may not fully appreciate the forms in which undue influence might come. During the consultation(s) minors should be given the opportunity to fully discuss how they came to their decision.

Consultants should attempt to identify any sources of stress and influence and should be particularly aware of the family and religious dynamics. To protect against information manipulation, such as where the risks of the underlying condition are minimized or the risks associated with treatment are exaggerated, it may be appropriate to ask the minors what types of information they have been exposed to, and to clarify any inaccuracies. While such clarifications may persuade the minor by appeal to reason, consultants and medical professionals should be careful to avoid manipulation or coercion of their own.

Two questions remain: how voluntary does the given decision need to be; and how certain do the consultants (or judges if it comes to that) need to be in their assessment that a given minor's decision to refuse life-saving treatment was voluntary. It should be clear that no test for assessing voluntariness will be perfect, and those making assessments will never know for sure whether they got it right.

Borrowing from the context of competency assessments, we might say that the level of voluntariness necessary to make the decision rises with the risk associated with it.[75] On this account, a higher level of voluntariness would be required to refuse life-saving treatment (risk of death), as compared to refusing a flu shot. Beauchamp and Childress counter that the level of risk is only relevant to the question of what evidentiary standard is applied.[76]

The difference is not semantic. Given that influence cannot be removed completely, the level of voluntariness required speaks to what amount of influence may be exerted over the decision maker while remaining compatible with substantial autonomy. The higher the risk, the less influence we ought to permit. An evidentiary standard, on the other hand, speaks to how confident we need to be in our voluntariness assessment, but the level of risk associated with the decision is still relevant.[77]

The choice of evidentiary standard reflects an attempt to allocate the risk of error in the most defensible way. Where the risk of getting it wrong is death, we ought to impose the heightened, clear and convincing evidence standard so as "to adjust the risk of error to favor the less perilous result."[78] This suggests that both a high level

---

[75] Buchanan & Brock, supra note 20, at 55.
[76] Beauchamp & Childress, supra note 17, at 117.
[77] Id.
[78] Conservatorship of Wendland, 28 P.3d 151, 170 (Cal. 2001); see also *Cruzan v. Director, Missouri Department of Health*, 497 U.S. 261, 282–3 (1990). It is worth raising, though space prevents full

of voluntariness and a heightened evidentiary standard should be applied when minors seek to refuse life-saving medical treatment based on their asserted religious beliefs. This is consistent with states like Illinois that require clear and convincing evidence to establish a minor's maturity more generally.[79]

CONCLUSION

In situations in which parents are not permitted to refuse life-saving medical treatment on behalf of their older children, the argument is sometimes made that it is, in fact, the minor's own decision. Certain jurisdictions permit such minors to rebut the presumption of incompetence, which reflects the view that some minors have sufficient capacity to make autonomous decisions regarding their medical care. But the existing case law and literature pay insufficient attention to the extent to which minors may be impermissibly influenced when making the asserted decision.

Refusals of life-saving blood transfusions by Jehovah's Witnesses were used in this chapter as a vehicle to highlight the problem, but these issues are implicated in any situation where third parties serve as a controlling interference that prevents independent thinking by the minor.[80] There is no question that forcing individuals to undergo treatment against their asserted wishes is not ideal. It is also unfortunate that children might need to be separated from their parents in order to fully assess the independence of the decisions being made. But the alternative – allowing minors to die based on decisions that are not truly their own – seems even more so.

---

exploration here, that imposition of this heightened standard, with its goal of erring on the side of preserving life, itself reflects a societal judgment regarding the merits of Jehovah's Witness beliefs. After all, Witnesses would argue that the more perilous result is eternal damnation. Indeed, this serves as a justification in favor of presuming competence when adult Jehovah's Witnesses refuse blood transfusions.

[79] In re E.G., 549 N.E.2d 322, 326–7 (1989).
[80] Muramoto Part 2, supra note 74, at 300. These issues could also be implicated in the nonminor context such as where a husband attempts to influence the decision of his wife regarding a blood transfusion. But again, when dealing with adult decision makers, competence is presumed and the person challenging competence would have the burden to rebut the presumption.

PART VIII

Religion and Reproductive Health Care

Introduction

Mindy Jane Roseman

In the United States, rights to privacy require state and federal authorities to respect individuals' decision making surrounding when, whether, or if at all to have children, and to some extent refrain from obstructing acts following on those decisions. Precisely because decisions about family formation are so personal, the internal faith-based beliefs that may guide such decision making also garner state respect as an aspect of free exercise of religion. The chapters in Part VIII map out the terrain muddled by these competing state obligations.

First, B. Jessie Hill considers religious motivation in decision making around contraception, and in particular refusals of employers to provide the full range of birth control mandated by the Affordable Care Act. Next, I. Glenn Cohen examines four matters where access to assisted reproductive technology may be impeded by the religious beliefs of service providers and others. And finally, Dov Fox takes up the issue of the status of products of conception – zygote, embryo, or fetus.

Roiling beneath much of the legal debate concerning privacy, religion, and reproductive health and rights and is the definition of when life begins. Who counts as a person for the purposes of the enjoyment and protection of civil and constitutional rights? The United States Supreme Court in *Roe v. Wade* chose not to speculate about "this most sensitive and difficult question."[1] Is such a definition a matter for reason, science and/or faith? All three chapters in this part engage with this issue.

Both Fox and Cohen squarely consider the consequences. Fox invitingly finds no US constitutional infirmity in a state choosing to respect "unborn life" insofar as the Establishment Clause goes. "This is not to say such laws do not have other constitutional problems; just that religion is not one," he explains. This is because Fox construes the Establishment clause to forbid state promotion or entanglement with transcendental aspects of religion, but not with those aspects that religion shares with secular ethics, such as living a good life. In other words, a law would have to express

---

[1] *Roe v. Wade*, 410 U.S. 113, 160 (1973).

more transcendent than secular purpose for it to run afoul of the Establishment Clause. Respecting potential life is as much a part of common secular values as it is divine reverence; thus, according to Fox, it passes Establishment Clause muster.

Cohen, while not directly addressing Establishment Clause jurisprudence, does analyze the legal arguments bolstering the embryo adoption and personhood movements, as well as pre-embryo disposition cases. He views claims made for the personhood status of zygotes and embryos as fundamentally religious in nature. Unlike Fox, who attends to the ideology underlying personhood, Cohen is concerned with the political strategy animating legislative attempts to define life, or impute the status of a child on an embryo or pre-embryo for adoption purposes. He sees these legal maneuvers as part of an anti-abortion agenda, inspired, ironically, by Justice Blackmun's throw-away line in *Roe v. Wade*, that is, that recognition of a fetal right to life vitiates the abortion right. Cohen does not think any claims for personhood will outweigh the right to be free from compelled gestation. At the very least, as a practical matter, religious encroachments into reproductive decision making, in Cohen's analysis, can be reasonably dodged and quelled.

Hill's chapter, with its focus on religious refusals to provide goods and services, does not engage directly with the question of when life begins. The individuals and employers who object to providing insurance coverage for certain forms of contraception do, however, and they do so on religious grounds. They believe, as a tenet of their faith, that life begins at conception and that certain oral contraceptives act as abortifacients. This is the familiar terrain of *Hobby Lobby* and its progeny. Hill re-examines the deference and accommodation government must grant to the free exercise of religion, implicitly asking how far the government can go in regulating our thoughts, or in compelling us to act against our beliefs. She concludes that whatever duty the government owes to respect and protect religious belief and exercise, the "government cannot commandeer the private decision making process around contraception, abortion, and fertility." Privacy jurisprudence permits the government to facilitate deliberation on, inform, perhaps persuade, and even favor certain outcomes. But government cannot compel any resultant decision. Hill, therefore, argues that accommodations for religious beliefs do unconstitutionally burden privacy and reproductive self determination when they selectively exempt employers from providing insurance coverage: giving them a pass when oral contraceptives and IUDs are prescribed for the purposes of family planning, but not when they are prescribed for medical uses (e.g., acne). Hill views such legislative tailoring to intrude on a woman's private reproductive decision making and in effect dictate to her what reasons are worthy. This is tantamount to coercion, not persuasion.[2]

---

[2] A blanket exemption, she notes, would be less repugnant to the woman's decision making, but perversely, would make it more difficult for her to obtain subsidized contraception.

One area that the chapters touch on only briefly, but that is ripe for further exploration, is the issue of discrimination. Cohen in his discussion of the refusal to provide assisted reproductive technology (ART) services to gay couples and single women suggests that recourse to arguments from faith may be pre-textual. Cohen sees in such refusals blatant discrimination against the desire to form a non-heteronormative family. The one case where a provider denied ART services to a gay couple found the action to be discrimination on the basis of sexual orientation. Fox suggests that discriminatory effects compromising women's rights to equality and liberty would result should the personhood status of zygotes, embryos, and fetuses be recognized. Hill raises the specter of government regulation of intimate decision making beyond insurance subsidies for contraception; it looms in legislation banning abortions for reasons of sex selection or fetal anomaly (ostensibly to prevent discrimination on the basis of sex and disability), opening the door to possible other incursions. This is not to say that assertions of faith are insincere; it does, however, suggest that more thought might be given to the standard of judicial review.

All three chapters in this part tend towards optimism in terms of preserving a right to privacy large enough to encompass women's (and men's) rights to decide on when, whether, if, and how many children to have; neither accessing contraception or abortion (up to some point in fetal development) seems to be in jeopardy. There may be more cause for concern. The organized Catholic and evangelical Christian churches have been staunchly opposed to the constitutional morality that infuses reproductive and sexual self-determination. And as all the authors admit, there are good arguments that would deny same-sex couples access to ART, would exempt employers from covering insurance costs for contraception, and would permit a personhood law or constitutional amendment. The terrain linking religion and reproductive health may be well-trodden, but it is far from being well-settled.

24

Regulating Reasons

Governmental Regulation of Private Deliberation in Reproductive Decision Making

B. Jessie Hill

The law often has something to say about what constitutes a legally acceptable reason for certain conduct. Indeed, sometimes the motivation for a person's actions can make the difference between legality and illegality. For example, a hate crime is one that is committed because of illicit bias; a crime that is not committed out of such a motivation cannot constitute a hate crime. Similarly, under the Religious Freedom Restoration Act (RFRA) and the Religious Land Use and Institutionalized Persons Act (RLUIPA), actions that are taken for religious reasons are specially protected, whereas the same actions could be outlawed when driven by secular reasons.

But constitutional law has marked some areas off-limits for governmental regulation of individual decision making. For example, at the same time that religious reasons are valorized, they are also protected by a zone of noninterference, as courts largely defer to individuals on the content of their beliefs. And, perhaps most notably, in recognizing a right to reproductive privacy, the Supreme Court has suggested that the government cannot commandeer the private decision-making process around contraception, abortion, and fertility. Indeed, as Professor Carol Sanger has argued, the right to noninterference in reproductive decision making arguably implies a right to noninterference with the decision making *process* as well.[1] Similarly, parents may be said to enjoy a degree of governmental deference to their decision-making processes, because the constitutional right of parents to direct the upbringing of their children forbids courts from substituting their understanding of the child's best interests for the parents'.[2] Thus, in the absence of abuse or neglect, parents are free to make important decisions for their children based on almost any reasoning whatsoever.

---

[1] Carol Sanger, *Seeing and Believing: Mandatory Ultrasound and the Path to a Protected Choice*, 56 UCLA L. Rev. 351, 387 (2008).
[2] *Troxel v. Granville*, 530 U.S. 57, 72–3 (2000) (plurality opinion).

In this chapter, I briefly consider the legal and constitutional significance of religious motivations in private decision making in the context of reproductive health care. In particular, this chapter considers two fundamental questions. First, under current constitutional doctrine, may the government regulate the *reasons* for certain reproductive health care decisions, given that reproductive health care decision making is protected by a constitutional privacy right? This question is raised, for example, by recent legislative attempts in the United States to regulate decision making in the abortion context by declaring certain reasons for terminating a pregnancy – for example, fetal anomaly or sex selection – to be criminal. After concluding that the government may not declare that certain reasons for engaging in constitutionally protected conduct are legally inappropriate, this chapter then asks the second question: what are the implications of this private decision making right when it conflicts with another's right to protection for religiously motivated decisions? For example, may states empower employers to selectively deny contraceptives coverage for employees based on the reason for the contraceptive use? This chapter concludes that the right to private decision making, due to its more significant constitutional standing, should trump religious rights when they conflict.

1. LAW'S REGULATION OF PRIVATE DECISION MAKING

Sometimes legal consequences turn on the reasons why an individual engages in certain conduct. On the most basic level, criminal prohibitions generally specify a particular state of mind (mens rea) that is required for liability to attach. But the requirement of a particular level of intent, which is ubiquitous in law, is slightly different from a legal condition that requires government actors to examine a private individual's reasons or motivations for acting before deciding whether a particular consequence attaches. The latter sort of legal condition is less common.

But it is not unheard of. For example, the Religious Freedom Restoration Act (RFRA) privileges religious motivations for engaging in particular conduct (or refusing to engage in particular conduct) over nonreligious reasons, providing that the federal government must satisfy strict scrutiny when its laws substantially burden religious exercise.[3] This means that conduct such as ingesting a controlled substance may be permissible when it is engaged in for religious reasons, but not when it is done for secular reasons.[4] Thus, where RFRA (or a similar law) applies, religious motivations might make otherwise-illicit conduct legal.

---

[3] 42 U.S.C. § 2000bb-1. The federal RFRA binds only the federal government; 21 states also have laws analogous to RFRA that bind state and local governments. See National Conference of State Legislatures, *State Religious Freedom Restoration Acts*, available at www.ncsl.org/research/civil-and-criminal-justice/2016-state-religious-freedom-restoration-act-legislation.aspx (last visited March 13, 2017) [https://perma.cc/46FS-57ZE] (listing state religious freedom laws enacted as of 2015).

[4] See, e.g., *Gonzales v. O Centro Espírita Beneficente União do Vegetal*, 546 U.S. 418 (2006).

In other contexts, by contrast, the government is specifically disabled from distinguishing between licit and illicit reasons for particular conduct. As this section argues, the constitutional right to privacy is generally understood to encompass a right to autonomous decision making – that is, a right to make certain personal, private decisions without government interference as to the reasons such decisions were made. This prohibition on government regulation of private reasons, though not often referenced explicitly by courts, may be inferred from the existence of a domain of decision making autonomy. In some cases, an individual's right to private decision making may clash with another's right to act in particular ways for religious reasons under RFRA and related laws. This potential conflict and its resolution are discussed further in Section 2.

A. The Constitutional Privacy Right

Since *Griswold v. Connecticut*,[5] the right to make reproductive health care decisions has been framed in terms of a right to privacy. While privacy is a protean concept, in the Fourteenth Amendment substantive due process context, it has largely included both a sense of spatial sanctity and decision-making autonomy.[6] The latter aspect of privacy most directly implicates the government's ability to influence, and pass judgment on, the reasons on which individuals rely for their most important and intimate decisions. *Roe v. Wade*, for example, focused on the woman's "decision," her "choice," and her right to engage in "consultation" with her physician.[7] And as the joint opinion in *Planned Parenthood v. Casey* famously declared, "At the heart of liberty is the right to define one's own concept of existence, of meaning, of the universe, and of the mystery of human life. Beliefs about these matters could not define the attributes of personhood were they formed under compulsion of the State."[8] This language not only highlights the protected nature of the decision-making process but also suggests, by using transcendental terminology, that the reasoning process itself may draw upon religious or spiritual beliefs. Thus, although the "undue burden" standard established by *Casey* for reviewing abortion restrictions seemingly focuses primarily on the outcome of the challenged regulation – whether it places a "substantial obstacle" in the woman's path and prevents her from accessing an abortion that she has chosen – it is nonetheless embedded in a broader privacy framework that connects it to the concept of decisional autonomy.[9]

[5] 381 U.S. 479 (1965).
[6] *Id.* at 485 ("Would we allow the police to search the sacred precincts of marital bedrooms for telltale signs of the use of contraceptives?"); *Planned Parenthood of Se. Pennsylvania v. Casey*, 505 U.S. 833, 851 (1992).
[7] *Roe v. Wade*, 410 U.S. 113, 153 (1973).
[8] *Casey*, 505 U.S. at 851.
[9] *Casey*, 505 U.S. at 877–8.

Given this decisional autonomy framework, the possibility that the government might regulate the reasons for which an abortion may be obtained contradicts *Roe*'s reasoning, as well as *Casey*'s. As Jaime King points out, the Supreme Court's reasoning in *Roe* and *Casey* emphasized the burdens of unwanted pregnancy as the rationale for protecting reproductive choice, but at no point did the Court suggest that only certain reasons for not wanting the pregnancy were valid ones.[10] Thus, if we are relying on a decisional privacy theory for protecting abortion rights, "[a] woman's thought process surrounding the decision of whether and when to have a child, with whom, and for what reasons should not be dissected by the government into valid and invalid reasons once they have entered her mind."[11]

At the same time, it is worth noting that *Roe* rejected the proposition that a woman "is entitled to terminate her pregnancy at whatever time, in whatever way, and *for whatever reason* she alone chooses."[12] Another complicating fact is that the Supreme Court has emphasized that the government has a role to play in ensuring that the woman's decision is well-informed, and beyond that, has gone so far as to insist that the state can try to persuade the woman to choose childbirth over abortion.[13] This suggests that the Supreme Court believes the state's role may extend beyond merely giving the woman factual information to actually putting a thumb on the scale of her deliberations. Indeed, recent cases, which have by and large upheld ideological "informed consent" requirements, may be seen to confirm this conclusion.[14] Finally, in relation to reason-based abortion prohibitions, one might also argue that the state has interests in prohibiting abortion for particular reasons that override the

---

[10] Jaime Staples King, *Not This Child: Constitutional Questions in Regulating Noninvasive Prenatal Genetic Diagnosis and Selective Abortion*, 60 UCLA L. Rev. 2, 33–4 (2012); see also Rosamund Scott, *Prenatal Screening, Autonomy and Reasons: The Relationship Between the Law of Abortion and Wrongful Birth*, 11 Med. L. Rev. 265, 277–8 (2003). In countries outside the United States where abortion is not governed by a privacy-rights framework, governmental regulation based on reasons for which an abortion is sought is much more prevalent. See generally Scott, supra, at 266–8 (contrasting U.S. and English abortion law); Daniela Reitz & Gerd Richter, *Current Changes in German Abortion Law*, 19 Cambridge Q. Healthcare Ethics 334, 334–5 (2010) (discussing German abortion law).

[11] King, supra note 10, at 33.

[12] *Roe v. Wade*, 410 U.S. 113, 153 (1973). Moreover, the Court itself treated certain reasons as special in *Roe* when it insisted that post-viability abortions must be available only to protect the life or health of the pregnant woman. Id. at 164–5. However, one might explain this reason-based regulation of abortion by suggesting that the "health exception" for postviability abortions applies in a context where the woman no longer has a real privacy right, because the state's interest in fetal life is compelling after viability. The exception is arguably motivated, instead, by concerns about the woman's right to bodily integrity – avoiding state-imposed harms to her health – rather than the woman's privacy right to make reproductive decisions.

[13] *Casey*, 505 U.S. at 878.

[14] See, e.g., *Texas Med. Providers Performing Abortion Servs. v. Lakey*, 667 F.3d 570, 573 (5th Cir. 2012); *Planned Parenthood v. Rounds*, 653 F.3d 662 (8th Cir. 2011). But see *Stuart v. Camnitz*, 774 F.3d 238 (4th Cir. 2014).

woman's right to choose, such as in protecting the integrity of the medical profession and of potential life by forbidding "eugenic" abortions that symbolically degrade disabled individuals or send the message that one gender is to be preferred to another.[15]

Nonetheless, much as the Supreme Court may appear to accept a role for the state in encouraging deliberation, the structure and logic of the decisional privacy right run counter to the notion that the government may actually *control* or *commandeer* the individual's reasoning process. The fact that religious or spiritual beliefs may form part of the reasoning process, as implied by *Casey*, may further strengthen the notion that the deliberation itself must be immune from governmental interference, because, as discussed below, religious beliefs are likewise specially immunized from legal control. There is, therefore, a difference between deliberation-forcing mechanisms, such as reasonable informed consent requirements, and coercion, such as taking abortion off-limits altogether when it is sought for certain reasons. And although courts have sometimes upheld even ideological speech requirements, such laws do not cross the line into directing the result or the path of the woman's deliberations, as opposed to seeking to influence them.[16]

This logic places on questionable constitutional ground the recent spate of laws, proposed and enacted, forbidding abortions for particular reasons, such as sex selection or fetal anomaly. Several states have recently adopted such reason-based bans on abortion, raising the specter of further reason-based regulation of reproductive health decisions in the future.[17] Because they not only regulate conduct protected by the constitutional right to privacy but also the deliberative process, these laws should be found unconstitutional under the *Roe-Casey* line of cases.

Of course, the reproductive health care context is not the only one in which this decision-making privacy right is relevant. It also extends to other familial privacy contexts, such as the right of parents to direct the upbringing of their children. In *Troxel v. Granville*, for example, the Supreme Court expressed strong disapproval of a Washington statute that allowed trial courts to substitute their judgment as to a child's best interests for the parent's in visitation matters. As the Court explained, "the Due Process Clause does not permit a State to infringe on the fundamental right of parents to make child rearing decisions simply because a state judge believes a 'better' decision could be made"; the courts do not have authority to scrutinize a fit parent's decision-making process so closely.[18]

---

[15] Rachel Rebouché, *Testing Sex*, 49 U. Rich. L. Rev. 519, 565–8 (2015).

[16] See, e.g., *Planned Parenthood Minn. v. Rounds*, 530 F.3d 724, 735–6 (8th Cir. 2008) (upholding a requirement that a physician inform a woman seeking an abortion "[t]hat the abortion will terminate the life of a whole, separate, unique, living human being").

[17] See, e.g., *Complaint, Planned Parenthood of Ind. & Ky. v. Comm'r, Indiana State Dep't of Health*, No. 15-CV-763 (S.D. Ind. April 7, 2016) (challenging a 2016 Indiana law banning abortion based on a diagnosis of fetal disability).

[18] *Troxel v. Granville*, 530 U.S. 57, 72–3 (2000).

Religious beliefs, too, appear to be protected by a sort of privacy right, which – as in the context of reproductive decision making – prevents the government from interfering in the deliberative process. In *Burwell v. Hobby Lobby*, the Supreme Court took an extremely deferential stance toward the plaintiffs' beliefs, in that it declined to examine closely the connection between the asserted religious belief – that abortion and complicity in abortion are morally wrong – and the conduct the plaintiffs wished to avoid – providing their employees with health care coverage that included contraceptives that the plaintiffs characterized as abortifacients.[19] Likewise, when applying the "ministerial exception," which protects religious organizations from liability in certain hiring and firing decisions and which is required by the Free Exercise and Establishment Clauses of the First Amendment, courts may not examine the actual reason for the employment decision to determine whether it is in fact religious, or whether it is a pretext for discrimination.[20] Thus, under both RFRA and the constitutionally grounded ministerial exception, there is a zone of privacy around religious deliberation, grounded at least in part in the First Amendment, similar to the zone of privacy that protects familial and reproductive decision making under the Fourteenth Amendment.

B. Statutory and Constitutional Protection for Religious Reasons

An extensive literature discusses whether religious reasons should be given preference over non religious reasons for particular conduct.[21] Largely, the debate centers on the problem of religious exemptions. For example, should individuals who wish to avoid military service based on their religious scruples be entitled to an exemption, while individuals who object to military service based on secular beliefs, or even based on fear of losing their lives, are not exempt? This question has been understood to have implications for both the Establishment Clause and Free Exercise Clause.[22]

The Supreme Court appeared to reject the privileging of religious reasons for conduct in *Employment Division v. Smith*, holding that no exemption is required from neutral, generally applicable laws, even when the individual's motive for engaging in prohibited conduct is religious.[23] As explained in this volume's Introduction, *Smith*'s

---

[19] *Burwell v. Hobby Lobby*, 134 S. Ct. 2751, 2778–9 (2014).
[20] *Hosanna-Tabor Evangelical Lutheran Church & Sch. v. E.E.O.C.*, 132 S. Ct. 694, 709 (2012).
[21] See, e.g., Christopher Lund, Religion Is Special Enough, __ Va. L. Rev. __ (forthcoming 2017); Micah Schwartzman, *What If Religion Is Not Special?*, 79 U. Chi. L. Rev. 1351, 1355 (2012); Andrew Koppelman, *How Shall I Praise Thee? Brian Leiter on Respect for Religion*, 47 San Diego L. Rev. 961, 965 (2010).
[22] See, e.g., Christopher L. Eisgruber and Lawrence G. Sager, *Religious Freedom and the Constitution* 51–77 (2007).
[23] 494 U.S. 872 (1990).

holding deviated from the prior approach to the Free Exercise Clause, according to which religious motivations were specially privileged, requiring the government either to satisfy strict scrutiny or to exempt religiously motivated conduct from generally applicable laws if they were sufficiently burdensome to individuals' religious exercise. After *Smith*, as far as the Constitution is concerned, religious reasons are on essentially the same plane as secular reasons, including conscientious reasons, for engaging in or refusing to engage in particular conduct. However, although the Court in *Smith* rejected the constitutional basis for privileging religious motivations over secular ones, it left the door open for legislatures to do so. In fact, Justice Scalia's majority opinion emphasized that legislatures could decide to grant religiously based exemptions and, most likely, would do so in many cases.[24] The Court's rejection of the requested religious exemption in *Smith* indicated only that the Free Exercise Clause of the Constitution did not *require* a religious exemption.

Outside the constitutional context, however, both the federal Religious Freedom Restoration Act and its state-law analogs still prioritize religious reasons over secular ones. If a generally applicable law substantially burdens an individual's or organization's religious exercise without being necessary to advance a compelling government interest, the law mandates an exemption. Thus, in *Burwell v. Hobby Lobby*, the Hobby Lobby corporation's religiously motivated objection to certain contraceptive drugs entitled it to an exemption from the federal mandate requiring employers to provide insurance coverage for those drugs – an exemption that Hobby Lobby could not have claimed if it had objected on purely secular grounds.[25]

C. Summary: When May the Government Regulate Reasons?

Some conclusions can now be drawn about when, and to what extent, the government may regulate the reasons for engaging in particular conduct. First, though there is no federal constitutional imperative to do so, the government may *choose* to privilege religious reasons over nonreligious reasons for engaging in conduct that is otherwise prohibited (or refusing to engage in conduct that is otherwise required). Although deciding to privilege religious over nonreligious reasons seems to invite governmental inquiry into the nature of the individual's religious beliefs (in order to determine whether the special legal dispensation applies), that inquiry is simultaneously limited by a general attitude of deference toward religious reasoning. The government may not examine religious reasoning processes too closely or distinguish between religious and secular reasons in ways that a religious institution or individual would not. This deference itself derives, at least in part, from

[24] Id. at 890.
[25] Hobby Lobby, 134 S. Ct. at 2759.

constitutional concerns, based either in the right to privacy or in the religion clauses of the Constitution.[26]

Second, in a domain of activity that is protected by a constitutional privacy right – such as reproductive decision making and parental decision making – the government may act to force deliberation and *perhaps* may insert its own views into the deliberative process, to some extent. The limits on its ability to do the latter are still somewhat unclear. It generally may not, however, distinguish between valid and invalid reasons in a way that coerces individual choice, in the absence of a compelling interest. Indeed, though the contours of the substantive due process right to privacy are unclear, the ability to deliberate and make decisions without coercive governmental judgments as to what are appropriate and inappropriate reasons is surely at the core of the right.

2. THE CONFLICT BETWEEN RELIGIOUS RIGHTS AND PRIVACY RIGHTS: THE CASE OF REASON-BASED CONTRACEPTION REGULATIONS

One person's right to privacy with respect to the deliberative process has the potential to conflict with another person's right to act based on religious motivations. In such cases, because privacy rights enjoy greater constitutional status, they should prevail. This section will give a brief illustration of this conflict and explain how it ought to be resolved, based on an interpretation of existing doctrine. Importantly, the extant cases on privacy and the religion clauses align with this framework and need not be extended in order to support it.

One potential area of conflict is between employees who wish to use employer-subsidized contraception for family planning purposes and employers who have religious objections to allowing their employees to access contraception for this reason, but not for other reasons, such as to treat a medical condition. In both cases, the law both governs the parties' respective entitlements and creates the potential for a conflict between individual rights to privacy and to religious freedom.

About half of the states require insurers in the state to provide coverage for contraceptives.[27] These state-law contraceptive coverage mandates are separate from the regulation passed during the Obama Administration requiring contraceptive

---

[26] Cf. Seana Valentine Shiffrin, *What Is Really Wrong with Compelled Association?*, 99 Nw. U. L. Rev. 839 (2005).
[27] National Conference of State Legislatures, *Insurance Coverage for Contraception Laws*, available at www.ncsl.org/research/health/insurance-coverage-for-contraception-state-laws.aspx (last visited March 13, 2017) (stating that at least 26 states require insurers to cover contraception if they cover other prescription drugs) [https://perma.cc/22QK-LEFK].

coverage under the Affordable Care Act, and they apply independently of it.[28] There are some differences between the state laws and the Obama era federal mandate; for example, the state laws do not generally exempt employers with fewer than fifty employees or grandfathered plans. Perhaps more importantly, because these mandates are enforced by state governments rather than the federal government, the federal RFRA – construed in *Hobby Lobby* to require an accommodation for employers that object on religious grounds – does not apply to them.[29] Nonetheless, in many of these states, religious employers may still be able to access insurance plans without contraceptive coverage, either because the state contraceptive coverage laws also have religious exemptions written into them, or because those exceptions are available via state RFRA analogs.

But there is yet another twist. In a handful of states, employers may opt out of providing insurance coverage of contraceptives for contraceptive purposes but not for therapeutic purposes.[30] For example, Arizona law, which requires insurers to provide contraceptive coverage if they cover other prescription drugs, also provides that "a religiously affiliated employer may require that the corporation provide a contract without coverage for [contraceptives]."[31] However, it goes on to specify that the insurance policy "shall not exclude coverage for prescription contraceptive methods ordered by a health care provider with prescriptive authority for medical indications other than for contraceptive, abortifacient, abortion or sterilization purposes."[32] Similarly, North Carolina law allows religious employers to offer plans without contraceptive coverage but does not exempt them from covering "prescription drugs ordered by a health care provider with prescriptive authority for reasons other than contraceptive purposes, or for prescription contraception that is necessary to preserve the life or health of a person covered under the plan."[33] Presumably, these sorts of provisos would cover women who seek contraceptive drugs for purposes of avoiding or curing particular medical conditions (such as certain skin conditions or menstrual disorders) as well as women who need contraception because pregnancy would be life-threatening or harmful to their health. At least in the latter scenario, it seems clear that such provisos distinguish between valid and invalid reasons for the same reproductive conduct.

---

[28] Kara Loewentheil, *The Satanic Temple, Scott Walker, and Contraception: A Partial Account of Hobby Lobby's Implications for State Law*, 9 Harv. L. & Pol'y Rev. 89, 113 (2015).

[29] For a thorough discussion of state contraceptive coverage laws and their continuing importance after *Hobby Lobby*, see Loewentheil, supra note 28.

[30] See, e.g., Ariz. Rev. Stat. §§20–826(Z); Cal. Health & Safety Code § 1367.25(d); Conn. Gen. Stat. Ann. § 38a-503e(d); N.C. Gen. Stat. Ann. § 58-3-178(e). A more complete listing of such statutes may be found in Loewentheil, supra note 72, at 103 n.68.

[31] Ariz. Rev. Stat. Ann. § 20–826(Y)-(Z).

[32] Ariz. Rev. Stat. Ann. § 20–826(Z).

[33] N.C. Gen. Stat. Ann. § 58-3-178(e).

While presumably intended to ensure that women's physical health is protected while safeguarding the religious freedom of employers, such provisions nonetheless have the effect of regulating the reasons for which women may engage in constitutionally protected conduct. Women working for religious employers who take advantage of these exceptions may access covered contraception if it is necessary to avoid harm to their health but not if they wish to engage in family planning. According to the framework outlined here, laws that distinguish between acceptable and unacceptable reasons for choosing contraception would be unconstitutional. Similarly to the selective abortion bans discussed above, they allow the employer to dictate the terms of the woman's reproductive decision, interfering with the woman's deliberative process as clearly as if the law itself denied women contraceptive access for certain reasons and not others. By empowering employers to privilege certain grounds of decision over others, the government picks and chooses among the reasons a woman may or may not have access to contraception. Because the privacy right related to contraceptives is constitutionally protected and the religious right – the right to be exempt from a generally applicable health insurance mandate because of one's religious beliefs – is not, the woman's right to choose contraception without regard to the reason should trump.[34]

There may appear to be a conceptual difficulty here, however. If the woman does not have a positive constitutional right to employer-provided contraception – and surely she does not – then how can she have a constitutional right to access privately subsidized contraception for any reason she chooses? The contraception provisions are arguably different from the reason-based abortion bans in that the abortions bans are criminal prohibitions, not mere withdrawals of government-mandated subsidies. If the regulation is targeting a government-mandated benefit, by contrast, and if the benefit is one to which the woman has no pre-existing entitlement, why is the government forbidden from delineating the extent of her entitlement by designating certain reasons and not others sufficient to trigger the benefit? Moreover, both private health insurers and government benefit programs regularly deem certain health conditions worthy of insurance coverage and others not; they may cover drugs when they are needed for certain conditions but not for others.

The analysis presented in Section 1 should answer this objection. Although the constitutional right to engage in the underlying conduct – contraceptive use – is not directly burdened by the state law, the right to engage in such conduct *for any reason* – the right to an autonomous deliberative process, free of government coercion – is directly and substantially burdened by a law that differentiates between

---

[34] Moreover, the fact that the woman's deliberations may themselves implicate her religious or spiritual beliefs further bolsters the constitutional claim. The government must not examine those beliefs too closely or distinguish between religious and secular beliefs in a way the individual would not.

acceptable and unacceptable reasons for contraceptive use. With laws protecting contraceptive access only for therapeutic reasons, the state is essentially declaring that some reasons are strong enough to overcome an employer's religious scruples and others are not. If this means the state is willing to protect women against certain harms that would be imposed by granting religious exemptions (such as severe physical risks caused by dangerous pregnancies), but not against others (such as the usual physical risks of pregnancy, and the emotional and social harms of unintended pregnancy), then the state is allowing nonconstitutional religious rights to overcome the woman's constitutional right to choose her own reasons for her reproductive health care decisions. This interference with private deliberation in the context of reproductive decision making does not occur when governmental or private benefit programs simply limit their overall scope or choose to cover some conditions but not others based on considerations such as the cost-benefit tradeoff.

Ironically, one consequence of this analysis is that laws providing blanket exemptions from contraceptive coverage are on firmer constitutional ground than more carefully tailored exemptions. A blanket exemption allowing religious employers to opt out from covering contraceptives would not unconstitutionally privilege certain reasons over others and, therefore, would not burden the constitutional right to deliberate autonomously, because it would not distinguish between valid and invalid reasons. But is this result correct or desirable?

There are several responses to this concern. First, although this result seems counter-intuitive, it may nonetheless be the correct one based on existing constitutional doctrine. Once the government begins carefully tailoring exemptions, problems can ensue. For example, a statute with a narrowly drafted religious exemption that excludes certain religious groups while protecting others would be more problematic than one with no exemption. Second, it is not the goal of this chapter to suggest that provisions distinguishing between different uses for contraception should be challenged in court. I argue that those laws are likely unconstitutional, but I leave to others the strategic decision whether they should be challenged on this ground. Finally, it is worth considering the political implications of a decision requiring states to exempt all religious employers from covering contraception in all circumstances, even when it is needed to protect the woman's health, or none at all. It is possible that the result would be that the practice of covering oral contraceptives for nonfamily-planning purposes would continue but without the sanction of law; employers and insurers could continue to make the distinction between therapeutic and nontherapeutic contraception, but through private, internal policies.[35] Since no

---

[35] For example, Catholic employers generally do not have a problem with covering contraception for "therapeutic," as opposed to family-planning, purposes. According to the Catholic doctrine of double effect, certain forbidden actions may be considered morally licit if they are done with the intention of achieving a permissible goal. See, e.g., *Brief for the Appellees, Zubik v. Burwell*, 778 F.3d 422 (3d

law would be implicated, there would be no state action and no constitutional problem. On the other hand, there might be value in highlighting the conflict between religious beliefs and private reproductive decision making in this context. It is worth considering, perhaps in a more public way, whether the distinction between therapeutic and nontherapeutic contraception is one that the government should make and whether the government should be deciding which uses of contraception are sufficient to outweigh an employer's religious claims. Currently, this debate is submerged by *Hobby Lobby* and the post-*Hobby Lobby* discourse, which treats religious exemptions from contraceptives coverage as an all-or-nothing issue.

CONCLUSION

The essence of the privacy right is a right against government interference with the reasons for which an individual chooses to engage in protected conduct – not just the right to engage in the conduct itself. Although the government may seek to force deliberation, to share information, and possibly even to influence the decision-making process in some ways, it cannot cross the line from influence to coercion. Moreover, the right to privacy in reproductive decision making must be understood to have privileged constitutional status, such that it should override individual religious claims in the case of a conflict. With respect to state-law religious exemptions from contraceptive coverage requirements that distinguish among reasons for using contraception, for example, a conflict is clearly presented between one person's religious rights and another's right to private and autonomous deliberation. According to the framework presented here, it is unacceptable for states to make such distinctions.

Cir. 2015), available at 2014 WL 3778380, at 6 ("Catholic teaching, however, allows the plans to, and the plans do, provide contraceptives and other hormone therapies when used for non-contraceptive, medically-necessary purposes."); Leonard J. Nelson, III, *God and Woman in the Catholic Hospital*, 31 J. Legis. 69, 103–104 (2004).

25

Religion and Reproductive Technology

I. Glenn Cohen

This chapter will examine four particular intersections of religion and reproductive technology. The first involves religiously motivated denials of service, in particular as they pertain to single individuals and gay and lesbian couples. The second involves embryo adoption, where the largest providers of the service in the United States are religious organizations. The third is a bit of a dog that didn't bark (at least so far): the "personhood movement" and its attempts to gain state constitutional protection for zygotes, embryos, and fetuses. Finally, the chapter will close by discussing relatively new attempts by religious organizations to bring forward objections to embryo destruction in pre-embryo disposition disputes between private individuals.

1. RELIGIOUSLY MOTIVATED DENIALS OF SERVICE

Laws in many parts of the world restrict access to reproductive technology by gays and lesbians; for instance, Italy's Law 40 confines use of reproductive technologies to infertile women of "potentially fertile age" who are married or part of a "stable" heterosexual couple, which indirectly burdens LGBTQ Assistive Reproductive Technology (ART) users by prohibiting the use of donated sperm or eggs.[1] France's 1994 law regulating reproductive technologies confines ART access to "heterosexual couples who ... are married or have lived together for at least two years prior to the reproductive procedure" and are of child-bearing age.[2]

---

[1] I. Glenn Cohen, *Regulating Reproduction: The Problem with Best Interests*, 96 Minn. L. Rev. 423, 450 (2011) (citing Rachel Anne Fenton, *Catholic Doctrine versus Women's Rights: The New Italian Law on Assisted Reproduction*, 14 Med. L. Rev. 73, 73 (2006)).

[2] Id. at 452 (citing Radhika Rao, *Equal Liberty: Assisted Reproductive Technology and Reproductive Equality*, 76 Geo. Wash. L. Rev. 1457, 1474 (2008); Patrick Roger, *Blocage Sur L'adoption Par Les Couples Homosexuels* [Ban on Adoption by Homosexual Couples], Le Monde (Fr.) (January 27, 2006, 4:56 PM), available at www.lemonde.fr/societe/article/2006/01/26/blocage-sur-l-adoption-par-les-couples-homosexuels_734791_3224.html [https://perma.cc/AE6M-96PY]).

In the United States no law explicitly bars gays, lesbians, or single individuals from accessing ARTs. Instead much of the access denial occurs due to individual provider choice. For example, a 2005 study found that one-fifth of U.S. ART treatment providers would refuse to provide services to a woman without a partner, 48 percent were "[v]ery or extremely likely to turn away" a gay couple that employed a surrogate, and 17 percent would turn away a lesbian couple seeking to achieve pregnancy with donor insemination.[3] The "Best Interests of the Child" refrain was a very common reason for their denials, with 62 percent and 64 percent of the practitioners agreeing with the statements "[i]t is wrong for me to help bring a child into the world to be cared for by a parent who would be unfit in some way" and "I have the responsibility to consider a parent's fitness before helping them conceive a child," respectively.[4]

When one scratches deeper, the "best interests of children" argument often (but not always) has a religious frame. Some socially conservative institutes have pressed for restrictions on gay family formation in the wake of same-sex marriage.[5] Attempts at religious "conscience clause" protections sometimes explicitly cover assisted reproductive technologies and LGBT communities: the Americans United for Life "model healthcare refusal act specifically includes not only abortion, contraception, and sterilization, but also 'artificial insemination [and] assisted reproduction' services vital to lesbian and gay family formation."[6] A similar intertwining of religious opposition to abortion and ARTs is evident in the discussion of personhood below.

As far as I am aware, however, there has only been one significant legal case in which an ART provider relied on explicitly religious reasons to deny access, and the denial was to a lesbian or gay individual seeking reproductive technologies. Guadalupe T. Benitez, a lesbian who lived with her partner, Joanne Clark, in San Diego County, sought to use intrauterine insemination to become pregnant. She was being seen by North Coast Women's Medical Care Group. Only one member of the group, Dr. Fenton, was licensed to perform the procedure using fresh sperm (there was some confusion about whether she wanted fresh sperm from a friend or frozen sperm from a bank), but "he refused to prepare donated fresh sperm for

---

[3] Andrea D. Gurmankin et al., *Screening Practices and Beliefs of Assisted Reproductive Technology Programs*, 83 Fertility & Sterility 61, 61–5 (2005).
[4] Id. at 61–5. See also Ryan E. Lawrence et al., *Obstetrician–Gynecologists' Beliefs About Assisted Reproductive Technologies*, 116 Obstetrics & Gynecology 127, 127 (2010).
[5] Douglas NeJaime, Forum, *Griswold's Progeny: Assisted Reproduction, Procreative Liberty, and Sexual Orientation Equality*, 124 Yale L.J. 340 (2015) (citing Elizabeth Marquardt et al., *My Daddy's Name Is Donor: A New Study of Young Adults Conceived Through Sperm Donation*, Inst. for Am. Values (2010), available at http://americanvalues.org/catalog/pdfs/Donor_FINAL.pdf [http://perma.cc/4T7N-ZLJW]; Elizabeth Marquardt, *One Parent or Five: A Global Look at Today's New Intentional Families*, Inst. for Am. Values 27 (2011), available at http://americanvalues.org/catalog/pdfs/one_parent_or_five.pdf [http://perma.cc/VR22-X3D5]).
[6] Id.

Benitez because of his religious objection." Two of his colleagues had no religious objection but neither was licensed to prepare fresh sperm, so Dr. Fenton referred Benitez to a physician outside of the North Coast practice.[7]

Benitez eventually brought suit against North Coast on several grounds, but most importantly for our purposes, alleged violation of California's Unruh Civil Rights Act, an antidiscrimination law that applies "to business establishments that offer to the public accommodations, advantages, facilities, privileges, or services."[8] At the time the denial of service occurred, the Act did not explicitly cover sexual orientation discrimination (although an amendment passed after Dr. Fenton's refusal but before the California Supreme Court's decision in the case explicitly added protection against that type of discrimination), but several courts in the state had previously treated it as a prohibited ground of discrimination.[9] North Coast complained that imposing liability under the Act for denying services would violate their *federal* constitutional First Amendment rights to freedom of religion and free speech. The court applied the U.S. Supreme Court's decision in *Employment Division v. Smith*, and found the Unruh Act to be a "neutral and valid law of general applicability" and thus the medical group had no federal Constitutional defense.[10] The court also rejected the medical group's argument that this was a "hybrid" claim combining speech and religion rights that should be treated differently.[11]

The court then considered the same defense under *California's* constitutional law. The court refused to spell out the exact standard of review for a challenge based on religious freedom, but instead held that even assuming the most generous standard to the defendants – strict scrutiny – applied, they must lose. Even if the law's prohibition against sexual orientation discrimination would substantially burden the defendants' religious beliefs,

> [t]he Act furthers California's compelling interest in ensuring full and equal access to medical treatment irrespective of sexual orientation, and there are no less restrictive means for the state to achieve that goal. To avoid any conflict between their religious beliefs and the state Unruh Civil Rights Act's antidiscrimination provisions, defendant physicians can simply refuse to perform the IUI medical procedure at issue here for any patient of North Coast, the physicians' employer.[12]

---

[7] *N. Coast Women's Care Med. Grp., Inc. v. San Diego Cty. Superior Court*, 189 P.3d 959, 963–4 (Cal. 2008).
[8] Id. at 964–5 (citing Civ. Code, § 51, subd. (a)).
[9] Id. As I will discuss more fully below, there was also a factual dispute in the case as to whether the discrimination was based on sexual orientation or marital status, which is relevant to the coverage of the Act. Id. at 970.
[10] Id. at 966 (relying on *Employment Div. v. Smith*, 494 U.S. 872 (1990)).
[11] Id. at 967.
[12] Id. at 968.

On remand, the court indicated that the physicians were free to present evidence that the reason for their discrimination against Benitez was not her sexual orientation but her *marital status*, which was not a protected ground under the Unruh Act.[13]

Let me make three observations about this case.

First, as noted earlier, this seems to be the only major legal case in the United States involving denials of ART services to lesbians, gays, or single individuals. Without putting too much stock into a negative finding, it might suggest that: (i) such denials happen infrequently, in part perhaps because members of those communities seek out providers comfortable serving them on the front end; or, (ii) such denials happen with some regularity, but (a) most patients are willing to accept the referral to another provider and not bring suit, or, (b) in relatively few states do sexual orientation anti-discrimination laws provide redress and a viable lawsuit for these denials. Given the evidence of denial of services to LGBTQ individuals discussed above, I suspect some combination of (a) and (b) are afoot, but we lack conclusive evidence.

Second, one might wonder whether the result of *North Coast* should change under the federal Religious Freedom Restoration Act (RFRA) or state equivalents. Such statutes typically require applying strict scrutiny.[14] *North Coast* held that the religious claims of the provider would not prevail even assuming *arguendo* that strict scrutiny applies, so the result would seem to hold even under these statutes. That said, strict scrutiny analysis is undoubtedly fact-specific and, given different (or even similar) facts, a court motivated to favor religious liberty in another state might come out differently.

Third, *North Coast*'s holding is very much framed in the doctrinal mode of equal protection (albeit not the federal constitutional provision), with the Court suggesting the clinic could level-up (provide the same service to LGBTQ patients and heterosexuals that it provides to other types of patients) or level-down (provide it to no patients), but not draw the distinction that it did. This is very much the route taken by scholars like Radhika Rao, who have argued for equality-based protections for reproductive technology use.[15] There is, however, another path that relies on a claim that denials of access to reproductive technologies violate a right that sounds more in substantive due process, as John Robertson is perhaps best known for arguing.[16] Others have expressed doubts about the federal constitutional bona fides of

---

[13] Id. at 970.
[14] See, e.g., Tex. Civ. Prac. & Rem. Code § 110.005 (2015); Conn. Gen. Stat. § 52-571b(b) (2016); 71 Pa. Cons. Stat. § 2404(b) (2016).
[15] Radhika Rao, *Equal Liberty: Assisted Reproductive Technology and Reproductive Equality*, 76 Geo. Wash. L. Rev. 1457, 1485–6 (2008).
[16] John A. Robertson, Children of Choice: Freedom and the New Reproductive Technologies 39–40 (1994).

such a right.[17] In any event, to succeed in such an argument one would have to locate a state action (at least in terms of the federal constitution, not necessarily for many state constitutions), which may be wanting in some of these cases – there does not appear to be a governmental actor, rule, or intertwinement. As applied to gays, lesbians, and single individuals, such an argument also faces the additional question of whether the federal constitution, if it protects rights related to reproductive technology use at all, protects only a negative liberty right for the *infertile* as opposed to the "dysfertile" – such as gays, lesbians, and single individuals who face social rather than medical infertility.[18]

2. EMBRYO ADOPTION

As part of in vitro fertilization (IVF), many prospective parents fertilize more eggs to produce more pre-embryos than they intend to immediately implant because the technology often requires multiple attempts to reach a successful pregnancy.[19] When excess pre-embryos are produced, couples typically cryopreserve them. The result is that, by some estimates, there are currently more than one million cryopreserved embryos in America, though the exact number is contested.[20]

Christian groups have had a major role in pressing for so-called "embryo adoption" as an option for the disposition of these embryos.[21] While individuals with dispositional authority over excess embryos are free to donate them to other known individuals or allow their clinic to anonymously provide them to other unknown individuals, this form of embryo *donation* is to be contrasted with embryo *adoption*. Nightlight Christian Adoptions Agency, one of the key actors in this space, which runs the so-called "Snowflakes" program, has described the donation-adoption distinction as follows:

---

[17] E.g., I. Glenn Cohen, *The Constitution and the Right Not to Procreate*, 60 Stan. L. Rev. 1135, 1195 n.244 (2008).

[18] Lisa C. Ikemoto, *The In/Fertile, the Too Fertile, and the Dysfertile*, 47 Hastings L.J. 1007, 1008–9 (1996).

[19] While the term is not without controversy, a pre-embryo typically refers to a fertilized ovum up to fourteen days of its existence before implantation in the uterus.

[20] See, e.g., Geoffrey P. Lomax & Alan O. Trounson, *Correcting misperceptions about cryopreserved embryos and stem cell research*, 31 Nature Biotechnology 288–90 (2013); Snow et al., *Contesting estimates of cryopreserved embryos in the United States*, 33 Nature Biotechnology, 909 (2015).

[21] June Carbone & Naomi Cahn, *Embryo Fundamentalism*, 18 Wm. & Mary Bill Rts. J. 1015, 1029–30 (2010). Some view the very term itself as one fueled by the anti-abortion movement as an attempt to connote the notion of embryonic personhood. See Susan L. Crockin & Gary A. Debele, *Ethical Issues in Assisted Reproduction: A Primer for Family Law Attorneys*, 27 J. Am. Acad. Matrim. Law. 289, 308 (2015).

"Embryo donation" is a program fertility clinics offer. Although some programs may vary, embryo donation differs from adoption in that the receiving family does not have a home study prepared, the donor families are anonymous, and there is no contact between the families before or after birth, even through an intermediary. Snowflakes goes beyond the embryo donation provided by fertility clinics by offering the safeguards and education available in a traditional adoption. A home study is prepared on the adopting family that includes screening and education. The placing family is able to select an adopting family (as opposed to the doctor in a clinic making the selection of a family), they will know if a child(ren) is born from the adopted embryos. The placing family may also delegate this responsibility to Nightlight, a licensed adoption agency. Our program recognizes the importance of counseling all parties involved. Most importantly, at Nightlight we recognize the personhood of embryos and we treat them as precious pre-born children.[22]

The agency claims to have facilitated 500 embryo adoptions.[23] As Naomi Cahn and June Carbone have noted, the support for the embryo adoption movement comes largely from the pro-life movement, and, indeed, in 2001 President George W. Bush embraced the concept and spoke specifically about Nightlife's Snowflakes program in his State of the Union address, discussing its importance in "ensuring 'our society's most vulnerable members are protected and defended at every stage of life' and securing federal funds to promote a movement, the transfer of embryos for reproductive purposes."[24] At least at an earlier time in its history (the topic is no longer covered on its website), "the Snowflakes program specifically prohibit[ed] selective abortion at any stage and for any reason after multiple embryo transfer" such that "'adopting families' are required to agree not to selectively reduce the number of fetuses when multiple pregnancies occur."[25] There are reasons to doubt such agreements would be legally enforceable, but they may serve as informal commitment devices nonetheless. To my knowledge, there have been no reported cases in which LGBTQ couples or single individuals have sought to use the Nightlife embryo adoption service, but although the website explicitly disclaims only serving Christians, the program is undeniably religiously motivated and there are reasons to doubt LGBTQ individuals would pass the home study visit.[26]

In March 2009, Georgia became the first state to pass a law specifically pertaining to embryo adoption, the Option of Adoption Act (OAA), which was viewed by some "as a victory for anti-abortion groups who want the law to recognize embryos in

---

[22] *Frequently Asked Questions*, Nightlight Christian Adoptions, available at www.nightlight.org/faqs/#b3 [https://perma.cc/K656-RWWV] (last visited May 26, 2016).
[23] Id.
[24] Carbone & Cahn, supra note 21, at 1030.
[25] Jaime E. Conde, *Embryo Donation: The Government Adopts A Cause*, 13 Wm. & Mary J. Women & L. 273, 286 (2006).
[26] Supra note 22.

their earliest stages of development as people."[27] In addition, the state of Louisiana requires by statute any pre-embryo renounced by the genetic parents to be made available for adoptive implantation.[28] The state of Oklahoma has also passed a statute regarding embryo adoption requiring that written consent to receive (and thus assume parentage over) the embryo be "executed and acknowledged by both the husband and wife, by the physician who is to perform the technique, and by a judge of the court having adoption jurisdiction" in the state.[29] The statute also legitimates any child born through embryo adoption as though it were a child born to the receiving parents through coital reproduction.

All-in-all, embryo adoption represents two facets of the interplay of religion and reproductive technology: first, it is a situs for religion to *facilitate* use of reproductive technology – unusual given that, more often, religious groups oppose such use – albeit while introducing some restrictions on abortions and potentially access by same-sex couples or single individuals. Second, these programs have received more attention for their rhetorical influence – the idea that by importing the language of adoption for embryos, they are an attempt to emphasize the personhood of the early embryo in line with some of the strategies of the anti-abortion movement, and in particular religious beliefs.

3. THE RISE OF PERSONHOOD MOVEMENTS

While the first two examples – denials of ART services and embryo adoption – involve a more subtle pressure point by religious organizations on reproductive technology policy, the next two examples discussed herein are much more direct.

In *Roe v. Wade*, Justice Blackmun wrote that "[i]f this suggestion of [fetal] personhood is established, the appellant's case [arguing in favor of women's choice], of course, collapses, for the fetus' right to life would then be guaranteed specifically by the [Fourteenth] Amendment."[30]

The "personhood movement" has taken this ball and run with it in a series of states and legal policy-making tools. "While the language and form of these proposals vary from state to state (legislative bills in some states versus ballot initiatives voted on directly by the public in others), each essentially attempts to secure

---

[27] Polina M. Dostalik, *Embryo "Adoption"? The Rhetoric, the Law, and the Legal Consequences*, 55 N.Y.L. Sch. L. Rev. 867, 889 (2011) (quoting Georgia Passes First Embryo Adoption Act, Embryo Adoption Awareness Ctr., available at www.embryoadoption.org/news/27.cfm). For the statute itself, see Ga. Code Ann. § 19-8-40 et seq (2009).
[28] 73 LA R.S. 9:130 (2016).
[29] 10 Okl. St. Ann. § 556 (2016).
[30] *Roe v. Wade*, 410 U.S. 113, 156–7 (1973).

legal rights for pre-born human beings starting from the moment of fertilization or conception."[31]

The movement's main organizing force is Personhood USA, a national organization that "identifies itself as a non-profit Christian ministry that serves the pro-life community by assisting local groups to initiate citizen, legislative, and political action focusing on the ultimate goal of the pro-life movement: personhood rights for all innocent humans," and is dedicated to "moving churches and the culture to make the dehumanization and murdering of preborn children unthinkable."[32]

Personhood USA has proposed ballot initiatives in Colorado, North Dakota, and Mississippi, all of which failed, though the Mississippi proposed constitutional amendment (which, full disclosure, I campaigned against in the pages of the *New York Times*) looked for a time to have had broad support.[33] They have also proposed state statutes in eleven states in 2012, none of which made it into law, a 2011 North Dakota bill that passed in the House but failed in the Senate, and federal legislation in 2011 sponsored by now-Speaker Paul Ryan, which did not come up for a vote.[34]

A key strategy of those opposed to the Personhood movements, including me, is to drive a wedge between the antiabortion aims of the movement and its effects on reproductive technology, on the theory that some portion of those opposing abortion use approve of the use of reproductive technologies. Take the Mississippi proposed state constitutional amendment, which defines a person as "every human being from the moment of fertilization, cloning, or the functional equivalent thereof."[35] As Jonathan Will and I have argued, the word conception was ambiguous and could mean at least four different things: penetration of the egg by a sperm, assembly of the new embryonic genome, successful activation of that genome, and implantation of the embryo in the uterus. The first occurs immediately; the last occurs approximately two weeks after insemination (or, in the case of embryos created through in vitro fertilization that do not get implanted, never). Thus, on some reasonable readings of the amendment, certain forms of birth control, stem cell derivation, and the

---

[31] Maya Manian, *Lessons from Personhood's Defeat: Abortion Restrictions and Side Effects on Women's Health*, 74 Ohio St. L.J. 75, 79 (2013).
[32] Jonathan F. Will, *Beyond Abortion: Why the Personhood Movement Implicates Reproductive Choice*, 39 Am. J.L. & Med. 573, 580 (2013).
[33] Rachana Pradhan & Jennifer Haberkorn, *Personhood Movement Loses Twice*, Politico (November 5, 2014, 12:00 AM), available at www.politico.com/story/2014/11/personhood-movement-north-dakota-colorado-112552 [https://perma.cc/CU46-TPXX]; Will, supra note 32, at 584–6; I. Glenn Cohen & Jonathan F. Will, *Op-Ed, Mississippi's Ambiguous 'Personhood' Amendment*, N.Y. Times (October 31, 2011), available at www.nytimes.com/2011/10/31/opinion/mississippis-ambiguous-personhood-amendment.html [https://perma.cc/CD3C-5L4Q].
[34] Manian, supra note 31, at 82–3.
[35] E.g., Cohen & Will, supra note 33.

destruction of embryos created through in vitro fertilization would seem impermissible, whereas on other equally reasonable readings they are not.[36]

I lack a front-row seat to the Personhood movement's strategy sessions. If the goal was simply to provide the Supreme Court an opportunity to overrule *Roe v. Wade* and its progeny, a constitutional amendment that directly addressed *only* abortion would seem to me to be a more sure-fire way to get success at the ballot box, for example defining a "person" as "every fertilized egg implanted in a uterus." One interesting reality is that while prohibitions on *abortion* rather than ART may be more attractive at the ballot box, when it comes to the likely constitutionality of such a prohibitions, the reverse is almost certainly true. *Roe* and its progeny certainly protect a right to be and not to be a *gestational* parent, but it is much less certain whether they protect ARTs that do not involve gestating an embryo created through intercourse rather than in vitro fertilization, for reasons I have discussed elsewhere.[37]

4. PRE-EMBRYO DISPOSITION DISPUTES

The same religious influences behind the personhood movement have recently spilled over into so-called "pre-embryo disposition cases." As discussed earlier, there are many embryos cryopreserved in America. As part of the informed consent process for IVF and/or cryopreservation, ART clinics typically ask patients to specify their dispositional preferences for cryopreserved embryos in the event of particular circumstances like divorce or death of one of the partners. They typically offer options for the use of the embryos by a specified partner, donation to research, or thawing and discarding the remaining pre-embryos.

Given the lengthy duration of cryopreservation, many courts in the United States (as well as in Europe, Israel, and elsewhere) have faced a recurring fact pattern: reproductive and romantic partners dissolve their relationship (most typically through divorce) and one party wants to use the frozen embryos over the objections of the other.[38] Courts and legislatures have struggled with what to do with these cases that seemingly pit one partner's right to procreate against the other's right not to procreate.

---

[36] Id.
[37] See generally, I. Glenn Cohen, *The Constitution and the Rights Not to Procreate*, 60 Stan. L. Rev. 1135 (2008).
[38] See, e.g., *Szafranski v. Dunston*, 34 N.E.3d 1132 (Ill. App. Ct. 2015); *Davis v. Davis*, 842 S.W.2d 588 (Tenn. 1992); *Kass v. Kass*, 696 N.E.2d 174 (N.Y. 1998); *A.Z. v. B.Z.*, 725 N.E.2d 1051 (Mass. 2000); *J.B. v. M.B.*, 783 A.2d 707 (N.J. 2001); *Litowitz v. Litowitz*, 48 P.3d 261 (Wash. 2002); *Roman v. Roman*, 193 S.W.3d 40 (Tex. Ct. App. 2006); In re Marriage of Dahl & Angle, 194 P.3d 384 (Or. Ct. App. 2008); *Reber v. Reiss*, 42 A.3d 1131 (Pa. Super. Ct. 2012).

In a recent case, however, the Thomas More Law Center asked a court in Missouri to consider the embryo a "child" and therefore make a decision on disposition that favors the best interests of the "child." The Thomas More Law Center describes itself as a national nonprofit public interest law firm, based in Ann Arbor, Michigan. The mission of the Thomas More Law Center is to: "Preserve America's Judeo-Christian heritage; Defend the religious freedom of Christians; Restore time-honored moral and family values; Protect the sanctity of human life; Promote a strong national defense and a free and sovereign United States of America."[39]

As the brief itself puts it, "Missouri law specifically recognizes that life begins at conception. This Amicus Brief challenges the holding from the Circuit Court of the County of St. Louis that failed to recognize that an embryo is a life and failed to treat this life as a child under" the child custody statute of the state.[40] The amicus relies on a Missouri statute that reads

1. The general assembly of this state finds that:
   (1) The life of each human being begins at conception;
   (2) Unborn children have protectable interests in life, health, and well-being;
   (3) The natural parents of unborn children have protectable interests in the life, health, and well-being of their unborn child.
2. Effective January 1, 1988, the laws of this state shall be interpreted and construed to acknowledge on behalf of the unborn child at every stage of development, all the rights, privileges, and immunities available to other persons, citizens, and residents of this state, subject only to the Constitution of the United States, and decisional interpretations thereof by the United States Supreme Court and specific provisions to the contrary in the statutes and constitution of this state.
3. As used in this section, the term "unborn children" or "unborn child" shall include all unborn child or children or the offspring of human beings from the moment of conception until birth at every stage of biological development.[41]

The Thomas More law center argued that this section gives a gloss on the correct interpretation of the term "child" in the state statutes governing custody and thus, as they put it in one of their argument headings "[r]equires that Unborn Children, Including Embryos, Receive the Same Legal Protections as Post-Birth Children and Adults."[42] This, then, lead the amicus to suggest that "[b]ecause the embryos in this

---

[39] Thomas More L. Ctr., available at www.thomasmore.org [https://perma.cc/ASX9-CGAD] (last visited May 19, 2016).
[40] Brief of Amicus Curiae the Thomas More Law Center in Support of Appellant at 1, *Mcqueen v. Gadberry*, No. ED103138 (Mo. Ct. App. E.D. filed December 22, 2015).
[41] Mo. Ann. Stat. § 1.205 (2016).
[42] Supra note 40, at 5.

case constitute 'children' within the meaning of Missouri's child-custody statutes, the circuit court erred by failing to allocate their custody based on the best interests of the children (i.e., the embryos)," and the court should remand for a custody determination.[43]

Left unsaid is the suggestion that taking such a perspective would likely lead to a ruling against embryo destruction in favor of embryo use.

That is a likely, though perhaps not inevitable, conclusion from adopting that perspective, as I have suggested elsewhere.[44] If one thought pre-embryos were the kinds of entities that have interests, it would seem that such interests would naturally be served by their implantation and hopefully eventual birth in most cases.[45]

There may be a series of questions between recognition of these entities as interest-holding and the view that this mandates a "must-implant rule" – questions about the slack between having interests and having the ability to make moral claims, for example. But the most important open question would be how to resolve cases in which a claim on behalf of the preembryo to have its best interests promoted faces a conflict with the genetic mother's interest in reproductive autonomy. Here it is useful to distinguish genetic and gestational motherhood. Although it is settled law that the interests of the pre-embryo will not trump a mother's right to refuse or discontinue gestation (before viability), it is unsettled whether the mother has a right not to be a *genetic* parent when that is unbundled from gestational parenthood. In other words, the constitutional analysis of a must-gestate rule will be different from the constitutional analysis of a must-make-available-for-others-to-implant rule, a kind of forced embryo adoption.[46]

I was skeptical the court would adopt the argument being offered by the Thomas More Law Center in this case, largely because I did not think the state had through its statutes made a clear assertion the pre-embryos are an entity that have a best-interests kind of claim to be implanted. The Missouri Court of Appeals ultimately rejected the argument 2–1, although did so by suggesting that a contrary holding would violate the father's right not to procreate.[47] This is an argument I am skeptical of, as addressed later. In any event, the best-interests argument may be deployed by personhood advocates in other cases.

Should a state explicitly adopt through statute a requirement that all fertilized embryos must be either implanted by the couple or made available for embryo

---

[43] Supra note 40, at 13.
[44] The following is derived from I. Glenn Cohen, *The Right Not to Be a Genetic Parent?*, 81 S. Cal. L. Rev. 1115, 1131–2 (2008).
[45] There may be "lives not worth living" involving Tay Sachs or Lesch-Nyhan syndrome on the margins.
[46] I. Glenn Cohen, *The Constitution and the Rights Not to Procreate*, 60 Stan. L. Rev. 1135 (2008).
[47] Mcqueen v. Gadberry, No. ED103138 (Mo. Ct. App. E.D. nov 15, 2016), available at www2.courthousenews.com/wp-content/uploads/2016/11/Embryos.pdf

adoption, it is unclear how a constitutional challenge would or should go. I am skeptical whether the best reading of the Constitution and existing precedents provides women a constitutionally protected right not to be a genetic parent when it is unbundled from gestational parenthood. I have argued elsewhere that the existing precedents are plausibly read to only provide a right against forced gestation, not forced genetic parenthood without gestation, and there may be advanced waiver of any such right through fertilizing pre-embryos to begin with, among other potential problems.[48]

CONCLUSION

In this chapter I have examined four instances where objections from religious quarters are manifested in access to reproductive technologies. One could find others, including the prominence of discourse on "playing G-d" language in fights over mitochondrial replacement therapy, gene editing, and the like, though sometimes this phrase may be used as a secular metonymy.[49]

Some of these instances, especially the denial of services, have long histories, but I do think most people who write in these areas have a sense that these disputes are "heating up." Why? Let me offer two related possibilities, while accepting that they are still speculative: first, the LGBTQ community's win on gay marriage in the United States has moved the frontier for resistance to gay family making. This is a good target because of the very private and peripheral status of reproductive technologies for heterosexuals in American society, due to the shame and quiet that still surrounds infertility. Opponents can potentially play on the distinctions between infertility and dysfertility in reproductive technology litigation. Second, abortion remains a wedge issue in our increasingly polarized political environment, and attempts to regulate abortion have swept in (sometimes to the movement's disadvantage) reproductive technologies.

Going forward, reproductive technology use is likely to continue to be a major place of conflict between religion, law, and medicine. Those who seek to avoid such restrictions on reproductive technology use might benefit from a "coming-out-of-the-closet" type movement, building a coalition between LGBTQ and non-LGBTQ users of these technologies. It is very powerful to know that it is not some hypothetical person but one's sister or co-worker who is being aggrieved.

---

[48] Id.
[49] See, e.g., James Gallagher, *MPs Say Yes to Three Person-Babies*, BBC News (February 3, 2015), available at www.bbc.com/news/health-31069173 [https://perma.cc/A9GF-RZ8C]; Lisa M. Krieger, *Biologist's Gene-Editing Kit lets DIYers Play God at Kitchen Table*, Chicago Tribune (January 29, 2016, 9:06 AM), available at www.chicagotribune.com/lifestyles/health/sc-gene-editing-kit-health-0203-20160203-story.html [https://perma.cc/9FT2-FY7V].

26

Religion and the Unborn Under the First Amendment

Dov Fox

Assisted reproduction, stem cell research, and abortion are among the primary social controversies in which religion tends to play a conspicuous role. A prominent objection to state restrictions on practices like these holds that they implicate judgments about nascent human life that hew too closely to religion under First Amendment principles governing the separation of church and state. I argue in this chapter that this Establishment Clause challenge trades on a misunderstanding of religion and its relationship to ideas about the unborn. It conflates four influences thought of as "religious." The first three – compulsions of faith, promises of salvation, and obedience to God – may not be endorsed by government. But there is a fourth influence, involving larger visions about what makes society good, that legitimately animates state action. And it is this fourth influence, I will show, that best explains most efforts to protect fetuses and embryos.

This is not to say such laws do not have other constitutional problems; just that religion is not one. Reproductive restrictions that nevertheless infringe liberty and equality guarantees do not necessarily violate free speech, that is, even if large numbers of people support them based on their faith. This chapter makes three chief contributions. First, it supplies a long-missing defense of the Supreme Court's cursory holding in *Harris v. McRae* that federal funding preferences for childbirth over abortion do not violate the First Amendment.[1] Second, it resolves the church-state case against laws ranging from fetal pain bans and mandatory ultrasounds to Pro-Life license plates and personhood amendments. Third, it offers original reflections on religious pluralism, democratic legitimacy, and constitutional contestation that

---

[1] *Harris v. McRae*, 448 U.S. 297, 319 (1980).

Thanks for valuable insights to David Dow, Doug Laycock, Holly Fernandez Lynch, Justin Murray, Michael Perry, Steven Smith, Micah Schwartzman, Mike Seidman, Horacio Specter, Nelson Tebbe, Peter Wenz, and participants at the Petrie-Flom Center conference on Law, Religion, and Health in the United States at Harvard Law School.

meaningfully implicate a range of controversies that reach beyond the treatment of potential life.

1. THE ESTABLISHMENT CLAUSE CHALLENGE

The First Amendment limits the kinds of values that government may endorse by forbidding any "law respecting an establishment of religion."[2] State action may promote only those values that qualify as duly secular under constitutional principles governing the separation of church and state.[3] The Supreme Court has designated the state's "potential life" interest in expressing respect for embryos and fetuses as at least a valid exercise of its police power to legislate social mores, and, at least when it is invoked later in pregnancy, the canonical kind of interest capable of overriding even fundamental rights.[4] That interest is legitimate, however, only so long as it reflects ideals and attitudes that are secular rather than religious. Government cannot, "consistent with our Establishment Clause," *Roe's*[5] author Justice Harry Blackmun wrote in *Casey*, regulate even modest reproductive regulations that promote "a theological or sectarian interest."[6]

This view captures the refrain that government cannot take sides on religion.[7] Leading judges and scholars deem it a principal reason why laws designed to protect the unborn are unconstitutional. "[T]hat the[ir] intensely divisive character ... reflects the deeply held religious convictions of many" led Justice John Paul Stevens to ascribe to them a "theological basis" with "no identifiable secular purpose."[8] Professor Ronald Dworkin has, in a similar vein, argued that efforts to protect the unborn innately "command one essentially religious" "interpretation of the sanctity of life" over others.[9] Likewise, David Richards maintains that arguments

---

[2] U.S. Const. amend. I; *Everson v. Bd. of Educ.*, 330 U.S. 1, 14–15 (1947) (incorporating the Establishment Clause against the states as a liberty protected by the Due Process Clause of the Fourteenth Amendment).
[3] See *McCreary Cty. v. Am. Civil Liberties Union of Ky.*, 545 U.S. 844, 860 (2005).
[4] See *Gonzales v. Carhart*, 550 U.S. 124, 158 (2007); Dov Fox, Interest Creep, 82 Geo. Wash. L. Rev. 273, 303–11 (2014).
[5] *Roe v. Wade*, 410 U.S. 113 (1973).
[6] *Planned Parenthood of Se. Pa. v. Casey*, 505 U.S. 833, 932 (1992) (Blackmun, J., concurring in part and dissenting in part).
[7] Cf. id. at 850 ("Some of us as individuals find abortion offensive to our most basic principles of morality, but that cannot control our decision. Our obligation is to define the liberty of all, not to mandate our own moral code.").
[8] *Webster v. Reprod. Health Servs.*, 492 U.S. 490, 571, 566–7 (1989) (Stevens, J., concurring and dissenting in part). For discussion, see John M. Breen, *Abortion, Religion, and the Accusation of Establishment: A Critique of Justice Stevens' Opinions in Thornburgh, Webster, and Casey*, 39 Ohio N.U.L. Rev. 823, 831–4 (2014).
[9] Ronald Dworkin, *Life's Dominion* 165 (1993). See also Ronald Dworkin, *Freedom's Law* 104–10 (1996).

against abortion come from irreducibly religious premises.[10] Professor Carol Sanger suggests that the "culture of life" claim that these laws rely on "comes straight from the Vatican."[11] And Professor Naomi Cahn has written that "[t]he nature of the view" about "the moral status of embryos" or fetuses "stems from religiously based beliefs that are ... designed to divide rather than create conciliation."[12] Laws restricting abortion, *in vitro* fertilization (IVF), and stem cell research violate the Establishment Clause, this argument goes, because they endorse values that are "religious."[13] The claim is not that efforts to express respect for the unborn are not strong enough to override individual rights; it is that they are illicit and so never justified, even for modest regulations. Religion is on this view a poisonous tree that makes any fruit derived from it forbidden, whatever its more particular shape or color.

Professor Laurence Tribe, who would later repudiate this objection with little explanation,[14] advanced a sophisticated version of it shortly after *Roe*.[15] What makes reproductive regulations impermissible, Tribe had argued, is not just that they tend to divide people along religious lines;[16] or that they presuppose "isolated answers to 'ultimate' questions" about the decisive value of human life;[17] or even that they enjoy support of religious teachings or church involvement.[18] The problem for Tribe was rather something like all of these difficulties at once. The influence that Catholics and Evangelical Christians hold over abortion restrictions, he argued, make such

---

[10] See David A. J. Richards, *Toleration and the Constitution* 264 (1986).
[11] Carol Sanger, *Infant Safe Haven Laws: Legislating in the Culture of Life*, 106 Colum. L. Rev. 753, 807 (2006).
[12] Naomi R. Cahn, *Test Tube Families: Why the Fertility Market Needs Legal Regulations*, 185–6 (2009).
[13] See Peter S. Wenz, *Abortion Rights As Religious Freedom* (1992); David Dow, *The Establishment Clause Argument for Choice*, 20 Golden Gate U.L. Rev. 479, 495–8 (1990); Larry Pittman, *Embryonic Stem Cell Research and Religion: The Ban on Federal Funding as a Violation of the Establishment Clause*, 68 U. Pitt. L. Rev. 131, 135 (2006); Edward Rubin, *Sex, Politics, and Morality*, 47 Wm. & Mary L. Rev. 1, 40–6 (2005); Paul Simmons, *Religious Liberty and Abortion Policy: Casey as "Catch-22"*, 42 J. Church & State 69 (2000); Huseina Sulaimanee, Note, *Protecting the Right to Choose: Regulating Conscience Clauses in the Face of Moral Obligation*, 17 Carodozo J.L. & Gender 417, 431 (2011).
[14] Compare Laurence H. Tribe, *American Constitutional Law* 1293 (2d. ed. 1988), and Laurence H. Tribe, *Abortion: The Clash of Absolutes* 116 (1990). I am not privy to the reasons that led Tribe to change this view on the Establishment Clause.
[15] See Laurence Tribe, *Foreword: Toward a Model of Roles in the Due Process of Life and Law*, 87 Harv. L. Rev. 1 (1973).
[16] *Lemon v. Kurtzman*, 403 U.S. 602, 622 (1971) ("Political division along religious lines" has played little role in Establishment Clause analysis since once thought "one of the principal evils against which the First Amendment was intended to protect.").
[17] See, e.g., *Malnak v. Yogi*, 592 F.2d 197, 208–209 (1979) (Adams, J., concurring in the judgment) ("Certain isolated answers to 'ultimate' questions ... are not necessarily 'religious' answers, because they lack the element of comprehensiveness.").
[18] See *Lemon*, 403 U.S. at 613.

Religion and the Unborn Under the First Amendment 375

limits on the destruction of early life tantamount to "a statement of religious faith" about its status.[19] When "the views of organized religious groups have come to play a pervasive role in an entire subject's legislative consideration for reasons intrinsic to the subject matter itself," those laws are unconstitutional, he wrote, unless they can be shown, as they could not in this case, "to serve a compelling purpose that can be defined, and defended as applicable, in terms generally regarded to be wholly secular."[20] He suggested that *Roe's* recognition of "the highly charged and distinctly sectarian religious controversy" surrounding abortion supported its rejection of fetal personhood, although it never referenced the Establishment Clause.[21] More recently, scholars have gone farther than Tribe initially had to suggest that the Supreme Court in fact "implicitly relies upon [these very] First Amendment-type arguments to justify abortion rights."[22]

The Supreme Court has for its part rejected the Establishment Clause challenge to abortion laws, just once, in a single paragraph.[23] *Harris v. McRae* involved the constitutionality of the Hyde Amendment, an appropriations rider that forbids states from using Medicaid funds to help poor women obtain abortion, while leaving those federal resources available to support the cost of childbirth.[24] That the law's funding restrictions "coincide with the religious tenets of the Roman Catholic Church" that regard the unborn as people, the majority held, "does not, without more, contravene the Establishment Clause."[25] For reasons articulated below, I believe that holding is right.[26] But the Court has never elaborated what role religion would have to play in an abortion law to invalidate it as a church-state violation. *McRae* said only that the funding law's "value judgment favoring childbirth over abortion" reflects "'traditionalist' values towards abortion" more than "the views of any particular religion."[27] It declined to say what "traditionalist" values consist of, however, and has never since clarified what qualities make them constitutionally permissible.[28]

---

[19] Tribe, supra note 15, at 23.
[20] Id. at 23–4.
[21] Id. at 22.
[22] Justin Murray, *Exposing the Underground Establishment Clause in the Supreme Court's Abortion Cases*, 23 Regent U.L. Rev. 1, 4 (2010).
[23] *Harris v. McRae*, 448 U.S. 297, 319. ("[A] statute [does not] violate[] the Establishment Clause because it 'happens to coincide or harmonize with the tenets of some or all religions.'" (quoting *McGowan v. Maryland*, 366 U.S. 420, 442 (1961)).
[24] Hyde Amendment, Pub. L. No. 96–123, § 109, 93 Stat. 923 (1979).
[25] *McRae*, 448 U.S. at 319–20.
[26] See Douglas Laycock, 1 *Collected Works on Religious Liberty: Overviews and History* 683–4 (2010).
[27] Id. at 314 (quoting *Maher v. Roe*, 432 U.S. 464, 474 (1977)), 319–20.
[28] The reference to "traditionalist" values in *McRae* appears to come from the district court's opinion, *McRae v. Califano*, 491 F. Supp. 630 (E.D.N.Y. 1980), which explained that "explicit disapproval of abortion in most cases reflects a general and long held social view." Id. at 741. That such views are not

2. WHAT MAKES "RELIGIOUS" PURPOSES IMPERMISSIBLE

The Court's most recent articulation of what the Constitution forbids with respect to establishment emphasizes the social meaning of government action. *McCreary County v. ACLU* held that impermissibly religious laws "manifest a purpose to favor one faith over another, or adherence to religion generally."[29] The Court reasoned that "Although a legislature's stated reasons will generally get deference the secular purpose required has to be genuine, not a sham, and not merely secondary to a religious objective."[30] The determination of whether a law's apparent (rather than actual) purpose is secular versus religious does not, under this approach, look to whether the drafters intended to endorse religion by enacting a particular law. Instead, it asks whether the law sends a message that endorses religion in the relevant sense. The "eyes that look to purpose belong" to neither believer nor skeptic, Justice Souter explained, but "an 'objective observer,'" who is informed of the law's "text, legislative history, and implementation."[31] The *McCreary* test concerns not just perceived social meanings as *either* religious *or* secular, but which, as between them, tend to *predominate* in controversies that involve shades of both. It asks whether an objective, informed observer – a citizen uninvolved in the dispute but knowledgeable about the political context surrounding it – would interpret its central or primary purpose as more saliently religious in the impermissible sense. What makes a law's perceived meaning illicit in this way, I will argue, is that the religious influence that it expresses is not temporal but *transcendent*, in the sense that it derives from authorities or it aims toward goals that go beyond the material universe or human experience.[32] Would the objective observer, in other words, see its purpose as more about the here and now, or more about a time and space beyond our own?

Paradigmatic of the transcendent meanings the First Amendment forbids are laws whose apparent purpose is adoption of holy belief or practice, or obedience to divine command, or the pursuit of salvation.[33] These transcendent objectives take form in what is commonly referred to as theology or religious ritual. Why should the state be barred from legislating in ways that send the message it is trying to force faith, secure conformity with God's directives, or save souls? John Locke's answer was that

---

unduly religious leaves open the possibility they are unconstitutional for equality reasons or otherwise that are independent of the Establishment Clause. See infra notes 39–40 and accompanying text.

[29] 545 U.S. 844, 860 (2005).
[30] Id. at 864.
[31] Id. at 862.
[32] See Martin Riesebrodt, *The Promise of Salvation: A Theory of Religion* 76–78 (2010).
[33] Cf. *Engel v. Vitale*, 370 U.S. 421, 431-32 (1962) (arguing that under the Establishment Clause, "religion is too personal, too sacred, too holy, to permit its 'unhallowed perversion' by a civil magistrate" (quoting James Madison, Memorial and Remonstrance Against Religious Assessments (1785), reprinted in 2 The Writings of James Madison 183, 187 (Galliard Hunt, ed., 1901)).

such laws would be dubious and futile: dubious because the route to piety, deference, or heaven "is not better known to the magistrate than to private persons";[34] and futile because religious goods cannot be achieved by force but only sincere and willing belief or practice.[35] The modern legal reply is that efforts to promote faith, obedience, or salvation cannot be justified without resort to spiritual convictions or authorities that, though "as real as life to some may be incomprehensible to others."[36] These concerns discredit state action that an objective observer would perceive as dependent on religious injunction or revelation or paths to the afterlife that are hard to explain plausibly in other ways. Consider mandates of school prayer or Sabbath observance. Such laws violate the Establishment Clause under *McCreary* because the competent interpreter would perceive their purpose as promoting faith, obedience, or salvation: namely, messages that transcend everyday life. Messages that are transcendent in this sense impart spiritual or otherworldly purposes that go beyond the apparent goal of helping people live healthier or happier, more rewarding or fulfilled lives in this world.[37]

But these supernatural purposes do not, as Professor Steve Smith points out, exhaust those state interests that sound in the register of religion.[38] Prominent among such religiously resonant goals are judgments about which understandings and aspirations are worth seeking if people are to live well. Consider questions that the government routinely answers: Should public funds be used for outdoor parks or parking lots? Should the state invest in open spaces and public transportation to make it easier for people from different classes to come together rather than stay apart? Should it encourage people to use their leisure time reading books or buying things? Restrict economic activity to preserve the environment? Give tax breaks to people who marry rather than cohabitate? Redistribute wealth or not? These are unavoidably value-based questions. And they may be informed by what Professor Smith describes as "the sorts of teachings, practices, sensibilities, and communal experience and formation that are commonly associated with 'religion.'"[39] But they

---

[34] John Locke, "A Letter Concerning Toleration," in *John Locke, Second Treatise of Government* 130 (Dover ed. 2002).

[35] See id. at 118–19.

[36] *United States v. Ballard*, 322 U.S. 78, 86–7 (1944).

[37] This account of nonestablishment as barring only official expression of apparently transcendent purposes would immunize government endorsement of beliefs or practices shared by group members who "identify as a Buddhist or a Jew" but "do not happen to subscribe to conceptions of theistic beings or spiritual forces." Nelson Tebbe, *Nonbelievers*, 97 VA. L. Rev. 1111, 1135 (2011) (arguing that their broader association with established religions would "be enough to win [them] legal protection").

[38] Steven D. Smith, "The Constitution and the Goods of Religion," in *Dimensions of Goodness* 321, 333 (V. Hosle ed., 2013).

[39] Id. at 331.

are the kinds of questions that states can and do answer all the time in seeking to promote a society in which people lead good lives. Sometimes these answers are illegitimate, as when they intend bare "desire to harm a politically unpopular group"[40] or if their effect is to undermine the rights of protected class members "to enjoy equal citizenship stature."[41] The reasons that promotions of the good like this are illegitimate, however, have nothing to do with religious establishment. The violation of equal protection guarantees is a discrete basis for forbidding certain among such policies, separate from the claim with which I am concerned here, namely, that those policies are unduly influenced by "religion."

Value judgments relating to matters of sex, race, family, and nature spring from a complex mix of moral, cultural, political, economic, and indeed religious sources. For many if not most people of faith, their thinking about how life should be lived or how society should be arranged is predictably informed by "religion," and the apparent purpose of laws designed to promote the good in the here-and-now may reflect that influence. Such purposes differ from faith, obedience, or salvation in that they will not, in most cases, be susceptible to the futility or public reason problems discussed above that afflict the illicit purposes of forced faith, divine mandates, or the afterlife. Certainly, the reason that some people of faith object to same-sex marriage, contraception access, or transgender rights relies on the revealed word of God. But not necessarily. The way to tell the difference is to ask whether understanding their views in secular terms would force believers to alienate themselves from their deepest convictions. This approach is the best way to understand Justice Antonin Scalia's insight that the Supreme Court "surely would not strike down a law providing money to feed the hungry or shelter the homeless if it could be demonstrated that, but for the religious beliefs of the legislators, the funds would not have been approved."[42] Whatever else might be true about such a law, it would not tell an objective observer that the government is trying to secure people's faith, obedience, or salvation. Rather, it would express valid efforts to promote desirable ways of being and doing. The mere influence of religious sensibilities does not make this kind of apparent purpose impermissible, or by itself a basis to invalidate an otherwise valid law.

---

[40] See, e.g., *United States v. Windsor*, 133 S. Ct. 2675, 2693 (2013) (defining animus against gays and lesbians); *City of Cleburne v. Cleburne Living Ctr., Inc.*, 473 U.S. 432, 446–7, 450 (1985) (similar for animus against people with disabilities).

[41] *Gonzales v. Carhart*, 550 U.S. 124, 172 (2007) (Ginsburg, J., dissenting).

[42] *Edwards v. Aguillard*, 482 U.S. 578, 615 (1987) (Scalia, J., dissenting). Justice Scalia's hypothetical found a real-world analogue in a failed referendum to make Alabama's tax system less regressive on the explicit ground that the existing system was unchristian. See Susan Pace Hamill, *An Argument for Tax Reform Based on Judeo-Christian Ethics*, 54 Ala. L. Rev. 1 (2002).

3. IS RESPECT FOR THE UNBORN "RELIGIOUS"?

On the foregoing account of the endorsement test, the First Amendment question for a state effort to protect embryos and fetuses is: Would an informed and reasonable observer understand its expression of respect for the unborn as trying to save people's souls or force compliance with divine dictates? Or is that central purpose, perceived in context, more plausibly aligned with moral, social, and cultural values? Whether state action imparts a verboten transcendent meaning is less a function of any religious motives lawmakers may have than whether a plausible and familiar secular justification is available. I argue that just such a justification is available for most regulations of reproduction. This does not prove they are ultimately constitutional, or that the state's interests in them outweigh any countervailing rights. It is just to say the First Amendment does not invalidate them in the way the Establishment Clause challenge holds.

The value of respect for unborn life that animates limited protection for embryos or fetuses draws meaning and force from Catholic and Evangelical Christian orthodoxy and advocacy. And religion can, of course, inform people's respect for the unborn. But many believe that the fetus each of us began as is, like cadavers, a powerful symbol of the human narrative that commands our respect.[43] Others think embryos – as genetically unique and complete entities with the potential, one day, if enabled to develop to feel pain, have thoughts, and experience relationships – merit respect as things of creative wonder or beauty, similar in this sense to the animals, artworks, and landscapes the law protects, though they have no rights.[44] These widely shared reasons to value nascent life give valid, even if not always all-things-considered, sufficient justification for limits on the use of embryos for trivial purposes or treatment of fetuses in callous ways. That neither of these familiar grounds for respect involves anything impermissibly religious is enough to shore up the duly secular social meaning of many reproductive regulations designed to protect the unborn.

What about people of faith who sincerely profess to support restrictions on abortion or stem cell research to help secure eternal life or enforce God's command that His creations never be destroyed? That *some* people argue from salvation or obedience does not mean those laws send an impermissibly religious message. Believers' convictions about the "sanctity" of life, of course informed by scripture and tradition, will, even so, tend to reflect their vision of what makes society good: that it protects the most vulnerable, for example, or stands in awe of life from its very

---

[43] See John A. Robertson, Symbolic Issues in Embryo Research, Hastings Ctr. Rep., January–February 1995, 37, 37.
[44] See Dov Fox, *Retracing Liberalism and Remaking Nature: Designer Children, Research Embryos, and Featherless Chickens*, 24 Bioethics 170, 172 (2010).

beginning. The process of interpreting what, according to scripture, is the right way to value the unborn is itself likely guided by readers' broader visions about how to live well.[45] This helps to explain why some adherents or denominations read the Bible to ban any practice that destroys embryos or fetuses, while others read it to allow that the unborn be used for suitably worthy purposes, even ones that require their destruction.[46] These rival scriptural interpretations about the proper treatment of the unborn reflects believers' broader understandings about what is good for society.

Nor is it likely that these broader valuations of the unborn reduce to belief that the divine forbids its destruction or that preserving it promotes salvation. This is not just pretext "aimed at making it appear that the ... law would have been enacted even in the absence of the religious premises."[47] The God that most devout people in America today believe in, Stephen Smith observes, is not arbitrary or inscrutable, but wise and loving; He wants people to live and society to be organized in certain ways *because* those are good ways of being.[48] Believers who say they oppose abortion or stem cell research in part because the Bible teaches respect for the unborn are not dishonest or deluded. But their self-consciously religious reasons for valuing the unborn are informed by acceptable ideas about the good. Most might resist that their interpretation of religious commands is informed by broader understandings about the good life. But this would help explain why many obey some decrees but not others, like bans on eating pork or wearing clothes that mix wool and linen. It is, on this picture of religion, a mistake to think that efforts to protect the unborn characteristically impart ideas the state may not advance. For most laws that safeguard embryos and fetuses, the message they send most plausibly reflects a value of respect that finds familiar expression in constitutionally permissible judgments about living well in the here-and-now that do not violate church-state separation even when they are informed by religious beliefs and practices.

A closer question under First Amendment analysis is posed by restrictions on reproductive conduct that protect prenatal life categorically from the moment it exists.[49] Take efforts to confer the privileges of (state) personhood upon the union of sperm and egg.[50] To review, the issue is not whether such bills are either motivated

---

[45] See Smith, supra note 37, at 334–5.
[46] See generally Susan Quilliam, *Catholics for Choice*, J. Fam. Planning Repro. Health Care 74 (2015).
[47] Michael J. Perry, *Why Political Reliance on Religiously Grounded Morality Does Not Violate the Establishment Clause*, 42 Wm. & Mary L. Rev. 663, 673 (2001).
[48] See Smith, supra note 37, at 335.
[49] See Kent Greenawalt, 2 *Religion and the Constitution: Establishment and Fairness* 528–9 (2008).
[50] See S. Res. 420, 152nd Gen. Assemb., Reg. Sess. (Ga. 2013), available at www.legis.ga.gov/Legislation/en-US/display/20132014/SR/420; S.J. Res. 10, 85th Gen. Assemb., Reg. Sess. (Iowa 2013), available at coolice.legis.iowa.gov/linc/85/external/SJR10_Introduced.pdf; Mississippi Right to Life Initiative, available at www.sos.ms.gov/elections/initiatives/InitiativeInfo.aspx?IId=41; North Dakota

by religion or entangled with it. It is whether their ostensible "acceptance of the belief" *Roe* eschewed, namely, "that [rights-bearing] life begins at conception" is impermissibly transcendent.[51] The view that single-cell life is more than just valuable but inviolate certainly is a church-decreed tenet of faith. But that view can also be credibly defended by the secular fact of biological equivalence over time. This is the argument that every child or adult is the same individual who, at an earlier stage, was a zygote who emerged at fertilization as a new, genetically unique being.[52] This claim that genetic similarity entitles the earliest human life to categorical protection is the kind of ideal about the good life that I have argued the First Amendment does not forbid. Now, I would emphatically reject such personhood bills as bad policy that deprives people, especially women, of equal standing and control over their reproductive lives, besides unconstitutional violations of Fourteenth Amendment rights to abortion and contraception.[53] But I would not say that their message is transcendent in a way that violates the Establishment Clause.

CONCLUSION

The Establishment Clause challenge to many reproductive regulations is premised on a mistake. It fails to distinguish *impermissibly* religious reasons to preserve embryos or fetuses – to promise salvation, compel faith, or obey God – from *permissibly* religious reasons that reflect less transcendent visions about what makes society good: that, like our bodies after we die, nascent life embodies the worth of persons; or that, like majestic nature or history, it inspires a sense of wonder that calls for limits on its treatment. That these kinds of reasons to protect the unborn may be informed by faith gives no basis for objection under the First Amendment, for they do not pose the usual problems about autonomy, futility and public reason. I have tried to give a new defense of the Supreme Court's distinction between traditionalist and religious reasons to regulate reproductive conduct and to show why reading *McRae* together with *McCreary* in this way need not cast church-state suspicion on personhood laws that protect life absolutely from conception.

Initiative, available at http://ballotpedia.org/North_Dakota_%22Life_Begins_at_Conception%22_Amendment,_Measure_1_(2014); Colorado Personhood Initiative, available at http://ballotpedia.org/Colorado_Definition_of_%22Personhood%22_Initiative,_Amendment_67_(2014).

[51] *Roe v. Wade*, 410 U.S. 113, 150 (1973).
[52] See Robert P. George & Christopher Tollefsen, *Embryo: A Defense of Human Life Hardcover* (2008). Even those who granting fetal personhood based on this equivalency rationale might argue that abortion restrictions unlawfully discriminate against women by compelling them alone to give of their bodies and liberty to support another. See Judith Jarvis Thomson, *A Defense of Abortion*, 1 Phil. & Pub. Aff. (1971); Donald Regan, *Rewriting Roe v. Wade*, 77 Mich. L. Rev. 1569 (1979).
[53] See Jonathan Will, *Beyond Abortion: Why the Personhood Movement Implicates Reproductive Choice*, 39 Am. J. Law & Med. 573, 582–3 (2013).

PART IX

Religion, Law, and Public Health

Introduction

Ahmed Ragab

The deep history of public health (and even the history of health care in different societies before the concept of "public health" emerged) has been intractably connected to religion and religious institutions. Hospitals, asylums, leprosaria, and other institutions of collective medical care were often either directly supported by, or indirectly inspired by, religious institutions and authorities in different regions around the world.[1] Religious events like pilgrimages constituted some of the earliest instances in which medical practitioners, state officials, and religious figures had to deal with large masses of people and with the resulting health issues. Also, many historians look at missionary medicine as the foreparent of global health. Of course, the history of missionary medicine, and of missions in general, is wrapped in exploitation and marginalization of native populations, and is deeply connected to colonialism. Medicine and health interventions served as means to conquer, recruit, and convert and to further integrate native populations in the Americas, Africa, Asia and Australia under colonial/Christian powers.

While contemporary public and global health take different approaches to populations' health, religion continues to play an important role – sometimes as a tool for public health interventions and at other times as a condition for the formulation of particular policies. For instance, the World Health Organization (WHO) pioneered and supported a religious-based antismoking program in different parts of the Middle East and the Islamic World.[2] It also sponsored faith-based initiatives

---

[1] For more details, see generally Peregrine Horden, *The Earliest Hospitals in Byzantium, Western Europe and Islam*, 35 J. of Interdisciplinary Hist. 361 (2005); Peregrine Horden, *Hospitals and Healing from Antiquity to the Later Middle Ages* (2008); Ahmed Ragab, *The Medieval Islamic Hospital: Medicine, Religion and Charity* (2015).

[2] See generally Samer Jabbour & Fouad Mohammad Fouad, *Religion-Based Tobacco Control Interventions: How Should WHO Proceed?*, 82 Bulletin of World Health Org. 891 (2004); Mustafa H. Sucakli et al., *Religious Officials' Knowledge, Attitude, and Behavior Towards Smoking and the New Tobacco Law in Kahramanmaras, Turkey*, 11 BMC Pub. Health 602 (2011).

concerning maternal and child health in sub-Saharan Africa to varying degrees of success.[3] At the same time, the faith-based views of the Bush Administration and of the Catholic Church and a number of other faith-based organizations affected HIV-prevention programs in many parts of Africa. Faith-based organizations, and the faith-based approach of the Bush administration, favored a focus on abstinence and faith as the main strategy for HIV-prevention. These policies diverted funding from other approaches, mainly CNN (Condoms, Needles, Negotiations), which focused more on prevention without intervening in moral or religious choices of individuals.[4]

Finally, religious views and traditions are afforded legal protections and privileges that may impact public health. These legal protections and privileges present the more sustained manner in which religion and religious beliefs come in contact with issues related to public health and, therefore, merit closer and deeper investigation. The chapters in this part engage precisely in this discussion.

The chapters attempt to investigate how religion, law, and public health interact, what challenges emerge, and how they can be addressed. The chapters look at cases that carry different significances for public health. In Michele Goodwin's *Race, Religion and Masculinity*, we look at HIV, which, until recently, constituted an epidemic and public health crisis before it appeared to come somewhat under control. Goodwin reminds us that this blunting of the scourge of HIV is only true for white patients and white LGBTQ communities and that the disease continues to ravage communities of color, particularly African-American communities. She looks at how religion impacts the spread of this disease.[5] Aileen Maria Marty, Elena Maria Marty-Nelson, and Eloisa C. Rodriguez-Dod address public health crises related to the disposal of human cadavers, with Ebola as the most obvious example. They look at how religion impacts critical and time-sensitive efforts to defend the population against a raging outbreak.[6] Jay Wexler's *When Religion Pollutes* addresses one of the more recent concerns of public health, namely the environment. He looks at how religious practices impact efforts to limit pollution and to mitigate its health effects.[7]

At the heart of all three chapters, we are faced with questions about the nature of religion: given the diversity of traditions and practices in contemporary society

---

[3] See, e.g., Mariana Widmer et al., *The Role of Faith-Based Organizations in Maternal and Newborn Health Care in Africa*, 114 Int'l J. of Gyn. & Obstetrics 218, 218 (2011).

[4] On these different approaches and the impact of faith in HIV-prevention strategies, see generally Nathan Grills, *The Paradox of Multilateral Organizations Engaging with Faith-based Organizations*, 15 Global Governance 505 (2009); Jenny Trinitapoli, *Religious Teachings and Influences on the ABCs of HIV Prevention in Malawi*, 69 Soc. Sci. & Med. 199 (2009); Victor Agadjanian, *Gender, Religious Involvement, and HIV/AIDS Prevention in Mozambique*, 61 Soc. Sci. & Med. 1529 (2005).

[5] Ch. 27, this volume.

[6] Ch. 28, this volume.

[7] Ch. 29, this volume.

(and in these chapters as well), how can we think about religion in abstract terms and what does "religion" mean? What the chapters show is that religion cannot be simply reduced to inherited traditions, specific holy books, or even the many oral traditions in different parts around the world. Instead, religion needs to be seen as a lived practice that impacts people's lives on a daily basis. As these chapters demonstrate, religion is, in fact, a component of community-making that allows particular groups of people to find shared spaces, confidence, and trust. Particularly for minority communities and marginalized groups, religion and religious institutions serve as anchoring points that hold communities together. Religion is not the only glue, but is an important ingredient.

In thinking about religion as part of community-making social processes, one can understand better the influence of particular religious traditions and practices on their followers. As Goodwin's chapter, for example, describes, the Black Church has played and continues to play a significant role in the Civil Rights struggle of African Americans in America. As a result of a long history of marginalization and exclusion and a deep mistrust of the State and of authorities, which is justified by police violence against black men among other examples, the Black Church emerged as the anchor to this community and an important trustworthy space. In some cases, as shown in the chapter, the community, centered here around the Church, may ostensibly espouse homophobic or misogynistic views. While these views are not necessarily shared by individual congregants, belonging to the community remains of vital importance. This can result in many of the problems, which Goodwin examines, and that follow from congregants' need to "pass" as heterosexual to maintain their membership in their community. In the same way, the indigenous traditions in different parts of Africa, which Marty et al. explore, constitute the backbone for communities that were constantly under attack from colonial powers and from the postcolonial state and are often outside the modernization efforts of the postcolonial state. The symbolism of "kidnapping" the dead becomes all the more important when seen within the context of land acquisition and marginalization. Similarly, even if they constitute environmental and health hazards, ritual practices of minority religious communities (the focus of Wexler) continue to be important for the survival of the community itself in the face of invading powerful cultural currents or emerging xenophobia, racism, and antisemitism.

The chapters reveal another important layer in the interplay of religion, law, and public health. The majority of these cases make evident a significant degree of mistrust between individuals and communities, on one hand, and the State and public health authorities, on the other. This mistrust has important historical and contemporary reasons. Goodwin shows how the Centers for Disease Control (CDC)'s efforts continue to be rooted in a paradigm of uncovering and outing people to, presumably, protect others with less attention to closeted MSM (men who have sex with men) in the community or to other ailments and problems affecting the community in general. This approach occurs in the context of longstanding mistrust between minority communities and the State in the United States. Marty et al. show how states' general negligence and lack of respect and understanding in dealing with burial rituals led to versions of civil disobedience regarding Ebola containment. While the people suffered the immediate consequences of the disease, they did not trust what the government or international health organizations tried to do. When seen in the context of a history of medical experiments in West Africa and the lack of a capable health system or infrastructure, this degree of mistrust can be better understood. Finally, Wexler's subjects are faced with mercury in the food that they buy in stores, lead in the walls of their homes and dangerous pollution produced by richer and more powerful entities, with the State generally unable to intervene. For them, efforts to modify their ritual practices with no similar focus on far more dangerous pollutants and health risks can be seen as largely disingenuous and difficult to sympathize with.

Across these diverse contexts, the chapters in this part engage in important and difficult conversations about what it means to belong to a religious community, how these communities affect people, and how individuals understand their belonging to these communities in relation to their health.

27

Race, Religion, and Masculinity

The HIV Double Bind

Michele Goodwin

We cannot promote any more pastors that allowing [sic] homosexuals to run their church, to be over their children, we must step back and tell them ... you are my enemy. Anybody that is an enemy of God is an enemy of mine ... The fight is on!

— Pastor Roland Caldwell, (signatory to amicus brief opposing gay marriage in Michigan)

In the early morning hours of June 12, 2016, nearly 50 patrons at a gay nightclub in Orlando, Florida were murdered in a relentless hail of bullets. Dozens more were severely injured and will likely suffer the trauma of that fateful evening for their lifetimes. The tragedy sparked important conversations and debates about terrorism, immigration, and gun policy. However, while attention turned to whether the attack represented international terrorism or homegrown domestic terrorism, some from religious communities suggested that the horrific assault was a message about the evils of homosexuality. Baptist minister, Roger Jimenez, explained to his church, "I think Orlando, Florida is a little safer tonight. The tragedy is that more of them didn't die," and asked his congregants if they were "sad that 50 pedophiles were killed today?"[1] Similarly disparaging comments were posted by a Florida prosecutor and numerous others on social media.[2]

---

[1] Brendan Gauthier, *Sacramento Pastor: Orlando Mass Shooting Victims "Deserve What They Got,"* Salon (June 14, 2016), available at www.salon.com/2016/06/14/sacramento_pastor_orlando_mass_shooting_victims_deserve_what_they_got/ [https://perma.cc/L88R-3XC9].

[2] Lisa Fieldstadt, *Florida Official Kenneth Lewis Suspended Over Anti-Orlando Facebook Post,* NBC News (June 18, 2016), available at www.nbcnews.com/storyline/orlando-nightclub-massacre/florida-official-kenneth-lewis-suspended-over-anti-orlando-facebook-post-n594966 [https://perma.cc/96XQ-NQ4M].

I would like to thank my research assistant Mariah Lindsay. © Michele Goodwin

Despite legal progress advancing marriage equality, stigma associated with homosexuality and the broader LGBTQ communities remains entrenched within the United States, and particularly within some religious communities.[3] Indeed, shame continues to be associated with the human immunodeficiency syndrome (HIV)[4] and acquired immune deficiency virus (AIDS)[5] within African-American religious communities. However, HIV stigmatization and shaming within U.S. ethnic communities is largely overlooked in legal and bioethical scholarship. Few scholars explore these important intersections, despite the fact that HIV and AIDS continue to uniquely and disproportionately impact communities of color, particularly among African Americans.

Notwithstanding great strides in public awareness,[6] the treatment of the disease, and the dramatic decline in the deaths of white, gay men since the horrific peak in the 1980s, alarming racial disparities persist.[7] According to government data, African Americans "have the most severe burden of HIV of all racial/ethnic groups in the United States."[8]

For example, the Centers for Disease Control (CDC) report that African Americans account for nearly half "of the more than one million people estimated to be living with HIV in the United States."[9] They accounted for 44 percent "of all new HIV infections."[10] The reach of the disease extends throughout the African American population; no subgroup is spared. Among youth, the CDC warns, "African American youth are particularly affected."[11] The organization cites a disquieting trend: almost 21,000 infections occur yearly among African Americans. Of those cases, 34 percent occur among Black youth. In fact, "black youth represent more than half (57 percent) of all new HIV infections among young people aged 13 to 24" and "these numbers underscore the need to reach a new generation with effective HIV prevention programs and messages."[12]

---

[3] Jack Jenkins, After Orlando, *Faith Leaders Are Starting to Take Ownership of Religious Homophobia*, Think Progress (June 15, 2016), available at http://thinkprogress.org/lgbt/2016/06/15/3788927/faith-leaders-condemn-homophobia/ [https://perma.cc/3E9E-3SJF].

[4] HIV causes a condition in humans that results in a progressive degeneration of the immune system.

[5] This chronic immune system disease is caused by HIV.

[6] HIV & AIDs now claim "national awareness days." April 10 is National Youth HIV & AIDS Awareness Day. May 18 is HIV Vaccine Awareness Day. See HIV/AIDs Awareness Days, AIDS.gov, available at www.aids.gov/news-and-events/awareness-days/ [https://perma.cc/YV7H-E5U5] (last visited April 6, 2016, 6:13 PM).

[7] HIV Among African Americans, Ctr. for Disease Control & Prevention (February 4, 2016), available at www.cdc.gov/hiv/group/racialethnic/africanamericans/ [https://perma.cc/D2SF-GGJU].

[8] Id.

[9] Id.

[10] See CDC Fact Sheet: HIV Among African American Youth, Ctr. for Disease Control & Prevention 1, 1 (2014), available at www.cdc.gov/nchhstp/newsroom/docs/factsheets/archive/cdc-youth-aas-508.pdf [https://perma.cc/2V47-FJA9].

[11] Id.

[12] Id.

The CDC's stark data on racial disparities and HIV reflects an even deeper and worrisome problem, because African Americans comprise only 13 percent of the United States population.[13] What accounts for this trend? Some scholars and pundits point to African American men who have sex with men (MSM) as a viable explanation. Notwithstanding the fact that these men may not identify as homosexual or bisexual, they do acknowledge engaging in sexual intercourse with other men. For example, among African Americans aged 13–24, males experience the higher rates of infection (more so than any other ethnic or racial demographic).[14] Contemporary rates of HIV infection among Black MSM is eleven times higher than that of white male counterparts.[15] It is four times higher than Latino/Hispanic males.[16]

Closer scrutiny of the CDC's research reveals that young African American MSM comprise 86 percent "of new infections" among Black males aged 13–24.[17] That is, within the same age cohort, MSM youth experience dramatically higher rates of HIV infection. Generally, however, "Black males account for more new infections (4,800 in 2010) than any other subgroup of MSM by race/ethnicity and age."[18] The urgency to address this matter from a social policy perspective manifests in perhaps the most startling and problematic data yet. A 2008 study of nearly two-dozen major U.S. cities revealed that greater than 70 percent of African American MSM were unaware of their infections.[19]

The concerns about HIV/AIDS in African American communities must be understood to impact youth of both sexes, particularly as the rate of new infections among young Black women is twenty times higher than that of their white female counterparts.[20] According to the Black Women's Health Imperative, "Every 35 minutes, a woman tests positive for HIV in this country."[21] They note, however, that "the impact of HIV among Black women and girls is even more startling … Nationally, [they] account for 66% of new cases of HIV among women."[22] The majority of these young women "are infected through heterosexual contact."[23]

As troubling as these statics are, such racial disparities lurk in the shadows of heralded achievements in the identification and treatment of HIV/AIDS. So, what

---

[13] Sonia Rastogi et al., *The Black Population: 2010*, U.S. Census Bureau 1, 3 (2011), available at www.census.gov/prod/cen2010/briefs/c2010br-06.pdf [https://perma.cc/KX8G-24P6].
[14] See *CDC Fact Sheet: HIV Among African American Youth*, supra note 10, at 2.
[15] Id. at 1.
[16] Id.
[17] Id.
[18] Id.
[19] Id.
[20] Id.
[21] *HIV/AIDS*, Black Women's Health Imperative, available at www.bwhi.org/issues-and-resources/black-women-and-hiv-aids [https://perma.cc/78P3-WPE4] (last visited April 6, 2016, 6:39 PM).
[22] Id.
[23] Id.

are we missing? And, importantly, what can be done? How should this problem be understood? Can law have an answer without first examining social and religious contexts?

This chapter informs from a unique and sensitive space – that is, the desire to bring greater awareness to a public health matter of indisputably crisis proportions, while also attempting to do so in a manner that takes seriously longstanding fears among African Americans that their communities are stereotyped and pathologized in medical, legal, and social ways that are particularly penetrating and harsh.[24] It argues that efforts to achieve acceptance and approval within their religious communities may result in African American gay men and women suppressing their sexual identities. In turn, this suppression of identity may also be accompanied by efforts to cover homosexuality through stereotypical acts of masculinity and overt heterosexual sex and relationships that, when unprotected, could threaten the health of both partners. This covering may also include homophobia. This chapter frames this tension to cover or closet behavior as a double-bind that implicates the "Black church" and pits spiritual health and identity against individual autonomy and health.[25]

1. RACE, SEX, AND PERFORMING MASCULINITY

Black same gender loving individuals have been beaten so terribly by "the saints" and "the ain'ts" that we have had no other choice but to turn to alcohol, drugs, and elicit sexual behavior for comfort (even though those things only offer temporary relief before making our problems worse – and we know it!). The church has preached hate, and meted out abuse so long that they have made the very "lifestyle" we are said to live the only place we have to go for acceptance and love.

– Tuan N' Gai, Operation Rebirth

In May 2014, the conservative Thomas More Law Center joined forces with African-American clergy to oppose gay marriage in Michigan. The Center filed an amicus brief on behalf of more than 100 African-American ministers in Ohio and Michigan

---

[24] Sandhya Someshekhar, *The Disturbing Reason Some African American Patients May Be Undertreated For Pain*, Washington Post (April 4, 2016) (reporting disturbing findings from a study where "[r]esearchers at the University of Virginia quizzed white medical students and residents to see how many believed inaccurate and at times 'fantastical' differences about the two races – for example, that blacks have less sensitive nerve endings than whites or that black people's blood coagulates more quickly. They found that fully half thought at least one of the false statements presented was possibly, probably or definitely true."). Id.

[25] This project takes seriously that the African American community is not monolithic. Moreover, it recognizes the diversity among religious faiths worshiped among African Americans. The use of terms "Black church," "African American church," and "Black community," references the unique and deep affinities in those communities among African Americans. The terminology acknowledges these terms as reflecting the ways in which many African Americans locate the church and their lives.

who sought to overturn a federal judge's ruling that Michigan's ban on gay marriage was illegal.[26] In their brief, the ministers claimed, "comparing the dilemmas of same-sex couples to the centuries of discrimination faced by Black Americans is a distortion of our country's cultural and legal history."[27] They said, "the fact that American media or other factions erroneously characterize the traditional meaning of 'marriage' as being on par with the civil rights deprivations of Black Americans does not make it so."[28] The ministers forged seductive arguments in their brief, pointing to the fact that race is immutable and homosexuality is not, and asserting "a person's sexuality ... [is] not their state of being or even an immutable aspect of who they are, as race is."[29] They pointed out that slavery's distinct and brutal legacy resulted in the murder of thousands of African Americans and that type of torture and discrimination extended well into Jim Crow, with lynchings in the south and northern racial segregation, wage discrimination, and social polarization. Yet, lurking beneath their argument was not simply a question about states having "no responsibility to promote any person's" sexuality.

Rather, homophobia and insensitivity to gay men and women motivated the ministers' amicus brief and subsequent press conferences and rallies. As one member of the group, Reverend Stacey Swimp, voiced at a press conference, marriage between gay men and women would "destroy the backbone of our society."[30] Another minister, Pastor Roland Caldwell, dramatically proclaimed, "the fight is not only on the inside. The fight is also in the church ... we gotta tell the preachers that are standing up for homosexuality that either you're with God or you're against Him ... We cannot promote anymore preachers who promote sin."[31] Others called for "tak[ing] our

---

[26] Kate Abbey-Lambertz, *Coalition of Black Pastors Speaks Out Against Gay Marriage*, Huffington Post (May 15, 2014, 4:04 PM), available at www.huffingtonpost.com/2014/05/15/black-pastors-gay-marriage-michigan_n_5332496.html [https://perma.cc/G9LU-NCUF].

[27] Brief for the Coalition of Black Pastors from Detroit, Outstate Michigan, & Ohio as Amici Curiae Supporting Petitioners, *DeBoer v. Snyder*, 772 F.3d 388 (2014) (No. 12-cv-10285), available at http://big.assets.huffingtonpost.com/black-pastors-amicus-brief-mich-gay-marriage.pdf [https://perma.cc/J9U4-7T7A], at 5.

[28] Id. at 11.

[29] Id. at 3.

[30] Niraj Warikoo, *Conservative Christian Groups Join Legal Fight to Keep Michigan's Gay Marriage Ban*, Detroit Free Press 1, 1 (May 14, 2014), available at www.micatholic.org/assets/files/advocacy/updates/2014/20140514-MCCAmicusDetroitPastors.pdf [https://perma.cc/KXD9-Z2VD]; see also Niraj Warikoo, *Religious leaders' reactions to gay marriage ruling mixed*, Detroit Free Press (June 26, 2015), available at www.freep.com/story/news/2015/06/26/religious-same-sex-marriage-reaction/29328951/ [https://perma.cc/R7HW-RTCW] (discussing Reverend Swimp's comment after the Supreme Court ruling in *Obergefell* that the decision "will destroy the very fabric of our society.").

[31] Tonya Garcia, *Detroit Pastors File Legal Brief Against Same-Sex Marriage, Say Civil Rights Comparison Is Wrong*, Madame Noire (May 16, 2014), available at http://madamenoire.com/430428/detroit-pastors-file-legal-brief-against-same-sex-marriage-say-its-wrong-to-compare-it-to-civil-rights/ [https://perma.cc/76RX-FA74].

nation back."[32] And the president of a ministerial alliance, Reverend James Crowder, proclaimed, "God does not agree with this kind of behavior," admonishing homosexuality as "despicable, and an abomination."[33]

This type of potent remonstrance of gay congregants (and homosexuals as a whole) must be understood in context. These ministers represented 100 congregations in the upper-Midwest – not a few isolated and fringe religious groups or cults. Sadly, these ministers reflect a core version of the mainstream in Black communities. Their sharp warnings about pain, suffering, and rejection in the present and afterlife for homosexuals and trans individuals suggests that if gay men and women attended those churches they would be unwelcome or shamed if their sexual identities were to become known. Could the force of religion and religious dogma of the sort described above play a key role in the rate of HIV/AIDS infection and the spread of the virus in African American communities?

A. The Double Bind

To say there is such a thing as a gay Christian is saying there's an honest thief. Today, we look back with scorn at those who twisted the law to make marriage serve a racist agenda, and I believe our descendants will look back the same way at us if we yield to the same kind of pressure a radical sexual agenda is placing on us today.

– Bishop Gilbert A. Thompson Jr., pastor of New Covenant Christian Church in Cambridge, Massachusetts

During the last half of the twentieth century, double-bind theory described "the psychological impasse created when contradictory demands are made on an individual"[34] with vulnerable social status or with weaker power within a relationship. The contradictory demands are such that, no matter which command is followed, the response will inevitably be construed as incorrect. According to the renowned critical psychologist and existentialist researcher R.D. Laing, the double bind is a "meta-communicative tangle" where "the 'victim' is caught in a tangle of paradoxical injunctions ... in which he cannot do the right thing."[35]

In the double bind, the disempowered actor operates without a true or unburdened choice, because whichever directive is followed invites negative consequences. The classic clinical examples apply to psychoanalytic clinical research on schizophrenia that involves patterns of communications, primarily at the interpersonal level. A common example is that of the secretly abused child who is told to

---

[32] Id.
[33] Id.
[34] *American Heritage Dictionary* 538 (2000).
[35] R.D. Laing, *Self and Others* 144 (1971).

hug her abuser (often by the abuser). Failure to provide the hug could result in severe punishment later. However, surrendering the hug also demoralizes the child and causes an internal psychological trauma.

The central tenet of the theory is that the disempowered actor feels trapped and afraid – unable to satisfy those to whom they desire to feel closeness or respect; to preserve their own respect they become an outcast and are punished. To accommodate the behavior expected by others, they lose or compromise themself, causing anxiety and psychological harm.

The double bind's utility to examining the intersections of race, religion, and homosexuality seems particularly pertinent, especially given high rates of HIV/AIDS in Black communities. In this context, the proof of not being homosexual is not simply asexuality, but proven or robust heterosexual intimacy carried out by public relationships with often-unknowing women. Failure to demonstrate masculinity in this context could result in shaming, stigmatization, and being cast out of the church and with that, the broader community. For example, one researcher explains that Black men who have sex with other men yet portray a heterosexual lifestyle by being married or having girlfriends "may actually be using a specific stress-coping mechanism."[36]

Professor Malenbranche notes that, "in the face of persistent racism and other forms of social oppression, Black [men who have sex with men] who view being gay as a lifestyle associated with effeminate behavior, displacement from the Black community, and HIV may consciously choose not to identify as such."[37] Malenbranche posits that what may be in operation in these cases "are efforts to survive in a society that places unique and often burdensome demands on Black men's "collective mental health.""[38] That stress, or the "double bind," is likely linked to a significant cohort of African-American men not only remaining closeted, but also donning the lives of heterosexuals by engaging in opposite-sex relationships.[39]

For Black gay men in particular, the double bind is illustrated by the Black church seeming to embrace all its congregants but disciplining and shaming its gay membership, imposing silence and "don't-ask-don't-tell," norms, which contribute in part to HIV/AIDS becoming a "secret epidemic." In essence, the directive is "come unto us, but leave your disease, lifestyle, and identity at home."[40] Indeed, a study

---

[36] David Malebranche, *The Truth About the "Down Low,"* Am. Psychol. Ass'n, (April 2011).
[37] Id.
[38] Id.
[39] Benoit Denizel-Lewis, *Double Lives On The Down Low*, N.Y. Times Magazine (August 3, 2003), available at www.nytimes.com/2003/08/03/magazine/double-lives-on-the-down-low.html?pagewanted=all [https://perma.cc/G473-QVDZ] (observing, "For African-Americans, facing and addressing the black AIDS crisis would require talking honestly and compassionately about homosexuality – and that has proved remarkably difficult, whether it be in black churches, in black organizations or on inner-city playgrounds.").
[40] *The Greatest Taboo: Homosexuality in Black Communities* 117 (Delroy Constantine-Simms ed., 2001).

by researchers Anthony Lemelle and Juan Battle found a direct link between Black churches and negative attitudes toward Black gay men. Their study concluded that those negative attitudes impacted health.[41]

B. Bridge Transmission Theory and Masculinity

Homophobia and even hypocrisy in Black churches might possibly exacerbate HIV and AIDS in Black communities by driving homosexuality underground while encouraging heterosexual intimacy by men who are gay. Indeed, it may be this heterosexual intimacy – a strange result of homophobia among Black ministers – that imperils Black women's health. For example, AIDS is the leading cause of death among Black women aged 25–34.[42] Because most of these women attribute their disease to heterosexual contact, some researchers and commentators are beginning to suggest, albeit with only preliminary data, that Black men who have sex with other Black men also engage in sexual activity with African American women and thereby infect them.[43] Professor David Malebranche, refers to this as "bisexual bridge" transmission.[44]

Professor Malebranche explains that bisexual bridge transmission describes the theory that "compromising down-low Black men" [bring] HIV from the Black MSM community to Black heterosexual women."[45] He goes on to explain that the theory posits that "since some bisexual men do not disclose their same-sex behavior to their female sexual partners, they must be HIV-positive and not be using condoms."[46]

Yet, if closeted sexual behavior is not unique to Black communities, can bridge theory offer a meaningful analysis? That is, if white men also engage in closeted behavior, why are the rates of transmission comparatively low among white women? A 2014 study conducted by The Foundation for AIDS Research reveals that, "health care outcomes [are] worse among black MSM with HIV than white MSM with

---

[41] Anthony J. Lemelle, Jr. & Juan Battle, *Black Masculinity Matters in Attitudes Toward Gay Males*, 47 J. of Homosexuality 39 (2004), available at www.usc.edu/student-affairs/glbss/PDFS/BlackMenMasculinity.pdf [https://perma.cc/N5PE-M2AP].

[42] CDC Fact Sheet: HIV Among African American Youth, supra note 10, at 1.

[43] Brandon Ambrosino, *Why Some Black Men Prefer the Down Low and What It Says About the Black Church in America*, Washington Post (September 4, 2015), available at www.washingtonpost.com/national/religion/why-some-black-men-prefer-the-down-low-and-what-it-says-about-the-black-church-in-america/2015/09/04/59788754-533b-11e5-b225-90edbd49f362_story.html [https://perma.cc/FS5K-UWW3].

[44] Malebranche, supra note 36.

[45] Id.

[46] Id.

HIV," because "32 percent of all black MSM in the U.S. were living with HIV [in 2010], compared with only 8 percent of white MSM."[47]

In part, CDC data informs us that Black men who fit a certain cohort are infected but undiagnosed, and, when diagnosed, may not be receiving antiretroviral therapies. Another clue to this enigma might be greater awareness of HIV and AIDS status among white men who have sex with men. As the CDC reports, a very high percentage of Black men do not know their positive status. They are untested and engage in unprotected sex with men and women. Thus, answering why Black men fail to test for HIV is an important next step for research.

Beyond testing, why else might the transmission rates of HIV to Black women be so high? A potential answer may relate to insufficient use of prophylactics among Black MSMs. A failure to use condoms may seem an obvious answer to the high transmission rates of HIV from Black gay men to heterosexual women, but the reasons for it are not. Could the failure or refusal to use condoms relate to projecting masculinity? Again, more research is necessary to further tease out these questions and analyze responses.

Lastly, social stigma may shackle Black men to a closeted fate that opts for masculinity even when doing so might be reckless. One author calls this, "the burden of black male racial performance." This burden entails proving "what constitutes your maleness and Blackness."[48] Indeed, the burden of proving masculinity – or performing it in Black communities – may be so overwhelming that it extends beyond homosexuality. In other words, "racialized gender performances [may be] used to assign a manly or unmanly status to black men, statuses that are taken as signs of sexuality."[49]

In a 2015 article in the *Washington Post*, Brandon Ambrosino argues that the down-low or bisexual bridge is not a "secret."[50] However, what may be shocking is the hypocrisy of traditional African-American churches. As one prominent African American comedian explained, "If you ever need a boyfriend, you could come to a [Church of God in Christ] convention and leave with two or three, and some of the best sex you've ever had ... I know from experience."[51] To place the comedian's comments in perspective, the Church of God in Christ "is the largest Pentecostal denomination in the U.S. and a predominantly African American church."[52] Jeffrey

---

[47] *New Study Shows Dire Consequences from Elevated HIV Cases Among Black Gay Men in the U.S.*, AMFAR, available at www.amfar.org/racial-disparities/ [https://perma.cc/2W4Q-PWR6].
[48] Vershawn Young, *Compulsory Homosexuality and Black Masculine Performance*, 7 Poroi (2011), available at http://dx.doi.org/10.13008/2151–2957.1095 [https://perma.cc/Q762-3EFN].
[49] Id. See also Roderick Ferguson, *Manliness and Its Discontents: The Black Middle Class and the Transformation of Masculinity, 1900–1930*, 58 Am. Q. 213 (2006).
[50] Ambrosino, supra note 43.
[51] Id.
[52] Id.

McCune suggests that African American churches are a "social space of high constraint, which produces the necessity for this secret," and that it is the churches that "require black men to be [Down Low], which is code for closeted and engaged in heterosexual intimacy.[53]

In essence, what Ambrosino and McCune describe reflects a deep complicity that extends beyond traditional African-American religious spaces, such as "the church" to include African-American women who may intentionally or not also invest in a complex psychology that perpetuates the myth of Black male masculinity. Sadly, even teens suffer the consequences of these sexuality norms. The dramatic rates of infection in African-American communities, coupled with the fact that only 21 percent of Black youth who are infected are prescribed antiretroviral treatment (and less than 20 percent have their virus stabilized) underscore the need for urgent and comprehensive approaches to tackling this problem and asking challenging questions.[54]

2. AIDS, HOMOPHOBIA, AND THE POWER OF BLACK MINISTRIES

One prominent news organization recently featured a story, "Blacks, Gays and The Church: A Complex Relationship,"[55] which made the case, "fairly or not, African-Americans have become the public face of resistance to same-sex marriage, owing to their religious beliefs and the outspoken opposition of many black pastors."[56] Arguably, this deeply entrenched resistance and war against homosexuality is not merely abstract, but also a battle against individual homosexuals, including those who live within Black communities and closet themselves in African-American churches. For Black gay men and women, mainstream incentives to "come out" may pale in comparison to the safety and security of remaining closeted.

Ultimately, sex is at the center of this double bind and public health problem. The behavior of those who engage in "down low" sex or "toss the salad" (another euphemism for dating heterosexually and sleeping homosexually) in order to maintain cultural and social legitimacy and privilege is not surprising. On one hand, if homosexuals or men on the "down low" reveal their sexual identities or sexuality, they stand the risk of being alienated and ostracized within their church communities and, by extension, an important part of the larger Black communities. On the other hand, perhaps what is at stake for them is something more. To the extent that salvation is offered only through religious contact controlled by Black

---

[53] Id.
[54] CDC Fact Sheet: HIV Among African American Youth, supra note 11, at 1.
[55] Corey Dade, *Blacks, Gays and the Church: A Complex Relationship*, National Public Radio (May 22, 2012), available at www.npr.org/2012/05/22/153282066/blacks-gays-and-the-church-a-complex-relationship [https://perma.cc/F7Y8-LUXM].
[56] Id.

pastors, one must fit through the pastor's needle in order to gain the gates of heaven. Thus, efforts to prevent, treat, and engage in HIV and AIDS intervention strategies cannot be properly addressed in law, medicine, or public health without a more nuanced understanding of cultural and racial politics, particularly in religious institutions. For example, Black religious institutions serve social, political, and economic as well as religious roles in African-American communities.[57] According to religious scholar, Dr. Charles Taylor, "[t]he church was more than a safe house," and its importance to the African-American community "can not be overstated."[58] The Black church is significant in the life of the Black community for political, economic, social, cultural and spiritual reasons. It is the single most identified and stable institution within the African-American experience.[59]

Alienation from these important religious institutions imposes a particularly stigmatizing and heavy burden for Blacks who are gay and MSM. It is a type of burden that may be very difficult for white Americans to comprehend – even those who study religion and health. A more sophisticated set of tools is necessary to appropriately and thoughtfully craft solutions to address HIV and AIDS in African-American communities. In light of religious homophobia, who would dare to even advocate for sexual equality in light of the risks of banishment from the intimate confines of community and church? What homosexual, bisexual, or "down-low" man would choose to reveal his sexuality by "coming out"?

The impact of public condemnation from Black ministers is that those suffering from HIV/AIDS remain fearful, closeted, and silent. Nearly 15 years ago, the September 2002 issue of *AIDS Impact*, a publication by the Office of Minority Health in the U.S. Department of Health and Human Services, highlighted the Black church and HIV.[60] The issue described one of a number of encounters in which Black parishioners, even women, suffer alienation, humiliation, and rejection by their churches. Tiffany White described a lonely journey with her Black church, the first place she turned to when she learned about her HIV status.[61] "I loved my church and it loved me. But it didn't love my disease. I told one of the other parishioners after worship and by the next week, I could see that a lot of people

---

[57] J.S. Mattis, *The Role of Religion and Spirituality in the Coping Experience of African American Women: A Qualitative Analysis*, 26 Psychol. Women Q. 308 (2002); Omar M. McRoberts, *Streets of Glory: Church and Community in a Black Urban Neighborhood* (2005).

[58] Charles Taylor, *The Black Church and Juneteenth: A Celebration of Freedom*, 19 (2002).

[59] C. Eric Lincoln, Lawrence H. Mamiya, *The Black Church in the African American Experience*, 7 (1990) (noting that Black churches "were one of the few stable and coherent institutions to emerge from slavery").

[60] See, e.g., Aimee Swartz, *HIV Impact*, Off. Minority Health, U.S. Dep't Health & Hum. Servs. (September/October 2002), available at http://files.eric.ed.gov/fulltext/ED472031.pdf [https://perma.cc/M8JZ-H345].

[61] Id.

were looking at me funny."[62] By the next week, her pew was empty. Within a month, she was replaced as the Sunday school teacher. According to White, "no one said anything. They aren't mean people, they just aren't loving either."[63]

Ms. White's experience is echoed by others in a study conducted by Jacob Levenson, who chronicled the lives of African Americans living with AIDS in southern states. His study provides an informative cultural lens to the problem. For example, Levenson reports that many of the people he encountered and interviewed were so stigmatized and shamed that they were unable to inform others about their HIV status. The narratives, involving teenage girls, young men right out of college, and others, offered a glimpse into the lives of those who understood all too well that any acknowledgment of their illness would result shaming and banishment from their churches.[64] As Levinson notes: "It didn't take an epidemiologist to see that rural Alabama was a potential tinderbox for an AIDS epidemic. It had some of the worst rates of gonorrhea, syphilis, and chlamydia in the country; those diseases, the Centers for Disease Control said, helped facilitate HIV transmission."[65] Could this double bind help to explain why African Americans experience the highest rates of AIDS infection among all U.S. populations?[66]

Intragroup silence and covering likely contribute to some degree to the escalating spread of sexual diseases among youth and adults in the African-American community. Kenji Yoshino speaks of covering as being a secondary aspect of closeting behavior. To silence the disempowered is not enough, as acceptance within the desired group also means disavowing certain relationships and behaviors and appearing to assimilate within the dominant culture. For Black gay men, assimilation and "covering" are expressed through stereotypically "manly" acts and donning the guise of heterosexuality. As described earlier, this means being "on the down-low." Sadly, the rapid spread of AIDS and its devastating effects in African-American communities are undeniable. Most tragically, HIV and AIDS are preventable.

CONCLUSION

The tales of homophobia in Black religious institutions speak directly to the question about the role of religion in health care policy and bioethics. Few other examples of the double bind in health and religion are as clear as the case of HIV/AIDS and the church. As the single most established institution within the Black community, engaging religious leaders in the battle against HIV and AIDS is essential.

---

[62] Id.
[63] Id.
[64] See, e.g., Jacob Levenson, *The Secret Epidemic: The Story of AIDS and Black America* (2004).
[65] Id.
[66] HIV Among African Americans, supra note 7.

28

The Intersection of Law, Religion, and Infectious Disease in the Handling and Disposition of Human Remains

Aileen Maria Marty, Elena Maria Marty-Nelson, and Eloisa C. Rodriguez-Dod

The cultural imperative to bury one's dead is rooted in thousands of years of civilization. The description, in the Iliad, of King Priam infiltrating the Greek camp at night, to beg Achilles to return his son Hector's body for burial is still considered one of the most powerful scenes in western literature.[1]

Not even death may stop a pathogen.[2] Recent outbreaks of highly contagious infectious diseases highlight the pressing need for effective laws governing human remains. Existing laws are inconsistent and underdeveloped in ways that jeopardize public health and conflict with religious beliefs regarding care of the body. These issues become critically important when death results from a highly contagious and highly lethal disease.

In times of crisis, without thoughtful and carefully crafted laws in place, governments may haphazardly impose methods of handling and disposing of bodies as emergency measures. These mandates, no matter how well intentioned, may unnecessarily impinge on personal rights and deeply held religious beliefs. In turn, the mandates risk civil disobedience, increased distrust of government, and unintended serious consequences, including further spread of infectious disease.

This chapter proceeds as follows. Section 1 discusses the significant risk of transmission of infectious diseases from contact with human remains or their bodily fluids. This section illustrates, through the lens of the West Africa Ebola crisis, that the risk is heightened when religious death rituals require close contact with the dead.

---

[1] *Emeagwali v. Brooklyn Hosp. Ctr.*, 815 N.Y.S.2d 494 (Sup. Ct. 2006).

[2] "Diseases have long traveled with patients, and as the phenomena of medical tourism and the more general globalization of health care grow, these problems are likely to grow as well." I. Glenn Cohen, *Traveling Patients, Traveling Disease: Ebola Is Just the Tip of the Iceberg*, OUPblog (December 14, 2014), available at http://blog.oup.com/2014/12/ebola-travel-globalization-disease [https://perma.cc/475H-PF53]; see also Aileen M. Marty, *Recognizing Ebola Is the Key to Prevention*, N.Y. Times (October 2, 2014), available at www.nytimes.com/roomfordebate/2014/10/02/how-to-stop-the-spread-of-ebola/recognizing-ebola-is-the-key-to-prevention [https://perma.cc/65CZ-FR7X].

Section 2 analyzes the varying laws in the United States governing the handling and disposition of human remains during public health emergencies. This section suggests that the United States is not immune to transmission of infections through religious death rituals and explains how disregarding community mores in the United States could conflict with public health goals during a major epidemic. Section 3 calls for clear guidance in the United States before the next major epidemic. The chapter concludes with a call for interdisciplinary collaboration to formulate protocols and processes that are scientifically valid and respectful of religious beliefs.

1. TRANSMISSION OF INFECTIOUS DISEASES FROM HUMAN REMAINS

Dead bodies can and do transmit infections. Knowledge that cadavers can be deadly precedes our awareness of germ theory by thousands of years.[3] Accounts of ancient Greeks purposely dropping cadavers into water supplies of their adversaries[4] and medieval armies catapulting cadavers into enemy fortresses provide evidence of early recognition that dead bodies spread disease.[5] The ancients recognized that not only the bodies, but also the clothing and other materials of the deceased, could be contagious.[6]

Fortunately, other than at a funeral service or a scene of an accident, people in the United States rarely encounter a dead body.[7] Nonetheless, when a person dies from a highly contagious infectious disease, the pathogens on the remains could pose a public health threat, particularly when religious practices call for contact with the dead body.[8]

Deaths from infectious diseases differ from most mass casualties not involving infectious agents. Although both scenarios are tragic, the concerns regarding the spread of disease from human remains are very different. In most natural

---

[3] Germ Theory, Encyclopædia Britannica, available at www.britannica.com/EBchecked/topic/230610/germ-theory [https://perma.cc/KR9G-RHQT] (last visited February 13, 2016).
[4] Daniel J. Dire, CBRNE – *Biological Warfare Agents*, Medscape, available at http://emedicine.medscape.com/article/829613-overview [https://perma.cc/B7YB-FMNJ] (last updated September 2, 2015).
[5] James W. Martin et al., "History of Biological Weapons: From Poisoned Darts to Intentional Epidemics," in *Medical Aspects of Biological Warfare* 1, 2 (Zygmunt F. Dembek ed., 2007).
[6] See, e.g., Russell Hopley, *Contagion in Islamic Lands: Reponses from Medieval Andalusia and North Africa*, 10 J. Early Mod. Cultural Stud. 45, 55 (2010) (citation omitted); see also *Ebola (Ebola Virus Disease): Q&As on Transmission*, CDC, available at www.cdc.gov/vhf/ebola/transmission/qas.html [https://perma.cc/5F6U-YBQE] (last updated November 24, 2015) ("Ebola on dry surfaces, such as doorknobs and countertops, can survive for several hours; however, virus in bodily fluids (such as blood) can survive up to several days at room temperature.")
[7] T. D. Healing et al., *The Infection Hazards of Human Cadavers*, 5(5) Communicable Disease Rep. R61, R61 (1995).
[8] Pentecostalism, BBC, available at www.bbc.co.uk/religion/religions/christianity/subdivisions/pentecostal_1.shtml [https://perma.cc/EWB5-ZPJD] (last updated July 2, 2009).

noninfectious catastrophes (e.g., hurricanes, floods, and earthquakes), cadavers pose only a limited health threat, because most of the common commensal organisms on the body die quickly as the internal temperature drops and the body desiccates.[9]

By contrast, the risk of infection from cadavers is significant during a natural or deliberate outbreak of an infectious disease. If deaths result from highly lethal contagious pathogens, cadavers can become serious public health threats. Risks escalate when such cadavers contain high levels of contagious pathogens on the surface or when the death results from an infection that releases a high concentration of contagious bodily fluid, such as diarrheal fluids from cholera. Moreover, the cadaver may have fleas, lice, or other vectors that could transfer to a living person in close proximity, bite that person, and transmit the deadly infection.

Ebola and its close relative Marburg are perfect examples of highly contagious pathogens that exist in high concentrations on the surface of cadavers and on bodily fluids. Thus, touching the body is potentially lethal. Ominously, the Ebola virus is transmitted principally by direct physical contact with an infected person or the person's body fluids during the later stages of illness or after death.[10] From a scientific and safety perspective, anyone handling a cadaver from an infected body should correctly use appropriate personal protective equipment (PPE), be well-trained in the procedure of using PPE, and use universal precautions, such as ultraviolet germicidal irradiation.[11]

These ideal scientific practices, however, often directly conflict with religious beliefs and potentially violate moral values and cultural customs. The World Health Organization (WHO) reported that at least 20 percent of Ebola cases from the West-African outbreak resulted from improper burial practices.[12] The religious practice of ritual purification by cleaning the body and washing it, typically using pieces of cloth to clean bodily orifices with an ungloved hand, was a clear means of Ebola transmission.[13]

Laws applied hastily in attempts to curtail spreading highly infectious disease from cadavers, particularly during religious death rituals, might not be effective

[9] Claude de Ville de Goyet, *Stop Propagating Disaster Myths*, 356 Lancet 762, 762 (2000); Sarah Tomkins, *Priam's Lament: The Intersection of Law and Morality in the Right to Burial and Its Need for Recognition in Post-Katrina New Orleans*, 12 UDC L. Rev. 93, 106 (2009).

[10] Carrie F. Nielsen et al., *Improving Burial Practices and Cemetery Management During an Ebola Virus Disease Epidemic – Sierra Leone, 2014*, 64(1) Morbidity & Mortality Wkly. Rep. 20 (2015), available at www.cdc.gov/mmwr/preview/mmwrhtml/mm6401a6.htm [https://perma.cc/U4J2-FEBL].

[11] Chetan Jinadatha at al., *Disinfecting Personal Protective Equipment with Pulsed Xenon Ultraviolet as a Risk Mitigation Strategy for Health Care Workers*, 43 Am. J. Infection Control 412, 413 (2015).

[12] *New WHO Safe and Dignified Burial Protocol – Key to Reducing Ebola Transmission*, WHO (November 7, 2014), available at www.who.int/mediacentre/news/notes/2014/ebola-burial-protocol/en/ [https://perma.cc/FVU3-EVGQ].

[13] See WHO, *Guidelines on Hand Hygiene in Health Care* 11–22 (2009), available at www.ncbi.nlm.nih.gov/books/NBK144013/pdf/TOC.pdf [https://perma.cc/DPG5-MNS7].

and may backfire. The need for community buy-in and respect for religious beliefs became evident during the West Africa Ebola crisis. For example, after Liberian President Ellen Johnson Sirleaf decreed that the bodies of Ebola victims had to be cremated, rather than buried, many people became so distressed that they kept their sick relatives home and performed secret burials.[14] These clandestine burials, using religious practices of washing and dressing the bodies, led to a surge of Ebola cases.[15] Similarly, when President Ernest Bai Koroma of Sierra Leone banned public celebrations or gatherings and private burials, major protests erupted.[16]

When laws curtail religious practices, civil disobedience can exacerbate the spread of infectious disease, particularly where religion plays a significant role in the community. The United States is a religious nation, with recent studies reporting slightly over 76 percent of the population identifying as religiously affiliated.[17] Thus, religious practices concerning the deceased should be considered not just in West Africa, but also in the United States, when crafting measures to prevent the spread of infectious disease.

2. INTERSECTION OF U.S. LAWS GOVERNING INFECTIOUS HUMAN REMAINS AND RELIGIOUS DEATH PRACTICES

Are U.S. laws governing the handling and disposal of infectious human remains coherent and consistent for effective implementation during a public health emergency? Do these laws appropriately balance the need to curtail the spread of deadly infectious diseases from cadavers with religious beliefs? As evidenced from the West Africa Ebola crisis, laws governing handling infectious human remains that are not carefully tailored to garner community acceptance may trigger civil disobedience, which could, paradoxically, hasten the spread of disease.

---

[14] *Ebola Cremation Ruling Prompts Secret Burials in Liberia*, Guardian (October 24, 2014, 2:31 PM), available at www.theguardian.com/world/2014/oct/24/ebola-cremation-ruling-secret-burials-liberia [https://perma.cc/UW4C-KW4H].

[15] Helene Sandbu Ryeng, *A Safe Burial for an Ebola Victim in Liberia*, UNICEF (February 9, 2015), available at www.unicef.org/infobycountry/liberia_79760.html [https://perma.cc/J7HA-AJWV].

[16] Mohamed Massaquoi, *In Kailahun: Bondo Women Demand Right to Bury Dead Sowie*, Concord Times (January 27, 2015), available at http://slconcordtimes.com/in-kailahun-bondo-women-demand-right-to-bury-head-sowie/ [https://perma.cc/JH4H-ZRMS]; see also *Sierra Leone Bans Christmas Celebrations, Cites Ebola*, Voice of America (December 13, 2014, 3:27 PM), available at www.voanews.com/content/sierra-leone-bans-public-christmas-celebrations/2557792.html [https://perma.cc/3L4T-CRW5].

[17] *America's Changing Religious Landscape*, Pew Research Center, available at www.pewforum.org/2015/05/12/americas-changing-religious-landscape/ [https://perma.cc/3E7H-GNDH] (last visited April 23, 2016).

A. Overlapping Authority in the United States

In the United States, federal, state, and local governments have broad and overlapping authority to prevent the spread of infectious disease. The federal government's authority in this area is generally based on the Commerce Clause, the Necessary and Proper Clause, and the General Welfare Clause under Article 1 of the U.S. Constitution.[18] The states' public health authority derives from "the police powers granted by their constitutions and reserved to them by the Tenth Amendment to the U.S. Constitution."[19] In the United States, federal and state authorities have a long history of competing for primacy during public health emergencies. During the 1918 Spanish flu epidemic, for example, U.S. federal authorities "often found themselves fighting state and local authorities as well as epidemics – even when they had been called in by these authorities."[20] As a practical matter, partly because of resource allocation at the federal level, coupled with the need for local co-ordination and implementation, both the federal government and the states are critical actors in public health.

The federal government exercises much of its authority for protecting the public from infectious disease through its various agencies, including the Centers for Disease Control and Prevention (CDC). When the Director of the CDC determines that measures taken by state health authorities are "insufficient to prevent the spread of any of the communicable diseases from such State or possession to any other State or possession, he/she may take such measures to prevent such spread of the diseases as he/she deems reasonably necessary..."[21]

Despite this authority, the CDC generally shows deference to, and acknowledges the frontline role of, individual states during public health emergencies. This deference was apparent following the attacks on September 11, 2001, and the anthrax exposures shortly thereafter. At that time, the CDC turned to the Centers for Law and the Public's Health to draft a model Act that states could adopt to assist in the "prevention, detection, management, and containment of public health emergencies," including bioterrorism and epidemics.[22] The final draft of the Model State Emergency Health Powers Act (MSEHPA) was released on December 21, 2001.

---

[18] U.S. Const. art. I, § 8, cl. 1, 3, 18.
[19] Jared P. Cole, Cong. Res. Serv., RL33201, Federal and State Quarantine and Isolation Authority (2014).
[20] *The Great Pandemic*, U.S. Dep't. Health & Hum. Services, available at www.flu.gov/pandemic/history/1918/life_in_1918/healthservice/index.html [https://perma.cc/57WT-L2VJ] (last visited April 22, 2016).
[21] 42 C.F.R. § 70.2 (2016).
[22] The Model State Emergency Health Powers Act (MSEHPA), Ctrs. for Law and the Pub.'s Health, available at www.publichealthlaw.net/ModelLaws/MSEHPA.php [https://perma.cc/R3Q7-DGSV] (last updated January 27, 2010).

The preamble to MSEHPA provides that it attempts to strike a balance to "contain emergency health threats without unduly interfering with civil rights and liberties."[23] Despite some criticism, a majority of states adopted at least some of the provisions of MSEHPA. The MSEHPA framework applies in times of a "public health emergency." MSEHPA provides that the term "public health emergency" includes "an occurrence or imminent threat of an illness or health condition that: (1) is believed to be caused by . . . : (i) bioterrorism; [or] (ii) the appearance of a novel or previously controlled or eradicated infectious agent or biological toxin," where there is a high probability of "a large number of deaths," "a large number of serious or long-term disabilities," or "widespread exposure to an infectious or toxic agent that poses a significant risk of substantial future harm."[24]

MSEHPA includes provisions for the safe disposal of human remains during public health emergencies. The general authority to adopt reasonable and necessary measures for handling human remains is found in Section 504(a). That section provides a nonexclusive list of measures, such as burial, cremation, interment, and disinterment of human remains. When the public health emergency is attributable to a contagious disease, Section 504(c) provides specific guidance. It permits authorities "to order the disposal of any human remains of a person who has died of a contagious disease through burial or cremation within twenty-four (24) hours after death."[25] This specific authority is qualified, however, by language within Section 504(c) providing that the authorities take into account, "to the extent possible, religious, cultural, family, and individual beliefs of the deceased person or his or her family" in disposing of the human remains.

Despite MSEHPA, states are not uniform in their laws regarding disposal of infectious human remains. Not all states adopted MSEHPA. Several states that adopted many of MSEHPA's other provisions did not adopt Section 504. Moreover, some states that adopted the general provision of Section 504 did not adopt Section 504(c) dealing with infectious bodies or omitted the qualifying language concerning respect for religious beliefs.

For example, South Carolina and Wyoming appear to have provisions similar to Section 504 of MSEHPA, giving the state health authorities significant latitude for the safe disposal of human remains during public health emergencies within 24 hours.[26] Neither, however, includes the language in Section 504(c) accommodating religious beliefs. Although Ohio's statute provides for disposal within 24 hours, it varies significantly from MSEHPA with regard to religious accommodations. Ohio's statute expressly prohibits a public or church funeral for a person who died from a

[23] Id.
[24] Id.
[25] Id. at § 504(c).
[26] S.C. Code Ann. § 44-4-320 (2016); Wyo. Stat. Ann. § 35-1-241 (2015).

communicable disease and forbids taking the cadaver into any church or other public place.[27] By contrast, a few states – Iowa, New Jersey, New Mexico, Oklahoma, and Oregon – expressly track the language of Section 504(c) providing for accommodation of religious beliefs.[28] Even if a state's version of MSEHPA does not specifically include the religious consideration provision, other laws in those states may afford the surviving family members similar consideration for their religious beliefs.

B. Respecting Religious Death Practices

The free exercise of religion is guaranteed under the First Amendment of the U.S. Constitution. In addition, the Restoration of Freedom of Religion Act of 1993 (RFRA) provides certain religious exemptions from federal laws for religious practices.[29] Many states also have their own version of RFRA or religious freedom provisions in their state constitutions.[30] All these religious rights must be analyzed in light of the state's interest in protecting the public from deadly infectious diseases. The U.S. Supreme Court made clear in *Jacobson v. Commonwealth of Massachusetts*, a case involving enforcement of a mandatory smallpox vaccine, that certain government interests may trump religious objections.[31] When public health is the compelling interest, the U.S. Supreme Court has further stated that "the right to practice religion freely does not include liberty to expose the community" to infectious disease.[32] Generally, under the federal and state RFRAs, when a government's directive would burden a person's exercise of religion, the government would need to show that its mandate is in furtherance of a compelling interest and is the least restrictive means of furthering that interest.[33] Preventing a major epidemic would almost invariably be a compelling interest. A government using the least restrictive means, thus, would likely withstand a challenge.

Nevertheless, for practical reasons, when dealing with laws that curtail religious death rituals, the government's least restrictive alternative should attempt to accommodate various religious practices. One of the painful lessons learned from the West

---

[27] Ohio Rev. Code Ann. § 3707.19 (2016).
[28] Iowa Code § 135.144 (2015); N.J. Stat. Ann. § 26:13-7 (2015); N.M. Stat. Ann. § 12-10A-6 (2015); Okla. Stat. tit. 63, § 6502 (2015); Or. Rev. Stat. § 433.449 (2015).
[29] 42 U.S.C.A. § 2000bb-1 (2015).
[30] See Eugene Volokh, *Religious Law (Especially Islamic Law) in American Courts*, 66 Okla. L. Rev. 431, 441 (2014).
[31] *Jacobson v. Commonwealth of Massachusetts*, 197 U.S. 11, 25 (1905).
[32] *Prince v. Massachusetts*, 321 U.S. 158, 166–7 (1944) (citing *People v. Pierson*, 68 N.E. 243 (N.Y. 1903)).
[33] "Though all of the sixteen state RFRAs adopt a compelling-interest test, they differ in what they require as a threshold – that is, they differ in what a plaintiff must initially show in order to trigger the government's obligation to demonstrate a compelling interest." Christopher C. Lund, *Religious Liberty After Gonzales: A Look at State RFRAs*, 55 S.D. L. Rev. 466, 478 (2010).

African Ebola crisis is that emergencies test communities' respect for government and that, when laws curtail religious practices, civil disobedience can exacerbate the spread of infectious disease. The risk of civil disobedience in these situations may be heightened when laws affecting religious practices are inconsistent.

In the United States during the Spanish flu epidemic, there was resistance to health measures that were "seen as inconsistent, burdensome, or contrary to common sense or deeply held values."[34] In attempts to stop the spread of the Spanish flu, the federal, state, and local authorities imposed differing mandates. The various restrictions included church closures and bans on public gatherings and funerals. Community protests emerged, and both lay and religious leaders argued "that an exclusively medical perspective of human suffering ignored a more spiritual one, depriving residents of solace."[35] One of the most devastating issues was the failure to respect social mores in regards to burial practices when hospitals and mortuaries were overwhelmed. In particular, the emergency measure of mass graves[36] was deemed to undermine the sense of propriety and religious beliefs. A recent U.S. Department of Defense (DOD) study of the Spanish flu "uncovered repeated examples of social concerns and anxieties associated with the mandated delay of funeral arrangements" and restrictions on attendance at funerals.[37] The report noted that the "emotional strain of not being able to dispose of the dead promptly, and in accordance with cultural and religious customs, has the power to create social distress and unrest" in the community.[38]

These problems are not confined to history. United States emergency preparedness laws, including state versions of MSEHPA, continue to suffer from inconsistency. Moreover, with regard to the handling of human remains during an epidemic and the intersection of religious rights, state laws vary greatly. Several states' statutes regarding disposal of human remains during an epidemic expressly require consideration of religious beliefs, whereas others are silent. In addition, some states have religious freedom provisions, such as found in state RFRAs, which may also apply to disposal of human remains. This overlapping and confusing legal system for handling infectious human remains during an epidemic could prove difficult to

---

[34] Monica Schoch-Spana, *Implications of Pandemic Influenza for Bioterrorism Response* 1412 (2000), available at http://cid.oxfordjournals.org/content/31/6/1409.full.pdf [https://perma.cc/BDU4-FXMA].

[35] Id.

[36] *New Jersey expressly permits temporary mass burials during a public health emergency*, N.J. Stat. Ann. § 26:13-7(1).

[37] Howard Markel et al., *A Historical Assessment of Nonpharmaceutical Disease Containment Strategies Employed by Selected U.S. Communities During the Second Wave of the 1918–1920 Influenza Pandemic* 137, 137 (2006), available at http://chm.med.umich.edu/wp-content/uploads/sites/20/2015/01/DTRA-Final-Influenza-Report.pdf [https://perma.cc/V24C-Y33P].

[38] Id.

implement, be viewed as arbitrary, and, ultimately, hamper attempts to curtail the spread of infection.

For example, if a state prohibits religious death rituals, relatives of the deceased may refuse to deliver a body to health authorities and, instead, attempt home burials. This may occur where the public health authority requires cremation, in contravention of religious beliefs. Even more troubling, perhaps, is a scenario where relatives of a dying person cross state lines to permit the infectious person to die in a state that would accommodate religious death rituals. Unfortunately, these scenarios are quite plausible. In the United States, there are a myriad of religious customs regarding death that are deemed critical for the survivors and for the deceased's safe transfer into the afterlife. Prohibiting families from performing such rites is viewed as a spiritual peril to the deceased, the family, and the community. As the DOD warned in its study of the Spanish flu, strict mandates that prohibit community practices may inflame groups, incite violence, and thereby spread the disease further.[39]

3. GUIDANCE FOR DISPOSITION OF HUMAN REMAINS BEFORE THE NEXT MAJOR EPIDEMIC

As is evident from the Spanish flu epidemic in the United States and the recent West African Ebola crisis, failure to properly prepare for the handling of vast numbers of dead bodies in thoughtful ways can significantly hinder efforts to combat the spread of infectious disease. In light of the critical importance of community acceptance of emergency measures, the United States should devise procedures for disposal of human remains that are clear and respectful of religious practices before the next major epidemic.

The international community has developed protocols on proper disposal of infectious bodies that could be helpful to the United States in crafting such procedures. Recognizing that containment of infectious disease requires worldwide cooperation, the WHO's 194 member states adopted the revised International Health Regulations (IHR). The IHR provides a framework for coordinating a response to a "public health emergency of international concern" (PHEIC).[40] Acknowledging that infectious human remains constitute a public health risk, the IHR expressly provides that the WHO recommendations may address the use of health measures to ensure the safe handling of human remains.

In accordance with IHR, in August 2014, the WHO declared the West African Ebola outbreak a PHEIC and issued recommendations.[41] Those recommendations

---

[39] Id. at 22.
[40] *International Health Regulations*, WHO 1-2 (2d ed. 2005).
[41] Statement on the 1st Meeting of the IHR Emergency Committee on the 2014 Ebola Outbreak in West Africa, WHO (August 8, 2014), available at http://who.int/mediacentre/news/statements/2014/ebola-20140808/en/ [https://perma.cc/CHQ9-HFRX].

recognized the risk from burial practices and provided that States with Ebola "should ensure funerals and burials are conducted by well-trained personnel, with provision made for the presence of the family and cultural practices, and in accordance with national health regulations, to reduce the risk of Ebola infection."[42]

Because unsafe cultural and religious burial practices continued, in October 2014, the WHO issued a 12-step protocol containing more specific guidance for culturally sensitive burials.[43] According to the protocol, the burial team should include a religious representative to work with the family to determine how to conduct a dignified burial in the particular social and religious context. The burial team should apprise the deceased's family about the procedure and inform them of their "religious and personal rights to show respect for the deceased."[44] With respect to Christian and Muslim decedents, the protocol identifies procedures for dignified burial. Recognizing the import of religious rituals of bathing or touching the body, the protocol specifies that Christian burials may include sprinkling blessed water over the body and reading scripture. For Muslim burials, the protocol provides for a dry ablution instead of an ablution performed with water and the use of white, rather than dark-colored, body bags to represent the burial shroud.

In January 2015, the WHO convened a meeting of more than 150 participants, which discussed the critical importance of community engagement and communication in breaking the chains of transmission of Ebola. The report from that meeting ("Taking Stock Report") noted that: "Many of the cultural practices which have enabled the transmission of [Ebola] have been curtailed during the emergency, but it is felt that these changes, such as changes in funeral practices, should be maintained in the long term, as it is uncertain where this disease may recur."[45] Significantly, the report provided the following key recommendations and action points for safe burials[46]:

Recommendations	Action Points
Increase capacity for dead body management	Consider research on local customs and funeral rites and anthropological studies recommended to understand local culture.
Establish teams in charge of safe burials	
Update safe burial protocols with regard to religious practice	Disseminate existing guidelines or articles. Train and equip National teams to perform safe burials activities
Identify safe burials sites	

[42] Id.
[43] *Field Situation: How to Conduct Safe and Dignified Burial of a Patient Who Has Died from Suspected or Confirmed Ebola Virus Disease*, WHO (October 2014), available at http://apps.who.int/iris/bitstream/10665/137379/1/WHO_EVD_GUIDANCE_Burials_14.2_eng.pdf [https://perma.cc/FUM9-CUVY].
[44] Id.
[45] WHO, *Ebola Virus Disease Preparedness: Taking Stock and Moving Forward* 9 (2015).
[46] Id. at 32.

In addition to the WHO, the CDC also has provided some guidelines on culturally sensitive burials, albeit on a limited basis. For example, during the West Africa Ebola crisis, the CDC issued guidelines to be used in West Africa with regard to the disposition of human remains. The CDC's guidelines were not as detailed as the WHO protocol for culturally sensitive burials, but did, however, suggest the need for safe respectful burials. The CDC's December 2014 pamphlet titled "Ebola Must Go: Bury All Dead Bodies Safely" noted that government-imposed safe burial practices may be "very difficult for the family and the community" and that safe burial teams should "talk to the family members about the different ways they can pay respect without touching the body."[47] The pamphlet further provided that a religious leader could attend the burial. Concerning the Ebola outbreak in Sierra Leone, the CDC published a report documenting the need for "plans to effectively and safely handle the bodies of persons who have died from Ebola, and to execute these plans in a dignified and respectful manner that honors the deceased, their families, and their communities."[48] The report noted that "[r]apidly scaling up of safe, dignified burial practices and focusing on increasing community acceptance of safe burials during an Ebola epidemic could interrupt transmission substantially."[49]

The CDC's observations regarding cultural and religious sensitivities in West Africa do not appear to have been incorporated in the CDC's U.S. guidelines concerning safe handling of human remains of Ebola victims in the United States.[50] What might be the reason for the difference between the CDC's West Africa guidelines and its U.S. guidelines? One reason could be that the CDC assumes that most of the Ebola deaths in the United States "would likely occur within a hospital setting."[51] Accordingly, its guidance on safe handling of Ebola victims in the United States is directed to "[p]ersonnel who perform postmortem care in U.S. hospitals and mortuaries."[52] Perhaps because of the assumption regarding hospital deaths, the CDC guidelines do not specifically include the culturally sensitive protocols suggested by the WHO.

Is the CDC too optimistic about the capacity of U.S. hospitals to handle mass casualties during the next major epidemic? If hospitals become overwhelmed or

---

[47] *Ebola Must Go: Bury All Dead Bodies Safely*, CDC (December 23, 2014), available at www.cdc.gov/vhf/ebola/pdf/bury-body-safely.pdf [https://perma.cc/BYC6-D7MC].

[48] Nielsen, supra note 10 (citation omitted).

[49] Id.

[50] CDC, *Interim Guidance for Managing Patients with Suspected Viral Hemorrhagic Fever in U.S. Hospitals* (May 19, 2005), available at www.cdc.gov/vhf/ebola/pdf/vhf-interim-guidance.pdf [https://perma.cc/2MH6-L3JY].

[51] *Guidance for Safe Handling of Human Remains of Ebola Patients in U.S. Hospitals and Mortuaries*, CDC, available at www.cdc.gov/vhf/ebola/healthcare-us/hospitals/handling-human-remains.html [https://perma.cc/XD7E-M9JD] (last updated February 11, 2015).

[52] Id.

if travel restrictions and quarantines are imposed, management of the contagious disease may require home isolation as occurred during the Spanish flu. Recognizing these possibilities, the United States should develop culturally and religiously sensitive procedures for handling human remains during a public health emergency. The United States should review and borrow from the WHO's twelve-step protocol and the CDC's guidance on safe burials that it developed for West Africa. These procedures should be carefully tailored for adoption in the United States and its various religiously diverse communities.

CONCLUSION

The U.S. procedures for handling infectious human remains should not only be scientifically valid, but should also be consistent and sufficiently flexible to accommodate varying religious practices. Strictly science-based policies, isolated from the reality of how people might react on an emotional and spiritual basis during a public health emergency, are likely to fail. The goal of devising a scientifically valid system for disposal of human remains that is religiously and culturally sensitive may be more readily achieved if the process for designing such a system includes the collaboration of religious and community leaders, scholars, scientists, and policymakers. Some of the groundwork for developing such an interdisciplinary and collaborative process can already be found in hospital programs dealing with their patients' religious diversity. Several hospitals have recognized that the "time of death – the hours before and the hours after – is embedded in meanings and rules for different religious groups making it a prime example of the importance of cultural and religious competencies."[53] Thus, these hospitals have taken steps to bridge "the gap between medical institutions and the cultural and religious communities of their patients."[54]

Similarly, U.S. policymakers need to bridge the cultural competency gap and use collaborative processes to ensure effective implementation of public health emergency measures. As Professor Jay Wexler astutely notes, "collaboration might help persuade religious believers to alter their practices" in beneficial ways "without either unduly harming the religious community or forcing the offending practices underground where they potentially cannot be reached by regulation at all."[55]

---

[53] *Hospitals in a New Era*, Harvard University, available at http://pluralism.org/encounter/todays-challenges/hospitals-in-a-new-era/ [https://perma.cc/EZG4-H8U3] (last visited April 22, 2016).
[54] Id.
[55] Jay Wexler, Ch. 29.

29

When Religion Pollutes

How Should Law Respond When Religious Practice Threatens Public Health?

Jay Wexler

In recent years, clashes between the values of certain religious traditions and norms of the secular state – anti-discrimination, gender equality, relatively comprehensive health care, and so on – have become more pronounced and politically (and legally) charged.[1] There is another way, however, less recognized but still important, in which certain religious traditions have come into conflict with the secular state. This involves religious practices that harm the environment, bringing religion into conflict with the state's secular goals of protecting its natural resources and the health of its citizens.

Although numerous religious practices exist that pollute the environment and place stress on health care systems around the world, I focus here on two examples from the United States: the ritualistic use of mercury by practitioners of Caribbean religions such as Santeria and Voodoo in cities such as Miami and New York, and the resistance of Old Order Amish in Pennsylvania and elsewhere to the protection of waterways from agricultural runoff pollution caused by their farming and sanitary practices. In both cases, religious beliefs and practices have polluted the environment and threatened public health (in the former, mercury poisoning has caused neurological damage to children living in homes where rituals have taken place; in the latter, E. coli and other dangerous substances have entered water supplies), and the EPA has engaged the religious communities to try and reach solutions.

In this article, I consider how the state should respond when faced with a conflict between deeply held religious beliefs and environmental protection. I suggest that the government must tread carefully with religious groups if it wants to appropriately balance the interests of public health and environmental protection with religious

---

[1] See generally *Burwell v. Hobby Lobby*, 134 S.Ct. 275(2014); Stephen Prothero, *Indiana Needs to Balance Gay, Religious Rights*, USA Today, March 30, 2015.

This article is adapted from my book, *When God Isn't Green: A World-Wide Journey to Places Where Religious Practice and Environmentalism Collide* (Beacon Press 2016).

freedom. Specifically, the state must be extraordinarily careful in using law as a heavy-handed weapon to promote its interests and should first attempt to defuse conflicts through approaches such as promoting education, engaging in collaborative efforts with religious communities, and seeking technological solutions.

1. RELIGION AND THE ENVIRONMENT

The relationship between religion and the environment has always been extremely complicated. On the one hand, many believe that organized religion, and particularly Christianity, has historically been unfriendly toward the environment. In his classic 1966 lecture before the American Association for the Advancement of Science entitled "The Historical Roots of Our Ecological Crisis," historian Lynn White, Jr. surely spoke for many when he laid the blame for much of the world's environmental problems at the feet of Christianity. "Christianity, in absolute contrast to ancient paganism and Asia's religions," White wrote, "not only established a dualism of man and nature but also insisted that it is God's will that man exploit nature for his proper ends."[2] Echoes of this attitude toward nature abound today: the religious right's skepticism of science; an Alabama official's claim that the EPA's coal regulations interfered with a "gift from God";[3] the *Resisting the Green Dragon* DVD series put out by a conservative Christian group that denies the importance of climate change and decries the environmental movement as "one of the greatest threats to society and the church today."[4]

On the other hand, religion has done a lot of good for the environment, particularly lately. For one thing, many Eastern religions, particularly Buddhism and Taoism, as well as other traditions that treat natural objects as sacred (Shintoism, for example, and Native American religions) are largely environment-friendly. Secondly, contrary to claims that Christianity teaches humans to assert *dominion* over the environment, many Christian believers interpret the Bible to require that humans act as *stewards* of nature. For example, former pastor and presidential candidate Mike Huckabee has publicly cited his Biblical beliefs as support for his view that "we should see to it that our care for the environment enhances not only its aesthetic value but preserves the resources themselves for future generations."[5]

---

[2] Lynn White, Jr., *The Historical Roots of Our Ecological Crisis*, Science, March 1967, 1203–7.
[3] Stan Diel, *Pray God Blocks EPA Plan, Chief Regulator of Alabama Utilities Tells Consumers* (July 28, 2014, 2:13 PM), available at www.al.com/news/index.ssf/2014/07/post_14.html [https://perma.cc/RRW5-7F3Q].
[4] See Resisting the Green Dragon, available at www.resistingthegreendragon.com/ [https://perma.cc/79PN-VUM7] (last visited May 27, 2016).
[5] Mike Huckabee on Environment, OntheIssues.org, available at www.ontheissues.org/2016/Mike_Huckabee_Environment.htm [https://perma.cc/NW86-T3YS] (last updated March 12, 2016).

Finally, over the past three decades, a number of organized religious groups have begun enthusiastically promoting environmental values. For example, acting under the umbrella of a secular organization known as the Alliance of Religions and Conservation, a dozen faiths from around the world have co-operated in spreading environmental education in rural areas, promoting environmentally friendly pilgrimages, and planting trees in Africa.[6] In the United States, some of the loudest voices clamoring for action on climate change come from the Christian evangelical community, many members of which have signed formal commitments to fight global warming.[7] Indeed, the overall narrative of recent years is probably that organized religion has recognized the importance of protecting the environment and is acting accordingly.

Yet, even as religions begin to embrace environmental values, we find throughout the world instances in which particular religious practices harm the environment. In Colombia, demand for the palm fronds used in Palm Sunday celebrations almost rendered extinct a rare and beautiful parrot.[8] In Israel, bonfires to mark the holiday of Lag B'Omer fill the air with dangerous smoke.[9] In South Africa and Zimbabwe, members of the Shembe religion – a mixture of Christian and Zulu traditions – drape themselves in leopard pelts during spiritual dances; the demand for pelts has a serious effect on wild leopard populations.[10] In India, Hindus throw half-burnt corpses into the Ganges River and immerse thousands of enormous plaster-of-Paris idols of the elephant god Ganesh into rivers, lakes, and oceans.[11] In Bangladesh, Hindus celebrate the Festival of Light by sacrificing tens of thousands of turtles annually, while Buddhists in Taiwan and elsewhere engage in "mercy release," in which they release millions of small animals (birds, turtles, frogs) into inappropriate environments and then capture and release them once more, killing thousands in the process.[12]

2. CONFLICTS BETWEEN RELIGIOUS PRACTICES AND ENVIRONMENTAL PROTECTION

Investigating instances like *these*, and thinking about what we might do about *them*, is the aim of this article. One interesting example involves the religious use

---

[6] See generally Alliance of Religions and Conservation, available at www.arcworld.org/ [https://perma.cc/9QDV-E68V] (last visited May 27, 2016).
[7] See David Wheeler, *Greening for God: Evangelicals Learn to Love Earth Day*, Atlantic (April 18, 2012).
[8] See Susan McGrath, *Parrot Conservation Changes a Catholic Tradition*, Audubon (March–April 2012).
[9] See Ron Friedman, Lag B'Omer *Takes its Fiery Toll*, The Times of Israel (April 29, 2013).
[10] See Nkepile Mabuse & Vanessa Ko, *Wild Leopards Threatened by Religious Tradition in Africa*, CNN (September 17, 2012), 10:37 PM), available at www.cnn.com/2012/09/16/world/africa/leopards-shembe-south-africa/ [https://perma.cc/7UTF-24NK].
[11] See, e.g., Sarika Bansal, *Ganesh Chaturthi: India's Toxic Festival*, Guardian (September 22, 2010); Marc Abrahams, *God-Awful Pollution of India's Waters*, Guardian (April 30, 2012).
[12] Elizabeth Hsu, *"Release of Life" Religious Practice Spurs Big Business*, Taiwan News (October 2, 2009).

of mercury. Mercury is an element that people generally do not want to mess with. Touching or eating mercury or, most dangerously, breathing in the vapors that it releases, can be extremely dangerous, potentially causing respiratory problems and damage to the nervous system. Given the perils of inhaling mercury vapors, it might be surprising to learn that some religious believers sprinkle the metal inside their homes to ward off evil spirits. The practice puts at risk not only current residents but also future ones, as mercury can stay in fabrics and carpets for up to a decade, releasing dangerous vapors.

Back in 1989, Arnold Wendroff, a middle-school chemistry teacher in Brooklyn, was teaching his students about the periodic table. When he asked if they knew what mercury was used for, he fully expected them to mention thermometers. Instead, one of his students answered that his mother, a Santeria practitioner originally from Puerto Rico, sprinkled it around their apartment to fend off witches. Concerned and curious, Wendroff became a one-man watchdog of the ritualistic use of mercury. He learned that many practitioners of Caribbean religions like Santeria, Palo, and Voodoo believe mercury brings good luck and wards off evil spirits. In U.S. cities with substantial populations of these believers – New York, Chicago, Miami, and elsewhere – practitioners purchase capsules containing a small amount of liquid mercury from so-called botanicals, which are basically stores that sell religious paraphernalia, and then do things like sprinkle it on floors, furniture, or car interiors, mop the floor with it, burn it in candles, mix it with perfume, or even swallow it. Because mercury vapors are so dangerous to inhale, many of the people who will inhale the vapors are children (who are closer to the ground than their parents), and mercury remains dangerous for so long, Wendroff concluded that the ritualistic use of mercury posed a significant health hazard that the government needed to address.[13]

Through Wendroff's efforts, the EPA became aware of the problem in the early 1990s and started considering whether to take action. The agency has several statutes that it could have used to regulate the ritual use of mercury inside homes, most importantly the Toxic Substances Control Act ("TSCA"), which allows the agency to take a wide variety of regulatory actions against substances that pose an unreasonable risk to the environment or public health.[14] EPA considered using the TSCA but

---

[13] See Emily Yehle, *EPA Weighs Threats Posed by Mercury Used in Religious Rituals*, N.Y. Times (May 18, 2011); Lauryn Schroeder et al., *Ritualistic Use of Mercury Remains a Mystery – but Health Effects Aren't*, Medill Reports (March 14, 2013), available at http://news.medill.northwestern.edu/chicago/news.aspx?id=219201 [https://perma.cc/PY29-6KTQ]; Leonora LaPeter & Paul de la Garza, *Mercury in Rituals Raises Alarms*, St. Petersburg Times Online (January 26, 2004), available at www.sptimes.com/2004/01/26/news_pf/Hillsborough/Mercury_in_rituals_ra.shtml [https://perma.cc/Q444-C88B]. For a piece written by Wendroff himself, see Arnold P. Wendroff, *Magico-Religious Mercury Use in Caribbean and Latino Communities: Pollution, Persistence, and Politics*, 7 Envtl. Prac. 87 (2005).

[14] Toxic Substances Control Act, 15 U.S.C. §2601 et seq. (1976).

decided against it, opting instead to work with states and municipalities to spread the word about the dangers of mercury through education and community outreach.

Unsatisfied, Wendroff continued to pressure the EPA and others, and in 1999, the agency established a formal "Task Force on Ritualistic Uses of Mercury," complete with subcommittees on issues like clinical research, environmental monitoring, and community outreach. The Task Force conducted research, held conference calls, interviewed interested parties, and held a public forum in 2001 where it heard from all sorts of people, including representatives of various Caribbean religious groups, who almost uniformly recommended against the EPA targeting specific religions for regulation. In 2002, the Task Force issued a hefty 111-page report summarizing its activities and conclusions. Again, decision makers rejected the possibility of direct regulation in lieu of softer approaches, such as reaching out into the community, encouraging alternatives, and engaging in further research.[15]

In the wake of the Task Force's Report, Wendroff continued to call for further efforts to address the indoor religious mercury problem. In 2005, he asked the Office of the Inspector General at EPA to "determine whether EPA had adequately investigated whether [indoor religious mercury] contamination poses an environmental health threat and, if so, had substantively acted to address its dangers."[16] The Office concluded that the EPA had acted properly and did not recommend further action.[17] It did, however, release a report on its investigation "to further emphasize that the ritual use of mercury poses a health risk."[18] This final conclusion does seem to be accurate. A 2011 article, for instance, reported on the case of a three-year-old who suffered mercury poisoning when her family moved into a Rhode Island apartment that had been the site of ritual mercury use by a former tenant many years earlier.[19]

No less than the air we breathe, human beings require clean water to live safe and healthy lives. Yet, even as recently as the early 1970s, the waterways of the United States were horribly polluted. Factories discharged toxic substances into the nation's rivers. Municipalities dumped untreated sewage into the rivers. Fish died in record numbers. Most watersheds were unusable for swimming or other recreation.[20] Lake Erie was declared dead; the Hudson River contained bacterial levels over a hundred times greater than what is considered safe.[21] When Cleveland's Cuyahoga River,

---

[15] EPA Task Force on Ritualistic Use of Mercury, Report, December 2002, available at www.epa.gov/superfund/community/pdfs/mercury.pdf [https://perma.cc/25AX-2LXM].

[16] EPA Office of Inspector General, *Public Liaison Report, EPA Is Properly Addressing the Risks of Using Mercury in Rituals*, Report No. 2006-P-00031 (August 31, 2006).

[17] Id.

[18] Id.

[19] See Yehle, supra note 13.

[20] See James Salzman, *Why Rivers No Longer Burn: The Clean Water Act is One of the Great Successes in Environmental Law*, Slate (December 10, 2012).

[21] Id.

containing "no visible life, not even low forms such as leeches and sludge worms," burst into flames in 1969,[22] it became clear to many that the federal government had to step in and do something. Over Richard Nixon's veto, Congress enacted the Clean Water Act in 1972, and slowly the nation's waters started improving.[23]

For a variety of reasons, including ease of enforcement as well as the strength of the nation's farming lobby, the Clean Water Act distinguishes between "point source" pollution, which basically means pollution that comes from a specific, easily identifiable source like the end of a pipe, and so-called "nonpoint source" pollution, which generally refers to pollution from runoff, particularly from agriculture. The Act thoroughly and strictly regulates point source pollution, but leaves nonpoint source pollution primarily to the states.[24] As a result, the country has made great strides in reducing the amount of point source pollution in our waters, while agricultural runoff and other nonpoint source pollution continue to cause significant problems.[25]

Realizing that something has to be done about these problems, states, localities, and to some degree the EPA have begun, in recent years, to focus more on ways to reduce nonpoint source pollution. Some state and local governments, for example, have begun urging or requiring farmers and other creators of nonpoint pollution (timber harvesters, construction managers, etc.) to take affirmative steps to reduce the amount of nonpoint source pollution generated and to reduce the possibility that the pollution will make it into waterways.[26] These measures include things like installing fences, moving activities back some distance from waterways, restoring eroded areas, and other so-called "best management practices."[27] Although these requirements have not always been strictly enforced, environmental officials have increasingly been investigating farms and other sites to ensure that the rules are being followed. In addition to imposing fines for violations, the government also often works together with farmers and other polluters to educate them about the dangers of runoff pollution and to fund pollution-reduction projects when necessary.[28]

But what should the government do with farmers whose religious beliefs counsel them against working with the government, taking government money, or developing technological solutions to problems? Consider the plain-sect, old order Amish

---

[22] Id (quoting the Federal Water Pollution Control Administration).
[23] Id.
[24] Id.
[25] Id.
[26] See New Hampshire Department of Environmental Services, *Best Management Practices to Control Nonpoint Source Pollution: A Guide for Citizens and Town Officials* (January 2004).
[27] See F. Abbas & A. Fares, *Best Management Practices to Minimize Non-point Source Pollution in Agriculture*, Soil & Crop Management (June 2009).
[28] See Lara B. Fowler, Matthew B. Royer, & Jamison E. Colburn, *Addressing Death by a Thousand Cuts: Legal and Policy Innovations to Address Nonpoint Source Runoff*, Choices (October 3, 2013).

of Lancaster County, Pennsylvania. Amish families own over half of the 5000-or-so dairy farms in the county – the county that is the worst contributor to the terrible pollution that plagues the Chesapeake Bay. Lancaster County generates over 60 million pounds of cow manure every year, much of which makes its way to the Bay, "reducing oxygen rates, killing fish and creating a dead zone that has persisted since the 1970s."[29] As a result of this pollution, the Bay's blue crabs are in such bad shape and so hungry that they have started eating each other.[30] In 2009, a group of environmental investigators visited two dozen-or-so Amish farms and found that most of them were not managing their manure properly and that, as a result, a large number of nearby wells were contaminated with E. coli, nitrates, or possibly both.[31]

Environmental officials have been trying to work with these Amish farmers to implement pollution control measures – such as building fences around their farms, larger pits to store manure, and buffers between their farms and nearby rivers and streams – but they have not been greeted with open arms.[32] The Amish are famously resistant to change, skeptical of the government, and wary of taking money from others. They were generally not happy to see the EPA, especially when the agency first arrived in 2009. It certainly did not help that the agency originally lacked sensitivity to the unique situation of the Amish; according to one non-Amish farmer, "they came in here with guns ablazing and really tried to hammer some people hard."[33]

When the government started taking a more cooperative approach, however, it met with more success. Many Amish farmers accepted funds to modernize their operations and reduced manure pollution from their livestock. Even so, taking such steps remains controversial within the Amish community.[34] In one 2011 article, a farmer who accepted money from the federal government did not want his full name printed in the paper "because he was afraid his neighbors might see the story and criticize him for taking federal money."[35]

A similar problem arose with the extremely conservative Swartzentruber Amish in Pennsylvania, who have been reluctant to employ required technology to reduce the risk of water contamination from human feces.[36] The Swartzentrubers may

---

[29] Sindya N. Bhanoo, *Amish Farming Draws Rare Government Scrutiny*, N.Y. Times (June 9, 2010).
[30] See Brian Winter, *Scientists, Amish to Fight Chesapeake Bay Pollution*, USA Today (February 2, 2010).
[31] See Banhoo, supra note 29.
[32] See Amanda Pertaka, *Amish Farmers in Chesapeake Bay Watershed Find Themselves in EPA's Sights*, N.Y. Times (October 10, 2011).
[33] Id.
[34] See id.
[35] Id.
[36] See Associated Press, *Embattled Amish Set in Cambria County Moving to Upstate New York*, TRIB Live (November 24, 2012, 11:16 AM), available at http://triblive.com/home/3016359-74/amish-county-swartzentrubers-moving-sewage-state-pennsylvania-swartzentruber-york-cambria [https://perma.cc/NF8P-9RNR].

seem familiar to those who follow disputes involving law and religion because in 2003 a group of them ran into trouble when they refused to put reflective orange triangles on their buggies, as required by state law. After a prolonged legal battle, the group convinced the Pennsylvania courts to let them use gray tape instead.[37] This is not a group, in other words, that would cave at the first sight of a state sewage official.

When Pennsylvania sewage officials came to Swartzentruber properties in 2008, they found numerous violations of the state sewage codes. The tanks were too small, were made out of the wrong materials, and lacked electronic monitoring equipment. Sewage was overflowing, untreated, and emptied onto the ground.[38] Neighbors worried, understandably, that their well water might become contaminated.[39] The sewage authorities told the Swartzentrubers to modernize or else. The Swartzentrubers refused; according to one member of the group, "They're enforcing stuff that's against our religion."[40] A judge even sentenced one member of the sect to jail for ninety days for failing to comply.[41]

Nor are these conflicts limited to Pennsylvania. Disputes involving sewage requirements have made it to courts in Michigan and Ohio.[42] An Ohio municipal judge, for instance, found in favor of the state's Board of Health, which had required an Amish man to install an off-lot septic system with electricity, on the grounds that "the state's interest in preventing the discharge of untreated septic/sewage from being washed downstream in the surface waters and into the groundwater is compelling."[43]

As for the Pennsylvania Swartzentrubers, most left the state for New York, where they expect more lenient treatment.[44] Moving states to avoid sewage regulations may seem radical, but this example serves as a poignant reminder of the importance of religion to many people. As an attorney for one of the sewage agencies said: "I remember going to the [Amish] house ... and the wife came out and said, 'You're going to keep me from going to heaven. Whose fault is it going to be that I'm going to hell?'"[45]

---

[37] See *Pennsylvania Superior Court Rules: Amish Can Stick with Reflective Tape on Buggies*, ACLU (October 21, 2003), available at www.aclu.org/news/pennsylvania-superior-court-rules-amish-can-stick-reflective-tape-buggies [https://perma.cc/9X6N-ZU2L].
[38] See Sean Hamill, *Religious Freedom vs. Sanitation Rules*, N.Y. Times, June 13, 2009.
[39] See id.
[40] Id.
[41] See id.
[42] See generally *Ohio v. Bontrager*, 897 N.E. 2d 244 (Newton Falls Municipal Court 2008); *Beechy v. Central Michigan District Health Dept.*, 475 F.Supp.2d 671 (E.D. Mich. 2007)
[43] Bontrager, supra note 42.
[44] See Associated Press, supra note 36.
[45] Hamill, supra note 38.

3. RESOLVING THE CONFLICT: SOME OBSERVATIONS

The government has an enormous range of options at its disposal to deal with environmental problems, and finding the right one is no easy matter. For one thing, there is the question of which level of government should play the lead role – federal, state, or local. Once that decision has been made (along with the corollary decision of what subsidiary roles the other levels of government should play), the critical question becomes whether to proceed through traditional command-and-control regulation on the one hand or softer approaches on the other, such as disclosure of information, investment in new technologies, market-based systems such as cap and trade, education to raise consciousness, and the like. If a command-and-control regulation is appropriate, the next question might be whether that regulation will take the form of a design requirement or a performance standard? If a performance standard is chosen, should the standard should be keyed primarily (or exclusively) to health benefits, or will costs to industry be taken into account? The details of any of these specific approaches can be nearly endless.

Ordinarily, the cause of environmental damage is human activity motivated by some sort of economic interest: manufacturing, development, transportation, and so on. Recreation – driving, fishing, riding off-road vehicles on pristine lands, and so on – is another primary source of environmental harm. Government officials are quite used to developing regulatory approaches to address environmental harms caused by these activities. Environmental harm caused by religious beliefs or practices, however, is somewhat different. Religion is primarily neither recreational nor commercial (though it can involve aspects of both). How, then, should the government's approach when addressing religious causes of environmental harm compare to its approach when addressing environmental harm caused by commercial or recreational activities? What might be the same, and what might differ?

First of all, the government need not take a hands-off approach simply because a particular type of water or air pollution is a by-product of religious practice as opposed to economic or recreational activity. The government has a compelling interest, to use the language of constitutional law, in protecting the public's health and the nation's natural resources from environmental harm, regardless of the source of that harm.

Second, if the government does address an environmental harm that is caused by a religious belief or practice, it must take a general approach to preventing the harm rather than target religion specifically. The Supreme Court has made clear that the Constitution does not prohibit the government from imposing burdens, even significant ones, on religious practice if it proceeds through neutral laws of general applicability,[46] but that the government may not single out religion for specific

---

[46] *Employment Division v. Smith*, 494 U.S. 872, 885 (1990).

regulation.[47] In *Church of Lukumi Babalu Aye v. City of Hialeah*, the Court held that the city of Hialeah, Florida, had violated the First Amendment's Free Exercise Clause by prohibiting the Santeria practice of animal sacrifice in a way that made clear that the city was not concerned generally about protecting animals from harm but rather only with protecting them from a disfavored religious practice.[48]

Therefore, if the government were to take measures to address the mercury problem discussed earlier it would need to address the use of mercury in homes generally rather than focusing on the religious use of mercury in homes. Of course, as a federal agency, the EPA also would need to satisfy the requirements of the Religious Freedom Restoration Act, meaning that it could not impose a significant burden on religion without satisfying the statute's stringent narrow tailoring requirement (indeed, from a purely strategic perspective, the presence of RFRA might counsel in favor of state and local governmental units addressing environmental harms caused by religious practice, at least in states which lack their own RFRAs or analogous constitutional standards).

Third, the government should not justify regulating a religious practice by claiming that the practice is inauthentic, unnecessary to believers, or not reflective of how real members of the tradition practice their faith. It can be tempting to justify regulating a religious practice because that practice is not how *most* practitioners practice their religion. Not all Santeria believers sprinkle mercury around their apartments. Not all Amish refuse to build sufficiently large sewage tanks. So why should the government worry about those who do?

There are several reasons why the government should not go down this road. For one thing, who is to say that one way of practicing any particular religious faith is true and other ways are not true? Religious believers regularly disagree about what their faith requires – consider, just as examples, the difference between reform, conservative, and orthodox Judaism; whether the Episcopalian Church should allow gay ministers; and whether, as some Buddhists believe but others do not, laypeople as well as monks can reach enlightenment. The division of religious faiths into schools, the creation of sects, and the presence of schisms within faith traditions are indelible features of religious communities. Even if it were theoretically possible to say that some interpretations of a religious tradition are wrong, an outsider to the tradition, and particularly the government, should not be the one deciding the matter. How many Jews, for example, regardless of what particular stripe of Judaism they might belong to, would agree to allow a Catholic, a Zoroastrian, a secular scholar, or a government official decide what counts as true Judaism? Why should it be any different when the Amish or Santeria are involved? Finally, determining that some

---

[47] *Church of Lukumi Babalu Aye v. Hialeah*, 508 U.S. 520, 537–8 (1993).
[48] Id., at 537.

practice does not *really* represent the beliefs of a religious faith is not necessary to justify regulation to protect the environment. As I have explained earlier, the government may generally impose regulations even if those regulations happen to burden a religious practice. But the justification for that regulation should be to protect the environment and the public's health; the state should not rely in any way on a judgment about what constitutes a genuine or authentic religious practice.

Fourth, in implementing regulations or other actions intended to protect the environment, the state should try to minimize or mitigate any burdens on religious practice to the extent possible. Regulating those who practice their religion is very different from regulating, for example, a business that is producing nickel-washers for sale in the marketplace. Regulating the nickel producer may cause the business to earn less money, but it will not affect the way that the producer fundamentally relates to what he or she believes is most meaningful in life. Regulating how a believer practices their religion does exactly that. Moreover, religious practices are often as important for communities of believers as they are for the individuals who partake in them. Regulations that interfere with religious practice, therefore, may have serious effects not only on individuals but also on religious communities. The story of the Swartzentruber Amish, who dispersed from Pennsylvania to take up residence elsewhere, illustrates this phenomenon. While regulation may be justified, government officials should remember these costs to religion from regulation and to try to reduce them where possible.

This fourth point leads directly to the fifth and final one, which is that, when deciding between top-down, law-heavy, command-and-control approaches and more flexible approaches to reducing the environmental impact from religious practices, the government should err on the side of the latter. More flexible approaches are less burdensome on regulated parties and offer more autonomy in determining how to proceed, both of which are desirable features when it comes to balancing religious freedom rights with environmental protection. In particular, collaboration between agencies and the regulated parties – communication, negotiation, and information exchange – would seem appropriate in many of these cases. Collaboration between the government and regulated parties to address environmental harms is a well-established method of approaching environmental problems in a variety of contexts, and may perhaps be becoming increasingly important. In areas such as land management, protection of endangered species, and pollution control, collaborative efforts have proven effective in addressing particularly complex environmental problems.[49] In the context of religious practice, collaboration might help persuade

---

[49] See generally, e.g., David J. Sousa & Christopher McGrory Klyza, *New Directions in Environmental Policy Making: An Emerging Collaborative Regime or Reinventing Interest Group Liberalism*, 47 Nat. Res. J. 377 (2007); Francisco Zamora-Arroyo, Osvel Hinojosa-Huerta, Edith Santiago, Emily Brott, & Peter Culp, *Collaboration in Mexico: Renewed Hope for the Colorado River Delta*, 8

religious believers to alter their practices in ways beneficial to environmental protection without either unduly harming the religious community or forcing the offending practices underground where they potentially cannot be reached by regulation at all. In large part, the relevant agencies took this approach in both the Amish nonpoint source and the Santeria mercury contexts and should be applauded for working with the relevant communities to reduce the impact of their religious practices.

Balancing religious freedom and environmental protection is no easy matter. The government should take both sides of the equation seriously and work together with stakeholders to find the most appropriate way of protecting the environment and the public's health without excessively imposing upon religious freedom.

Nev. L.J. 871 (2008); Antony Cheng, *Build it and They Will Come? Mandating Collaboration in Public Lands Planning and Management*, 46 Nat. Res. J. 841 (2006); Daniel Kemmis & Matthew McKinney, *Collaboration and the Ecology of Democracy*, 12 Sustainable Dev. L. & Pol'y 46 (2001).

Index

abortion, xix, 113, 116, 117, 119, 120, 122, 123, 146, 179, 189–90, 191–92, 237, 243, 244, 245, 246, 247, 248–50, 251–55, 283, 313, 334, 350–52. *See also* personhood movement
  emergency termination, 30–32, 191–92, 253–55
  obstetrics training programs, 51–52
  professional conscientious objection, 188
  restrictions and the Establishment Clause, 372–81
  selective ban, 349, 352, 357
Affordable Care Act, xvii, 115, 134, 136, 140, 199, 216, 230–31, 236, 240, 252, 314
  actuarial fairness, 148–49
  'Cadillac tax', 166
  contraception provisions, 10, 43, 64, 72, 81, 231, 232, 233, 235, 237, 238, 239, 241, 256, 356. *See also* contraception, coverage litigation
  employer mandate, 4, 162–63, 166
  health care sharing ministries, 144–45, 150, 151–53
  health exchanges, 4, 72, 153, 163, 165, 166
  individual mandate, 29
  philosophical basis, 150–51
  social solidarity, 148
Alito, Samuel, 58, 80, 82, 127–28, 129–30, 210, 234
Alliance Defending Freedom, 45
American Association of Christian Counselors, 280, 281, 283
American Catholic Psychology Association, 279
American Civil Liberties Union, 30–31, 32, 34, 35, 192, 254
American Counseling Association, 260, 264, 265, 267
American Medical Association, 179
American Pharmacists Association, 50

American Psychological Association, 179, 259, 260, 266, 267, 268, 270, 272
Americans with Disabilities Act, 55, 71
Americans United for Life, 361
Americans United for the Separation of Church and State, 34
Amish, 316, 416–18
anthrax, 403
Aristotle, 106
artificial insemination, 122
assisted suicide. *See* end-of-life treatment
assistive reproductive technology. *See also* personhood movement
  denial of service, 360–64
  embryo adoption, 364–66
  Europe, 360
  pre-embryo disposition disputes, 368–71
  restrictions and the Establishment Clause, 372–81

Baby Rena, 306
Barriocanal v. Gibbs, 194
Becket Fund for Religious Liberty, 44–45, 68
Belloti v. Baird, 334
Benedict XVI, 94, 97, 100
Black church, 387–98
Blackmun, Harry, 50, 346, 366, 373
Blagojevich, Rod, 51
Bob Jones University v. United States, 74
Brennan, William, 128, 222
Buchanan, Pat, 40
Buddhism, 412, 413
Burwell v. Hobby Lobby, 2, 4, 5–6, 21–23, 29, 30, 34, 35, 42, 43, 44–45, 53, 55–56, 59, 60–61, 62–63, 71, 72, 73, 74, 81–85, 103–4, 108, 112, 124, 125, 127–30, 136–37, 158, 159, 160, 199,

423

Burwell v. Hobby Lobby (cont.)
    203, 204, 206, 208, 210, 211, 216,
    236–37, 353, 354, 356, 359
Bush, George H.W., 39
Bush, George W., 365

Cardwell v. Bechtol, 334
Caribbean mercury rituals, 413–15, 420
Catholic Church
    abortion, 30–32, 41–43, 116, 117, 191–92, 245, 246,
        253, 254, 375
    contraception, 41–43, 117, 125, 245
    contractual impositions on non-Catholic
        health care providers, 113–24
    disclosure of health care restrictions, 189
    end-of-life treatment, 33, 114
    Ethical and Religious Directives for Catholic
        Health Care Services, 114, 115, 116, 117, 118,
        119, 122, 123, 130, 131, 247, 253
    health care mission, 49, 87, 90–102, 243
        charity, 93–94, 97
        corporate religion, 97–101
        governance structure, 94–96
        history, 140
        mission integrity, 125–37
        pluralism of employees, 96–97, 115
    HIV prevention, 384
    homosexuality, 263
    local health care monopolies, 32–33, 123,
        243, 246
    psychology profession, 278
    sterilization, 190, 244
Catholic Health Association, 66, 125, 132–33, 134
Catholics for Choice, 43
Centers for Disease Control and Prevention,
    403, 409–10
Christian Association for Psychological Studies,
    279, 280
Christian Healthcare Ministries, 144
Christian Scientists, 29–30, 152
Church Amendment, 243, 244, 246, 250, 251, 313
*Church of Lukumi Babalu Aye v. City of
    Hialeah*, 419–20
Clean Water Act, 416
Clinton, Bill, 34, 39
Clinton, Hillary, 167
Coalition for the Free Exercise of Religion, 38, 40
Coates-Snow Amendment, 251
community benefit standard, 125–26, 131–34
conscience, 103–12
    burden on third parties, 208–14
        undue hardship standard, 212–14, 215–29

classical conception, 105–7
complicity in sin, 42–45
conflation with religion, 104, 107–9
'corporate', 109–12, 160–61
determining substantial burden, 204–8
natural person, 104, 112
sincerity of religious objections, 65–70, 157
statutory conscience protections, 120–21,
    123–24, 242–57
    institutional disclosure, 246–48
    super conscience clauses, 251–53
Constitution
    Article 1, 403
    First Amendment, xvi, 4, 50, 55, 75, 76, 79, 121,
        154, 178, 185, 186, 215, 219, 229, 265, 297,
        315, 317, 353
    Establishment Clause, 13, 55, 61, 74,
        199, 200, 209–10, 217, 221–23, 226,
        261, 372–81
    Free Exercise Clause, 3, 5, 25, 26, 36–37, 53,
        55, 58, 60, 61, 70, 73, 77, 78, 309, 340, 341,
        353–54, 362, 405
    Fourteenth Amendment, 39, 350, 353, 366. *See
        also* privacy rights
    Tenth Amendment, 403
contraception, xix, 30, 53–59, 146, 245
    benefits for women, 70–71
    conflation with abortion, 68–70
    coverage litigation, 2, 4–7, 21–24, 62–74, 81–86,
        90, 127–30, 156–57, 203, 204, 206–8, 210,
        211, 216, 231–41, 256–57, 353. *See also
        Burwell v. Hobby Lobby; Zubik v. Burwell*
    emergency, 24–27, 51, 117, 120, 122, 190
contractual religious restrictions on health
    care, 113–24
Corp. of Presiding Bishop v. Amos, 55, 61, 128
Council of Social Work Education's Commission
    on Accreditation, 268
Crider v. University of Tennessee, 226–27
cuius regio, 238–39
Culture Wars, 40–46, 90, 91, 202
    Religious Right, 42–46
    Republican Party, 44
Cutter v. Wilkinson, 210

Danbury Baptists, 235
death penalty, 50–51, 205
DeBoer v. Snyder, 390–91
Department of Health and Human Services, 4–5,
    6, 133, 134, 135, 248, 252
*Diagnostic and Statistical Manual of Mental
    Disorders*, 286–87, 322

Index

disposal of hazardous human remains, 399–410
  religious dissent, 401–2, 406, 407
  US laws, 402–5, 406–7
    legal protection for death rituals, 405

Ebola, 401–2, 407–9
Eden Foods, Inc. v. Sebelius, 66
EEOC v. Townley, 227–28
Emergency Medical Treatment and Labor Act (EMTALA), 148, 254, 255
eminent domain, 234
Employee Retirement Income Security Act (ERISA), 164
employer-sponsored health insurance, 154–68
  history, 162–63
  privilege v. entitlement, 163
  regressive distribution of benefits, 163–64
  religious conflict, 161–62
  risk pooling, 164
  stagnant pay, 163
Employment Division v. Smith, xvi, 3, 4, 26, 37–38, 39, 309, 310, 312, 353–54, 362
end-of-life treatment, 33, 120, 123, 169, 247
  assisted suicide, xix, 119, 312, 313
  euthanasia, 52
  spiritual, 318
  withdrawal of life support, 114, 188
environment, 411–22
  Amish waterway pollution, 405–18
  Caribbean mercury rituals, 416–18
  regulatory collaboration with religious groups, 419–22
  religious attitudes, 412–13
Environmental Protection Agency
  coal regulations, 412
  mercury rituals, 414–15, 420
  waterway pollution, 416, 417
epidemics, 399–410
Estate of Thornton v. Caldor, 61

Falwell, Jerry, 42
feudalism, 230–31, 235, 236–37, 239–41
Focus on the Family, 281
Francis (Pope), 100
Fuller seminary, 279

Genetic Information Nondiscrimination Act, 148
Georgetown University, 66
Gillette v. United States, 54
Ginsburg, Ruth Bader, 23, 29, 58, 82, 83, 84, 85, 127, 128–29, 208
Good News Club v. Milford, 284, 285–86, 287

Grace Schools v. Burwell, 84–85
Griswold v. Connecticut, 350

Harris v. McRae, 375
health care sharing ministries, 144–53. *See also under* Affordable Care Act
  actuarial fairness, 149
  operating principles, 144–47
  philosophical basis, 151–52
  social solidarity, 149
  stability, 152–53
Hinduism, 413
HIV/AIDS and African Americans, 387–98
Holt v. Hobbs, 44, 80–81, 218
Home School Legal Defense Association, 34
Hosanna-Tabor v. EEOC, 55, 58, 61, 79–80, 234–35
Huckabee, Mike, 412
Hyde Amendment, 313, 375

Illinois Conscience Act, 25
in vitro fertilization, 27–28, 122
individual choice, xvii, xix, xx
insanity defense, 319–31
  distinguishing disorder from extremism, 322–25
  insanity standard, 325–27
  islamophobia, 328–30
  raising the defense, 327–28
Insanity Defense Reform Act, 325
Internal Revenue Code, 162
International Health Regulations, 407–8
Islam, 323–24, 327–30
  extremism, 319–21, 322, 323–24, 327–28

Jacobson v. Commonwealth of Massachusetts, 405
Jefferson, Thomas, 235–36
Jehovah's Witnesses
  blood transfusion, 30, 219, 292, 335, 336–37, 340, 342
  renunciation of autonomy, 337–38, 340
John Paul II, 100
Johnson v. Kokemoor, 194
Julea Ward Freedom of Conscience Act, 265–66

Kagan, Elena, 58, 80
Keeton v. Anderson-Wiley, 264–65
Kennedy, Anthony, 23, 24, 59
King v. Burwell, 232
King v. Christie, 276, 281
knowledge communities, 173–86
  constitutive characteristics, 175–79, 182–84
  external outliers, 181–82

knowledge communities (*cont.*)
  internal outliers, 180–81
  professional–client relationship, 184–85
Korte v. Sebelius, 314

labor unions, 236
LGBT, xvi, 158, 179, 216
  access to assistive reproductive
    technology, 360–64
  conversion therapy, 173, 181, 264–65, 267
    Establishment Clause objections, 283–87
    as religious v. medical activity, 278–83
  counselors with religious objections, 263–75
    disclosure, 274
    legislation, 265–66
    limited certification, 273–74
    litigation, 263–65
    referral, 270–72
    training programs, 272–73
  marriage and family-making, 371
  views of counseling profession, 266–67
Locke, John, 376

Madison, James, 60
Magna Carta, 234
March for Life v. Burwell, 210
Marshall, Thurgood, 222
McCreary County v. ACLU, 376, 377
McDaniel v. Essex International, 228
Means v. US Conference of Catholic Bishops, 30–31
Medicaid, 142, 148, 164, 219
Medicare, 142, 164, 313
Medi-Share, 144, 145–46, 147, 149, 151–52
minors refusing treatment, 332–44
  autonomy, 335
    assessment of, 341–44
  mature minor doctrine, 334–35, 337, 340, 341
  parental rights, 333
  undue influence, 338–40
Model State Emergency Health Powers Act, 403–5, 406
Moore v. Regents of the University of California, 196

National Association of Evangelicals, 34
National Association of Nouthetic Counselors, 280
National Federation of Independent Businesses v. Sebelius, 231–32
National Labor Relations Board v. Noel Canning, 55

National Right to Life Committee, 39
Native American religion, 37, 412
New Jersey Declaration of Death Act, 297–98
New York Department of Health, 298
New York State Task Force on Life and the Law, 298
Nightlight Christian Adoptions Agency, 364–65
Nixon, Richard, 416
North Coast Women's Health Group v. San Diego Superior Court, 362–63
Notre Dame University, 66–67, 237, 239, 240

Obama, Barack, 236
Obergefell v. Hodges, 259

pacifism, 205, 207
palliative sedation, 188
Parham v. J.R., 333
Paul VI, 41
personhood movement, 366–68, 380–81
Personhood USA, 367
pharmacies, 24–27
Pickup v. Brown, 276, 281
Planned Parenthood v. Casey, 39, 350, 351, 352, 373
President's Council on Bioethics, 304
Prince v. Massachusetts, 405
privacy rights, 348–59
  protection from governmental interference, 350–53
  conflict with religious reasons, 353–59
professional conscientious objection, 169–98. *See also* knowledge communities
  disclosure of objection, 184–85, 187–98
  personal interests disclosure common law, 196–97
  standard risk-and-benefit disclosure common law, 193–96
Protos v. Volkswagen of America, 223–24
Provena Covenant Medical Center v. Director of Revenue, 131–33

Religious Freedom Restoration Act, 124, 127, 128, 199, 204, 208
  federal, 3–4, 5–6, 7, 22, 23, 28, 45–46, 55–56, 61, 63, 64, 65, 66, 73, 74, 76, 77, 78, 80, 82, 83, 84, 90, 127, 154, 155, 156, 157, 158, 161, 208–9, 212, 231, 232, 234, 237, 238, 240, 241, 309, 348, 349, 350, 353, 354, 356, 363, 405, 420
  enactment, 34, 38–40

state, 3, 28, 76, 77, 121, 154, 309–12, 314, 315, 317, 354, 356, 363, 405, 406
  Arizona, 310, 311
  Idaho, 310, 311
  Indiana, 34
  Oklahoma, 310, 311
  Pennsylvania, 311
Religious Land Use and Institutionalized Persons Act, 61, 76, 77, 78, 80, 218, 234, 348
Reno, Janet, 39
Roberts, John, 59, 79, 234–35
Roe v. Wade, 39, 243, 345, 346, 351, 352, 366, 375, 381
Rosenberger v. University of Virginia, 284
Ryan, Paul, 367

Samaritan Ministries, 144, 145–46, 149, 151–52
Sanders, Bernie, 167
Scalia, Antonin, 7, 37, 85, 354, 378
Seventh-day Adventists, 48, 49, 54, 225, 228
sexual orientation change efforts. *See* LGBT, conversion therapy
Shembe, 413
Sherbert v. Verner, 26–27, 36–37, 40, 54–55, 61
Shinto, 295, 412
single-payer insurance, 167
Sotomayor, Sonia, 23, 81, 85–86
Souter, David, 376
Southern Baptist Convention, 41
Southern Baptist Theological Seminary, 278
Spanish flu, 403, 406, 410
sterilization, 113, 116, 119, 120, 190, 244, 313
Stevens, John Paul, 373
Stormans, Inc. v. Wiesman, 25–27
Supreme Court of Canada, 341

Taoism, 412
Thomas Aquinas, 106, 107, 110
Thomas v. Review Board of the Indiana Employment Security Division, 238
Thomas, Clarence, 79
Title VII, 50, 55, 201, 217, 220, 221, 222, 223, 224, 225, 226, 297

Tocqueville, Alexis de, 236
Tooley v. Martin-Marietta Corp., 225–26
Toxic Substances Control Act, 414
Troxel v. Granville, 352
TWA v. Hardison, 220–23

Uniform Determination of Death Act, 294, 295–96, 299
United States v. Ewing, 326
United States v. Lee, 61
Unruh Civil Rights Act (California), 362–63
US Conference of Catholic Bishops, 30–31, 39, 72, 100

vaccination, 28–29
  MMR and autism, xvii, 180

Ward v. Polite, 264, 269
Watch Tower Bible and Tract Society, 337
Welch v. Brown, 276, 283
Weldon Amendment, 251, 252, 253
Wendroff, Arnold, 414–15
Wheaton College v. Burwell, 68
Wieland, Paul, 240
Wisconsin v. Yoder, 316
withholding futile treatment, 188, 291, 306–18
  brain death, 290, 293–305
    accommodation for religious objection, 298–305
    exemption for religious objection, 297–98, 305
    scientific criticism of definition, 304
  medical futility statutes, 308–17
    compelling state interest, 312–17
    Free Exercise Clause, 309
    religious burden, 309–12
World Health Organization, 383, 401, 407–9, 410
Worldwide Church of God, 220

Zubik v. Burwell, 7, 23–24, 53–54, 57–58, 64, 75, 85–86, 135–36, 203, 204, 207, 213, 216, 233–34, 242, 253, 256–57
Zubik v. Sebelius, 135